RELATIONS, TRANSFORMATIONS AND STATISTICS

H. A. Elliott

Associate Director

Service for Admission to College and University

Ottawa, Ontario

K. D. Fryer

Associate Dean, Faculty of Mathematics

University of Waterloo

Waterloo, Ontario

J. C. Gardner

Superintendent of Schools

The Carleton Board of Education

Ottawa, Ontario

Norman J. Hill

Head of Mathematics Department

St. Mary's Collegiate and Vocational Institute

St. Mary's, Ontario

RELATIONS, TRANSFORMATIONS AND STATISTICS

ELLIOTT
FRYER
GARDNER
HILL

Holt, Rinehart and Winston of Canada, Limited
Toronto

CONTENTS

FUNCTION AS A MAPPING

1.1. Relations

"Chris is the brother of Peter."

"Three is greater than two."

Each of these sentences involves a *binary* relation, which associates *two* objects. (All the relations considered in this chapter are binary.) Consider the sentence

$$x > y, \quad \text{where} \quad x, y \in I.$$

This sentence defines a relation. The values $x = 5$, $y = -2$ satisfy this inequality, and we say that the *ordered pair* $(5, -2)$ is a member of the solution set of the inequality. The pairs $(-2, -3)$, $(1, 0)$ are also members of the solution set, but $(-1, 1)$ and $(3, 5)$ are not members.

Consider the set

$$A = \{ (x, y) \mid x > y, \quad x, y \in I \}.$$

We see that any ordered pair belonging to A satisfies the defining sentence of the relation. Conversely, any ordered pair that satisfies the defining sentence of the relation belongs to A. Thus, we may consider the relation to be the set A itself. In general, we call any set of ordered pairs a relation.

The set of all first components, x, of the ordered pairs in a relation is called the *domain* of the relation. The set of all second components, y, of the ordered pairs in a relation is called the *range* of the relation. For the relation above whose defining sentence is

$$x > y, \quad x, y \in I,$$

the domain is the set of integers, I, and the range is also I.

1

We may interpret *a relation as a subset of a Cartesian product.* Consider the Cartesian product $A \times B$ ("*A* cross *B*") where $A = \{1, 2, 3\}$ and $B = \{7, 8, 9\}$. Recall that $A \times B$ is the set of all ordered pairs (x, y) such that $x \in A$ and $y \in B$. Thus, nine ordered pairs may be formed; that is,

$$A \times B = \{(1, 7), (1, 8), (1, 9), (2, 7), (2, 8), (2, 9), (3, 7), (3, 8), (3, 9)\}.$$

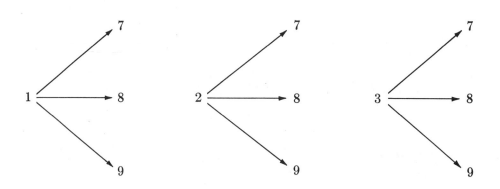

Figure 1.1

The relation whose defining sentence is

$$y = x + 5, \quad x \in A, \quad y \in B,$$

consists of the pairs $(2, 7)$ and $(3, 8)$. We may write

$$\{(x, y) \mid y = x + 5, x \in A, y \in B\} = \{(2, 7), (3, 8)\}.$$

Naming the set $\{(2, 7), (3, 8)\}$ as S, we say that S is a relation in $A \times B$.

Example 1.

(a) If $M = \{1, 2, 3, 4, 5\}$, list the members of the relation in $M \times M$ defined by

$$x^2 + y^2 < 25.$$

(b) List the members of (i) the domain, (ii) the range, of this relation.

Solution:

(a) By trial, we find the relation is described by the set P where

$$P = \{(1,1), (1,2), (1,3), (1,4), (2,1), (2,2), (2,3), (2,4), (3,1), (3,2), (3,3), (4,1), (4,2)\}.$$

(b) (i) The domain $D_P = \{1, 2, 3, 4\}$.
(ii) The range $R_P = \{1, 2, 3, 4\}$.

Example 2. Low temperature readings on a certain January 4 are given by the following table.

Ottawa	$-10°F$
Kingston	$-5°F$
Toronto	$0°F$
London	$5°F$
Windsor	$10°F$

List the ordered pairs in the relation defined by the sentence "City x has a lower temperature than city y". What are the domain and range of the relation?

Solution: If the relation involves the set T, then

$T = \{$(Ottawa, Kingston), (Ottawa, Toronto), (Ottawa, London),
(Ottawa, Windsor), (Kingston, Toronto), (Kingston, London),
(Kingston, Windsor), (Toronto, London), (Toronto, Windsor),
(London, Windsor)$\}$

$D_T = \{$Ottawa, Kingston, Toronto, London$\}$

$R_T = \{$Kingston, Toronto, London, Windsor$\}$.

EXERCISE 1.1

1. State the domain and range of the relations described by the following sets.
   (a) $\{(3, 2), (3, 1), (3, 0)\}$ 　　　　　(b) $\{(4, 5), (5, 6), (6, 7), (7, 8)\}$
   (c) $\{(x, y) \mid x, y \in N$ and $x + y < 6\}$ 　(d) $\{(x, y) \mid x, y \in I$ and $xy = 4\}$

2. State which of the ordered pairs listed belong to the relation indicated.
   (a) $\{(x, y) \mid x, y \in Re$ and $x^2 > y^3\}$; $(1, \frac{1}{2}), (-4, 2), (1, -5), (0, -1), (\sqrt{5}, \pi)$
   (b) $\{(x, y) \mid x, y \in Re$ and $\mid y \mid > x + 2\}$; 　$(-3, 0), (100, 98), (\sqrt{2}, \sqrt{\pi}),$
   $(-\frac{1}{3}, -\frac{1}{5}), (\sqrt{61}, 5)$.

3. List the ordered pairs in $M \times N$ if
   $$M = \{-2, 0, 2\} \quad \text{and} \quad N = \{3, 5, 7, 9\}.$$

4. What is (a) the intersection, (b) the union of M and N in question (3)?

5. From $M \times N$ in question (3), select the ordered pairs (a, b) such that
   $$a = b - 5.$$
   If the relation thus defined is denoted by P, list the members of D_P and R_P.

6. What is the domain of the relations in $I \times I$ defined by the following sentences?
   (a) $y = \dfrac{5}{x}$ 　　　　　　　　(b) $y = \dfrac{x + 2}{x + 1}$
   (c) $y = \dfrac{3}{x^2 - 4}$ 　　　　　　　(d) $y = \dfrac{5}{x^2 + 2}$

(e) $y = \sqrt{x}$ (f) $y = |x|$

(g) $y = \dfrac{x}{x^2 - x - 6}$ (h) $y = 2^x$

(i) $y = -x^2$ (j) $y^2 = -x$

7. List four members for each of the following infinite sets. In each case, the relation is a subset of $Re \times Re$.

   (a) $\{(a, b) \mid ab < 4\}$ (b) $\{(r, s) \mid s = 3r + 1\}$
   (c) $\{(p, q) \mid q = 0\}$ (d) $\{(x, y) \mid x < 4 \text{ and } y = x\}$
   (e) $\{(a, b) \mid 3 < a < 5\} \cap \{(a, b) \mid b = a^2\}$
   (f) $\{(x, y) \mid y = |x|\} \cap \{(x, y) \mid |x| \le 2\}$

1.2.   Graphs of Relations

If both the domain and range of a relation are subsets of Re, the graph of the relation is the set of points whose co-ordinates are the ordered pairs in the relation.

Example 1.   Draw the graph of the relation whose defining sentence is

$$x^2 + y^2 = 25, \quad x, y \in I.$$

Solution: The pairs of integers that satisfy this equation are $(0, 5)$, $(0, -5)$, $(5, 0)$, $(-5, 0)$, $(3, 4)$, $(-3, 4)$, $(3, -4)$, $(-3, -4)$, $(4, 3)$, $(-4, 3)$, $(4, -3)$ and $(-4, -3)$; the graph is shown in Figure 1.2.

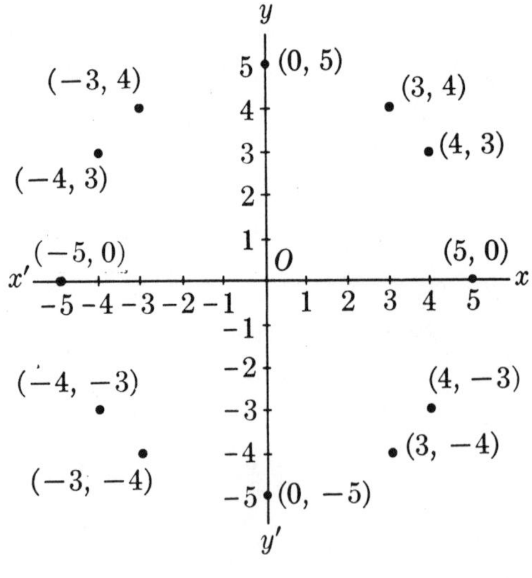

Figure 1.2

Example 2. Draw the graphs of the relations in $Re \times Re$ defined by

(i) $x^2 + y^2 = 25$,   (ii) $x^2 + y^2 < 25$,   (iii) $x^2 + y^2 \geq 25$.

Solution:

(i) Referring to our solution for Example 1, we see that the graph of $x^2 + y^2 = 25$ includes all those points shown in Figure 1.3(i) and is a circle with centre at the origin and radius 5.

(ii) The graph of $x^2 + y^2 < 25$ contains all those points that lie inside the circle in (i) above. The required region is shown shaded in Figure 1.3(ii). The circle itself is shown as a broken line to indicate that it is not part of the required graph.

(iii) The graph of $x^2 + y^2 \geq 25$ consists of the points on the circle in (i) and the points outside the circle. Figure 1.3 (iii) shows only part of the graph.

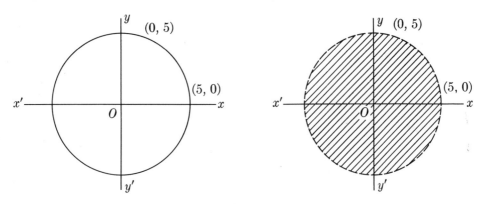

Figure 1.3 (i)   Figure 1.3 (ii)

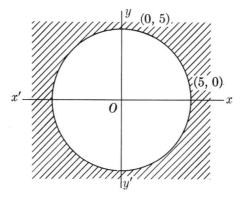

Figure 1.3 (iii)

EXERCISE 1.2

1. State the condition on the co-ordinates of a point (x, y) for the point to lie in the (a) first, (b) second, (c) third, (d) fourth quadrant.

2. State, if possible, the x- and y-intercepts of the graphs defined by the following sentences. $(x, y \in Re)$

   (a) $x + y = 1$ (b) $2x + y = 5$ (c) $y = x^2$

   (d) $y - 1 = 3(x - 2)^2$ (e) $x^2 + y^2 = 30$ (f) $xy = 0$.

3. Describe in words the graphs of each of the following relations in $Re \times Re$.

   (a) $\{(x, y) \mid y = 4\}$ (b) $\{(x, y) \mid x = -2\}$

   (c) $\{(x, y) \mid y = 0\}$ (d) $\{(x, y) \mid x = 0\}$

   (e) $\{(x, y) \mid y > 0\}$ (f) $\{(x, y) \mid x > 0\}$

   (g) $\{(x, y) \mid y > 0 \text{ and } x > 0\}$ (h) $\{(x, y) \mid y < 0 \text{ and } x < 0\}$

4. Given that the domain for each relation is $\{-4, -2, 0, 2, 4\}$, list the ordered pairs and draw the graph of the following.

   (a) $\{(a, b) \mid b = a^2\}$ (b) $\{(x, y) \mid y = |x|\}$

   (c) $\{(m, n) \mid n = 2m + 1\}$ (d) $\{(s, t) \mid t = -s\}$

5. Graph the relations in $Re \times Re$ defined by the following sentences.

   (a) $5x + 3y = 15$ (b) $y = x^2$ (c) $x - y = 2$ (d) $x - y < 2$

   (e) $x - y > 2$ (f) $y = |x|$ (g) $y > |x|$ (h) $y < |x|$

   (i) $|x - y| < 2$

6. Draw the graphs of the following relations in $Re \times Re$.

   (a) $\{(x, y) \mid 3x - 2y > 6\} \cap \{(x, y) \mid 3x - 2y < 12\}$

   (b) $\{(x, y) \mid x^2 + y^2 \leq 25\} \cap \{(x, y) \mid y \geq x\}$

   (c) $\{(x, y) \mid -x^2 \leq y \leq x^2\}$

   (d) $\{(x, y) \mid (x - 1)^2 + (y + 2)^2 < 4\}$

   (e) $\{(x, y) \mid x^2 + 2x + y^2 - 2y \leq 23\}$

   (f) $\{(x, y) \mid x^2 + y^2 < 16\} \cap \{(x, y) \mid |x - y| < 2\}$

   (g) $\{(x, y) \mid |x - y| \leq 3\} \cap \{(x, y) \mid 3y > x\} \cap \{(x, y) \mid 3y < 2x\}$

   (h) $\{(x, y) \mid x^2 - 4nx + y^2 < 1 - 4n^2, n \in I\}$

   (i) $\{(x, y) \mid x^2 + y^2 = 1, y = nx, n \in I\}$

   (j) $\{(x, y) \mid x^2 + y^2 \leq 16\} \cap \{(x, y) \mid x^2 - 12x + y^2 + 11 \leq 0\}$

7. Graph in $I \times I$ the relation defined by

$$x^4 + y^4 \leq 256.$$

1.3. Function as a Mapping

Consider the graphs of the two relations shown in Figure 1.4

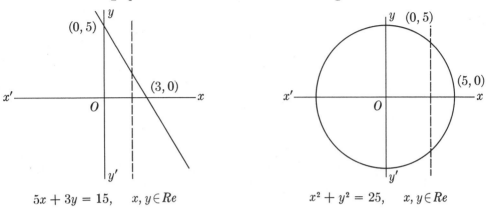

$$5x + 3y = 15, \quad x, y \in Re$$

$$x^2 + y^2 = 25, \quad x, y \in Re$$

Figure 1.4

Note that, in the ordered pairs that satisfy $5x + 3y = 15$, *for each value of x there is exactly one value of y. No two ordered pairs in the relation have the same first element. Such a relation is called a function. A line drawn parallel to the y-axis meets the graph in, at most, one point.*

Note that, in the ordered pairs that satisfy $x^2 + y^2 = 25$, some values of x are paired with more than one value of y. It is possible to find two ordered pairs in the relation that have the same first element. Such a relation is *not* a function. A line drawn parallel to the y-axis may intersect the graph in more than one point.

We may say that *a function is a relation in which each element in the domain is paired with one and only one element in the range.*

Consider the function whose defining sentence is

$$y = x + 2, \quad 0 \leq x \leq 3, \quad x \in I.$$

The graph of this function is shown in Figure 1.5.

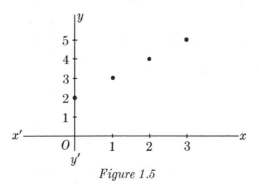

Figure 1.5

This same function may also be graphed in a different way by using two vertical number lines as in Figure 1.6.

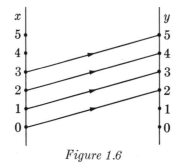

Figure 1.6

Figure 1.6 suggests that a function is a *mapping*. Each value of x is carried to or mapped onto its corresponding value of y. We may say that the function maps the elements of the domain *onto* the elements of the range. The function f graphed in Figure 1.6 is written as

$$f : x \rightarrow x + 2 \,,$$

which is read as "the function f maps the number x onto the number $x + 2$." Any element $x + 2$ of the range is called the *image* of the corresponding element x of the domain. The symbol used to represent the image of x is $f(x)$, read as "f at x" or "f of x". In the example we have been discussing, $f(x) = x + 2$. Sometimes we write

$$f : x \rightarrow f(x)$$

to stress the fact that x is mapped onto its image $f(x)$ by the function f. Note that each value of x in the domain and its image $f(x)$ constitute an ordered pair $(x, f(x))$. The set of all such ordered pairs involved in the function f is identical with the set of ordered pairs obtained from our earlier definition of function as a special type of relation.

Sometimes we use the notation

$$f : A \rightarrow B$$

to stress the fact that a function maps the members of one set into those of another. In this notation, the function we have been discussing would be written in the form

$$f : \{0, 1, 2, 3\} \rightarrow \{2, 3, 4, 5\}, \quad f(x) = x + 2 \,.$$

In the notation

$$f : x \rightarrow f(x) \,,$$

the domain of f may be stated explicitly; if it is not, it is simply $\{x \mid f(x) \text{ is defined}\}$.

For example, if the function f is defined by

$$f : x \to \frac{1}{x}, \qquad f \text{ is in } Re \times Re,$$

the domain of f is $Re - \{0\}$, that is, $\{x \mid x \in Re, x \neq 0\}$.

In the notation

$$f : A \to B,$$

the domain of f is A. (Occasionally, we call f a mapping from A to B.)

The reader should have no difficulty in distinguishing these two notations for a function; it is always clear whether the arrow is preceded and followed by sets or individual elements.

Example 1. For the function

$$k : x \to x^2, \qquad x \in Re,$$

find $k(2), k(1), k(0), k(-1), k(-2)$.

Solution: If
$$k(x) = x^2,$$
then
$$k(2) = 4,$$
$$k(1) = 1,$$
$$k(0) = 0,$$
$$k(-1) = 1,$$
$$k(-2) = 4.$$

Note that $k(x) = k(-x)$. The graph of the function k is symmetric with respect to the y-axis.

Note: The function

$$f : Re \to Re, \qquad f(x) = x + 2$$

maps the set Re *onto* the set Re; i.e., each element of the second set is the image of an element of the first set. Such a function is sometimes called *surjective*. (See Figure 1.7(i).) The function

$$f : Re \to Re, \qquad f(x) = x^2,$$

as in Example 1 above, maps the set Re *into* Re but not *onto* Re; the set of image points is not Re but a proper subset of Re, namely, the set of nonnegative real numbers. (We may say that this function is not a surjective mapping from Re to Re). (See Figure 1.7(ii) on the following page.)

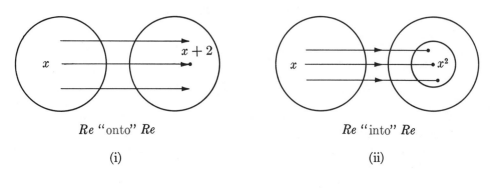

Re "onto" Re   Re "into" Re

(i)   (ii)

Figure 1.7

EXERCISE 1.3

1. If $g(x) = 2x - 5$, $x \in Re$, state the value of each of the following.
   (a) $g(1)$ (b) $g(0)$ (c) $g(-1)$ (d) $g(\sqrt{2})$
   (e) $g(13)$ (f) $g(-40)$ (g) $g(2x)$ (h) $g(x+1)$
   (i) $g[g(x)]$ (j) $g(k)$ (k) $g(x+a)$ (l) $g(\pi^2)$

2. What is the image of -1 under each of the following mappings?   ($x \in Re$)
   (a) $f : x \rightarrow -x$ (b) $g : x \rightarrow x$
   (c) $h : x \rightarrow 3x - 5$ (d) $m : x \rightarrow -x^3$
   (e) $s : x \rightarrow x^{2n}$ (f) $t : x \rightarrow (-x)^3$
   (g) $u : x \rightarrow (3x)^2$ (h) $v : x \rightarrow -\sqrt{x^2}$

3. Determine which of the following mappings are functions. List the sets of ordered pairs illustrated.

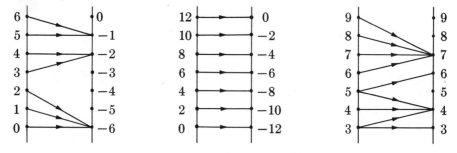

4. Which of the mappings shown below are functions?   Explain.

(a)

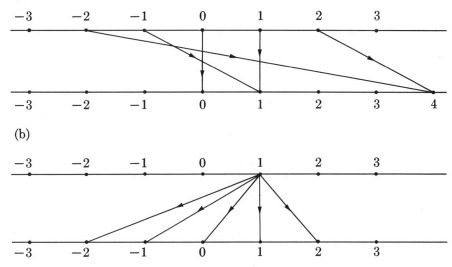

(b)

5. Given that $-3 < x < 3$, $x \in I$, illustrate the following functions as mappings into the set of real numbers.

(a) $f : x \rightarrow 3x$

(b) $f : x \rightarrow 5 - x$

(c) $f : x \rightarrow \dfrac{3}{x}$, $x \neq 0$

(d) $f : x \rightarrow x^2 - 4$

6. Find the range for each of the mappings in question 5.

7. Given that the domain for each of the following mappings is $\{-3, -2, -1, 0\}$, graph the function using two vertical number lines in each case.

(a) $g : x \rightarrow 5x - 2$

(b) $h : x \rightarrow -x^2$

(c) $q : a \rightarrow (a + 1)^2$

(d) $r : b \rightarrow (2b - 1)^2$

8. The domain of a function g is $\{x \mid -2 \leq x \leq 3, x \in Re\}$.   Find the range if

(a) $g(x) = x^3$,

(b) $g(x) = \mid x \mid$.

9. For functions f and g, $f(x) = 7 - x$ and $g(x) = (x - 1)^2$.   Find the members of $\{x \mid f(x) = g(x)\}$.

10. List five ordered pairs in each of the following functions and graph each function, using cartesian co-ordinates.

(a) $f = \{(x, y) \mid y = 3x^2 - 12x + 17,$ $x = 0, 1, 2, 3, 4\}$

(b) $g = \{(a, b) \mid ab = 8,$ $a \in Re^+\}$

(c) $h = \{(m, n) \mid n = 3 + \mid m + 1 \mid,$ $m \in I\}$

(d) $k = \{(x, k(x)) \mid x - 2k(x) = 5,$ $x \in Re^+\}$.

11. f is a function such that, for all real numbers x and y,
$$f(x) + f(y) = f(x + y) .$$
(a) Prove that $f(0) = 0$.   (Set $x = y = 0$.)
(b) Prove that $f(y) = -f(-y)$ for all $y \in Re$.

12. If s is a function such that for all real numbers t and u,
$$s(t - u) = s(t) \cdot s(u) ,$$
show that the range of s must be either $\{0\}$ or $\{1\}$.

13. List the mappings in question (2) that map the first set onto the second (that is, the surjective mappings).   Consider Re to be the second set.

If
$$f : A \to B ,$$
and C is a subset of A, we define $f(C)$, the image of C, by
$$f(C) = \{f(c) \mid c \in C\} .$$
Find the images of the following sets under the given mappings.

14. $f : Re \to Re$, $f(x) = x + 1$, $\{x \mid 0 \le x \le 1\}$

15. $f : Re \to Re$, $f(x) = 2x^2$, $\{x \mid -1 \le x \le 3\}$

16. $f : Ra \to Ra$, $f(x) = -7x$, I

17. If $f : A \to B$, where $A \subset B$, and if $a \in A$ has the property that
$$f(a) = a ,$$
a is said to be a fixed point.   What are the fixed points, if any, of the following functions?
(a) $f : Re \to Re$, $f(x) = x^2$
(b) $f : Re \to Re$, $f(x) = x + 1$
(c) $f : Re - \{1\} \to Re$, $f(x) = \dfrac{x}{1 - x}$
(d) $f : Re \to Re$, $f(x) =$ the least integer not less than x .

1.4.   Inverse of a Relation

Consider the relation
$$A = \{(1, 4), (2, 5), (3, 6), (4, 7)\} .$$

Interchanging the components of each ordered pair, we obtain the relation
$$B = \{(4, 1), (5, 2), (6, 3), (7, 4)\} .$$

A and B are *inverse relations*. B is the inverse of A and the symbol used is A^{-1} ("inverse of A" or "A inverse").   We may also write $A = B^{-1}$, since A is the inverse of B.

DEFINITION. A^{-1}, the inverse of a relation A, is the relation obtained by interchanging the components of each ordered pair in A.

Figure 1.8 shows the graph of relation A and its inverse, A^{-1}.

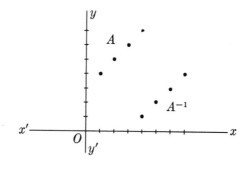

Figure 1.8

Note that the inverse of a relation is a relation. We have been discussing the function, which is a special type of relation. Consider the following mapping f and its inverse f^{-1}, which is also a function. The mapping $f : x \rightarrow 2x + 1$ is shown in Figure 1.9.

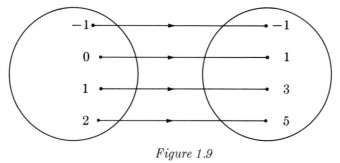

Figure 1.9

The ordered pairs in f are $(-1, -1)$, $(0, 1)$, $(1, 3)$ and $(2, 5)$. If the arrows are reversed as in Figure 1.10 the inverse of f is obtained.

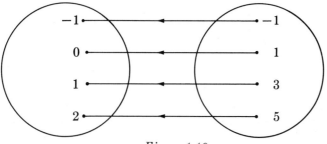

Figure 1.10

The inverse, f^{-1}, has as its ordered pairs

$$(-1, -1), (1, 0), (3, 1), (5, 2).$$

If we write the defining sentence of f as

$$y = 2x + 1$$

then the defining sentence for f^{-1} is found by interchanging x and y.

$$x = 2y + 1$$

or

$$y = \frac{x - 1}{2}.$$

Using the notation which corresponds to

$$f : x \rightarrow 2x + 1,$$

we have

$$f^{-1} : x \rightarrow \frac{x - 1}{2}.$$

Is the inverse of a function always a function?   Consider Example 1 below.

Example 1.   List the ordered pairs in the inverses of each of the following functions. Is the inverse a function?
  (a) $M = \{(2, 5), (3, 6), (4, 7)\}$
  (b) $N = \{(4, 2), (5, 2), (6, 3)\}.$

Solution:
  (a) $M^{-1} = \{(5, 2), (6, 3), (7, 4)\}.$

M^{-1} is a function because no two pairs have the same first element.

  (b) $N^{-1} = \{(2, 4), (2, 5), (3, 6)\}.$

N^{-1} is not a function because two pairs have the same first element.
In general, the inverse of a function is not always a function.
    In Example 1, the relation M is defined by the sentence

$$y = x + 3.$$
$$M = \{(x, y) \mid y = x + 3\}.$$

The ordered pairs in M are such that each second component is found by *adding* 3 to the first component.   In the inverse, M^{-1}, each second component is found by *subtracting* three from the first component.   That is, if the defining sentence for M is

$$y = x + 3,$$

then the defining sentence for M^{-1} is

$$x = y + 3,$$

or

$$y = x - 3.$$

Hence, $M^{-1} = \{(x, y) \mid y = x - 3\}$.

Example 2. What is the defining sentence of the inverse of the function S, where

$$S = \{(x, y) \mid y = 5x - 4\} ?$$

Solution: Interchange the variables x and y. The defining sentence for S^{-1} is

$$x = 5y - 4$$

or

$$y = \frac{x + 4}{5}.$$

Hence,

$$S^{-1} = \left\{(x, y) \,\middle|\, y = \frac{x + 4}{5}\right\}.$$

Note that, if $(2, 6)$ is a member of a function then, $(6, 2)$ is a member of its inverse. We say that $(6, 2)$ is the *mirror image* of $(2, 6)$. We can show that the "mirror" is the line $y = x$; that is, show that the graph of the function and its inverse are symmetric with respect to the line $y = x$.

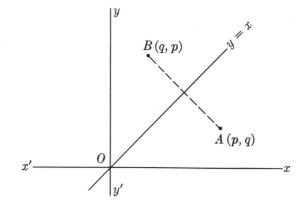

Figure 1.11

In Figure 1.11,

$$\text{Slope } AB = \frac{q - p}{p - q} = -1.$$

Since the slope of the line $y = x$ is 1, then AB is perpendicular to the line $y = x$. Also, the co-ordinates of the midpoint of AB are

$$\left(\frac{p+q}{2}, \frac{p+q}{2}\right)$$

and these co-ordinates satisfy the equation $y = x$. Hence, this midpoint lies on $y = x$ and $y = x$ is the perpendicular bisector of the line AB.

In general, the graph of the inverse of a relation is the mirror image in the line $y = x$, of the graph of the relation.

EXERCISE 1.4

1. List the ordered pairs in the mappings
   (i) $f : x \rightarrow 5x + 2$
   (ii) $f : x \rightarrow x^3$
   (iii) $f : x \rightarrow |x|$
   if $x \in I$ and $|x| \leq 2$.

2. List the ordered pairs in the inverse of each mapping in question (1). Is the inverse a function in each case? Explain.

3. $$A = \{(4, 3), (5, 3), (6, 3)\} .$$
   List the pairs in A^{-1}. Is A^{-1} a function? Explain.

4. State the defining equation for the inverse of each of the following relations.
   (a) $\{(x, y) \mid 2y = 3x + 1\}$ (b) $\{(x, y) \mid y = x^3\}$
   (c) $\{(a, b) \mid b = a - 3\}$ (d) $\{(s, t) \mid s^2 - t^2 = 16\}$.

5. The following pairs are members of g where
   $$g = \{(x, y) \mid y = 2x - 5\} .$$
   State the missing component in each pair.
   (a) $(7, ?)$ (b) $(?, 9)$ (c) $(\frac{1}{2}, ?)$
   (d) $(?, 7)$ (e) $(?, 0)$ (f) $(0, ?)$

6. In question (5), what is the defining sentence for g^{-1}? Is g a function? Is g^{-1} a function? Explain. If each of the pairs in question (5) is considered as a member of g^{-1}, state the missing component.

7. How is the inverse of the function
   $$f : x \rightarrow x$$
   related to f?

8. (a) For any function f, what is the inverse of f^{-1}?
   (b) What is the intersection of f and f^{-1} if
   $$f : x \rightarrow x + 3?$$

9. In which of the cases illustrated below are A and B inverse functions?

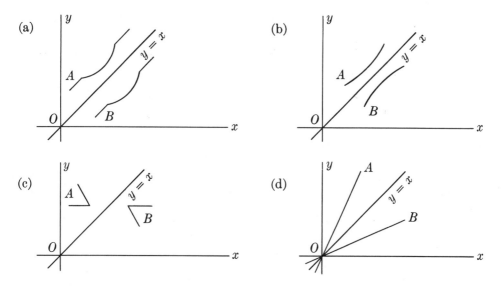

(a)

(b)

(c)

(d)

10. Graph the function
$$f = \{(0,0),\ (1,1),\ (2,4),\ (3,9)\}$$
its inverse, f^{-1} and the line $y = x$. Is f^{-1} a function?

11. Graph the function
$$f = \{(x, y) \mid y = x^2,\ x \in Re,\ |x| \leq 3\}.$$
Graph the inverse of f. Is f^{-1} a function?

12. Repeat question (11) with
$$y = x^3$$
as the defining equation.

13. (a) Graph $f : x \to \dfrac{3}{x+2}$

(b) Find the domain and range of f in $Re \times Re$.

(c) Find the domain and range of f^{-1}.

(d) Is f^{-1} a function? Explain.

14. If
$$f : A \to B$$
and $b \in A$, we define $f^{-1}(b)$, the inverse image of b, by
$$f^{-1}(b) = \{a \mid a \in A \text{ and } f(a) = b\}.$$
Find the inverse images of the following points, under the given mappings.

(a) $f : Re \to Re,\ f(x) = x^2;\ 1, 0, -3$

(b) $f : N \to Re,\ f(x) = 3x + 4;\ 13, 2$

15. If
$$f : A \to B$$
and D is a subset of B, we define $f^{-1}(D)$, the inverse image of D, by
$$f^{-1}(D) = \{a \mid a \in A \text{ and } f(a) \in D\}.$$
Find the inverse images of the following sets, under the given mappings in $Re \times Re$

(a) $f : x \to x^2$, $\{x \mid 0 < x < 1\}$

(b) $f : x \to$ the least integer not less than x, $\{x \mid -1.5 < x \le 3.7\}$.

1.5.   One-to-One Mappings

Consider the mapping
$$f : x \to x^2.$$

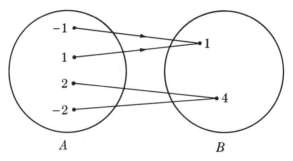

Note that, in the mapping f from domain A to range B, *two* elements of A are mapped onto *one* element of B.

Now consider the mapping
$$g : x \to 2x + 5.$$

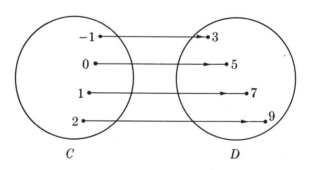

If g is a mapping from the domain C to the range D, we note that each distinct element of C is mapped onto a separate and distinct element of D. Such a mapping or function is called *one-to-one*. (The mapping f is described as many-to-one.) Consider the one-to-one mapping g and its inverse, g^{-1}. Both are graphed in Figure 1.12.

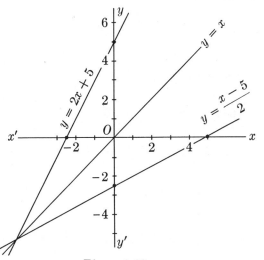

Figure 1.12

The inverse, g^{-1}, defined by

$$x = 2y + 5$$

or

$$y = \frac{x - 5}{2}$$

is also a function.   The mapping

$$f : x \rightarrow x^2$$

and its inverse f^{-1} are graphed in Figure 1.13. In this case, the inverse of f is not a function.

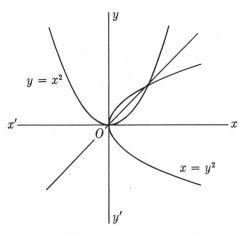

Figure 1.13

Note that the inverse of a many-to-one mapping is not a function.   In general, although we shall not prove the fact, it can be shown that *the inverse of a function (or mapping) $f : A \to B$ is a function, if and only if, f is one-to-one.* In such a case, the inverse f^{-1} is also one-to-one.

Example 1.   For the function f defined by

$$y = x^2 - 4x + 5, \quad x \in Re, \quad x \geq 2,$$

find

    (a)   the range of f,

    (b)   the defining equation of f^{-1},

    (c)   the domain and range of f^{-1}.   Also sketch the graph of f^{-1}.

Solution:

    (a)   If
$$y = x^2 - 4x + 5,$$
$$y - 1 = x^2 - 4x + 4,$$
$$y - 1 = (x - 2)^2.$$

If $x \geq 2$, the range of f is $\{y \mid y \geq 1\}$.

    (b)
$$y = x^2 - 4x + 5$$

       or

$$y - 1 = (x - 2)^2$$

is the defining equation for f, the defining equation for f^{-1} is

$$x - 1 = (y - 2)^2.$$

    (c)   Here, since $(y - 2)^2$ is nonnegative,

$$x - 1 \geq 0$$

    and

$$x \geq 1.$$

The domain of f^{-1} is $\{x \mid x \geq 1\}$ and the range is $\{y \mid y \geq 2\}$.

Note: The domain of f is the range of f^{-1} and the range of f is the domain of f^{-1}.

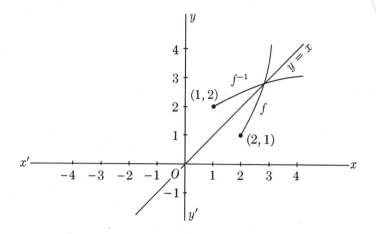

Figure 1.14

Note: A one-to-one mapping is said to be *injective*. A mapping that is both injective and surjective is said to be *bijective*.

EXERCISE 1.5

1. State the inverse of each of the following functions.
    (a) $\{(2, 6), (3, 4), (4, 1), (5, 0)\}$
    (b) $\{(0, 1), (4, 0)\}$
    (c) $\{(-4, 3), (4, 5), (-6, 0)\}$

If, for each of the following functions f, the image $f(x)$ is defined by the given equation, find (a) the range if the domain is as indicated, (b) an equation for $f^{-1}(x)$, (c) the domain and range of f^{-1}.

2. $f(x) = 5x - 4$, $\quad x \in Re$

3. $f(x) = \dfrac{3x - 5}{2}$, $\quad x \in Re$

4. $f(x) = \sqrt{x^2 - 16}$, $\quad x \in Re, x \geq 4$

5. $f(x) = \dfrac{1}{1 - x}$, $\quad x \in Re, x \neq 1$

6. $f(x) = x^2 - 6x + 9$, $\quad x \in Re, x \geq 3$

7. $f(x) = x^2 - 3$, $\quad x \in Re, x \geq \sqrt{3}$

Graph the following functions. In each case, state the range.

8. $f = \{(x, f(x)) \mid f(x) = -x, \quad x \leq 4\}$

9. $g = \{(x, g(x)) \mid g(x) = x^3, \quad x \leq 3\}$

10. $h = \{(x, h(x)) \mid h(x) = (x - 3)^2, \quad 0 \leq x \leq 6\}$

11. Graph the inverse of each function in questions (8) to (10). Is the inverse in each case a function?

12. For the mappings in questions (2) to (10), list those that are one-to-one (injective).

13. If the graph of a function is symmetric with respect to the line $y = x$, what relationship exists between the graph of the function and the graph of its inverse?

14. If f is a general linear function in Re defined by $y = ax + b$, show that f^{-1} is also a linear function.

15. Compare the relations defined by the following with their inverses $(x, y \in Re)$.
    (a) $x^2 + y^2 = 25$ (b) $xy = 8$.

16. In question (15) (a) and (b) what is the intersection of f and f^{-1}?

Chapter Summary

Cartesian product, ordered pair, relation, domain, range · Functions—Graphs of relations and functions · Function as a mapping · Inverse of a relation · Inverse of a function · One-to-one mappings

REVIEW EXERCISE 1

1. List the ordered pairs in $A \times B$ if
$$A = \{5, 4, 3\} \quad \text{and} \quad B = \{2, 7, 3, 1\}.$$

2. In question (1), what is (a) the intersection, (b) the union of A and B?

3. If $f(x) = |x| - 5$, state the value of
   (a) $f(2)$ (b) $f(-2)$ (c) $f(\frac{1}{2})$
   (d) $f[f(x)]$ (e) $f(x^2)$ (f) $f(a - b)$, $a < b$

4. If $x \in Re$ find the domain and the range for each of the following functions.
   (a) $f : x \to x^2 - 2$ (b) $f : x \to \dfrac{8}{x}$
   (c) $f : x \to 2\sqrt{x}$ (d) $f : x \to 1 + |x|$
   (e) $f : x \to - |x|$ (f) $f : x \to \dfrac{1}{x^2 + 5}$

5. Use two horizontal number lines to draw the mappings in questions 4(a), 4(b), and 4(d), if $|x| \leq 4$ and $x \in I$.

6. Use a Cartesian co-ordinate system to draw the graphs of the functions in 4(e) and 4(f) if $|x| \leq 3$.

7. Which of the following mappings is a function?   Explain.

(a)   (b)

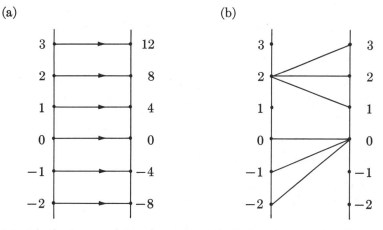

8. What is the image of 4 under each of the following mappings?
   (a) $p : x \rightarrow \sqrt{x}$ (b) $q : x \rightarrow 3x - 10$
   (c) $r : x \rightarrow \sqrt{x^2 + 9}$ (d) $s : x \rightarrow x^{2/3}$
   (e) $t : x \rightarrow x^0$ (f) $u : x \rightarrow x^2 - 4x + 5$

9. List the pairs in B^{-1} if
$$B = \{(2, 3), (7, 4), (8, 5)\}$$
Is B^{-1} a function?   Explain.

10. Graph the following functions over Re.   In each case, state the range.
    (a) $f = \{(x, y) \,|\, y = -2x, |x| \leq 3\}$
    (b) $g = \{(x, y) \,|\, y = x^2 - 8x + 14, |x| \leq 7\}$

11. Graph the inverse of each function in question (10).   Is the inverse in each case a function?

12. Draw the graphs of the following relations in $Re \times Re$.
    (a) $\{(x, y) \,|\, 5x - 4y > 0\} \cap \{(x, y) \,|\, 5x - 4y < 20\}$
    (b) $\{(x, y) \,|\, -(x - 2)^2 \leq (y - 5) \leq (x - 2)^2\}$

13. For the functions m and n, $m(x) = x^2 - 5x + 3$, and $n(x) = 51 - 3x$.   Find the members of the set $\{x \,|\, m(x) = n(x)\}$.

14. For relation g, $g(x) = \sqrt{x}$.   Find an expression for $g^{-1}(x)$.   Find three points on the graph of g and the corresponding points on the graph of g^{-1}.   Find the midpoint of the line joining each of the three pairs of points and show that the midpoint lies on the line $y = x$.

15. Sketch the graphs of g and g^{1-} in question (14).   On a separate set of axes, sketch the graph of h where $h(x) = -\sqrt{x}$ and the graph of h^{-1}.

16. For the function (in $Re \times Re$)
$$t : x \rightarrow x^2 - 12x + 25,$$
find the domain and range.   Also find the domain and range of t^{-1}.

17. For the mapping $f : x \rightarrow \dfrac{5}{x^2 + 5}$,
   (a) draw the Cartesian graph for $|x| \leq 5$,
   (b) find the domain and range of f in $Re \times Re$,
   (c) on the same set of axes, graph f^{-1},
   (d) find the domain and range of f^{-1}.
   (e) Is f^{-1} a function?   Explain.

18. Draw the graph of the region defined by
$$\{(x, y) \mid y > 3x^2, \ x \in Re\} \cap \{(x, y) \mid 2y < x + 5, \quad x \in Re\}.$$

19. If
$$f : A \rightarrow B,$$
C and D are subsets of A, and H and G are subsets of B, prove each of the following.
   (i) $f(C \cup D) = f(C) \cup f(D)$
   (ii) $f(C \cap D)$ is a subset of $f(C) \cap f(D)$.
   (iii) $f^{-1}(G \cup H) = f^{-1}(G) \cup f^{-1}(H)$
   (iv) $f^{-1}(G \cap H) = f^{-1}(G) \cap f^{-1}(H)$
Give an example of a function for which the inclusion of (ii) is proper.

20. In the notation of the previous question, prove that D is a subset of $f^{-1}(f(D))$ and that $f(f^{-1}(H))$ is a subset of H.   Give examples of functions for which the inclusions are proper.

Chapter **2**

SECOND DEGREE RELATIONS
IN THE PLANE

2.1.   The Circle

From our definition of a circle as a set of points in a plane that are a constant distance from a given point in the plane, we can, by using a rectangular co-ordinate system, develop an equation for the circle.   Let $P(x, y)$ be any point in the plane.

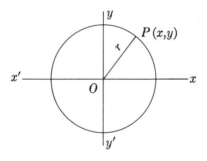

Figure 2.1

$P(x, y)$ lies on the circle with centre at the origin and radius r units if, and only if, $OP = r$.   Therefore,

$$\sqrt{x^2 + y^2} = r \quad \text{or} \quad x^2 + y^2 = r^2.$$

Therefore, the equation of the circle is $x^2 + y^2 = r^2$.

Example 1. Find an equation of the circle with radius $3/2$ units and centre at the origin.

Solution: The equation of the circle is

$$x^2 + y^2 = \tfrac{9}{4},$$

or, with integral coefficients,

$$4x^2 + 4y^2 = 9.$$

25

Example 2.   Find the radius of the circle represented by

$$25x^2 + 25y^2 = 8 .$$

Solution: An equation equivalent to the given equation is

$$x^2 + y^2 = \tfrac{8}{25} .$$

Therefore, the radius of the circle is $\sqrt{\tfrac{8}{25}}$ units or $\tfrac{2}{5}\sqrt{2}$ units.

We have previously studied the relation

$$C = \{(x, y) \mid x^2 + y^2 = 25, \quad x, y \in Re\} .$$

Let us sketch the graph of C by determining the intercepts, the domain, the range, and any symmetry that exists.

Intercepts

In the relation $\qquad\qquad x^2 + y^2 = 25 ,$

if
$$y = 0 ,$$
then
$$x^2 = 25 , \qquad\text{and}$$
and
$$x = \pm 5 .$$

if
$$x = 0 ,$$
then
$$y^2 = 25 ,$$
and
$$y = \pm 5 .$$

Therefore, the x-intercepts are ± 5.   The points $(5, 0)$ and $(-5, 0)$ are on the graph. The y-intercepts are ± 5.   The points $(0, 5)$ and $(0, -5)$ are on the graph.

We have established that the four points shown in Figure 2.2 are on the graph.

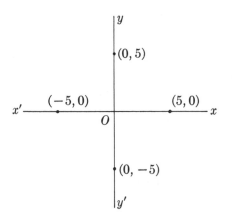

Figure 2.2

Domain

If
$$x^2 + y^2 = 25 \,,$$
then
$$y^2 = 25 - x^2 \,,$$
and
$$y = \pm\sqrt{25 - x^2} \,.$$

For $y \in Re$,
$$25 - x^2 \geq 0$$
and
$$x^2 \leq 25 \,;$$
therefore,
$$|\,x\,| \leq 5 \,.$$

The domain of the relation is $\{x \in Re \mid \ |\,x\,| \leq 5\}$.

Range

Similarly,
$$x^2 = 25 - y^2 \,,$$
and
$$x = \pm\sqrt{25 - y^2} \,.$$

For $x \in Re$, $|\,y\,| \leq 5$.   The range of the relation is $\{y \in Re \mid \ |\,y\,| \leq 5\}$.

We now know that the graph is confined to that region of the plane bounded by and inside the broken lines in Figure 2.3.

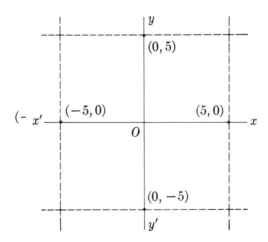

Figure 2.3

Symmetry

In the equation

$$x^2 + y^2 = 25 ,$$

if we replace x by $-x$ *or* if we replace y by $-y$, the equation is unchanged and so the graph is symmetrical with respect to the y-axis and the x-axis.

In the equation

$$x^2 + y^2 = 25 ,$$

if x is replaced by $-x$ *and* y by $-y$, the equation is unchanged and, therefore, the graph is symmetrical with respect to the origin.

Checking for symmetry enables us to sketch the graph quickly. For each point plotted in the first quadrant, we can immediately plot its *reflection* in the axis of symmetry or in the origin.

For $$x^2 + y^2 = 25 ,$$

a suitable table of values is

x	3	4
y	4	3

From the points $(3, 4)$ and $(4, 3)$, we can plot 6 other points by symmetry, as shown in Figure 2.4.

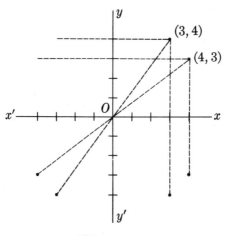

Figure 2.4

It appears that the complete graph of relation C is a circle with centre the origin and radius 5 as shown in Figure 2.5.

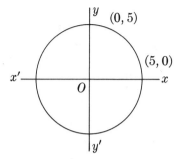

Figure 2.5

It should be noted that, if the graph of a relation is symmetrical about both the x-axis and the y-axis, it is symmetrical about the origin. The converse of this statement is not necessarily true. For example, the graph of $xy = 8$ is symmetrical about the origin but not symmetrical about either axis. Check by applying the three tests above. See question 5(h) in Exercise 2.1.

Example 3.   Sketch the graph of

$$\{(x, y) \mid x^2 + y^2 < 25, \quad x > 0, \quad y < 0, \quad x, y \in Re\}.$$

Solution: The solution set of $\{(x,y) \mid x^2 + y^2 < 25, x,y \in Re\}$ is the set of all points inside the circle, whose equation is $x^2 + y^2 = 25$. The solution set of $\{(x,y) \mid x > 0, y < 0, x,y \in Re\}$ is the set of all points in the fourth quadrant not including the co-ordinate axes. The required solution set is the intersection of these two sets and is shown in Figure 2.6.

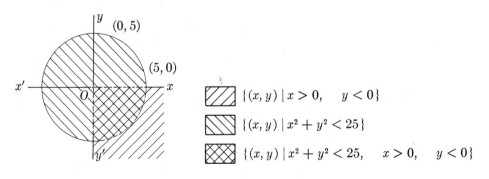

Figure 2.6

EXERCISE 2.1

1. State equations for circles with centre at the origin and the following radii.

   (a) 4   (b) $\dfrac{3}{5}$ (c) $2\sqrt{2}$ (d) $\dfrac{1}{\sqrt{3}}$ (e) $\dfrac{1}{4}\sqrt{7}$

2. Find equations for the circles, centre $(0,0)$, which pass through the following points.

   (a) $(5, 12)$ (b) $(1, 2)$ (c) $(0, 3\sqrt{3})$

   (d) $(-2, -5)$ (e) $(4, 5)$ (f) $(-6, -8)$

3. What are the radii of the circles represented by the following equations?

   (a) $x^2 + y^2 = 49$ (b) $x^2 + y^2 = 12$

   (c) $4x^2 + 4y^2 = 81$ (d) $25x^2 + 25y^2 = 18$

4. For each of the following, find the intercepts, domain, and range, and sketch the graph $(x, y \in Re)$.

   (a) $x^2 + y^2 = 4$ (b) $3x^2 + 3y^2 = 1$

   (c) $25x^2 + 25y^2 = 64$ (d) $x^2 + y^2 = 6$

5. Apply the three tests for symmetry of Section 2.1 to determine what symmetry, if any, is possessed by the graphs of each of the following.

   (a) $4x^2 + 9y^2 = 36$ (b) $y = 3x^2$

   (c) $y = x^3$ (d) $3x + 5y = 15$

   (e) $y^2 = 4x - 16$ (f) $x^2 - y^2 = 4$

   (g) $y = |x|$ (h) $xy = 8$

6. For each of the following points, determine whether it is outside, inside, or on the circle defined by $x^2 + y^2 = 25$.

   (a) $(-5, 0)$ (b) $(-1, -4.5)$ (c) $(4, -3)$

   (d) $(-1, 2\sqrt{6})$ (e) $(1, 2\sqrt{6})$ (f) $(4, 3.5)$

7. Sketch the graphs of the relations defined by the following inequalities $(x, y \in Re)$.

   (a) $x^2 + y^2 > 1$ (b) $x^2 + y^2 \le 9$

   (c) $x^2 + y^2 \le 4,\ x < 0,\ y > 0$ (d) $4x^2 + 4y^2 < 9,\ y < x$

8. Sketch the graphs of the following relations $(x, y \in Re)$.

   (a) $\{(x, y) \mid x^2 + y^2 \ge 16\} \cap \{(x, y) \mid y > 2x - 4\}$

   (b) $\{(x, y) \mid x^2 + y^2 < 25\} \cap \{(x, y) \mid 4x^2 + 4y^2 > 9\}$

   (c) $\{(x, y) \mid x^2 + y^2 < 1\} \cup \{(x, y) \mid x^2 + y^2 \ge 4\}$

   (d) $\{(x, y) \mid x^2 + y^2 \le 25\} \cap \{(x, y) \mid x^2 + y^2 \ge 4\} \cap \{(x, y) \mid x < 0,\ y < 0\}$

9. For each of the following determine the intercepts, the domain, and the range; discuss the symmetry and sketch the graph $(x, y \in Re)$.

(a) $\{(x, y) \mid x^2 + y^2 = 16, \ |x| > 1\}$

(b) $\{(x, y) \mid x^2 + y^2 - 4y = 5\}$ (Complete the square of the terms in y.)

(c) $\{(x, y) \mid x^2 + 2x + y^2 = 8\}$

2.2.   Circle Problems Solved by Analytic Methods (Supplementary)

Example 1.   A chord of the circle $x^2 + y^2 = 65$ is represented by $3x - y + 5 = 0$. Find the length of the chord.

Solution: If
$$3x - y + 5 = 0,$$
then
$$y = 3x + 5.$$
Therefore, at the end-points of the chord,
$$x^2 + (3x + 5)^2 = 65,$$
or
$$10x^2 + 30x - 40 = 0,$$
$$x^2 + 3x - 4 = 0,$$
$$(x + 4)(x - 1) = 0.$$

Hence, $x = -4$ or $x = 1$, and $y = -7$ or $y = 8$.   Therefore, the endpoints of the chord are $(-4, -7)$ and $(1, 8)$.   The length of the chord is
$$\sqrt{(1 + 4)^2 + (8 + 7)^2} = 5\sqrt{10}.$$

Example 2.   Find the length of the tangent drawn from the point $A\,(16, 12)$ to the circle whose equation is $x^2 + y^2 = 100$.

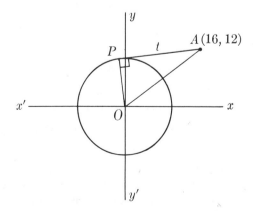

Solution: Suppose that t units is the length of the tangent AP where P is the point of contact. $\angle APO = 90°$;
thus,

$$t^2 = AO^2 - OP^2$$
$$= (16 - 0)^2 + (12 - 0)^2 - 100$$
$$= 256 + 144 - 100$$
$$= 300 .$$

Therefore,
$$t = 10\sqrt{3} .$$

The length of the tangent AP is $10\sqrt{3}$ units.

EXERCISE 2.2

1. A chord of the circle $x^2 + y^2 = 36$ joins the point of intersection of the circle and the x-axis to a point of intersection of the circle and the y-axis.
   Find the length of the perpendicular from the centre of the circle to such a chord.

√2. A circle, centre the origin, passes through $A(2, \sqrt{21})$ and $B(-\sqrt{21}, 2)$.
   Find an equation of the circle and show that the perpendicular bisector of chord AB passes through the centre of the circle.

3. For each of the following circles, the co-ordinates of the midpoint of a chord are given.   Find the length of the chord and an equation of the chord.
   (a) $x^2 + y^2 = 25$ $(0, 4)$ (b) $x^2 + y^2 = 25$ $(1, 2)$
   (c) $4x^2 + 4y^2 = 57$ $(-2, \frac{5}{2})$ (d) $x^2 + y^2 = 16$ $(5, 6)$

4. There is no solution in question 3(d).   Explain.

5. In each of the following, the equation of a circle and the co-ordinates of a point not on the circle are given.   Find the length of the tangent from the given point.
   √(a) $x^2 + y^2 = 25$ $(6, 5)$ (b) $4x^2 + 4y^2 = 81$ $(6.5, 7)$
   √(c) $x^2 + y^2 = 3$ $(-3, 7)$ (d) $x^2 + y^2 = 169$ $(11, 20)$
   √(e) $x^2 + y^2 = 100$ $(3, 4)$

6. There is no solution in question 5(e).   Explain.

7. Develop a formula for the length of a tangent from $A(x_1, y_1)$ to the circle defined by $x^2 + y^2 = r^2$.   Is there any restriction on x_1 and y_1?   Explain.

8. Use the result of question (7) to calculate the lengths of the tangents in question (5).

9. A and A' are the points of intersection of the circle represented by $x^2 + y^2 = r^2$ and the x-axis.   If $P(m, n)$ is any point on the circle, prove that angle APA' is a right angle.   State this result in general terms.

✓ 10. Find an equation for the circle with centre $(2, 1)$ and radius 5 units.

✓ 11. For the circle in question (10), find the length of the tangent drawn to the circle from the point $(-5, 7)$.

2.3.   The Parabola

In an earlier course, we have studied the relation

$$P = \{(x, y) \mid y = ax^2, \quad x \in Re, \quad a > 0\}.$$

Let us sketch the graph of P by determining the intercepts, domain, range, and any symmetry that exists.

Intercepts

In the relation

$$y = ax^2,$$

if		if
$y = 0,$		$x = 0,$
then	and	then
$x = 0,$		$y = 0.$

The only x-intercept is zero and the only y-intercept is zero.   The origin lies on the graph of P and is the only point of either axis to do so.

Domain

Since $y = ax^2$, there is a real value of y for all $x \in Re$.   The domain is Re.

Range

Since $x^2 = \dfrac{y}{a}$, then $x = \pm\sqrt{\dfrac{y}{a}}$. For real values of x, we have $y \geq 0$. The range is $\{y \mid y \in Re, y \geq 0\}$. It now appears that the graph is confined to the region shaded in Figure 2.7.

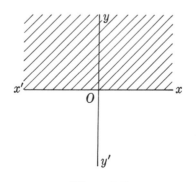

Figure 2.7

Symmetry

In $y = ax^2$, when x is replaced by $-x$, the equation is unchanged, and therefore the graph is symmetrical with respect to the y-axis. Replacing y by $-y$ or replacing both x by $-x$ and y by $-y$ changes the equation, and therefore, symmetry with respect to the x-axis and symmetry with respect to the origin do not exist.

For each point plotted in the first quadrant, we may plot its reflection in the y-axis. That is, each point (x,y) in the first quadrant has an image or reflection $(-x,y)$ in the second quadrant. The graph, which is shown in Figure 2.8, is a parabola opening upward, with its vertex at the origin and its axis of symmetry is the y-axis.

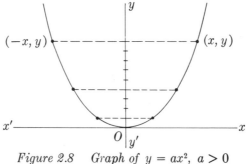

Figure 2.8   Graph of $y = ax^2$, $a > 0$

Now suppose $a < 0$. The discussion above may be repeated without change except for the fact that the range is $\{y \mid y \leq 0, y \in Re\}$ since $x = \pm \sqrt{\dfrac{y}{a}}$ and $a < 0$. The graph is a *parabola* opening downward, vertex at the origin and the y-axis as the axis of symmetry. See Figure 2.9.

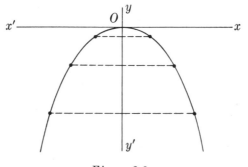

Figure 2.9

Imagine a line passing through a fixed point in space and tangent to a circle whose plane is perpendicular to the line joining its centre to the fixed point (Figure 2.10). The locus of points on all such lines through the fixed point is a surface called a right circular cone.

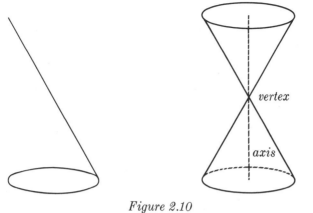

Figure 2.10

We say that the cone is a surface generated by a line passing through a fixed point (vertex) and touching a circle whose plane is perpendicular to the line (axis) joining its centre to the fixed point. As shown in Figure 2.10, the cone consists of two nappes, one above and one below the vertex.

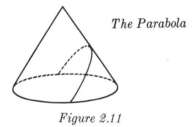

The Parabola

Figure 2.11

The curve of intersection of a right circular cone by a plane is called a conic section or, sometimes, a conic. If the cutting plane is parallel to the generating line (Figure 2.11), the conic is called a parabola. This is the curve we have studied from an analytic point of view in this section. Under the assumption of negligible air resistance, any ball thrown or kicked is found to follow a parabolic path. The path of a projectile or missile near the surface of the earth is also parabolic. If a load is uniformly distributed along the bridge, the cable of a suspension bridge assumes a parabolic form.

The laminated arches that support the roofs in many modern buildings and also the supporting arches of bridges are often parabolic.

EXERCISE 2.3

For the relations defined by each of the following, find the intercepts, domain, range, and symmetry, and sketch the graph.

1. $y = -x^2$
2. $y = 4x^2$
3. $y = \frac{1}{4}x^2$
4. $2y = 5x^2$
5. $x^2 = -8y$
6. $x^2 = 16y$

Use the solutions for questions (1) to (6) above to sketch the regions defined by the following inequalities.

7. $y > 4x^2$ 8. $y > 4x^2,$ $x > 0$ 9. $x^2 < -8y$

10. $x^2 < -8y,$ $x < 0$ 11. $y > \frac{1}{4}x^2,$ $y < 4x^2$ 12. $y < 4x^2,$ $-8y < x^2$

13. The point with co-ordinates $(8, -8)$ is on the graph defined by
$$-ky = x^2 .$$
What is the value of k?

14. Describe the graph defined by $x^2 = my$ when m is replaced by zero. (This graph is called a degenerate parabola.) Can you give a geometric interpretation by referring to Figure 2.9?

15. By analogy to the graph of
$$y = 4x^2 ;$$
that is,
$$y - 0 = 4(x - 0)^2 ,$$
sketch the graph of
$$y - 2 = 4(x - 1)^2 .$$

16. Sketch the graph defined by $y = 3x^2 - 12x + 7.$ First reduce the equation to the form $y - d = a(x - m)^2.$

17. Repeat question (16) for $y = -4x^2 - 24x - 34.$

18. As a increases from zero through positive values, describe the change that takes place in the graph defined by $y = ax^2.$

2.4.   The Ellipse

Let us sketch the graph of the relation E where
$$E = \{(x, y) \mid 4x^2 + 9y^2 = 36, \quad x, y \in Re\} .$$

Intercepts

In
$$4x^2 + 9y^2 = 36 ,$$
if
$$y = 0 ,$$
then
$$x^2 = 9 ,$$
and
$$x = +3 \quad \text{or} \quad -3 .$$

The x-intercepts are ± 3 and the points $(3, 0)$ and $(-3, 0)$ are on the graph.

In the equation
$$4x^2 + 9y^2 = 36 ,$$
if
$$x = 0 ,$$
then
$$y^2 = 4 ,$$
and
$$y = +2 \quad \text{or} \quad -2 .$$

The y-intercepts are ± 2 and the points $(0, 2)$ and $(0, -2)$ are on the graph.

Domain

Since
$$4x^2 + 9y^2 = 36 ,$$
then
$$9y^2 = 36 - 4x^2 ,$$
and
$$3y = \pm \sqrt{36 - 4x^2} .$$
For real values of y,
$$36 - 4x^2 \geq 0 ,$$
so that
$$4x^2 \leq 36 ,$$
and
$$x^2 \leq 9 ,$$
and
$$|x| \leq 3 .$$
The domain is $\{x \mid x \in Re, \ -3 \leq x \leq 3\}$.

Range

Since
$$4x^2 + 9y^2 = 36 ,$$
then
$$4x^2 = 36 - 9y^2 ,$$
and
$$2x = \pm \sqrt{36 - 9y^2} .$$
For real values of x,
$$36 - 9y^2 \geq 0 ,$$
so that
$$9y^2 \leq 36 ,$$
and
$$y^2 \leq 4 ,$$
and
$$|y| \leq 2 .$$
The range is $\{y \mid y \in Re, \ -2 \leq y \leq 2\}$.

We now know that the graph is restricted to the shaded rectangular region in Figure 2.12.

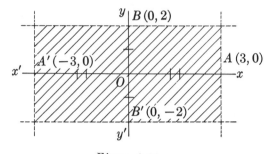

Figure 2.12

Symmetry

The equation $4x^2 + 9y^2 = 36$ is unchanged when x is replaced by $-x$.   The graph is symmetric with respect to the y-axis.

The equation is unchanged when y is replaced by $-y$.   The graph is symmetric with respect to the x-axis.

The equation is also unchanged when x is replaced by $-x$ *and* y by $-y$. The graph must be symmetric with respect to the origin.

It will be sufficient to plot points in the first quadrant. Points in the other three quadrants may be determined by symmetry (Figure 2.13). A table of values precedes the figure. Some values of y in the table are approximate. The graph is called an *ellipse* with centre at the origin.

x	y
0	2
1	1.9
2	1.5
2.5	1.1
3	0

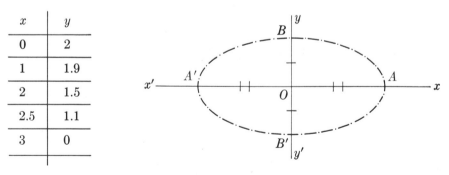

Figure 2.13

In the ellipse, the line segment AA' is called the *major axis* and the line segment BB' the *minor axis*.   The line segment OA or OA' is called the *semi-major axis* and the line segment OB or OB' the *semi-minor axis*.   The point O is called the *centre* and the points A and A', which are the end-points of the major axis, are called the *vertices* of the ellipse.

Consider the equation $4x^2 + 9y^2 = 36$. If both members are divided by 36, we obtain

$$\frac{x^2}{9} + \frac{y^2}{4} = 1 \, ,$$

or

$$\frac{x^2}{3^2} + \frac{y^2}{2^2} = 1 \, .$$

Note that the denominators on the left side are the squares of the x-and y-intercepts. Similarly, any relation whose defining equation is of the form

$$\frac{x^2}{a^2} + \frac{y^2}{b^2} = 1$$

(where a and b are unequal positive real numbers and $a > b$) has as its graph the ellipse shown in Figure 2.14.

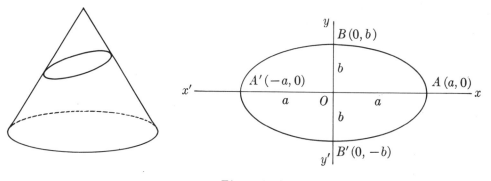

Figure 2.14

We say that the semi-major axis is a units in length and that the semi-minor axis is b units in length. The origin is the centre of the ellipse. An ellipse is sometimes referred to as a central conic.

The Ellipse

When a cutting plane cuts entirely across one nappe of a cone, the conic section obtained is the ellipse.

The orbits of the planets, including our own, are ellipses. Man-made satellites travel around the earth in elliptical orbits. The question of elliptical orbits for the planets (versus circular orbits) was the subject of bitter debate during the Renaissance. Consult an encyclopedia or other reference work for articles on Galileo and Kepler.

The arches of bridges are frequently constructed in the form of semi-ellipses.

Elliptical gears are used in machines such as power machines, where slow and powerful motion is needed during a part of each revolution.

EXERCISE 2.4

For the relations defined by each of the following, find the intercepts, domain, range, symmetry, and sketch the graph.

1. $16x^2 + 25y^2 = 400$ 2. $12x^2 + 25y^2 = 300$

3. $x^2 + 9y^2 = 9$ 4. $2x^2 + 5y^2 = 40$

5. $\dfrac{x^2}{3} + y^2 = 1$ 6. $\dfrac{x^2}{64} + \dfrac{y^2}{9} = 1$

7. For each of the ellipses sketched in questions (1) to (6), state
    (a) the lengths of the semi-major and semi-minor axes,
    (b) the co-ordinates of the vertices.

Use the solution for questions (1) to (6) above to sketch the regions defined by the following inequalities.

8. $16x^2 + 25y^2 < 400$ 9. $x^2 + 9y^2 > 9$

10. $16x^2 + 25y^2 < 400,\ x < 0$ 11. $2x^2 + 5y^2 \geq 40,\quad x > 0,\quad y < 0$

12. $x^2 > y,\quad 16x^2 + 25y^2 < 400$ 13. $x^2 + y^2 > 1,\quad \dfrac{x^2}{64} + \dfrac{y^2}{9} < 1$

14. The point whose co-ordinates are $(2, -3)$ is on the graph of the relation defined by $9x^2 + ky^2 = 54$.   What is the value of k?

15. Describe the ellipse with centre at the origin and both semi-axes equal to 4. What is the equation of this ellipse?

16. Are the points whose co-ordinates are given outside, inside, or on the ellipse defined by
$$4x^2 + 9y^2 = 36?$$
    (a) $(-2, -1)$ (b) $(3, -2)$ (c) $(-1, 1.5)$ (d) $\left(-2, -\dfrac{2\sqrt{5}}{3}\right)$

17. By analogy to the graph of
$$\frac{x^2}{a^2} + \frac{y^2}{b^2} = 1\,,$$
    that is,
$$\frac{(x - 0)^2}{a^2} + \frac{(y - 0)^2}{b^2} = 1$$
    sketch the graph of $\dfrac{(x - 3)^2}{25} + \dfrac{(y - 1)^2}{16} = 1$.

18. Repeat question (17) for $\dfrac{(x + 5)^2}{4} + \dfrac{(y + 1)^2}{1} = 1$.

2.5.   The Hyperbola

Let us sketch the graph of relation H where

$$H = \{(x, y) \mid 4x^2 - 9y^2 = 36, \quad x, y \in Re\} .$$

Intercepts

In the equation
$$4x^2 - 9y^2 = 36 ,$$
if
$$y = 0 ,$$
then
$$x^2 = 9 ,$$
and
$$x = +3 \text{ or } -3 .$$

The x-intercepts are ± 3 and the points $(3, 0)$ and $(-3, 0)$ are on the graph.

In the equation
$$4x^2 - 9y^2 = 36 ,$$
if
$$x = 0 ,$$
then
$$y^2 = -4 .$$

There is no real value of y that satisfies this equation.   There are no y-intercepts and the graph has no points on the y-axis.

Domain

Since
$$4x^2 - 9y^2 = 36 ,$$
then
$$9y^2 = 4x^2 - 36 ,$$
and
$$3y = \pm\sqrt{4x^2 - 36} .$$
For real values of y,
$$4x^2 - 36 \geq 0 ,$$
so that
$$4x^2 \geq 36 ,$$
and
$$x^2 \geq 9 ,$$
and
$$|x| \geq 3 .$$

The domain is $\{x \mid x \in Re, x \geq 3 \text{ or } x \leq -3\}$.

Range

Since

$$4x^2 - 9y^2 = 36\,,$$

then

$$4x^2 = 9y^2 + 36, \quad \text{and} \quad 2x = \pm\sqrt{9y^2 + 36}\,.$$

For real values of x,

$$9y^2 + 36 \geq 0\,.$$

Since $9y^2 + 36 \geq 0$ for all $y \in Re$, the range is Re. We now know that the graph is restricted to the shaded region in Figure 2.15.

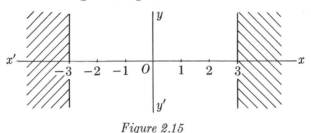

Symmetry.

Figure 2.15

Since the equation

$$4x^2 - 9y^2 = 36$$

is unchanged when x is replaced by $-x$, the graph is symmetric with respect to the y-axis. Since the equation is unchanged when y is replaced by $-y$, the graph is symmetric with respect to the x-axis.   The equation is also unchanged when x is replaced by $-x$ *and y is replaced by* $-y$ so that the graph must be symmetric with respect to the origin.

It is sufficient to plot points in the first quadrant. Points in the other three quadrants may be determined by symmetry. A table of values precedes Figure 2.16. Some values of y in the table are approximate.

x	y
3	0
3.5	1.2
4	1.8
5	2.7

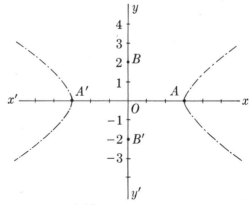

Figure 2.16

The graph is called a *hyperbola* with centre at the origin. If we divide both members of the defining equation by 36, we obtain

$$\frac{x^2}{9} - \frac{y^2}{4} = 1, \quad \text{or} \quad \frac{x^2}{3^2} - \frac{y^2}{2^2} = 1.$$

Note that, as in the case of the ellipse, the denominator of the first term is the square of the x-intercept.

The line segment AA' is called the *transverse axis* of the hyperbola and the points A and A' are the vertices of the curve.

The denominator of the second term locates for us the points $B(0, 2)$ and $B'(0, -2)$ on the y-axis. While there are no y-intercepts, the segment BB' of the y-axis is called the *conjugate axis* of the hyperbola.

Similarly, any relation whose defining equation is of the form

$$\frac{x^2}{a^2} - \frac{y^2}{b^2} = 1$$

(where a and b are positive real numbers) has as its graph the hyperbola shown in Figure 2.17.

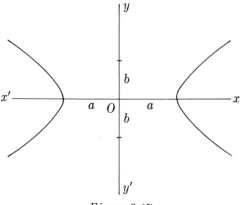

Figure 2.17

The semi-transverse axis is a units in length and the semi-conjugate axis is b units in length. The hyperbola, like the ellipse and the circle, is a central conic.

The Hyperbola

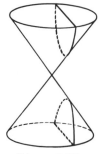

Figure 2.18

If both nappes of a right circular cone are cut by the same plane, the resulting conic section is a hyperbola.   The parabola, ellipse, and hyperbola were named and studied thoroughly by the ancient Greek geometers.   Using synthetic methods they discovered many properties of these curves, including the definitions of the conics which we shall use in the next chapter.

The hyperbola is the graph of many relations in science, for example Boyle's Law, which relates the volume of a gas to its pressure if the temperature is constant.

The properties of the hyperbola are important in modern navigation systems such as Loran.   Further reference will be made to this in the next chapter.

EXERCISE 2.5

For the relations defined by each of the following, find the intercepts, domain, range, symmetry, and sketch the graph.

1. $16x^2 - 25y^2 = 400$

2. $25x^2 - 4y^2 = 100$

3. $5x^2 - y^2 = 20$

4. $\dfrac{x^2}{20} - \dfrac{y^2}{49} = 1$

5. $4x^2 - y^2 = 1$

6. $x^2 - y^2 = 25$

7. For each of the hyperbolas in questions (1) to (6), state

   (a) the lengths of the semi-transverse and semi-conjugate axes,

   (b) the co-ordinates of the vertices.

8. The hyperbola in question (6) is called an equilateral hyperbola.   Suggest the reason for this name.

Use the solutions for questions (1) to (6) above to sketch the regions defined by the following inequalities.

9. $16x^2 - 25y^2 < 400$

10. $5x^2 - y^2 > 20$

11. $16x^2 - 25y^2 < 400, \quad x, y < 0$

12. $\dfrac{x^2}{20} - \dfrac{y^2}{49} > 1, \quad x > 0$

13. $4x^2 - y^2 < 1, \quad x^2 + y^2 < 1$

14. $x^2 < y, \quad x^2 - y^2 < 25$

15. The point whose co-ordinates are $(\frac{3}{2}, -2\sqrt{2})$ is on the graph of the relation defined by $4x^2 - ky^2 = 1$.   What is the value of k?

16. Describe the graph defined by

$$\frac{x^2}{16 - m} + \frac{y^2}{9 - m} = 1$$

when   (a) $m < 9$,   (b) $9 < m < 16$.

17. By comparison with the graph of

$$\frac{x^2}{a^2} - \frac{y^2}{b^2} = 1, \quad \text{that is,} \quad \frac{(x-0)^2}{a^2} - \frac{(y-0)^2}{b^2} = 1,$$

sketch the hyperbola defined by

$$\frac{(x-3)^2}{25} - \frac{y^2}{16} = 1.$$

18. Repeat question (17) for

$$\frac{(x+4)^2}{49} - \frac{(y-5)^2}{64} = 1.$$

2.6.   Another Defining Equation for the Hyperbola

Example 1.   Sketch the graph of the relation

$$H_1 = \{(x, y) \mid xy = 36, x, y \in Re\}.$$

Solution:

Intercepts.   Replacing either x or y by 0 in $xy = 36$ does not produce a value for the other variable.   There are no x- or y-intercepts.

Domain.   Since

$$xy = 36,$$

$$y = \frac{36}{x}.$$

Real values of y are produced by all $x \in Re$ except zero.   The domain is $\{x \mid x \in Re, x \neq 0\}$.

Range.   Since

$$xy = 36,$$

$$x = \frac{36}{y}.$$

Real values of x correspond to all $y \in Re$ except zero.   The range is $\{y \mid y \in Re, y \neq 0\}$.

Symmetry.   The equation $xy = 36$ is changed when x is replaced by $-x$. The graph is not symmetric with respect to the y-axis. The equation is also changed when y is replaced by $-y$. The graph is not symmetric with respect to the x-axis. The equation is unchanged when x is replaced by $-x$ *and* y is replaced by $-y$. The graph is symmetric with respect to the origin.

Since $xy = 36$, x and y are both positive or both negative. Symmetry about the origin means that each point plotted in the first quadrant has its reflection in the third quadrant. The required graph, preceded by a table of values, is shown in Figure 2.19

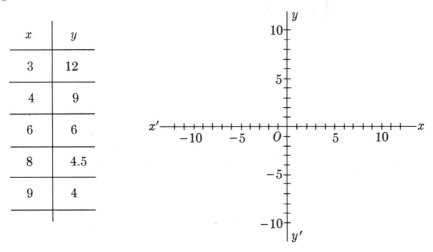

x	y
3	12
4	9
6	6
8	4.5
9	4

Figure 2.19

The graph is a hyperbola. It is actually an equilateral hyperbola such as that defined by $x^2 - y^2 = 25$. The transverse axis lies on the line lying in the first and third quadrants and bisecting the angle between the co-ordinate axes.

Example 2.   Sketch the graph of the relation

$$L = \{ (x, y) \mid 4x^2 - 9y^2 = 0, \quad x, y \in Re \} .$$

Solution:

Intercepts.   In the equation $4x^2 - 9y^2 = 0$,

if   if

$\qquad y = 0 ,$ $\qquad x = 0 ,$

then   and   then

$\qquad x = 0 .$ $\qquad y = 0 .$

The x- and y-intercepts are both zero.   The origin is on the graph.

Domain.   If

$$4x^2 - 9y^2 = 0 ,$$

then

$$9y^2 = 4x^2 ,$$

and

$$3y = \pm 2x .$$

For real values of y, we see that $2x$ must be real and this is true for all $x \in Re$. The domain is Re.

Range.   Similarly, $2x = \pm 3y$.   The range is Re.

Symmetry.   Applying the three tests for symmetry to the equation $4x^2 - 9y^2 = 0$ shows that the graph is symmetric with respect to both axes and the origin.   This symmetry allows us to plot points in the second, third, and fourth quadrants as reflections of first quadrant points.

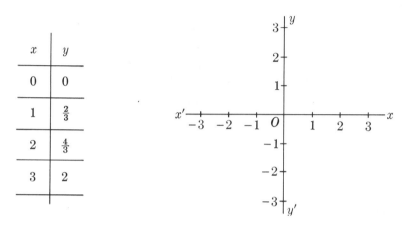

x	y
0	0
1	$\frac{2}{3}$
2	$\frac{4}{3}$
3	2

Figure 2.20

The graph, shown in Figure 2.20, is a pair of straight lines through the origin. *Note:* The defining equation of the relation L may be written as

$$(2x - 3y)(2x + 3y) = 0.$$

Therefore,

$$2x - 3y = 0 \quad \text{or} \quad 2x + 3y = 0.$$

Hence, if the co-ordinates of a point (x, y) satisfy the equation $4x^2 - 9y^2 = 0$ they must satisfy one or the other of $2x - 3y = 0$ or $2x + 3y = 0$.   Conversely, it must also be true that a point whose co-ordinates satisfy one or the other of $2x - 3y = 0$ or $2x + 3y = 0$ has co-ordinates that satisfy $4x^2 - 9y^2 = 0$.   Therefore, the graph of L is the graph of

$$\{(x, y) \mid 2x - 3y = 0 \quad \text{or} \quad 2x + 3y = 0\}.$$

The graph of L is then the pair of straight lines defined by

$$2x - 3y = 0 \quad \text{and} \quad 2x + 3y = 0.$$

Such a pair of straight lines is called a degenerate conic.   The cutting plane passes through the vertex of the cone.

Example 3.   Sketch the graph of the relation

$$\{ (x, y) \mid x^2 - 5x + 6 = 0 \} .$$

Solution: The defining equation may be rewritten as

$$(x - 2)(x - 3) = 0 .$$

Therefore, $x - 2 = 0$ or $x - 3 = 0$. The graph (Figure 2.21) is the two parallel straight lines defined by

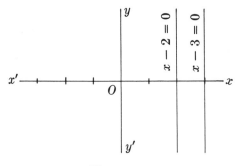

Figure 2.21

EXERCISE 2.6

Sketch the graphs of the relations defined by the following equations.

1. $xy = 4$ 2. $xy = -4$

3. $xy = \frac{25}{2}$ 4. $4x^2 - y^2 = 0$

5. $x^2 - 8x + 12 = 0$ 6. $x^2 - xy - 12y^2 = 0$

7. $8x^2 + 2xy - 15y^2 = 0$ 8. $(x - 3)^2 + 3(x - 3) + 2 = 0$

9. $3x^2 + 8xy - 35y^2 = 0$ 10. $y^2 - 4y - 45 = 0$

11. Compare the graph in question (3) with that of $x^2 - y^2 = 25$ (question (6) in Exercise 2.5). What appears to be an analogous conclusion for the graphs of $\qquad\qquad x^2 - y^2 = a^2$ and $xy = \dfrac{a^2}{2}$?

Use the solutions for questions (1) to (10) to assist in the constructions of the graphs of the following inequalities.

12. $xy < 4$ 13. $4x^2 - y^2 \geq 0$

14. $x - 6 < 0$ and $x - 2 > 0$ 15. $x^2 - 8x + 12 > 0$

16. $y - 9 > 0$ or $y + 5 < 0$ 17. $xy < 4$ and $x^2 + y^2 < 25$

18. Using the same set of axes, sketch the graphs of
$$4x^2 - y^2 = 0$$
and
$$4x^2 - y^2 = 4 .$$

19. Repeat question (17) for $16x^2 - 25y^2 = 0$ and $16x^2 - 25y^2 = 400$. Can you suggest an alternative method for drawing the hyperbola? The lines defined by
$$4x \pm 5y = 0$$
are called the *asymptotes* of the hyperbola.

Chapter Summary

The equation of a circle · Analytic methods for circle problems (supplementary) · Graphs of the circle, parabola, ellipse, and hyperbola · Conics as sections of a right circular cone · The corresponding inequalities and their graphs · The equilateral hyperbola defined by $xy = k$ · Pairs of straight lines

REVIEW EXERCISE 2

1. State equations for circles with centre at the origin and the following radii.
   (a) 10   (b) $\frac{4}{9}$ (c) $\sqrt{5}$ (d) $\frac{1}{3}\sqrt{13}$

2. Find equations for the circles, centre $(0, 0)$, that pass through the following points.
   (a) $(8, -6)$ (b) $(-2\sqrt{5}, 3)$ (c) $(\sqrt{14}, -2)$

3. Find the radii of the circles represented by the following equations.
   (a) $4x^2 + 4y^2 = 25$ (b) $x^2 + y^2 = 28$
   (c) $6x^2 + 6y^2 = 35$ (d) $50x^2 + 50y^2 = 1$

4. Apply the three tests for symmetry used in this chapter to determine what symmetry, if any, is possessed by the graphs of each of the following.
   (a) $x^2 + y^2 = 1$ (b) $x^2 - y^2 = 25$
   (c) $y = 3x^2$ (d) $y = x^5$
   (e) $xy = -32$ (f) $y = |x| + 2$
   (g) $x^2 = 3y - 15$ (h) $4x^2 + 25y^2 = 1$

Sketch the graphs of the relations defined by each of the following.

5. $x^2 + y^2 = 100$ 6. $50x^2 + 50y^2 = 81$

7. $x^2 + y^2 - 2y = 8$ 8. $x^2 + y^2 < 9, x < 0, y > 0$

9. $y = -4x^2$ 10. $x^2 = 10y$

11. $y > -4x^2, \quad x^2 + y^2 < 25$

12. $x^2 > -\dfrac{y}{4}, \quad y < 4x^2$

13. $x^2 + 4y^2 = 20$

14. $\dfrac{x^2}{81} + \dfrac{y^2}{9} = 1$

15. $x^2 + 4y^2 < 20, \quad x < 0, y < 0$

16. $\dfrac{x^2}{81} + \dfrac{y^2}{9} > 1, \quad x^2 + y^2 < 144$

17. $\dfrac{x^2}{16} - \dfrac{y^2}{100} = 1$

18. $x^2 - y^2 = 4$

19. $xy = -25$

20. $x^2 - y^2 < 4, \quad x^2 + y^2 > 1$

21. $x^2 - 6x + 5 = 0$

22. $x^2 - 6x + 9 = 0$

23. $64x^2 - 25y^2 = 0$

24. $3x^2 - 10xy - 8y^2 = 0$

25. $64x^2 - 25y^2 > 0, \quad x^2 + y^2 < 16$

26. $xy > 8, \quad \dfrac{x^2}{25} + \dfrac{y^2}{16} < 1$

If the point whose co-ordinates are indicated is on the graph of the relation whose defining equation is given, find the value of k.

27. $x^2 + y^2 = k, \quad (1, \sqrt{2})$

28. $x^2 = -ky, \quad (4, -1)$

29. $25x^2 + ky^2 = 300, \quad (2, 5\sqrt{2})$

30. $\dfrac{x^2}{40} - \dfrac{y^2}{50} = k, \quad (4\sqrt{10}, 2\sqrt{5})$

31. We have called a pair of straight lines, such as those defined by $4x^2 - 9y^2 = 0$, a degenerate conic. Under what geometric conditions would the degenerate conic be (a) a single straight line, (b) a single point?

32. Given the equation

$$\frac{x^2}{30 - m} + \frac{y^2}{m - 5} = 1,$$

find the set of values of m for which the equation defines
(a) an ellipse, (b) a hyperbola.

Chapter 3

GEOMETRIC DEFINITIONS OF CONICS
TANGENTS TO CONICS

3.1. Focus-Directrix Definition

In Chapter 2, we sketched the conic sections by studying their defining equations. In this chapter, we will develop these same equations using the definition of a conic section as our initial concept.

DEFINITION. A conic section is the set of points in a plane, such that the ratio of the distance of each member of the set from a fixed point (*focus*) to its distance from a fixed line (*directrix*) is constant.

This constant ratio is called the *eccentricity* and is denoted by *e*.

Using the definition, we will examine the general equation of a conic section, the effects of changing the value of the eccentricity and the effect of specifying particular values for it.

The definition requires a fixed point and a fixed line. Once we have selected them, we may then place our co-ordinate axes in any suitable position. It would seem useful to place the fixed point on an axis and the fixed line parallel to an axis in order to simplify the resulting equation.

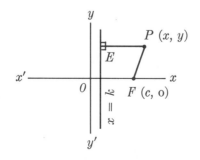

Given: A point $F(c,0)$ and line $x = k$ with PE perpendicular to the line.

51

Required: To develop an equation of a conic section with focus F, directrix the line $x = k$, and eccentricity e.

Solution: P (x,y) is any point on the conic if and only if

$$\frac{PF}{PE} = e.$$

$$PF = e. \, PE$$

$$\sqrt{(x\text{-}c)^2 + y^2} = e\sqrt{(x\text{-}k)^2}$$

Hence,
$$x^2 - 2cx + c^2 + y^2 = e^2 \, (x^2 - 2kx + k^2)$$
$$x^2 - 2cx + c^2 + y^2 = e^2x^2 - 2ke^2x + k^2e^2$$
$$(1 - e^2) \, x^2 + 2 \, (ke^2 - c) \, x + y^2 = k^2e^2 - c^2$$

$$(1)$$

By specifying certain values in this general equation, we should be able to obtain various simplified forms of the equation. Since the eccentricity e may be any ratio, we first substitute values for e.

A   In (1), let $e = 1$ so that $2 \, (k - c) \, x + y^2 = k^2 - c^2$.

The constant term may now be eliminated if we let $k = \pm \, c$.

If $k = +c$, the equation becomes $y^2 = 0$ (the x-axis) which is a trivial solution but, nevertheless, is a degenerate conic with a point on the directrix as focus.

If $k = -c$, the equation becomes $-4cx + y^2 = 0$,
$$y^2 = 4cx \text{ (parabola)}.$$

B   In (1), let $e \neq 1$ and $c = e^2k$ (chosen in order to eliminate the x-term).

Then,
$$(1 - e^2) \, x^2 + y^2 = k^2e^2 - e^4k^2,$$
$$(1 - e^2) \, x^2 + y^2 = k^2e^2 \, (1 - e^2),$$

or

$$\frac{x^2}{k^2e^2} + \frac{y^2}{k^2e^2 \, (1 - e^2)} = 1.$$

$$(2)$$

Now let $k^2e^2 = a^2$ with $a > 0$,

Hence

$$\frac{x^2}{a^2} + \frac{y^2}{a^2 \, (1 - e^2)} = 1.$$

Since $e \neq 1$, then $e < 1$ or $e > 1$.

Suppose $\qquad e < 1, 1 - e^2 > 0.$

Let $\qquad\qquad\qquad a^2 (1 - e^2) = b^2 \qquad (b > 0)$

Then (2) becomes $\qquad\qquad \dfrac{x^2}{a^2} + \dfrac{y^2}{b^2} = 1 \qquad$ (ellipse)

Suppose $\qquad e > 1, 1 - e^2 < 0.$

Let $\qquad\qquad\qquad a^2 (1 - e^2) = - b^2 \ (b > 0)$

Then (2) becomes

$$\frac{x^2}{a^2} - \frac{y^2}{b^2} = 1 \qquad \text{(hyperbola)}$$

EXERCISE 3.1

1. (a) What is the result in equation (2) of the development in Section 3.1 if $e = 0$?
   (b) What problems occur if we let $e = 0$ in (2)?
2. When we let $e = 1$ we obtained the equation of a parabola. Write a definition of a parabola using this concept.
3. When we let $e = 1$ and $k = - c$ we obtained the equation of a parabola with vertex at the origin. Using this result, sketch the graph of $y^2 = 4cx$ showing the focus and directrix with
   (a) $c > 0$, and (b) $c < 0$.
4. State the equation of the directrix of the ellipse and hyperbola after we let $k^2 e^2 = a^2$. How many directrices are possible in each case?

3.2. The Parabola

To obtain the equation of the parabola, we let $e = 1$ and $k = - c$ in the general equation (1) of a conic section. Hence we may define a parabola as follows:

DEFINITION. *A parabola* is the set of points in a plane each of which is equidistant from a fixed point (focus) and a fixed line (directrix),

or more simply,

> *A parabola* is a conic section with eccentricity 1.

From the development in Section 3.1 we see that if the focus of a parabola is $(p,0)$ and the equation of the directrix is $x = -p$ (or $x + p = 0$), the equation of the parabola is $y^2 = 4px$. Generally p is used in place of c in the parabola.

To develop the equation of a parabola with focus $F(0,p)$ and directrix $y + p = 0$ we will use the definition above.

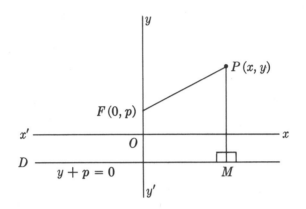

Figure 3.1

Theorem. An equation of the parabola with focus on the y-axis at $F(0, p)$, $p > 0$, and directrix the line defined by $y + p = 0$ is $x^2 = 4py$.

Proof: In Figure 3.1, if $P(x,y)$ is *any* point on the parabola, then

$$PF = PM, \qquad \text{(definition)}$$

thus,

$$\sqrt{(x-0)^2 + (y-p)^2} = y + p,$$

or

$$x^2 + y^2 - 2py + p^2 = y^2 + 2py + p^2,$$

or

$$x^2 = 4py.$$

Conversely, if $P(x, y)$ is a point whose co-ordinates satisfy $x^2 = 4py$, then, on reversing the steps above, we obtain

$$x^2 + y^2 - 2py + p^2 = y^2 + 2py + p^2$$

and

$$\sqrt{x^2 + (y-p)^2} = \sqrt{(y+p)^2}.$$

Thus,

$$\sqrt{x^2 + (y-p)^2} = |y + p|$$
$$= y + p \qquad (y \geq 0 \text{ and } p > 0).$$

Therefore,

$$PF = PM.$$

Hence, $P(x, y)$ represents those and only those points that are equidistant from F and the line defined by $y + p = 0$. The equation of the parabola is therefore $x^2 = 4py$. This equation is called the standard form of the equation of the parabola opening upward with vertex at the origin and focus at $F(0, p)$, $p < 0$.

Similarly, it may be shown that the standard form of the equation of the parabola opening downward with vertex at the origin and focus at $F(0, p)$, $p < 0$, is $x^2 = 4py$.

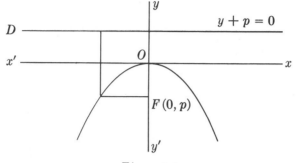

Figure 3.2

Note that the value of p may be obtained by calculating one quarter of the coefficient of y in the standard form of the equation, and with this value of p we may write the co-ordinates of the focus and the equation of the directrix.

Example 1.   Find the co-ordinates of the focus and the equation of the directrix for the parabola defined by

$$x^2 = 25y .$$

Solution: From

$$x^2 = 25y ,$$
$$p = \tfrac{25}{4} .$$

The co-ordinates of the vertex are $(0, \tfrac{25}{4})$ and the equation of the directrix is

$$y + \tfrac{25}{4} = 0 ,$$

or, with integral coefficients,

$$4y + 25 = 0 .$$

Example 2.   Find an equation of the parabola with vertex at the origin and focus at $F(0, -\tfrac{1}{8})$.

Solution: Since $p = -\tfrac{1}{8}$, replacing p by $-\tfrac{1}{8}$ in the equation $x^2 = 4py$, we obtain

$$x^2 = -\tfrac{1}{2}y ,$$

or

$$2x^2 + y = 0 .$$

EXERCISE 3.2

For the parabolas defined by the following equations state (i) the co-ordinates of the focus, (ii) the equation of the directrix, (iii) the ordinate of the point whose abscissa is -2.

1. $x^2 = 8y$

2. $5x^2 = 12y$

3. $x^2 = -\frac{15}{4}y$

4. $25x^2 = -y$

State equations for the parabolas defined by the following.

5. vertex $(0,0)$, focus $(0,-4)$

6. vertex $(0,0)$, directrix $y - 5 = 0$

7. focus $(0,3)$, directrix $y + 3 = 0$

8. vertex $(0,0)$, focus $(0,\frac{15}{2})$

Calculate values of p so that the parabola defined by

$$x^2 = 4py$$

will pass through the given point.

9. $(2,1)$ 10. $(-1,-1)$ 11. $(6,-9)$ 12. $(-6,-9)$

13. Prove the following theorem:
    An equation of the parabola with focus on the x-axis at $F(p,0)$, $p > 0$, and directrix the line defined by
    $$x + p = 0$$
    is
    $$y^2 = 4px.$$

14. Prove the theorem:
    An equation of the parabola with focus on the x-axis at $F(p,0)$, $p < 0$, and directrix the line defined by
    $$x + p = 0$$
    is
    $$y^2 = 4px.$$

For the parabolas defined by the following equations state (i) the co-ordinates of the focus, (ii) the equation of the directrix, and (iii) the abscissa of the point whose ordinate is 5.

15. $y^2 = 20x$

16. $4y^2 = -15x$

17. $y^2 = -\frac{1}{8}x$

18. $10y^2 = 25x$

State equations for the parabolas defined by the following.

19. vertex $(0,0)$, directrix $x - 10 = 0$

20. vertex $(0,0)$, focus $(-\frac{1}{3},0)$

21. focus $(\frac{7}{5},0)$, directrix $5x + 7 = 0$

22. vertex $(0,0)$, focus $(-\frac{5}{8},0)$

Calculate values of p so that the parabola defined by
$$y^2 = 4px$$
will pass through the point given in each of questions 23-26.

23. $(-8, 4)$ 24. $(-8, -4)$

25. $(10, 2\sqrt{5})$ 26. $(-2, -\frac{1}{4})$

27. Obtain an equation for the parabola with vertex at the origin, focus on the x-axis, opening to the right, if the focus is on the line whose equation is
$$4x - 7y - 12 = 0$$

28. Repeat question (27) given that the required parabola opens downward from the origin.

29. The line segment that joins the focus and any point on the parabola is a focal radius. Show that if $P_1(x_1, y_1)$ is a point on the parabola defined by $y^2 = 4px$, $p > 0$, the length of the focal radius is $p + x_1$ units.

30. Obtain an equation for the parabola with vertex at (1,2) and focus at (5,2).

31. Obtain an equation for the parabola with vertex at $(p, 0)$, $p > 0$ and focus at $(0, 0)$.

3.3. The Ellipse

To obtain the equation of an ellipse in Section 3.1, we had $e < 1$, $c = e^2k$, $a^2 = k^2e^2$, and $b^2 = a^2(1 - e^2)$ with $a > 0$, $b > 0$. Let us examine the effect of these substitutions.

Since
$$a^2 = k^2e^2$$
$$k^2 = \frac{a^2}{e^2}$$
$$k = \pm \frac{a}{e}.$$

Hence the equation of the directrix is $x = \frac{a}{e}$ or $x = -\frac{a}{e}$.

Also,
$$c = e^2k \text{ and } k = \pm \frac{a}{e}.$$

When
$$k = \frac{a}{e}, c = \frac{e^2a}{e} = ae$$

When
$$k = -\frac{a}{e}, c = -ae.$$

Hence there are two possible foci for the same ellipse $(ae,0)$ and $(-ae,0)$. Note that $a > 0$ and $e > 0$, hence $ae > 0$ and $-ae < 0$.

When the focus is $(ae,0)$, the directrix is $x = \dfrac{a}{e}$.

When the focus is $(-ae,0)$, the directrix is $x = -\dfrac{a}{e}$.

Since $b^2 = a^2(1 - e^2)$, and $c = ae$.

Then
$$e = \frac{c}{a},$$

and
$$b^2 = a^2\left(1 - \frac{c^2}{a^2}\right),$$
$$b^2 = a^2 - c^2,$$

or
$$a^2 = b^2 + c^2.$$

Conventionally, we agree that $c > 0$ as well as $a > 0$ and $b > 0$. Hence foci are $(\pm c,0)$ or $(\pm ae,0)$.

In summary, for the ellipse $\dfrac{x^2}{a^2} + \dfrac{y^2}{b^2} = 1$.

$$a^2 = b^2 + c^2.$$

Foci are $F(c,0)$ and $F'(-c,0)$

$$e = \frac{c}{a}.$$

Directrices are
$$x \pm \frac{a}{e} = 0.$$

Example.   Construct a sketch-graph of an ellipse with one focus at $F(6,0)$ and eccentricity $\dfrac{3}{4}$ showing foci and directrices.

Solution:
$$c = 6 \text{ and } e = \frac{c}{a} = \frac{3}{4}.$$

Hence
$$\frac{6}{a} = \frac{3}{4} \text{ and } a = 8,$$
$$b^2 + c^2 = a^2,$$
$$b^2 + 36 = 64,$$
$$b^2 = 28.$$
$$b = +2\sqrt{7}\ (b > 0)$$

Directrices are

$$x = \pm \frac{a}{e}$$

$$x = \pm \frac{8}{\frac{3}{4}}$$

$$x = \pm \frac{32}{3}.$$

x—intercepts are ± 8, y—intercepts are $\pm 2\sqrt{7}$.

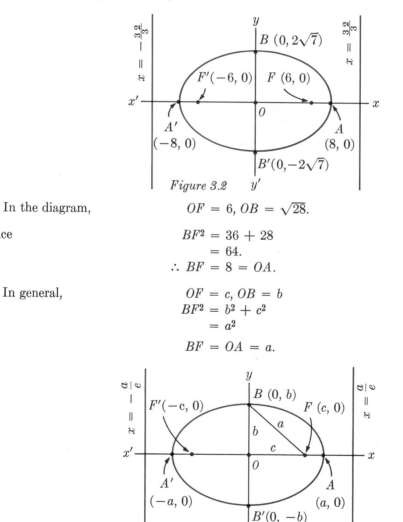

Figure 3.2

In the diagram, $OF = 6, OB = \sqrt{28}.$

Hence $BF^2 = 36 + 28$
$$= 64.$$
$$\therefore BF = 8 = OA.$$

In general, $OF = c, OB = b$
$$BF^2 = b^2 + c^2$$
$$= a^2$$

$$BF = OA = a.$$

Figure 3.3

The Pythagorean relationship between a, b, c is now apparent in the diagram and $\triangle BOF$ is known as the *abc* triangle.

Also, $e < 1$, $\dfrac{a}{e} > a > c$ and the positions of the foci, vertices (A and A') and directrices are as shown in the diagram.

EXERCISE 3.3

For the ellipses defined by the following equations, state (i) the co-ordinates of the foci, (ii) the equations of the directrices, (iii) the eccentricity.

1. $\dfrac{x^2}{25} + \dfrac{y^2}{16} = 1$ 2. $x^2 + 4y^2 = 36$

3. $\dfrac{x^2}{20} + \dfrac{y^2}{16} = 1$ 4. $3x^2 + 5y^2 = 15$

Calculate equations for the ellipses, centre $(0, 0)$, defined by the following.

5. focus at $(-5, 0)$, equation of directrix $x = 20$

6. focus at $(2, 0)$, $e = \dfrac{1}{3}$

7. vertex at $(5, 0)$, $e = \dfrac{3}{5}$

8. vertex at $(-7, 0)$, equation of directrix $x = \dfrac{28}{3}$

9. Obtain an equation for the ellipse with centre at the origin and foci on the x–axis, given that an equation of the directrix is

$$x = 10,$$

and that one focus lies on the line

$$5y = 10x - 16.$$

10. Obtain an equation for the ellipse with one focus at $(2, 1)$, one vertex at $(5, 1)$, and centre at $(1, 1)$.

3.4.   The Hyperbola

As with the ellipse, we will examine the effect of the substitution made in Section 3.1, to obtain the equation of the hyperbola

$$\frac{x^2}{a^2} - \frac{y^2}{b^2} = 1.$$

To obtain this equation we had $e > 1$, $c = e^2k$, $a^2 = k^2e^2$, and $a^2(1 - e^2) = -b^2$ with $a > 0$, $b > 0$.

Using the same arguments as with the ellipse, we again obtain the results:

Equations of directrices are $$x = \pm \frac{a}{e}$$

Co-ordinates of foci are $$(\pm c, 0) = (\pm ae, 0)$$

$$e = \frac{c}{a}.$$

The one difference is that in the Pythagorean relationship we have

$$a^2 (1 - e^2) = - b^2$$
$$a^2 \left(1 - \frac{c^2}{a^2}\right) = - b^2$$
$$a^2 - c^2 = - b^2$$
$$c^2 = a^2 + b^2.$$

In this case, $c > a$, and $c > b$.

Since $e > 1$, and $c > a$, then $c > a > \dfrac{a}{e}$.

The graph has x–intercepts $\pm a$ and no y–intercepts and is symmetrical about the origin.

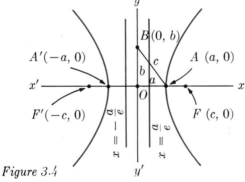

Figure 3.4

Consider the point $B (0, b)$ on the y–axis in the diagram.

$$OB = b, OA = a.$$

Then $$AB^2 = a^2 + b^2.$$

Hence $$AB = c = OF.$$
$\triangle OAB$ is the acb triangle of the hyperbola.

Note: Since the ellipse and hyperbola are symmetrical about the origin they are known as central conics.

Example 1.   For the hyperbola defined by $9x^2 - 25y^2 = 225$, state (i) the co-ordinates of the foci, (ii) the equations of the directrices, and (iii) the eccentricity.

Solution: $9x^2 - 25y^2 = 225$ may be written as

$$\frac{x^2}{25} - \frac{y^2}{9} = 1.$$

Hence
$$a^2 = 25; \, b^2 = 9.$$
$$c^2 = a^2 + b^2$$
$$= 34$$
$$c = \sqrt{34}.$$
$$e = \frac{c}{a} = \frac{\sqrt{34}}{5}$$

Hence
$$\frac{a}{e} = (5).\frac{5}{\sqrt{34}}$$
$$= \frac{25}{\sqrt{34}}.$$

Foci are $(\pm \sqrt{34}, 0).$

Directrices are $x = \pm \dfrac{25}{\sqrt{34}}$

or $\sqrt{34}x = \pm 25.$

Eccentricity is $\dfrac{\sqrt{34}}{5}.$

Example 2.   Obtain an equation of the hyperbola with one directrix $5x + 9 = 0$, and one focus at $(5, 0)$.

Solution: Since $5x + 9 = 0$

$$x = -\tfrac{9}{5}$$
$$\frac{a}{e} = \frac{9}{5} \text{ and } c = 5.$$

Hence
$$\frac{a}{\frac{c}{a}} = \frac{9}{5}.$$

∴
$$\frac{a^2}{c} = \frac{9}{5}$$
$$\frac{a^2}{5} = \frac{9}{5}$$
$$a^2 = 9$$
$$a^2 + b^2 = c^2$$
$$9 + b^2 = 25$$
$$b^2 = 16.$$

Hence equation of hyperbola is

$$\frac{x^2}{9} - \frac{y^2}{16} = 1.$$

EXERCISE 3.4

For the hyperbolas defined by the following equations, state (i) the co-ordinates of the foci, (ii) the equations of the directrices, (iii) the eccentricity.

1. $\dfrac{x^2}{64} - \dfrac{y^2}{28} = 1$

   2. $16x^2 - 9y^2 = 144$

3. $x^2 - 9y^2 = 9$

   4. $4x^2 - 5y^2 = 20$

Find equations for the hyperbolas, centre $(0, 0)$, defined by the following.

5. focus at $(5, 0)$, vertex at $(-3, 0)$

6. vertex at $(2, 0)$, equation of directrix $x = \frac{8}{5}$

7. focus at $(-13, 0)$, equation of directrix $x = \frac{13}{4}$

8. focus at $(5\frac{1}{2}, 0)$, $e = \frac{11}{7}$

Find values of k so that the central conics determined by the following equations pass through the given point.

9. $4x^2 - y^2 = k$, $(8, -5)$

   10. $16x^2 - ky^2 = 72$, $(-3, 3)$

11. $kx^2 + 25y^2 = 100$, $(5, 1)$

   12. $kx^2 + 3ky^2 = 20$, $(2, -4)$

13. Find an equation for the hyperbola, centre the origin, and foci on the $x-$ axis, given that $e = \sqrt{2}$ and that one focus lies on the line defined by

$$2y - 3x = 6.$$

14. Find an equation for the hyperbola with a focus at $(3, -4)$, the corresponding directrix given by

$$4x + 3 = 0,$$

and with both foci lying in the line

$$y = -4.$$

$$e = \tfrac{3}{2}.$$

3.5.   Alternative Definitions for the Ellipse and Hyperbola

Conics have many interesting geometrical properties other than the ones we have previously developed.   In particular, there are two simple geometrical properties, one for the ellipse and one for the hyperbola, of such a fundamental nature that if a curve has one of these properties it *must* be an ellipse or hyperbola; these properties *characterize* the ellipse or hyperbola.   In fact, these properties can be used as alternative definitions of the ellipse and hyperbola.   First, we consider the case of the ellipse.

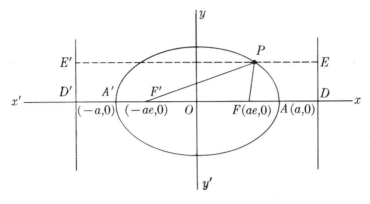

Figure 3.5

If P is any point on the ellipse in Figure 3.5, then PF and PF' are called the focal radii and

$$PF = e \cdot PE \text{ and } PF' = e \cdot PE' \, ;$$

therefore,

$$
\begin{aligned}
PF + PF' &= e \cdot (PE + PE') \\
&= e \, (EE') \\
&= e \, (DD') \\
&= e \cdot 2OD \\
&= e \cdot \frac{2a}{e} \\
&= 2a \, .
\end{aligned}
$$

Note that the sum of the focal radii is constant for any point P on the ellipse and that the constant sum is equal to the length of the major axis, $2a$. This fact suggests the following alternative definition.

DEFINITION.   An ellipse is a set of points such that the sum of the distances from each point to two fixed points (the foci) is a constant.

Theorem.   An equation of the ellipse with centre the origin, foci on the x-axis at $(\pm c. 0)$, and with sum of the focal radii $2a \, (a > c)$, is of the form

$$\frac{x^2}{a^2} + \frac{y^2}{b^2} = 1 \, ,$$

where $b^2 = a^2 - c^2$.

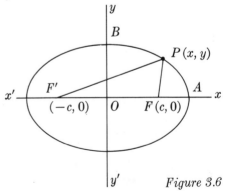

Figure 3.6

Proof: If $P(x, y)$ is any point on the ellipse (Figure 3.6), then

$$PF + PF' = 2a.$$

Therefore,

$$\sqrt{(x-c)^2 + y^2} + \sqrt{(x+c)^2 + y^2} = 2a,$$

or

$$\sqrt{(x-c)^2 + y^2} = 2a - \sqrt{(x+c)^2 + y^2}.$$

Squaring both members of the equation, we find

$$x^2 - 2cx + c^2 + y^2 = 4a^2 - 4a\sqrt{(x+c)^2 + y^2} + x^2 + 2cx + c^2 + y^2$$

or

$$a\sqrt{(x+c)^2 + y^2} = a^2 + cx.$$

On squaring again, we obtain

$$a^2(x^2 + 2cx + c^2 + y^2) = (a^2 + cx)^2,$$

or

$$a^2x^2 + 2a^2cx + a^2c^2 + a^2y^2 = a^4 + 2a^2cx + c^2x^2,$$

or

$$x^2(a^2 - c^2) + a^2y^2 = a^2(a^2 - c^2).$$

But

$$a^2 - c^2 = a^2 - (ae)^2$$
$$= a^2(1 - e^2)$$
$$= b^2.$$

Replacing $a^2 - c^2$ by b^2, we find that the equation becomes

$$\frac{x^2}{a^2} + \frac{y^2}{b^2} = 1.$$

Conversely, if $P(x, y)$ is any point with co-ordinates satisfying this equation, it may be shown that

$$PF + PF' = 2a.$$

Therefore, the equation of the ellipse is

$$\frac{x^2}{a^2} + \frac{y^2}{b^2} = 1.$$

The major and minor axes have lengths $2a$ and $2b$ units respectively, (a and b are considered to be positive).

Example 1.   Find an equation for the ellipse with one focus at $(-4, 0)$ and the semi-minor axis 6 units in length.

Solution:

$$c = 4 \; ; b = 6 \, .$$
$$a^2 = b^2 + c^2 = 52 \, .$$

An equation of the required ellipse is

$$\frac{x^2}{52} + \frac{y^2}{36} = 1 \, .$$

Let us now consider the case of the hyperbola.

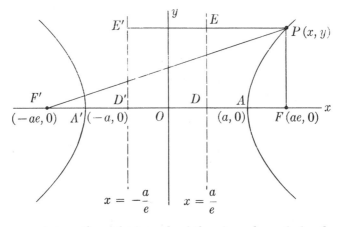

If P is any point on the right branch of the above hyperbola, then

$$PF' - PF = e \cdot PE' - e \cdot PF$$
$$= e \, (PE' - PE)$$
$$= e \cdot EE'$$
$$= e \cdot DD'$$
$$= e \cdot \frac{2a}{e}$$
$$= 2a \, .$$

If P is on the left branch of the hyperbola,

$$PF' - PF = -2a \, .$$

Therefore, in both cases,

$$|\, PF' - PF \,| = 2a \, .$$

The constant absolute value of the difference between the focal radii is equal to $2a$, the length of the transverse axis. The discussion above suggests the following alternative definition.

DEFINITION. A hyperbola is a set of points in a plane such that the absolute value of the difference of the distances from each point to two fixed points (the foci) is a constant.

Theorem. An equation of the hyperbola with centre the origin, foci on the x-axis at $(\pm c, 0)$, and with difference between the focal radii $2a\,(a < c)$ is of the form

$$\frac{x^2}{a^2} - \frac{y^2}{b^2} = 1 \,.$$

The proof of this theorem is required in Exercise 3.5, question (17).

Example 2. For the hyperbola defined by

$$4x^2 - 9y^2 = 36 \,,$$

state the values of a, b, c, and state the co-ordinates of the foci.

Solution: The defining equation may be written as

$$\frac{x^2}{9} - \frac{y^2}{4} = 1 \,;$$

therefore,

$$a = 3, \quad b = 2 \,,$$

and

$$\begin{aligned}
c &= \sqrt{a^2 + b^2} \\
&= \sqrt{9 + 4} \\
&= \sqrt{13} \,.
\end{aligned}$$

The foci have co-ordinates $(\pm \sqrt{13}, 0)$.

EXERCISE 3.5

1. State the standard form of the equation of the ellipse with centre $(0, 0)$, foci on the x-axis, and

    (a) $a = 5$, $b = 3$ (b) $a = 8$, $c = 6$

    (c) one focus at $(-6, 0)$, sum of focal radii $= 14$

    (d) y-intercept $= 12$, sum of focal radii $= 52$

2. State equations for the hyperbolas with centre $(0, 0)$, foci on the x-axis, and

    (a) $a = 6$, $b = 3$ (b) $a = 4$, $c = 5$

(c)   one focus at $(-10, 0)$, difference between focal radii 16

(d)   semi-conjugate axis 3 units in length, one focus at $(6, 0)$

Find equations for the central conics with centre $(0, 0)$, and foci on the x-axis, in the following cases.

3.   Major axis 26 units in length and one focus at $(-12, 0)$

4.   An ellipse passing through $A(7, 0)$ and $B(0, 4)$

5.   An ellipse passing through $(3, 2)$ and $(1, 4)$

6.   An ellipse passing through $(3, 2\sqrt{3})$ and $(\sqrt{21}, 2)$

7.   Semi-transverse axis 6 units in length and one focus at $(10, 0)$

8.   One vertex at $(-\sqrt{14}, 0)$, semi-conjugate axis $\sqrt{22}$ units in length

9.   A hyperbola passing through $(-5, 2)$ and $(7, 10)$

10.   A hyperbola passing through $(-8, 6)$ and $(4, -2)$

Find the semi-axes, foci, and eccentricity for the following:

11. $25x^2 - 9y^2 = 225$ 12. $x^2 + 4y^2 = 16$

13. $x^2 - y^2 = 32$ 14. $25x^2 + 169y^2 = 4225$

15. $3x^2 - 16y^2 = 48$ 16. $64x^2 + 144y^2 = 1$

17.   Prove that an equation of the hyperbola with centre the origin, foci on the x-axis at $(\pm c, 0)$, and with difference between the focal radii $2a\,(a < c)$ is of the form
$$\frac{x^2}{a^2} - \frac{y^2}{b^2} = 1 \,.$$

18.   Find an equation for the ellipse, centre $(0, 0)$, foci on the x-axis, such that the length of the major axis is four times the length of the minor axis and the point $(-3, 2)$ is on the ellipse.

19.   Find an equation satisfied by the co-ordinates of the points that divide the ordinates of the points on the circle defined by $x^2 + y^2 = 25$ in the ratio 3:2.

20.   Find an equation satisfied by the co-ordinates of all points $P(x, y)$ such that the distance from $P(x, y)$ to $(1, 1)$ is one-half the distance from P to the y-axis.

21.   Find an equation satisfied by the co-ordinates of the points that bisect the ordinates of points on the hyperbola defined by
$$16x^2 - 9y^2 = 144 \,.$$

22. The line segments joining $P(x, y)$ to $F(5, 0)$ and $F'(-5, 0)$ have slopes whose product is 4. Find an equation satisfied by the co-ordinates of P and graph the relation defined by this equation.

23. The focal radii definition of the hyperbola is used in range-finding to locate a hidden object. Suppose listening posts are at points F and F' that are 600 feet apart. The report of an enemy gun is heard at F' 0.1 seconds later than at F. Find an equation for the hyperbola on which the gun must be located. (Assume sound travels 1100 feet per second.) In actual practice, a second hyperbola is determined by a second pair of listening posts and the gun is located at an intersection of the two curves.

24. Show that, if a man hears the sound of a rifle firing at the same time that he hears the bullet hit its target, he must be on the branch of a hyperbola for which the target is the closer focus and the rifle is the focus farther from him.

25. In the Loran navigation system, two transmitters sending out signals replace the listening posts in (23) above. The difference in time of reception of the signals allows the navigator of a ship (or plane) to locate his vessel on a hyperbola. A second pair of signals permits him to find his exact position at an intersection of two hyperbolas. If the two transmitters are 400 miles apart and time difference in reception of the two signals indicates that a ship is 150 miles farther from one transmitter than the other, find an equation for the hyperbola on which the ship must lie.

3.6. Equations of the Conics in the Other Standard Positions

In Section 3.2 and Exercise 3.2 we developed the equation of the parabola in four standard positions. Our conclusions may be summarized as in Figure 3.7.

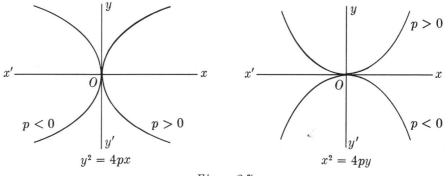

Figure 3.7

Our study of the ellipse has been restricted to the ellipse with centre at the origin and foci on the x-axis. Let us examine the corresponding ellipse with foci on the y-axis.

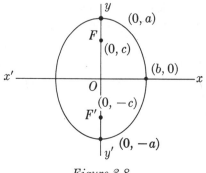

Figure 3.8

The major axis is now a segment of the y-axis and the vertices are at $(0, a)$ and $(0, -a)$. If the foci are $F(0, c)$ and $F'(0, -c)$ and $c < a$, it may be shown that the equation of the ellipse is

$$\frac{x^2}{b^2} + \frac{y^2}{a^2} = 1 .$$

(The proof of this theorem is required in Exercise 3.6, question (21).)

Example 1.   Find an equation of the ellipse with centre $(0, 0)$, foci on the y-axis, $c = 2\sqrt{3}$, $a = 4$.

Solution:

$$b^2 = a^2 - c^2$$
$$= 16 - 12$$
$$= 4 .$$

Therefore, an equation of the ellipse is

$$\frac{x^2}{4} + \frac{y^2}{16} = 1 ,$$

or

$$4x^2 + y^2 = 16.$$

Note that, as in the case of the ellipse with foci on the x-axis, when the equation is in standard form with foci on the y-axis,

$$\frac{x^2}{b^2} + \frac{y^2}{a^2} = 1 ,$$

the denominators of the left member may be associated with the squares of the x- and y-intercepts.

In considering relations that have hyperbolas as their graphs, we have also restricted our discussion to curves with foci on the x-axis. If the hyperbola has foci on the y-axis at $(0, c)$ and $(0, -c)$, and vertices at $(0, a)$ and $(0, -a)$, where $c > a$, it may be shown that the equation representing this conic is

$$\frac{x^2}{b^2} - \frac{y^2}{a^2} = -1 .$$

The graph is shown in Figure 3.9 and a proof is required in Exercise 3.6, question (23).

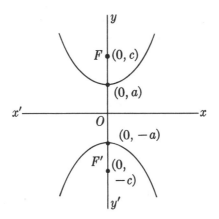

Figure 3.9

Example 2. State the values of a, b, c, e and locate the foci of the hyperbola defined by

$$\frac{x^2}{16} - \frac{y^2}{49} = -1 .$$

Solution:

$$c^2 = a^2 + b^2$$
$$= 49 + 16$$
$$= 65 .$$

Therefore,

$$a = 7, \quad b = 4, \quad c = \sqrt{65} ,$$

and

$$e = \frac{c}{a} = \frac{\sqrt{65}}{7} .$$

The foci have co-ordinates $(0, \pm\sqrt{65})$.

Note that, for the hyperbola with foci on the x-axis, it is convenient to remember the equation as

$$\frac{x^2}{(\text{length of semi-axis on } x\text{-axis})^2} - \frac{y^2}{(\text{length of semi-axis on } y\text{-axis})^2} = 1.$$

The equation of the hyperbola with foci on the y-axis may be remembered as

$$\frac{x^2}{(\text{length of semi-axis on } x\text{-axis})^2} - \frac{y^2}{(\text{length of semi-axis on } y\text{-axis})^2} = -1.$$

Example 3.   Find an equation for the hyperbola with its centre at $(0,0)$, and foci on the y-axis if points with co-ordinates $(2, -5)$ and $(-5, 10)$ are on the graph.
Solution: Since the equation is of the form

$$\frac{x^2}{b^2} - \frac{y^2}{a^2} = -1$$

and $(2, -5)$ is on the graph, then

$$\frac{4}{b^2} - \frac{25}{a^2} = -1 \tag{1}$$

and similarly, since $(-5, 10)$ is also on the graph, then

$$\frac{25}{b^2} - \frac{100}{a^2} = -1, \tag{2}$$

$(1) \times 4$
$$\frac{16}{b^2} - \frac{100}{a^2} = -4, \tag{3}$$

$(2) - (3)$
$$\frac{9}{b^2} = 3,$$
$$b^2 = 3.$$

Replacing b^2 by 3 in (1), we obtain

$$\frac{4}{3} - \frac{25}{a^2} = -1,$$

$$\frac{25}{a^2} = \frac{7}{3},$$

$$a^2 = \frac{75}{7}.$$

The equation is

$$\frac{x^2}{3} - \frac{y^2}{\frac{75}{7}} = -1,$$

or

$$25x^2 - 7y^2 = -75 .$$

The equilateral hyperbola

$$x^2 - y^2 = a^2 ,$$

a special case of the hyperbola with foci on the x-axis, has been discussed in Section 2.6. We may extend our discussion to

$$x^2 - y^2 = - a^2 ,$$

the equilateral hyperbola with foci on the y-axis.

Example 4. State the lengths of semi-axes, eccentricity, and co-ordinates of vertices and foci, for the hyperbola defined by

$$x^2 = y^2 - 25 .$$

Solution: Since

$$x^2 = y^2 - 25 ,$$

$$\frac{x^2}{25} - \frac{y^2}{25} = -1 .$$

The length of each semi-axis is 5 units. The co-ordinates of the vertices are $(0, \pm 5)$.

$$c^2 = a^2 + b^2$$
$$= 50 .$$

Therefore, $c = \sqrt{50}$. The eccentricity $e = \frac{\sqrt{50}}{5}$, that is, $\sqrt{2}$, and the co-ordinates of the foci are $(0, \pm 5\sqrt{2})$.

EXERCISE 3.6

For the ellipses defined by the following equations, find (i) the co-ordinates of the vertices, (ii) the foci, (iii) the eccentricity, and (iv) sketch the curve.

1. $25x^2 + 4y^2 = 100$ 2. $9x^2 + y^2 = 9$

3. $4x^2 + 3y^2 = 12$ 4. $81x^2 + 16y^2 = 1$

Find an equation for the ellipse with centre at the origin, given the following:

5. Foci $(0, \pm 4)$, $a = 5$ 6. Foci $(0, \pm 6)$, $e = \frac{1}{3}$

7. Vertices $(0, \pm 5)$, $e = \frac{1}{5}$ 8. Foci $(\pm 15, 0)$, $a = 17$

9. Find an equation for the ellipse with centre $(0, 0)$ and foci on the x-axis that passes through $(5, -2)$ and $(2, 4)$.

10. Find an equation for the ellipse with centre $(0,0)$ and foci on the y-axis which passes through $(1, -4)$ and $(-3, 2)$.

For the hyperbolas defined by the following equations, find (i) the co-ordinates of the vertices, (ii) the foci, (iii) the eccentricity, and (iv) sketch the curve.

11. $25x^2 - 9y^2 = -225$ 12. $9y^2 - 4x^2 = 36$

13. $x^2 - y^2 = -4$ 14. $3y^2 - x^2 = 9$

Find an equation for the hyperbola with centre the origin, given the following:

15. Foci $(0, \pm 5)$, length of conjugate axis 8 units

16. Vertices $(0, \pm 4)$, $e = \frac{3}{2}$

17. Foci $(0, \pm\sqrt{34})$, semi-transverse axis $3\sqrt{2}$ units

18. Foci $(0, \pm 2\sqrt{6})$, hyperbola equilateral

19. Find an equation for the hyperbola with centre $(0,0)$ and foci on the x-axis which passes through $(5, -2)$ and $(7, 10)$.

20. Find an equation for the hyperbola with centre $(0,0)$ and foci on the y-axis that passes through $(4, -3)$ and $(\frac{1}{4}, \sqrt{2})$.

21. Prove that an equation of the ellipse with centre the origin, foci at $(0, \pm c)$, and sum $2a\,(a > c)$ of the focal radii of any point on the curve has the form

$$\frac{x^2}{b^2} + \frac{y^2}{a^2} = 1 .$$

22. Develop the equation in question (21) using the fact that the ratio of the distance from $P(x,y)$ on the ellipse to the focus $F(0, ae)$ to the distance from P to the line $y = \frac{a}{e}$ is equal to a constant $e(e < 1)$.

23. Prove that an equation of the hyperbola with centre the origin, foci at $(0, \pm c)$, and difference $2a(a < c)$ of the focal radii of any point, has the form

$$\frac{x^2}{b^2} - \frac{y^2}{a^2} = -1.$$

24. Develop the equation in question (23), using the alternative focus-directrix definition.

25. Find an equation satisfied by the co-ordinates of all points that are twice as far from the line

$$y = 8$$

as they are from the point $(0, 2)$.

26. Find an equation for the hyperbola, centre $(0,0)$, with one focus at $(0, -10)$ and the equation of the corresponding directrix

$$9y + 40 = 0 .$$

27. Prove that the eccentricity of an equilateral hyperbola is $\sqrt{2}$.

28. Prove that the length of the line segment joining any point on the equilateral hyperbola defined by $x^2 - y^2 = a^2$ to its centre is a mean proportional between the focal radii drawn to that point.

29. The arch of a bridge is in the form of a segment of an equilateral hyperbola. The arch is 24 feet high, its base is 72 feet wide.   Find the height of the arch at a point 8 feet from the midpoint of the base.

3.7.   Intersection of Lines with Conics

If a line intersects a conic, we may find the co-ordinates of the points of inter-section by solving the linear-quadratic system formed by the defining equations of the line and the conic.

Example 1.   Find the co-ordinates of the points of intersection of the line defined by $5x - y - 20 = 0$ and the parabola defined by $y^2 = 50x$.

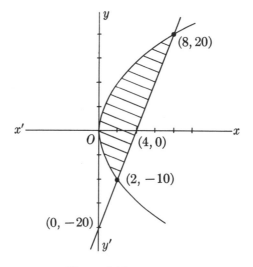

Figure 3.10

Solution: Let a point of intersection be $P(x, y)$.   As P lies on both the line and the parabola, its co-ordinates satisfy both their equations.   From the equation of the line, we obtain

$$5x - y - 20 = 0,$$
$$50x = 10y + 200.$$

Substituting for x in the equation of the parabola, we obtain an equation for the ordinate of a point of intersection.

$$y^2 = 10y + 200,$$
$$y^2 - 10y - 200 = 0,$$
$$(y - 20)(y + 10) = 0;$$

hence,

$$y = 20 \text{ or } -10.$$

Now

$$x = \frac{y + 20}{5}.$$

Therefore,

$$x = \frac{20 + 20}{5}$$
$$= 8,$$

or

$$x = \frac{-10 + 20}{5}$$
$$= 2.$$

The co-ordinates of the points of intersection are $(8, 20)$ and $(2, -10)$. These points are shown in Figure 3.10.

Example 2.   Sketch the graph of

$$\{(x, y) \mid 5x - y - 20 \leq 0 \text{ and } y^2 \leq 50x, \quad x, y \in Re\}.$$

Solution: Consider the inequality

$$5x - y - 20 \leq 0.$$

At the origin,

$$5x - y - 20 = 0 - 0 - 20 < 0.$$

Hence, the inequality is satisfied in the closed half-plane containing the origin and bounded by the line

$$5x - y - 20 = 0.$$

(The reader will recall that a region is *closed* if its boundary is included in the region.)

The point $(1, 1)$ satisfies the inequality $y^2 \leq 50x$.

Hence, this inequality is satisfied by the closed region containing the point $(1, 1)$

and bounded by the parabola
$$y^2 = 50x .$$

The set of points satisfying both inequalities is the intersection of the regions found in the two preceding paragraphs (Figure 3.10).

Example 3.   Sketch the graph of

$$\{(x, y) \mid 4x^2 + 9y^2 > 36 \text{ and } 16x^2 + y^2 < 16, \quad x, y \in Re\} .$$

Solution: Equations associated with these inequalities are

$$\frac{x^2}{9} + \frac{y^2}{4} = 1 , \tag{1}$$

and

$$\frac{x^2}{1} + \frac{y^2}{16} = 1 . \tag{2}$$

Figure 3.11 illustrates the ellipses defined by (1) and (2).

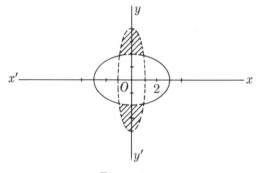

Figure 3.11

The required region is made up of the two areas shaded in Figure 3.11. The boundaries are not included. These areas contain all the points which are outside the ellipse defined by (1) and inside the ellipse defined by (2).

Note: The origin is a convenient "test point" for the inequalities in Example 3 and many other examples.

EXERCISE 3.7

Find the co-ordinates of the points of intersection of the graphs defined by the following equations.

1. $y^2 = 4x, \ x^2 = 4y$
2. $y^2 = 8x, \ 3y = 8 - 4x$
3. $x^2 + 4y^2 = 40, \ x + 2y = 8$
4. $4x^2 + 9y^2 = 36, \ 3x^2 + y^2 = 9$

5. $16x^2 + 25y^2 = 400$, $x^2 = -\frac{45}{16}y$ 6. $16x^2 - 5y^2 = 80$, $16x^2 - 25y^2 = -400$.

7. $3x^2 - y^2 = 2$, $x + y - 2 = 0$ 8. $5x^2 - 4y^2 = -24$, $y^2 = 8x$

Use the solutions for questions (1) to (8) to sketch the graphs of the following $(x, y \in Re)$.

9. $\{(x, y) \,|\, y^2 < 4x, \ x^2 < 4y\}$

10. $\{(x, y) \,|\, y^2 < 8x, \ 3y > 8 - 4x\}$

11. $\{(x, y) \,|\, x^2 + 4y^2 < 40\} \cap \{(x, y) \,|\, x + 2y > 8\}$

12. $\{(x, y) \,|\, x^2 + 4y^2 < 40\} \cup \{(x, y) \,|\, x + 2y > 8\}$

13. $\{(x, y) \,|\, 4x^2 + 9y^2 \leq 36, \ 3x^2 + y^2 \geq 9\}$

14. $\{(x, y) \,|\, 16x^2 + 25y^2 \leq 400, \ x^2 \leq -\frac{45}{16}y\}$

15. $\{(x, y) \,|\, 16x^2 - 5y^2 \leq 80, \ 16x^2 - 25y^2 > -400\}$

16. $\{(x, y) \,|\, 3x^2 - y^2 < 2, \ x + y - 2 < 0, \ x > 0, \ y > 0\}$

17. $\{(x, y) \,|\, y^2 < 8x, \ 5x^2 - 4y^2 < -24\}$

18. $\{(x, y) \,|\, y^2 < 8x \ \text{or} \ 5x^2 - 4y^2 < -24\}$

19. A square with sides parallel to the co-ordinate axes is inscribed in the ellipse $16x^2 + 9y^2 = 400$. Find the co-ordinates of its vertices and its area.

20. A line segment MN is always situated such that M is on the x-axis and N is on the y-axis. Find the equation satisfied by the co-ordinates (x, y) of point P where P is 4 inches from M and MN is 16 inches long.

21. Find the eccentricity of an ellipse if the lines joining a focus to the extremities of the minor axis are perpendicular.

22. Find an equation of the locus of the middle points of chords of an ellipse drawn from the positive end of the major axis.

23. (a) Any member of a family of chords with slope m intersects the ellipse $b^2x^2 + a^2y^2 = a^2b^2$ at (x_1, y_1) and (x_2, y_2).
    Express X and Y, the co-ordinates of the mid-point of the chord, in terms of x_1, y_1, x_2, and y_2.

    (b) Use the fact that (x_1, y_1) and (x_2, y_2) are points on the ellipse to show that
    $$\frac{y_2 + y_1}{x_2 + x_1} = -\frac{b^2(x_2 - x_1)}{a^2(y_2 - y_1)}$$
    and hence,
    $$\frac{Y}{X} = -\frac{b^2}{a^2 m}$$
    or
    $$Y = -\frac{b^2}{a^2 m}X.$$

(c) The line whose equation was developed in (b) is the *diameter* of the ellipse which bisects chords with slope m. Note that all diameters pass through the centre of the conic.

(d) For the ellipse with equation

$$16x^2 + 9y^2 = 144 \,,$$

find an equation for the diameter bisecting chords with slope $\frac{1}{2}$.

3.8.   Equations of Tangents

In Figure 3.12, the line defined by

$$5x - y - 20 = 0$$

intersects the parabola

$$y^2 = 50x$$

in two distinct points. The line (AB_1 in Figure 3.12) is a secant of the parabola.

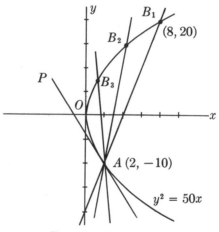

Figure 3.12

AP is the limiting position of the secant AB_n where the length of the chord AB_n approaches zero. AP is called the tangent to the parabola at point A. A similar definition may be given for the tangent at any point on a curve.

DEFINITION.   The tangent to a curve at a point A on the curve is the limiting position of a secant AB_n where $\{B_n\}$ is a set of points on the curve such that the length of the chord AB_n approaches zero.

When we say that the length of AB_n approaches zero, we mean that AB_n eventually becomes *and remains* as small as we please. More formally, we say that for any $\epsilon > 0$ there exists an N such that, for all $n \geq N$, the length of AB_n is less than ϵ.

How may we obtain the equation of the tangent at $A\,(2, -10)$ in the above example? When we solved the equation $5x - y - 20 = 0$ with $y^2 = 50x$ we obtained a quadratic in y which had two distinct roots.

Referring to Figure 3.12, we see that as the length AB_n approaches zero, the two distinct roots become very close to each other in value and in the limiting case, the two roots become equal. Recall that, if the roots

$$x = \frac{-b \pm \sqrt{b^2 - 4ac}}{2a}$$

of

$$ax^2 + bx + c = 0$$

are equal, then the discriminant $b^2 - 4ac$ must be zero. Now, in our example, we may use

$$y + 10 = m(x - 2)$$

to represent the family of lines all of which pass through $(2, -10)$. Let us solve the equation for the intersection of this line and the curve and insist on equal roots.

If

$$y + 10 = mx - 2m, \tag{1}$$

and

$$y^2 = 50x \tag{2}$$

then

$$y + 10 = \frac{my^2}{50} - 2m,$$

$$50y + 500 = my^2 - 100m,$$

$$my^2 - 50y - 100m - 500 = 0.$$

For equal roots, the discriminant is zero; that is,

$$2500 - 4(m)(-100m - 500) = 0,$$

$$25 + 4m(m + 5) = 0,$$

$$4m^2 + 20m + 25 = 0,$$

$$(2m + 5)^2 = 0;$$

therefore,

$$m = -\tfrac{5}{2}.$$

The equation of the required tangent is

$$y + 10 = -\frac{5}{2}(x - 2);$$

therefore,
$$2y + 20 = -5x + 10 \,,$$
or
$$5x + 2y + 10 = 0 \,.$$

The following example shows how the same method will produce the equation of a tangent to a conic if the slope is given.

Example 1. Find equations for the tangents with slope 2 to the ellipse defined by

$$x^2 + 2y^2 = 18 \,. \tag{1}$$

Solution: The equation of the family of lines with slope 2 is

$$y = 2x + b \,. \tag{2}$$

Solving (1) and (2), we obtain

$$x^2 + 2\,(4x^2 + 4bx + b^2) = 18 \,;$$
therefore,
$$9x^2 + 8bx + (2b^2 - 18) = 0 \,.$$
For equal roots,
$$64b^2 - 4\,(9)\,(2b^2 - 18) = 0 \,,$$
$$8b^2 - 9\,(b^2 - 9) = 0 \,,$$
$$b^2 = 81 \,,$$
$$b = \pm 9 \,.$$
The equations of the required tangents are
$$y = 2x + 9 \text{ and } y = 2x - 9 \,.$$

EXERCISE 3.8

For the conic whose equation is given, find an equation for the tangent at the given point.

1. $x^2 + y^2 = 25$, $(3, -4)$ 2. $x^2 = 8y$, $(4\sqrt{2}, 4)$

3. $16x^2 + y^2 = 20$, $(-1, 2)$ 4. $4x^2 - y^2 = 75$, $(5, 5)$

Find equations for tangents to the given conics with the given slope.

5. $x^2 + y^2 = 4$, $m = -\frac{1}{2}$ 6. $y^2 = -12x$, $m = -\frac{3}{4}$

7. $x^2 + 2y^2 = 22$, $m = \frac{1}{3}$ 8. $16x^2 - 2y^2 = -1$, $m = 2$

For the conics whose equations are given, find equations for the tangents from the given external point.

9. $x^2 + y^2 = 10$, $(4, -2)$ 10. $x^2 = 4y$, $(4, -5)$

11. $x^2 + 4y^2 = 4$, $(2, -1)$ 12. $3x^2 - y^2 = 3$, $(3, 5)$

13. For what value of k will the line defined by $3x + y = k$ be a tangent to the curve defined by $2x^2 - y^2 = 14$?

14. Repeat question (9), representing the co-ordinates of the point of contact as (x_1, y_1), setting up two equations in x_1 and y_1, and solving these equations.

15. Repeat questions (10) to (12), using the method of question (14).

16. Prove that an equation of the tangent at (x_1, y_1) to the parabola $y^2 = kx$ is

$$y_1 y = \frac{k}{2} (x + x_1).$$

17. Find the co-ordinates of the points of contact of the lines with slope $\sqrt{3}$ that are tangents to the ellipse defined by $4x^2 + 3y^2 = 5$.

18. Repeat question (16) for $x^2 = ky$.

19. Use the result of question (18) to obtain the required equation in question (2).

20. If P, Q, and R are three points on the parabola defined by $y^2 = kx$ and if the ordinates of P, Q, and R form a geometric sequence, prove that the tangents at P and R meet on a vertical line through Q.

21. (a) Find the co-ordinates of the points of contact of the tangents in question (9).

(b) Find an equation of the chord of contact in (a), that is, the chord joining the points of contact.

(c) Is it possible to obtain the equation of the chord of contact directly from the equation of the circle and the co-ordinates of the external point?

(d) State a general formula for the equation of the chord of contact for tangent drawn from (x_1, y_1) to $x^2 + y^2 = r^2$. The external point and the chord of contact are called *pole* and *polar* with respect to each other.

22. (a) Write the equation of a line passing through the point $P(2, 1)$ and having slope k. Express the condition that this line be a tangent to the parabola whose equation is

$$y = x^2$$

as a quadratic equation in k.

(b) Let the roots of the quadratic equation be k_1 and k_2. Find $k_1 + k_2$ and

$k_1 k_2$, without solving the quadratic equation.

(c) Show that the tangents from P to the parabola have points of contact $\left(\dfrac{k_1}{2}, \dfrac{k_1^2}{4}\right)$ and $\left(\dfrac{k_2}{2}, \dfrac{k_2^2}{4}\right)$

(d) Show that the equation of the chord of contact is $\dfrac{4y - k_1^2}{2x - k_1} = k_2 + k_1$.

Use your answer to part (b) to show that the equation of the chord of contact is
$$y = 4x - 1.$$

23. (a) Show that the chord of contact for the parabola whose equation is
$$y = ax^2$$
and the point $P(x_1, y_1)$ is given by the equation
$$y + y_1 = 2ax_1 x.$$

(b) Find the point of intersection of the tangents at the intersections of the line.
$$y = 4x + 2$$
with the conic
$$y = 3x^2.$$

24. For the circle of question 21(d) and the parabola of question 23(a) show that, if the polar of P_1 passes through P_2, the polar of P_2' passes through P_1.

25. Show that the chord of contact for a parabola and a point on its directrix passes through the focus of the parabola.

26. (a) For the ellipse defined by $x^2 + 4y^2 = 25$, find an equation for the diameter that bisects chords with slope $\frac{3}{8}$.

(b) Find the co-ordinates of the end points of the diameter in (a).

(c) Show that the tangents at the end points in (b) are parallel to the original family of chords.

27. Let $P_1(x_1, y_1)$ lie on the conic

$$Ax^2 + 2Fxy + By^2 + 2Gx + 2Hy + K = 0.$$

Show that the line with equation

$$Ax_1 x + F(x_1 y + y_1 x) + By_1 y + G(x + x_1) + H(y + y_1) + K = 0$$
is a tangent to the conic at P_1.

28. The points $P(1, 2)$, $Q(1, -2)$ and $R\left(\dfrac{3\sqrt{2}}{4}, \sqrt{2}\right)$ lie on the conic with equation $16x^2 + y^2 = 20$. Show that, for the triangle PQR, the tangents at the vertices meet the opposite sides in collinear points.

29. The points $A(0, 0)$, $B(\frac{1}{2}, \frac{1}{2})$, $C(1, 2)$, $D(2, 8)$, $E(3, 18)$, and $F(5, 50)$ form an irregular hexagon inscribed in the conic $y = 2x^2$. Show that the points of intersection of opposite sides are collinear.

30. State the theorems suggested in the preceding two questions in general form. Is there any relationship between them?

3.9. Asymptotes of a Hyperbola

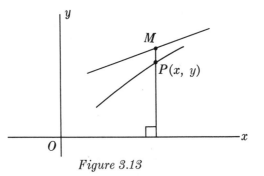

Figure 3.13

DEFINITION. If $P(x, y)$ is any point on a hyperbola with foci on one of the co-ordinate axes, and the ordinate of P is produced to meet a fixed straight line at M, this straight line is called an asymptote of the hyperbola if the difference between the ordinates of P and M approaches zero as x increases indefinitely.

Example 1. Show that the line defined by $2x - 5y = 0$ is an asymptote of the hyperbola whose equation is $4x^2 - 25y^2 = 100$.

Solution: If $P(x,y)$ is any point on the hyperbola, M is the point located by producing the ordinate of P. (See Figure 3.14.) Since $4x^2 - 25y^2 = 100$, the

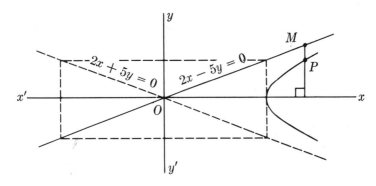

Figure 3.14

ordinate of P is given, for any value of x, by the equation

$$y = \tfrac{1}{5}\sqrt{4x^2 - 100}$$
$$= \tfrac{2}{5}\sqrt{x^2 - 25}$$

The ordinate of M is $\tfrac{2}{5}x$ and the difference in ordinates of M and P is

$$\tfrac{2}{5}x - \tfrac{2}{5}\sqrt{x^2 - 25}$$

So that we may study the value of this expression as x increases indefinitely, we multiply it by a rational number equal to 1.

$$\tfrac{2}{5}x - \tfrac{2}{5}\sqrt{x^2 - 25} = (\tfrac{2}{5}x - \tfrac{2}{5}\sqrt{x^2 - 25}) \frac{\tfrac{2}{5}x + \tfrac{2}{5}\sqrt{x^2 - 25}}{\tfrac{2}{5}x + \tfrac{2}{5}\sqrt{x^2 - 25}}$$

$$= \frac{\tfrac{4}{25}x^2 - \tfrac{4}{25}(x^2 - 25)}{\tfrac{2}{5}x + \tfrac{2}{5}\sqrt{x^2 - 25}}$$

$$= \frac{4}{\tfrac{2}{5}x + \tfrac{2}{5}\sqrt{x^2 - 25}}$$

We now have a fraction with a constant numerator and with a denominator that increases indefinitely as x increases indefinitely. Therefore,

$$\frac{4}{\tfrac{2}{5}x + \tfrac{2}{5}\sqrt{x^2 - 25}}$$

approaches zero as x increases indefinitely and the difference in the ordinates of P and M also tends to zero. Thus, the line whose equation is $2x - 5y = 0$ is an asymptote of the hyperbola.

Note that, if the constant term in the equation of the hyperbola is replaced by zero, we obtain the equations of the asymptotes. If

$$4x^2 - 25y^2 = 0,$$

then

$$(2x - 5y)(2x + 5y) = 0,$$

and

$$2x - 5y = 0 \text{ or } 2x + 5y = 0.$$

For the hyperbola represented by

$$\frac{x^2}{a^2} - \frac{y^2}{b^2} = 1,$$

if

$$\frac{x^2}{a^2} - \frac{y^2}{b^2} = 0,$$

then
$$\left(\frac{x}{a} - \frac{y}{b}\right)\left(\frac{x}{a} + \frac{y}{b}\right) = 0 \,,$$
and
$$\frac{x}{a} - \frac{y}{b} = 0 \quad \text{or} \quad \frac{x}{a} + \frac{y}{b} = 0 \,;$$
that is,
$$y = \frac{b}{a}x \quad \text{or} \quad y = -\frac{b}{a}x \,.$$

Theorem: The lines whose equations are $y = \frac{b}{a}x$ and $y = -\frac{b}{a}x$ are the asymptotes of the hyperbola with equation
$$\frac{x^2}{a^2} - \frac{y^2}{b^2} = 1 \,.$$

The proof of this theorem is required in Exercise 3.9, question (9).

Example 2.   Find equations for the asymptotes of the hyperbolas defined by

(i) $9x^2 - 4y^2 = -1$ (ii) $x^2 - 5y^2 = 20$.

Solution:

(i) Replace the constant term by zero

If
$$9x^2 - 4y^2 = 0,$$
$$(3x + 2y)(3x - 2y) = 0.$$

Equations of the asymptotes are

$$3x + 2y = 0 \text{ and } 3x - 2y = 0.$$

(ii)

If
$$x^2 - 5y^2 = 0,$$
then
$$(x + \sqrt{5}y)(x - \sqrt{5}y) = 0.$$

Equations of the asymptotes are

$$x + \sqrt{5}y = 0 \text{ and } x - \sqrt{5}y = 0.$$

EXERCISE 3.9

State equations for the asymptotes of hyperbolas defined by each of the following equations.

1. $64x^2 - 144y^2 = 1$ 2. $x^2 - y^2 = 25$

3. $49x^2 - y^2 = 16$

4. $4x^2 - 4y^2 = -45$

5. $14x^2 - 25y^2 = 3600$

6. $144x^2 - 25y^2 = -3600$

7. Sketch the hyperbolas in (5) and (6) and their asymptotes. Each hyperbola is said to be *conjugate* with respect to the other.

8. Prove that $y = 2x$ is an asymptote of the hyperbola defined by $4x^2 - y^2 = 49$.

9. Prove that $y = \dfrac{b}{a}x$ and $y = -\dfrac{b}{a}x$ represent asymptotes of the hyperbola defined by $\dfrac{x^2}{a^2} - \dfrac{y^2}{b^2} = 1$.

10. Find equations for the asymptotes of the hyperbola defined by $x^2 - y^2 = -81$. Compare the equations with those in question (2). What special property is possessed by the asymptotes of any equilateral hyperbola? For this reason, an equilateral hyperbola is said to be rectangular.

11. Explain how the asymptotes of a hyperbola may be used as an aid in sketching the graph of the hyperbola itself.

12. Prove that an asymptote of a hyperbola does not intersect the curve.

13. Sketch the hyperbola defined by $xy = 32$. Find equations for its asymptotes. State the equations of (i) the conjugate hyperbola and (ii) its asymptotes.

14. Find an equation of the hyperbola which passes through the point with co-ordinates $(2, -1)$ and has the line defined by $y = -\frac{4}{5}x$ as an asymptote.

Chapter Summary

Focus-directrix definitions of parabola $(e = 1)$, ellipse $(e < 1)$, hyperbola $(e > 1)$ · Constant sum and difference definitions for the ellipse and hyperbola · Equations of the conics in the other standard positions.

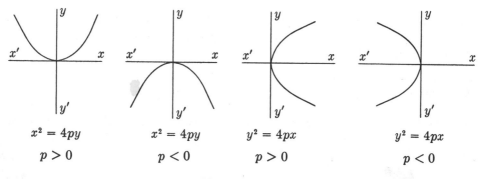

$$x^2 = 4py \qquad x^2 = 4py \qquad y^2 = 4px \qquad y^2 = 4px$$
$$p > 0 \qquad\quad p < 0 \qquad\quad p > 0 \qquad\quad p < 0$$

The Parabola

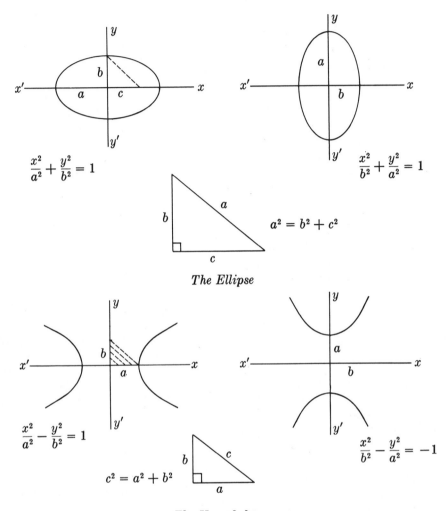

The Ellipse

The Hyperbola

Asymptotes of a hyperbola (Supplementary) · Intersections of lines with conics · Intersections of conics with conics · Regions defined by inequalities · Equations of tangents to particular conics.

REVIEW EXERCISE 3

For the parabolas defined by the following equations, state (i) the co-ordinates of the focus, (ii) the equation of the directrix, (iii) the abscissa of the point whose ordinate is 2.

1. $3x^2 = 8y$
2. $y^2 = \frac{3}{2}x$
3. $x^2 = \frac{15}{4}y$
4. $3y^2 = -14x$

5. Find an equation for the parabola with vertex at the origin and opening downward if the focus is on the line whose equation is

$$5x - 3y - 15 = 0.$$

Find equations for the ellipses with centres at (0,0) defined by the following.

6. Focus at (4,0), equation of directrix $x = 10$

7. Vertex at $(-10,0)$, $e = \frac{2}{5}$

8. Vertex at (5,0), equation of directrix $x = 8$

Find equations for the hyperbolas centre (0,0), defined by the following.

9. Focus at (0,5), $e = \frac{5}{3}$

10. Vertex at $(0,-8)$, equation of directrix $y = -2$

11. Vertex at $(0, \frac{3}{2})$, $e = \sqrt{2}$ ·

Find equations for the central conics, centre (0,0), and the following.

12. Ellipse, one focus at (3,0), sum of focal radii 10

13. Hyperbola, $e = 3$, foci on y-axis, difference between focal radii 10

14. Ellipse, vertex at (0,5), equation of directrix $y = 8$

15. Hyperbola, difference between focal radii $\frac{15}{2}$, focus at $(0,-8)$ ·

16. Hyperbola, foci on x-axis, passing through $(-4,2)$ and (8,6)

17. Ellipse, foci on y-axis, passing through $(\sqrt{3},-2)$ and $(1,2\sqrt{3})$

18. Equilateral hyperbola, one focus at (0,10) ↙

Construct the graphs of the following sets of points $(x,y \in Re)$.

19. $\{(x,y) \mid x + y < 1, y^2 < 4x\}$

20. $\{(x,y) \mid x + y > 1 \text{ or } y^2 < 4x\}$

21. $\{(x,y) \mid x^2 + y^2 \geq 1, 16x^2 + 25y^2 \leq 400\}$

22. $\{(x,y) \mid x^2 < y\} \cup \{(x,y) \mid x^2 < -y\}$

23. $\{(x,y) \mid x + y > 1, x^2 + 25y^2 = 25, x > 0, y > 0\}$

24. For the circle defined by $x^2 + y^2 = 13$, find an equation of the tangent at (2,3).

25. For the parabola defined by $y^2 = -16x$, find an equation of the tangent with slope 2.

26. Show that the line defined by $2x - y = 8$ is tangent to the parabola represented by $x^2 = 8y$ and find the co-ordinates of the point of contact.

27. Find a value of k so that the line represented by $y = 4x + k$ will be tangent to the parabola defined by $y^2 = -20x$.

28. Find equations for the tangents from $(-4, -3)$ to the hyperbola defined by

$$\frac{x^2}{64} - \frac{y^2}{36} = 1 .$$

29. The distance between the towers of a suspension bridge is 800 feet. The lowest point on the cables is 120 feet below the tops of the towers. Assume that the form of the cables is parabolic and find an equation for the parabola.

30. Show that an equation of the tangent with slope m to the parabola with equation $y^2 = 4px$ is $y = mx + \dfrac{p}{m}$.

31. Repeat question (30) for $x^2 = 4py$.

32. Use the result of question (31) to write an equation for the tangent with slope $\frac{1}{2}$ to the parabola whose equation is $3x^2 = 8y$.

33. Find the area of the isosceles right-angled triangle inscribed in the parabola defined by $y^2 = kx$ $(k < 0)$ and having the vertex of the right angle at the origin.

34. Find an equation for the tangent common to the parabolas defined by

$$y^2 = 4x \text{ and } x^2 = 32y .$$

35. (a) Any member of a family of chords with slope m intersects the hyperbola whose equation is

$$\frac{x^2}{a^2} - \frac{y^2}{b^2} = 1$$

at the points $P_1(x_1, y_1)$ and $P_2(x_2, y_2)$. Let the mid-point of $P_1 P_2$ be $P(X, Y)$. Express X and Y in terms of x_1, x_2, y_1, and y_2.

(b) Use the fact that P_1 and P_2 lie on the hyperbola to show that

$$\frac{y_1 + y_2}{x_1 + x_2} = \frac{b^2 (x_1 - x_2)}{a^2 (y_1 - y_2)} ,$$

and hence that

$$Y = \frac{b^2}{a^2 m} X .$$

(c) For the hyperbola with equation

$$3x^2 - 4y^2 = 12 ,$$

find an equation for the diameter bisecting chords with slope 10.

36. (a) The polar of P_1 (x_1, y_1) with respect to the ellipse

$$\frac{x^2}{a^2} + \frac{y^2}{b^2} = 1$$

is the line

$$\frac{x_1 x}{a^2} + \frac{y_1 y}{b^2} = 1.$$

(b) Verify this fact for the ellipse

$$3x^2 + 4y^2 = 12$$

and the point (1,2).

(c) Show that the polar of a point on the diameter of the ellipse in part (a) is parallel to the family of chords that determines the diameter.

(d) Find the point of intersection of the tangents at the points of intersection of the ellipse

$$x^2 + 2y^2 = 40$$

with the line

$$2y - 3x = 4.$$

37. State equations for the asymptotes of the hyperbolas defined by each of the following equations.

(a) $25x^2 - 16y^2 = -1$ (b) $36x^2 - y^2 = 5$

(c) $x^2 - y^2 = -16$ (d) $5x^2 - y^2 = 2$

(e) $81x^2 - 169y^2 = 117$ (f) $xy = 20$

38. Find an equation for the hyperbola which passes through the point whose co-ordinates are $(3, -\frac{1}{2})$ and has the line defined by $3x + 8y = 0$ as an asymptote.

39. Let a point $P_1(x_1, y_1)$ lie on the hyperbola

$$\frac{x^2}{a^2} - \frac{y^2}{b^2} = 1.$$

Draw a line through P_1 parallel to the y-axis to intersect the nearer asymptote at Q and the farther asymptote at Q'. Let the perpendicular from P_1 to the nearer asymptote be $P_1 R$ and to the farther asymptote be $P_1 R'$. Let the lengths of $P_1 Q$, $P_1 Q'$, $P_1 R$ and $P_1 R'$ be d, d', p and p' respectively. Let each asymptote make an angle θ with the x-axis.

(a) Show that

$$p = d \cos\theta$$

and that

$$p' = d' \cos\theta.$$

(b) Express d and d' in terms of a, b, and x.

(c) Show that
$$dd' = b^2$$

(d) Show that
$$pp' = \frac{a^2 b^2}{a^2 + b^2} .$$

40. (a) The polar of $P_1(x_1, y_1)$ with respect to the hyperbola
$$\frac{x^2}{a^2} - \frac{y^2}{b^2} = 1$$

is the line
$$\frac{x_1 x}{a^2} - \frac{y_1 y}{b^2} = 1 .$$

(b) Verify this fact for the hyperbola
$$2x^2 - 5y^2 = 20$$

and the point $(2, 3)$.

(c) Show that an asymptote to a hyperbola cannot be a polar of any point, with respect to the hyperbola.

41. Show that the polar of a point on the diameter of a hyperbola is parallel to the system of chords that determine the diameter.

42. For the circle, parabola, ellipse, and hyperbola show that the point of intersection of the polars of two points is the pole of the line joining the two points.

Chapter 4

TRANSLATIONS IN THE PLANE

4.1. The Mapping (x,y) ⟶ (x + h, y + k)

In a first study of a function as a mapping, one of the simplest mappings would be

$$x \to x + 1, \quad (x \in Re).$$

For clarity, this mapping is often represented geometrically on two number lines as follows:

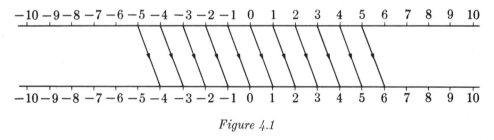

Figure 4.1

In Figure 4.1, the line segments with arrows illustrate the mapping

$$x \to x + 1, \quad x \in I, \ -5 \le x \le +5.$$

If we tried to draw all the arrows for $x \to x + 1$ in the domain $x \in Re$, we could not exhibit the arrows separately.

The mapping above,

$$x \to x + 1 \quad x \in I, \ -5 \le x \le +5,$$

as illustrated, maps points on one number line onto points on a second number line. If we now consider points in a region of the Cartesian plane, say (x, y), where $x, y \in I$, $-5 \le x \le +5$ and $-5 \le y \le +5$, we can map this set of points onto another set of points in the plane by means of a mapping such as

$$x \to x + 1, \ y \to y - 1.$$

In practice, for clarity, we often draw two Cartesian planes, or, more precisely, portions of them, on the same sheet of paper, just as we used two number lines in Figure 4.1.

Thus, we illustrate the mapping

$$x \rightarrow x + 1, \quad y \rightarrow y - 1, \quad x, y \in I, \quad -5 \leq x \leq 5, \quad -5 \leq y \leq 5,$$

in Figure 4.2.

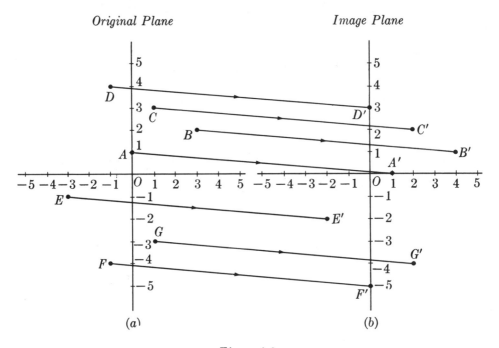

Figure 4.2

We have inserted only a few of the line segments with arrows that join corresponding points in the two planes. The diagram becomes much too confusing if we try to insert too many such line segments.

Using the terminology that we developed in Chapter 1 for functional mappings in one variable, we say that A' is the *image* of A under the mapping

$$x \rightarrow x + 1, \quad y \rightarrow y - 1;$$

similarly, B' is the image of B, and so on. To each point in the first Cartesian plane, (a), there corresponds a unique point in the second Cartesian plane, (b).

If we return to the consideration of the single-variable mapping

$$x \rightarrow x + 1, \quad x \in I,$$

we see that it maps the set of integers onto the set of integers. In this sense, it maps the points given by integers on a number line onto the points given by integers on the same number line. This mapping is shown in Figure 4.3, where it is illustrated by four arrows.

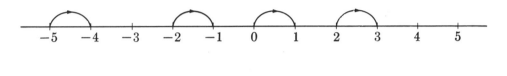

Figure 4.3

In the same sense, the two dimensional mapping

$$x \rightarrow x + 1, \quad y \rightarrow y - 1, \quad x, y \in I,$$

maps the set of ordered pairs of integers onto the set of ordered pairs of integers. Thus, the mapping maps the points given by ordered pairs of integers in a Cartesian plane onto the points given by ordered pairs of integers in the same Cartesian plane. This mapping is shown in Figure 4.4, where we have illustrated the mapping of some particular points by arrows.

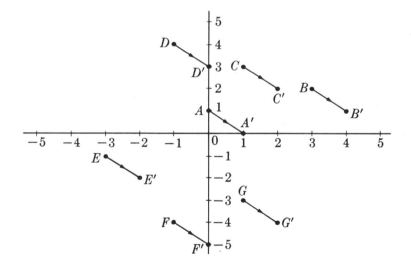

Figure 4.4

The decision on whether to use a two-plane or a single-plane representation is usually made on the basis of which diagram illustrates the situation more clearly.

If we examine Figure 4.4, we see that all the arrows connecting the original points with their images are parallel line segments of the same length and direction. Such a mapping is called a *uniform translation* or, more simply, a *translation*. If the original set of points and the axes are drawn on a sheet of rigid transparent plastic, we see that a movement of the sheet by the translation indicated by any one of the arrows, and without any rotation, will move all the original points into coincidence with their corresponding image points. Note that we are actually moving a "model" of the mathematical concept, not the mathematical points.

The above conclusions, reached on the basis of a few points, remain valid for all points in the case of the mapping

$$x \rightarrow x + 1, \quad y \rightarrow y - 1, \quad x, y \in Re.$$

If we use the two plane representation, we see that to any point in the *original plane* (the first plane) there corresponds a unique point in the *image plane* (the second plane). If we use the single plane representation, we see that each point in the plane has a unique image point in the plane. In more algebraic terms, we may say that the ordered pair (x, y) is transformed onto its image $(x + 1, y - 1)$ by the mapping

$$(x, y) \rightarrow (x + 1, y - 1) \quad x, y \in Re.$$

DEFINITION.   The mapping

$$(x, y) \rightarrow (x + h, y + k), \quad x, y \in Re,$$

maps a given ordered pair (x, y) uniquely onto its image $(x + h, y + k)$. Such a mapping is called a *translation*.

Example 1. Find the images of the points $A(2, 1)$, $B(4, 3)$, $C(-2, 5)$, $D(-6, 1)$, $E(-2, -4)$, $F(0, -3)$, $G(3, -4)$ under the translation

$$(x, y) \rightarrow (x - 2, y + 3)$$

and showing the corresponding points in sketch graphs.

Solution:

$$A(2, 1) \rightarrow A'(2 - 2, 1 + 3) = A'(0, 4)$$
$$B(4, 3) \rightarrow B'(2, 6)$$
$$C(-2, 5) \rightarrow C'(-4, 8)$$
$$D(-6, 1) \rightarrow D'(-8, 4)$$
$$E(-2, -4) \rightarrow E'(-4, -1)$$
$$F(0, -3) \rightarrow F'(-2, 0)$$
$$G(3, -4) \rightarrow G'(1, -1)$$

We may use a two-plane or a single-plane representation.

Two-Plane Representation

Original Plane *Image Plane*

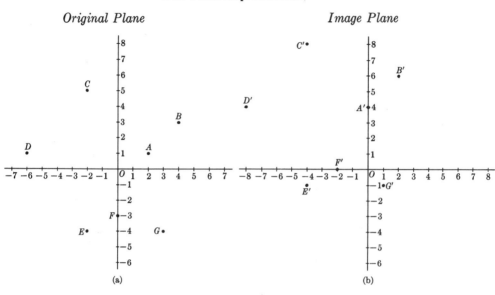

(a) (b)

Single-Plane Representation

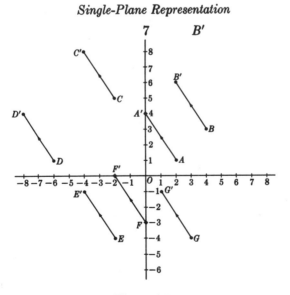

Figure 4.5

Example 2.   Find images of $A(-3, -2)$, $B(-1, 0)$, $C(0, 1)$, $D(2, 3)$, $E(4, 5)$, under the translation

$$(x, y) \rightarrow (x + 1, \ y - 2) .$$

Sketch the corresponding points.

Solution:

$$A(-3, -2) \rightarrow A'(-2, -4) ,$$
$$B(-1, 0) \rightarrow B'(0, -2) ,$$
$$C(0, 1) \rightarrow C'(1, -1) ,$$
$$D(2, 3) \rightarrow D'(3, 1) ,$$
$$E(4, 5) \rightarrow E'(5, 3)$$

We note that the points $ABCDE$ lie on a line and that the points $A'B'C'D'E'$ lie on a line with the same slope.

Two-Plane Representation

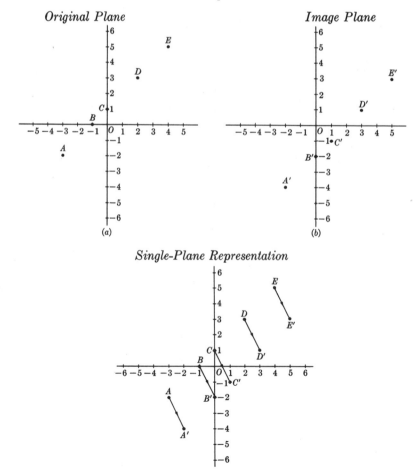

(a)
(b)

Single-Plane Representation

EXERCISE 4.1

1. Find the images of the points
$$A(3, -5), \quad B(-4, 3), \quad C(-2, -5), \quad D(3, 2)$$
under the following translations.
   (a) $(x, y) \rightarrow (x + 1, \ y + 2)$ (b) $(x, y) \rightarrow (x - 2, \ y + 4)$
   (c) $(x, y) \rightarrow (x + 3, \ y - 2)$ (d) $(x, y) \rightarrow (x - 3, \ y - 5)$
   Show the corresponding points on sketch graphs.

2. Find the images of the points
$$A(-2, -1), \quad B(0, 2), \quad C(2, 5), \quad D(6, 11)$$
under the following translations.
   (a) $(x, y) \rightarrow (x - 1, \ y + 1)$ (b) $(x, y) \rightarrow (x - 2, \ y - 3)$
   (c) $(x, y) \rightarrow (x + 2, \ y - 3)$ (d) $(x, y) \rightarrow (x + 4, \ y + 6)$
   Show the corresponding points on sketch graphs.

3. Find the images of the points
$$A(3, -2), \quad B(4, 1), \quad C(-2, 2), \quad D(-3, -1)$$
under the translations
   (a) $(x, y) \rightarrow (x - 4, y - 1)$,   (b) $(x, y) \rightarrow (x + 3, y + 1)$.
   Sketch the graphs of the points. What geometric figure is formed by $ABCD$? What geometric figure is formed by the corresponding sets of image points?

4. Find the images of the points
$$A(1, 2), \quad B(-2, 4), \quad C(-1, -2)$$
under the translations
   (a) $(x, y) \rightarrow (x - 1, y - 2)$,   (b) $(x, y) \rightarrow (x + 1, y + 2)$.
   Sketch the graphs of the points. What geometric figures are formed by ABC and by the image points? Do these figures appear to be congruent?

4.2.   Invariance of Length and Angle under a Translation

If we consider the graphs in Example 1 of the previous section, we see that the two figures $ABCDEFG$ and $A'B'C'D'E'F'G'$ appear to be congruent. If they are, then
$$AB = A'B', \quad BC = B'C', \text{ etc.,}$$
and
$$\angle ABC = \angle A'B'C', \quad \angle BCD = \angle B'C'D', \text{ etc.}$$

We now investigate this question more precisely.

Example 1. $A(2, 1)$, $B(4, 3)$, $C(-2, 5)$ have images $A'(0, 4)$, $B'(2, 6)$, $C'(-4, 8)$ under the translation

$$(x, y) \rightarrow (x - 2, y + 3) .$$

Show that $AB = A'B'$, $BC = B'C'$, $CA = C'A'$ and $\angle ABC = \angle A'B'C'$.

Solution:

$$AB^2 = (4 - 2)^2 + (3 - 1)^2$$
$$= 2^2 + 2^2$$
$$= 8 ,$$

and

$$A'B'^2 = (2 - 0)^2 + (6 - 4)^2$$
$$= 2^2 + 2^2$$
$$= 8 ,$$

Thus,

$$AB^2 = A'B'^2;$$

therefore,

$$AB = A'B' .$$

Similarly,

$$BC^2 = 6^2 + 2^2 = 40 ,$$
$$B'C'^2 = 6^2 + 2^2 = 40 .$$
$$BC = B'C' ,$$

and

$$CA^2 = 4^2 + 4^2 = 32 ,$$
$$C'A'^2 = 4^2 + 4^2 = 32 .$$

Therefore,

$$CA = C'A' ,$$

Slope of $AB = m_1 = \frac{2}{2} = 1 .$

Slope of $BC = m_2 = -\frac{2}{6} = -\frac{1}{3} .$

Hence,

$$\tan (\angle ABC) = \frac{1 + \frac{1}{3}}{1 + 1(-\frac{1}{3})} = \frac{\frac{4}{3}}{\frac{2}{3}} = 2 .$$

Slope of $A'B' = m_1' = \frac{2}{2} = 1 .$

Slope of $B'C' = m_2' = -\frac{2}{6} = -\frac{1}{3} .$

$$\tan (\angle A'B'C') = \frac{1 + \frac{1}{3}}{1 + 1(-\frac{1}{3})} = \frac{\frac{4}{3}}{\frac{2}{3}} = 2 .$$

Therefore,

$$\angle ABC = \angle A'B'C' .$$

Thus we have established for this translation that the length of a typical line segment is unchanged and so is the angle between two typical line segments. Mathematicians use the word *invariant* to describe this changelessness.

We note that, in fact, AB is equal to $A'B'$ and AB is parallel to $A'B'$. As BC is parallel to $B'C'$, the angle between AB and BC must be equal to the angle between $A'B'$ and $B'C'$.

In general, if the translation is

$$(x, y) \rightarrow (x + h, \, y + k),$$

then any line segment PQ and its image $P'Q'$ are equal and **parallel**. Let P be the point (a, b) and Q the point (c, d); then P' is $(a + h, \, b + k)$ and Q' is $(c + h, \, d + k)$.

$$PQ^2 = (c - a)^2 + (d - b)^2$$
$$= [(c + h) - (a + h)]^2 + [(d + k) - (b + k)]^2$$
$$= P'Q'^2 \, ;$$

therefore,

$$PQ = P'Q'.$$

$$\text{Slope of } PQ = \frac{d - b}{c - a}$$
$$= \frac{(d + k) - (b + k)}{(c + h) - (a + h)}$$
$$= \text{slope of } P'Q'.$$

Thus, we have established that the length of any line segment is invariant under a translation and that the slope of any line is also an invariant under a translation.

If we consider a third point $R(e, f)$, we can show in the same way that

$$QR = Q'R' \quad \text{and} \quad RP = R'P'$$

Thus,

$$\triangle PQR \equiv \triangle P'Q'R',$$

and from this

$$\angle PQR = \angle P'Q'R'.$$

The angle between any two lines is therefore an invariant under a translation. We could also show this invariance by calculating the slope of QR and $Q'R'$ and then finding the angle between PQ and QR, and $P'Q'$ and $Q'R'$.

The following example illustrates the effect of these invariant properties for a simple polygon under translation.

Example 2. $\triangle ABC$, with vertices $A(-1, 0)$, $B(1, 0)$, $C(0, \sqrt{3})$, is equilateral. Show that the mapping

$$(x, y) \rightarrow (x + \sqrt{2}, \, y - \sqrt{5})$$

produces an image triangle $A'B'C'$ that is congruent to $\triangle ABC$ and therefore equilateral. Show both triangles on a single plane representation.

Solution:

$A \rightarrow A'$ is
$$(-1, 0) \rightarrow (-1 + \sqrt{2}, \, -\sqrt{5}) \, ;$$
$B \rightarrow B'$ is
$$(1, 0) \rightarrow (1 + \sqrt{2}, \, -\sqrt{5}) \, ;$$
and $C \rightarrow C'$ is
$$(0, \sqrt{3}) \rightarrow (\sqrt{2}, \sqrt{3} - \sqrt{5}) \, .$$
$$AB^2 = [1 - (-1)]^2 \, ;$$
$$AB = 2 \, .$$

Hence,
$$A'B'^2 = [(+1 + \sqrt{2}) - (-1 + \sqrt{2})]^2 + [(-\sqrt{5}) - (-\sqrt{5})]^2$$
$$= 2^2 \, ,$$
and
$$A'B' = 2 \, .$$

Thus,
$$AB = A'B'$$
$$BC^2 = (0 - 1)^2 + (\sqrt{3} - 0)^2$$
$$= 1 + 3 \, ,$$
and
$$BC = 2 \, .$$
$$B'C'^2 = [\sqrt{2} - (1 + \sqrt{2})]^2 + [\sqrt{3} - \sqrt{5} - (-\sqrt{5})]^2$$
$$= 1 + 3 \, ,$$
and
$$B'C' = 2 \, .$$

Hence,
$$BC = B'C' \, .$$

Similarly,
$$CA = C'A' \, .$$

Therefore,
$$\triangle ABC \equiv \triangle A'B'C'$$

and $\triangle ABC$ is equilateral; hence, $\triangle A'B'C'$ is equilateral.

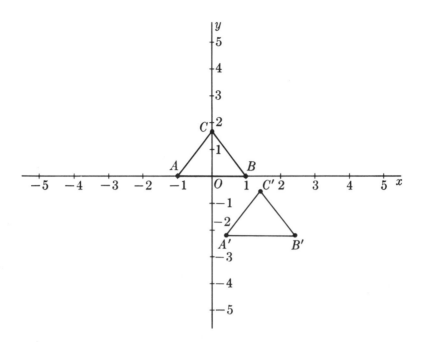

EXERCISE 4.2

1. Find the lengths of the line segments AB, BC, CA if A is $(2, 1)$, B is $(6, 1)$, and C is $(6, 4)$. If A', B', C' are the image points of A, B, C, under the translation

$$(x, y) \rightarrow (x - 2, \, y - 1) \,,$$

find the lengths of $A'B'$, $B'C'$, $C'A'$. Verify that

$$AB = A'B', \qquad BC = B'C', \qquad CA = C'A'.$$

2. In question (1), find the slope of AC and show that $A'C'$ has the same slope.

3. $A(0, 0)$, $B(2, 1)$, $C(3, 5)$ are three points, and A', B', C', are their respective images under

$$(x, y) \rightarrow (x - 3, \, y - 5) \,.$$

Verify that

$$\angle BAC = \angle B'A'C'$$

and that

$$\angle ACB = \angle A'C'B' \,.$$

4. Find and graph the image points of $A(2, 1)$, $B(0, 3)$, and $C(-1, 2)$ under the transformation

$$(x, y) \rightarrow (x + 2, \, y - 1) \,.$$

Show that the two triangles are congruent.

4.3.   The Equation of the Image of the Line $y = mx + b$

So far, we have considered the mapping of isolated points and line segments in a given Cartesian plane and have plotted the results of a translation in an image Cartesian plane.   In order to distinguish easily between co-ordinates in the two planes, we shall use (x, y) for the co-ordinates of a point in the original plane and (u, v) for the image point in the image plane.

We first note that, if (u, v) is the image point of (x, y), the general translation mapping may be written

$$(x, y) \rightarrow (x + h, y + k) = (u, v),$$

and hence

$$u = x + h, \quad v = y + k.$$

These equations express the relation between the co-ordinates in the original plane and the co-ordinates in the image plane.

In the original plane, the x-axis is the line on which y is equal to zero; that is, its equation is $y = 0$.   In the new plane, therefore, it is mapped onto the line with the equation $v = k$ in the image plane.   Similarly, the y-axis is $x = 0$ in the original plane, and it is mapped onto the line with the equation $u = h$ in the image plane. This mapping of the axes is illustrated in Figure 4.6.

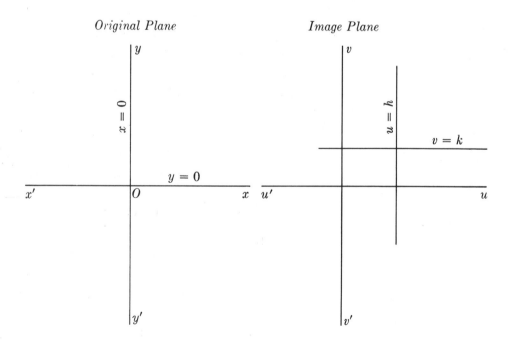

Figure 4.6

Note that the images of the axes in the original plane intersect at (h, k) in the image plane.

Let us now consider a line through the origin $(0, 0)$ in the original plane, for example, the line

$$y = 2x \, .$$

Example 1 in Section 4.2 indicated that points on a line are translated into points on a line with the same slope. We can verify this fact by plotting some points on $y = 2x$, for example $(0, 0)$, $(1, 2)$, $(2, 4)$, and their images in the image plane. Thus we see that the image of the line $y = 2x$ passes through the point (h, k), the image of the origin in the image plane, and has slope 2. The equation of such a line in the image plane where the co-ordinates are u and v is

$$v - k = 2(u - h) \, ,$$

as shown in Figure 4.7 for $(h, k) = (2, 1)$

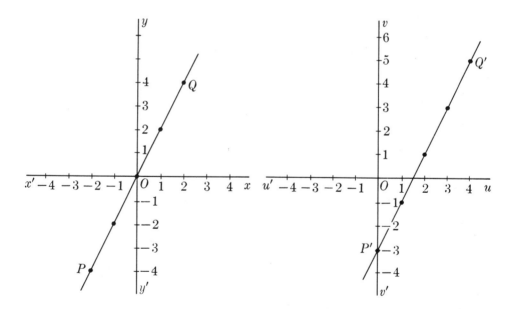

Figure 4.7

We have marked the image points P' and Q' corresponding to the points P and Q.

We notice immediately that we may obtain the equation of the image line

$$v - k = 2(u - h)$$

by using

$$u = x + h, \quad v = y + k,$$

to obtain

$$x = u - h, \quad y = v - k,$$

and then substituting these values in

$$y = 2x.$$

We may also represent this mapping on a single plane by superimposing the uv-axes (shown in colour) on the xy-axes (shown in black), as we have done in Figure 4.8. In this case, $(h, k) = (2, 1)$ and the original line given by $y = 2x$ is translated into the image line given by $v - 1 = 2(u - 2)$.

As the uv-axes and xy-axes coincide in the single-plane representation the equation of the image line in the single plane may be written as

$$y - 1 = 2(x - 2).$$

Thus, in the single-plane representation the original line given by

$$y = 2x$$

is translated by

$$(x, y) \rightarrow (x + 2, y + 1)$$

into the image line given by

$$y - 1 = 2(x - 2).$$

The graph of the single-plane representation is shown in Figure 4.8, where again we have marked corresponding points P, Q and P', Q'.

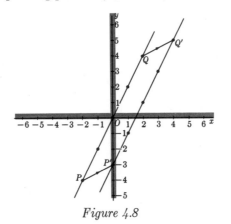

Figure 4.8

We shall now apply a similar analysis to a line that does not pass through the origin.

Example 1. Find the image of the line given by the equation

$$y = 3x - 2$$

under the translation

$$(x, y) \rightarrow (x - 1, y + 1) = (u, v).$$

Solution:

$$u = x - 1, \quad v = y + 1;$$

therefore,

$$x = u + 1, \quad y = v - 1.$$

The image of

$$y = 3x - 2$$

is given by

$$v - 1 = 3(u + 1) - 2,$$
$$v - 1 = 3u + 3 - 2,$$
$$v = 3u + 2.$$

We may verify that this line is indeed the equation of the image line in the uv-plane, the image plane, by the following procedure. The line

$$y = 3x - 2$$

passes through the points

$$(0, -2) \quad \text{and} \quad (1, 1).$$

The images of these points are

$$(0 - 1, -2 + 1) \quad \text{and} \quad (1 - 1, 1 + 1),$$

that is,

$$(-1, -1) \quad \text{and} \quad (0, 2).$$

We easily verify that the line

$$v = 3u + 2$$

passes through these two image points, and hence that

$$v = 3u + 2$$

is the equation of this image line.

Example 2.   Find a translation

$$(x, y) \rightarrow (x + h, y + k)$$

that simplifies the equation of a line

$$y = 4x + 3 \quad \text{to} \quad y = 4x$$

in a single-plane representation.

Solution: Let the mapping be

$$(x, y) \rightarrow (x + h, y + k) = (u, v) \,;$$

then

$$u = x + h \,, \quad v = y + k \,;$$

therefore,

$$x = u - h \,, \quad y = v - k \,.$$

Substituting in $y = 4x + 3$, we obtain

$$v - k = 4(u - h) + 3 \,,$$
$$v = 4u + k - 4h + 3 \,.$$

If

$$k - 4h + 3 = 0 \,,$$

then the equation on the uv-plane becomes

$$v = 4u \,,$$

Suitable values for h and k are

$$h = 0 \,, \quad k = -3 \,,$$
$$h = \tfrac{3}{4} \,, \quad k = 0 \,,$$
$$h = 1 \,, \quad k = 1 \,,$$

and

$$h = 2 \,, \quad k = 5 \,,$$

amongst others.   Thus,

$$(x, y) \rightarrow (x + 1, y + 1)$$

is a suitable translation to simplify the equation

$$y = 4x + 3$$

to

$$y = 4x$$

in the single-plane representation.

Other suitable translations are

$$(x, y) \rightarrow (x, y - 3) ,$$
$$(x, y) \rightarrow (x + \tfrac{3}{4}, y) ,$$

and

$$(x, y) \rightarrow (x + 2, y + 5) .$$

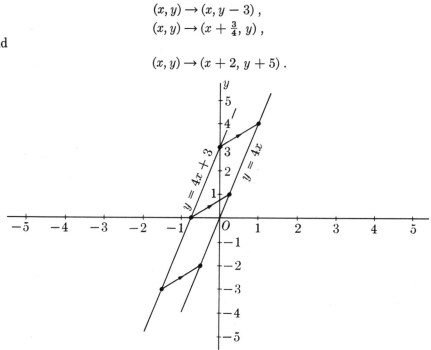

We show the single-plane representation for the mapping of

$$\{x, y) \mid y = 4x + 3\} \rightarrow \{(x, y) \mid y = 4x\}$$

by the translation

$$(x, y) \rightarrow (x + 1, y + 1) .$$

EXERCISE 4.3

Find the image of the line determined by each of the following equations under the translation stated, and sketch the graph in both planes.

1. $y = 3x$; $(x, y) \rightarrow (x - 2, y + 1) = (u, v)$

2. $y = -2x$; $(x, y) \rightarrow (x + 1, y + 3) = (u, v)$

3. $y = 4x + 1$; $(x, y) \rightarrow (x + 1, y + 3) = (u, v)$

4. $\dot{y} = 2x - 3$; $(x, y) \rightarrow (x - 1, y + 1) = (u, v)$

5. $y = 2 - x$; $(x, y) \rightarrow (x - 2, y) = (u, v)$

6. $2y = 3x - 5$; $(x, y) \rightarrow (x - 1, y + 1) = (u, v)$

7. $2y = 3x - 5$; $(x, y) \rightarrow (x + 1, y + 4) = (u, v)$

8. $y = 2 - x$; $(x, y) \rightarrow (x, y + 2) = (u, v)$

9. $y = 2 - x$; $(x, y) \rightarrow (x - 1, y + 1) = (u, v)$

10. $y = 2x - \pi$; $(x, y) \rightarrow (x, y + \pi) = (u, v)$

Find suitable translations $(x, y) \rightarrow (x + h, \ y + k)$ that simplify the following equations for lines to the form $y = cx$ in a single-plane representation; give *at least two* such translations in each case. Show the positions of the original and image lines in a single-plane representation.

11. $y = 2x + 3$ 12. $y = 4x - 1$

13. $2y = 5x - 7$ 14. $3y = 1 - 4x$

15. $2x + 3y = 5$ 16. $2x - 3y = 4$

17. $\dfrac{x}{2} + \dfrac{y}{3} = 1$ 18. $\dfrac{y}{\sqrt{2}} = \dfrac{x}{\pi} + \dfrac{3}{\pi\sqrt{2}}$

19. Can the slope of a line, given by the value of m in the equation
$$y = mx + b,$$
be changed by a translation?

20. Can the intercepts of a line on the co-ordinate axes be changed by a translation?

21. (a) Find the image in the uv-plane of the region consisting of the points below the line
$$x + 2y = 5$$
under the translation
$$x \rightarrow x + 2, \ y \rightarrow y - 1.$$
Is this region the same as the region consisting of the points below the image of the line?

(b) Make a similar comparison for points to the left of the line
$$3x + 2y = 7$$
under the translation
$$x \rightarrow x + 1, \ y \rightarrow y + 3.$$

22. Generalize the results of the previous question for an arbitrary line under an arbitrary translation.

23. Find the images of the given regions under the given translations. Sketch the original region and its image.

(a) $x > 0, y < 0$; $x \rightarrow x + 1, y \rightarrow y - 1$

(b) $3y - 2x \le 6, 2x - y < 2$; $x \rightarrow x - 3, y \rightarrow y + 7$

(c) $y - x < 1, x + 2y > 2, 3x + 2y < 6$; $x \rightarrow x - 5, y \rightarrow y - 3$

4.4.   Geometric Invariance of a Locus under a Translation

In Section 4.2, we saw that the length of a line segment and the angle between two line segments were invariant under a translation.   In the last section, we found that the image of a line under a translation is a line.   Each of these statements is equivalent to the statement that, in the cases considered, the image of the geometric figure under a translation is a congruent geometric figure.   In fact, this statement is true for any geometric figure under a translation.

If the original geometric figure is a polygon, we can prove the congruency of its image under a translation by dividing the polygon into triangles and then proving that each triangle transforms into a congruent triangle.

Proof: Let ABC be any triangle in the original plane and $A'B'C'$ be its image under a translation.   Then,

$$\left. \begin{aligned} AB &= A'B' , \\ BC &= B'C' , \\ CA &= C'A' . \end{aligned} \right\} \text{ invariance of length}$$

Therefore,

$$\triangle ABC \equiv \triangle A'B'C' .$$

A rigorous proof for any curve is more difficult.   However, we can fix the relative positions of *any* three points on a curve by a triangle and we see that the three corresponding points after the translation have the same relative positions. This makes reasonable the conclusion that the geometric character of any figure is invariant under a translation.   Thus a circle translates into a circle of the same radius; an ellipse translates into an ellipse of the same dimensions; and a square translates into a square of the same size.

Example 1.   Find the image of the parallelogram $ABCD$, for the points $A\,(0,0)$, $B(2,0)$, $C(1,3)$, $D(3,3)$ under the translation

$$(x, y) \to (x - 2 , y - 2) .$$

Show that the image is a parallelogram.

Solution:

$$A\,(0,0) \to A'(-2 , -2)$$
$$B\,(2,0) \to B'(0, -2)$$
$$C(1,3) \to C'(-1,1)$$
$$D(3,3) \to D'(1,1)$$

$$\text{Slope of } A'B' = \frac{-2 - (-2)}{0 - (-2)} = 0 .$$

$$\text{Slope of } C'D' = \frac{1 - 1}{1 - (-1)} = 0 .$$

Therefore,
$$A'B' \parallel C'D' .$$
Similarly,
$$A'D' \parallel B'C' .$$
Hence, $A'B'C'D'$ is a parallelogram.

Example 2.   Find the equation of the image of the circle

$$x^2 + y^2 = 9$$

under the translation

$$(x, y) \rightarrow (x + 1, y - 2) .$$

Solution: The given circle has radius 3 units and centre at $(0, 0)$ in the xy-plane. The point $(0, 0)$ in the xy-plane has the image $(1, -2)$ in the uv-plane under the given translation.   The radius is invariant under the translation.   Therefore, the image is a circle with centre at $(1, -2)$ and radius 3 units.

Let (u, v) be any point on this circle; then

$$\text{length of the radius} = \sqrt{(u - 1)^2 + (v - (-2))^2} .$$

Therefore,
$$(u - 1)^2 + (v + 2)^2 = 3^2 ,$$
$$u^2 - 2u + 1 + v^2 + 4v + 4 = 9 ,$$

or

$$u^2 + v^2 - 2u + 4v - 4 = 0$$

is the equation of the image circle in the uv-plane.

In a single-plane representation, the image circle has the equation

$$x^2 + y^2 - 2x + 4y - 4 = 0 .$$

This mapping of the circle is shown in the diagram.

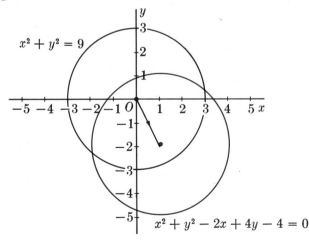

Alternative Solution:

$$(x, y) \rightarrow (x + 1, y - 2) = (u, v).$$

Therefore,

$$x + 1 = u, \quad y - 2 = v,$$

and

$$x = u - 1, \quad y = v + 2.$$

Substituting in the equation of the given circle, we have

$$(u - 1)^2 + (v + 2)^2 = 9,$$

$$u^2 - 2u + 1 + v^2 + 4v + 4 = 9.$$

Therefore,

$$u^2 + v^2 - 2u + 4v - 4 = 0$$

is the equation of the image circle in the uv-plane.

EXERCISE 4.4

1. The points $A(0, 0)$, $B(3, 0)$, $C(3, 3)$, and $D(0, 3)$ determine a square. What are the co-ordinates of the images A', B', C', and D' under the translation

$$(x, y) \rightarrow (x - \tfrac{3}{2}, y - \tfrac{3}{2})?$$

Verify that the image figure is also a square with sides 3 units.

2. Verify that the image of the circle whose equation is

$$x^2 + y^2 = 25$$

under the translation

$$(x, y) \rightarrow (x + 2, y - 1)$$

is a congruent circle.

3. Use a translation $(x, y) \rightarrow (u, v)$ to show that

$$x^2 + y^2 - 6x + 8y = 0$$

is the equation of a circle of radius 5 units. Where is the centre of the circle in the xy-plane? Where is the centre in the uv-plane? Which translation (or translations) reduces the equation to the form

$$u^2 + v^2 = 25?$$

For each of the following equations of circles, find a translation that maps the centre onto the origin, and find the equation of the image circle. Sketch the graphs of both circles and show the mapping for the centres.

4. $x^2 + y^2 - 6x + 4y + 12 = 0$

5. $x^2 + y^2 - 4x - 6y - 18 = 0$

6. $x^2 + y^2 + 6x - 8y - 24 = 0$

7. $x^2 + y^2 - 24x - 10y = 0$

8. $x^2 + y^2 + 4\sqrt{2}x + 2y = 0$

9. The lines with the equations
$$y = 2x + 1 \quad \text{and} \quad 2y = 3x + 3$$
intersect at the point $(1, 3)$.   Find a translation that reduces them to
$$v = 2u \quad \text{and} \quad 2v = 3u$$
respectively in the uv-plane.   Use this translation to show that the line determined by
$$4x + 2y = 10$$
passes through the point of intersection of the first two lines.

10. Show that the effect of the translation
$$(x, y) \rightarrow (x + 1, y - 2) = (u, v)$$
followed by the translation
$$(u, v) \rightarrow (u - 2, v + 3) = (s, t)$$
is equivalent to the single translation
$$(x, y) \rightarrow (x - 1, y + 1) = (s, t)$$
for

(a) the points
$$(2, 3), (-1, 4), (0, 0),$$

(b) the line given by
$$x + 2y = 1,$$

(c) the circle
$$x^2 + y^2 = 4.$$

4.5.   The Images of the Conic Sections under a Translation

As we have noted, the geometric character of a curve is unchanged under a translation.   Therefore,

an ellipse translates into an ellipse,

an hyperbola translates into an hyperbola,

and

a parabola translates into a parabola.

Example 1. Find the image of the ellipse

$$\frac{x^2}{9} + \frac{y^2}{4} = 1$$

under the translation

$$(x, y) \rightarrow (x + 3, y - 2) = (u, v) .$$

Solution:

$$(x, y) \rightarrow (x + 3, y - 2) = (u, v) ;$$

therefore,

$$x + 3 = u, \quad y - 2 = v ,$$

and

$$x = u - 3, \quad y = v + 2 .$$

Therefore,

$$\frac{(u - 3)^2}{9} + \frac{(v + 2)^2}{4} = 1 ,$$

$$4(u^2 - 6u + 9) + 9(v^2 + 4v + 4) = 36 ,$$

or

$$4u^2 + 9v^2 - 24u + 36v + 36 = 0$$

is the equation of the image ellipse in the uv-plane.

In a single-plane representation the image ellipse is

$$4x^2 + 9y^2 - 24x + 36y + 36 = 0 ,$$

as shown in the diagram.

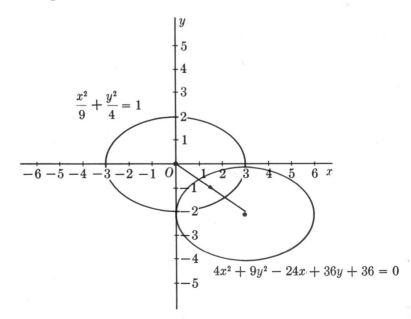

Example 2. Use the transformation

$$(x, y) \rightarrow (x - 1, y + 1) = (u, v)$$

to show that

$$x^2 + 2y^2 - 2x + 4y - 5 = 0$$

is the equation of an ellipse.

Solution:

$$x^2 + 2y^2 - 2x + 4y - 5 = 0,$$
$$x^2 - 2x + 2y^2 + 4y = 5,$$
$$(x^2 - 2x + 1) + 2(y^2 + 2y + 1) = 8,$$
$$\frac{(x - 1)^2}{8} + \frac{(y + 1)^2}{4} = 1.$$

But

$$x - 1 = u \quad \text{and} \quad y + 1 = v;$$

therefore,

$$\frac{u^2}{8} + \frac{v^2}{4} = 1.$$

This equation is the standard equation of an ellipse of semi-axes $2\sqrt{2}$ and 2, with its centre at the origin in the uv-plane.

Translations leave geometric loci invariant; hence,

$$x^2 + 2y^2 - 2x + 4y - 5 = 0$$

is the equation of an ellipse in the xy-plane.

Two-Plane Representation

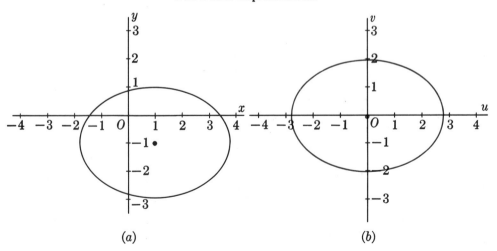

(a)   (b)

Figure 4.9

Note that the semi-axes of this ellipse must also be $2\sqrt{2}$ and 2, and the centre must be at the image of the origin of the uv-plane in the xy-plane, that is, at the point $(1, -1)$ in the xy-plane.

Single-Plane Representation

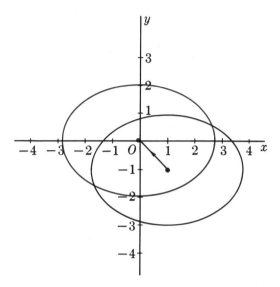

EXERCISE 4.5

Find the images of each of the curves determined by the following equations under the translations stated. State the type of curve determined by the equation in each case.

1. $y^2 - 4x + 8 = 0;$ $(x, y) \rightarrow (x - 2, y)$

2. $y^2 - 2x^2 - 2y + 6x = 12;$ $(x, y) \rightarrow (x - \frac{3}{2}, y - 1)$

3. $x^2 - 4y^2 + 8x + 24y = 20;$ $(x, y) \rightarrow (x + 4, y - 3)$

4. $2x^2 + 3y^2 - 12x + 12y + 24 = 0;$ $(x, y) \rightarrow (x - 3, y + 2)$

5. $9x^2 - 4y^2 + 54x - 8y - 41 = 0;$ $(x, y) \rightarrow (x + 3, y + 1)$

6. $3x^2 - y^2 + 6x + 4y - 1 = 0;$ $(x, y) \rightarrow (x + 1, y - 2)$

7. $4x^2 + 32x - 4y - 16 = 0;$ $(x, y) \rightarrow (x + 4, y + 20)$

8. $x^2 + 4y^2 - 10x + 12y - 20 = 0;$ $(x, y) \rightarrow (x - 5, y + \frac{3}{2})$

9. $4x^2 + 9y^2 + 24x - 36y + 36 = 0;$ $(x, y) \rightarrow (x + 3, y - 2)$

10. $9y^2 - 4x^2 - 18y + 8x - 8 = 0;$ $(x, y) \rightarrow (x - 1, y - 1)$

4.6.   Simplification of Quadratic Relations by Translations

In the previous section, we have seen how a certain transformation may simplify a given quadratic relation. In Example 2, the given translation

$$(x, y) \to (x - 1, y + 1) = (u, v)$$

simplified $\{(x, y) \mid x^2 + 2y^2 - 2x + 4y - 5 = 0\}$

in the xy-plane to

$$\left\{(u, v) \,\middle|\, \frac{u^2}{8} + \frac{v^2}{4} = 1\right\},$$

in the uv-plane and hence we showed that the graph was an ellipse.
In this section, we illustrate how to find a translation that will perform the simplification.   Basically, the method involves *completion of the square.*

Example 1. Find a translation that will eliminate the first degree terms from the equation

$$25x^2 - 16y^2 + 100x + 32y - 316 = 0 \,.$$

Solution:
$$25x^2 - 16y^2 + 100x + 32y = 316 \,,$$
$$25x^2 + 100x - (16y^2 - 32y) = 316 \,,$$
$$25(x^2 + 4x) - 16(y^2 - 2y) = 316 \,,$$
$$25(x^2 + 4x + 4) - 16(y^2 - 2y + 1) = 316 + 100 - 16 \,,$$
$$25(x + 2)^2 - 16(y - 1)^2 = 400 \,.$$

If $$x + 2 = u \,, \quad y - 1 = v \,,$$

then
$$25u^2 - 16v^2 = 400 \,.$$

The required translation is

$$(x, y) \to (x + 2, y - 1) = (u, v) \,.$$

Note that the graph of the equation is a hyperbola with semi-axes 4 and 5; the equation in standard form is

$$\frac{u^2}{4^2} - \frac{v^2}{5^2} = 1 \,.$$

This image under the translation

$$(x, y) \to (x + 2, y - 1)$$

is the hyperbola

$$\frac{x^2}{4^2} - \frac{y^2}{5^2} = 1$$

in the single-plane representation.

Example 2. Simplify

$$x^2 + 6x - 8y + 25 = 0$$

by a translation and identify the character of the curve. Show both the original curve and the image curve in a single-plane representation.

Solution:

$$(x^2 + 6x) - 8y + 25 = 0,$$
$$(x^2 + 6x + 9) = 8y - 25 + 9,$$
$$(x + 3)^2 = 8(y - 2).$$

Put $$u = x + 3, \quad v = y - 2;$$
then

$$u^2 = 8v$$

in the uv-plane. Therefore, in a single-plane representation, the image is given by

$$x^2 = 8y.$$

The image curve is a parabola with $x = 0$ for its axis, its vertex at $(x, y) = (0, 0)$, and opening towards positive values of y. Hence the original graph is a parabola with

$$x + 3 = 0$$

as its axis, its vertex at $(-3, 2)$ and opening towards positive values of y.

EXERCISE 4.6

For each of the following equations, find a translation that reduces the equation to the form

$$ax^2 + by^2 = c \quad \text{or} \quad y^2 = 4ax \quad \text{where } a, b, c \in I.$$

State the type of conic section represented in each case.

1. $y^2 + 4x - 4y + 8 = 0.$

2. $4x^2 + 32x - 4y - 13 = 0.$

3. $y = 4x - x^2.$

4. $x^2 - 6x - 4y + 8 = 0.$

5. $x^2 - y^2 + 12x + 4y + 16 = 0.$

6. $3x^2 + 4y^2 + 12x + 6y + 7 = 0.$

7. $4x^2 + y^2 + 12x - 10y + 14 = 0.$

8. $x^2 - y^2 + 8x - 14y - 35 = 0.$

9. $9x^2 + 4y^2 + 36x - 24y + 36 = 0.$

10. $4x^2 - 9y^2 - 8x + 72y - 104 = 0.$

11. By examining the pattern of the results in questions (1) to (10), can you form a rule for the type of curve that is given by an original equation of the form

$$ax^2 + by^2 + 2gx + 2fy + c = 0$$

when   (i) $ab = 0$,
   (ii) $ab > 0$,
   (iii) $ab < 0$?

12. The mapping
$$(x, y) \to (x + h, y + k)$$
reduces
$$ax^2 + by^2 + 2gx + 2fy + c = 0$$

to a standard form for a conic.   Find the values of h and k in terms of a, b, g, and f.   Verify that

(a)   if $ab = 0$ the conic is a parabola,

(b)   if $ab > 0$ the conic is an ellipse,

(c)   if $ab < 0$ the conic is a hyperbola.

Chapter Summary

The general translation $(x, y) \to (x + h, y + k) = (u, v)$ · Invariance of length and angle under translation · Invariance of locus shape under translation · Simplification of quadratic relations by translations

REVIEW EXERCISE 4

1. Find the images of the points
$$A\,(2, 6), \quad B\,(1, 1), \quad \text{and} \quad C\,(-3, -19)$$
under the translation
$$(x, y) \to (x + 2, y - 4)\,.$$
Show that (a) A, B, C are collinear, (b) the images A', B', C' are collinear, and (c) the slope of the line is invariant under the translation.

2. What geometric figure is formed by the points
$$A\,(3, 4), \quad B\,(0, 0), \quad \text{and} \quad C\,(6, 0)\;?$$
Find the images of A, B, and C under the translation
$$(x, y) \to (x - 4, y - 2)$$
and prove that ABC and $A'B'C'$ are congruent.

3. Find the images of the points
$$A\,(2, \sqrt{3}), \quad B\,(1, 1) \quad \text{and} \quad C\,(5, -\sqrt{3})$$
under the translation
$$(x, y) \to (x - 2, y - \sqrt{3})\,.$$
Show that angle ABC = angle $A'B'C'$.

4. (a) Show that the image of the line whose equation is
$$y = 5x - 4$$
under the translation
$$(x, y) \rightarrow (x - 3, y + 4) = (u, v)$$
is the line whose equation is
$$v = 5u + 15 \,.$$

(b) Verify that
$$v = 5u + 15$$
is the equation of the image line by finding two points that lie on the original line and then finding the equation of the line that passes through the images of these two points.

5. Find the equation of the image of the line determined by
$$3y = 2x - 7$$
under the translation
$$(x, y) \rightarrow (x + 4, y - 5) = (u, v) \,.$$

Find suitable translations
$$(x, y) \rightarrow (x + h, y + k)$$
that simplify the following equations for lines to the form
$$y = kx \,.$$
Find at least one such translation in each case and show the original and the image lines in a single-plane representation.

6. $y = 4x - 3$ $\qquad\qquad\qquad$ 7. $2x + y = 5$

8. $\dfrac{x}{3} + \dfrac{y}{4} = 1$ $\qquad\qquad\qquad$ 9. $\sqrt{3}y = \sqrt{2}x + \sqrt{3}$

10. Find the image in the uv-plane of the region determined by
$$3x - 5y < 15$$
under the translation
$$(x, y) \rightarrow (x - 2, y - 1) \,.$$
Sketch the region in the xy- and uv-planes.

11. (a) Sketch the region consisting of the points under the line whose equation is
$$x - 3y + 3 = 0 \,.$$

(b) Find the equation in the uv-plane of the image of the line in (a) under the translation
$$(x, y) \rightarrow (x - 1, y + 2) \,.$$

Is the region consisting of the points under the line determined in (b) the same region as the region which is the image of the region in (a)?

12. Verify that the image of the circle whose equation is
$$4x^2 + 4y^2 = 25$$
under the translation
$$(x, y) \rightarrow (x + 3, y - 2)$$
is a congruent circle.

13. For the circle determined by
$$x^2 + y^2 - 10x + 6y + 22 = 0 \,.$$
find a translation that maps the centre onto the origin, and find the equation of the image circle. Show the graphs of both circles in a single-plane representation.

14. Repeat question (13) for
$$4x^2 + 4y^2 - 4x + 12y = 15 \,.$$

15. Find the image of the conic determined by
$$4x^2 - 9y^2 + 32x + 18y + 19 = 0$$
under the translation
$$(x, y) \rightarrow (x + 4, y - 1) \,.$$
Name and describe the conic.

16. Repeat question (15) for
$$x^2 + 4y^2 + 8x - 6y + 12 = 0$$
and the translation
$$(x, y) \rightarrow (x + 4, y - \tfrac{3}{4}) \,.$$

For each of the following equations, find a translation that reduces the equations to the form
$$ax^2 + by^2 = c \quad \text{or} \quad y^2 = 4ax$$
where a, b, $c \in I$.   Identify the conic section represented in each case.

17. $y^2 + 4x - 8y + 28 = 0$ 18. $3x^2 + 4y^2 - 30x - 8y + 67 = 0$

19. $3x^2 + y^2 - 18x + 10y - 10 = 0$ 20. $16x^2 + 7y^2 - 32x + 28y - 68 = 0$

21. $4x^2 - 12x - 16y + 1 = 0$

22. Show that the effect of the translation
$$(x, y) \rightarrow (x - 4, y - 2) = (u, v)$$
followed by the translation
$$(u, v) \rightarrow (u + 5, v + 1) = (s, t)$$
is equivalent to the single translation
$$(x, y) \rightarrow (x + 1, y - 1) = (s, t)$$
for (a) the line $5x - y = 4$, (b) the circle $4x^2 + 4y^2 = 49$, and (c)   the hyperbola $2x^2 - 9y^2 = 18$.

Chapter 5

REFLECTIONS AND DILATATIONS

5.1. Reflections of Points and Polygons

In the previous chapter we have seen that under translations, distances and angles remain invariant, as does the order of the points on a geometric figure, such as, for example, a polygon or a curve. There are other mappings under which distances, angles or both remain invariant; an interesting example is the *reflection* transformation. An example of a reflection transformation is given by

$$(x, y) \to (-x, y) .$$

If we consider the images of three points

$$A (1, 2), \qquad B (3, 4), \text{ and } C (2, 5)$$

under such a transformation, we see that the image points are

$$A' (-1, 2), \qquad B' (-3, 4), \text{ and } C' (-2, 5) .$$

The two triangles ABC and $A'B'C'$ are shown in Figure 5.1.

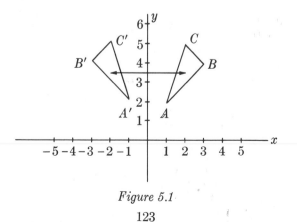

Figure 5.1

123

We easily establish that

$$AB^2 = (3-1)^2 + (4-2)^2 = 4 + 4 = 8\,,$$

and

$$A'B'^2 = (-3+1)^2 + (4-2)^2 = 4 + 4 = 8\,,$$

so that

$$AB = A'B'\,.$$

Also,

$$\text{slope of } AB = m_1 = \frac{4-2}{3-1} = 1\,,$$

$$\text{slope of } AC = m_2 = \frac{5-2}{2-1} = 3\,;$$

hence,

$$\tan \angle BAC = \frac{3-1}{1+3} = \tfrac{1}{2}\,.$$

and similarly

$$\tan \angle B'A'C' = \tfrac{1}{2}\,.$$

Therefore,

$$\angle BAC = \angle B'A'C'\,.$$

However, although the lengths of line segments and the sizes of angles are preserved, under this transformation, there is an important difference from the translations. *The directions are changed.* Thus, if we proceed around $\triangle ABC$ from A to B to C back to A (i.e., counterclockwise) the interior is on the left; while for $\triangle A'B'C'$ the interior is on the right if we proceed from A' to B' to C' and back to A' (i.e., clockwise). Thus, we may say that the order of the vertices is reversed by a reflection. The reader should check that this reversal of order does not occur under translations.

If we use an analogue from geometrical optics and consider a plane mirror to be placed along the y-axis perpendicular to the page, then the reflection or mirror image of $\triangle ABC$ appears to be $\triangle A'B'C'$. This analogy is the reason for the name of this type of transformation.

The transformation

$$(x,\, y) \rightarrow (-x,\, y)$$

is a reflection in the y-axis.

The transformation

$$(x,\, y) \rightarrow (x,\, -y)$$

is another reflection transformation and this time the axis of reflection is the x-axis as shown in Figure 5.2.

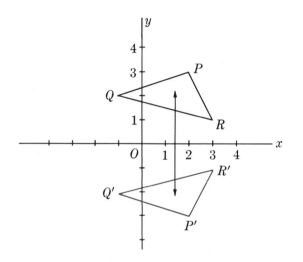

Figure 5.2

Again the order of the points $P'Q'R'$ is the reverse of the order of PQR, if we traverse the triangles so that the interior is on the left in each case.

Note that, in Figure 5.1,

$$\triangle A'B'C' \text{ is the image of } \triangle ABC$$

and

$$\triangle ABC \text{ is the image of } \triangle A'B'C'$$

under the reflection

$$(x, y) \rightarrow (-x, y) \,.$$

In Figure 5.2,

$$\triangle P'Q'R' \text{ is the image of } \triangle PQR$$

and

$$\triangle PQR \text{ is the image of } \triangle P'Q'R'$$

under the reflection

$$(x, y) \rightarrow (x, -y) \,.$$

This reciprocity between image and original is not true in general for translations.

Let us now look at what happens if we use more than one reflection and in particular study the effect on direction of two reflections.

Figure 5.3(a) shows the double reflection, the reflection

$$(x, y) \rightarrow (-x, y)$$

followed by

$$(x, y) \rightarrow (x, -y) \,.$$

Figure 5.3(b) shows the double reflection, the reflection

$$(x, y) \rightarrow (x, -y)$$

followed by

$$(x, y) \rightarrow (-x, y) \,.$$

In each case, the result is equivalent to the transformation

$$(x, y) \rightarrow (-x, -y) \,.$$

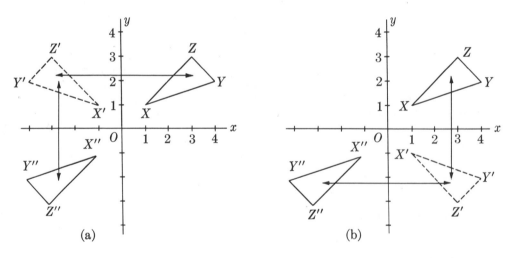

(a)   (b)

Figure 5.3

When we consider the transformation

$$(x, y) \rightarrow (-x, -y)$$

as a mathematical reflection in the origin, we are defining a reflection in the origin as follows:

Given the point P and the origin O, let us extend the line PO beyond O to P' so that $PO = OP'$. Then P' is the reflection of P in the origin. Figure 5.4 illustrates the reflection of $\triangle XYZ$ in the origin, the image being $X''Y''Z''$.

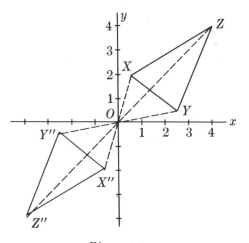

Figure 5.4

We note that the double reflection, or a reflection in the origin, leaves the interior of the triangle on the same side (the left in this case) of the paths XYZ and $X''Y''Z''$. Each of the two reflections reverses the order (see Figure 5.3) and the final result of the two reflections is the preservation of the order.

EXERCISE 5.1

1. (a) Find the images of the three points $P(3, 2)$, $Q(7, 3)$, and $R(4, 0)$ under the transformation
$$(x, y) \rightarrow (x, -y) .$$
   (b) Sketch the original and image triangles.
   (c) Prove that the triangles are congruent.
   (d) What is the equation of the axis of reflection for this transformation?

2. (a) Find images A', B', C', of the three points $A(3, 5)$, $B(1, 2)$, and $C(8, 1)$ by a reflection in the origin.   Plot the six points.
   (b) Show that $\angle ABC = \angle A'B'C'$.
   (c) Check to show that the order of the vertices in triangles ABC and $A'B'C'$ has been preserved by this reflection.   Contrast this result with the result in question (1).   Explain.

3. (a) Find the co-ordinates of A', B', and C', the images of $A(4, 8)$, $B(4, 2)$, and $C(7, 2)$ under the reflection transformation $(x, y) \rightarrow (-x + 6, y)$. Plot the six points.

   (b) What is the axis of reflection for this mapping?

4. (a) Find images corresponding to the points $M(1, 0)$, $N(2, 1)$, and $P(7, 4)$ under the reflection transformation $(x, y) \rightarrow (y, x)$.

   (b) Plot the six points. Sketch the axis of reflection for this transformation and state its equation.

5. (a) Under the transformations F and F followed by G, where $F : (x, y) \rightarrow (x, -y)$ and $G (x, y) \rightarrow (-x, y)$, find a first and second set of images for the points $A(1, 9)$, $B(3, 6)$, and $C(5, 3)$.

   (b) Show that the collinearity of A, B, and C is preserved in each transformation.

   (c) What are the axes of reflection for the transformations in (a)?

   (d) What single reflection transformation is equivalent to the two reflections in (a)?

6. (a) Under the transformations given by S and S followed by T, where $S : (x, y) \rightarrow (x, -y)$ and $T : (x, y) \rightarrow (-x - 2, y)$, find a final set of images for the points A, B, and C of question (5).

   (b) What is the axis of reflection for the second reflection in 6(a)?

   (c) Use mapping notation to describe a single transformation equivalent to the two reflections in (a).

   (d) In which point could the transformation in (c) be considered as a reflection?

7. (a) Under the transformations V followed by W and W followed by V, where $V : (x, y) \rightarrow (x + 1, y - 3)$ and $W : (x, y) \rightarrow (-x, -y)$, find final sets of images of $A(3, 1)$, $B(-6, -1)$, and $C(2, -4)$.

   (b) Show that, if A, B, and C are collinear and B is between A and C, B remains between A and C after a reflection in an axis or the origin.

5.2. Reflections of Lines and Curves

The invariance of the lengths of line segments and angles under reflection implies the invariance of polygons, and consequently of all geometric loci, including curves under reflection. However, we must remember that the order of the points on a curve is reversed by each reflection. We shall now examine the reflections of some lines and conics.

When we wished to find the effect of translations on the equations of various curves we used a two-plane representation at first. After the equation had been transformed from one in x and y to one in u and v, we returned to a single-plane representation.

If we do the same for the reflection

$$(x, y) \rightarrow (-x, y) = (u, v),$$

we see that

$$u = -x, \quad v = y,$$

and so that

$$x = -u, \quad y = v$$

is the required substitution in a given equation in x and y.   For example, the line given by the equation

$$x + y = 1 \qquad \text{in the } xy\text{-plane}$$

becomes the line given by the equation

$$-u + v = 1 \qquad \text{in the } uv\text{-plane.}$$

Therefore, in the single plane representation, the image line is given by

$$-x + y = 1.$$

Thus, we can pass from the original equation to the image equation by replacing x by $-x$ and y by y without using the two plane representation first. The reader should contrast this situation with the case of translation.

Example 1.

(a)   Apply the reflections,

$$\text{(i)} \quad R_1 : (x, y) \rightarrow (-x, y)$$

$$\text{(ii)} \quad R_2 : (x, y) \rightarrow (x, -y)$$

to the line

$$3x + 4y = 12.$$

(b)   Find the result of the reflection R_1 followed by R_2 and show that the result is that given by the reflection

$$R_3 : (x, y) \rightarrow (-x, -y).$$

(c)   Show that R_3 is also the result of the reflection R_2 followed by R_1. Show the various lines on one Cartesian plane.

Solution:

    (a) (i) Under the reflection

$$R_1 : (x, y) \to (-x, y) \,,$$

x is replaced by $-x$ and y by y; that is, y is unchanged.   Therefore, the line

$$l = \{(x, y) \mid 3x + 4y = 12\} \,,$$

under the reflection R_1, becomes

$$\begin{aligned} l_1 &= \{(x, y) \mid 3(-x) + 4y = 12\} \\ &= \{(x, y) \mid -3x + 4y = 12\} \,. \end{aligned}$$

    (ii) Similarly, the line

$$l = \{(x, y) \mid 3x + 4y = 12\} \,,$$

under the reflection R_2,
becomes the line

$$\begin{aligned} l_2 &= \{(x, y) \mid 3x + 4(-y) = 12\} \\ &= \{(x, y) \mid 3x - 4y = 12\} \,. \end{aligned}$$

    (b) If the reflection R_2

is applied to the line l_1, it becomes

$$\begin{aligned} l_3 &= \{(x, y) \mid -3x + 4(-y) = 12\} \\ &= \{(x, y) \mid -3x - 4y = 12\} \,. \end{aligned}$$

If the reflection

$$R_3 : (x, y) \to (-x, -y)$$

is applied to the line l, it becomes the line

$$\{(x, y) \mid 3(-x) + 4(-y) = 12\} = \{(x, y) \mid -3x - 4y = 12\}$$
$$= l_3 \,.$$

    (c) Similarly, the reflection R_1 applied to the line l_2 gives the line

$$\{(x, y) \mid 3(-x) - 4y = 12\} = \{(x, y) \mid -3x - 4y = 12\}$$
$$= l_3 \,.$$

We note that we could have used a two-plane representation by writing

$$R_1 : (x, y) \to (-x, y) = (u, v) \,,$$

so that the reflection of the line

$$l = \{ (x, y) \mid 3x + 4y = 12 \} \text{ in the } xy\text{-plane}$$

becomes the line

$$l'_1 = \{ (u, v) \mid -3u + 4v = 12 \} \text{ in the } uv\text{-plane.}$$

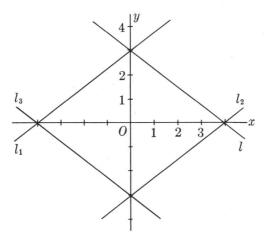

Example 2.   Find the image of

$$x^2 + 2xy + y^2 = 4(x - y)$$

under the reflection

$$(x, y) \rightarrow (-x, y) .$$

Solution: Under the reflection, x is replaced by $-x$ and y by y, so that the image equation is given by

$$(-x)^2 + 2(-x)y + y^2 = 4(-x - y) ,$$
$$x^2 - 2xy + y^2 = -4(x + y) .$$

EXERCISE 5.2

1. Apply the reflection
$$R_1 : (x, y) \rightarrow (-x, y)$$
to the line whose equation is
$$2x + 3y = -6,$$
and apply the reflection
$$R_2 : (x, y) \rightarrow (x, -y)$$
to the image under R_1. Show that the final result is also obtained by applying the reflection
$$R_3 : (x, y) \rightarrow (-x, -y)$$
to the original line. Show the original lines and the two image lines in a single-plane representation.

2. Under the reflection
$$R : (x, y) \rightarrow (-x, -y)$$
find the image of the point of intersection of the lines whose equations are
$$7x - 3y = -21 \quad \text{and} \quad 3x + 6y = 8.$$
Sketch the two original and two image lines in a single-plane representation.

3. A circle has its centre at $(0, 5)$ and radius 5 units. Find the equation of the image circle under the reflection
$$R : (x, y) \rightarrow (x, -y)$$
Show both circles in one Cartesian plane.

4. Find the region that is the image of the region defined by
$$2x + 3y < -6$$
under the reflection
$$R : (x, y) \rightarrow (-x, y).$$

5. Find the region which is the image of the region defined by
$$x^2 + y^2 \leq 16, \ 3x + 5y \geq 15$$
under the reflection
$$R : (x, y) \rightarrow (x, -y).$$
Sketch the original region and its image in a single-plane representation.

6. Find defining equations for the region that is the image of the region defined by
$$x + y > 2, \ x + y < 6,$$
under the reflection
$$R : (x, y) \rightarrow (-x, -y).$$
Show both regions on one Cartesian plane.

7. (a) Find the image of the hyperbola $x^2 - y^2 = 16$ under the reflections
   (i) $R_1 : (x, y) \rightarrow (-x, y)$,
   (ii) $R_2 : (x, y) \rightarrow (x, -y)$,
   (iii) $R_3 : (x, y) \rightarrow (-x, -y)$.

   (b) Find the image of the hyperbola $xy = 8$ under the reflections (i) R_1, (ii) R_2, (iii) R_3.

   (c) How many different hyperbolas are involved in part (b)?   Sketch them on one Cartesian plane.

8. Find the equation of, and sketch the image of the ellipse
$$\frac{(x + 4)^2}{16} + \frac{y^2}{9} = 1$$
under the reflection
$$R : (x, y) \rightarrow (-x, y) \,.$$

9. (a) Find the equation of the image of the parabola
$$y^2 = 4(x - 2)$$
under the reflection
$$R : (x, y) \rightarrow (-x + 2, y) \,,$$

   (b) Sketch the original parabola and its image in a single-plane representation.

   (c) State the equation of the axis of reflection.

10. (a) Apply in turn the reflections
$$R_1 : (x, y) \rightarrow (y, x) \,,$$
$$R_2 : (x, y) \rightarrow (-y, -x) \,,$$
to the ellipse
$$\frac{(x - 12)^2}{144} + \frac{y^2}{25} = 1 \,.$$

   (b) How many *different* ellipses are involved?   Sketch them in a single-plane representation.   Show on the graph the axes of reflection.

11. Find the image of the graph of
$$y = \frac{6}{x^2 + 2}$$
under the reflection
$$R : (x, y) \rightarrow (x, -y) \,.$$
Show both original and image on one Cartesian plane.

12. Find the image of the region
$$y > \frac{6}{x^2 + 2}, \quad x^2 + y^2 < 9 \,,$$
under the transformation in question (11).   Sketch the original region and its image on one Cartesian plane.

5.3.   Dilatations of Polygons

In all the transformations we have studied so far, lengths and angles have been invariant. We shall now consider some elementary transformations under which lengths or angles or both are not invariant.

Example 1.   Find the image points of

$$A\,(1,1) \quad B\,(-1,1) \quad \text{and} \quad C\,(0,-1)$$

under the transformation

$$(x, y) \rightarrow (3x, 3y)\,.$$

Show the original and image points on one Cartesian plane.

Solution:

> The point $A\,(1,1)$ has the image $A'(3,3)\,.$
> The point $B\,(-1,1)$ has the image $B'(-3,3)\,.$
> The point $C\,(0,-1)$ has the image $C'(0,-3)\,.$

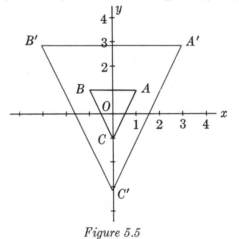

Figure 5.5

If we form the triangles ABC and $A'B'C'$ in Figure 5.5, we see immediately that they are similar. Thus, the transformation

$$(x, y) \rightarrow (3x, 3y)$$

preserves the angles of the triangles; that is, the angles are invariant under the transformation. Also, the length of AB is 2 units and of $A'B'$ 6 units, so that the ratio of the sides of the triangles is

$$\frac{A'B'}{AB} = \frac{B'C'}{BC} = \frac{C'A'}{CA} = \frac{3}{1}\,.$$

It would appear, therefore, that the coefficient of x or y (when the coefficients are equal) gives the amplification of the transformation. Such a transformation is called a homogeneous isotropic dilatation, which means that the amplitude of the stretching is the same at all points of the plane and in all directions.

The general homogeneous isotropic dilatation transformation is given by

$$(x,y) \rightarrow (ax, ay), \quad a \in Re^+$$

and a is the amplification of the dilatation.

A more general transformation, which changes lengths, is

$$(x, y) \rightarrow (ax, by), \quad a, b \in Re^+, \quad a \neq b.$$

Such a transformation also changes angles in general, as we can show in the following examples.

Example 2. Find the images, A' and B', of $A(2,4)$ and $B(-4,2)$ under the transformation

$$(x, y) \rightarrow (\tfrac{1}{2}x, \tfrac{3}{2}y).$$

Show the original and image points on one Cartesian plane. Show that

$$\angle AOB \neq \angle A'OB',$$

where O is the origin of the co-ordinate system.

Solution:

The image of $A(2,4)$ is $A'(1,6)$.
The image of $B(-4,2)$ is $B'(-2,3)$.

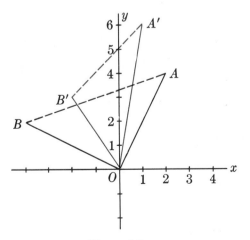

Figure 5.6

The slope of $OA = m_1 = 2$ and the slope of $OB = m_2 = -\frac{1}{2}$. The numbers m_1 and m_2 are negative reciprocals; therefore,

$$\angle AOB = 90°,$$

and the slope of $OA' = m_1' = 6$, and the slope of $OB' = m_2' = -\frac{3}{2}$.
Thus,

$$\tan \angle A'OB' = \left| \frac{6 - (-\frac{3}{2})}{1 + 6(-\frac{3}{2})} \right|$$

$$= \left| \frac{6 + 1.5}{1 - 9} \right|$$

$$= \frac{7.5}{8}$$

$$= .9375.$$

Hence,

$$\angle A'OB' \simeq 43°.$$

Therefore, $\angle AOB \neq \angle A'OB'$.

We note that some angles are invariant; for example, if C is the point $(2, 0)$ and D the point $(0, 2)$, then the images are $C'(1, 0)$ and $D'(0, 3)$, so that

$$\angle COD = \angle C'OD' = 90°.$$

If, in Figure 5.6, we form the triangles AOB and $A'O'B'$, we see that the two triangles are neither congruent nor similar. We should expect this result, as the transformation has changed both lengths and angles. However, the two figures are both triangles. In general under dilatations, an n-gon (a polygon of n sides) remains an n-gon with no change in n, the number of sides.

Example 3. Using the points of Example 2, find the ratios $OA : OA'$, $OB : OB'$ and $AB : A'B'$.

Solution:

$$OA^2 = 2^2 + 4^2 \qquad\qquad OA'^2 = 1^2 + 6^2$$
$$= 4 + 16 \qquad\qquad\qquad = 1 + 36$$
$$= 20, \qquad\qquad\qquad\quad = 37,$$
$$OA = \sqrt{20}. \qquad\qquad\qquad OA' = \sqrt{37}.$$

Therefore,

$$OA : OA' = \sqrt{20} : \sqrt{37}.$$

$$OB^2 = (-4)^2 + 2^2 \qquad\qquad OB'^2 = (-2)^2 + 3^2$$
$$= 16 + 4 \qquad\qquad\qquad = 4 + 9$$
$$= 20\,, \qquad\qquad\qquad\quad = 13\,,$$
$$OB = \sqrt{20}\,. \qquad\qquad\qquad OB' = \sqrt{13}\,.$$

Therefore,

$$OB : OB' = \sqrt{20} : \sqrt{13}\,.$$

$$AB^2 = (-4 - 2)^2 + (2 - 4)^2 \qquad A'B'^2 = (-2 - 1)^2 + (3 - 6)^2$$
$$= 6^2 + 2^2 \qquad\qquad\qquad = 3^2 + 3^2$$
$$= 36 + 4 \qquad\qquad\qquad = 9 + 9$$
$$= 40\,, \qquad\qquad\qquad\quad = 18\,,$$
$$AB = \sqrt{40}\,. \qquad\qquad\qquad A'B' = \sqrt{18}\,.$$

Therefore,

$$AB : A'B' = \sqrt{40} : \sqrt{18}\,.$$

The reader should verify that, if C is the point $(3, 6)$ and C' its image, then $OC : OC' = \sqrt{20} : \sqrt{37}$ and that O, A and C, are collinear and so are O, A', and C'. This result illustrates the fact that the ratio of the lengths of line segments in a given direction is independent of the length of the line segments. The ratio of the lengths of line segments in any given direction is called the *amplification* in that direction.

The dilatation

$$(x, y) \rightarrow (ax, by), \quad a, b \in Re^+, \quad a \neq b$$

is homogeneous but not isotropic; that is, the amplification is the same at every point in the plane but not the same in all directions.

EXERCISE 5.3

1. (a) The points $A(1, 1)$, $B(-1, 1)$, $C(-1, -1)$, and $D(1, -1)$ are vertices of a square. Find image points for these vertices under the homogeneous, isotropic dilatation

$$D : (x, y) \rightarrow (4x, 4y)\,.$$

   (b) Calculate slopes to show that

$$\angle AOD = \angle A'OD'\,.$$

   (c) Repeat (b) by showing that O, A, A' and O, D, D' are collinear.

2. Repeat question (1) for a congruent square centred at $E(6, 8)$ rather than at $O(0, 0)$.

3. (a) Find the image of the square in question (1) under the homogeneous, nonisotropic dilatation

$$D_1 : (x, y) \rightarrow (2x, \tfrac{1}{2}y).$$

(b) Sketch the original square and its image in a single-plane representation.

(c) Identify the image figure. Show that

$$\angle AOD \neq \angle A'OD'.$$

4. (a) The vertices of an isosceles triangle are $A(1, 0)$, $B(-1, 0)$, and $C(0, -\sqrt{3})$. Find the vertices of the image triangle under the dilatation,

$$D : (x, y) \rightarrow (\sqrt{3}x, \sqrt{3}y).$$

(b) Sketch both triangles in one Cartesian plane.

(c) Prove that the triangles ABC and $A'B'C'$ are similar.

5. (a) Find the image of the triangle in question 4(a) under the dilatation

$$D_1 : (x, y) \rightarrow \left(2x, \frac{y}{3}\right).$$

(b) Sketch the original triangle and its image.

(c) Show that the new image triangle $A''B''C''$ is isosceles but not similar to $\triangle ABC$.

6. The points $M(2, 2)$, $O(0, 0)$, $N(-3, 3)$, $P(-3, -2)$, and $Q(2, -2)$ are the vertices of a pentagon. Find the co-ordinates of the vertices of the image of this pentagon under the dilatation

$$D : (x, y) \rightarrow (3x, 3y).$$

Sketch both pentagons in a single plane representation.

7. (a) Find the image of the original pentagon in question (6) under the dilatation

$$D_1 : (x, y) \rightarrow (3x, 2y)$$

(b) Sketch the original pentagon and the image under D_1 in a single-plane representation.

(c) Show that $MQ \parallel M''Q''$ and $OM \nparallel O''M''$.

5.4. Dilatations of Lines and Curves

In the previous section and exercise, we observed that the number of sides of a polygon was unchanged under a dilatation but that the shape was changed. As a consequence a line remains a line under a dilatation, but one curve may be changed into a curve of a different type. For example, a circle can be changed into an ellipse. However, a closed curve (*e.g.*, an ellipse) cannot be changed into an open curve (*e.g.*, a parabola or hyperbola) by a finite dilatation.

Example 1. Find the equation of the image of the line $3x + 4y = 6$ under the transformation

$$(x, y) \rightarrow (3x, 2y) = (u, v) .$$

Draw a two-plane diagram and a single-plane diagram of the original line and its image.

Solution: For the transformation,

$$3x = u \quad \text{and} \quad 2y = v ;$$

therefore,

$$x = \tfrac{1}{3}u \quad \text{and} \quad y = \tfrac{1}{2}v .$$

Substituting for x and y in

$$3x + 4y = 6,$$

we obtain the transformed equation

$$3\left(\tfrac{1}{3}u\right) + 4\left(\tfrac{1}{2}v\right) = 6 .$$

Hence, the equation of the image line is

$$u + 2v = 6 .$$

In the single-plane representation, the uv- and xy-axes coincide, and we may write the image equation as

$$x + 2y = 6 .$$

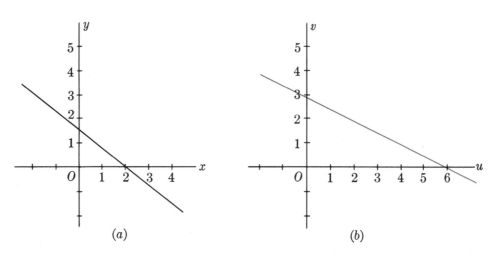

(a) $\qquad\qquad\qquad\qquad\qquad$ (b)

Two-Plane Representation

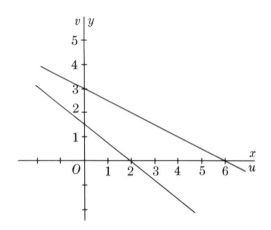

Single-Plane Representation

To verify the correctness of these equations, we may find the intercept points of the original line and the images of these points and check that the images do lie on the image line.   The line

$$3x + 4y = 6$$

passes through $(2, 0)$ and $(0, \frac{3}{2})$.   The image points are $(6, 0)$ and $(0, 3)$ respectively.

The line

$$u + 2v = 6$$

passes through $(6, 0)$ and $(0, 3)$ as required, or, in the single plane representation, the line

$$x + 2y = 6$$

passes through $(6, 0)$ and $(0, 3)$.

Example 2. Find the equation of the image of

$$\frac{x^2}{9} + \frac{y^2}{4} = 1$$

under the transformation

$$(x, y) \rightarrow \left(\frac{x}{3}, \frac{y}{2}\right) = (u, v).$$

Identify both the original and image curves.   Draw a two-plane diagram and a single-plane diagram.

Solution: For the transformation

$$\frac{x}{3} = u \quad \text{and} \quad \frac{y}{2} = v \; ;$$

hence,

$$x = 3u \quad \text{and} \quad y = 2v \, .$$

Therefore the equation becomes, in the uv-plane,

$$\frac{(3u)^2}{9} + \frac{(2v)^2}{4} = 1 \, ,$$

$$\frac{9u^2}{9} + \frac{4v^2}{4} = 1 \, ,$$

$$u^2 + v^2 = 1 \, .$$

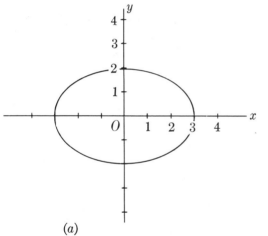

(a)

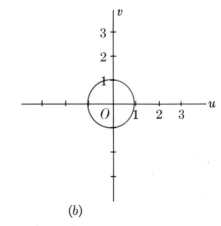

(b)

Two-Plane Representation

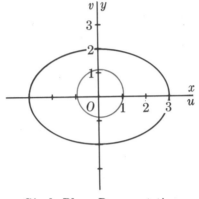

Single-Plane Representation

The original curve is an ellipse centred at O with semi-major axis 3 units on the x-axis and semi-minor axis 2 units. The image curve is a circle of unit radius with centre at O.

EXERCISE 5.4

1. (a) Find equations of the images of the line
$$x + y + 1 = 0$$
    under the dilatations
$$D_1 : (x, y) \rightarrow (2x, 2y) = (u, v)$$
    and
$$D_2 : (x, y) \rightarrow (2x, 4y) = (s, t) .$$

    (b) Sketch the three lines involved in both a three-plane representation and a single-plane representation.

2. (a) Find the image of the circle whose equation is
$$x^2 + y^2 = 1$$
    under the dilatations
$$D_1 : (x, y) \rightarrow (3x, 3y) = (u, v)$$
    and
$$D_2 : (x, y) \rightarrow (3x, 5y) = (s, t) .$$

    (b) Sketch the original circle and the two images of (a) in both a three-plane and single-plane representation.

3. (a) Find the image of the circle whose equation is
$$x^2 - 2x + y^2 + 6y = -1$$
    under the dilatation D_1 of question (2).

    (b) Find the centre of the image circle and the image of the centre of the original circle of (a).

4. (a) Find the image of the parabola

$$x^2 = -y$$

under the dilatation

$$D : (x, y) \rightarrow (\tfrac{1}{2}x, \tfrac{1}{5}y) = (u, v) .$$

Sketch the original and image graphs in one Cartesian plane.

(b) Find the co-ordinates of the focus of both the original parabola and its image.

5. Find the equation of the image of

$$\frac{x^2}{49} + \frac{y^2}{576} = 1$$

under the transformation

$$(x, y) \rightarrow (x, \tfrac{7}{24}y) = (u, v) .$$

Identify both original and image curves and sketch them in a single-plane representation.

6. Repeat question (5) but precede the transformation of question (5) by the translation

$$T : (x, y) \rightarrow (x - 8, y + 4) .$$

7. (a) Find the images of the hyperbola whose equation is

$$\frac{x^2}{9} - \frac{y^2}{16} = 1$$

under each of the transformations

$$D_1 : (x, y) \rightarrow \left(x, \frac{y}{2} \right) = (u, v)$$

and

$$D_2 : (x, y) \rightarrow \left(\frac{x}{3}, \frac{y}{4} \right) = (m, n) .$$

(b) Sketch the three curves involved in a single-plane representation.

8. (a) Translate the hyperbola whose equation is

$$\frac{(x + 4)^2}{25} - \frac{(y - 3)^2}{49} = -1$$

so that the image hyperbola is centred at the origin.

(b) Find the image of the transformed hyperbola in (a) under the dilatation

$$(x, y) \rightarrow \left(2x, \frac{y}{7} \right) .$$

9. (a) Find the image of the ellipse
$$2x^2 + \sqrt{3}xy + y^2 = 5$$
under the rotation mapping
$$(x,\ y) \to \left(\frac{1}{2}x - \frac{\sqrt{3}}{2}y,\ \frac{\sqrt{3}}{2}x + \frac{1}{2}y\right).$$

(b) To the transformed ellipse in (a) apply the dilatation
$$(x,\ y) \to \left(\frac{x}{2\sqrt{2}},\ \frac{y}{\sqrt{10}}\right) = (u,\ v).$$
Find the lengths of the semi-axes of the resulting curve.

(c) Show the three ellipses involved in a single-plane representation.

10. (a) Apply a suitable transformation to the conic represented by
$$6x^2 + 24xy - y^2 - 12x + 26y + 11 = 0$$
to remove the xy-term.

(b) To the transformed hyperbola in part (a) apply the translation
$$(x,\ y) \to \left(x + \frac{7}{5},\ y + \frac{1}{5}\right).$$

(c) Identify the conic.   Find its eccentricity.

(d) To the conic obtained in (b) apply the dilatation
$$(x,\ y) \to \left(\frac{x}{\sqrt{2}},\ \frac{y}{\sqrt{3}}\right).$$
Describe the image.   Find its eccentricity.

11. Find the image of the graph of
$$y = \frac{-5}{x^2 + 1}$$
under the transformation
$$(x,\ y) \to \left(\frac{x}{2},\ y\right).$$
Sketch both graphs in a single-plane representation.

Chapter Summary

Reflection transformations · Invariance of length and angle · Change in direction under a reflection · Reflections of lines and conics · Dilatation transformations · Change in length and/or angle · Amplitude of a dilatation. General homogeneous isotropic dilatation
$$(x,\ y) \to (ax,\ ay), \quad a \in Re^+.$$
General homogeneous dilatation
$$(x,\ y) \to (ax,\ by), \quad a,\ b \in Re^+,\ a \neq b.$$
Dilatations of lines and conics.

REVIEW EXERCISE 5

1. (a) Find images for the points $A\,(4,\,1)$, $B\,(6,\,5)$, and $C\,(9,\,-1)$ under the transformation
$$(x,\,y) \rightarrow (-x,\,y)\,.$$
   (b) Prove that $\angle BAC = \angle B'A'C'$.

2. (a) Find the image of $y = |x|$ under the reflection $(x,\,y) \rightarrow (x,\,-y)$
   (b) Sketch the original and image graphs in a single-plane representation.
   (c) Use the three points $(4,\,4)$, $(0,\,0)$ and $(-2,\,2)$ with their images to show that order has been reversed by this reflection.

3. Find the images of the points $P\,(-1,\,5)$, $Q\,(0,\,3)$, and $R\,(6,\,7)$ under the transformation
$$(x,\,y) \rightarrow (x,\,-y-2)\,.$$
Sketch the six points involved. State the axis of reflection for this transformation.

4. Under the reflection
$$(x,\,y) \rightarrow (-x,\,-y)\,,$$
find the image of triangle ABC where A is $(2,\,-1)$, B is $(1,\,-3)$, and C is $(6,\,-5)$. Sketch the two triangles in a single-plane representation and show that they are congruent by calculating lengths of corresponding sides.

5. Find the image of the region defined by $x - y + 1 < 0$, $x + 5y - 5 > 0$, $x < 5$ under the reflection $(x,\,y) \rightarrow (x,\,-y)$.
Sketch both regions in a single-plane representation.

6. Find the image of the region defined by $4x^2 + y^2 \leq 36$, $2x + y \geq 6$ under the transformation $(x,\,y) \rightarrow (-x,\,-y)$.
Show both regions in one Cartesian plane.

7. Find the equation of the image of the conic $9x^2 - 16y^2 = 144$ under the transformation $(x,\,y) \rightarrow (x,\,-y-8)$.
Sketch both original and image in a single-plane representation. State the equation of the axis of reflection for this transformation.

8. (a) Sketch the equilateral hyperbola $xy = 8$ and its reflection in the x-axis both on one Cartesian plane.
   (b) Sketch the circle $x^2 + y^2 = 8$ on the same set of axes.
   (c) Shade in the region defined by
$$x^2 + y^2 \geq 8,\quad |xy| \leq 8\,.$$

9. The points $A\,(0,4)$, $B\,(0,\,-4)$, $C\,(6,\,-4)$, and $D\,(6,4)$ are vertices of a rectangle. Find the vertices of a rectangle which is the image of the original rectangle under the dilatation $(x,\,y) \rightarrow (\frac{3}{2}x,\,\frac{3}{2}y)$
Show that the rectangles are similar.

10. (a) Find the image of the rectangle in (9) under the dilatation

$$(x,\ y) \rightarrow \left(\frac{x}{2},\ 2y\right)$$

   (b) Prove that the original rectangle and its new image are not similar.

   (c) Sketch the three rectangles of questions (9) and (10) in one Cartesian plane.

11. Repeat question (9) if the original rectangle is first moved to the left so that its centre is at $(-3,\ 0)$. Show that the angle between the diagonals remains constant under the homogeneous, isotropic dilatation of (9).

12. Find the vertices of the image of an isosceles triangle with vertices at $P(5,0)$, $Q(5,-6)$, and $R(9,-3)$ under the dilatation

$$(x,\ y) \rightarrow (3x,\ 3y).$$

   Sketch the two triangles in a single-plane representation. Show that the image triangle is isosceles and similar to the original.

13. Find the image of the isosceles triangle in (12) under the dilatation

$$(x,\ y) \rightarrow \left(\frac{x}{2},\ \frac{y}{3}\right).$$

   Show that the image triangle is isosceles but not similar to the original.

14. (a) Find the images of an ellipse whose equation is $4x^2 + 25y^2 = 100$ under the dilatations

$$D_1 : (x,\ y) \rightarrow \left(\frac{x}{2},\ \frac{y}{2}\right) = (u,\ v)\ ,$$

$$D_2 : (x,\ y) \rightarrow \left(\frac{x}{5},\ \frac{y}{2}\right) = (u,\ v)\ .$$

   (b) Show the original ellipse and its images in a single-plane representation.

15. Find the equation for the image of the conic $x^2 - y^2 = -25$ under the dilatation

$$(x,\ y) \rightarrow (4x,\ 4y) = (u,\ v).$$

   Describe the image conic and sketch both original and image in a single-plane representation.

16. Repeat question (15) if the dilatation is

$$(x,\ y) \rightarrow \left(\frac{x}{2},\ \frac{y}{3}\right) = (u,\ v)\ .$$

17. By a suitable rotation transformation, remove the xy-term from

$$11x^2 - 6xy + 3y^2 - 18 = 0\ .$$

   Describe the conic and sketch it in a single-plane representation. Also find the equation of the reflection of the original conic in the original y-axis and sketch this image in the same Cartesian plane.

Chapter 6

TRIGONOMETRIC FUNCTIONS

6.1. Definition of the Trigonometric Functions

In an earlier course, we learned that the trigonometric functions may be defined by reference to a co-ordinate system. We choose a point $P(x, y)$ on the circle with centre at the origin and radius r. A counterclockwise rotation from a fixed initial ray OA to a final ray OP determines a unique angle θ. The unit of measurement is the radian or the degree.

The measure of the angle, in either unit, is a real number, and π radians $= 180°$.

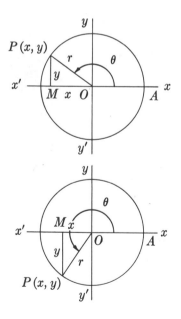
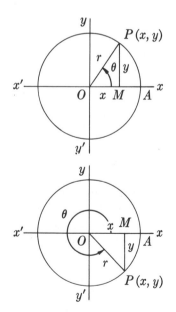

Figure 6.1

147

The values of the trigonometric functions (θ in radians, $0 \le \theta \le 2\pi$) are then defined by the following equations.

sine of $\theta = \sin \theta = \dfrac{y}{r}$,   cosecant of $\theta = \csc \theta = \dfrac{r}{y}(y \ne 0)$,

cosine of $\theta = \cos \theta = \dfrac{x}{r}$,   secant of $\theta = \sec \theta = \dfrac{r}{x}(x \ne 0)$,

tangent of $\theta = \tan \theta = \dfrac{y}{x}(x \ne 0)$,   cotangent of $\theta = \cot \theta = \dfrac{x}{y}(y \ne 0)$.

In Section 6.2, we shall show that these are true functions defined in the usual way.

It follows from these definitions that the sine, cosine, and tangent functions (along with their reciprocal functions) are positive in the quadrants indicated in Figure 6.2 (the CAST diagram).

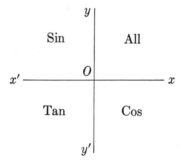

Figure 6.2

Example 1.   Find the values of (a) $\cos 43°$, (b) $\sec 135°$, (c) $\tan 220°$, (d) $\sin 345°$.

Solution:
  (a) From the tables, $\cos 43° \simeq .7314$.
  (b) Sec $135°$ is negative (CAST rule).

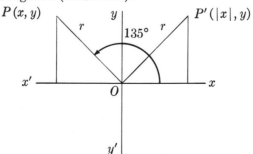

From the diagram,

$$\sec 135° = \sec (180° - 45°)$$
$$= -\sec 45°$$
$$\simeq -1.414 .$$

(tables)

(c)

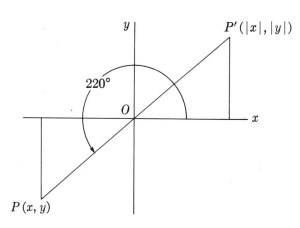

From the diagram,

$$\tan 220° = \tan (180° + 40°)$$
$$= \tan 40°$$
$$\simeq .8391 .$$

(tables)

(d)

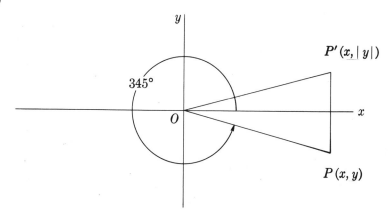

$$\sin 345° = \sin (360° - 15°)$$
$$= -\sin 15°$$
$$\simeq -.2588 .$$

(tables)

Example 2. Without using tables, find the values of cos 45° and tan $\frac{\pi}{4}$.

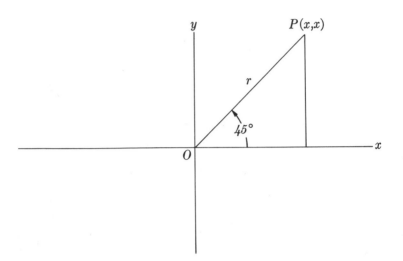

Solution: If the point P has co-ordinates (x, x), then $OP = x\sqrt{2}$ (Pythagoras). In this isosceles right-angled triangle, angle xOP has 45 as its measure in degrees (or $\frac{\pi}{4}$ in radians). Therefore,

$$\cos 45° = \frac{x}{r}$$

$$= \frac{1}{\sqrt{2}},$$

and

$$\tan \frac{\pi}{4} = \frac{x}{x}$$

$$= 1 .$$

Let us extend our definitions beyond those given for $0 \leq \theta \leq 2\pi$. It is important to do so because in practice we deal with angles whose measure in degrees may be 400 or 5000. Our own planet rotates through 360° in one day, 720° in two days, and so on. Any rotating object moves through angles that increase with time. The diagram shows what we mean by an angle of 400°. Our definitions of the trigonometric functions for $0 \leq \theta \leq 2\pi$ imply that the values of these functions for 400° are the same as the values for the coterminal angle 40°. The ray OP is a common coterminal ray.

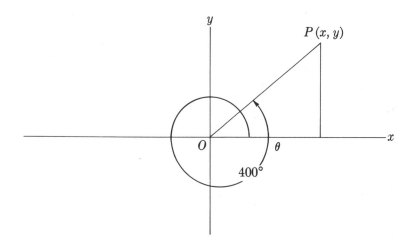

Similarly, the values of the trigonometric functions of $-505°$ (a clockwise rotation) are identical with those for its coterminal angle, $215°$.

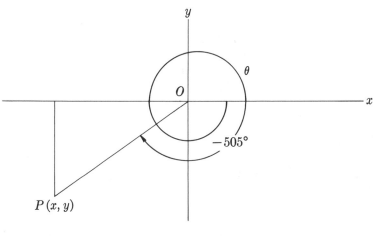

Note that

$$215° = -505° + 720°$$
$$= -505° + 2(360)°.$$

In general, to find the trigonometric functions of any angle θ, we add or subtract multiples of $2\pi(360°)$ until we obtain an angle ϕ between 0 and $2\pi(0°$ and $360°)$. Then, any trigonometric function of θ has the same value as the trigonometric function of the coterminal angle ϕ.

Example 3. Find the values of (a) tan 820°, (b) sin (−1100°).

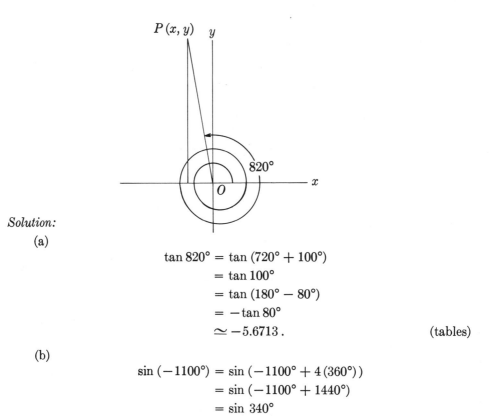

Solution:
(a)

$$\tan 820° = \tan (720° + 100°)$$
$$= \tan 100°$$
$$= \tan (180° − 80°)$$
$$= −\tan 80°$$
$$\simeq −5.6713 . \qquad \text{(tables)}$$

(b)

$$\sin (−1100°) = \sin (−1100° + 4\,(360°))$$
$$= \sin (−1100° + 1440°)$$
$$= \sin 340°$$
$$= \sin (360° − 20°)$$
$$= −\sin 20°$$
$$\simeq −.3420 . \qquad \text{(tables)}$$

EXERCISE 6.1

Use tables to find the following values of trigonometric functions.

1. $\sin 48°$

2. $\cos 100°$

3. $\tan 17°$

4. $\sin 228°$

5. $\cos 260°$

6. $\tan 343°$

7. $\tan \frac{1}{12}\pi$

8. $\sin \frac{3}{5}\pi$

9. $\cos \left(−\frac{1}{18}\pi\right)$

10. $\tan \frac{25}{12}\pi$

11. $\sin \frac{18}{5}\pi$

12. $\cos \frac{19}{18}\pi$

13. $\sin 523°$

14. $\cos 837°$

15. $\tan (−395°)$

16. $\sin (−125°)$

17. $\cos 430°$

18. $\tan 1510°$

Without using tables, find the following values.

19. $\cos 60°$

20. $\sec 45°$

21. $\tan 60°$

22. $\sin 120°$

23. $\cos 225°$

24. $\cot 300°$

25. $\csc (-60°)$

26. $\sin 945°$

27. $\cos (-750°)$

28. $\tan \dfrac{3\pi}{4}$

29. $\sin\left(-\dfrac{7\pi}{3}\right)$

30. $\csc\left(-\dfrac{2\pi}{3}\right)$

31. $\cos(-\tfrac{33}{4}\pi)$

32. $\cot \tfrac{13}{6}\pi$

33. $\sec \tfrac{17}{3}\pi$

Find, to the nearest degree, two angles θ, $0° \le \theta \le 360°$, for the following values of each trigonometric function.

34. $\sin \theta = .4511$

35. $\cos \theta = .8457$

36. $\tan \theta = 1.0724$

37. $\cos \theta = .6820$

38. $\sin \theta = -.7641$

39. $\tan \theta = -2.0511$

40. $\sec \theta = 1.374$

41. $\csc \theta = 3.924$

42. $\cot \theta = -.2155$

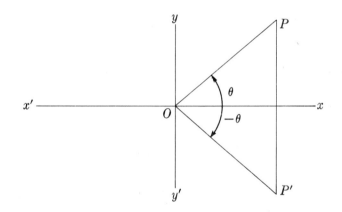

43. Referring to the diagram above, prove that
$$\sin (-\theta) = -\sin \theta .$$
$-\theta$ is a negative fourth quadrant angle and θ is the corresponding positive acute angle.

44. As in question (43) prove (a) $\cos (-\theta) = \cos \theta$, (b) $\tan (-\theta) = -\tan \theta$. Similar results may be obtained in all four quadrants and hence are true for any angle θ.

45. Use the results of questions (43) and (44) to find the following values.
   (a) $\sin (-60°)$
   (b) $\cos (-130°)$
   (c) $\tan (-200°)$
   (d) $\cos (-1540°)$
   (e) $\tan (-30°)$
   (f) $\sec (-1000°)$

6.2.   Domain, Range, and Graph of the Sine and Cosine Functions

Consider the function that we have called "sine".   Each angle θ determines one and only one final ray OP. The ratio $\sin \theta$ is independent of the radius of the circle but is determined by the angle θ.   Thus, for each θ, there is exactly one value of $\sin \theta$. The set of ordered pairs $(\theta, \sin \theta)$ satisfies the requirement for the set to be a function, namely, that no two pairs have the same first element.

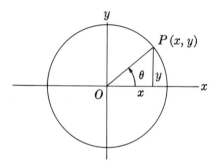

Figure 6.3

In Figure 6.3, if P (x, y) is any point on a unit circle with centre $(0, 0)$, then

$$\frac{x}{1} = \cos \theta ,$$

or

$$x = \cos \theta ,$$

and

$$y = \sin \theta .$$

By the theorem of Pythagoras,

$$x^2 + y^2 = 1 ,$$

or

$$\cos^2\theta + \sin^2\theta = 1 .$$

Now

$$x^2 \geq 0, \quad \text{since} \quad x \in Re ;$$

therefore,

$$y^2 \leq 1 ;$$

that is,

$$\sin^2\theta \leq 1 ,$$

and

$$-1 \leq \sin \theta \leq 1 .$$

From our discussion, we conclude that the range for the sine function is the set of real numbers between -1 and $+1$, including the real numbers -1 and $+1$ themselves.

In summary, the sine function is defined by

$$f(\theta) = \sin \theta, \quad \theta \in Re,$$

and the range is such that

$$|f(\theta)| \leq 1.$$

Similarly, the cosine function is defined by

$$f(\theta) = \cos \theta, \quad \theta \in Re,$$

and the range is such that

$$|f(\theta)| \leq 1.$$

Returning to Figure 6.3, an examination of the ordinate of P as θ increases from 0 to 2π shows that y or $\sin \theta$ changes from 0 to 1 to 0 to -1 and back to 0. These values are incorporated in the following table of values.

θ	0	$\frac{\pi}{4}$	$\frac{\pi}{2}$	$\frac{3\pi}{4}$	π	$\frac{5\pi}{4}$	$\frac{3\pi}{2}$	$\frac{7\pi}{4}$	2π	$\frac{9\pi}{4}$	$\frac{5\pi}{2}$	$\frac{11\pi}{4}$	3π	$\frac{13\pi}{4}$	$\frac{7\pi}{2}$	$\frac{15\pi}{4}$	4π
$\sin \theta$.	0	$\frac{1}{\sqrt{2}}$	1	$\frac{1}{\sqrt{2}}$	0	$-\frac{1}{\sqrt{2}}$	-1	$-\frac{1}{\sqrt{2}}$	0	$\frac{1}{\sqrt{2}}$	1	$\frac{1}{\sqrt{2}}$	0	$-\frac{1}{\sqrt{2}}$	-1	$-\frac{1}{\sqrt{2}}$	0

This table produces the points plotted in the right half of the graph in Figure 6.4. Similar values may be calculated for $-4\pi \leq \theta \leq 0$ and points plotted for the left half of the graph. We have used θ as the abscissa and $\sin \theta$ as the ordinate, and have joined the points by straight line segments. Despite this lack of accuracy, we can see the repeating or periodic nature of the sine function.   The function takes all its values for $0 < \theta \leq 2\pi$ and this interval of 2π is called the period of the function.

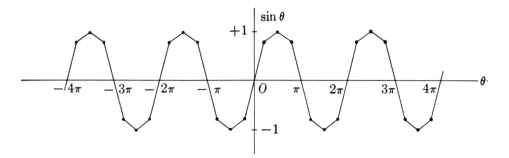

Figure 6.4

By plotting points obtained by calculating values for sin θ at, say, 15° intervals for θ, we may obtain the more accurate smooth curve shown in Figure 6.5.

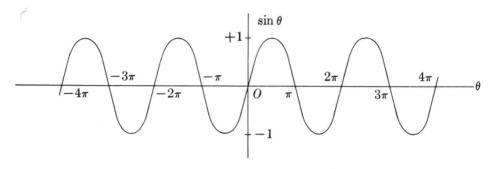

Figure 6.5

A similar graph for the cosine function is shown in Figure 6.6.

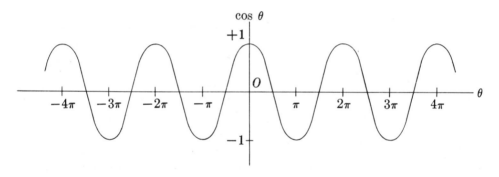

Figure 6.6

Note that the graph of the cosine function can be made to coincide with the graph of the sine function if we "move" the cosine curve a distance $\frac{\pi}{2}$ to the right parallel to the θ-axis.   That is,

$$\sin 90° \; = \cos 0°,$$
$$\sin 180° = \cos 90°,$$

and, in general,

$$\sin \theta = \cos\left(\theta - \frac{\pi}{2}\right), \quad \theta \in Re.$$

We may also write

$$\cos \theta = \sin\left(\theta + \frac{\pi}{2}\right), \quad \theta \in Re.$$

From Figure 6.5, the maximum value of $\sin \theta$ is 1 and this maximum occurs when

$$\theta = \cdots, -\frac{7\pi}{2}, -\frac{3\pi}{2}, \frac{\pi}{2}, \frac{5\pi}{2}, \frac{9\pi}{2}, \cdots.$$

The minimum of -1 occurs when

$$\theta = \cdots, -\frac{5\pi}{2}, -\frac{\pi}{2}, \frac{3\pi}{2}, \frac{7\pi}{2}, \frac{11\pi}{2}, \cdots.$$

The function takes zero values for

$$\theta = \cdots, -2\pi, -\pi, 0, \pi, 2\pi, \cdots.$$

We have defined period from a consideration of the graph in Figure 6.5; let us examine it in a slightly different way.

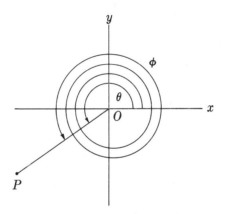

Suppose that θ and ϕ are angles which differ by an integral multiple of 2π radians, as in the diagram above. Then these angles have the same final ray OP, hence the same value of the sine function. But

$$\phi = \theta + 2n\pi, \quad n \in I;$$

therefore,

$$\sin (\theta + 2n\pi) = \sin \theta.$$

Similarly, it may be shown that

$$\cos (\theta + 2n\pi) = \cos \theta.$$

DEFINITION. The period of the sine or cosine function is 2π; that is, $\sin \theta = \sin (\theta + 2n\pi)$ and $\cos \theta = \cos (\theta + 2n\pi)$, for all $\theta \in Re, n \in I$.
The period of a function f is the least positive real number, say T, for which the statement "$f(\theta) = f(\theta + T)$, for all $\theta \in Re$" is true.

EXERCISE 6.2

1. Construct a table of values for $\cos \theta$ from $0°$ to $360°$ at intervals of $15°$ for θ. Use the table to draw the graph of the cosine function for $-360° \leq \theta \leq 360°$.

2. From the graph in question (1), find the following.
   (a) The maximum value of $\cos \theta$.
   (b) The values of θ for which the maximum occurs.
   (c) The minimum value of $\cos \theta$.
   (d) The values of θ for which the minimum occurs.
   (e) The values of θ for which $\cos \theta = 0$.

3. Prove that, if θ and ϕ are two angles such that
$$\phi = \theta + 2n\pi, \quad n \in I,$$
$$\cos \phi = \cos (\theta + 2n\pi) = \cos \phi, \quad \theta \in Re.$$

4. What symmetry, if any, is possessed by (a) the sine function, (b) the cosine function?

5. Use the property of periodicity to give four values for θ so that $\sin \theta$ is equal to each of the following.
   (a) 0   (b) $-.5$ (c) .7071   (d) -1

6. Repeat question (5) so that $\cos \theta$ is equal to each of the following.
   (a) $-\dfrac{1}{\sqrt{2}}$ (b) $\dfrac{1}{2}$ (c) $-.8660$ (d) $-.7660$

7. Consider the graphs of the sine and cosine functions in the interval $0 \leq \theta \leq 2\pi$. For what values of θ, if any, in this interval is each of the following equations a true statement?
   (a) $\sin \theta = \cos \theta$ 45, 225°   (b) $\sin \theta = -\cos \theta$ θ = 135°, 315°
   (c) $\sin \theta + \cos \theta = 1$ θ=0°, 90°, 365 (d) $\sin \theta + \cos \theta = 2$ no value
   (e) $\sin \theta + \cos \theta = -3$ no value   (f) $\sin \theta = \cos \theta - 1$ θ=0°, 270°, 360°

8. The amplitude of a periodic function is one half the difference between the maximum and minimum ordinates. What is the amplitude of (a) the sine function $(\sin \theta)$, (b) the cosine function $(\cos \theta)$?

9. Repeat question (8) for the functions defined by (a) $y = 3 \sin x$, (b) $y = k \cos x$.

10. Prove that, for any value of θ,
$$\sin (\theta + 2n\pi) = \cos \left(\theta - \frac{\pi}{2}\right).$$

6.3.   Other Trigonometric Functions and Their Graphs

The tangent function whose value is given by $\tan \theta = \dfrac{y}{x}$, $x \neq 0$, has a domain that excludes those values for θ for which $x = 0$.   These are

$$\theta = \cdots, \; -\frac{3\pi}{2}, \; -\frac{\pi}{2}, \frac{\pi}{2}, \frac{3\pi}{2}, \frac{5\pi}{2}, \cdots.$$

The domain of the tangent function is

$$\left\{ \theta \; \middle| \; \theta \in Re, \; \theta \neq \frac{\pi}{2} + n\pi, \; n \in I \right\}$$

and the range is Re, as there is no restriction on $\dfrac{y}{x}$ when x is not zero.

The following table of values has been used to construct the portion of the graph in Figure 6.7 for which $-\dfrac{\pi}{2} < \theta < \dfrac{\pi}{2}.$ In this interval of π, the function takes all real values. The period of the tangent function is π; that is,

$$\tan (\theta + n\pi) = \tan \theta, \quad n \in I.$$

θ	$-\dfrac{\pi}{2}$	$-\dfrac{\pi}{3}$	$-\dfrac{\pi}{4}$	$-\dfrac{\pi}{6}$	0	$\dfrac{\pi}{6}$	$\dfrac{\pi}{4}$	$\dfrac{\pi}{3}$	$\dfrac{\pi}{2}$
$\tan \theta$	not defined	$-\sqrt{3}$	-1	$-\dfrac{1}{\sqrt{3}}$	0	$\dfrac{1}{\sqrt{3}}$	1	$\sqrt{3}$	not defined

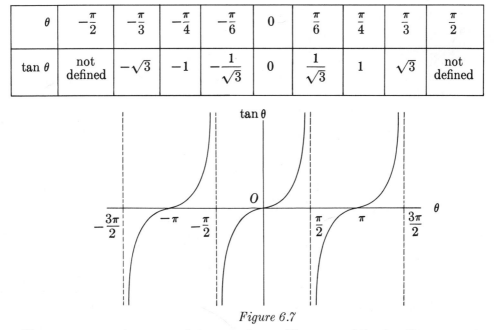

Figure 6.7

There are no maximum or minimum values.   The zeros of the function occur at

$$\theta = \cdots, \; -2\pi, \; -\pi, 0, \pi, 2\pi, \cdots.$$

The cotangent, secant and cosecant functions are called reciprocal functions with respect to the tangent, cosine, and sine functions respectively. (Why?) The graphs of these functions are required in Exercise 6.3. In this exercise, it may be helpful to remember the identities

$$\cot x = \frac{1}{\tan x}, \quad \sec x = \frac{1}{\cos x}, \quad \text{and} \quad \csc x = \frac{1}{\sin x}, \quad \text{in constructing tables of}$$

values.

EXERCISE 6.3

1. Using a table of values similar to that in Section 6.3 for tan θ, construct the graph of the cotangent function for

$$-\frac{3\pi}{2} < \theta < \frac{3\pi}{2}.$$

2. (a) Name the maximum and minimum values, if any, of the cotangent function.

   (b) State the domain and range of the function.

   (c) Name the values of θ at which the zeros of the function occur.

   (d) What is the period of the cotangent function?

   (e) Use the property of periodicity to name four values of θ for which $\cot \theta = 1$.

3. Calculate a suitable table of values and draw the graph of the secant function defined by
$$f(\theta) = \sec \theta \quad \text{for} \quad 0 \leq \theta \leq 2\pi.$$

4. Repeat question (2) for the secant function.

5. Repeat question (3) for the cosecant function defined by
$$f(\theta) = \csc \theta \quad \text{for} \quad 0 < \theta < 2\pi.$$

6. Repeat question (2) for the cosecant function.

7. How does the graph of $y = 3 \tan x$ differ from the graph of $y = \tan x$?

8. How does the graph of $y = \frac{1}{2} \sec x$ differ from the graph of $y = \sec x$?

9. How does the graph of $y = \sec \frac{x}{2}$ differ from the graph of $y = \sec x$?

10. Draw a graph of the function $y = \sin^2 x$ for $0 \leq x \leq 2\pi$.

11. Draw a graph of the function $y = \cos^2 x$ for $-2\pi \leq x \leq 2\pi$.

6.4.   Amplitude, Periodicity, and Phase Shift

If we apply the transformation $(\theta,y) \to (\theta,ay)$ to the graph of $y = \sin \theta$ we have

$$(\theta,y) \to (\theta,ay) = (u,v)$$

$$u = \theta, v = ay$$

$$\theta = u, y = \frac{v}{a}$$

and the equation in the uv-plane is

$$\frac{v}{a} = \sin u$$

$$v = a \sin u.$$

Hence the equation of the image is $y = a \sin \theta$.

The transformation is a nonisotropic dilatation although we may refer to it more informally as a "vertical stretch".

Figure 6.8 shows the graphs of $y = \sin \theta$ and $y = 2.5 \sin \theta$. The latter is obtained by applying the transformation $(\theta, y) \to (\theta, 2.5y)$ to the graph of $y = \sin \theta$.

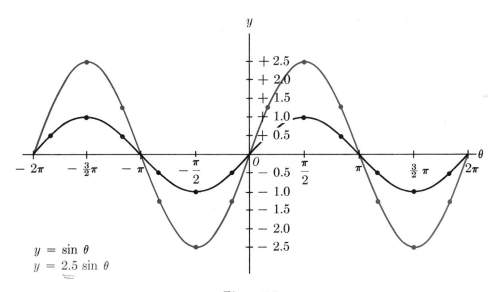

$y = \sin \theta$
$y = 2.5 \sin \theta$

Figure 6.8

If we draw the graphs for other values of a, we observe similar results: $|y| < a$ for all values of the argument θ and $|y| = a$ only at the maxima and minima.

In these cases we notice also that the graph of $a \sin \theta$ is very much like that of $\sin \theta$. It has zeros for the same values of the argument θ (..., -2π, $-\pi$, 0, $+\pi$, $+2\pi$, ...) and its maxima and minima occur at the same values of the argument θ. The distinction between the two graphs is that the value of y for any given value of θ is greater; in fact, it is a times as great. In particular, the maxima and minima are a times as far from the θ-axis. We might say that the graph of $a \sin \theta$ is the graph of $\sin \theta$ with the ordinate magnified, or amplified, to use a term from sound rather than sight. Thus a is an amplification factor; it is used very frequently in science and is called simply *the amplitude*.

DEFINITION.   If $y = a \sin \theta$, then $|a|$ is called the amplitude of the function.

Note that *the amplitude is one half of the difference between the maximum and minimum values,* and this is often the practical definition used in physics. The amplitude of a vibration is very important in physics. For example, in sound, the changes in amplitude cause the changes in the volume of a sound, and in radio, the changes in amplitude of radio waves are used to receive signals on the A.M. (Amplitude Modulation) band of a radio set.

Another transformation that we have applied to various graphs is the transformation $(x,y) \rightarrow \left(\dfrac{x}{k}, y. \right)$ From the graph of $y = R(x)$, this transformation produces the graph of $y = R(kx)$ and is a "horizontal stretch".

In the same way we can obtain the graph of $y = \sin 3\theta$ from the graph of $y = \sin \theta$ by first sketching the graph of $y = \sin \theta$ and applying the transformation $(\theta, y) \rightarrow \left(\dfrac{\theta}{3}, y \right)$ to that graph.

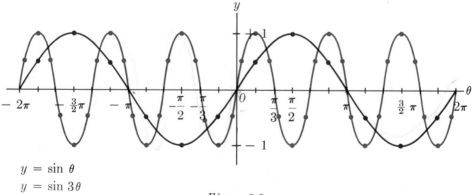

$y = \sin \theta$
$y = \sin 3\theta$

Figure 6.9

We see that the amplitude is not changed; it is *one* in both cases. However the maxima and minima are closer together when $k = 3$ than when $k = 1$, and the same applies to the zeros. In fact the whole graph has been *squeezed* in the direction parallel to the θ-axis. Therefore, the periods of the two functions must be different.

DEFINITION. The *period*, in θ, of the sine function, $\sin k\theta$, is the difference in the value of θ between two adjacent zeros of $y = \sin k\theta$ at which y changes sign from negative to positive as θ increases.

If we examine Figure 6.9, we see that for $y = \sin 3\theta$, the period is $\dfrac{2\pi}{3}$, and for $y = \sin \theta$, the period is 2π.

Note that if θ alone is the argument of the sine function, we usually shorten the phrase 'the period in θ' to merely 'the period'.

Thus the period in θ is only one third as great for $y = \sin 3\theta$ as for $y = \sin \theta$. Alternatively, we could say that $y = \sin 3\theta$ repeats 3 times as rapidly when θ increases as does $y = \sin \theta$.

When we sketch the graphs for other values of k in the exercises, we will see in every case the period in θ is $\dfrac{2\pi}{k}$.

DEFINITION (ALTERNATE). The period, in θ, of the sine function $\sin k\theta$ is $\dfrac{2\pi}{k}$.

A third transformation that we will consider in this section is the translation $(x,y) \to (x - a, y)$. This translation produces a "shift" parallel to the x-axis and from the graph of $y = R(x)$ we obtain the graph of $y = R(x + a)$. If $a > 0$, each point on the graph of $y = R(x + a)$ can be obtained by translating a point on the graph of $y = R(x)$ a units to the left. Similarly if $a < 0$, each point on the graph of $y = R(x + a)$ can be obtained by translating a point on the graph of $y = R(x)$ a units to the right. In the same way the graph of $y = \sin(\theta + d)$ may be obtained from the graph of $y = \sin \theta$ by the translation $(\theta,y) \to (\theta - d,y)$.

In Figure 6.10 we have obtained the graph of $y = \sin\left(\theta + \dfrac{\pi}{3}\right)$ from the graph of $y = \sin x$ by means of the translation $(\theta,y) \to \left(\theta - \dfrac{\pi}{3},y\right)$.

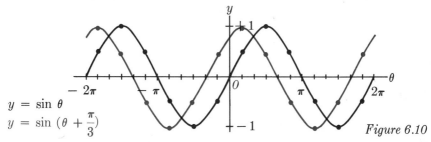

$y = \sin \theta$

$y = \sin\left(\theta + \dfrac{\pi}{3}\right)$

Figure 6.10

DEFINITIONS. If $y = \sin(\theta + d)$, then the constant angle d is called the phase angle of the function with respect to $y = \sin \theta$.

The relative shift of the curve $y = \sin(\theta + d)$ with respect to $y = \sin \theta$ is called a phase shift.

Generally the range of d is restricted so that $-\pi \le d \le \pi$.

(If $y = \cos(\theta + d)$, then d is the phase angle of the function with respect to $y = \cos \theta$.)

If we examine the two graphs shown we see that the zeros of $y = \sin \theta$ are $\{..., -2\pi, -\pi, 0, \pi, 2\pi, ...\}$, and the zeros of $y = \sin\left(\theta + \dfrac{\pi}{3}\right)$ are $\left\{..., -\dfrac{7\pi}{3}, -\dfrac{4\pi}{3}, -\dfrac{\pi}{3}, \dfrac{2\pi}{3}, \dfrac{5\pi}{3}, ...\right\}$. Thus the phase angle, $\dfrac{\pi}{3}$, determines the displacement of the zeros of $y = \sin\left(\theta + \dfrac{\pi}{3}\right)$ with respect to those of $y = \sin \theta$. This displacement is most easily calculated by finding the value of θ for which the argument is zero; this zero is at $\theta + \dfrac{\pi}{3} = 0$, that is, $\theta = -\dfrac{\pi}{3}$, and the phase shift is $\dfrac{\pi}{3}$ to the left.

In the general case of $y = \sin(\theta + d)$, the phase shift is given by $\theta = -d$, which is the condition for the argument of the sine function to be zero.

If d is positive $\left(\text{in our example } d = \dfrac{\pi}{3}\right)$, the function $y = \sin(\theta + d)$ is said to *lead* the function $y = \sin \theta$; the corresponding zeros of $y = \sin(\theta + d)$ occur *before or to the left* of the zeros of $y = \sin \theta$.

If d is negative, then $y = \sin(\theta + d)$ is said to *lag* the function $y = \sin \theta$.

Note that in this terminology

$$y = \cos \theta = \sin\left(\theta + \frac{\pi}{2}\right) \qquad \text{leads } y = \sin \theta \text{ by } \frac{\pi}{2},$$

and

$$y = \sin \theta = \cos\left(\theta - \frac{\pi}{2}\right) \qquad \text{lags } y = \cos \theta \text{ by } \frac{\pi}{2}.$$

Note also that a lead by π has the same effect as a lag by π; $\sin \theta$ and $\sin(\theta \pm \pi)$ are said to be in *antiphase*.

EXERCISE 6.4

1. Sketch the graph of $y = 2 \cos \theta$ for $-2\pi \le \theta \le 2\pi$.
2. Sketch the graph of $y = \cos 4\theta$ for $0 \le \theta \le \pi$.
3. Sketch the graph of $y = \cos\left(\theta + \dfrac{\pi}{2}\right)$ for $-2\pi \le \theta \le 2\pi$.
4. State the amplitude of each of the following:
   (a) $y = 2 \sin \theta$ (b) $y = \frac{1}{2} \cos \theta$ (c) $y = 2\pi \sin \theta$

5. State the period of each of the following:

  (a) $y = \sin 4\theta$ (b) $y = \cos \dfrac{\theta}{3}$ (c) $y = \cos \pi\theta$

6. Sketch the graphs of each of the following for $-4\pi \le \theta \le 4\pi$:

  (a) $y = 2 \sin \theta$ (b) $y = \sin \dfrac{\theta}{3}$ (c) $y = 2 \sin \dfrac{\theta}{3}$

7. Sketch the graphs of each of the following for $-2\pi \le \theta \le 2\pi$:

  (a) $y = \frac{1}{2} \cos \theta$ (b) $y = \cos\left(\theta - \dfrac{\pi}{3}\right)$ (c) $y = \frac{1}{2} \cos\left(\theta - \dfrac{\pi}{3}\right)$

8. Sketch the graph of $y = 3 \sin(2\theta - \pi)$ for $-2\pi \le \theta \le 2\pi$.
9. State the amplitude, period and phase shift of each of the following:

  (a) $y = 4 \sin\left(3\theta + \dfrac{\pi}{2}\right)$ (b) $y = \dfrac{1}{3} \cos 2\left(\theta - \dfrac{\pi}{2}\right)$.

6.5.   The Transformation $(\theta,y) \rightarrow (a\theta + b, cy + d)$

The three transformations of the previous section together with a fourth trans-formation have all been studied in Chapters 4 and 5. We will now summarize these transformations and study the effect of applying all or some of them to the graph of a trigonometric function.

1. If the transformation $(\theta,y) \rightarrow (\theta,ay)$ is applied to the graph of $y = f(\theta)$, the image is the graph of $y = af(\theta)$; a vertical stretch by a factor of a. Note that the "stretch" is actually a compression if $a < 1$.

2. If the transformation $(\theta,y) \rightarrow \left(\dfrac{\theta}{k},y\right)$ is applied to the graph of $y = f(\theta)$, the

  image is the graph of $y = f(k\theta)$; a horizontal stretch by a factor of $\dfrac{1}{k}$. Again

  the "stretch" is actually a compression if $k > 1$.

3. If the translation $(\theta,y) \rightarrow (\theta - d,y)$ is applied to the graph of $y = f(\theta)$, the image is the graph of $y = f(\theta + d)$; a translation of $-d$ units parallel to the x-axis.

4. If the translation $(\theta,y) \rightarrow (\theta, y + d)$ is applied to the graph of $y = f(\theta)$, the image is the graph of $y = f(\theta) + d$; a translation of d units parallel to the y-axis.

We will now use these transformations to sketch the graph of $y = 3 \sin\left(2\theta + \dfrac{\pi}{2}\right) + 2$

This may be rewritten in the form

$$y - 2 = 3 \sin 2 \left(\theta + \frac{\pi}{4} \right).$$

Starting with the graph of $y = \sin \theta$ we must, by one or more transformations, obtain the graph of $y - 2 = 3 \sin 2 \left(\theta + \frac{\pi}{4} \right)$ as the final image. In practice, we apply the "stretch" transformations first and can apply both together if both are necessary. This can be followed by applying both translations together if both are necessary.

Starting with $$y = \sin \theta$$

we apply the transformation

$$(\theta,y) \rightarrow \left(\frac{\theta}{2}, 3y \right) = (u,v).$$

Hence $$u = \frac{\theta}{2}, v = 3y$$

and $$\theta = 2u, y = \frac{v}{3},$$

and the graph of $y = \sin \theta$ has as its image the graph of

$$\frac{v}{3} = \sin 2u$$

or $$v = 3 \sin 2u.$$

This will produce a horizontal stretch by a factor of $\frac{1}{2}$ and a vertical stretch by a factor of 3 or a period of π and an amplitude of 3.

Now apply the transformation

$$(u,v) \rightarrow \left(u - \frac{\pi}{4}, v + 2 \right)$$
$$= (r,s)$$

to the graph of $$v = 3 \sin 2u.$$

Hence $$r = u - \frac{\pi}{4}, s = v + 2$$

$$u = r + \frac{\pi}{4}, v = s - 2$$

and the graph of

$$v = 3 \sin 2u$$

has as its image the graph of

$$s - 2 = 3 \sin 2\left(r + \frac{\pi}{4}\right).$$

This will produce a translation of $-\dfrac{\pi}{4}$ in the u or θ direction and a translation of 2 units in the v or y direction.

Replacing s by y and r by θ, the final result is the graph of

$$y - 2 = 3 \sin 2\left(\theta + \frac{\pi}{4}\right).$$

Note that u and r are dummy variables replacing θ in the transformations in order to avoid confusion. Similarly v and s are dummy variables replacing y.

The three stages of the graphing are shown in the following diagrams.

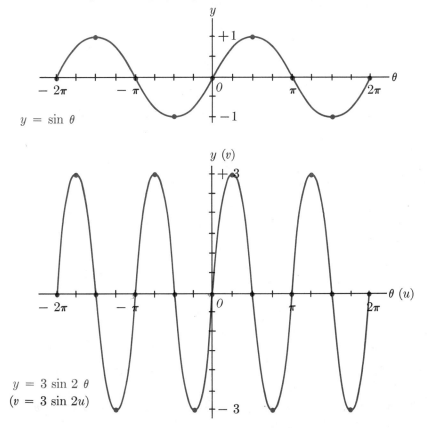

$y = \sin \theta$

$y = 3 \sin 2\,\theta$
$(v = 3 \sin 2u)$

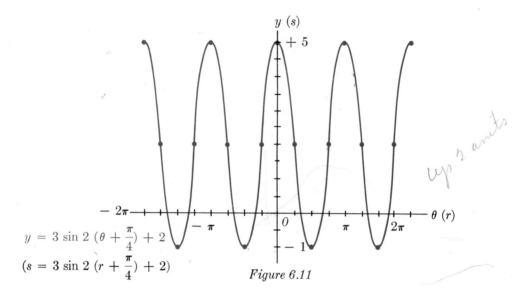

$$y = 3 \sin 2 \left(\theta + \frac{\pi}{4}\right) + 2$$

$$(s = 3 \sin 2 \left(r + \frac{\pi}{4}\right) + 2)$$

Figure 6.11

Note that in the construction of the graph of

$$y = 3 \sin 2\left(\theta + \frac{\pi}{4}\right) + 2$$

we first used the transformation

$$(\theta, y) \rightarrow \left(\frac{\theta}{2},\ 3y\right) \qquad = (u, v)$$

so that

$$u = \frac{\theta}{2}, \qquad v = 3y.$$

This was followed by the transformation

$$(u, v) \rightarrow \left(u - \frac{\pi}{4},\ v + 2\right) = (r, s)$$

so that

$$r = u - \frac{\pi}{4}, \qquad s = v + 2.$$

Hence

$$r = \frac{\theta}{2} - \frac{\pi}{4}, \qquad s = 3y + 2$$

and the complete transformation is $(\theta, y) \rightarrow \left(\dfrac{\theta}{2} - \dfrac{\pi}{4},\ 3y + 2\right)$.

This has produced a graph similar in shape to the graph of $y = \sin \theta$ but with an amplitude of 3, a period of π, a phase shift of $-\dfrac{\pi}{4}$, and a vertical shift of 2 units.

By comparison, the general transformation

$$(\theta,y) \rightarrow (a\theta + b, cy + d)$$

will produce a graph of a trigonometric function with an amplitude of c, a period of $2\pi a$, a phase shift of $+ b$, and a vertical shift of d.

The graph obtained by this transformation will be the graph of

$$y = cf\left[\dfrac{1}{a}(\theta - b)\right] + d$$

where f is a trigonometric function.

EXERCISE 6.5

1. Sketch the graphs of each of the following for $- 2\pi \le \theta \le 2\pi$:

   (a) $y = 2 \sin 3\theta$
   (b) $y = \frac{1}{2} \cos 2\theta$

   (c) $y = \sin 3\left(\theta + \dfrac{\pi}{4}\right)$
   (d) $y = 2 \cos\left(2\theta - \dfrac{2\pi}{3}\right)$

   (e) $y = 3 \cos \frac{1}{2}(\theta + \pi)$
   (f) $y = \frac{3}{2} \sin(3\theta - \pi)$

   (g) $y = 2 \sin\left(\theta - \dfrac{\pi}{2}\right) + 1$
   (h) $y = 4 \cos 3\left(\theta - \dfrac{\pi}{2}\right) - 3$

   (i) $y = \frac{1}{2} \sec 2\left(\theta + \dfrac{\pi}{4}\right)$
   (j) $y = 3 \csc \frac{1}{2}\left(\theta - \dfrac{\pi}{3}\right) + 1$.

2. Apply the following transformations to the graph of $y = \sin \theta$ $(-2\pi \le \theta \le 2\pi)$ and sketch the image-graphs.

   (a) $(\theta,y) \rightarrow \left(\theta + \dfrac{\pi}{2}, y\right)$
   (b) $(\theta,y) \rightarrow \left(\dfrac{\theta}{2} - \dfrac{\pi}{3}, 2y\right)$

   (c) $(\theta,y) \leftrightarrow (2\theta - \pi, y + 1)$
   (d) $(\theta,y) \rightarrow \left(\dfrac{\theta}{3} + \dfrac{\pi}{2}, 3y - 2\right)$.

3. Apply the following transformations to the graph of $y = \cos \theta$ $(-2\pi \le \theta \le 2\pi)$ and sketch the image-graphs.

   (a) $(\theta,y) \rightarrow (2\theta,y)$
   (b) $(\theta,y) \rightarrow (\theta,3y)$

   (c) $(\theta,y) \rightarrow \left(\dfrac{\theta}{2} + \dfrac{\pi}{3}, 2y\right)$
   (d) $(\theta,y) \rightarrow \left(\dfrac{\theta}{3} + \pi, 2y + 2\right)$.

Chapter Summary

If (x,y) is any point in the plane and $r^2 = x^2 + y^2$ $(r > 0)$ then

$$\sin \theta = \frac{y}{r} \qquad \cos \theta = \frac{x}{r} \qquad \tan \theta = \frac{y}{x}$$

$$\csc \theta = \frac{r}{y} \qquad \sec \theta = \frac{r}{x} \qquad \cot \theta = \frac{x}{y}$$

$\sin (180° - \theta) = \sin \theta$	$\cos (180° - \theta) = -\cos \theta$	$\tan (180° - \theta) = -\tan \theta$
$\sin (180° + \theta) = -\sin \theta$	$\cos (180° + \theta) = -\cos \theta$	$\tan (180° + \theta) = \tan \theta$
$\sin (360° - \theta) = -\sin \theta$	$\cos (360° - \theta) = \cos \theta$	$\tan (360° - \theta) = -\tan \theta$
$\sin (- \theta) = -\sin \theta$	$\cos (- \theta) = \cos \theta$	$\tan (- \theta) = -\tan \theta$

$\sin 0 = 0$	$\cos 0 = 1$	$\tan 0 = 0$
$\sin \frac{\pi}{6} = \frac{1}{2}$	$\cos \frac{\pi}{6} = \frac{\sqrt{3}}{2}$	$\tan \frac{\pi}{6} = \frac{1}{\sqrt{3}}$
$\sin \frac{\pi}{4} = \frac{1}{\sqrt{2}}$	$\cos \frac{\pi}{4} = \frac{1}{\sqrt{2}}$	$\tan \frac{\pi}{4} = 1$
$\sin \frac{\pi}{3} = \frac{\sqrt{3}}{2}$	$\cos \frac{\pi}{3} = \frac{1}{2}$	$\tan \frac{\pi}{3} = \sqrt{3}$
$\sin \frac{\pi}{2} = 1$	$\cos \frac{\pi}{2} = 0$	$\tan \frac{\pi}{2}$ is undefined

The sine and cosine functions of θ exist in the domain of the set of real numbers, Re, and are subject to the inequalities $-1 \le \sin \theta \le 1$ and $-1 \le \cos \theta \le 1$, respectively.

The domain of the functions defined by $y = \csc \theta$ and $y = \tan \theta$ is $\{\theta \in Re \mid \theta \ne n\pi, n \in I\}$.

The domain of the functions defined by $y = \sec \theta$ and $y = \cot \theta$ is

$$\left\{ \theta \in Re \;\middle|\; \theta \ne \frac{(2n-1)\pi}{2}, n \in I \right\}.$$

The range of $y = \sec \theta$ and $y = \csc \theta$ is $\{ y \in Re \mid y \le -1 \text{ or } y \ge 1 \}$.

The range of $y = \tan \theta$ and $y = \cot \theta$ is Re.

$\sin (- \theta) = -\sin \theta$, $\cos (- \theta) = \cos \theta$, $\tan (- \theta) = -\tan \theta$.

The functions $\sin \theta$, $\cos \theta$, $\csc \theta$ and $\sec \theta$ are periodic with period 2π.

The functions $\tan \theta$ and $\cot \theta$ are periodic with period π.

The zeros of $\sin \theta$ are $\{ \ldots, -2\pi, -\pi, 0, \pi, 2\pi, \ldots \} = \{n\pi, n \in I\}$.

The zeros of $\cos \theta$ are $\left\{ \ldots, -\frac{3\pi}{2}, -\frac{\pi}{2}, \frac{\pi}{2}, \frac{3\pi}{2}, \ldots \right\} = \left\{ \left(\frac{2n-1}{2} \right) \pi, n \in I \right\}$.

The zeros of $\tan \theta$ are $\{ \ldots, -2\pi, -\pi, 0, \pi, 2\pi, \ldots \} = \{ n\pi, n \in I \}$.

The zeros of $\cot \theta$ are $\left\{ \ldots, -\dfrac{3}{2}\pi, -\dfrac{1}{2}\pi, \dfrac{1}{2}\pi, \dfrac{3}{2}\pi, \ldots \right\} = \left\{ \dfrac{(2n-1)\pi}{2}, n \in I \right\}.$

There are no zeros of $\csc \theta$ and $\sec \theta$.

$\sin \theta = 1$ when $\theta = \left\{ \ldots, -\dfrac{3\pi}{2}, \dfrac{\pi}{2}, \dfrac{5\pi}{2}, \ldots \right\} = \left\{ \left(2n + \dfrac{1}{2}\right)\pi, n \in I \right\}.$

$\sin \theta = -1$ when $\theta = \left\{ \ldots, -\dfrac{5\pi}{2}, -\dfrac{\pi}{2}, \dfrac{3\pi}{2}, \ldots \right\} = \left\{ \left(2n - \dfrac{1}{2}\right)\pi, n \in I \right\}.$

$\cos \theta = 1$ when $\theta = \{ \ldots, -2\pi, 0, 2\pi, \ldots \} = \{ 2n\pi, n \in I \}.$

$\cos \theta = -1$ when $\theta = \{ \ldots, -3\pi, -\pi, \pi, 3\pi, \ldots \} = \{ (2n+1)\pi, n \in I \}.$

For the function determined by $y = a \sin (\theta + d)$,

a is the amplitude, 2π is the period in θ, and d is the phase angle.

For the functions determined by $y = a \sin (k\theta + d)$ and $y = a \cos (k\theta + d)$

a is the amplitude, $\dfrac{2\pi}{k}$ is the period in θ, d is the phase angle, and the phase

shift in θ is $-\dfrac{d}{k}$.

If the transformation $(\theta, y) \to (a\theta + b, cy + d)$ is applied to the graph $y = f(x)$ where f is a trigonometric function, the image is the graph of

$$y = cf \left[\dfrac{1}{a} (\theta - b) \right] + d.$$

REVIEW EXERCISE 6

1. Express each of the following angles in radian measure (in terms of π):
   (a) 150°   (b) − 330°   (c) 750°
   (d) − 1225°   (e) 3600°   (f) 450°.

2. Express each of the following angles in degree measure:
   (a) $\dfrac{5\pi}{4}$ (b) $-\dfrac{7\pi}{6}$ (c) $\dfrac{53\pi}{4}$ (d) − 30π.

3. Without using tables, evaluate each of the following:
   (a) $\cos 150°$ (b) $\sin (-330°)$ (c) $\tan 750°$
   (d) $\sin \dfrac{53\pi}{4}$ (e) $\cot 3600°$ (f) $\sec \left(-\dfrac{7\pi}{6}\right).$

4. State the amplitude, period, and phase shift of each of the following:
   (a) $y = \sin \theta$ (b) $y = 2 \cos 3\theta$
   (c) $y = \dfrac{5}{2} \cos 3 \left(\theta - \dfrac{\pi}{2} \right)$ (d) $y = 4 \sin \left(3\theta + \dfrac{\pi}{2} \right)$
   (e) $y = 4 \sin 3 \left(\theta + \dfrac{\pi}{2} \right)$ (f) $y = 2 \cos \dfrac{1}{2} (\theta - 2\pi)$

(g) $y = \dfrac{1}{3} \left[\sin 4 \left(\theta - \dfrac{\pi}{3} \right) \right] + 2$ (h) $y = 5 \left[\cos \left(4\theta - \dfrac{\pi}{3} \right) \right] - 3.$

5. Sketch the graphs of each of the following for $-2\pi \le \theta \le 2\pi$:

    (a) $y = 3 \sin \theta$ (b) $y = \cos 3\theta$

    (c) $y = 2 \cos \dfrac{\theta}{2}$ (d) $y = \dfrac{1}{2} \sin (2\theta - \pi)$

    (e) $y = 4 \cos 3 \left(\theta + \dfrac{\pi}{4} \right)$ (f) $y = 4 \cos 3 \left(\theta + \dfrac{\pi}{4} \right) + 4$

6. Apply the following transformations to the graphs of $y = \sin \theta$ and $y = \cos \theta$ and sketch the images for $-2\pi \le \theta \le 2\pi$:

    (a) $(\theta,y) \to (\theta, y + 2)$ (b) $(\theta,y) \to \left(\theta + \dfrac{\pi}{2}, y \right)$

    (c) $(\theta,y) \to (2\theta, y)$ (d) $(\theta,y) \to (2\theta - \pi, 3y)$

    (e) $(\theta,y) \to \left(\dfrac{\theta}{2} - \dfrac{\pi}{3}, 2y + 1 \right)$ (f) $(\theta,y) \to \left(\dfrac{2\theta}{3} + \dfrac{\pi}{3}, 2y + \dfrac{3}{2} \right).$

7. Show that (a) $\sin \theta = 0$ for $\{ \theta \mid \theta = n\pi, n \in I \}$,

        (b) $\sin \theta = 1$ for $\left\{ \theta \mid \theta = \left(2n + \dfrac{1}{2} \right)\pi, n \in I \right\}$,

        (c) $\sin \theta = -1$ for $\left\{ \theta \mid \theta = \left(2n - \dfrac{1}{2} \right)\pi, n \in I \right\}$.

8. Show that (a) $\cos \theta = 1$ for $\{ \theta \mid \theta = 2n\pi, n \in I \}$,

        (b) $\cos \theta = -1$ for $\{ \theta \mid \theta = (2n + 1)\pi, n \in I \}$,

        (c) $\cos \theta = 0$ for $\left\{ \theta \mid \theta = \left(n + \dfrac{1}{2} \right)\pi, n \in I \right\}$.

9. Show that (a) $\sin \theta = \dfrac{1}{2}$ for $\left\{ \theta \mid \theta = \left(2n + \dfrac{1}{6} \right)\pi, n \in I \right\}$,

        (b) $\tan \theta = 1$ for $\left\{ \theta \mid \theta = \left(n + \dfrac{1}{4} \right)\pi, n \in I \right\}$,

        (c) $\cos^2\theta = \dfrac{3}{4}$ for $\left\{ \theta \mid \theta = \left(n + \dfrac{1}{6} \right)\pi, n \in I \right\}$,

        (d) $\sin^4\theta = 1$ for $\left\{ \theta \mid \theta = \left(n + \dfrac{1}{2} \right)\pi, n \in I \right\}$,

        (e) $\tan^2\theta = 1$ for $\left\{ \theta \mid \theta = \left(\dfrac{n}{2} + \dfrac{1}{4} \right)\pi, n \in I \right\}$.

10. Find the minimum and maximum values of the following functions and state for which values of θ they occur.

    (a) $1 + \sin \theta$

    (b) $2 - 3 \cos 5\theta$

    (c) $2^{\cos \theta}$

    (d) $\cos (\cos \theta)$

    (e) $7 + 2 \cos (\sin \theta)$

Chapter 7

TRIGONOMETRIC FUNCTIONS
OF COMPOUND ANGLES

7.1. Functions of $A + B$, $A,B \in Re$

We shall develop an identity for the cosine of the sum of two real numbers (or of the sum of the measures of two angles) in terms of the cosines of the separate real numbers (or angles).

Consider the unit circle in Figure 7.1. $R(1, 0)$ is on the x-axis; P is located

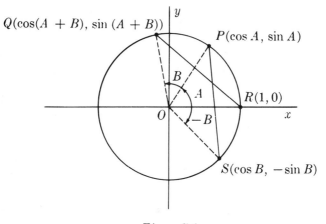

Figure 7.1

by a positive rotation from the initial ray OR through angle A, and Q by a further rotation through angle B. S is located by a negative rotation from OR through angle B. Since chords RQ and PS subtend equal angles $A + B$ at the centre of the circle,

$$RQ = PS;$$

$$\sqrt{[\cos(A + B) - 1]^2 + [\sin(A + B) - 0]^2} = \sqrt{(\cos A - \cos B)^2 + (\sin A + \sin B)^2}.$$

Squaring each member of the equation and expanding, we obtain

$$\cos^2(A + B) - 2 \cos (A + B) + 1 + \sin^2(A + B)$$
$$= \cos^2 A - 2 \cos A \cos B + \cos^2 B + \sin^2 A + 2 \sin A \sin B + \sin^2 B.$$

Therefore, using the identity $\cos^2\theta + \sin^2\theta = 1$ for $\theta = A$ and $\theta = A + B$, we obtain

$$2 - 2 \cos (A + B) = 2 - 2 \cos A \cos B + 2 \sin A \sin B,$$

and thus

$$\cos (A + B) = \cos A \cos B - \sin A \sin B.$$

Note that A and B are any two angles or real numbers.

Example 1. Without using tables, find $\cos 105°$.

Solution:

$$\cos 105° = \cos (60° + 45°)$$
$$= \cos 60° \cos 45° - \sin 60° \sin 45°$$
$$= \frac{1}{2} \cdot \frac{1}{\sqrt{2}} - \frac{\sqrt{3}}{2} \cdot \frac{1}{\sqrt{2}}$$
$$= \frac{1 - \sqrt{3}}{2\sqrt{2}} = \frac{\sqrt{2} - \sqrt{6}}{4}.$$

The above formula for $\cos (A + B)$ is true for all A and B; therefore, we may replace B by $-B$.
Since

$$\cos (A + B) = \cos A \cos B - \sin A \sin B,$$

then

$$\cos [A + (-B)] = \cos A \cos (-B) - \sin A \sin (-B).$$

Now,

$$\sin (-B) = -\sin B \text{ and } \cos (-B) = \cos B.$$

Therefore,

$$\cos (A - B) = \cos A \cos B + \sin A \sin B.$$

Example 2. Without using tables, find a value for $\cos 15°$.

Solution:

$$\cos 15° = \cos (60° - 45°)$$
$$= \cos 60° \cos 45° + \sin 60° \sin 45°$$

$$= \frac{1}{2} \cdot \frac{1}{\sqrt{2}} + \frac{\sqrt{3}}{2} \cdot \frac{1}{\sqrt{2}}$$

$$= \frac{1 + \sqrt{3}}{2\sqrt{2}}$$

$$= \frac{\sqrt{2} + \sqrt{6}}{4} \, .$$

Example 3.   Prove that $\cos (90° - \theta) = \sin \theta$.

Solution:

$$\cos (90° - \theta) = \cos 90° \cos \theta + \sin 90° \sin \theta$$
$$= 0 + \sin \theta$$
$$= \sin \theta \, .$$

Therefore,

$$\cos (90° - \theta) = \sin \theta \, .$$

Example 4.   Prove that $\cos \theta = \sin (90° - \theta)$.

Solution: Since

$$\cos (90° - x) = \sin x \, ,$$

(proved in Example 3) we replace x by $90° - \theta$, and thus have

$$\cos[90° - (90° - \theta)] = \sin (90° - \theta) \, ,$$
$$\cos \theta = \sin (90° - \theta) \, ,$$

as required.

Let us use the results of Examples 3 and 4 to develop a formula for the sine of the sum of two angles.   Since it has been established that, for all x and y,

$$\cos (x - y) = \cos x \cos y + \sin x \sin y \, ,$$

we may replace x by $90°$ and y by $A + B$ and thus obtain

$$\cos [90° - (A + B)] = \cos [(90° - A) - B]$$
$$= \cos (90° - A) \cos B + \sin (90° - A) \sin B$$
$$= \sin A \cos B + \cos A \sin B \, .$$

But

$$\cos [90° - (A + B)] = \sin (A + B) \, ;$$

therefore,

$$\sin (A + B) = \sin A \cos B + \cos A \sin B \, .$$

Now, in this last result, let us replace B by $-B$.

$$\sin [A + (-B)] = \sin A \cos (-B) + \cos A \sin (-B) \, ,$$

and therefore,

$$\sin (A - B) = \sin A \cos B - \cos A \sin B \, .$$

Example 5. Without using tables, find the values of sin 75°.

Solution:

$$\sin 75° = \sin (45° + 30°),$$

$$= \sin 45° \cos 30° + \cos 45° \sin 30°$$

$$= \frac{1}{\sqrt{2}} \cdot \frac{\sqrt{3}}{2} + \frac{1}{\sqrt{2}} \cdot \frac{1}{2}$$

$$= \frac{\sqrt{3} + 1}{2\sqrt{2}}$$

$$= \frac{\sqrt{6} + \sqrt{2}}{4}.$$

We may obtain a formula for the tangent of the sum of two angles as follows:

$$\tan x = \frac{\sin x}{\cos x}, \quad \cos x \neq 0,$$

and so if

$$x = A + B,$$

$$\tan (A + B) = \frac{\sin (A + B)}{\cos (A + B)}$$

$$= \frac{\sin A \cos B + \cos A \sin B}{\cos A \cos B - \sin A \sin B}.$$

Dividing numerator and denominator of the right member of this equality by $\cos A \cos B$, we obtain

$$\tan (A + B) = \frac{\dfrac{\sin A \cos B}{\cos A \cos B} + \dfrac{\cos A \sin B}{\cos A \cos B}}{\dfrac{\cos A \cos B}{\cos A \cos B} - \dfrac{\sin A \sin B}{\cos A \cos B}}$$

$$= \frac{\tan A + \tan B}{1 - \tan A \tan B}.$$

Note that we need the restrictions that $\cos A \neq 0$, $\cos B \neq 0$ (why?), and $A + B$ be not an odd multiple of $\dfrac{\pi}{2}$ to ensure that $\tan (A + B)$ be defined.

Similarly, we may show that

$$\tan (A - B) = \frac{\tan A - \tan B}{1 + \tan A \tan B}.$$

Example 6. Without using tables, find the value of $\tan \dfrac{7}{12} \pi$.

Solution:

$$\tan \frac{7}{12} \pi = \tan \left(\frac{\pi}{3} + \frac{\pi}{4} \right)$$

$$= \frac{\tan \dfrac{\pi}{3} + \tan \dfrac{\pi}{4}}{1 - \tan \dfrac{\pi}{3} \tan \dfrac{\pi}{4}}$$

$$= \frac{\sqrt{3} + 1}{1 - \sqrt{3}}$$

$$= \frac{(1 + \sqrt{3})^2}{1 - 3}$$

$$= -\frac{1}{2}(4 + 2\sqrt{3})$$

$$= -(2 + \sqrt{3}) .$$

EXERCISE 7.1

Use one of the formulae developed in Section 7.1 to find the value of each of the following.

1. $\sin 105°$
2. $\sin \dfrac{7\pi}{12}$
3. $\sin 210°$
4. $\tan \dfrac{\pi}{12}$
5. $\cos 75°$
6. $\tan 195°$

If x and y are acute angles such that $\sin x = \frac{2}{3}$ and $\cos y = \frac{5}{13}$ find the value of each of the following.

7. $\sin (x + y)$
8. $\cos (x + y)$
9. $\tan (x + y)$
10. $\cot (x + y)$
11. $\sin (x - y)$
12. $\cos (x - y)$
13. $\sin 2(x - y)$
14. $\cos 2(x - y)$
15. $\tan (x - y)$

Use the formulae of Section 7.1 to prove the following statements.

16. $\sin (180° - \theta) = \sin \theta$
17. $\sin (180° + \theta) = -\sin \theta$
18. $\cos (180° - \theta) = -\cos \theta$
19. $\cos (180° + \theta) = -\cos \theta$
20. $\tan (180° - \theta) = -\tan \theta$
21. $\tan (180° + \theta) = \tan \theta$

22. $\sin\left(\dfrac{\pi}{2}+\theta\right)=\cos\theta$ 　　　　23. $\cos\left(\dfrac{\pi}{2}+\theta\right)=-\sin\theta$

24. $\cos\left(\dfrac{3\pi}{2}+\theta\right)=\sin\theta$ 　　　　25. $\tan\left(\dfrac{3\pi}{2}+\theta\right)=-\cot\theta$

26. Expand $\cos(90°+x)=\cos[90°-(-x)]$ to show that
$$-\sin x=\sin(-x).$$

27. Show that
$$\cos x=\cos(-x).$$

28. Show that
$$-\tan x=\tan(-x).$$

Find a value for each of the following without using tables.

29. $\cos(-105°)$ 　　　　30. $\sin(-15°)$ 　　　　31. $\tan(-165°)$

32. $\sin(-\tfrac{11}{12}\pi)$ 　　　　33. $\cos(-\tfrac{5}{12}\pi)$ 　　　　34. $\tan(-\tfrac{4}{3}\pi)$

Find a simpler expression for each of the following.

35. $\sin 75°\cos 45°+\cos 75°\sin 45°$

36. $\cos\left(A+\dfrac{\pi}{4}\right)\cos A-\sin\left(A+\dfrac{\pi}{4}\right)\sin A$

37. $\cos A\cos A-\sin A\sin A$

38. $\cos\left(-\dfrac{\pi}{4}\right)\cos\left(-\dfrac{\pi}{12}\right)-\sin\left(-\dfrac{\pi}{4}\right)\sin\left(-\dfrac{\pi}{12}\right)$

39. $\cos(A+B)+\cos(A-B)$ 　　　　40. $\cos(A+B)-\cos(A-B)$

41. $\sin(A+B)+\sin(A-B)$ 　　　　42. $\sin(A+B)-\sin(A-B)$

43. Find expressions for $\cot(A+B)$ and $\cot(A-B)$ in terms of $\cot A$ and $\cot B$.

44. If m, n, and θ are real numbers, prove that there is a real number ϕ such that
$$m\sin\theta+n\cos\theta=\sqrt{m^2+n^2}\,\sin(\theta+\phi).$$

7.2. Sum and Difference Formulae

From the previous section, we know that,

$$\sin(A+B)=\sin A\cos B+\cos A\sin B,$$

and

$$\sin(A-B)=\sin A\cos B-\cos A\sin B.$$

From these equations we obtain

$$\sin (A + B) + \sin (A - B) = 2 \sin A \cos B, \tag{1}$$

and

$$\sin (A + B) - \sin (A - B) = 2 \cos A \sin B. \tag{2}$$

If we replace $A + B$ by x and $A - B$ by y, then,

$$A + B = x,$$
$$A - B = y,$$

and

$$2A = x + y,$$
$$2B = x - y.$$

Hence,

$$A = \frac{x + y}{2},$$

and

$$B = \frac{x - y}{2}.$$

Therefore, from (1)

$$\sin x + \sin y = 2 \sin \frac{x + y}{2} \cos \frac{x - y}{2}$$

and, from (2)

$$\sin x - \sin y = 2 \cos \frac{x + y}{2} \sin \frac{x - y}{2}$$

Example 1. Express $\sin 2x - \sin 4x$ in product form.

Solution:

$$\sin 2x - \sin 4x = 2 \cos \frac{2x + 4x}{2} \sin \frac{2x - 4x}{2}$$
$$= 2 \cos 3x \sin (-x)$$
$$= -2 \cos 3x \sin x.$$

Example 2. Calculate the value of $\sin 75° + \sin 15°$.

Solution:

$$\sin 75° + \sin 15° = 2 \sin \frac{90°}{2} \cos \frac{60°}{2}$$
$$= 2 \sin 45° \cos 30°$$
$$= 2 \left(\frac{1}{\sqrt{2}} \right) \left(\frac{\sqrt{3}}{2} \right)$$
$$= \frac{\sqrt{3}}{\sqrt{2}}$$
$$= \frac{\sqrt{6}}{2}.$$

EXERCISE 7.2

1. Using the formulae for $\cos (A + B)$ and $\cos (A - B)$, establish formulae for $\cos x + \cos y$ and $\cos x - \cos y$.

2. Express each of the following in product form.
   (a) $\sin 6x + \sin 2x$ (b) $\cos 6x + \cos 2x$
   (c) $\sin A - \sin 2A$ (d) $\cos A - \cos 2A$
   (e) $\sin 5\theta + \sin 3\theta$ (f) $\cos 5\theta + \cos 3\theta$
   (g) $\sin (A + B) - \sin A$ (h) $\cos (A + B) - \cos A$

3. Calculate the values of
   (a) $\sin 75° - \sin 15°$,   (b) $\cos 75° - \cos 15°$,
   (c) $\sin 15° - \sin 105°$,   (d) $\cos 15° - \cos 105°$.

7.3. Angle Between Two Lines

An interesting application of the formula for $\tan (A + B)$ lies in finding the angle between two lines.

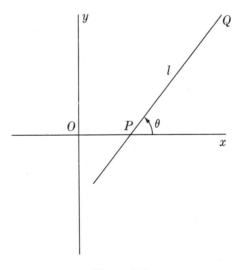

Figure 7.2

If line l intersects the x-axis at P and if Q is a point on l in the first or second quadrant, then angle xPQ, measured in a positive sense, is the angle that line l makes with the x-axis. This angle of inclination is denoted by θ in the diagram above. In Figure 7.3, l_1 and l_2 are lines whose angles of inclination are θ_1 and θ_2.

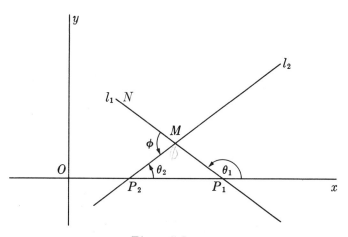

Figure 7.3

We define the angle between l_1 and l_2 as the acute angle at M, the point of intersection.

In Figure 7.3

$$\theta_1 - \theta_2 > 90° \quad \text{and} \quad \angle NMP_2 \text{ is the acute angle } \phi.$$

and, in triangle MP_1P_2,

$$\angle P_1MP_2 = \theta_1 - \theta_2.$$

Hence,

$$\phi = 180 - (\theta_1 - \theta_2).$$

and

$$\begin{aligned}
\tan \phi &= \tan [180 - (\theta_1 - \theta_2)] \\
&= -\tan (\theta_1 - \theta_2) \\
&= \tan[-(\theta_1 - \theta_2)] \\
&= \tan (\theta_2 - \theta_1) \\
&= \frac{\tan \theta_2 - \tan \theta_1}{1 + \tan \theta_2 \tan \theta_1}.
\end{aligned}$$

But

$$\tan \theta_1 = m_1$$

and

$$\tan \theta_2 = m_2$$

where m_1 and m_2 are the slopes of l_1 and l_2.

Hence,

$$\begin{aligned}
\tan \phi &= \frac{m_2 - m_1}{1 + m_2 m_1} \\
&= \frac{m_2 - m_1}{1 + m_1 m_2}
\end{aligned}$$

Suppose as in Figure 7.4,

$$\theta_1 - \theta_2 < 90° \text{ and } \angle P_2 M P_1 \text{ is acute.}$$

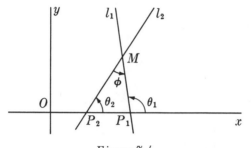

Figure 7.4

Then,

$$\theta_1 = \theta_2 + \phi ,$$

or

$$\phi = \theta_1 - \theta_2 ,$$

and, as in the previous case,

$$\tan \phi = \tan (\theta_1 - \theta_2)$$

Using the same methods as in the previous case, we find

$$\tan \phi = \frac{m_1 - m_2}{1 + m_1 m_2} .$$

Hence, in either case the acute angle ϕ is given by $\tan \phi = \left| \dfrac{m_1 - m_2}{1 + m_1 m_2} \right| .$

The formula for $\tan \phi$ is applicable unless $m_1 m_2 = -1$, that is, $m_2 = -\dfrac{1}{m_1} .$

In this case, $l_1 \perp l_2$ and $\tan \phi$ is undefined; the angle between l_1 and l_2 is 90° Thus, if $m_1 m_2 = -1$, the two lines are perpendicular.

Example 1.   Find the angle between the lines defined by

$$3x + y = 15 ,$$

and

$$3x - 2y + 6 = 0 .$$

Solution: If

$$3x + y = 15 \quad \text{defines } l_1 ,$$

and

$$3x - 2y + 6 = 0 \quad \text{defines } l_2 ,$$

then

$$m_1 = -3 ,$$

and

$$m_2 = \tfrac{3}{2} .$$

The angle ϕ, between l_1, and l_2 is given by

$$\tan \phi = \left| \frac{m_2 - m_1}{1 + m_2 m_1} \right|$$

$$= \left| \frac{\frac{3}{2} - (-3)}{1 + (\frac{3}{2})(-3)} \right|$$

$$= \left| \frac{\frac{9}{2}}{-\frac{7}{2}} \right|$$

$$= \frac{9}{7}$$

$$\simeq 1.29 \,.$$

Therefore,

$$\phi \simeq 52° \,. \qquad\qquad\qquad \text{(tables)}$$

Example 2. Find the angle between l_1 defined by

$$x - 2y + 5 = 0 \,,$$

and l_2 defined by

$$4x - 3y - 8 = 0 \,.$$

Solution:

$$m_1 = \tfrac{1}{2} \quad \text{and} \quad m_2 = \tfrac{4}{3} \,.$$

$$\tan \phi = \left| \frac{m_2 - m_1}{1 + m_2 m_1} \right|$$

$$= \left| \frac{\frac{4}{3} - \frac{1}{2}}{1 + (\frac{4}{3})(\frac{1}{2})} \right|$$

$$= \frac{\frac{5}{6}}{\frac{10}{6}}$$

$$= \tfrac{1}{2} \,.$$

Therefore, $\phi \simeq 27° \,.$

The acute angle between l_1 and l_2 is approximately 27°.

EXERCISE 7.3

Find (to the nearest degree) the acute angle between the two lines defined by the following pairs of equations.

1. $3x - 2y + 8 = 0, \quad x - y - 4 = 0$

2. $5x - 8y - 10 = 0, \quad x - 3y - 5 = 0$

3. $14x - 12y - 1 = 0,   3x + y - 8 = 0$

4. $4x - 8y + 17 = 0,   4x + 3y + 5 = 0$

5. $3y - 4x = 2,   x = 7y$

6. Find the acute angle between the line through $(-2, -1)$ and $(5, 7)$, and the line through $(11, -1)$ and $(7, 4)$.

7. If the angle from a line whose slope is $\frac{1}{4}$ to a second line with greater slope m_2 is $45°$, find m_2.

8. If $\phi = 30°$ and $m_2 = 2$, find m_1 (as an irrational number in its simplest form).

9. Two lines intersect at the point whose co-ordinates are $(3, 7)$.   The angle between l_1 and l_2 is $45°$ and an equation for l_1 is
$$x + 3y - 12 = 0.$$
Find an equation for l_2 if its slope is positive.

10. Show that the tangent of the acute angle between the lines whose slopes are $\sqrt{2}$ and $\sqrt{3}$ is $\frac{1}{5}(4\sqrt{2} - 3\sqrt{3})$.

7.4.   Formulae for sin 2θ, cos 2θ, tan 2θ

The formulae numbered (1), (2), and (3) below are three of those that we developed in Section 7.1. They permit us to develop formulae for $\sin 2\theta$, $\cos 2\theta$, and $\tan 2\theta$, in terms of $\sin \theta$, $\cos \theta$, and $\tan \theta$ respectively,

$$\sin (A + B) = \sin A \cos B + \cos A \sin B \tag{1}$$
$$\cos (A + B) = \cos A \cos B - \sin A \sin B \tag{2}$$
$$\tan (A + B) = \frac{\tan A + \tan B}{1 - \tan A \tan B} \tag{3}$$

From (1), replacing B by A, we obtain

$$\sin (A + A) = \sin A \cos A + \cos A \sin A,$$

or

$$\sin 2A = 2 \sin A \cos A.$$

From (2), replacing B by A, we obtain

$$\cos (A + A) = \cos A \cos A - \sin A \sin A,$$

or

$$\cos 2A = \cos^2 A - \sin^2 A.$$

Since

$$\sin^2 A + \cos^2 A = 1,$$

we may write

$$\cos 2A = 1 - \sin^2 A - \sin^2 A,$$

and hence

$$\cos 2A = 1 - 2 \sin^2 A \,,$$

or

$$\cos 2A = \cos^2 A - (1 - \cos^2 A)\,,$$

and hence

$$\cos 2A = 2 \cos^2 A - 1\,.$$

From (3), replacing B by A, we obtain,

$$\tan (A + A) = \frac{\tan A + \tan A}{1 - \tan A \tan A}\,,$$

Therefore,

$$\tan 2A = \frac{2 \tan A}{1 - \tan^2 A}\,.$$

The formulae of this section and those of Section 7.1 allow us to prove many other identities. Consider the following examples.

Example 1. Develop a formula for $\sin 3A$ in terms of $\sin A$.

Solution:

$$\begin{aligned}
\sin 3A &= \sin (A + 2A) \\
&= \sin A \cos 2A + \cos A \sin 2A \\
&= \sin A (1 - 2 \sin^2 A) + \cos A (2 \sin A \cos A) \\
&= \sin A - 2 \sin^3 A + 2 \sin A (1 - \sin^2 A)\,.
\end{aligned}$$

Therefore,

$$\sin 3A = 3 \sin A - 4 \sin^3 A\,.$$

Example 2. Prove that, for $\theta \in Re$, $\quad \theta \neq (2n + 1)\pi, \quad n \in I$

$$\frac{\sin \theta}{1 + \cos \theta} = \tan \frac{\theta}{2}\,.$$

Solution:

$$\frac{\sin \theta}{1 + \cos \theta} = \frac{2 \sin \dfrac{\theta}{2} \cos \dfrac{\theta}{2}}{1 + (2 \cos^2 \dfrac{\theta}{2} - 1)}$$

$$= \frac{2 \sin \dfrac{\theta}{2} \cos \dfrac{\theta}{2}}{2 \cos \dfrac{\theta}{2} \cos \dfrac{\theta}{2}}$$

$$= \tan \frac{\theta}{2}\,.$$

Thus,

$$\frac{\sin \theta}{1 + \cos \theta} = \tan \frac{\theta}{2}\,.$$

Example 3 .   Find a value of $\cos 22\frac{1}{2}°$ without using tables.
Solution:

$$\cos 2A = 2 \cos^2 A - 1,$$

$$\cos 45° = 2 \cos^2 22\frac{1}{2}° - 1,$$

$$2 \cos^2 22\frac{1}{2}° = 1 + \frac{1}{\sqrt{2}}$$

$$= \frac{\sqrt{2} + 1}{\sqrt{2}}$$

$$= \frac{2 + \sqrt{2}}{2},$$

$$\cos 22\frac{1}{2}° = \sqrt{\frac{2 + \sqrt{2}}{4}}$$

$$= \frac{1}{2} \sqrt{2 + \sqrt{2}}.$$

$22\frac{1}{2}°$ is a first quadrant angle; thus, $\cos 22\frac{1}{2}° > 0$.

EXERCISE 7.4

Change each of the following to an equivalent expression in terms of half the given angles.

1. $\cos 4A$

2. $\sin 4A$

3. $\tan 4A$

4. $\sin 12A$

5. $\cos 12A$

6. $\sin 10\pi$

7. $\cos \dfrac{\pi}{4}$

8. $\cos \dfrac{7\pi}{2}$

9. $\tan 240°$

10. If

$$\sin A = \tfrac{5}{13}$$

and

$$0 < A < \frac{\pi}{2},$$

find $\sin 2A$, $\cos 2A$, $\tan 2A$.   In which quadrant does $2A$ lie?

11. Repeat question (10), given that

$$\cos A = \frac{1}{\sqrt{5}}$$

and

$$0 < A < \frac{\pi}{2}.$$

12. Develop a formula for cos $3A$ in terms of cos A.

13. If
$$\cos A = \frac{4}{5}$$
and
$$0 < A < \frac{\pi}{2},$$
find cos $3A$.

14. Develop formulae for cot $2A$ in terms of (a) tan A, (b) cot A.

15. If
$$\cos \theta = \tfrac{4}{5}, \quad 0 < \theta < \frac{\pi}{2}$$
find values for $\cos \dfrac{\theta}{2}$ and $\sin \dfrac{\theta}{2}$.

16. If
$$\sin x = \tfrac{\sqrt{3}}{2},$$
find values for $\cos \dfrac{x}{2}$ and $\sin \dfrac{x}{2}$.

17. Prove
$$\sin \frac{\theta}{2} = \pm \sqrt{\frac{1 - \cos \theta}{2}}.$$
Why do we use positive and negative signs?

18. Develop formulae for $\cos \dfrac{\theta}{2}$ and $\tan \dfrac{\theta}{2}$ from the formula in question (17).

Prove the following identities. State any necessary restriction on the variables involved.

19. $\cos 2x = \cos^4 x - \sin^4 x$

20. $\sqrt{2}\ \sqrt{1 - \cos 2x} = 4 \sin \dfrac{x}{2} \cos \dfrac{x}{2}$

21. $\left(\cos \dfrac{\theta}{2} - \sin \dfrac{\theta}{2}\right)^2 = 1 - \sin \theta$

22. $\sin 2B = 1 - 2 \sin^2 \left(\dfrac{\pi}{4} - B\right)$

*
23. $\dfrac{1 + \sin y}{\cos y} = \dfrac{1 + \tan \dfrac{y}{2}}{1 - \tan \dfrac{y}{2}}$

24. $\dfrac{2}{1 + \cos A} = \sec^2 \dfrac{A}{2}$

25. $\tan \dfrac{\theta}{2} = \dfrac{1 - \cos \theta}{\sin \theta}$

26. $\tan A = \pm \sqrt{\dfrac{1 - \cos 2A}{1 + \cos 2A}}$

27. $\dfrac{\sin y \cos y}{1 - 2 \sin^2 y} = \dfrac{1}{\cot y - \tan y}$

28. $\cos \dfrac{5x}{2} \cdot \cos \dfrac{x}{2} + \sin \dfrac{5x}{2} \cdot \sin \dfrac{x}{2} = \cos 2x$

29. $\sin \dfrac{7\pi}{4} \cdot \cos \dfrac{3\pi}{4} - \cos \dfrac{7\pi}{4} \cdot \sin \dfrac{3\pi}{4} = 0$

30. $\cos x + \cos 2x + \cos 3x = \cos 2x(1 + 2 \cos x)$

*31. $2(\cos^4 A + \sin^4 A) = 1 + \cos^2 2A$ 32. $\sin 3y + \sin y = 2 \sin 2y \cos y$

33. Explain the restriction on θ in Example 2 of Section 7.4.

7.5.   Addition of Sine and Cosine Functions

If we wish to construct the graph of $y = \sin \theta + \cos \theta$, we could construct a table
of values and, from this, draw the graph.   However,

$$\sin \theta + \cos \theta = \sin \theta + \sin (90° - \theta)$$
$$= 2 \sin \frac{90°}{2} \cos \frac{2\theta - 90°}{2}$$
$$= 2 \sin 45° \cos (\theta - 45°)$$
$$= 2(\tfrac{1}{\sqrt{2}}) \cos (45° - \theta)$$
$$= \sqrt{2} \sin (90° - 45° + \theta)$$
$$= \sqrt{2} \sin (\theta + 45°) .$$

We note that the graph is sinusoidal; that is, it has the same shape as the graph of
the sine function.   The amplitude is $\sqrt{2}$, the period is 2π, and the phase angle is 45°
or $\dfrac{\pi}{4}$.

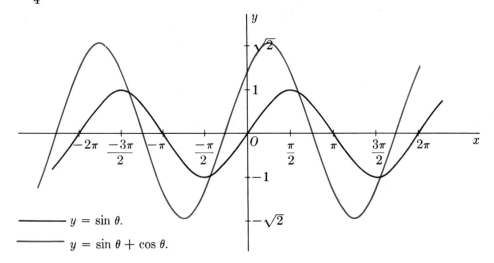

——— $y = \sin \theta$.

——— $y = \sin \theta + \cos \theta$.

Figure 7.5

A more general function formed from the sine and cosine functions is the function determined by $y = a \sin \theta + b \cos \theta$. The example above is the special case obtained when $a = b = 1$.

From the special case we see that

$$\sqrt{2} \sin (\theta + 45°) = \sqrt{2} \ (\sin \theta \cos 45° + \cos \theta \sin 45°)$$
$$= (\sqrt{2} \cos 45°) \sin \theta + (\sqrt{2} \sin 45°) \cos \theta \,.$$
$$= \sin \theta + \cos \theta \,.$$

This suggests that in the general case we might try to find two numbers k and ϕ such that

$$a \sin \theta + b \cos \theta = k \cos \phi \sin \theta + k \sin \phi \cos \theta$$
$$= k \sin (\theta + \phi) \,.$$

If these numbers exist, we must have

$$a = k \cos \phi \text{ and } b = k \sin \phi \,.$$

By squaring and adding, we obtain

$$a^2 + b^2 = k^2 \cos^2 \phi + k^2 \sin^2 \phi$$
$$= k^2 \,,$$

and by elimination of k we obtain

$$\frac{b}{a} = \frac{\sin \phi}{\cos \phi}$$
$$= \tan \phi \,.$$

Example 1. Find k and ϕ so that

$$4 \sin \theta + 3 \cos \theta = k \sin (\theta + \phi) \,.$$

Solution:
$$k^2 = 4^2 + 3^2$$
$$= 25$$

Therefore,
$$k = 5 \,,$$

and
$$\tan \phi = \frac{3}{4}$$

Hence,
$$\phi \simeq 37°$$

Therefore,
$$4 \sin \theta + 3 \cos \theta = 5 \sin (\theta + 37°) \,.$$

In Figure 7.6(a), we show the graphs of $y = 4 \sin \theta$ and $x = 3 \cos \theta$ and in Figure 7.6(b) we show the graph of

$$y = 4 \sin \theta + 3 \cos \theta$$
$$= 5 \sin (\theta + 37°).$$

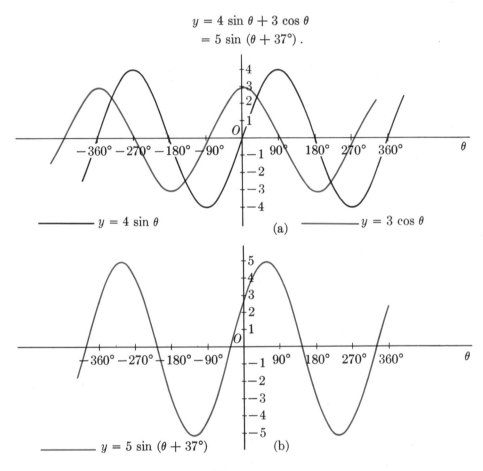

$y = 4 \sin \theta$ (a) $y = 3 \cos \theta$

$y = 5 \sin (\theta + 37°)$ (b)

Figure 7.6

EXERCISE 7.5

1. Find the period and amplitude of the following functions.
   - (a) $\sin \theta + \sqrt{3} \cos \theta$
   - (b) $-3 \sin \theta + 4 \cos \theta$
   - (c) $5 \sin x + 12 \cos x$
   - (d) $2 \sin x - \cos x$
   - (e) $\sin 2\theta + \sqrt{3} \underset{\text{cos}}{\sin} 2\theta$
   - (f) $\sin 3\pi x + 2 \cos 3\pi x$

2. In the preceding question, find the phase angle of the functions in (a) to (d) with respect to both sine and cosine functions.

3. In question (1), sketch the graphs of parts (a) to (f).

Chapter Summary

Compound angle formulae:

$$\cos (A \pm B) = \cos A \cos B \mp \sin A \sin B$$
$$\sin (A \pm B) = \sin A \cos B \pm \cos A \sin B$$
$$\tan (A \pm B) = \frac{\tan A \pm \tan B}{1 \mp \tan A \tan B}$$
$$\sin 2x = 2 \sin x \cos x$$
$$\cos 2x = \cos^2 x - \sin^2 x$$
$$= 2 \cos^2 x - 1$$
$$= 1 - 2 \sin^2 x$$
$$\tan 2x = \frac{2 \tan x}{1 - \tan^2 x}$$

Sum and difference formulae:

$$\sin x + \sin y = 2 \sin \frac{x+y}{2} \cos \frac{x-y}{2}$$
$$\sin x - \sin y = 2 \cos \frac{x+y}{2} \sin \frac{x-y}{2}$$
$$\cos x + \cos y = 2 \cos \frac{x+y}{2} \cos \frac{x-y}{2}$$
$$\cos x - \cos y = -2 \sin \frac{x+y}{2} \sin \frac{x-y}{2}$$

If a line l_1 has slope m_1 and a line l_2 has slope m_2, then the acute angle ϕ between l_1 and l_2 is given by

$$\tan \phi = \left| \frac{m_1 - m_2}{1 + m_1 m_2} \right|.$$

The equation

$$a \sin \theta + b \cos \theta = k \sin (\theta + \phi),$$

where

$$k^2 = a^2 + b^2,$$

and

$$\tan \phi = \frac{b}{a}.$$

REVIEW EXERCISE 7

1. Find the acute angle between the line whose equation is
$$x - 4y - 2 = 0,$$
   and the line whose equation is
$$4x + 4y - 17 = 0.$$

2. Find the acute angle between the line that passes through $(7, -1)$ and $(4, 8)$ and the line that has a slope of $1/2$ and a y-intercept of 5.

3. Show that the tangent of one of the angles between the lines whose slopes are $\sqrt{3}$ and $1/\sqrt{3}$ is $-1/\sqrt{3}$.

4. Find the value of sin 120° by expanding sin 2(60°).

Prove the following identities.

5. $\sin 5\theta \cos \theta + \cos 5\theta \sin \theta = \sin 6\theta$

6. $\cos \dfrac{7\pi}{2} \cos \dfrac{3\pi}{2} + \sin \dfrac{7\pi}{2} \sin \dfrac{3\pi}{2} = 1$

7. $\cos^2 x + \cos^2 y - 1 = \cos(x + y)\cos(x - y)$

8. $\cos(m + n) + \cos(m - n) = 2\cos m \cos n$

9. $\sin(m + n) + \sin(m - n) = 2\sin m \cos n$

10. $\tan(x + y + z) = \dfrac{\tan x + \tan y + \tan z - \tan x \tan y \tan z}{1 - \tan x \tan y - \tan x \tan z - \tan y \tan z}$

11. $\cos(\pi + \theta) + \cos(\pi - \theta) = -2\cos \theta$

12. $\dfrac{\sin 2A}{\sin A} - \dfrac{\cos 2A}{\cos A} = \dfrac{1}{\cos A}$

13. $\cos 2x = \dfrac{1 - \tan^2 x}{1 + \tan^2 x}$

14. $\sin(\pi + \theta) + \cos\left(\dfrac{\pi}{2} - \theta\right) + \tan\left(\dfrac{\pi}{2} + \theta\right) = -\cot \theta$

15. $\sin 3A - \sin A = 2\sin A - 4\sin^3 A$.

16. $\cos 3A + \cos A = 4\cos^3 A - 2\cos A$.

17. State the period, amplitude, and phase angle, and draw the graphs of each of the following.
    (a) $\sqrt{3}\sin \theta + \cos \theta$.   (b) $\sqrt{3}\sin \theta - \cos \theta$.
    (c) $4\sin \theta - 3\cos \theta$.   (d) $2\sin \theta + 2\cos \theta$.

Chapter 8

ROTATIONS IN THE PLANE

8.1. The Mapping
$(x, y) \rightarrow (x \cos \theta - y \sin \theta, \; x \sin \theta + y \cos \theta)$

If we consider a two plane representation of the transformation

$$(x, y) \rightarrow \left(x \cos \frac{\pi}{4} - y \sin \frac{\pi}{4}, \; x \sin \frac{\pi}{4} + y \cos \frac{\pi}{4} \right) = (u, v),$$

that is

$$(x, y) \rightarrow \left(\frac{x}{\sqrt{2}} - \frac{y}{\sqrt{2}}, \; \frac{x}{\sqrt{2}} + \frac{y}{\sqrt{2}} \right) = (u, v),$$

we see that

$$(0, 0) \rightarrow (0, 0),$$

$$(1, 0) \rightarrow \left(\frac{1}{\sqrt{2}}, \; \frac{1}{\sqrt{2}} \right),$$

$$(0, 1) \rightarrow \left(-\frac{1}{\sqrt{2}}, \; \frac{1}{\sqrt{2}} \right),$$

$$(-1, 0) \rightarrow \left(-\frac{1}{\sqrt{2}}, \; -\frac{1}{\sqrt{2}} \right),$$

and

$$(0, -1) \rightarrow \left(\frac{1}{\sqrt{2}}, \; -\frac{1}{\sqrt{2}} \right).$$

The two-plane representation of the transformation of these points is shown in Figure 8.1.

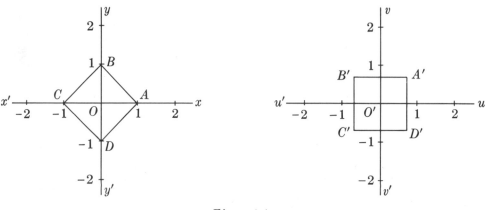

Figure 8.1

We see immediately that each of the original points O, A, B, C, D in the xy-plane is mapped onto a unique image point O', A', B', C', D' in the uv-plane. Obviously, *any* given point (a, b) in the xy-plane is mapped onto a unique image point $\left(\dfrac{a}{\sqrt{2}} - \dfrac{b}{\sqrt{2}}, \dfrac{a}{\sqrt{2}} + \dfrac{b}{\sqrt{2}}\right)$ in the uv-plane.

Thus, the transformation

$$(x, y) \rightarrow \left(\frac{x}{\sqrt{2}} - \frac{y}{\sqrt{2}}, \frac{x}{\sqrt{2}} + \frac{y}{\sqrt{2}}\right)$$

maps the points in the xy-plane onto corresponding points in the uv-plane and the correspondence is one-to-one.   (See Exercise 8.1, question (7).)

As in the case of the translations, we can use a one-plane representation if we make the xy-axes and uv-axes coincide. Figure 8.2 shows the same points as Figure 8.1 under this transformation.

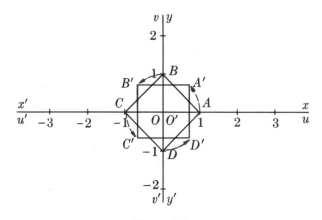

Figure 8.2

This last diagram seems to indicate that the effect of the transformation on the square $ABCD$ is the *rotation* of the square about the origin O through an angle of $\frac{\pi}{4}$ into the congruent square $A'B'C'D'$. (Verify that $ABCD$ and $A'B'C'D'$ are congruent squares.) This rotation does indeed occur and the effect of the transformation is the rotation of the original plane through an angle of $\frac{\pi}{4}$ about the origin, which is a fixed point for the transformation and, in fact, is the only fixed point.

The general transformation of this kind is

$$P \rightarrow P',$$
$$(x, y) \rightarrow (x \cos \theta - y \sin \theta, \ x \sin \theta + y \cos \theta) = (u, v).$$

We see that, for this transformation,

$$OP^2 = (x - 0)^2 + (y - 0)^2$$
$$= x^2 + y^2,$$

and

$$OP'^2 = (u - 0)^2 + (v - 0)^2$$
$$= (x \cos \theta - y \sin \theta)^2 + (x \sin \theta + y \cos \theta)^2$$
$$= x^2 \cos^2 \theta - 2xy \cos \theta \sin \theta + y^2 \sin^2 \theta + x^2 \sin^2 \theta$$
$$\quad + 2xy \sin \theta \cos \theta + y^2 \cos^2 \theta$$
$$= x^2 (\cos^2 \theta + \sin^2 \theta) + y^2 (\sin^2 \theta + \cos^2 \theta)$$
$$= x^2 + y^2$$
$$= OP^2.$$

Thus, the transformation is such that the distance of any point from the origin is constant under the transformation. Also, if we consider two points $P(a, b)$ and $Q(c, d)$ and their image points $P'(a', b')$ and $Q'(c', d')$, then

$$a' = a \cos \theta - b \sin \theta, \ b' = a \sin \theta + b \cos \theta$$

and

$$c' = c \cos \theta - d \sin \theta, \ d' = c \sin \theta + d \cos \theta.$$

Therefore,

$$PQ^2 = (a - c)^2 + (b - d)^2,$$

and

$$P'Q'^2 = (a' - c')^2 + (b' - d')^2$$
$$= [(a - c) \cos \theta - (b - d) \sin \theta]^2 + [(a - c) \sin \theta + (b - d) \cos \theta]^2$$
$$= (a - c)^2 (\cos^2 \theta + \sin^2 \theta) + (b - d)^2 (\sin^2 \theta + \cos^2 \theta)$$
$$= PQ^2.$$

Thus, the lengths of line segments are invariant under the transformation.

These two results together show that any point on a circle with its centre at the origin is mapped into another point on the same circle and that the distance the point is "moved" on the circle is the same for each point on the circle.   Such a "motion" is produced by a rigid counterclockwise rotation of the plane through an angle θ about the origin as the centre of rotation.   For this reason, the transformation is called a rotation.

DEFINITION.   The mapping

$$(x, y) \rightarrow (x \cos \theta - y \sin \theta, \ x \sin \theta + y \cos \theta), \quad x, y, \theta \in Re$$

is a one-to-one mapping called a *rotation*.   The rotation is counterclockwise through the angle θ radians; the centre of rotation is $(0, 0)$.

Example.   Find the image points of some typical points on the line $y = x$ under the transformation

$$(x, y) \rightarrow (\tfrac{\sqrt{3}}{2}x - \tfrac{1}{2}y, \ \tfrac{1}{2}x + \tfrac{\sqrt{3}}{2}y) \ .$$

Using a single-plane representation, illustrate this mapping as a rotation of the line $y = x$ through an angle of $30°$.   Indicate also the image of the half plane $x > y$.

Solution: Under the transformation

$$(x, y) \rightarrow (\tfrac{\sqrt{3}}{2}x - \tfrac{1}{2}y, \ \tfrac{1}{2}x + \tfrac{\sqrt{3}}{2}y)$$

we obtain the following correspondences:

$$(0, 0) \rightarrow (0, 0) \ ,$$

$$(1, 1) \rightarrow \left(\frac{\sqrt{3} - 1}{2}, \ \frac{1 + \sqrt{3}}{2} \right),$$

$$(2, 2) \rightarrow (\sqrt{3} - 1, \ 1 + \sqrt{3}) \ ,$$

$$(-1, -1) \rightarrow \left(\frac{-\sqrt{3} + 1}{2}, \ \frac{-\sqrt{3} - 1}{2} \right),$$

$$(-2, -2) \rightarrow (-\sqrt{3} + 1, \ -\sqrt{3} - 1) \ .$$

Thus, the image points lie on a line through the origin with slope $\dfrac{1 + \sqrt{3}}{\sqrt{3} - 1}$.   The equation of the image line is

$$(\sqrt{3} - 1)y = (1 + \sqrt{3})x \ .$$

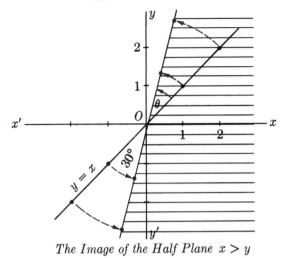

The Image of the Half Plane $x > y$

The slope of the original line, $y = x$, is 1, the slope of the image line is $\frac{1+\sqrt{3}}{\sqrt{3}-1}$.

Therefore, if ϕ is the angle between the lines, we have

$$\tan \phi = \frac{\dfrac{1+\sqrt{3}}{\sqrt{3}-1} - 1}{1 + \dfrac{1+\sqrt{3}}{\sqrt{3}-1}}$$

$$= \frac{\sqrt{3}+1-\sqrt{3}+1}{\sqrt{3}-1+1+\sqrt{3}}$$

$$= \frac{1}{\sqrt{3}},$$

$$\phi = \frac{\pi}{6} \text{ or } 30°.$$

EXERCISE 8.1

1. Find the images of the points
    $$A\,(4, 3), \quad B\,(-1, 3), \quad C\,(-1, -2), \quad D\,(4, -2),$$
    under the rotations

    (a) $(x, y) \rightarrow \left(\dfrac{x - y}{\sqrt{2}}, \dfrac{x + y}{\sqrt{2}} \right)$,

    (b) $(x, y) \rightarrow \left(\dfrac{-x - y}{\sqrt{2}}, \dfrac{x - y}{\sqrt{2}} \right)$,

    (c) $(x, y) \rightarrow \left(\dfrac{x}{2} - \dfrac{\sqrt{3}y}{2}, \dfrac{\sqrt{3}x}{2} + \dfrac{y}{2} \right)$,

    (d) $(x, y) \rightarrow (-y, x)$.

    State the angle of rotation in each case. Show the corresponding points in both two-plane and single-plane representations.

2. Find the images of the points
$$A(-2, -1), \quad B(0, 0), \quad C(2, 1), \quad D(6, 3),$$
under the rotations

(a) $(x, y) \rightarrow \left(\dfrac{\sqrt{3}x - y}{2}, \dfrac{x + \sqrt{3}y}{2}\right)$, (b) $(x, y) \rightarrow \left(\dfrac{x + y}{\sqrt{2}}, \dfrac{-x + y}{\sqrt{2}}\right)$,

(c) $(x, y) \rightarrow (-x, -y)$,   (d) $(x, y) \rightarrow \left(\dfrac{-x - \sqrt{3}y}{2}, \dfrac{\sqrt{3}x - y}{2}\right)$.

State the angle of rotation in each case and show the corresponding points in both two-plane and single-plane representations. What do you note about the set of given points and the set of image points?

3. The points A $(2, 3)$, $B(-1, +1)$, $C(0, -3)$, and $D(3, -1)$ determine a parallelogram $ABCD$. Find the length of the sides AB and AD. The parallelogram is transformed into another quadrilateral $A'B'C'D'$ by the rotation

$$(x, y) \rightarrow \left(\frac{x\sqrt{3} - y}{2}, \frac{x + y\sqrt{3}}{2}\right).$$

Show that $A'B'C'D'$ is also a parallelogram congruent to $ABCD$. Sketch the two parallelograms in a single plane.

4. The points $A(0, -\frac{\sqrt{3}}{3})$, $B(-\frac{1}{2}, \frac{\sqrt{3}}{6})$, and $C(\frac{1}{2}, \frac{\sqrt{3}}{6})$ determine an equilateral triangle with its centroid (point of intersection of the medians) at $(0, 0)$. Find two *different* rotations which transform $\triangle ABC$ into a congruent triangle coincident with $\triangle ABC$. State the mapping for each transformation in the standard form.

5. If $P(x, y)$ and $P'(u, v)$ are points in the plane such that
$$OP = OP',$$
and
$$\angle POP' = \theta,$$
show that
$$u = x \cos \theta - y \sin \theta$$
and
$$v = x \sin \theta + y \cos \theta.$$
(*Hint:* Let angle xOP be ψ and angle xOP' be ϕ and apply the formulae for the sine and cosine of the sum of two angles.)

6. If $P(x, y)$ and $P'(u, v)$ are points in the plane such that
$$u = x \cos \theta - y \sin \theta$$
and
$$v = x \sin \theta + y \cos \theta,$$
show that
$$\angle POP' = \theta.$$
(*Hint:* Find $\tan \angle POP'$.)

7. Given the mapping

$f: (x, y) \rightarrow (x \cos \theta - y \sin \theta, \, x \sin \theta + y \cos \theta) = (u, v), \qquad (x, y, \theta \in \text{Re})$

where (u, v) is the image of (x, y), show that

$$x = u \cos \theta + v \sin \theta \, ,$$
$$y = -u \sin \theta + v \cos \theta \, .$$

Now let

$g: (u, v) \rightarrow (u \cos \theta + v \sin \theta, \, -u \sin \theta + v \cos \theta)$

and show that $g(f(x, y)) = (x, y)$.

8.2. Geometric Invariance Under a Rotation

We have already shown that the distance between two points P and Q is unchanged or *invariant* under a rotation. If we also show that the angle between two intersecting line segments is invariant under a rotation then, as in the case of translations, any triangle, and so any polygon, is invariant under a rotation. As a closed curve may be considered to be the limit of a polygon as the number of sides is increased in a suitable way, it follows that any geometric figure remains invariant under a rotation.

Example 1. Show that the angle α between two line segments AB and BC is invariant under the rotational mapping

$$(x, y) \rightarrow (x \cos \theta - y \sin \theta, \, x \sin \theta + y \cos \theta) \, .$$

Solution: Let O be the origin of the co-ordinate system and, therefore, the centre of rotation.

Let A', B', C' be the image points of A, B, C respectively, $\alpha = \angle ABC$ and $\alpha' = \angle A'B'C'$.

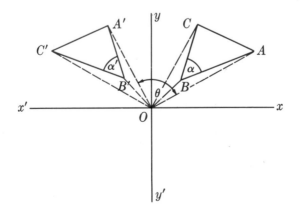

Using the results of Section 8.1 for the invariance of the lengths of line segments under a rotation, in $\triangle ABC$ and $\triangle A'B'C'$, we obtain

$$AB = A'B' , \; BC = B'C' , \; CA = C'A' ,$$

$$\triangle ABC \equiv \triangle A'B'C' ;$$

that is,

$$\angle ABC = \angle A'B'C' , \quad \alpha = \alpha' .$$

Example 2. Find the equation of the image of the line $y = 2x - 1$ under the rotation $(x, y) \rightarrow (.6x - .8y, .8x + .6y) = (u, v)$. Illustrate the line and its image in a single-plane representation.

Solution: The transformation gives the equations

$$.6x - .8y = u , \quad .8x + .6y = v$$

Hence, $$.36x + .64x = .6u + .8v$$

$$x = .6u + .8v \quad \text{and} \quad y = -.8u + .6v .$$

Therefore, the equation of the image line in the uv-plane is

$$(-.8u + .6v) = 2(.6u + .8v) - 1 ,$$
$$0 = 2u + v - 1 .$$

In the two-plane representation, we have following diagrams.

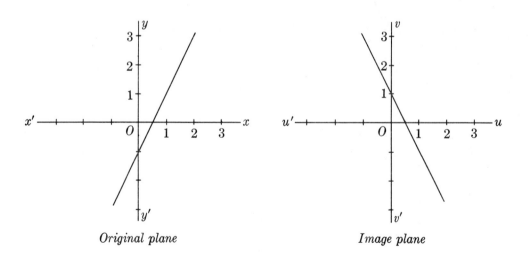

Original plane   Image plane

In the single-plane representation, we allow the uv-axes and the xy-axes to coincide and have the same scale.   In this case, the image line in the xy-plane has the equation

$$2x + y - 1 = 0 .$$

The original and image lines and the angle of rotation are shown in the following diagram.

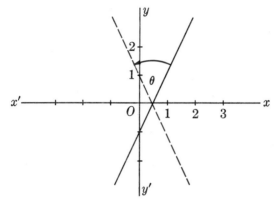

Example 3.   Find the image of the curve determined by the equation

$$9x^2 + 4xy + 6y^2 = 20$$

under the rotation

$$(x, \ y) \rightarrow \left(\frac{x - 2y}{\sqrt{5}}, \ \frac{2x + y}{\sqrt{5}} \right) = (u, \ v) .$$

Identify the curve and illustrate both the original and image curves on a single plane.   What is the *angle of rotation* (to the nearest degree)?   (By the *angle of rotation*, we mean the *angle between 0° and 360° through which all points of the original curve are rotated to produce the image curve.*)

Solution: The rotation determines

$$x - 2y = \sqrt{5}u ,$$
$$2x + y = \sqrt{5}v ,$$
$$4x + 2y = 2\sqrt{5}v .$$

Hence,

$$5x = \sqrt{5}u + 2\sqrt{5}v ,$$

$$x = \frac{u + 2v}{\sqrt{5}} ,$$

and

$$y = \frac{-2u + v}{\sqrt{5}} .$$

Therefore, the equation of the image curve is

$$9\left(\frac{u+2v}{\sqrt{5}}\right)^2 + 4\,\frac{(u+2v)\,(v-2u)}{5} + 6\left(\frac{v-2u}{\sqrt{5}}\right)^2 = 20\,,$$

$$9\,(u^2+4uv+4v^2) + 4\,(-2u^2+2v^2-3uv) + 6\,(v^2-4uv+4u^2) = 100\,,$$

$$(9-8+24)u^2 + (36-12-24)uv + (36+8+6)v^2 = 100\,,$$

$$25u^2 + 50v^2 = 100\,,$$

$$u^2 + 2v^2 = 4\,,$$

$$\frac{u^2}{4} + \frac{v^2}{2} = 1\,.$$

The curve is an ellipse with centre at the origin, semi-major axis 2 units long and semi-minor axis $\sqrt{2}$ units long. In the single-plane representation, the equation of the image ellipse is

$$\frac{x^2}{4} + \frac{y^2}{2} = 1\,.$$

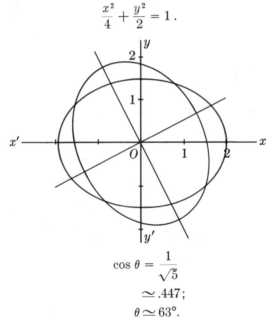

$$\cos\theta = \frac{1}{\sqrt{5}}$$

therefore,

$$\simeq .447\,;$$

$$\theta \simeq 63°.$$

The angle of rotation is approximately 63°.

EXERCISE 8.2

1. $A\,(\sqrt{3}, 1)$ and $B\,(\sqrt{3}, 3)$ are two points in the $x\,y$-plane. The rotation

$$(x,\,y) \rightarrow\ (\tfrac{\sqrt{3}}{2}x + \tfrac{1}{2}y,\ -\tfrac{1}{2}x + \tfrac{\sqrt{3}}{2}y)$$

is applied to the plane.

(a) Show that $\angle AOB$ is invariant under this rotation.

(b) Verify that all the sides and angles of $\triangle AOB$ are invariant under the rotation.

(c) Draw the original and image triangles in a single plane representation to common axes.

2. The four points $A(-\sqrt{2}, -\sqrt{2})$, $B(\sqrt{2}, -3\sqrt{2})$, $C(3\sqrt{2}, -\sqrt{2})$ and $D(\sqrt{2}, \sqrt{2})$ determine a quadrilateral.

   (a) Find the image points under the rotation
   $$(x,\ y) \rightarrow \left(\frac{x-y}{\sqrt{2}},\ \frac{x+y}{\sqrt{2}} \right).$$

   (b) Verify that both the original quadrilateral and the image quadrilateral are squares.

   (c) Draw the original and image squares in a single plane representation to common axes.

3. The points $A(2,0)$, $B(1,\sqrt{3})$, $C(-1,\sqrt{3})$, $D(-2,0)$, $E(-1,-\sqrt{3})$, $F(1,-\sqrt{3})$ define a polygon.

   (a) Find the image polygon under the rotation
   $$(x,\ y) \rightarrow \left(\frac{-x-\sqrt{3}y}{2},\ \frac{\sqrt{3}x-y}{2} \right).$$

   (b) Find four other rotations that map $ABCDEF$ onto itself.

   (c) Show that the polygon is a regular hexagon and indicate the symmetries of the rotations on a diagram.

In the following questions, find the equations of the images under the given rotation. Sketch the original and image figures on a single plane with the same set of axes. Identify the curve in each case.

4. $y = x$; $(x,\ y) \rightarrow \left(\dfrac{x-y}{\sqrt{2}},\ \dfrac{x+y}{\sqrt{2}} \right) = (u,\ v)$

5. $y = \sqrt{3}x$; $(x,\ y) \rightarrow \left(\dfrac{\sqrt{3}x-y}{2},\ \dfrac{x+\sqrt{3}y}{2} \right) = (u,\ v)$

6. $y = -x$; $(x,\ y) \rightarrow (-y,\ x) = (u,\ v)$

7. $y - x = 4$; $(x,\ y) \rightarrow \left(\dfrac{x-y}{\sqrt{2}},\ \dfrac{x+y}{\sqrt{2}} \right) = (u,\ v)$

8. $y + x + \sqrt{2} = 0$; $(x,\ y) \rightarrow \left(\dfrac{-x+y}{\sqrt{2}},\ \dfrac{-x-y}{\sqrt{2}} \right) = (u,\ v)$

9. $y = 4$; $(x,\ y) \rightarrow \left(\dfrac{3x-4y}{5},\ \dfrac{4x+3y}{5} \right) = (u,\ v)$

10. $\left.\begin{array}{l} 4x + 3y = 5 \\ 3x - 4y = -5 \end{array}\right\}$; $(x,\ y) \rightarrow \left(\dfrac{3x+4y}{5},\ \dfrac{3y-4x}{5} \right) = (u,\ v)$

11. $x^2 + y^2 = 4$; $(x, y) \rightarrow \left(\dfrac{x - 2y}{\sqrt{5}}, \dfrac{2x + y}{\sqrt{5}} \right) = (u, v)$

12. $5x^2 - 6xy + 5y^2 = 32$; $(x, y) \rightarrow \left(\dfrac{x - y}{\sqrt{2}}, \dfrac{x + y}{\sqrt{2}} \right) = (u, v)$.   Find the lengths

of the semi-axes and the co-ordinates of the foci of the image figure.

13. $3x^2 + 3y^2 - 6xy = -32$; $(x, y) \rightarrow \left(\dfrac{x + y}{\sqrt{2}}, \dfrac{-x + y}{\sqrt{2}} \right) = (u, v)$

14. $4y(y - \sqrt{3}x) + 3 = 0$; $(x, y) \rightarrow \left(\dfrac{\sqrt{3}x + y}{2}, \dfrac{-x + \sqrt{3}y}{2} \right) = (u, v)$.   Find the

eccentricity and the coordinates of the foci of the image figure.

15. $x^2 - 2xy + y^2 = x + y$; $(x, y) \rightarrow \left(\dfrac{x + y}{\sqrt{2}}, \dfrac{-x + y}{\sqrt{2}} \right) = (u, v)$.

16. $x^2 - y^2 = 4$; $(x, y) \rightarrow \left(\dfrac{x - y}{\sqrt{2}}, \dfrac{x + y}{\sqrt{2}} \right) = (u, v)$.

17. $xy = 4$; $(x, y) \rightarrow \left(\dfrac{x + y}{\sqrt{2}}, \dfrac{-x + y}{\sqrt{2}} \right) = (u, v)$.   Find the coordinates of the

vertices and the foci of the image figure.

18. $\dfrac{x^2}{16} + \dfrac{y^2}{9} = 1$; $(x, y) \rightarrow \left(\dfrac{4x - 3y}{5}, \dfrac{3x + 4y}{5} \right) = (u, v)$.

19. $x^2 = 2y$; $(x, y) \rightarrow \left(\dfrac{\sqrt{3}x - y}{2}, \dfrac{x + \sqrt{3}y}{2} \right) = (u, v)$.

20. $9x^2 - 24xy + 16y^2 = 20x + 15y$; $(x, y) \rightarrow \left(\dfrac{3x - 4y}{5}, \dfrac{4x + 3y}{5} \right) = (u, v)$.

In each of the following questions, find the image of the region under the given rotation. Sketch the original and image regions on a single plane with the same set of axes.

21. $x < 2$; $(x, y) \rightarrow \left(\dfrac{2x - 3y}{\sqrt{13}}, \dfrac{3x + 2y}{\sqrt{13}} \right) = (u, v)$.

22. $x > y, x \leq y + 1$; $(x, y) \rightarrow \left(\dfrac{-5x - 12y}{13}, \dfrac{12x - 5y}{13} \right) = (u, v)$.

23. $x > -1 - y, x < -1 + y, y < 1$;

$(x, y) \rightarrow \left(\dfrac{-x + \sqrt{7}y}{2\sqrt{2}}, \dfrac{-\sqrt{7}x - y}{2\sqrt{2}} \right) = (u, v)$.

8.3.   Simplification of Quadratic Relations by Rotations

In Example 3 of the previous section, the application of the rotation

$$(x, y) \rightarrow \left(\frac{x - 2y}{\sqrt{5}}, \frac{2x + y}{\sqrt{5}} \right)$$

reduced the equation

$$9x^2 + 4xy + 6y^2 = 20$$

to the simpler form

$$x^2 + 2y^2 = 4 ,$$

or

$$\frac{x^2}{4} + \frac{y^2}{2} = 1 .$$

The latter form of the equation is the equation of an ellipse in standard form; the transformed ellipse has its major axis along the x-axis, its minor axis is along the y-axis, and its centre at the origin $(0, 0)$.

Essentially the problem is that of transforming the general quadratic form

$$px^2 + qxy + ry^2$$

to the form of the sum or difference of two squares,

$$au^2 + bv^2 , \qquad a, b \in Re .$$

The solution is not quite as simple as in the case of translations and so we have to proceed more formally.

Example 1.   Determine a rotation which simplifies the equation

$$3x^2 + 2\sqrt{3}xy + 5y^2 = 36 ;$$

find the simplified equation and sketch the graphs of both equations to a common set of axes.

Solution: Apply the rotation

$$(x, y) \rightarrow (x \cos \theta - y \sin \theta, \ x \sin \theta + y \cos \theta) = (u, v) .$$

Then,

$$x \cos \theta - y \sin \theta = u ,$$
$$x \sin \theta + y \cos \theta = v ,$$

and, solving these two equations for x and y, we find

$$x = u \cos \theta + v \sin \theta$$

and

$$y = -u \sin \theta + v \cos \theta .$$

Substituting in the given equation, we obtain the transformed equation

$$3 (u \cos \theta + v \sin \theta)^2 + 2\sqrt{3} (u \cos \theta + v \sin \theta) (-u \sin \theta + v \cos \theta)$$
$$+ 5 (-u \sin \theta + v \cos \theta)^2 = 36,$$

or

$$u^2(3 \cos^2 \theta - 2\sqrt{3} \sin \theta \cos \theta + 5 \sin^2 \theta)$$
$$+ 2uv (3 \sin \theta \cos \theta - \sqrt{3} \sin^2 \theta + \sqrt{3} \cos^2 \theta - 5 \sin \theta \cos \theta)$$
$$+ v^2 (3 \sin^2 \theta + 2\sqrt{3} \sin \theta \cos \theta + 5 \cos^2 \theta)$$
$$= 36.$$

If the coefficient of uv is to be zero, which is the requirement for simplification, then

$$-2 \sin \theta \cos \theta - \sqrt{3} (\sin^2 \theta - \cos^2 \theta) = 0,$$
$$- \sin 2\theta + \sqrt{3} \cos 2\theta = 0,$$
$$\tan 2\theta = \sqrt{3}.$$

Any angle θ for which

$$\tan 2\theta = \sqrt{3}$$

will be a suitable rotation.   Let us choose the smallest positive such angle.

Therefore,

$$2\theta = 60°,$$
$$\theta = 30°.$$

Hence,

$$\sin \theta = \tfrac{1}{2} \quad \text{and} \quad \cos \theta = \tfrac{\sqrt{3}}{2}.$$

The simplified transformed equation is, therefore,

$$u^2 (3 \cdot \tfrac{3}{4} - 2\sqrt{3} \cdot \tfrac{\sqrt{3}}{2} \cdot \tfrac{1}{2} + \tfrac{5}{4}) + v^2 (3 \cdot \tfrac{1}{4} + 2\sqrt{3} \cdot \tfrac{\sqrt{3}}{2} \cdot \tfrac{1}{2} + \tfrac{15}{4}) = 36$$
$$u^2 (\tfrac{9}{4} - \tfrac{6}{4} + \tfrac{5}{4}) + v^2 (\tfrac{3}{4} + \tfrac{6}{4} + \tfrac{15}{4}) = 36$$
$$8u^2 + 24v^2 = 144$$
$$\frac{u^2}{18} + \frac{v^2}{6} = 1.$$

Hence, the simplified equation in the xy-plane for a single-plane representation is

$$\frac{x^2}{18} + \frac{y^2}{6} = 1.$$

This curve, which is the original curve with all points rotated 30° counterclockwise, is an ellipse with centre at (0, 0), a semi-major axis of length $3\sqrt{2}$ units along the x-axis and a semi-minor axis of length $\sqrt{6}$ units along the y-axis.

As a rotation of +30° transformed the original ellipse into the image ellipse, the original ellipse may be obtained from the image ellipse by a rotation of −30°, that is, by a clockwise rotation of the axes of the image ellipse through 30°.

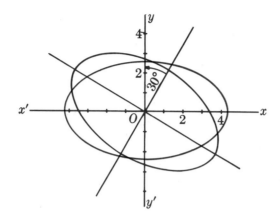

Example 2. Simplify the equation $x^2 + 4xy + 4y^2 + 12x - 6y = 6\sqrt{5}$ to a standard form by suitable transformations. For both the original and image conics, find the co-ordinates of the focus or foci and of the vertex or vertices and find an equation of a directrix.

Solution: We can always bring a conic into a standard position, with focus or foci on or parallel to the x- or y-axis, by a rotation through an angle less than 90°, say θ. If we apply a rotation $(x, y) \to (x \cos \theta - y \sin \theta, x \sin \theta + y \cos \theta) = (u, v)$, then

$$x = u \cos \theta + v \sin \theta,$$
$$y = -u \sin \theta + v \cos \theta,$$

and the equation of the curve becomes

$$(u \cos \theta + v \sin \theta)^2 + 4 (u \cos \theta + v \sin \theta)(-u \sin \theta + v \cos \theta)$$
$$+ 4(-u \sin \theta + v \cos \theta)^2 + 12 (u \cos \theta + v \sin \theta) - 6(-u \sin \theta + v \cos \theta)$$
$$= 6\sqrt{5},$$

$$u^2(\cos^2 \theta - 4 \sin \theta \cos \theta + 4 \sin^2 \theta)$$
$$+ uv (2 \sin \theta \cos \theta + 4 \cos^2 \theta - 4 \sin^2 \theta - 8 \sin \theta \cos \theta)$$
$$+ v^2 (\sin^2 \theta + 4 \sin \theta \cos \theta + 4 \cos^2 \theta)$$
$$+ u(12 \cos \theta + 6 \sin \theta) + v(12 \sin \theta - 6 \cos \theta)$$
$$= 6\sqrt{5}.$$

The coefficient of $uv = 0$, if

$$-6 \sin \theta \cos \theta + 4 (\cos^2\theta - \sin^2\theta) = 0 ;$$

that is, if

$$\tan 2\theta = +\tfrac{4}{3}.$$

Hence, 2θ is a first-quadrant angle and

$$\cos 2\theta = +\frac{3}{\sqrt{3^2 + 4^2}} = +\tfrac{3}{5}.$$

Therefore,

$$2 \cos^2\theta - 1 = +\tfrac{3}{5} \quad \text{and} \quad 1 - 2 \sin^2\theta = +\tfrac{3}{5}.$$

Thus,

$$\cos^2\theta = \tfrac{4}{5} \quad \text{and} \quad \sin^2\theta = \tfrac{1}{5},$$

$$\cos\theta = \tfrac{2}{\sqrt{5}} \quad \text{and} \quad \sin\theta = \tfrac{1}{\sqrt{5}},$$

and the rotation required is

$$(x,\, y) \rightarrow (\tfrac{2}{\sqrt{5}} x - \tfrac{1}{\sqrt{5}} y,\ \tfrac{1}{\sqrt{5}} x + \tfrac{2}{\sqrt{5}} y).$$

Therefore, the equation becomes

$$u^2(\tfrac{4}{5} - 4 \cdot \tfrac{1}{\sqrt{5}} \cdot \tfrac{2}{\sqrt{5}} + 4 \cdot \tfrac{1}{5}) + v^2(\tfrac{1}{5} + 4 \cdot \tfrac{1}{\sqrt{5}} \cdot \tfrac{2}{\sqrt{5}} + 4 \cdot \tfrac{4}{5}) + u(12 \cdot \tfrac{2}{\sqrt{5}} + 6 \cdot \tfrac{1}{\sqrt{5}})$$
$$+ v(12 \cdot \tfrac{1}{\sqrt{5}} - 6 \cdot \tfrac{2}{\sqrt{5}}) = 6\sqrt{5},$$

that is

$$\tfrac{25}{5} v^2 + \tfrac{30}{\sqrt{5}} u = 6\sqrt{5}$$
$$v^2 = -\tfrac{6}{\sqrt{5}} u + \tfrac{6\sqrt{5}}{5}$$
$$v^2 = -\tfrac{6}{\sqrt{5}}(u - 1).$$

Thus, if we now apply the translation

$$(u,\, v) \rightarrow (u - 1,\, v) = (s,\, t),$$

we obtain one of the standard forms of the parabola

$$t^2 = -\tfrac{6}{\sqrt{5}} s.$$

We can illustrate the three curves on a single-plane representation if we note that

$$x^2 + 4xy + 4y^2 + 12x - 6y = 6\sqrt{5}$$

is reduced by the rotation

$$(x,\, y) \rightarrow (\tfrac{2}{\sqrt{5}} x - \tfrac{1}{\sqrt{5}} y,\ \tfrac{1}{\sqrt{5}} x + \tfrac{2}{\sqrt{5}} y)$$

to

$$y^2 = -\tfrac{6}{\sqrt{5}}(x - 1)$$

which is in turn reduced by the translation

$$(x,\, y) \rightarrow (x - 1,\, y)$$

to

$$y^2 = -\tfrac{6}{\sqrt{5}} x.$$

In the st-plane, the focus is $(-\frac{3}{2\sqrt{5}}, 0)$, the vertex $(0, 0)$, and the directrix the line whose equation is $s = \frac{3}{2\sqrt{5}}$.
Observe that

$$u = s + 1, \quad v = t.$$

In the uv-plane, the focus is $(1 - \frac{3}{2\sqrt{5}}, 0)$, the vertex $(1, 0)$, and the directrix the line whose equation is $u = \frac{3}{2\sqrt{5}} + 1$.
Note that

$$x = \frac{2u + v}{\sqrt{5}}, \quad y = \frac{-u + 2v}{\sqrt{5}}.$$

In the xy-plane, the focus is

$$\left(\frac{2 - \frac{3}{\sqrt{5}}}{\sqrt{5}}, \frac{-1 + \frac{3}{2\sqrt{5}}}{\sqrt{5}} \right) = \left(\frac{2\sqrt{5} - 3}{5}, \frac{-2\sqrt{5} + 3}{10} \right).$$

The vertex in the xy-plane is $(\frac{2}{\sqrt{5}}, \frac{1}{\sqrt{5}})$.   In the xy-plane, the directrix is the line whose equation is

$$\frac{2}{\sqrt{5}}x - \frac{1}{\sqrt{5}}y = \frac{3}{2\sqrt{5}} + 1, \quad \text{or} \quad 4x + 2y = 3 + 2\sqrt{5}.$$

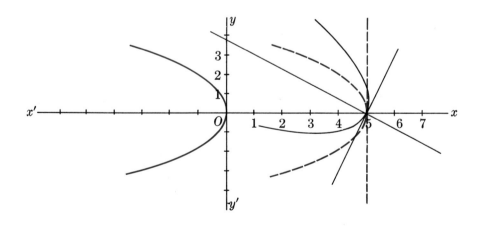

EXERCISE 8.3

In questions (1) to (10), find a suitable rotation which eliminates the xy-term in the given equation.   Sketch the original and image curve to the same set of axes in each case.

1. $x^2 - 2xy + y^2 = 12x + 12y$ 2. $x^2 + 2\sqrt{3}xy - y^2 = 4$

3. $3x^2 + 4\sqrt{3}xy - y^2 = 9$ 4. $17x^2 + 16xy + 17y^2 = 225$

5. $x^2 - 4xy + y^2 = 16$ 6. $xy = 9$

7. $3x^2 + 10xy + 3y^2 = 25$ 8. $25x^2 - 14xy + 25y^2 = 288$

9. $x^2 - 2xy + y^2 - 2x - 2y + 1 = 0$ 10. $x^2 + 2\sqrt{3}xy + 3y^2 + 4\sqrt{3}x + 4y = 0$

Reduce each of the following equations to a suitable standard form for a conic.

11. $x^2 + 4xy + y^2 + 6x - 12y = 0$

12. $5x^2 + 6xy + 5y^2 + 6x - 12y + 21 = 0$ 13. $x^2 - 2xy + y^2 + 5x = 0$

14. $x^2 + 6x - 3y + 6 = 0$ 15. $3x^2 - 2\sqrt{3}xy + y^2 + 4x - 4\sqrt{3}y = 0$

16. In questions (11) to (15), find the lengths of the semi-axes (if applicable) and the co-ordinates of the vertex or vertices of the conic in standard position. Find the co-ordinates of the vertex or vertices of the original conic.

17. (a) Show that if the rotation
$$(x, y) \rightarrow (x \cos \theta - y \sin \theta, \ x \sin \theta + y \cos \theta) = (u, v)$$
is applied to
$$ax^2 + 2hxy + by^2 + 2gx + 2fy + c = 0$$
the coefficient of the uv term is
$$(a - b) \sin 2\theta + 2h \cos 2\theta.$$
(b) Find the condition on 2θ which will make the coefficient of uv in (a) equal to zero.

18. Use the method suggested by 17(b) in question (15) to find $\sin \theta$ and $\cos \theta$.

19. If $a = b$ in 17(b), find the value of 2θ and hence of θ.   Use this conclusion to do question (1).

Chapter Summary

The mapping $(x, y) \rightarrow (x \cos \theta - y \sin \theta, \ x \sin \theta + y \cos \theta)$ · Rotations · Invariance of lengths of line segments and of angle under rotational mappings · Simplification of equations for quadratic relations by rotational mappings

REVIEW EXERCISE 8

1. Find the images of the points $M(2, -1)$, $N(3, 4)$, $P(0, 5)$, $Q(-1, -1)$, under the rotations.

   (a) $(x, y) \rightarrow \left(\dfrac{\sqrt{3}x - y}{2}, \dfrac{x + \sqrt{3}y}{2} \right)$

   (b) $(x, y) \rightarrow (-x, -y)$

   (c) $(x, y) \rightarrow \left(\dfrac{2x - y}{\sqrt{5}}, \dfrac{x + 2y}{\sqrt{5}} \right)$

   In each case, state the angle of rotation and show each point and its image in a single-plane representation.

2. Suppose that the origin, $A(5, 0)$, and $B(4, 3)$ are vertices of a triangle OAB. Find the co-ordinates of the vertices of a triangle $OA'B'$ which is the image of OAB under a rotation through an angle of 60°.

3. Find an equation for the line which is the image of $y = x$ after the plane has been rotated through 45°. Show both original and image lines in a single-plane representation.

Find the equations of the images under the following rotations. In each case, identify the curve and sketch both original and image figures in a single-plane representation.

4. $x + y + 5 = 0$; $(x, y) \rightarrow \left(\dfrac{x - y}{\sqrt{2}}, \dfrac{x + y}{\sqrt{2}} \right)$.

5. $y = \dfrac{3}{2}$; $(x, y) \rightarrow \left(\dfrac{4x - 3y}{5}, \dfrac{3x + 4y}{5} \right)$

6. $x^2 + y^2 = 9$; $(x, y) \rightarrow \left(\dfrac{x - 3y}{\sqrt{10}}, \dfrac{3x + y}{\sqrt{10}} \right)$

7. $xy = 8$; $(x, y) \rightarrow \left(\dfrac{x - y}{\sqrt{2}}, \dfrac{x + y}{\sqrt{2}} \right)$

8. $\dfrac{x^2}{4} - \dfrac{y^2}{25} = 1$; $(x, y) \rightarrow (-y, x)$

A point (x_1, y_1) is inside the ellipse with equation

$$\frac{x^2}{a^2} + \frac{y^2}{b^2} = 1$$

if and only if

$$\frac{x_1{}^2}{a^2} + \frac{y_1{}^2}{b^2} < 1.$$

If a plane is rotated, points inside an ellipse remain inside and points outside remain outside. Transform the following ellipses into standard form and determine whether the given points are inside the ellipse.

9. $3x^2 - 2xy + 3y^2 = 8$, $(0, \sqrt{2})$, $(-\frac{3\sqrt{2}}{2}, \frac{\sqrt{2}}{2})$

10. $66x^2 + 24xy + 59y^2 = 500$, $(\frac{-9}{5}, \frac{-13}{5})$ $(\frac{-11}{5}, \frac{-2}{5})$

In the following questions, find a suitable rotation that eliminates the xy term in the given equation. In each case, sketch the original and image curves in a single-plane representation.

11. $5x^2 + 4xy + 5y^2 - 9 = 0$ 12. $xy = -32$

13. $4x^2 + 12xy + 9y^2 = 52$ 14. $4x^2 - 20xy + 25y^2 - 15x - 6y = 0$

15. Using the method we developed in question (18), of Exercise 8.3, repeat question (13).

16. (a) Simplify the equation
$$6x^2 + 24xy - y^2 - 12x + 26y + 11 = 0$$
by first applying a suitable rotation to remove the xy-term and then applying a suitable translation to remove the first-degree terms in x and y.

    (b) Simplify the equation in part (a) by first applying a translation to eliminate the first-degree terms in x and y. (*Hint:* Let the translation be $u = x + h$, $v = y + k$. Express the conditions for the vanishing of the first-degree terms in u and v as equations in h and k.) Then apply a rotation to eliminate the xy-term.

    (c) Identify the graph of the relation. Show the original and all image graphs in (a) and (b) in a single-plane representation.

17. For the image of the mapping in question (16), find the lengths of the semi-axes and the foci of the conic involved in the transformation.

18. Remove the xy-term from the equation
$$6x^2 + 3xy + 2y^2 - 39 = 0$$
by a suitable rotation. Identify the conic and find its eccentricity and the co-ordinates of the foci in the image position. Find the co-ordinates of the foci in the original position.

Chapter 9

MATRICES AND LINEAR TRANSFORMATIONS

9.1. Definition of a Matrix

A *real matrix* is a rectangular array of real numbers aligned in rows (horizontally) and columns (vertically) and designated 2 x 2 (two rows, two columns), 2 x 3 (two rows, three columns), 3 x 3, etc., so as to indicate its dimensions. In this chapter and the next, we shall be concerned with matrices as mathematical objects; we shall introduce operations of addition and multiplication for matrices and shall consider the properties of these operations.

A 2×2 real matrix is a square array of real numbers, such as

$$\begin{bmatrix} 1 & 0 \\ 5 & -1 \end{bmatrix}, \quad \begin{bmatrix} 3 & \frac{1}{2} \\ 2 & -4 \end{bmatrix}, \quad \begin{bmatrix} \pi & 0 \\ 0 & 0 \end{bmatrix}, \quad \begin{bmatrix} 0 & 0 \\ 0 & 0 \end{bmatrix}.$$

In this text, we enclose the array in square brackets; other authors may use different symbols, such as parentheses or double bars.

A 2×2 real matrix consists of two rows and two columns of real numbers. In general, a 2×2 real matrix has the form

$$\begin{bmatrix} a_{11} & a_{12} \\ a_{21} & a_{22} \end{bmatrix} \}\text{rows}$$
$$\underbrace{\qquad}_{\text{columns}}$$

in which a_{ij} represents the real number in row i and column j; a_{12} is the entry or component in row 1 and column 2, etc. The two rows are

$$[a_{11} \quad a_{12}] \quad \text{and} \quad [a_{21} \quad a_{22}].$$

The two columns are

$$\begin{bmatrix} a_{11} \\ a_{21} \end{bmatrix} \quad \text{and} \quad \begin{bmatrix} a_{12} \\ a_{22} \end{bmatrix}.$$

Example 1.   Identify a_{11}, a_{12}, a_{21}, and a_{22} in the matrix

$$\begin{bmatrix} 3 & -1 \\ 0 & 5 \end{bmatrix}.$$

Solution:

$$a_{11} = 3; \quad a_{12} = -1; \quad a_{21} = 0; \quad a_{22} = 5.$$

A capital letter, A, B, C, etc., is often used to indicate a certain matrix; also, the matrix in which the element in row i and column j is a_{ij} is represented by the symbol $[a_{ij}]$.

An $m \times n$ real matrix is a rectangular array consisting of m rows and n columns of real numbers. (Such a matrix is said to have dimensions $m \times n$.)

$$\begin{bmatrix} 3 & 0 & -1 \\ 5 & 2 & 0 \end{bmatrix} \quad \text{is a } 2 \times 3 \text{ real matrix.}$$

$$\begin{bmatrix} 5 & -1 \\ 4 & \frac{1}{2} \\ -7 & 0 \end{bmatrix} \quad \text{is a } 3 \times 2 \text{ real matrix.}$$

$$\begin{bmatrix} 5 & 2 & -1 \\ 3 & 1 & 5 \\ 6 & 2 & 4 \end{bmatrix} \quad \text{is a } 3 \times 3 \text{ real matrix.}$$

$$[1 \quad 5] \quad \text{is a } 1 \times 2 \text{ real matrix.}$$

$$\begin{bmatrix} 1 \\ 5 \end{bmatrix} \quad \text{is a } 2 \times 1 \text{ real matrix.}$$

Note that vectors such as $(3, 5)$ and $(-1, 2, 4)$ may be considered as 1×2 and 1×3 real matrices, $[3 \quad 5]$ and $[-1 \quad 2 \quad 4]$. We refer to these vectors as row vectors; 2×1 and 3×1 real matrices such as

$$\begin{bmatrix} 3 \\ 5 \end{bmatrix} \quad \text{and} \quad \begin{bmatrix} -1 \\ 2 \\ 4 \end{bmatrix}$$

are called column vectors.

The components a_{ij} of a matrix are not necessarily real numbers. However, we shall restrict our attention in this course to real matrices, that is, matrices in which the components are real numbers.

We now consider what is meant by the equality of two matrices.

DEFINITION. Two matrices are equal if and only if

(i) they have the same dimensions (same number of rows and same number of columns)

and

(ii) corresponding components are equal.

$$\begin{bmatrix} a_{11} & a_{12} \\ a_{21} & a_{22} \end{bmatrix} = \begin{bmatrix} b_{11} & b_{12} \\ b_{21} & b_{22} \end{bmatrix}$$

iff $\begin{cases} a_{11} = b_{11}, & a_{12} = b_{12}, \\ a_{21} = b_{21}, & a_{22} = b_{22}. \end{cases}$

Example 4. Can $A = B$ or $B = C$ or $C = A$ if

$$A = \begin{bmatrix} 3 & -1 \\ 5 & 2 \end{bmatrix}, \quad B = \begin{bmatrix} x & -1 \\ 5 & y \end{bmatrix}, \quad C = \begin{bmatrix} 3 & -1 & 0 \\ 5 & 2 & 0 \end{bmatrix}?$$

Solution:

(i) $A = B$ iff $x = 3$ and $y = 2$.

(ii) $B \neq C$ since B and C do not have the same dimensions.

(iii) $C \neq A$ since C and A do not have the same dimensions.

EXERCISE 9.1

1. List a_{11}, a_{13}, and a_{22} (if they exist) for the following matrices.

(a) $\begin{bmatrix} 3 & -1 \\ 5 & 2 \end{bmatrix}$

(b) $\begin{bmatrix} 6 & -2 & 0 \\ 1 & 5 & -3 \end{bmatrix}$

(c) $\begin{bmatrix} 4 & 2 \\ -1 & 6 \\ 0 & 0 \end{bmatrix}$

(d) $[1 \quad 5 \quad 3 \quad 0]$

(e) $\begin{bmatrix} 5 \\ -1 \\ 3 \\ 6 \end{bmatrix}$

(f) $\begin{bmatrix} 4 & 0 & -1 \\ -3 & 5 & 0 \\ 0 & -2 & 4 \end{bmatrix}$

2. State the dimensions of the matrices in question (1). Are there any row or column vectors in question (1)?

3. Are any of the matrices in question (1) equal? Explain.

4. Under what conditions can $A = B$ if

$$A = \begin{bmatrix} 2 & a \\ -1 & 3 \end{bmatrix} \quad \text{and} \quad B = \begin{bmatrix} 2 & 5 \\ b & 3 \end{bmatrix}?$$

5. Under what conditions can $A = B$ if

$$A = \begin{bmatrix} 5 & -3 \\ b & 4 \end{bmatrix} \quad \text{and} \quad B = \begin{bmatrix} 5 & 3 \\ 5 & -a \end{bmatrix}?$$

6. If $A = [a_{ij}] = \begin{bmatrix} 5 & 3 \\ -1 & 2 \end{bmatrix}$ and $B = [b_{ij}] = \begin{bmatrix} 4 & 1 \\ -3 & -2 \end{bmatrix}$, find

(a) $a_{11}b_{11} + a_{12}b_{21}$,   (b) $a_{11}b_{12} + a_{12}b_{22}$,

(c) $a_{21}b_{11} + a_{22}b_{21}$,   (d) $a_{21}b_{12} + a_{22}b_{22}$.

7. Repeat question (6) for the matrices

$$A = [a_{ij}] = \begin{bmatrix} 5 & 0 \\ -1 & 4 \end{bmatrix} \quad \text{and} \quad B = [b_{ij}] = \begin{bmatrix} -3 & 2 \\ 2 & 3 \end{bmatrix}.$$

9.2. Addition of Matrices • Multiplication by a Real Number

What is meant by the addition of equidimensional matrices (matrices of the same shape)? The addition of two such matrices is performed by adding their corresponding components.

DEFINITION. If

$$A = \begin{bmatrix} a_{11} & a_{12} \\ a_{21} & a_{22} \end{bmatrix} \quad \text{and} \quad B = \begin{bmatrix} b_{11} & b_{12} \\ b_{21} & b_{22} \end{bmatrix},$$

then

$$A + B = \begin{bmatrix} a_{11} + b_{11} & a_{12} + b_{12} \\ a_{21} + b_{21} & a_{22} + b_{22} \end{bmatrix}.$$

This definition may be extended to the sum of two $m \times n$ matrices.

Example 1. Find $A + B$ if

$$A = \begin{bmatrix} 3 & -1 \\ 5 & 7 \end{bmatrix} \quad \text{and} \quad B = \begin{bmatrix} -4 & 1 \\ -3 & 5 \end{bmatrix}.$$

Solution:

$$A + B = \begin{bmatrix} 3 + (-4) & (-1) + 1 \\ 5 + (-3) & 7 + 5 \end{bmatrix}$$

$$= \begin{bmatrix} -1 & 0 \\ 2 & 12 \end{bmatrix}.$$

Note that under the above definition, the set of all 2×2 real matrices is closed under addition.

The product of a matrix and a real number is defined in terms of the multiplication of each component by a real number.

DEFINITION.   If k is a real number and

$$A = \begin{bmatrix} a_{11} & a_{12} \\ a_{21} & a_{22} \end{bmatrix},$$

then

$$kA = \begin{bmatrix} ka_{11} & ka_{12} \\ ka_{21} & ka_{22} \end{bmatrix}.$$

Again, this definition may be extended to the product of a real number and an $m \times n$ matrix.

Example 2.   Find $7A$ and $(-2)A$ if

$$A = \begin{bmatrix} -2 & 1 \\ 5 & 0 \end{bmatrix}.$$

Solution:

$$7A = \begin{bmatrix} 7 \times (-2) & 7 \times 1 \\ 7 \times 5 & 7 \times 0 \end{bmatrix}$$

$$= \begin{bmatrix} -14 & 7 \\ 35 & 0 \end{bmatrix}.$$

$$(-2)A = \begin{bmatrix} (-2) \times (-2) & (-2) \times 1 \\ (-2) \times 5 & (-2) \times 0 \end{bmatrix}$$

$$= \begin{bmatrix} 4 & -2 \\ -10 & 0 \end{bmatrix}.$$

EXERCISE 9.2

1. If

$$A = \begin{bmatrix} 4 & -1 \\ 5 & 2 \end{bmatrix}, \quad B = \begin{bmatrix} 0 & 3 \\ -7 & 1 \end{bmatrix}, \quad \text{and} \quad C = \begin{bmatrix} 4 & 4 \\ -2 & 1 \end{bmatrix},$$

find the following.

(a) $A + B$ (b) $B + C$ (c) $C + A$ (d) $B + A$
(e) $C + B$ (f) $A + C$ (g) $A + (B + C)$ (h) $(A + B) + C$

2. Repeat question (1) for

$$A = \begin{bmatrix} 5 & -1 \\ -1 & 3 \end{bmatrix}, \quad B = \begin{bmatrix} 2 & -7 \\ 5 & 0 \end{bmatrix}, \quad \text{and} \quad C = \begin{bmatrix} -5 & 4 \\ 1 & 6 \end{bmatrix}.$$

3. Find (a) $6A$ (b) $(-3)B$ (c) $\frac{1}{2}C$ for the matrices in question (2).

4. For the matrices in question (2), find
   (a) $3A + 2B$, (b) $(-2)A + 5C$, (c) $(-4)A + 2B + (-3)C$.

5. If

$$A = \begin{bmatrix} 3 & -2 \\ 1 & 5 \end{bmatrix}, \quad B = \begin{bmatrix} 4 & -1 \\ 3 & 0 \end{bmatrix}, \quad C = \begin{bmatrix} 2 & -2 \\ 5 & 1 \end{bmatrix}, \quad D = \begin{bmatrix} 0 & 5 \\ -3 & 1 \end{bmatrix},$$

   find the following.
   (a) $A + D$ (b) $A + (B + C)$ (c) $(A + B) + C$ (d) $3A + 2B$
   (e) $[A + 3B] + 2C$ (f) $3A + [(-2)B + D]$
   (g) $[5B + (-1)C] + 3D$ (h) $[A + 2B] + [3C + 4D]$

6. If

$$A = \begin{bmatrix} -1 & 2 \\ 7 & 5 \end{bmatrix}, \quad B = \begin{bmatrix} a & -b \\ -c & d \end{bmatrix}, \quad \text{and} \quad C = \begin{bmatrix} 2 & -2 \\ 1 & 1 \end{bmatrix},$$

   find a, b, c, and d so that
   (a) $A + B = C$, (b) $2A + (-3)B = C$, (c) $5C + (-a)A = 3B$.

7. Explain the statement "The set of all 2×2 real matrices is closed under multiplication by real numbers."

8. Assuming that the definition given for addition of 2×2 real matrices holds for any two equidimensional matrices, find $A + B$, where possible, for the following matrices.

   (a) $A = \begin{bmatrix} 3 & -1 & 5 \\ 2 & 0 & 4 \end{bmatrix}, \quad B = \begin{bmatrix} -3 & -1 & 2 \\ 6 & 4 & -3 \end{bmatrix}$

   (b) $A = \begin{bmatrix} 5 & -1 \\ -4 & 6 \\ 3 & 2 \end{bmatrix}, \quad B = \begin{bmatrix} 3 & 1 \\ 0 & -6 \\ -4 & 5 \end{bmatrix}$

   (c) $A = \begin{bmatrix} 5 & -2 \\ -1 & 3 \\ 6 & 0 \\ 7 & 1 \end{bmatrix}, \quad B = \begin{bmatrix} 0 & 0 \\ 0 & 0 \\ 0 & 0 \\ 0 & 0 \end{bmatrix}$

   (d) $A = \begin{bmatrix} 3 & 4 & -2 \\ -1 & 0 & 5 \\ 2 & 7 & -1 \end{bmatrix}, \quad B = \begin{bmatrix} 6 & -2 & 3 \\ -4 & 5 & -5 \\ 3 & -7 & 1 \end{bmatrix}$

   (e) $A = \begin{bmatrix} -1 & 2 & 3 \\ 3 & 0 & 6 \\ 5 & -4 & -1 \end{bmatrix}, \quad B = \begin{bmatrix} 2 & 3 & 0 \\ 4 & -4 & 0 \\ -1 & 6 & 0 \end{bmatrix}$

   (f) $A = \begin{bmatrix} -1 & 2 & 3 \\ 3 & 0 & 6 \\ 5 & -4 & -1 \end{bmatrix}, \quad B = \begin{bmatrix} 2 & 3 \\ 4 & -4 \\ -1 & 6 \end{bmatrix}$

9. Is the set of all (a) 3×3 matrices (b) 2×3 matrices (c) 3×5 matrices closed under addition?

9.3.   Properties of Addition of Matrices

The problems of Exercise 9.2 may have indicated some of the properties of addition of 2×2 real matrices. We will illustrate these properties by examples but leave their general proof to the reader.

Example 1.   Find $A + B$ and $B + A$ if

$$A = \begin{bmatrix} 6 & -1 \\ 2 & 4 \end{bmatrix} \quad \text{and} \quad B = \begin{bmatrix} -3 & 5 \\ 0 & 4 \end{bmatrix}.$$

Solution:

$$
\begin{aligned}
A + B &= \begin{bmatrix} 6 & -1 \\ 2 & 4 \end{bmatrix} + \begin{bmatrix} -3 & 5 \\ 0 & 4 \end{bmatrix} \\
&= \begin{bmatrix} 6 + (-3) & (-1) + 5 \\ 2 + 0 & 4 + 4 \end{bmatrix} \\
&= \begin{bmatrix} 3 & 4 \\ 2 & 8 \end{bmatrix}.
\end{aligned}
$$

$$
\begin{aligned}
B + A &= \begin{bmatrix} -3 & 5 \\ 0 & 4 \end{bmatrix} + \begin{bmatrix} 6 & -1 \\ 2 & 4 \end{bmatrix} \\
&= \begin{bmatrix} (-3) + 6 & 5 + (-1) \\ 0 + 2 & 4 + 4 \end{bmatrix} \\
&= \begin{bmatrix} 3 & 4 \\ 2 & 8 \end{bmatrix}.
\end{aligned}
$$

Notice that

$$A + B = B + A$$

for the matrices of this example.   This result is true in general.   Addition of 2×2 real matrices is commutative.

Example 2.   Find $(A + B) + C$ and $A + (B + C)$ if A and B are as in Example 1 and

$$C = \begin{bmatrix} 3 & -4 \\ -2 & 5 \end{bmatrix}.$$

Solution: Using the result from Example 1, we find that

$$
\begin{aligned}
(A + B) + C &= \begin{bmatrix} 3 & 4 \\ 2 & 8 \end{bmatrix} + \begin{bmatrix} 3 & -4 \\ -2 & 5 \end{bmatrix} \\
&= \begin{bmatrix} 6 & 0 \\ 0 & 13 \end{bmatrix}.
\end{aligned}
$$

Also,

$$
\begin{aligned}
A + (B + C) &= A + \left\{ \begin{bmatrix} -3 & 5 \\ 0 & 4 \end{bmatrix} + \begin{bmatrix} 3 & -4 \\ -2 & 5 \end{bmatrix} \right\} \\
&= \begin{bmatrix} 6 & -1 \\ 2 & 4 \end{bmatrix} + \begin{bmatrix} 0 & 1 \\ -2 & 9 \end{bmatrix} \\
&= \begin{bmatrix} 6 & 0 \\ 0 & 13 \end{bmatrix}.
\end{aligned}
$$

Notice that

$$(A + B) + C = A + (B + C)$$

for the matrices of this example. This result is also true in general. Addition of 2×2 real matrices is associative.

It is easily seen that the matrix

$$O = \begin{bmatrix} 0 & 0 \\ 0 & 0 \end{bmatrix}$$

is an additive identity under addition of 2×2 real matrices, since

$$\begin{bmatrix} a_{11} & a_{12} \\ a_{21} & a_{22} \end{bmatrix} + \begin{bmatrix} 0 & 0 \\ 0 & 0 \end{bmatrix} = \begin{bmatrix} a_{11} & a_{12} \\ a_{21} & a_{22} \end{bmatrix}.$$

It is left as an exercise (see question (10), Exercise 9.3) for the reader to show that this identity is unique.

Example 3. Find $A + (-1)A$ if

$$A = \begin{bmatrix} 3 & 6 \\ -2 & -5 \end{bmatrix}.$$

Solution:

$$(-1)A = \begin{bmatrix} -3 & -6 \\ 2 & 5 \end{bmatrix}.$$

$$A + (-1)A = \begin{bmatrix} 3 & 6 \\ -2 & -5 \end{bmatrix} + \begin{bmatrix} -3 & -6 \\ 2 & 5 \end{bmatrix}$$

$$= \begin{bmatrix} 0 & 0 \\ 0 & 0 \end{bmatrix}$$

$$= O.$$

We see that for this matrix A, the matrix (-1) A is the additive inverse; this result is also true in general. We refer to the additive inverse or negative of A as $-A$. The additive inverse of a matrix is unique (see question (11), Exercise 9.3).

Subtraction of matrix B from matrix A is defined as the addition of $-B$ to A.

$$A - B = A + (-B).$$

Example 4. Find $3A - 4B$ if

$$A = \begin{bmatrix} 3 & -1 \\ 1 & 5 \end{bmatrix} \quad \text{and} \quad B = \begin{bmatrix} -2 & -7 \\ 1 & 3 \end{bmatrix}.$$

Solution:

$$3A = \begin{bmatrix} 9 & -3 \\ 3 & 15 \end{bmatrix} \quad \text{and} \quad (-4)B = \begin{bmatrix} 8 & 28 \\ -4 & -12 \end{bmatrix}.$$

$$3A - 4B = 3A + (-4)B$$
$$= \begin{bmatrix} 9 & -3 \\ 3 & 15 \end{bmatrix} + \begin{bmatrix} 8 & 28 \\ -4 & -12 \end{bmatrix}$$
$$= \begin{bmatrix} 17 & 25 \\ -1 & 3 \end{bmatrix}.$$

Example 5. Show that $3(A + B) = 3A + 3B$ if

$$A = \begin{bmatrix} 7 & -1 \\ 2 & 4 \end{bmatrix} \quad \text{and} \quad B = \begin{bmatrix} -5 & 1 \\ -3 & 2 \end{bmatrix}.$$

Solution:

$$3A = \begin{bmatrix} 21 & -3 \\ 6 & 12 \end{bmatrix} \quad \text{and} \quad 3B = \begin{bmatrix} -15 & 3 \\ -9 & 6 \end{bmatrix}.$$

$$3A + 3B = \begin{bmatrix} 6 & 0 \\ -3 & 18 \end{bmatrix}.$$

$$A + B = \begin{bmatrix} 2 & 0 \\ -1 & 6 \end{bmatrix}.$$

$$3(A + B) = \begin{bmatrix} 6 & 0 \\ -3 & 18 \end{bmatrix}.$$

Therefore, $3(A + B) = 3A + 3B$ for these matrices A and B.

The result obtained in Example 5 is also true in general.

$$k(A + B) = kA + kB, \quad k \in Re.$$

EXERCISE 9.3

1. Verify the commutativity of addition of 2×2 real matrices by calculating
   (a) $A + B$ (b) $B + A$ (c) $A + C$ (d) $C + A$ (e) $B + C$ (f) $C + B$
   if

$$A = \begin{bmatrix} 1 & 7 \\ -3 & 5 \end{bmatrix}, \quad B = \begin{bmatrix} -3 & -3 \\ 5 & -2 \end{bmatrix}, \quad \text{and} \quad C = \begin{bmatrix} 4 & -2 \\ 1 & 7 \end{bmatrix}.$$

2. Prove that addition of 2×2 real matrices is commutative.

3. Use the matrices of question (1) to show that
$$(A + B) + C = A + (B + C).$$

4. Prove that addition of 2×2 real matrices is associative.

5. State the negatives of the matrices of question (1).

6. Find
    (a) $3A - 2B + C$ (b) $A - 5B - 2C$ (c) $3A - 4B - C$
    for the matrices A, B, and C of question (1).

7. Check that
    (a) $4(A + B) = 4A + 4B$ (b) $(-2)(B + C) = (-2)B + (-2)C$
    (c) $\frac{1}{2}(A + B) = \frac{1}{2}A + \frac{1}{2}B$ (d) $3(A + B + C) = 3A + 3B + 3C$
    for the matrices of question (1).

8. Prove that $k(A + B) = kA + kB$ if A and B are 2×2 real matrices and k is a real number.

9. Is the set of 2×2 real matrices closed under subtraction?

10. Show that the matrix

$$\begin{bmatrix} 0 & 0 \\ 0 & 0 \end{bmatrix}$$

is the unique additive identity in the set of 2×2 real matrices.

11. Show that $(-1)A$ is the unique additive inverse of A in the set of 2×2 real matrices.

9.4. Linear Transformations of the Plane

The system of equations

$$\left. \begin{matrix} u = 3x - 2y \\ v = 4x + y \end{matrix} \right\} \tag{1}$$

produces a mapping $(x, y) \to (u, v)$ of the set of ordered pairs (x, y) *into* or *onto* the set of ordered pairs (u, v) in the sense that, whenever a pair of values is assigned to x and y, a pair of values is produced for u and v. (The distinction between *into* and *onto* will be clear later on.)

Geometrically, the system of equations produces a mapping or transformation of the plane in the sense that, to every point P with co-ordinates (x, y), there corresponds a point Q with co-ordinates (u, v). We call Q the *image* of P under this mapping.

If we use a letter such as T to represent this transformation or mapping, we write

$$T\begin{bmatrix} x \\ y \end{bmatrix} = \begin{bmatrix} u \\ v \end{bmatrix}$$

to indicate that $\begin{bmatrix} x \\ y \end{bmatrix}$ is changed into or mapped onto $\begin{bmatrix} u \\ v \end{bmatrix}$, by the transformation T.

Thus, for the mapping T determined by equations (1),

$$T\begin{bmatrix} 2 \\ 1 \end{bmatrix} = \begin{bmatrix} 4 \\ 9 \end{bmatrix}$$

since
$$u = (3)(2) - (2)(1) = 4 ,$$
and
$$v = (4)(2) + (1)(1) = 9 .$$

We also write $(2, 1) \rightarrow (4, 9)$ to indicate that $(4, 9)$ is the image of $(2, 1)$. The latter notation may seem more useful in order to indicate that ordered pairs are mapped onto ordered pairs or points onto points, but the former notation will prove desirable in our further study of matrices.

It is apparent that every point P with co-ordinates (x, y) will have an image under this transformation T; we say that T is a transformation or mapping *of the* (entire) *plane.*

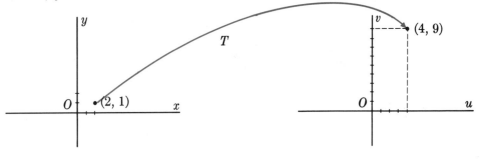

Example 1. Find the images of the points with the co-ordinates
  (a) $(0, 0)$ (b) $(1, 4)$ (c) $(-2, 3)$ (d) $(-1, -1)$
under the transformation T determined by equations (1), and show the images on a diagram.

Solution:

  (a) $T\begin{bmatrix} 0 \\ 0 \end{bmatrix} = \begin{bmatrix} 0 \\ 0 \end{bmatrix}$ (b) $T\begin{bmatrix} 1 \\ 4 \end{bmatrix} = \begin{bmatrix} -5 \\ 8 \end{bmatrix}$

  (c) $T\begin{bmatrix} -2 \\ 3 \end{bmatrix} = \begin{bmatrix} -12 \\ -5 \end{bmatrix}$ (d) $T\begin{bmatrix} -1 \\ -1 \end{bmatrix} = \begin{bmatrix} -1 \\ -5 \end{bmatrix}$

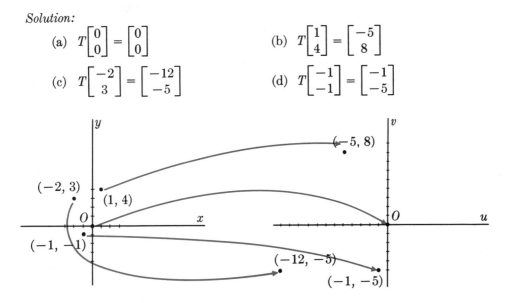

We see that the transformation T determined by equations (1) is a transformation of the entire plane; that is, it provides an image for each point in the xy-plane. Now we ask "Is every point of the uv-plane the image of some point in the xy-plane?" We consider a particular point in the following example.

Example 2. Is the point with co-ordinates $(5, -7)$ the image of some point in the xy-plane under the transformation T determined by equations (1)?

Solution: Rephrasing the question, we are asking if the system of equations

$$5 = 3x - 2y$$

$$-7 = 4x + y$$

has a real solution. Using our techniques for solving such a system, we find the solution set to be $\{(-\frac{9}{11}, -\frac{41}{11})\}$; that is, the point with co-ordinates $(-\frac{9}{11}, -\frac{41}{11})$ has as its image the point with co-ordinates $(5, -7)$ under the mapping T.

$$T \begin{bmatrix} -\dfrac{9}{11} \\ -\dfrac{41}{11} \end{bmatrix} = \begin{bmatrix} 5 \\ -7 \end{bmatrix}.$$

We now see that the question "Is every point of the uv-plane the image of some point under mapping T?" is equivalent to the question "Does the system of equations

$$a = 3x - 2y$$
$$b = 4x + y$$

have a real solution for every pair (a, b) of real numbers?" The answer is "Yes" and its justification is required in question (8). Exercise 9.4. At the same time, we shall see that the solution in each case is unique, so that each point in the uv-plane will be the image of exactly one point in the xy-plane. The mapping T provides a one-to-one correspondence between the points of the xy-plane and the points of the uv-plane. We also say that T is a one-to-one mapping of the xy-plane onto the uv-plane. Not all mappings have this character, as we shall see in the next section.

The basic ingredients of the transformation T are the coefficients of the variables in the system of equations, since

$u = 3x - 2y$	$\lambda = 3\alpha - 2\beta$	$m = 3r - 2s$	$X = 3V - 2W$
$v = 4x + y$	$\delta = 4\alpha + \beta$	$n = 4r + s$	$Y = 4V + W$

are all essentially the same transformation. Thus, the transformation is determined by the coefficients

$$\begin{matrix} 3 & -2 \\ 4 & 1 \end{matrix}.$$

In this way, we may associate a matrix with every such transformation; that is,

$$T \quad \begin{cases} u = 3x - 2y \\ v = 4x + y \end{cases}$$

corresponds to the matrix of coefficients

$$T = \begin{bmatrix} 3 & -2 \\ 4 & 1 \end{bmatrix}.$$

We use the same symbol T to refer to both the transformation and the matrix corresponding to the transformation but there should be no confusion.

Example 3.   Write the matrix associated with the transformation

$$R \quad \begin{cases} u = x + 3y \\ v = 2x + 4y \end{cases}.$$

Solution: The corresponding matrix is the matrix of coefficients

$$R = \begin{bmatrix} 1 & 3 \\ 2 & 4 \end{bmatrix}.$$

Example 4.   Write a linear transformation corresponding to the matrix

$$S = \begin{bmatrix} 3 & 4 \\ -1 & 2 \end{bmatrix}.$$

Solution: Such a linear transformation may be written as

$$u = 3x + 4y,$$
$$v = -x + 2y,$$

or as

$$m = 3r + 4s,$$
$$n = -r + 2s,$$

etc.

Finally, we point out that in this chapter we are restricting the examples mainly to transformations corresponding to 2×2 real matrices.

EXERCISE 9.4

1. For the transformation

$$T \quad \begin{cases} u = x + 3y \\ v = 2x - y \end{cases}$$

find the following.

(a) $T \begin{bmatrix} 0 \\ 0 \end{bmatrix}$ (b) $T \begin{bmatrix} 1 \\ 1 \end{bmatrix}$ (c) $T \begin{bmatrix} 2 \\ 3 \end{bmatrix}$ (d) $T \begin{bmatrix} -3 \\ 0 \end{bmatrix}$

(e) $T \begin{bmatrix} 5 \\ 0 \end{bmatrix}$ (f) $T \begin{bmatrix} 0 \\ -3 \end{bmatrix}$ (g) $T \begin{bmatrix} -1 \\ -5 \end{bmatrix}$ (h) $T \begin{bmatrix} 3 \\ -2 \end{bmatrix}$

Show these points and their images on a diagram.

2. For the transformation T in question (1), find the points whose images are the points with the following co-ordinates.

(a) (0, 0)   (b) (−1, 3)   (c) (5, 0)   (d) (−2, 4)

3. State the matrices corresponding to the following transformations.

(a) R $\begin{cases} u = 3x - y \\ v = 5x + 2y \end{cases}$ (b) S $\begin{cases} m = r + s \\ n = 2r - 3s \end{cases}$ (c) T $\begin{cases} \lambda = \alpha + 4\beta \\ \mu = 2\alpha + \beta \end{cases}$

(d) U $\begin{cases} u = x \\ v = y \end{cases}$ (e) V $\begin{cases} R = 3r \\ S = 5s \end{cases}$ (f) W $\begin{cases} \lambda = \alpha + \beta \\ \mu = 2\beta \end{cases}$

4. Write transformations corresponding to the following matrices.

(a) $\begin{bmatrix} 5 & -1 \\ 1 & 1 \end{bmatrix}$ (b) $\begin{bmatrix} 2 & -3 \\ 1 & 0 \end{bmatrix}$ (c) $\begin{bmatrix} 5 & 5 \\ -2 & 3 \end{bmatrix}$

(d) $\begin{bmatrix} 1 & -1 \\ 0 & 1 \end{bmatrix}$ (e) $\begin{bmatrix} 1 & 0 \\ 0 & 1 \end{bmatrix}$ (f) $\begin{bmatrix} 0 & 1 \\ 1 & 0 \end{bmatrix}$

5. For the transformations of question (3), find the following.

(a) $R \begin{bmatrix} -1 \\ 2 \end{bmatrix}$ (b) $S \begin{bmatrix} -1 \\ 0 \end{bmatrix}$ (c) $T \begin{bmatrix} 4 \\ 4 \end{bmatrix}$

(d) $U \begin{bmatrix} -2 \\ -3 \end{bmatrix}$ (e) $V \begin{bmatrix} -5 \\ 5 \end{bmatrix}$ (f) $W \begin{bmatrix} 0 \\ -3 \end{bmatrix}$

6. For the transformations of question (3), find (x, y), (r, s), etc., such that

(a) $R \begin{bmatrix} x \\ y \end{bmatrix} = \begin{bmatrix} 5 \\ 2 \end{bmatrix}$,   (b) $S \begin{bmatrix} r \\ s \end{bmatrix} = \begin{bmatrix} -2 \\ 4 \end{bmatrix}$,   (c) $T \begin{bmatrix} \alpha \\ \beta \end{bmatrix} = \begin{bmatrix} -1 \\ 0 \end{bmatrix}$,

(d) $U \begin{bmatrix} x \\ y \end{bmatrix} = \begin{bmatrix} 4 \\ -3 \end{bmatrix}$,   (e) $V \begin{bmatrix} r \\ s \end{bmatrix} = \begin{bmatrix} 1 \\ 1 \end{bmatrix}$,   (f) $W \begin{bmatrix} \alpha \\ \beta \end{bmatrix} = \begin{bmatrix} -2 \\ 3 \end{bmatrix}$.

7. If T is the transformation corresponding to the matrix

$$\begin{bmatrix} 3 & -2 \\ 1 & 2 \end{bmatrix}$$

find

(a) $T \begin{bmatrix} 4 \\ -5 \end{bmatrix}$,   (b) $\begin{bmatrix} x \\ y \end{bmatrix}$ such that $T \begin{bmatrix} x \\ y \end{bmatrix} = \begin{bmatrix} -3 \\ 2 \end{bmatrix}$.

8. If T is the transformation

$$T \quad \begin{cases} u = 3x - 2y \\ v = 4x + y \end{cases},$$

show that every point in the uv-plane is the image of a unique point in the xy-plane; that is, show that a unique ordered pair (x, y) exists such that $T \begin{bmatrix} x \\ y \end{bmatrix} = \begin{bmatrix} a \\ b \end{bmatrix}$ for every pair (a, b) of real numbers.

9. Repeat question (8) for the transformation T of question (7).

10. Explain what is meant by saying that the transformation

$$T \quad \begin{cases} u = 3x + 5y \\ v = 2x + y \end{cases}$$

is a one-to-one mapping of the xy-plane onto the uv-plane.   Show that it is.

9.5.   Linear Transformations of the Plane into the Plane

The linear transformations of the preceding section were all transformations of the xy-plane *onto* the uv-plane; that is, every point of the xy-plane had an image, and every point of the uv-plane was the image of some point under these transformations.   Further, the transformations were all one-to-one transformations of the plane onto the plane; that is, each point in the xy-plane had a unique image, and each point in the uv-plane was the image of exactly one point under these transformations.

Now consider the transformation

$$T \quad \begin{cases} u = 2x + y \\ v = 4x + 2y \end{cases}.$$

It is evident that every point in the xy-plane will have an image under this transformation so that T is a transformation *of* the xy-plane.   It is also evident that the images will be points with co-ordinates (u, v) such that $v = 2u$.   This means that all the image points will be on the line with equation $v = 2u$ in the uv-plane.

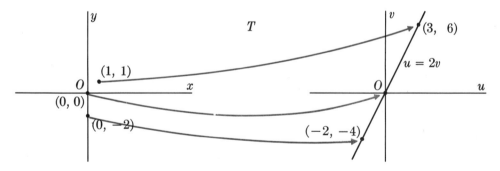

Under this transformation, it is obvious that not all points of the uv-plane will be image points.   Indeed, none of the points not on the line with equation $v = 2u$ will be image points.   This transformation does not provide a one-to-one correspondence between the points of the xy-plane and the points of the uv-plane. This is not a transformation of the plane onto the plane, but rather a transformation of the plane *into* the plane.

The matrix associated with this transformation is

$$T = \begin{bmatrix} 2 & 1 \\ 4 & 2 \end{bmatrix}.$$

Example 1. Show that

$$S \begin{cases} u = -2x + 3y \\ v = 6x - 9y \end{cases}$$

is a transformation of the plane *into* the plane.

Solution:

$$S \begin{bmatrix} x \\ y \end{bmatrix} = \begin{bmatrix} u \\ v \end{bmatrix} \quad \text{with } v = -3u .$$

Thus all image points lie on the line in the *uv*-plane with equation $v = -3u$; points not on this line will not be image points under this transformation. This transformation is a transformation of the plane into the plane. The matrix associated with this transformation is

$$S = \begin{bmatrix} -2 & 3 \\ 6 & -9 \end{bmatrix} .$$

Example 2.

(a) For the transformation S in Example 1, find $S \begin{bmatrix} 1 \\ -2 \end{bmatrix}$.

(b) Do any other points of the *xy*-plane have the image point found in (a)?

Solution:

(a)

$$S \begin{bmatrix} 1 \\ -2 \end{bmatrix} = \begin{bmatrix} -8 \\ 24 \end{bmatrix} .$$

(b) We readily check that

$$S \begin{bmatrix} 4 \\ 0 \end{bmatrix} = S \begin{bmatrix} 7 \\ 2 \end{bmatrix} = S \begin{bmatrix} 10 \\ 4 \end{bmatrix} = \begin{bmatrix} -8 \\ 24 \end{bmatrix} .$$

As a matter of fact, the question asked in part (b) of Example 2 is equivalent to asking "Is the solution of the system of equations

$$-2x + 3y = -8$$
$$6x - 9y = 24$$

unique; that is, is the system independent or dependent?" We know that the system does have a solution, namely $(1, -2)$, so that the system is consistent. We may replace the system by an equivalent reduced system of the form

$$-2x + 3y = -8 ,$$
$$0y = 0 .$$

Now we see that the system is dependent and has the solution set

$$\left\{ \left(\frac{3k + 8}{2}, k \right) \middle| k \in Re \right\} .$$

This solution set contains the particular solutions $(4, 0)$, $(7, 2)$, and $(10, 4)$ indicated in the previous page.

We also see that every point with co-ordinates $\left(\dfrac{3k + 8}{2}, k\right)$ is mapped onto the point $(-8, 24)$ by S. But these points are all points with co-ordinates (x, y) such that

$$x = \frac{3y + 8}{2},$$

that is, all points on the line $-2x + 3y = -8$. Thus this entire line is mapped onto the point $(-8, 24)$ by the transformation S.

Example 3. Find the set of points mapped onto the point $(1, -3)$ by the transformation S of Example 1.

Solution: The required set will consist of all points with co-ordinates (x, y) such that

$$-2x + 3y = 1 \quad \text{and} \quad 6x - 9y = -3 \,;$$

that is, all points on the line with equation $-2x + 3y = 1$. The solution set of the equation $-2x + 3y = 1$ is

$$\left\{\left(\frac{3k - 1}{2}, k\right) \middle| k \in Re\right\}.$$

We check our original statement by noting that

$$S\begin{bmatrix} \dfrac{3k - 1}{2} \\ k \end{bmatrix} = \begin{bmatrix} -2\left(\dfrac{3k - 1}{2}\right) + 3k \\ 6\left(\dfrac{3k - 1}{2}\right) - 9k \end{bmatrix}$$

$$= \begin{bmatrix} 1 \\ -3 \end{bmatrix}.$$

Example 4. Find the set of points mapped onto the point $(0, 0)$ by the transformation S of Example 1.

Solution: The set of points on the line whose equation is

$$-2x + 3y = 0$$

is the required set, since these points have co-ordinates (x, y) such that

$$u = -2x + 3y = 0$$

and

$$v = 6x - 9y = 0,$$

so that

$$T\begin{bmatrix} x \\ y \end{bmatrix} = \begin{bmatrix} 0 \\ 0 \end{bmatrix} \text{ for all such points } (x, y).$$

Finally, we note that under transformation S of Example 1,

line $-2x + 3y = -8$ is mapped onto point $(-8, 24)$;
line $-2x + 3y = 1$ is mapped onto point $(1, -3)$;
line $-2x + 3y = 0$ is mapped onto point $(0, 0)$.

In general, we see that the line whose equation is $-2x + 3y = k$ is mapped onto the point with co-ordinates $(k, -3k)$. Thus S is a many-to-one mapping of points of the xy-plane onto certain points of the uv-plane. Indeed, S sets up a one-to-one correspondence between the members of the family of parallel lines whose equations are $-2x + 3y = k$, $k \in Re$, and the points $(k, -3k)$ on the line $y = -3x$.

EXERCISE 9.5

Show that the following transformations are mappings of the xy-plane *into* the uv-plane.

1. R $\begin{cases} u = x - 2y \\ v = 3x - 6y \end{cases}$
2. S $\begin{cases} u = \frac{1}{2}x + y \\ v = x + 2y \end{cases}$
3. T $\begin{cases} u = -x + 4y \\ v = 2x - 8y \end{cases}$

4. U $\begin{cases} u = 3x - 2y \\ v = -x + \frac{2}{3}y \end{cases}$
5. V $\begin{cases} u = 3x - y \\ v = 6x - 2y \end{cases}$
6. W $\begin{cases} u = x + y \\ v = 4x + 4y \end{cases}$

7. X $\begin{cases} u = -x + \frac{1}{3}y \\ v = x - \frac{1}{3}y \end{cases}$
8. Y $\begin{cases} u = x + 2y \\ v = 0 \end{cases}$
9. Z $\begin{cases} u = 0 \\ v = 4x - y \end{cases}$

10. Find the set of points whose image under R is $R \begin{bmatrix} 1 \\ 1 \end{bmatrix}$.

11. Find the set of points whose image under T is $T \begin{bmatrix} -2 \\ 3 \end{bmatrix}$.

12. Find the set of points whose image under V is $V \begin{bmatrix} 5 \\ 0 \end{bmatrix}$.

13. Find the set of points whose image under X is $X \begin{bmatrix} -2 \\ 2 \end{bmatrix}$.

14. Find the set of points whose image under Z is $Z \begin{bmatrix} 1 \\ 2 \end{bmatrix}$.

15. The transformations in questions (1) to (9) set up one-to-one correspondences between the members of certain families of parallel lines and the points of a line. Find the family of parallel lines and the corresponding points for each of these transformations.

16. Under what algebraic condition on the coefficients will the transformation

$$T \begin{cases} u = ax + by \\ v = cx + dy \end{cases}$$

be a transformation of the xy-plane *into* the uv-plane?

9.6.   Transformations with Inverses

If a transformation T sets up a one-to-one correspondence between the points of the xy- and the uv-planes, that is, if T is a one-to-one transformation of the xy-plane onto the uv-plane, then there should be a corresponding one-to-one mapping T^* of the uv-plane onto the xy-plane. This mapping T^* should undo what mapping T does; that is, mapping T^* should be the inverse of mapping T.

Example 1.   If T is the transformation

$$T \quad \begin{cases} u = 3x - 2y \\ v = 4x + y \end{cases},$$

find a transformation T^* by solving for x and y in terms of u and v. Show that T^* is the inverse of mapping T in the sense that if T maps point P onto point P^*, then T^* maps point P^* onto point P.

Solution: The result of question (8), Exercise 9.4 shows that T is a one-to-one transformation of the xy-plane onto the uv-plane. We solve the system

$$3x - 2y = u$$
$$4x + y = v$$

in one of the usual ways, to obtain

$$T^* \quad \begin{cases} x = \tfrac{1}{11}u + \tfrac{2}{11}v \\ y = \tfrac{-4}{11}u + \tfrac{3}{11}v \end{cases}.$$

T^* is obviously a transformation of the uv-plane. Also, the image of point P with co-ordinates (a, b) under T is the point P^* with co-ordinates $(3a - 2b, 4a + b)$ since

$$T \begin{bmatrix} a \\ b \end{bmatrix} = \begin{bmatrix} 3a - 2b \\ 4a + b \end{bmatrix}.$$

We now find the image of point P^* under T^*; that is, we find

$$T^* \begin{bmatrix} 3a - 2b \\ 4a + b \end{bmatrix}.$$

But

$$\tfrac{1}{11}(3a - 2b) + \tfrac{2}{11}(4a + b) = a$$

and

$$\tfrac{-4}{11}(3a - 2b) + \tfrac{3}{11}(4a + b) = b,$$

so that

$$T^* \begin{bmatrix} 3a - 2b \\ 4a + b \end{bmatrix} = \begin{bmatrix} a \\ b \end{bmatrix}.$$

This proves that if T maps point P onto point P^*, then T^* maps P^* back onto P. We call T^* the inverse transformation of T; we normally use the symbol T^{-1} to represent the inverse transformation of T.

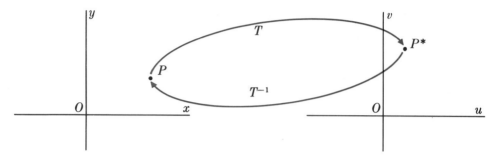

As specific examples, we note that

$$T\begin{bmatrix} 3 \\ 4 \end{bmatrix} = \begin{bmatrix} 1 \\ 16 \end{bmatrix} \quad \text{and} \quad T^{-1}\begin{bmatrix} 1 \\ 16 \end{bmatrix} = \begin{bmatrix} 3 \\ 4 \end{bmatrix};$$

$$T\begin{bmatrix} 5 \\ -2 \end{bmatrix} = \begin{bmatrix} 19 \\ 18 \end{bmatrix} \quad \text{and} \quad T^{-1}\begin{bmatrix} 19 \\ 18 \end{bmatrix} = \begin{bmatrix} 5 \\ -2 \end{bmatrix};$$

$$T\begin{bmatrix} 1 \\ 1 \end{bmatrix} = \begin{bmatrix} 1 \\ 5 \end{bmatrix} \quad \text{and} \quad T^{-1}\begin{bmatrix} 1 \\ 5 \end{bmatrix} = \begin{bmatrix} 1 \\ 1 \end{bmatrix}.$$

The transformations T and T^{-1} of this example both set up one-to-one correspondences between the sets of points of the xy- and uv-planes; T is a one-to-one transformation of the xy-plane onto the uv-plane and T^{-1} is a one-to-one transformation of the uv-plane onto the xy-plane.

Example 2. Find, if possible, the inverse transformation of the transformation

$$S \quad \begin{cases} u = x + 3y \\ v = 2x + 6y \end{cases}.$$

Solution: The transformation S does not produce a one-to-one correspondence between the points of the xy-plane and the points of the uv-plane. All points of the xy-plane have images which lie on the line $v = 2u$ in the uv-plane.

Indeed, S sets up a one-to-one correspondence between the members of the family of parallel lines $x + 3y = k$, $k \in Re$, and the points $(k, 2k)$ of the uv-plane. It seems reasonable then that, since the points of the line $x + 3y = k$ map onto the single point with co-ordinates $(k, 2k)$, there would be no way of knowing which point of the line to take as the image of the point with co-ordinates $(k, 2k)$ under an inverse transformation.

In addition, points not on the line $v = 2u$ would not have images under such an inverse transformation. Therefore it is clear that there can be no inverse for the transformation S.

The transformation

$$T \quad \begin{cases} u = ax + by \\ v = cx + dy \end{cases}$$

will have an inverse T^{-1} if and only if T is a one-to-one mapping of the xy-plane onto the uv-plane. We see the algebraic conditions on the coefficients a, b, c, d for T to have an inverse in the following theorem.

Theorem.   The transformation

$$T \quad \begin{cases} u = ax + by \\ v = cx + dy \end{cases}$$

has an inverse if and only if $ad - bc \neq 0$.

Proof: The transformation T has an inverse T^{-1} if and only if we can solve

$$u = ax + by, \quad v = cx + dy$$

for x and y in terms of u and v. We find that

$$x = \frac{du - bv}{ad - bc}, \quad y = \frac{-cu + av}{ad - bc}$$

and so this yields the desired transformation T^{-1} if and only if

$$ad - bc \neq 0 .$$

We conclude that T is a one-to-one mapping of the xy-plane onto the uv-plane if and only if $ad - bc \neq 0$.

Example 3.   Do the transformations

(a) $T \quad \begin{cases} u = 5x - 2y \\ v = -x + 3y \end{cases}$
        (b) $S \quad \begin{cases} u = 3x - y \\ v = -9x + 3y \end{cases}$

have inverses?

Solution:

(a)   Here $ad - bc$ has the value

$$(5)(3) - (-2)(-1) = 13 \neq 0 .$$

Therefore T has an inverse; T is a one-to-one mapping of the xy-plane onto the uv-plane.

(b)   Here $ad - bc$ has the value

$$(3)(3) - (-1)(-9) = 0 .$$

Therefore S does not have an inverse; S is a mapping of the xy-plane into the uv-plane.

EXERCISE 9.6

State which of the following transformations do not have inverses and find the inverses of the remaining transformations.

1. A $\begin{cases} u = x + 3y \\ v = 3x + y \end{cases}$

2. B $\begin{cases} u = 3x + 2y \\ v = x - y \end{cases}$

3. C $\begin{cases} u = 3x - y \\ v = x - 2y \end{cases}$

4. D $\begin{cases} u = 3x \\ v = 2y \end{cases}$

5. E $\begin{cases} u = 3y \\ v = 2x \end{cases}$

6. F $\begin{cases} u = x - y \\ v = -2x + 2y \end{cases}$

7. R $\begin{cases} u = x + 2y \\ v = 0 \end{cases}$

8. S $\begin{cases} u = x + y \\ v = 3x \end{cases}$

9. T $\begin{cases} u = 2y \\ v = 2x - 3y \end{cases}$

10. U $\begin{cases} u = 0 \\ v = 3x - y \end{cases}$

11. V $\begin{cases} u = 3x + y \\ v = 2x - y \end{cases}$

12. W $\begin{cases} u = -x + 3y \\ v = 4x - 12y \end{cases}$

13. For the transformations in questions (1) to (12) that have inverses, find the images of the points with the co-ordinates
    (a) $(1, 2)$ (b) $(-3, 0)$ (c) $(2, -5)$ (d) $(2, -4)$
    and show in each case that the inverse transformation maps the image onto the original point.

14. The transformations we have been studying are called linear transformations. The points $P_1(2, 3)$, $P_2(-4, 7)$, and $P_3(-1, 5)$ are collinear. Show that the images of P_1, P_2, and P_3 are collinear under the transformations of questions (1) to (6).

15. Show that if points $P_1(x_1, y_1)$, $P_2(x_2, y_2)$, and $P_3(x_3, y_3)$ are collinear, and T is the transformation
    $$T \quad \begin{cases} u = ax + by \\ v = cx + dy \end{cases},$$
    then $T(P_1)$, $T(P_2)$, and $T(P_3)$ are collinear points. What is the situation if $ad - bc = 0$?

9.7.   Products of Transformations

The transformation
$$T \quad \begin{cases} u = x - 2y \\ v = 2x + y \end{cases}$$

provides a one-to-one mapping of the xy-plane onto the uv-plane. ($ad - bc$ has the value 5.)   Similarly, the transformation

$$S \quad \begin{cases} r = 3u + v \\ s = u + 2v \end{cases}$$

provides a one-to-one mapping of the uv-plane onto the rs-plane.   ($ad - bc$ has the value 5.)   The transformation T maps every ordered pair (x, y) onto an ordered pair (u, v).

$$T \begin{bmatrix} x \\ y \end{bmatrix} = \begin{bmatrix} u \\ v \end{bmatrix}.$$

S maps every ordered pair (u, v) onto an ordered pair (r, s).

$$S \begin{bmatrix} u \\ v \end{bmatrix} = \begin{bmatrix} r \\ s \end{bmatrix}.$$

Then the performance of transformation T followed by the performance of transformation S has the total effect of mapping every ordered pair (x, y) onto an ordered pair (r, s), by using an intermediate step.

$$(x, y) \xrightarrow{\quad T \quad} (u, v) \xrightarrow{\quad S \quad} (r, s)$$

This combination of the two transformations T and S, namely transformation T followed by transformation S, is itself a transformation of the xy-plane into or onto the rs-plane.   We call such a combination of two transformations T and S the product ST of the two transformations.

The product ST of two transformations T and S is the transformation equivalent to that obtained by carrying out transformation T and following this with transformation S (note the apparent reversal of the normal order).   Then

$$ST \begin{bmatrix} x \\ y \end{bmatrix} = S \left(T \begin{bmatrix} x \\ y \end{bmatrix} \right) = S \begin{bmatrix} u \\ v \end{bmatrix} = \begin{bmatrix} r \\ s \end{bmatrix}.$$

Example 1. Find

(a) $ST \begin{bmatrix} 1 \\ 1 \end{bmatrix}$ (b) $ST \begin{bmatrix} -2 \\ 5 \end{bmatrix}$ (c) $ST \begin{bmatrix} 3 \\ -4 \end{bmatrix}$

for the transformations S and T of this section.

Solution:

(a) $ST \begin{bmatrix} 1 \\ 1 \end{bmatrix} = S \left(T \begin{bmatrix} 1 \\ 1 \end{bmatrix} \right) = S \begin{bmatrix} -1 \\ 3 \end{bmatrix} = \begin{bmatrix} 0 \\ 5 \end{bmatrix}.$

(b) $ST \begin{bmatrix} -2 \\ 5 \end{bmatrix} = S \left(T \begin{bmatrix} -2 \\ 5 \end{bmatrix} \right) = S \begin{bmatrix} -12 \\ 1 \end{bmatrix} = \begin{bmatrix} -35 \\ -10 \end{bmatrix}.$

(c) $ST \begin{bmatrix} 3 \\ -4 \end{bmatrix} = S \left(T \begin{bmatrix} 3 \\ -4 \end{bmatrix} \right) = S \begin{bmatrix} 11 \\ 2 \end{bmatrix} = \begin{bmatrix} 35 \\ 15 \end{bmatrix}.$

Example 2. Find $ST \begin{bmatrix} x \\ y \end{bmatrix}$ for the transformations S and T of this section.

Solution:

$$(x, y) \xrightarrow{\ T\ } (u, v) = (x - 2y, 2x + y) \,.$$

$$
\begin{aligned}
(u, v) \xrightarrow{\ S\ } (r, s) &= (3u + v, \ u + 2v) \\
&= [3\,(x - 2y) + (2x + y), \ x - 2y + 2(2x + y)] \\
&= (5x - 5y, \ 5x) \,.
\end{aligned}
$$

Therefore,

$$ST \begin{bmatrix} x \\ y \end{bmatrix} = \begin{bmatrix} 5x - 5y \\ 5x \end{bmatrix} \,.$$

The transformation ST is

$$ST \quad \begin{cases} r = 5x - 5y \\ s = 5x \end{cases} \,.$$

This provides a one-to-one mapping of the xy-plane onto the rs-plane since $ad - bc$ has the value 25.   We may now check the results in Example 1.

(a)

$$ST \begin{bmatrix} 1 \\ 1 \end{bmatrix} = \begin{bmatrix} 5 - 5 \\ 5 \end{bmatrix} = \begin{bmatrix} 0 \\ 5 \end{bmatrix} \,.$$

(b)

$$ST \begin{bmatrix} -2 \\ 5 \end{bmatrix} = \begin{bmatrix} -10 - 25 \\ -10 \end{bmatrix} = \begin{bmatrix} -35 \\ -10 \end{bmatrix} \,.$$

(c)

$$ST \begin{bmatrix} 3 \\ -4 \end{bmatrix} = \begin{bmatrix} 15 + 20 \\ 15 \end{bmatrix} = \begin{bmatrix} 35 \\ 15 \end{bmatrix} \,.$$

Example 3.   Find the product transformation AB for the transformations

$$B \begin{cases} u = x - 3y, \\ v = 2x + y, \end{cases} \qquad A \begin{cases} r = -u + 2v \\ s = 2u - 4v \end{cases} \,.$$

Solution: We express r and s in terms of x and y as follows.

$$r = -u + 2v = -(x - 3y) + 2\,(2x + y) = 3x + 5y \,,$$

$$s = 2u - 4v = 2\,(x - 3y) - 4\,(2x + y) = -6x - 10y \,.$$

Therefore,

$$AB \begin{bmatrix} x \\ y \end{bmatrix} = \begin{bmatrix} 3x + 5y \\ -6x - 10y \end{bmatrix} \,.$$

The transformation AB is

$$AB \quad \begin{cases} r = 3x + 5y \\ s = -6x - 10y \end{cases} \,.$$

EXERCISE 9.7

1. Find $S \begin{bmatrix} -1 \\ 1 \end{bmatrix}$ and $T \left(S \begin{bmatrix} -1 \\ 1 \end{bmatrix} \right)$ for the following transformations.

   (a) $S \begin{cases} u = 5x - y \\ v = x + 2y \end{cases}$ $T \begin{cases} r = 3u - v \\ s = u + v \end{cases}$

   (b) $S \begin{cases} u = 2x + 3y \\ v = x - y \end{cases}$ $T \begin{cases} r = 3u + 2v \\ s = -u + 2v \end{cases}$

   (c) $S \begin{cases} u = -x + 2y \\ v = 2x - 4y \end{cases}$ $T \begin{cases} r = -u + 4v \\ s = 3u - v \end{cases}$

   (d) $S \begin{cases} u = 3x + y \\ v = x - 5y \end{cases}$ $T \begin{cases} r = 2u - v \\ s = -6u + 3v \end{cases}$

2. Find $S \begin{bmatrix} 2 \\ -3 \end{bmatrix}$ and $T \left(S \begin{bmatrix} 2 \\ -3 \end{bmatrix} \right)$ for the transformations in question (1).

3. Find the products TS of the transformations in question (1). Check the results of questions (1) and (2) by finding $TS \begin{bmatrix} -1 \\ 1 \end{bmatrix}$ and $TS \begin{bmatrix} 2 \\ -3 \end{bmatrix}$ in each case.

4. Find the product transformation BA if A and B are the transformations
$$A \begin{cases} u = 3x - 2y \\ v = x + 3y \end{cases} \quad \text{and} \quad B \begin{cases} r = 3u + v \\ s = 2u - v \end{cases}$$

5. Find the inverse transformations A^{-1} and B^{-1} of the transformations in question (4).

6. Find the inverse $(BA)^{-1}$ of the transformation in question (4).

7. Find the product transformation $A^{-1}B^{-1}$ of the transformations in question (4). Compare the result with that in question (6).

8. Repeat questions (4) to (7) for the transformations
$$A \begin{cases} u = 5x + y \\ v = 2x \end{cases} \quad B \begin{cases} r = 3v \\ s = u + v \end{cases}.$$

Chapter Summary

Definition of 2×2 and $m \times n$ real matrices · Dimensions of a matrix · Entries or components of a matrix · Row and column vectors · Equality of matrices · Addition of matrices · Multiplication of a matrix by a real number · Properties of addition of matrices: commutativity, associativity, existence of identity, existence of inverses · Linear transformations of the plane · Associated matrices · One-to-one transformations of the plane onto the plane · Linear transformations of the plane into the plane · Transformations with inverses · Products of transformations · ST is the transformation equivalent to the result of performing transformation T first, followed by transformation S

REVIEW EXERCISE 9

1. State (i) a_{12}, (ii) b_{21}, (iii) b_{22}, and find $a_{21}b_{11} + a_{22}b_{21}$ if

$$A = \begin{bmatrix} a_{ij} \end{bmatrix} = \begin{bmatrix} 3 & -1 \\ 5 & 2 \end{bmatrix} \quad \text{and} \quad B = \begin{bmatrix} b_{ij} \end{bmatrix} = \begin{bmatrix} 4 & 0 \\ -1 & 3 \end{bmatrix}.$$

2. For the matrices A and B of question (1), find
   (a) $A + B$,   (b) $(-1)B$,   (c) $3A + 2B$.

3. Show that $A + B = B + A$ and $A + (B + C) = (A + B) + C$ for the matrices A and B of question (1) and

$$C = \begin{bmatrix} -5 & 4 \\ 1 & -7 \end{bmatrix}.$$

4. Find $A - B - C$ and $A - (B + C)$ for the matrices of question (3).

5. (a) Write a transformation T corresponding to the matrix
   $$\begin{bmatrix} -1 & 3 \\ 5 & 2 \end{bmatrix}.$$

   (b) Find $T \begin{bmatrix} -5 \\ 1 \end{bmatrix}$.

   (c) Find a and b such that
   $$T \begin{bmatrix} a \\ b \end{bmatrix} = \begin{bmatrix} -5 \\ 1 \end{bmatrix}.$$

   (d) Show that (x, y) exists such that
   $$T \begin{bmatrix} x \\ y \end{bmatrix} = \begin{bmatrix} m \\ n \end{bmatrix}$$
   for every ordered pair (m, n) of real numbers.

6. (a) Show that S is a transformation of the plane *into* the plane if
   $$S \quad \begin{cases} u = -x + 4y \\ v = 3x - 12y \end{cases}.$$

   (b) Show that S sets up a one-to-one correspondence between the members of a certain family of parallel lines and the points of a line.

7. Find the inverses of the following transformations (if possible).
   (a) $u = 3x + 2y$ (b) $u = 3x + y$ (c) $u = 3x + y$
       $v = 3x - 2y$ $v = 6x + y$ $v = 6x + 2y$

8. For the following transformations find
   (a) SR,   (b) $T(SR)$,   (c) TS,   (d) $(TS)R$.

   $R \begin{cases} u = 2x + y \\ v = 3x - y \end{cases}$ $S \begin{cases} r = 3u + 2v \\ s = 6u + v \end{cases}$ $T \begin{cases} w = 2r \\ z = 3s \end{cases}$

Chapter 10

MATRIX MULTIPLICATION

10.1. Definition of Matrix Multiplication

In this chapter, we shall reconsider "multiplication" of linear transformations and use it to define a corresponding multiplication of matrices. We shall then go on to study the properties and some of the applications of matrix multiplication.

We should point out that, although there are other possible ways of defining the product of two matrices, no use has been found for such definitions. On the other hand, the definition we shall give proves extremely useful.

In this section, we shall develop the rule for multiplying 2×2 real matrices. The method will apply in general whenever multiplication of matrices is possible.

We have seen that we have a one-to-one correspondence between 2×2 real matrices and transformations of the form

$$T \quad \begin{cases} u = ax + by \\ v = cx + dy \end{cases}.$$

Such a transformation corresponds to the matrix of coefficients

$$T = \begin{bmatrix} a & b \\ c & d \end{bmatrix}.$$

Then the transformations

$$T \quad \begin{cases} u = x - 2y \\ v = 2x + y \end{cases} \quad \text{and} \quad S \quad \begin{cases} r = 3u + v \\ s = u + 2v \end{cases}$$

correspond to the matrices

$$T = \begin{bmatrix} 1 & -2 \\ 2 & 1 \end{bmatrix} \quad \text{and} \quad S = \begin{bmatrix} 3 & 1 \\ 1 & 2 \end{bmatrix},$$

respectively.

In Section 9.7, we defined the product transformation ST of two such transformations T and S, and, in Example 2 of that section, we found the product of these particular transformations T and S to be the transformation

$$ST \quad \begin{cases} r = 5x - 5y \\ s = 5x \end{cases}.$$

This transformation corresponds to the matrix

$$\begin{bmatrix} 5 & -5 \\ 5 & 0 \end{bmatrix},$$

and we define this matrix to be the product ST of the matrices corresponding to the transformations S and T.   If

$$S = \begin{bmatrix} 3 & 1 \\ 1 & 2 \end{bmatrix} \quad \text{and} \quad T = \begin{bmatrix} 1 & -2 \\ 2 & 1 \end{bmatrix},$$

then

$$ST = \begin{bmatrix} 3 & 1 \\ 1 & 2 \end{bmatrix} \begin{bmatrix} 1 & -2 \\ 2 & 1 \end{bmatrix}$$

$$= \begin{bmatrix} 5 & -5 \\ 5 & 0 \end{bmatrix}.$$

DEFINITION. The product ST of two matrices S and T is the matrix of coefficients of the product transformation ST of the two linear transformations corresponding to S and T.

Example 1.   Find ST if

$$S = \begin{bmatrix} 5 & -1 \\ 2 & 3 \end{bmatrix} \quad \text{and} \quad T = \begin{bmatrix} 4 & 1 \\ -1 & 2 \end{bmatrix}.$$

Solution: Let $T = \begin{bmatrix} 4 & 1 \\ -1 & 2 \end{bmatrix}$ correspond to the transformation

$$T \quad \begin{cases} u = 4x + y \\ v = -x + 2y \end{cases}$$

and $S = \begin{bmatrix} 5 & -1 \\ 2 & 3 \end{bmatrix}$ correspond to the transformation

$$S \quad \begin{cases} r = 5u - v \\ s = 2u + 3v \end{cases}.$$

Then, by definition, ST corresponds to the product transformation.

$$r = 5(4x + y) - (-x + 2y) = 21x + 3y$$

and

$$s = 2(4x + y) + 3(-x + 2y) = 5x + 8y,$$

so that ST is the transformation

$$ST \quad \begin{cases} r = 21x + 3y \\ s = 5x + 8y \end{cases}.$$

Therefore, by our definition,

$$ST = \begin{bmatrix} 5 & -1 \\ 2 & 3 \end{bmatrix}\begin{bmatrix} 4 & 1 \\ -1 & 2 \end{bmatrix}$$

$$= \begin{bmatrix} 21 & 3 \\ 5 & 8 \end{bmatrix}.$$

Example 2.   Find TS for the matrices of Example 1.

Solution: Let $S = \begin{bmatrix} 5 & -1 \\ 2 & 3 \end{bmatrix}$ correspond to the transformation

$$S \quad \begin{cases} u = 5x - y \\ v = 2x + 3y \end{cases}$$

and $T = \begin{bmatrix} 4 & 1 \\ -1 & 2 \end{bmatrix}$ correspond to the transformation

$$T \quad \begin{cases} r = 4u + v \\ s = -u + 2v \end{cases}.$$

Then TS corresponds to the product transfomation.

$$r = 4(5x - y) + (2x + 3y) = 22x - y$$

and

$$s = -(5x - y) + 2(2x + 3y) = -x + 7y,$$

so that TS is the transformation

$$TS \quad \begin{cases} r = 22x - y \\ s = -x + 7y \end{cases}.$$

Therefore, by definition,

$$TS = \begin{bmatrix} 4 & 1 \\ -1 & 2 \end{bmatrix}\begin{bmatrix} 5 & -1 \\ 2 & 3 \end{bmatrix}$$

$$= \begin{bmatrix} 22 & -1 \\ -1 & 7 \end{bmatrix}.$$

We see from Examples 1 and 2 that matrices ST and TS are not equal, and we conclude that, in general, multiplication of matrices, as we have defined it, is not commutative. This does not mean that AB is never equal to BA; it is true that $AB = BA$ for certain matrices, but not for all matrices A and B.

EXERCISE 10.1

Find AB and BA for the following pairs of matrices.

1. $A = \begin{bmatrix} 5 & 1 \\ 0 & 1 \end{bmatrix}$, $B = \begin{bmatrix} -3 & 1 \\ 5 & 2 \end{bmatrix}$

2. $A = \begin{bmatrix} 3 & 3 \\ -1 & 2 \end{bmatrix}$, $B = \begin{bmatrix} 5 & 2 \\ 1 & 1 \end{bmatrix}$

3. $A = \begin{bmatrix} 1 & 0 \\ 0 & 1 \end{bmatrix}$, $B = \begin{bmatrix} 4 & -3 \\ 1 & 2 \end{bmatrix}$

4. $A = \begin{bmatrix} 1 & -1 \\ 2 & 5 \end{bmatrix}$, $B = \begin{bmatrix} 3 & -2 \\ 1 & 6 \end{bmatrix}$

5. $A = \begin{bmatrix} 3 & -2 \\ 4 & 1 \end{bmatrix}$, $B = \begin{bmatrix} \frac{1}{11} & \frac{2}{11} \\ \frac{-4}{11} & \frac{3}{11} \end{bmatrix}$

6. $A = \begin{bmatrix} 3 & 4 \\ 2 & 3 \end{bmatrix}$, $B = \begin{bmatrix} 3 & -4 \\ -2 & 3 \end{bmatrix}$

10.2.   Rule for Multiplication of Matrices

We find it convenient to develop a rule for multiplying 2×2 matrices rather than setting up the corresponding transformations each time as in the previous section. We consider two general matrices

$$A = \begin{bmatrix} a_{11} & a_{12} \\ a_{21} & a_{22} \end{bmatrix} \quad \text{and} \quad B = \begin{bmatrix} b_{11} & b_{12} \\ b_{21} & b_{22} \end{bmatrix}$$

and find their product, using the definition given in Section 9.7 for the product of the corresponding transformations.

Let

$$A = \begin{bmatrix} a_{11} & a_{12} \\ a_{21} & a_{22} \end{bmatrix}$$

correspond to the transformation

$$\begin{cases} u = a_{11}x + a_{12}y, \\ v = a_{21}x + a_{22}y, \end{cases}$$

and

$$B = \begin{bmatrix} b_{11} & b_{12} \\ b_{21} & b_{22} \end{bmatrix}$$

correspond to the transformation

$$\begin{cases} r = b_{11}u + b_{12}v \,. \\ s = b_{21}u + b_{22}v \end{cases}$$

Then matrix BA corresponds to the product transformation.

$$\begin{aligned} r &= b_{11}(a_{11}x + a_{12}y) + b_{12}(a_{21}x + a_{22}y) \\ &= (b_{11}a_{11} + b_{12}a_{21})x + (b_{11}a_{12} + b_{12}a_{22})y \end{aligned}$$

and

$$\begin{aligned} s &= b_{21}(a_{11}x + a_{12}y) + b_{22}(a_{21}x + a_{22}y) \\ &= (b_{21}a_{11} + b_{22}a_{21})x + (b_{21}a_{12} + b_{22}a_{22})y \,, \end{aligned}$$

so that the product transformation is

$$\begin{cases} r = (b_{11}a_{11} + b_{12}a_{21})x + (b_{11}a_{12} + b_{12}a_{22})y \\ s = (b_{21}a_{11} + b_{22}a_{21})x + (b_{21}a_{12} + b_{22}a_{22})y \end{cases} .$$

Therefore, by definition,

$$\begin{aligned} BA &= \begin{bmatrix} b_{11} & b_{12} \\ b_{21} & b_{22} \end{bmatrix} \begin{bmatrix} a_{11} & a_{12} \\ a_{21} & a_{22} \end{bmatrix} \\ &= \begin{bmatrix} b_{11}a_{11} + b_{12}a_{21} & b_{11}a_{12} + b_{12}a_{22} \\ b_{21}a_{11} + b_{22}a_{21} & b_{21}a_{12} + b_{22}a_{22} \end{bmatrix} . \end{aligned}$$

This formula may appear quite formidable as one for the product of the matrices B and A until we point out a fairly simple rule for obtaining the terms of the product matrix.

If we let BA be the matrix C, with

$$C = \begin{bmatrix} c_{11} & c_{12} \\ c_{21} & c_{22} \end{bmatrix},$$

we see that

(i) c_{11} is the sum of the products of corresponding terms of the *first* row of B and the *first* column of A;

$$[b_{11} \quad b_{12}] \begin{bmatrix} a_{11} \\ a_{21} \end{bmatrix} \quad column \ 1$$

row 1

that is,

$$c_{11} = b_{11}a_{11} + b_{12}a_{21};$$

(ii) c_{21} is the sum of the products of corresponding terms of the *second* row of B and the *first* column of A;

$$[b_{21} \quad b_{22}] \begin{bmatrix} a_{11} \\ a_{21} \end{bmatrix} \quad column \ 1$$

$$row \ 2$$

that is,

$$c_{21} = b_{21}a_{11} + b_{22}a_{21};$$

(iii) c_{12} is the sum of the products of corresponding terms of the *first* row of B and the *second* column of A;

$$[b_{11} \quad b_{12}] \begin{bmatrix} a_{12} \\ a_{22} \end{bmatrix} \quad column \ 2$$

$$row \ 1$$

that is,

$$c_{12} = b_{11}a_{12} + b_{12}a_{22};$$

(iv) c_{22} is the sum of the products of corresponding terms of the *second* row of B and the *second* column of A;

$$[b_{21} \quad b_{22}] \begin{bmatrix} a_{12} \\ a_{22} \end{bmatrix} \quad column \ 2$$

$$row \ 2$$

that is,

$$c_{22} = b_{21}a_{12} + b_{22}a_{22}.$$

The finding of the product matrix can be made even more mechanical by noting that the above results may be obtained for the product

$$\begin{bmatrix} b_{11} & b_{12} \\ b_{21} & b_{22} \end{bmatrix} \begin{bmatrix} a_{11} & a_{12} \\ a_{21} & a_{22} \end{bmatrix}$$

by picturing the first column of the right matrix picked up and placed horizontally above the left matrix as shown below.

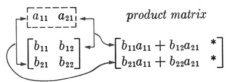

The sums of the products of corresponding elements for this row and the first and second rows of B then produce the terms of the first column of the product matrix as indicated.

Now picture the second column of the right matrix picked up and placed horizontally above the left matrix as shown below.

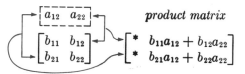

Again, the sums of the products of corresponding elements of this row and the first and second rows of B produce the terms of the second column of the product matrix as indicated.

Example 1. Find AB if

$$A = \begin{bmatrix} 3 & -1 \\ 3 & 4 \end{bmatrix} \quad \text{and} \quad B = \begin{bmatrix} 5 & 2 \\ -3 & 4 \end{bmatrix}.$$

Solution: The first column of AB is obtained as indicated in the following scheme

$$\begin{bmatrix} \boxed{5 \quad -3} \end{bmatrix} \quad \begin{bmatrix} 3 & -1 \\ 3 & 4 \end{bmatrix} \quad \begin{bmatrix} 15+3 & * \\ 15+(-12) & * \end{bmatrix}$$

and the second column of AB is obtained similarly.

$$\begin{bmatrix} \boxed{2 \quad 4} \end{bmatrix} \quad \begin{bmatrix} 3 & -1 \\ 3 & 4 \end{bmatrix} \quad \begin{bmatrix} * & 6+(-4) \\ * & 6+16 \end{bmatrix}$$

Therefore,

$$\begin{bmatrix} 3 & -1 \\ 3 & 4 \end{bmatrix}\begin{bmatrix} 5 & 2 \\ -3 & 4 \end{bmatrix} = \begin{bmatrix} 18 & 2 \\ 3 & 22 \end{bmatrix}.$$

Of course, in practice, the steps outlined in detail above are performed mentally.

Example 2. Find BA for the matrices A and B of Example 1.

Solution:

$$BA = \begin{bmatrix} 5 & 2 \\ -3 & 4 \end{bmatrix}\begin{bmatrix} 3 & -1 \\ 3 & 4 \end{bmatrix}$$

$$= \begin{bmatrix} 3(5)+3(2) & (-1)5+4(2) \\ 3(-3)+3(4) & (-1)(-3)+4(4) \end{bmatrix}$$

$$= \begin{bmatrix} 21 & 3 \\ 3 & 19 \end{bmatrix}.$$

Again we see that $AB \neq BA$ for the matrices A and B of Examples 1 and 2.

Example 3. If $A^2 = AA$, find A^2 if

$$A = \begin{bmatrix} 3 & 4 \\ -2 & 1 \end{bmatrix}.$$

Solution:

$$A^2 = AA = \begin{bmatrix} 3 & 4 \\ -2 & 1 \end{bmatrix}\begin{bmatrix} 3 & 4 \\ -2 & 1 \end{bmatrix}$$

$$= \begin{bmatrix} 3(3) + (-2)4 & 4(3) + 1(4) \\ 3(-2) + (-2)1 & 4(-2) + 1(1) \end{bmatrix}$$

$$= \begin{bmatrix} 1 & 16 \\ -8 & -7 \end{bmatrix}.$$

Finally, we see that, in the product matrix

$$\begin{bmatrix} b_{11} & b_{12} \\ b_{21} & b_{22} \end{bmatrix}\begin{bmatrix} a_{11} & a_{12} \\ a_{21} & a_{22} \end{bmatrix} = \begin{bmatrix} c_{11} & c_{12} \\ c_{21} & c_{22} \end{bmatrix},$$

we have

c_{ij} = the sum of the products of corresponding terms of the ith row of the left matrix and the jth column of the right matrix.

$$= b_{i1}a_{1j} + b_{i2}a_{2j}$$

$$= \sum_{k=1}^{2} b_{ik}a_{kj}.$$

Then, abbreviating A by $[a_{ij}]$ and B by $[b_{ij}]$, we may write

$$BA = [b_{ij}][a_{ij}]$$

$$= \left[\sum_{k=1}^{2} b_{ik}a_{kj}\right].$$

This definition may be extended to the product of matrices other than 2×2 matrices under certain conditions of compatibility of the two matrices.

Example 4. Assuming that it is possible to extend our rule of multiplication (taking sums of the products of elements of rows of the *left-hand matrix* and the corresponding elements of the columns of the *right-hand matrix*), find, if possible, AB and BA if

$$A = \begin{bmatrix} 3 & 1 & 2 \\ -1 & 4 & -3 \\ 2 & 3 & 0 \end{bmatrix} \quad \text{and} \quad B = \begin{bmatrix} 3 \\ -2 \\ 4 \end{bmatrix}.$$

Solution:

$$AB = \begin{bmatrix} 3 & 1 & 2 \\ -1 & 4 & -3 \\ 2 & 3 & 0 \end{bmatrix}\begin{bmatrix} 3 \\ -2 \\ 4 \end{bmatrix}$$

$$= \begin{bmatrix} 3(3) + 1(-2) + 2(4) \\ (-1)(3) + 4(-2) + (-3)(4) \\ 2(3) + 3(-2) + 0(4) \end{bmatrix} \cdot$$

$$= \begin{bmatrix} 15 \\ -23 \\ 0 \end{bmatrix} \cdot$$

$$BA = \begin{bmatrix} 3 \\ -2 \\ 4 \end{bmatrix} \begin{bmatrix} 3 & 1 & 2 \\ -1 & 4 & -3 \\ 2 & 3 & 0 \end{bmatrix} \cdot$$

Here, the rows of the left matrix contain only one element, while the columns of the right matrix contain three elements. It is impossible to multiply corresponding elements and so it is impossible to find BA.

EXERCISE 10.2

1. If

$$A = \begin{bmatrix} 2 & 2 \\ -1 & 4 \end{bmatrix} \quad \text{and} \quad B = \begin{bmatrix} -3 & 1 \\ 5 & -2 \end{bmatrix},$$

find

(a) AB,   (b) BA,   (c) A^2,   (d) B^2,   (e) $A^2 + A^2B$.

2. If

$$P = \begin{bmatrix} -1 & 5 \\ 2 & 4 \end{bmatrix} \quad \text{and} \quad Q = \begin{bmatrix} 3 & -2 \\ 5 & 1 \end{bmatrix},$$

find

(a) PQ,   (b) QP,   (c) P^2,   (d) P^3,   (e) P^4.

3. If

$$A = \begin{bmatrix} 1 & 1 \\ 0 & 4 \end{bmatrix}, \quad B = \begin{bmatrix} -3 & 1 \\ 1 & 4 \end{bmatrix}, \quad C = \begin{bmatrix} 3 & -1 \\ 4 & 2 \end{bmatrix},$$

find

(a) AB,   (b) BC,   (c) CA,   (d) $A^2 + B^2$,   (e) $A - BC$.

4. If

$$A = \begin{bmatrix} 3 & -2 \\ 5 & 4 \end{bmatrix} \quad \text{and} \quad I = \begin{bmatrix} 1 & 0 \\ 0 & 1 \end{bmatrix},$$

find

(a) AI,   (b) IA,   (c) I^2,   (d) A^2,   (e) A^2I.

5. If

$$A = \begin{bmatrix} 3 & -1 \\ 5 & -2 \end{bmatrix} \quad \text{and} \quad B = \begin{bmatrix} 0 & 1 \\ 1 & 0 \end{bmatrix},$$

find

(a) AB,   (b) BA,   (c) B^2,   (d) A^2,   (e) BA^2.

6. If

$$A = \begin{bmatrix} 3 & 4 \\ 2 & 3 \end{bmatrix} \quad \text{and} \quad B = \begin{bmatrix} 3 & -4 \\ -2 & 3 \end{bmatrix},$$

find AB and BA, and comment on the result.

7. Find the product AB, where possible, for the following A and B.

(a) $A = \begin{bmatrix} 3 & -1 \\ 5 & 2 \end{bmatrix}, \quad B = \begin{bmatrix} 6 \\ 2 \end{bmatrix}$

(b) $A = [1 \quad 5], \quad B = \begin{bmatrix} 3 & -2 \\ -1 & 5 \end{bmatrix}$

(c) $A = \begin{bmatrix} 3 \\ -2 \end{bmatrix}, \quad B = \begin{bmatrix} 4 & 0 \\ -1 & 0 \end{bmatrix}$

(d) $A = \begin{bmatrix} 6 & 4 \\ -1 & 2 \end{bmatrix}, \quad B = [3 \quad 1]$

(e) $A = \begin{bmatrix} 2 & 3 & -1 \\ 5 & 6 & 4 \end{bmatrix}, \quad B = \begin{bmatrix} 1 \\ 1 \\ 5 \end{bmatrix}$

(f) $A = [1 \quad 2 \quad -1], \quad B = \begin{bmatrix} 3 \\ -1 \\ 4 \end{bmatrix}$

(g) $A = \begin{bmatrix} 2 & 3 & -1 \\ 5 & 6 & 4 \end{bmatrix}, \quad B = \begin{bmatrix} 4 & -3 \\ 1 & 0 \\ 2 & 2 \end{bmatrix}$

(h) $A = [4 \quad 2 \quad -4], \quad B = \begin{bmatrix} 1 & -2 \\ 1 & 1 \\ 5 & 0 \end{bmatrix}$

(i) $A = \begin{bmatrix} -1 & 3 & 1 \\ 2 & 1 & 1 \\ 0 & 4 & 2 \end{bmatrix}, \quad B = \begin{bmatrix} -1 \\ 2 \\ 1 \end{bmatrix}$

(j) $A = \begin{bmatrix} -1 & 3 & 1 \\ 2 & 1 & 1 \\ 0 & 4 & 2 \end{bmatrix}, \quad B = \begin{bmatrix} 3 & 5 & 3 \\ -1 & 2 & 0 \\ 1 & 0 & -2 \end{bmatrix}$

8. If

$$A = \begin{bmatrix} 0 & 1 \\ 1 & 0 \end{bmatrix}, \quad B = \begin{bmatrix} 1 & 0 \\ 0 & -1 \end{bmatrix}, \quad C = \begin{bmatrix} 0 & 1 \\ 0 & 0 \end{bmatrix},$$

find A^2, B^2, and C^2. How do your results differ from those obtained in similar situations for the real numbers?

9. Is it possible to extend our rule of multiplication (multiplying elements of rows of the left matrix by elements of columns of the right matrix) to find the products AB and BA of two matrices if
    (a) A is a 2×2 matrix, B is a 2×1 matrix?
    (b) A is a 1×2 matrix, B is a 2×2 matrix?
    (c) B and A are both 3×3 matrices?
    (d) B is a 3×2 matrix, A is a 2×3 matrix?
    (e) B and A are both 3×2 matrices?

10. If B is an $m \times n$ matrix and A is an $r \times s$ matrix, under what condition will it be possible to form the product BA? the product AB?

10.3. Algebraic Properties of Multiplication of Matrices

In this section, we shall examine the algebraic properties of matrix multiplication as applied to the set of all 2×2 real matrices.

(1) *Closure* It is always possible to find the product of two 2×2 real matrices, although, as we have seen, it is not always possible to find the product of any two matrices. By our definition, the product of two 2×2 real matrices is again a 2×2 real matrix. Thus the set of all 2×2 real matrices is closed under matrix multiplication.

(2) *Commutativity* We have seen from a number of examples that multiplication of 2×2 real matrices is not commutative in general. It may be true that $AB = BA$ for some special matrices A and B, but, in general, $AB \neq BA$.

(3) *Associativity* Multiplication of 2×2 real matrices is associative; for all 2×2 real matrices A, B, and C,

$$A(BC) = (AB)C.$$

We shall not prove this statement but we shall check it in Example 1 and in the exercises.

Example 1. Show that $A(BC) = (AB)C$ if

$$A = \begin{bmatrix} 1 & -3 \\ 2 & 4 \end{bmatrix}, \qquad B = \begin{bmatrix} 1 & 1 \\ 3 & -2 \end{bmatrix}, \qquad C = \begin{bmatrix} 5 & 0 \\ -1 & 2 \end{bmatrix}.$$

Solution:

$$BC = \begin{bmatrix} 1 & 1 \\ 3 & -2 \end{bmatrix} \begin{bmatrix} 5 & 0 \\ -1 & 2 \end{bmatrix}$$

$$= \begin{bmatrix} 4 & 2 \\ 17 & -4 \end{bmatrix}.$$

$$A(BC) = \begin{bmatrix} 1 & -3 \\ 2 & 4 \end{bmatrix} \begin{bmatrix} 4 & 2 \\ 17 & -4 \end{bmatrix}$$

$$= \begin{bmatrix} -47 & 14 \\ 76 & -12 \end{bmatrix}.$$

$$AB = \begin{bmatrix} 1 & -3 \\ 2 & 4 \end{bmatrix} \begin{bmatrix} 1 & 1 \\ 3 & -2 \end{bmatrix}$$

$$= \begin{bmatrix} -8 & 7 \\ 14 & -6 \end{bmatrix}.$$

$$(AB)C = \begin{bmatrix} -8 & 7 \\ 14 & -6 \end{bmatrix} \begin{bmatrix} 5 & 0 \\ -1 & 2 \end{bmatrix}$$

$$= \begin{bmatrix} -47 & 14 \\ 76 & -12 \end{bmatrix}.$$

Therefore,

$$(AB)C = A(BC)$$

for these matrices A, B, and C.

(4) *Multiplicative Identity*   The matrix

$$I = \begin{bmatrix} 1 & 0 \\ 0 & 1 \end{bmatrix}$$

is the multiplicative identity for the set of 2×2 real matrices.   Certainly,

$$\begin{bmatrix} a & b \\ c & d \end{bmatrix} \begin{bmatrix} 1 & 0 \\ 0 & 1 \end{bmatrix} = \begin{bmatrix} a & b \\ c & d \end{bmatrix}$$

and

$$\begin{bmatrix} 1 & 0 \\ 0 & 1 \end{bmatrix} \begin{bmatrix} a & b \\ c & d \end{bmatrix} = \begin{bmatrix} a & b \\ c & d \end{bmatrix}$$

so that

$$AI = IA = A$$

for all 2×2 real matrices A.

(5) *Distributivity*   Multiplication of matrices is distributive over addition in the set of all 2×2 real matrices.   Again we shall not formally prove this statement but we shall check it in Example 2 and in the exercises.

Example 2.   Show that $A(B + C) = AB + AC$ for the matrices of Example 1.

Solution:

$$B + C = \begin{bmatrix} 1 & 1 \\ 3 & -2 \end{bmatrix} + \begin{bmatrix} 5 & 0 \\ -1 & 2 \end{bmatrix}$$

$$= \begin{bmatrix} 6 & 1 \\ 2 & 0 \end{bmatrix}.$$

$$A(B + C) = \begin{bmatrix} 1 & -3 \\ 2 & 4 \end{bmatrix} \begin{bmatrix} 6 & 1 \\ 2 & 0 \end{bmatrix}$$

$$= \begin{bmatrix} 0 & 1 \\ 20 & 2 \end{bmatrix}.$$

$$AB = \begin{bmatrix} 1 & -3 \\ 2 & 4 \end{bmatrix} \begin{bmatrix} 1 & 1 \\ 3 & -2 \end{bmatrix}$$

$$= \begin{bmatrix} -8 & 7 \\ 14 & -6 \end{bmatrix}.$$

$$AC = \begin{bmatrix} 1 & -3 \\ 2 & 4 \end{bmatrix} \begin{bmatrix} 5 & 0 \\ -1 & 2 \end{bmatrix}$$

$$= \begin{bmatrix} 8 & -6 \\ 6 & 8 \end{bmatrix}.$$

$$AB + AC = \begin{bmatrix} -8 & 7 \\ 14 & -6 \end{bmatrix} + \begin{bmatrix} 8 & -6 \\ 6 & 8 \end{bmatrix}$$

$$= \begin{bmatrix} 0 & 1 \\ 20 & 2 \end{bmatrix}.$$

Therefore,

$$A(B + C) = AB + AC$$

for these matrices A, B, and C.

(6) *Divisors of Zero*   We know that the product ab of two real numbers can equal zero if and only if at least one of a or b is zero. We say that the set of real numbers does not contain divisors of zero.   This is not true for the set of 2×2 real matrices. We recall that the zero matrix in this set is the matrix

$$O = \begin{bmatrix} 0 & 0 \\ 0 & 0 \end{bmatrix}.$$

This matrix is the additive identity in this set. It is possible to have $AB = O$ and yet neither A nor B be the zero matrix.   This is exemplified in Example 3. The set of 2×2 real matrices contains divisors of zero.

Example 3.   Find AB if

$$A = \begin{bmatrix} 2 & 3 \\ 4 & 6 \end{bmatrix} \quad \text{and} \quad B = \begin{bmatrix} -3 & 6 \\ 2 & -4 \end{bmatrix}.$$

Solution:

$$AB = \begin{bmatrix} 2 & 3 \\ 4 & 6 \end{bmatrix} \begin{bmatrix} -3 & 6 \\ 2 & -4 \end{bmatrix}$$

$$= \begin{bmatrix} 0 & 0 \\ 0 & 0 \end{bmatrix}$$

$$= O.$$

Note that $A \neq O$ and $B \neq O$.

EXERCISE 10.3

Find
(a) $A(BC)$,   (b) $(AB)C$,   (c) $A(B+C)$,   (d) $AB+AC$
for the following matrices A, B, and C.

1. $A = \begin{bmatrix} -1 & 1 \\ 5 & 2 \end{bmatrix}$, $B = \begin{bmatrix} 3 & -1 \\ -1 & 2 \end{bmatrix}$, $C = \begin{bmatrix} 3 & 1 \\ 0 & -2 \end{bmatrix}$

2. $A = \begin{bmatrix} 2 & -2 \\ 1 & 4 \end{bmatrix}$, $B = \begin{bmatrix} 3 & 1 \\ 4 & 1 \end{bmatrix}$, $C = \begin{bmatrix} 1 & 3 \\ 3 & 1 \end{bmatrix}$

3. $A = \begin{bmatrix} 5 & 3 \\ 3 & 2 \end{bmatrix}$, $B = \begin{bmatrix} 2 & -3 \\ -3 & 5 \end{bmatrix}$, $C = \begin{bmatrix} -1 & 0 \\ 5 & 2 \end{bmatrix}$

4. $A = \begin{bmatrix} 4 & 4 \\ -3 & 5 \end{bmatrix}$, $B = \begin{bmatrix} -3 & 5 \\ 2 & 1 \end{bmatrix}$, $C = \begin{bmatrix} 2 & 2 \\ 4 & 1 \end{bmatrix}$

5. If
$$A = \begin{bmatrix} 3 & 1 \\ -2 & 5 \end{bmatrix} \quad \text{and} \quad B = \begin{bmatrix} 5 & -3 \\ 2 & 1 \end{bmatrix},$$
   find
   (a) $A(AB)$,   (b) A^2B,   (c) $A(A+B)$,   (d) A^2+AB.

6. If
$$A = \begin{bmatrix} 5 & 0 \\ 2 & 0 \end{bmatrix},$$
   find a matrix $B \neq O$ such that $AB = O$.

7. If
$$A = \begin{bmatrix} 6 & -3 \\ 0 & 0 \end{bmatrix},$$
   find a matrix $B \neq O$ such that $AB = O$.

8. If
$$A = \begin{bmatrix} 4 & -2 \\ -2 & 1 \end{bmatrix},$$
   find a matrix $B \neq O$ such that $AB = O$.

9. If
$$A = \begin{bmatrix} a & 0 \\ 0 & b \end{bmatrix}, \quad B = \begin{bmatrix} c & 0 \\ 0 & d \end{bmatrix}, \quad \text{and} \quad C = \begin{bmatrix} e & 0 \\ 0 & f \end{bmatrix},$$
   where a, b, c, d, e, f are real numbers, prove that $A(BC) = (AB)C$.

10.4.   The Inverse of a Matrix

The identity matrix
$$I = \begin{bmatrix} 1 & 0 \\ 0 & 1 \end{bmatrix}$$

corresponds to the identity linear transformation

$$I \quad \begin{cases} u = x + 0y \\ v = 0x + y \end{cases},$$

the transformation that maps every point onto itself; that is,

$$I \begin{bmatrix} x \\ y \end{bmatrix} = \begin{bmatrix} x \\ y \end{bmatrix}.$$

Now if T is a linear transformation such that

$$T \begin{bmatrix} x \\ y \end{bmatrix} = \begin{bmatrix} u \\ v \end{bmatrix},$$

and if it is possible to find the inverse transformation T^{-1} such that

$$T^{-1} \begin{bmatrix} u \\ v \end{bmatrix} = \begin{bmatrix} x \\ y \end{bmatrix},$$

then the product $T^{-1}T$ is such that

$$T^{-1}T \begin{bmatrix} x \\ y \end{bmatrix} = T^{-1} \left(T \begin{bmatrix} x \\ y \end{bmatrix} \right) = T^{-1} \begin{bmatrix} u \\ v \end{bmatrix} = \begin{bmatrix} x \\ y \end{bmatrix};$$

that is,

$$T^{-1}T = I.$$

Similarly,

$$TT^{-1} \begin{bmatrix} u \\ v \end{bmatrix} = T \left(T^{-1} \begin{bmatrix} u \\ v \end{bmatrix} \right) = T \begin{bmatrix} x \\ y \end{bmatrix} = \begin{bmatrix} u \\ v \end{bmatrix},$$

so that again TT^{-1} is the identity linear transformation in the form

$$\begin{cases} x = u + 0v \\ y = 0u + v \end{cases}.$$

(Recall that we have already pointed out that the letters or variables or place-holders used are just dummies, so that the transformations

$$\begin{cases} u = x + 0y \\ v = 0x + y \end{cases} \quad \text{and} \quad \begin{cases} x = u + 0v \\ y = 0u + v \end{cases}$$

are essentially the same.)

If matrix T corresponds to transformation T and matrix S to transformation T^{-1}, then TS corresponds to TT^{-1} and ST to $T^{-1}T$ so that

$$TS = ST = I,$$

since I corresponds to the identity transformation.

S is the multiplicative inverse of T, and we use the symbol T^{-1} for this matrix. (Of course, T is also the inverse of S; $T = S^{-1}$.) Thus, a matrix will have an inverse if the corresponding linear transformation has an inverse.

Example 1.   Find the inverse of the matrix

$$T = \begin{bmatrix} 2 & -3 \\ 1 & 6 \end{bmatrix}.$$

Solution: Matrix T corresponds to the transformation

$$T \quad \begin{cases} u = 2x - 3y \\ v = x + 6y \end{cases}.$$

We may solve for x and y in terms of u and v and obtain the inverse transformation

$$T^{-1} \quad \begin{cases} x = \frac{2}{5}u + \frac{1}{5}v \\ y = -\frac{1}{15}u + \frac{2}{15}v \end{cases}.$$

According to our reasoning, the matrix

$$S = \begin{bmatrix} \frac{2}{5} & \frac{1}{5} \\ -\frac{1}{15} & \frac{2}{15} \end{bmatrix}$$

should be the inverse of T.   We check by multiplication.

$$TS = \begin{bmatrix} 2 & -3 \\ 1 & 6 \end{bmatrix} \begin{bmatrix} \frac{2}{5} & \frac{1}{5} \\ -\frac{1}{15} & \frac{2}{15} \end{bmatrix}$$

$$= \begin{bmatrix} 1 & 0 \\ 0 & 1 \end{bmatrix}$$

$$= I.$$

$$ST = \begin{bmatrix} \frac{2}{5} & \frac{1}{5} \\ -\frac{1}{15} & \frac{2}{15} \end{bmatrix} \begin{bmatrix} 2 & -3 \\ 1 & 6 \end{bmatrix}$$

$$= \begin{bmatrix} 1 & 0 \\ 0 & 1 \end{bmatrix}$$

$$= I.$$

Therefore, $S = T^{-1}$ by definition.

We may always find the inverse of a 2×2 real matrix by the method of Example 1, provided we can find the inverse of the corresponding transformation, and we have seen earlier that some transformations do not have inverses.   In the proof of the following theorem, we will apply the technique of Example 1 in general to see under what condition a 2×2 real matrix will have an inverse, and to see how to write the inverse immediately if it exists.

Theorem.   The matrix

$$T = \begin{bmatrix} a & b \\ c & d \end{bmatrix}$$

has an inverse

$$T^{-1} = \begin{bmatrix} \dfrac{d}{ad-bc} & \dfrac{-b}{ad-bc} \\ \dfrac{-c}{ad-bc} & \dfrac{a}{ad-bc} \end{bmatrix}$$

if and only if $ad - bc \neq 0$.

Proof: Matrix T corresponds to the transformation

$$T \quad \begin{cases} u = ax + by \\ v = cx + dy \end{cases}.$$

Then

$$cu = acx + bcy\,,$$
$$av = acx + ady\,,$$

and

$$av - cu = (ad - bc)\,y\,.$$

Also,

$$du = adx + bdy\,,$$
$$bv = bcx + bdy\,,$$

and

$$du - bv = (ad - bc)\,x\,.$$

Then

$$T^{-1} \quad \begin{cases} x = \dfrac{d}{ad-bc}\,u + \dfrac{-b}{ad-bc}\,v \\[2mm] y = \dfrac{-c}{ad-bc}\,u + \dfrac{a}{ad-bc}\,v \end{cases}$$

is the inverse transformation of T if and only if $ad - bc \neq 0$, as we saw in Section 9.6. We conclude that

$$T^{-1} = \begin{bmatrix} \dfrac{d}{ad-bc} & \dfrac{-b}{ad-bc} \\ \dfrac{-c}{ad-bc} & \dfrac{a}{ad-bc} \end{bmatrix}$$

is the inverse of T if and only if $ad - bc \neq 0$.

Check:

$$TT^{-1} = \begin{bmatrix} a & b \\ c & d \end{bmatrix} \begin{bmatrix} \dfrac{d}{ad-bc} & \dfrac{-b}{ad-bc} \\ \dfrac{-c}{ad-bc} & \dfrac{a}{ad-bc} \end{bmatrix}$$

$$= \begin{bmatrix} \dfrac{ad - bc}{ad - bc} & \dfrac{-ab + ab}{ad - bc} \\[2mm] \dfrac{cd - cd}{ad - bc} & \dfrac{-bc + ad}{ad - bc} \end{bmatrix} \qquad \text{(provided } ad - bc \neq 0)$$

$$= \begin{bmatrix} 1 & 0 \\ 0 & 1 \end{bmatrix}$$

$$= I \,.$$

The check that $T^{-1}T = I$ is left to the reader.   If $ad - bc = 0$, so that the matrix does not have an inverse, the matrix is said to be non-invertible; otherwise, the matrix is invertible.

Example 2.   Does the matrix

$$A = \begin{bmatrix} 5 & -4 \\ 1 & -2 \end{bmatrix}$$

have an inverse?   If so, find A^{-1}.

Solution: We note that for this matrix $ad - bc$ has the value $5\,(-2) - (-4)\,(1)$ $= -6$; hence, A^{-1} exists.   From our expression for A^{-1}, we see that

$$A^{-1} = \begin{bmatrix} \dfrac{-2}{-6} & \dfrac{4}{-6} \\[2mm] \dfrac{-1}{-6} & \dfrac{5}{-6} \end{bmatrix}$$

$$= \begin{bmatrix} \dfrac{1}{3} & \dfrac{-2}{3} \\[2mm] \dfrac{1}{6} & \dfrac{-5}{6} \end{bmatrix}.$$

Check:

$$AA^{-1} = \begin{bmatrix} 5 & -4 \\ 1 & -2 \end{bmatrix} \begin{bmatrix} \dfrac{1}{3} & \dfrac{-2}{3} \\[2mm] \dfrac{1}{6} & \dfrac{-5}{6} \end{bmatrix}$$

$$= \begin{bmatrix} 1 & 0 \\ 0 & 1 \end{bmatrix}$$

$$= I \,.$$

Thus, A^{-1} is the required inverse.

Example 3.   Find the inverse of the matrix

$$B = \begin{bmatrix} -1 & 4 \\ 2 & -8 \end{bmatrix}.$$

Solution: $ad - bc$ has the value $(-1)\,(-8) - (4)\,(2) = 0$.   This matrix does not have an inverse. B is a non-invertible matrix.

The technique used in the proof of the theorem of this section, that is, in the attempt to find the inverse of a linear transformation, may be used in general to determine under what conditions a given $m \times n$ matrix has an inverse.

EXERCISE 10.4

In questions (1) to (4), find the inverse of the corresponding linear transformation (as in Example 1) in order to find the inverse of the given matrix.

1. $\begin{bmatrix} 4 & -1 \\ -1 & 4 \end{bmatrix}$ 2. $\begin{bmatrix} -3 & 1 \\ 5 & 0 \end{bmatrix}$ 3. $\begin{bmatrix} 2 & 2 \\ -1 & 3 \end{bmatrix}$ 4. $\begin{bmatrix} 2 & -5 \\ 1 & 2 \end{bmatrix}$

Determine which of the following matrices have inverses and find the inverse when it exists.

5. $\begin{bmatrix} -1 & 3 \\ 5 & -15 \end{bmatrix}$ 6. $\begin{bmatrix} -1 & 3 \\ -15 & 5 \end{bmatrix}$ 7. $\begin{bmatrix} 1 & -3 \\ -15 & 5 \end{bmatrix}$ 8. $\begin{bmatrix} 1 & -3 \\ -5 & 15 \end{bmatrix}$

9. $\begin{bmatrix} 2 & 2 \\ -1 & 0 \end{bmatrix}$ 10. $\begin{bmatrix} 3 & 0 \\ 4 & 1 \end{bmatrix}$ 11. $\begin{bmatrix} 5 & 0 \\ 0 & 1 \end{bmatrix}$ 12. $\begin{bmatrix} 0 & 4 \\ -3 & 0 \end{bmatrix}$

13. $\begin{bmatrix} 5 & 0 \\ 0 & 0 \end{bmatrix}$ 14. $\begin{bmatrix} 1 & 1 \\ 1 & 1 \end{bmatrix}$ 15. $\begin{bmatrix} 1 & 1 \\ -1 & 1 \end{bmatrix}$ 16. $\begin{bmatrix} 4 & \frac{1}{2} \\ \frac{1}{3} & 1 \end{bmatrix}$

17. If a and d are nonzero, find the inverse of $\begin{bmatrix} a & 0 \\ 0 & d \end{bmatrix}$.

18. If b and c are nonzero, find the inverse of $\begin{bmatrix} 0 & b \\ c & 0 \end{bmatrix}$.

19. If $A = \begin{bmatrix} 1 & 1 \\ -2 & 4 \end{bmatrix}$ and $B = \begin{bmatrix} 3 & 2 \\ -1 & 4 \end{bmatrix}$,   find

    (a) AB (b) $(AB)^{-1}$ (c) A^{-1} (d) B^{-1}

    and check that $(AB)^{-1} = B^{-1}A^{-1}$ for these matrices.

20. If A, B, and AB all have inverses, prove that
$$(AB)^{-1} = B^{-1}A^{-1}.$$

10.5. The Linear Matrix Equation $AX = B$

We have mentioned earlier that a matrix may contain any number of rows and columns, and that one-rowed matrices, such as

$$[3 \quad 5], \quad [4 \quad 0 \quad -3], \quad [5 \quad 0 \quad 0 \quad 4],$$

are also called row vectors, and one-columned matrices, such as,

$$\begin{bmatrix} 2 \\ -3 \end{bmatrix}, \quad \begin{bmatrix} 5 \\ 3 \\ -1 \end{bmatrix}, \quad \begin{bmatrix} 4 \\ 2 \\ 0 \\ 1 \end{bmatrix},$$

are also called column vectors. Thus a row vector is a $1 \times n$ matrix and a column vector is an $m \times 1$ matrix.

In defining multiplication of matrices, we pointed out that the product AB of two matrices A and B could always be found if our technique of "applying columns of the right matrix to rows of the left matrix and multiplying corresponding elements" could be used. This definition implied certain restrictions on the dimensions of A and B.

Example 1. Find AB if

$$A = \begin{bmatrix} 5 & -1 \\ 3 & 2 \end{bmatrix} \quad \text{and} \quad B = \begin{bmatrix} 4 \\ -3 \end{bmatrix}.$$

Solution: By our technique for multiplying matrices,

$$AB = \begin{matrix} \boxed{\begin{matrix} 4 & -3 \end{matrix}} \\ \begin{bmatrix} 5 & -1 \\ 3 & 2 \end{bmatrix} \end{matrix} \begin{bmatrix} 4 \\ -3 \end{bmatrix} = \begin{bmatrix} 4(5) + (-3)(-1) \\ 4(3) + (-3)(2) \end{bmatrix} = \begin{bmatrix} 23 \\ 6 \end{bmatrix}.$$

Example 2. Find BA in Example 1.

Solution:

$$BA = \begin{bmatrix} 4 \\ -3 \end{bmatrix} \begin{bmatrix} 5 & -1 \\ 3 & 2 \end{bmatrix},$$

If we apply our multiplication technique, we arrive at the following.

The elements of a column of A do not pair off with the elements of a row of B; hence, the product BA does not exist.

Example 3. Find AX if

$$A = \begin{bmatrix} 5 & -1 \\ 3 & 2 \end{bmatrix} \quad \text{and} \quad X = \begin{bmatrix} x_1 \\ x_2 \end{bmatrix}.$$

Solution:

$$AX = \begin{bmatrix} 5 & -1 \\ 3 & 2 \end{bmatrix} \begin{bmatrix} x_1 \\ x_2 \end{bmatrix} = \begin{bmatrix} 5x_1 - x_2 \\ 3x_1 + 2x_2 \end{bmatrix}.$$

Example 4. Under what conditions will

$$\begin{bmatrix} 5x_1 - x_2 \\ 3x_1 + 2x_2 \end{bmatrix} = \begin{bmatrix} 4 \\ -7 \end{bmatrix}?$$

Solution: We know that two matrices are equal if and only if they have the same dimensions and corresponding components are equal.   These matrices are both 2×1 matrices and so are equal if and only if

$$5x_1 - x_2 = 4$$

and

$$3x_1 + 2x_2 = -7 \,.$$

We see now from the results of Examples 3 and 4 that the system of equations

$$5x_1 - x_2 = 4$$
$$3x_1 + 2x_2 = -7$$

is equivalent to the single linear matrix equation $AX = B$ with

$$A = \begin{bmatrix} 5 & -1 \\ 3 & 2 \end{bmatrix}, \qquad X = \begin{bmatrix} x_1 \\ x_2 \end{bmatrix}, \qquad \text{and} \qquad B = \begin{bmatrix} 4 \\ -7 \end{bmatrix};$$

that is,

$$\begin{bmatrix} 5 & -1 \\ 3 & 2 \end{bmatrix} \begin{bmatrix} x_1 \\ x_2 \end{bmatrix} = \begin{bmatrix} 4 \\ -7 \end{bmatrix}.$$

This result can be generalized; a system of linear equations can always be replaced by a single linear matrix equation.

Example 5.   Replace the system of equations

$$3x_1 - 7x_2 = 5$$
$$x_1 + 5x_2 = -3$$

by a single linear matrix equation.

Solution: Choose matrix A as the matrix of coefficients

$$A = \begin{bmatrix} 3 & -7 \\ 1 & 5 \end{bmatrix}.$$

Then

$$AX = \begin{bmatrix} 3 & -7 \\ 1 & 5 \end{bmatrix} \begin{bmatrix} x_1 \\ x_2 \end{bmatrix} = \begin{bmatrix} 3x_1 - 7x_2 \\ x_1 + 5x_2 \end{bmatrix},$$

so that the given system may be written as $AX = B$ with

$$A = \begin{bmatrix} 3 & -7 \\ 1 & 5 \end{bmatrix}, \qquad X = \begin{bmatrix} x_1 \\ x_2 \end{bmatrix}, \qquad \text{and} \qquad B = \begin{bmatrix} 5 \\ -3 \end{bmatrix};$$

that is,

$$\begin{bmatrix} 3 & -7 \\ 1 & 5 \end{bmatrix} \begin{bmatrix} x_1 \\ x_2 \end{bmatrix} = \begin{bmatrix} 5 \\ -3 \end{bmatrix}.$$

EXERCISE 10.5

1. Find the products of the following pairs of matrices.

(a) $\begin{bmatrix} -1 & 5 \\ 2 & 4 \end{bmatrix}$, $\begin{bmatrix} 3 \\ 4 \end{bmatrix}$ (b) $\begin{bmatrix} 5 & -1 \\ 3 & 2 \end{bmatrix}$, $\begin{bmatrix} 6 \\ -1 \end{bmatrix}$

(c) $\begin{bmatrix} 3 & 5 \\ -1 & 0 \end{bmatrix}$, $\begin{bmatrix} 2 \\ 7 \end{bmatrix}$ (d) $\begin{bmatrix} 5 & -1 \\ 3 & 2 \end{bmatrix}$, $\begin{bmatrix} 3 \\ 3 \end{bmatrix}$

(e) $\begin{bmatrix} 0 & -1 \\ 1 & 5 \end{bmatrix}$, $\begin{bmatrix} 3 \\ 2 \end{bmatrix}$ (f) $\begin{bmatrix} 0 & -1 \\ -1 & 0 \end{bmatrix}$, $\begin{bmatrix} 4 \\ 5 \end{bmatrix}$

(g) $\begin{bmatrix} 5 & 3 \\ -1 & 4 \end{bmatrix}$, $\begin{bmatrix} a \\ b \end{bmatrix}$ (h) $\begin{bmatrix} 3 & 2 \\ -2 & 3 \end{bmatrix}$, $\begin{bmatrix} x \\ y \end{bmatrix}$

(i) $\begin{bmatrix} 4 & 0 \\ -1 & 3 \end{bmatrix}$, $\begin{bmatrix} s \\ t \end{bmatrix}$ (j) $\begin{bmatrix} 6 & -1 \\ 4 & 5 \end{bmatrix}$, $\begin{bmatrix} m \\ n \end{bmatrix}$

2. Write the following systems of equations as single linear matrix equations.

(a) $6x_1 - x_2 = 3$
     $x_1 + 4x_2 = 5$

(b) $2x + 5y = 6$
     $x - 4y = -3$

(c) $3a + 2b = 5$
     $a - 6b = -2$

(d) $2m - 7n = 0$
     $5m + n = -3$

(e) $4r - s = 0$
     $r + 3s = 0$

(f) $5u - 2v = -1$
     $2u + 3v = 5$

3. For what values of k will $AU = V$ if

(a) $A = \begin{bmatrix} -3 & k \\ 2 & 4 \end{bmatrix}$, $U = \begin{bmatrix} 1 \\ 1 \end{bmatrix}$, $V = \begin{bmatrix} -5 \\ 6 \end{bmatrix}$?

(b) $A = \begin{bmatrix} 2 & 5 \\ -k & 2 \end{bmatrix}$, $U = \begin{bmatrix} 1 \\ 1 \end{bmatrix}$, $V = \begin{bmatrix} -5 \\ 0 \end{bmatrix}$?

(c) $A = \begin{bmatrix} 4 & 3k \\ -k & 5 \end{bmatrix}$, $U = \begin{bmatrix} 2 \\ 1 \end{bmatrix}$, $V = \begin{bmatrix} -1 \\ 11 \end{bmatrix}$?

4. If

$$A = \begin{bmatrix} 4 & 7 \\ -1 & 3 \end{bmatrix} \quad \text{and} \quad W = [1 \;\; 4],$$

find, if possible, the products WA and AW.

10.6. The Solution of AX = B

In this section, we consider the linear matrix equation $AX = B$. We show that this equation has a (unique) solution if the matrix A is invertible (has an inverse). Thus the linear matrix equation $AX = B$ compares with the real linear equation $ax = b$ $(a, b \in Re)$ which has a unique solution if a^{-1} exists.

Example 1.   Express the system of equations

$$3x_1 - x_2 = 5$$
$$2x_1 + 6x_2 = -3$$

as a linear matrix equation.

Solution: We may write this system as $AX = B$ with

$$A = \begin{bmatrix} 3 & -1 \\ 2 & 6 \end{bmatrix}, \qquad X = \begin{bmatrix} x_1 \\ x_2 \end{bmatrix}, \qquad \text{and} \qquad B = \begin{bmatrix} 5 \\ -3 \end{bmatrix},$$

that is,

$$\begin{bmatrix} 3 & -1 \\ 2 & 6 \end{bmatrix}\begin{bmatrix} x_1 \\ x_2 \end{bmatrix} = \begin{bmatrix} 5 \\ -3 \end{bmatrix}.$$

Example 2.   Find A^{-1} for the matrix A of Example 1.

Solution: $ad - bc$ has the value $3(6) - (-1)(2) = 20$; therefore A^{-1} exists.   We find that

$$A^{-1} = \begin{bmatrix} \frac{3}{10} & \frac{1}{20} \\ -\frac{1}{10} & \frac{3}{20} \end{bmatrix}.$$

Example 3.   Multiply both sides of the matrix equation in Example 1 *on the left* by A^{-1} from Example 2, and solve the resulting expression for x_1 and x_2.

Solution:

$$\begin{bmatrix} \frac{3}{10} & \frac{1}{20} \\ -\frac{1}{10} & \frac{3}{20} \end{bmatrix}\left(\begin{bmatrix} 3 & -1 \\ 2 & 6 \end{bmatrix}\begin{bmatrix} x_1 \\ x_2 \end{bmatrix}\right) = \begin{bmatrix} \frac{3}{10} & \frac{1}{20} \\ -\frac{1}{10} & \frac{3}{20} \end{bmatrix}\begin{bmatrix} 5 \\ -3 \end{bmatrix}.$$

Multiplication of matrices is associative, and so we may write

$$\left(\begin{bmatrix} \frac{3}{10} & \frac{1}{20} \\ -\frac{1}{10} & \frac{3}{20} \end{bmatrix}\begin{bmatrix} 3 & -1 \\ 2 & 6 \end{bmatrix}\right)\begin{bmatrix} x_1 \\ x_2 \end{bmatrix} = \begin{bmatrix} \frac{3}{10} & \frac{1}{20} \\ -\frac{1}{10} & \frac{3}{20} \end{bmatrix}\begin{bmatrix} 5 \\ -3 \end{bmatrix}.$$

The product matrix in parentheses is I (why?), and we have

$$\begin{bmatrix} 1 & 0 \\ 0 & 1 \end{bmatrix}\begin{bmatrix} x_1 \\ x_2 \end{bmatrix} = \begin{bmatrix} \frac{27}{20} \\ \frac{-19}{20} \end{bmatrix};$$

$$\begin{bmatrix} x_1 \\ x_2 \end{bmatrix} = \begin{bmatrix} \frac{27}{20} \\ \frac{-19}{20} \end{bmatrix},$$

and so $x_1 = \frac{27}{20}$ and $x_2 = \frac{-19}{20}$ (why?).   Thus

$$\left\{\left(\frac{27}{20}, \frac{-19}{20}\right)\right\}$$

is the solution set of the system of equations in Example 1.

The above examples show how a system of linear equations can be solved if the corresponding linear matrix equation $AX = B$ can be solved.

Theorem.   The linear matrix equation $AX = B$ can be solved if A^{-1} exists.

Proof: Suppose $AX = B$ and A^{-1} exists.   Then

$$A^{-1}(AX) = A^{-1}B.$$
$$(A^{-1}A)X = A^{-1}B.$$
$$IX = A^{-1}B.$$
$$X = A^{-1}B.$$

Thus $A^{-1}B$ is the solution of $AX = B$.

Check:

$$A(A^{-1}B) = (AA^{-1})B = IB = B.$$

Note that in the proof of the theorem, we were careful to multiply both members of the equation $AX = B$ *on the left* by A^{-1} to obtain $A^{-1}(AX) = A^{-1}B$. Remember that multiplication of matrices is not necessarily commutative so that if $A = B$, then $AC = BC$, but $AC \neq CB$ necessarily.

Example 4.   Use the method of this section to solve the system of equations

$$3x_1 + 5x_2 = 4,$$
$$2x_1 - x_2 = 0.$$

Solution: We write the system in the form $AX = B$.

$$\begin{bmatrix} 3 & 5 \\ 2 & -1 \end{bmatrix} \begin{bmatrix} x_1 \\ x_2 \end{bmatrix} = \begin{bmatrix} 4 \\ 0 \end{bmatrix},$$

and find

$$A^{-1} = \begin{bmatrix} \frac{1}{13} & \frac{5}{13} \\ \frac{2}{13} & \frac{-3}{13} \end{bmatrix}.$$

Then

$$\begin{bmatrix} \frac{1}{13} & \frac{5}{13} \\ \frac{2}{13} & \frac{-3}{13} \end{bmatrix} \begin{bmatrix} 3 & 5 \\ 2 & -1 \end{bmatrix} \begin{bmatrix} x_1 \\ x_2 \end{bmatrix} = \begin{bmatrix} \frac{1}{13} & \frac{5}{13} \\ \frac{2}{13} & \frac{-3}{13} \end{bmatrix} \begin{bmatrix} 4 \\ 0 \end{bmatrix}$$

and

$$\begin{bmatrix} x_1 \\ x_2 \end{bmatrix} = \begin{bmatrix} \frac{4}{13} \\ \frac{8}{13} \end{bmatrix},$$

so that $\{(\frac{4}{13}, \frac{8}{13})\}$ is the required solution.

Example 5.   Solve the system of equations

$$2x_1 - x_2 = 5,$$
$$-4x_1 + 2x_2 = -3.$$

Solution: If we write this system in the form $AX = B$ with

$$A = \begin{bmatrix} 2 & -1 \\ -4 & 2 \end{bmatrix},$$

we find that A^{-1} does not exist.   ($ad - bc$ has value 0.)   Hence, we cannot use the present method to solve this system.   We find, using other reasoning, that this system does not have a solution.

EXERCISE 10.6

Express the following systems of equations as linear matrix equations of the form $AX = B$, and solve the system if A^{-1} exists.

1. $3x_1 - 5x_2 = 3$
    $2x_1 + x_2 = 5$

2. $4x - y = 6$
    $x - 2y = -1$

3. $5a - 2b = -3$
    $2a + b = 4$

4. $3x_1 - x_2 = 7$
    $-12x_1 + 4x_2 = -3$

5. $3x_1 - x_2 = 7$
    $-12x_1 - 4x_2 = -3$

6. $4a + b = 0$
    $2a - b = -6$

7. $m + 5n = 6$
    $3m - 2n = -4$

8. $5s - 6t = 4$
    $3s - t = 0$

9. $6w - z = 2$
    $3w + 2z = 5$

10. $4a + 3b = m$
    $5a - 2b = n$

11. Show that the solution of $AX = B$ is unique if A^{-1} exists.

10.7.   An Alternate Method for Finding A⁻¹

The system of equations

$$3x - y = u$$
$$2x + 5y = v$$ (1)

can be written as the single linear matrix equation

$$\begin{bmatrix} 3 & -1 \\ 2 & 5 \end{bmatrix} \begin{bmatrix} x \\ y \end{bmatrix} = \begin{bmatrix} u \\ v \end{bmatrix},$$

and, indeed, in the form

$$\begin{bmatrix} 3 & -1 \\ 2 & 5 \end{bmatrix} \begin{bmatrix} x \\ y \end{bmatrix} = \begin{bmatrix} 1 & 0 \\ 0 & 1 \end{bmatrix} \begin{bmatrix} u \\ v \end{bmatrix}.$$ (2)

We shall illustrate in the following examples a general result which will enable us to establish an algorithm for finding the inverse of an invertible matrix.

Example 1. Interchange the equations of system (1) and write the resulting system as a single linear matrix equation as in (2).

Solution: If we interchange equations in (1), we obtain the following equivalent system.

$$2x + 5y = v \ .$$
$$3x - y = u \ .$$

The reader is asked to check that this system can be written as the single linear matrix equation

$$\begin{bmatrix} 2 & 5 \\ 3 & -1 \end{bmatrix} \begin{bmatrix} x \\ y \end{bmatrix} = \begin{bmatrix} 0 & 1 \\ 1 & 0 \end{bmatrix} \begin{bmatrix} u \\ v \end{bmatrix}.$$

Example 2. Multiply the second equation of system (1) by k, and write the resulting system as a single linear matrix equation as in (2).

Solution: If we multiply the second equation of (1) by k, we obtain the following equivalent system.

$$3x - y = u \ .$$
$$2kx + 5ky = kv \ .$$

The reader is asked to check that this system can be written as the single linear matrix equation

$$\begin{bmatrix} 3 & -1 \\ 2k & 5k \end{bmatrix} \begin{bmatrix} x \\ y \end{bmatrix} = \begin{bmatrix} 1 & 0 \\ 0 & k \end{bmatrix} \begin{bmatrix} u \\ v \end{bmatrix}.$$

Example 3. Add k times the first equation to the second equation in (1), and write the resulting system as a single linear matrix equation.

Solution: The resulting system is

$$3x - y = u$$
$$(2 + 3k)x + (5 - k)y = v + ku$$

The reader is asked to check that this system can be written as the single linear equation

$$\begin{bmatrix} 3 & -1 \\ 2 + 3k & 5 + (-1)k \end{bmatrix} \begin{bmatrix} x \\ y \end{bmatrix} = \begin{bmatrix} 1 & 0 \\ k & 1 \end{bmatrix} \begin{bmatrix} u \\ v \end{bmatrix}.$$

The examples above illustrate the following result. Any elementary row operation on a system of equations

$$ax + by = u$$
$$cx + dy = v \tag{3}$$

is performed simultaneously on the matrices of coefficients in the corresponding linear matrix equation

$$\begin{bmatrix} a & b \\ c & d \end{bmatrix}\begin{bmatrix} x \\ y \end{bmatrix} = \begin{bmatrix} 1 & 0 \\ 0 & 1 \end{bmatrix}\begin{bmatrix} u \\ v \end{bmatrix}. \tag{4}$$

Now perform, if possible, a sequence of elementary row operations on (3) so that (4) assumes the form

$$\begin{bmatrix} 1 & 0 \\ 0 & 1 \end{bmatrix}\begin{bmatrix} x \\ y \end{bmatrix} = \begin{bmatrix} e & f \\ g & h \end{bmatrix}\begin{bmatrix} u \\ v \end{bmatrix};$$

this corresponds to the system

$$\begin{aligned} x &= eu + fv \\ y &= gu + hv \end{aligned},$$

and so we will have inverted the system (3) and thus will have found the inverse of the original matrix.

$$\begin{bmatrix} a & b \\ c & d \end{bmatrix}^{-1} = \begin{bmatrix} e & f \\ g & h \end{bmatrix}.$$

This gives us the following rule.

Rule for Finding the Inverse of a Matrix

Let A be the matrix

$$A = \begin{bmatrix} a & b \\ c & d \end{bmatrix}.$$

Form the matrix

$$B = \begin{bmatrix} a & b & 1 & 0 \\ c & d & 0 & 1 \end{bmatrix}$$

by adjoining the matrices of coefficients in (4). Perform a sequence of row operations on B to obtain the following equivalent matrix.

$$C = \begin{bmatrix} 1 & 0 & e & f \\ 0 & 1 & g & h \end{bmatrix}.$$

Then

$$\begin{bmatrix} e & f \\ g & h \end{bmatrix} = A^{-1}.$$

It should be pointed out that an equivalent matrix of the form C is possible only when A has an inverse.

The reader should note carefully how this rule follows from the preceding discussion.

Example 4. Find the inverse of the matrix

$$A = \begin{bmatrix} 3 & -1 \\ 2 & 5 \end{bmatrix}.$$

Solution: Consider the matrix

$$B = \begin{bmatrix} 3 & -1 & 1 & 0 \\ 2 & 5 & 0 & 1 \end{bmatrix}.$$

We perform the following sequence of elementary row operations. (Note that such a sequence is not unique; there will be many possible sequences.)

$$B = \begin{bmatrix} 3 & -1 & 1 & 0 \\ 2 & 5 & 0 & 1 \end{bmatrix} \xrightarrow{\text{Add } (-1) \times \text{row (2) to row (1).}} \begin{bmatrix} 1 & -6 & 1 & -1 \\ 2 & 5 & 0 & 1 \end{bmatrix}$$

$$\xrightarrow{\text{Add } (-2) \times \text{row (1) to row (2).}} \begin{bmatrix} 1 & -6 & 1 & -1 \\ 0 & 17 & -2 & 3 \end{bmatrix}$$

$$\xrightarrow{\text{Multiply row (2) by } \frac{1}{17}.} \begin{bmatrix} 1 & -6 & 1 & -1 \\ 0 & 1 & \frac{-2}{17} & \frac{3}{17} \end{bmatrix}$$

$$\xrightarrow{\text{Add } 6 \times \text{row (2) to row (1).}} \begin{bmatrix} 1 & 0 & \frac{5}{17} & \frac{1}{17} \\ 0 & 1 & \frac{-2}{17} & \frac{3}{17} \end{bmatrix}$$

We conclude that

$$A^{-1} = \begin{bmatrix} \frac{5}{17} & \frac{1}{17} \\ \frac{-2}{17} & \frac{3}{17} \end{bmatrix}.$$

Check:

$$\begin{bmatrix} 3 & -1 \\ 2 & 5 \end{bmatrix}\begin{bmatrix} \frac{5}{17} & \frac{1}{17} \\ \frac{-2}{17} & \frac{3}{17} \end{bmatrix} = \begin{bmatrix} 1 & 0 \\ 0 & 1 \end{bmatrix}.$$

Example 5. Find the inverse of the matrix

$$A = \begin{bmatrix} 2 & -3 \\ -6 & 9 \end{bmatrix}.$$

Solution:

$$B = \begin{bmatrix} 2 & -3 & 1 & 0 \\ -6 & 9 & 0 & 1 \end{bmatrix} \xrightarrow{\text{Add } 3 \times \text{row (1) to row (2).}} \begin{bmatrix} 2 & -3 & 1 & 0 \\ 0 & 0 & 3 & 1 \end{bmatrix}$$

Now there is no sequence of row operations that will change the first two columns of this matrix into the desired form. We conclude that matrix A does not have an inverse. (Of course, we would recognize this immediately by checking that $ad - bc$ has the value $2(9) - (-3)(-6) = 0$ for this matrix.)

EXERCISE 10.7

Use the method of Section 10.7 to find inverses for the following matrices, where possible.

1. $\begin{bmatrix} 1 & 3 \\ 5 & 7 \end{bmatrix}$

2. $\begin{bmatrix} 0 & 1 \\ 2 & 3 \end{bmatrix}$

3. $\begin{bmatrix} 0 & 3 \\ 0 & -2 \end{bmatrix}$

4. $\begin{bmatrix} 3 & -6 \\ 1 & 4 \end{bmatrix}$

5. $\begin{bmatrix} 3 & -6 \\ 1 & 2 \end{bmatrix}$

6. $\begin{bmatrix} 3 & -6 \\ 1 & -2 \end{bmatrix}$

7. $\begin{bmatrix} \frac{1}{2} & \frac{1}{4} \\ -\frac{1}{4} & \frac{1}{2} \end{bmatrix}$

8. $\begin{bmatrix} -3 & 5 \\ -2 & 3 \end{bmatrix}$

9. $\begin{bmatrix} 6 & 0 \\ -3 & 2 \end{bmatrix}$

10.8.   The Function $x \longrightarrow Ax$

If A is a 2×2 matrix and $\mathbf{x}$ is a 2×1 matrix (a column vector with two entries), then the mapping

$$\mathbf{x} \rightarrow A\mathbf{x}$$

is a function whose domain is the set of all ordered pairs of real numbers written as column vectors.   The range is either this same set or a subset thereof.

From the definition of matrix multiplication, we know that, for given A and given $\mathbf{x}$, the product matrix $A\mathbf{x}$ is a unique column vector.   In the mapping $\mathbf{x} \rightarrow A\mathbf{x}$, there is a unique column vector $A\mathbf{x}$ corresponding to each column vector $\mathbf{x}$, and so this mapping is indeed a function.

Example 1.   State the domain and range of the function $\mathbf{x} \rightarrow A\mathbf{x}$ if

$$A = \begin{bmatrix} 3 & -1 \\ 2 & 1 \end{bmatrix}.$$

Solution: Let $A\mathbf{x} = \mathbf{y}$ with

$$\mathbf{x} = \begin{bmatrix} x_1 \\ x_2 \end{bmatrix} \quad \text{and} \quad \mathbf{y} = \begin{bmatrix} y_1 \\ y_2 \end{bmatrix}.$$

Then

$$\begin{bmatrix} y_1 \\ y_2 \end{bmatrix} = \begin{bmatrix} 3 & -1 \\ 2 & 1 \end{bmatrix}\begin{bmatrix} x_1 \\ x_2 \end{bmatrix} = \begin{bmatrix} 3x_1 - x_2 \\ 2x_1 + x_2 \end{bmatrix}$$

corresponds to the system of equations, that is, to the transformation

$$A \quad \begin{cases} y_1 = 3x_1 - x_2 \\ y_2 = 2x_1 + x_2 \end{cases}.$$

We now know that this transformation, and its corresponding matrix, have inverses if and only if $ad - bc \neq 0$. In this case, $ad - bc$ has the value $3(1) - (-1)(2) = 5$;

hence, the transformation A does have an inverse. Again, we know that this means that A is a one-to-one mapping of the set of ordered pairs (x_1, x_2) onto the set of ordered pairs (y_1, y_2), or a one-to-one mapping of the set of column vectors $\begin{bmatrix} x_1 \\ x_2 \end{bmatrix}$ onto the set of column vectors $\begin{bmatrix} y_1 \\ y_2 \end{bmatrix}$. Thus

$$\mathbf{x} \rightarrow A\mathbf{x} = \mathbf{y}$$

is a function with domain and range the set

$$\left\{ \begin{bmatrix} a \\ b \end{bmatrix} \mid a, \, b \in Re \right\},$$

that is, the set of all column vectors with two real components.

We have used the symbol V_2 to refer to the set of all row vectors with two components. We will use the symbol V_2' to refer to the set of all column vectors with two components;

$$V_2' = \left\{ \begin{bmatrix} a \\ b \end{bmatrix} \mid a, \, b \in Re \right\}.$$

Thus, in Example 1, V_2' is both the domain and the range of the function $\mathbf{x} \rightarrow A\mathbf{x}$.

Example 2.   Find the domain and range of the function $\mathbf{x} \rightarrow B\mathbf{x}$ if

$$B = \begin{bmatrix} 3 & -1 \\ -6 & 2 \end{bmatrix}.$$

Solution: Let $B\mathbf{x} = \mathbf{y}$ as in Example 1. Then $B\mathbf{x} = \mathbf{y}$ corresponds to the transformation

$$B \quad \begin{cases} y_1 = 3x_1 - x_2 \\ y_2 = -6x_1 + 2x_2 \end{cases}.$$

Neither the transformation B nor the corresponding matrix has an inverse, since $ad - bc$ has value 0. B is a mapping of the set V_2' *into itself.* Indeed, the image vectors, that is, the elements of the domain, will all be of the form

$$\begin{bmatrix} a \\ b \end{bmatrix}$$

with $b = -2a$.

The domain of the function $\mathbf{x} \rightarrow B\mathbf{x}$ is V_2' and the range is the subset

$$\left\{ \begin{bmatrix} a \\ b \end{bmatrix} \mid a, \, b \in Re, \, b = -2a \right\}$$

of V_2'.

Example 3. Show that $A(2\mathbf{x}) = 2A\mathbf{x}$, if

$$A = \begin{bmatrix} 4 & 3 \\ -1 & 2 \end{bmatrix} \quad \text{and} \quad \mathbf{x} = \begin{bmatrix} x_1 \\ x_2 \end{bmatrix}.$$

Solution:

$$2\mathbf{x} = 2\begin{bmatrix} x_1 \\ x_2 \end{bmatrix} = \begin{bmatrix} 2x_1 \\ 2x_2 \end{bmatrix}.$$

Hence

$$A(2\mathbf{x}) = \begin{bmatrix} 4 & 3 \\ -1 & 2 \end{bmatrix}\begin{bmatrix} 2x_1 \\ 2x_2 \end{bmatrix}$$

$$\begin{bmatrix} 8x_1 + 6x_2 \\ -2x_1 + 4x_2 \end{bmatrix}$$

$$= 2\begin{bmatrix} 4x_1 + 3x_2 \\ -x_1 + 2x_2 \end{bmatrix}$$

$$= 2\begin{bmatrix} 4 & 3 \\ -1 & 2 \end{bmatrix}\begin{bmatrix} x_1 \\ x_2 \end{bmatrix}$$

$$= 2A\mathbf{x}.$$

This result is true in general.   Restricting our attention to 2×2 real matrices A, we may say that

$$A(k\mathbf{x}) = kA\mathbf{x} \quad \text{if } k \in Re \text{ and } \mathbf{x} \in V_2'.$$

Example 4. Show that $A(\mathbf{x} + \mathbf{y}) = A\mathbf{x} + A\mathbf{y}$ if

$$A = \begin{bmatrix} 4 & 3 \\ -1 & 2 \end{bmatrix}, \quad \mathbf{x} = \begin{bmatrix} x_1 \\ x_2 \end{bmatrix}, \quad \mathbf{y} = \begin{bmatrix} y_1 \\ y_2 \end{bmatrix}.$$

Solution:

$$\mathbf{x} + \mathbf{y} = \begin{bmatrix} x_1 \\ x_2 \end{bmatrix} + \begin{bmatrix} y_1 \\ y_2 \end{bmatrix} = \begin{bmatrix} x_1 + y_1 \\ x_2 + y_2 \end{bmatrix}.$$

Hence,

$$A(\mathbf{x} + \mathbf{y}) = \begin{bmatrix} 4 & 3 \\ -1 & 2 \end{bmatrix}\begin{bmatrix} x_1 + y_1 \\ x_2 + y_2 \end{bmatrix}$$

$$= \begin{bmatrix} 4(x_1 + y_1) + 3(x_2 + y_2) \\ -(x_1 + y_1) + 2(x_2 + y_2) \end{bmatrix}$$

$$= \begin{bmatrix} (4x_1 + 3x_2) + (4y_1 + 3y_2) \\ (-x_1 + 2x_2) + (-y_1 + 2y_2) \end{bmatrix}$$

$$= \begin{bmatrix} 4x_1 + 3x_2 \\ -x_1 + 2x_2 \end{bmatrix} + \begin{bmatrix} 4y_1 + 3y_2 \\ -y_1 + 2y_2 \end{bmatrix}$$

$$= \begin{bmatrix} 4 & 3 \\ -1 & 2 \end{bmatrix}\begin{bmatrix} x_1 \\ x_2 \end{bmatrix} + \begin{bmatrix} 4 & 3 \\ -1 & 2 \end{bmatrix}\begin{bmatrix} y_1 \\ y_2 \end{bmatrix}$$

$$= A\mathbf{x} + A\mathbf{y}.$$

This result is also true in general.   Again restricting our attention to real matrices A, we may say that

$$A(\mathbf{x} + \mathbf{y}) = A\mathbf{x} + A\mathbf{y} \quad \text{if } \mathbf{x}, \mathbf{y} \in V_2'.$$

The properties

(i) $A(k\mathbf{x}) = kA\mathbf{x}$

(ii) $A(\mathbf{x} + \mathbf{y}) = A\mathbf{x} + A\mathbf{y}$

are called the *linear properties* of the function $\mathbf{x} \to A\mathbf{x}$.   They may be combined in the single property

(iii) $A(k\mathbf{x} + l\mathbf{y}) = kA\mathbf{x} + lA\mathbf{y}, \quad k, l \in Re, \mathbf{x}, \mathbf{y} \in V_2'.$

EXERCISE 10.8

1. State the domain and range of the function $\mathbf{x} \to A\mathbf{x}$ for the following matrices A.

(a) $\begin{bmatrix} 1 & 0 \\ 0 & 1 \end{bmatrix}$ (b) $\begin{bmatrix} -3 & 1 \\ 1 & 1 \end{bmatrix}$ (c) $\begin{bmatrix} 0 & 1 \\ 1 & 0 \end{bmatrix}$ (d) $\begin{bmatrix} 0 & 1 \\ 0 & 1 \end{bmatrix}$

(e) $\begin{bmatrix} 2 & 1 \\ -1 & 4 \end{bmatrix}$ (f) $\begin{bmatrix} 3 & -2 \\ 5 & 1 \end{bmatrix}$ (g) $\begin{bmatrix} -2 & 3 \\ 3 & -2 \end{bmatrix}$ (h) $\begin{bmatrix} 3 & -1 \\ -9 & 3 \end{bmatrix}$

2. For the matrices A of question (1), check that $A(-3\mathbf{b}) = (-3)A\mathbf{b}$ if

$$\mathbf{b} = \begin{bmatrix} 2 \\ -1 \end{bmatrix}.$$

3. For the matrices A in question (1), check that $A(\mathbf{b} + \mathbf{c}) = A\mathbf{b} + A\mathbf{c}$ if

$$\mathbf{b} = \begin{bmatrix} 2 \\ -1 \end{bmatrix} \quad \text{and} \quad \mathbf{c} = \begin{bmatrix} 3 \\ 0 \end{bmatrix}.$$

4. Prove that $A(k\mathbf{x}) = kA\mathbf{x}$ if $k \in Re$, $\mathbf{x} \in V_2'$, and A is a 2×2 real matrix.

5. Prove that $A(\mathbf{x} + \mathbf{y}) = A\mathbf{x} + A\mathbf{y}$ if $\mathbf{x}, \mathbf{y} \in V_2'$ and A is a 2×2 real matrix.

6. Prove algebraically that if $A(k\mathbf{x}) = kA\mathbf{x}$ and $A(\mathbf{x} + \mathbf{y}) = A\mathbf{x} + A\mathbf{y}$, then $A(k\mathbf{x} + l\mathbf{y}) = kA\mathbf{x} + lA\mathbf{y}$ for $k, l \in Re$.

7. Prove that if $A(k\mathbf{x} + l\mathbf{y}) = kA\mathbf{x} + lA\mathbf{y}$ for $k, l \in Re$, then $A(k\mathbf{x}) = kA\mathbf{x}$ and $A(\mathbf{x} + \mathbf{y}) = A\mathbf{x} + A\mathbf{y}$.

10.9.   Some Special Transformations

In this section, we shall consider some special linear transformations and their corresponding matrices.

We have already encountered the identity and the zero transformations corresponding to the matrices I and O.   We repeat them here for completeness.

(1) *The Identity Transformation and Identity Matrix*

The transformation

$$I \quad \begin{cases} u = x + 0y \\ v = 0x + y \end{cases}$$

or

$$I \begin{bmatrix} x \\ y \end{bmatrix} = \begin{bmatrix} x \\ y \end{bmatrix}$$

corresponds to the matrix

$$I = \begin{bmatrix} 1 & 0 \\ 0 & 1 \end{bmatrix}.$$

(2) *Zero Transformation and Zero Matrix*

The transformation

$$O \quad \begin{cases} u = 0x + 0y \\ v = 0x + 0y \end{cases}$$

or

$$O \begin{bmatrix} x \\ y \end{bmatrix} = \begin{bmatrix} 0 \\ 0 \end{bmatrix}$$

corresponds to the matrix

$$O = \begin{bmatrix} 0 & 0 \\ 0 & 0 \end{bmatrix}.$$

(3) *Rotations of the Plane*

We have also seen that the transformation

$$R_\theta \begin{bmatrix} x \\ y \end{bmatrix} = \begin{bmatrix} u \\ v \end{bmatrix}$$

given by the system of equations

$$\begin{cases} u = x \cos \theta - y \sin \theta \\ v = x \sin \theta + y \cos \theta \end{cases}$$

represents a rotation in the plane through angle θ. The corresponding matrix is

$$R_\theta = \begin{bmatrix} \cos \theta & -\sin \theta \\ \sin \theta & \cos \theta \end{bmatrix}.$$

For this matrix, $ad - bc$ has the value $\cos^2\theta + \sin^2\theta = 1$, and so an inverse transformation and matrix exists. Solving for x and y in terms of u and v yields

$$\begin{cases} x = u \cos \theta + v \sin \theta \\ y = -u \sin \theta + v \cos \theta \end{cases}.$$

The inverse transformation should represent a rotation through angle $-\theta$. We check that this is so by noting that the inverse matrix is

$$\begin{bmatrix} \cos \theta & \sin \theta \\ -\sin \theta & \cos \theta \end{bmatrix} = \begin{bmatrix} \cos (-\theta) & -\sin (-\theta) \\ \sin (-\theta) & \cos (-\theta) \end{bmatrix} = R_{-\theta}.$$

Example 1.   Find the images of the points $P_1(0,0)$, $P_2(1,0)$, and $P_3(1,1)$ under the transformation effecting a rotation of $90°$.   Draw the triangle $P_1P_2P_3$ and the image triangle $P_1'P_2'P_3'$ on the same diagram.

Solution: The required transformation is $R_{\pi/2}$ with

$$R_{\pi/2}\begin{bmatrix} x \\ y \end{bmatrix} = \begin{bmatrix} x\cos\frac{\pi}{2} - y\sin\frac{\pi}{2} \\ x\sin\frac{\pi}{2} + y\cos\frac{\pi}{2} \end{bmatrix};$$

that is,

$$R_{\pi/2}\begin{bmatrix} x \\ y \end{bmatrix} = \begin{bmatrix} -y \\ x \end{bmatrix}$$

Then

$$R_{\pi/2}\begin{bmatrix} 0 \\ 0 \end{bmatrix} = \begin{bmatrix} 0 \\ 0 \end{bmatrix}, \quad R_{\pi/2}\begin{bmatrix} 1 \\ 0 \end{bmatrix} = \begin{bmatrix} 0 \\ 1 \end{bmatrix}, \quad \text{and} \quad R_{\pi/2}\begin{bmatrix} 1 \\ 1 \end{bmatrix} = \begin{bmatrix} -1 \\ 1 \end{bmatrix}.$$

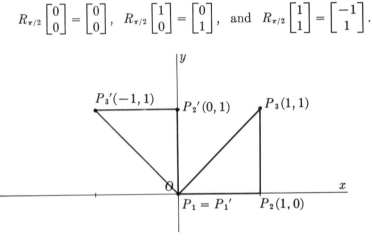

Note that the lengths of line segments are invariant under such a rotation.

(4)   *Uniform Magnification*

The transformation

$$M \quad \begin{cases} u = kx + 0y \\ v = 0x + ky \end{cases}$$

or

$$M\begin{bmatrix} x \\ y \end{bmatrix} = \begin{bmatrix} kx \\ ky \end{bmatrix}$$

is called a *uniform magnification*.   The images $M(P)$ and $M(Q)$ of two points P and Q determine a line segment whose length is kPQ.   The corresponding matrix is

$$\begin{bmatrix} k & 0 \\ 0 & k \end{bmatrix}.$$

(5)   *Magnification in the x-Direction*

$$M_x \quad \begin{cases} u = kx + 0y \\ v = 0x + y \end{cases}$$

or

$$M_x \begin{bmatrix} x \\ y \end{bmatrix} = \begin{bmatrix} kx \\ y \end{bmatrix}.$$

(See question (5), Exercise 10.9.)

(6)   *Magnification in the y-Direction*

$$M_y \quad \begin{cases} u = x + 0y \\ v = 0x + ky \end{cases}$$

or

$$M_y \begin{bmatrix} x \\ y \end{bmatrix} = \begin{bmatrix} x \\ ky \end{bmatrix}.$$

(See question (6), Exercise 10.9.)

Example 2.   Find the images of the points $P_1(0,0)$, $P_2(1,0)$, and $P_3(1,1)$ under the transformation effecting a magnification in the y-direction (let $k = 3$).   Show the triangles $P_1P_2P_3$ and $P_1'P_2'P_3'$ on the same diagram.

Solution: The transformation involved is M_y with $k = 3$.

$$M_y \begin{bmatrix} x \\ y \end{bmatrix} = \begin{bmatrix} x \\ 3y \end{bmatrix}.$$

Then

$$M_y \begin{bmatrix} 0 \\ 0 \end{bmatrix} = \begin{bmatrix} 0 \\ 0 \end{bmatrix}, \quad M_y \begin{bmatrix} 1 \\ 0 \end{bmatrix} = \begin{bmatrix} 1 \\ 0 \end{bmatrix}, \quad \text{and} \quad M_y \begin{bmatrix} 1 \\ 1 \end{bmatrix} = \begin{bmatrix} 1 \\ 3 \end{bmatrix}.$$

(7) *Projection Onto the x-Axis*

$$P_x \quad \begin{cases} u = x + 0y \\ v = 0x + 0y \end{cases}$$

or

$$P_x \begin{bmatrix} x \\ y \end{bmatrix} = \begin{bmatrix} x \\ 0 \end{bmatrix}.$$

(8) *Projection Onto the y-Axis*

$$P_y \quad \begin{cases} u = 0x + 0y \\ v = 0x + y \end{cases}$$

or

$$P_y \begin{bmatrix} x \\ y \end{bmatrix} = \begin{bmatrix} 0 \\ y \end{bmatrix}.$$

(9) *Reflection in the y-Axis*

$$R_y \quad \begin{cases} u = -x + 0y \\ v = 0x + y \end{cases}$$

or

$$R_y \begin{bmatrix} x \\ y \end{bmatrix} = \begin{bmatrix} -x \\ y \end{bmatrix}.$$

(See question (8), Exercise 10.9.)

(10) *Reflection in the x-Axis*

$$R_x \quad \begin{cases} u = x + 0y \\ v = 0x - y \end{cases}$$

or

$$R_x \begin{bmatrix} x \\ y \end{bmatrix} = \begin{bmatrix} x \\ -y \end{bmatrix}.$$

(See question (8), Exercise 10.9.)

Example 3.   Find the images of the points $P_1(0,0)$, $P_2(1,1)$, and $P_3(2,3)$ under the transformation effecting a reflection in the x-axis.   Show the triangles $P_1P_2P_3$ and $P_1'P_2'P_3'$ on the same diagram.

Solution: The transformation involved is R_x with

$$R_x \begin{bmatrix} x \\ y \end{bmatrix} = \begin{bmatrix} x \\ -y \end{bmatrix}.$$

Then

$$R_x \begin{bmatrix} 0 \\ 0 \end{bmatrix} = \begin{bmatrix} 0 \\ 0 \end{bmatrix}, \quad R_x \begin{bmatrix} 1 \\ 1 \end{bmatrix} = \begin{bmatrix} 1 \\ -1 \end{bmatrix}, \quad \text{and} \quad R_x \begin{bmatrix} 2 \\ 3 \end{bmatrix} = \begin{bmatrix} 2 \\ -3 \end{bmatrix}.$$

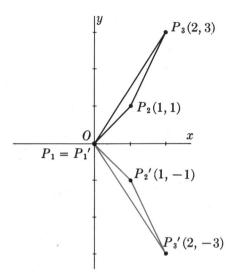

(11) *Reflection in the Origin*

$$R_O \quad \begin{cases} u = -x + 0y \\ v = 0x - y \end{cases}$$

or

$$R_O \begin{bmatrix} x \\ y \end{bmatrix} = \begin{bmatrix} -x \\ -y \end{bmatrix}.$$

(See question (8), Exercise 10.9.)

(12) *Shear in the x-Direction*

$$S_x \quad \begin{cases} u = x + ay \\ v = 0x + y \end{cases}$$

or

$$S_x \begin{bmatrix} x \\ y \end{bmatrix} = \begin{bmatrix} x + ay \\ y \end{bmatrix}.$$

(See question (9), Exercise 10.9.)

(13) *Shear in the y-Direction*

$$S_y \quad \begin{cases} u = x + 0y \\ v = ax + y \end{cases}$$

or

$$S_y \begin{bmatrix} x \\ y \end{bmatrix} = \begin{bmatrix} x \\ ax + y \end{bmatrix}.$$

(See question (9), Exercise 10.9.)

Example 4.   Find the images of the points $P_1(0,0)$, $P_2(1,0)$, and $P_3(1,1)$ under the transformation effecting a shear in the y-direction (let $a = 2$). Show the triangles $P_1P_2P_3$ and $P_1'P_2'P_3'$ on the same diagram.

Solution: The transformation involved is S_y with $a = 2$.

$$S_y \begin{bmatrix} x \\ y \end{bmatrix} = \begin{bmatrix} x \\ y + 2x \end{bmatrix}.$$

Then

$$S_y \begin{bmatrix} 0 \\ 0 \end{bmatrix} = \begin{bmatrix} 0 \\ 0 \end{bmatrix}, \qquad S_y \begin{bmatrix} 1 \\ 0 \end{bmatrix} = \begin{bmatrix} 1 \\ 2 \end{bmatrix}, \qquad \text{and} \qquad S_y \begin{bmatrix} 1 \\ 1 \end{bmatrix} = \begin{bmatrix} 1 \\ 3 \end{bmatrix}.$$

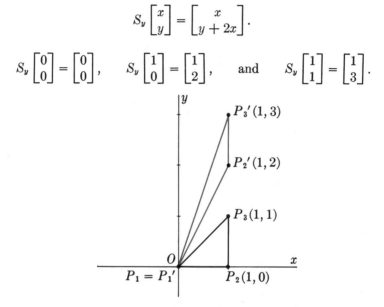

In addition to the preceding basic transformations, we have many combinations of them.

Example 5.   Find the transformation equivalent to a shear in the x-direction followed by a reflection in the x-axis.

Solution: The transformation is the product R_xS_x.

$$(x, y) \xrightarrow{\ S_x\ } (x + ky, y) \xrightarrow{\ R_x\ } (x + ky, -y)$$

Thus R_xS_x is the transformation

$$R_xS_x \quad \begin{cases} u = x + ky \\ v = 0x - y \end{cases}$$

and the corresponding matrix is

$$\begin{bmatrix} 1 & k \\ 0 & -1 \end{bmatrix}.$$

Example 6.   Find the transformation equivalent to a magnification in the y-direction followed by a projection onto the y-axis.

Solution: The transformation is the product $P_y M_y$.

$$(x, y) \xrightarrow{\quad M_y \quad} (x, ky) \xrightarrow{\quad P_y \quad} (0, ky)$$

We also write

$$P_y M_y \begin{bmatrix} x \\ y \end{bmatrix} = P_y \left(M_y \begin{bmatrix} x \\ y \end{bmatrix} \right) = P_y \begin{bmatrix} x \\ ky \end{bmatrix} = \begin{bmatrix} 0x + 0y \\ 0x + ky \end{bmatrix}.$$

Thus $P_y M_y$ is the transformation

$$P_y M_y \quad \begin{cases} u = 0x + 0y \\ v = 0x \ + ky \end{cases}$$

and the corresponding matrix is

$$\begin{bmatrix} 0 & 0 \\ 0 & k \end{bmatrix}.$$

EXERCISE 10.9

1. Write matrices corresponding to rotations of
   (a) 0°,   (b) 30°,   (c) 45°,   (d) 60°,
   (e) 90°,   (f) 120°,   (g) 180°,   (h) 270°.

2. (a) If $R_{\pi/6}$ is the matrix in question (1b) and $R_{\pi/3}$ is the matrix in question (1d), show that
   $$R_{\pi/6}^2 = R_{\pi/3}.$$
   (b) Show that
   $$R_{\pi/4}^2 = R_{\pi/2}.$$
   (c) Show that
   $$R_{\pi/3}^3 = R_{\pi}.$$

3. Find the images $T(P)$ of the points $P_1(0, 2)$, $P_2(-2, -1)$, $P_3(2, -1)$ under the transformation T effecting a rotation of 60°.   Draw the triangles $P_1 P_2 P_3$ and $T(P_1) T(P_2) T(P_3)$ on the same diagram.

4. Repeat question (3) if T is the transformation effecting a uniform magnification (let $k = 2$).   Compare the areas of the resulting triangles.

5. (a) Write the matrix corresponding to a magnification in the x-direction with
   (i) $k = 2$,   (ii) $k = -2$.

   (b) Find the images $T(P)$ of the points $P_1(1, 2)$, $P_2(3, 2)$, and $P_3(5, 7)$ under the transformation T effecting a magnification in the x-direction (let $k = 2$).   Draw the triangles $P_1 P_2 P_3$ and $T(P_1) T(P_2) T(P_3)$ and compare their areas.

   (c) Repeat part (b) using $k = -3$.

6. Repeat question (5) using the points $P_1(1, -3)$, $P_2(1, 5)$, and $P_3(2, 8)$ and their images under the transformation effecting a magnification in the y-direction with   (a) $k = 3$,   (b) $k = -1$.

7. Write matrices corresponding to
   (a) a projection onto the x-axis,   (b) a projection onto the y-axis.

8. (a) Write the matrices corresponding to a reflection in
      (i) the y-axis,   (ii) the x-axis,   (iii) the origin.
   (b) Find the images of the points $P_1(1, 3)$, $P_2(2, 5)$, $P_3(3, 7)$, under the transformation T effecting a reflection in the y-axis. Draw the two triangles involved.
   (c) Repeat part (b) if T is a reflection in the x-axis.
   (d) Repeat part (b) if T is a reflection in the origin.

9. (a) Write the matrix corresponding to
      (i) a shear in the x-direction,   (ii) a shear in the y-direction.
   (b) Find the images of the points $P_1(0, 0)$, $P_2(3, 0)$, $P_3(1, 4)$, under the shear
   $$T \quad \begin{cases} u = x + 3y \\ v = y \end{cases}.$$
   Draw the triangles determined by the two sets of points.
   (c) Repeat part (b) for the shear
   $$T \quad \begin{cases} u = x \\ v = -2x + y \end{cases}.$$

10. Find the transformation equivalent to a reflection in the x-axis followed by a magnification in the y-direction. State the matrix of the product transformation.

11. Find the transformation equivalent to a uniform magnification followed by a shear in the x-direction followed by projection onto the x-axis. State the matrix of the product transformation.

12. Find the transformation equivalent to a magnification in the y-direction followed by reflection in the origin followed by a shear in the x-direction. State the matrix of the product transformation.

13. Using the addition formulae for sine and cosine, show that
    $$R_\theta \, R_\phi = R_{\theta + \phi}.$$
    Interpret this result geometrically.

14. Use mathematical induction to show that
    $$\begin{bmatrix} 1 & 1 \\ 0 & 1 \end{bmatrix}^n = \begin{bmatrix} 1 & n \\ 0 & 1 \end{bmatrix}.$$
    Give a geometric interpretation of this result.

Chapter Summary

Multiplication of matrices defined in terms of the "multiplication" of the corresponding linear transformations

Rule for multiplication of matrices

Properties of matrix multiplication: (i) noncommutativity in general, (ii) associativity, (iii) existence of identity, (iv) distributivity

Divisors of zero

The inverse of a matrix

The linear matrix equation $AX = B$

The solution of the linear matrix equation $AX = B$

The inverse of a matrix using elementary row operations

The function $\mathbf{x} \rightarrow A\mathbf{x}$ · domain and range

Some special transformations: identity, zero, rotation, uniform magnification, magnification in the x- or y-direction, reflection in the x- or y-axis or the origin, projection onto the x- or y-axis, shear in the x- or y-direction

REVIEW EXERCISE 10

1. Write linear transformations A and B corresponding to the matrices
$$A = \begin{bmatrix} 5 & 2 \\ -3 & 4 \end{bmatrix} \quad \text{and} \quad B = \begin{bmatrix} 4 & 0 \\ -3 & 1 \end{bmatrix}$$
in such a way that the product transformation BA can be formed and hence the product BA of matrices B and A can be obtained.

2. Rework question (1) in such a way as to obtain AB.

3. Prove that AB does not always equal BA if A and B are 2×2 real matrices.

4. If
$$A = \begin{bmatrix} 3 & 3 \\ -1 & 2 \end{bmatrix}, \quad B = \begin{bmatrix} -3 & 5 \\ 2 & -1 \end{bmatrix}, \quad \text{and} \quad C = \begin{bmatrix} 2 & 0 \\ 0 & -3 \end{bmatrix},$$
find
   (a) AB,   (b) BC,   (c) CA,   (d) $A^2 + B^2 + C^2$.

5. If A is a 3×2 matrix, is it possible to form AB if B is
   (a) 3×2?   (b) 2×3?   (c) 3×3?   (d) 2×2?

6. Show that
   (a) $A(BC) = (AB)C$ (b) $A(B + C) = AB + AC$
   for the matrices of question (4).

7. Find AB if
$$A = \begin{bmatrix} 3 & -1 \\ -6 & 2 \end{bmatrix} \quad \text{and} \quad B = \begin{bmatrix} 1 & 0 \\ 3 & 0 \end{bmatrix}.$$
   What multiplicative property does this illustrate?

8. Find the inverse of the matrix
$$A = \begin{bmatrix} 4 & -1 \\ 3 & 6 \end{bmatrix}$$
   by finding the inverse of the corresponding transformation.

9. Given
$$A = \begin{bmatrix} 2 & 3 \\ -1 & 6 \end{bmatrix}, \quad B = \begin{bmatrix} 2 & -5 \\ 1 & 1 \end{bmatrix},$$
   find
   (a) A^{-1},   (b) B^{-1},   (c) AB,   (d) $(AB)^{-1}$.
   Show that $(AB)^{-1} = B^{-1}A^{-1}$.

10. Given
$$A = \begin{bmatrix} 4 & 4 \\ -1 & 3 \end{bmatrix}, \quad B = \begin{bmatrix} 5 & 0 \\ -1 & 1 \end{bmatrix},$$
    find
    (a) AB,   (b) $(AB)^{-1}$,   (c) B^{-1}.
    Show that $(AB)^{-1} A = B^{-1}$.

11. (a) If
$$A = \begin{bmatrix} 4 & 4 \\ -1 & 3 \end{bmatrix}, \quad \mathbf{r} = \begin{bmatrix} 5 \\ 5 \end{bmatrix}, \quad \mathbf{s} = \begin{bmatrix} 4 \\ 1 \end{bmatrix}, \quad \mathbf{t} = \begin{bmatrix} 0 \\ 5 \end{bmatrix},$$
    find
    (i) $A\mathbf{r}$,   (ii) $A\mathbf{s}$,   (iii) $A\mathbf{t}$.
    (b) Explain why it is impossible to find $\mathbf{r}A$.

12. Write the system
$$3x - 2y = 4$$
$$x + 5y = -3$$
    as a single linear matrix equation.

13. Show that
    (a) $A(3\mathbf{r}) = 3A\mathbf{r}$
    (b) $A(\mathbf{r} + \mathbf{s}) = A\mathbf{r} + A\mathbf{s}$
    (c) $A(2\mathbf{r} + 3\mathbf{s} - \mathbf{t}) = 2A\mathbf{r} + 3A\mathbf{s} - A\mathbf{t}$
    for the matrices of question (11).

Chapter 11

MATHEMATICS OF INVESTMENT

11.1. Simple Interest

If we purchase a $500, 5% government bond, we receive 5% of $500 or $25 each year as an interest payment for the use of our money. At the end of the period for which the bond is issued, our $500 would be returned as the particular bond issue was redeemed. With a savings bond, although not with other bonds, we may redeem the bond at any time during its life.

In the example given, the $500 originally lent is known as the *principal*, the 5% per annum is known as the *rate*, and the $25 per annum received for the use of the money is the annual *interest*. In such a case, since the annual interest is always calculated on the principal, we are receiving *simple interest*. For our bond, if held for 10 years, the total amount received over this period would be the return of our $500 at the end of the period plus 10 interest payments of $25 each, a total of $750. This sum is known as the *amount*.

If $1 is invested for one year at a rate of 5% per annum simple interest, the interest earned will be $.05, and the amount at the end of the year will be $1(1+.05). Therefore, if $500 is invested for one year at a rate of 5% per annum simple interest, the amount at the end of the year will be $500(1 + .05). If the $1 is invested for two years, the interest earned will be $2(.05) and the amount will be $[1 + 2(.05)]. Therefore, on $500, the amount will be $500[1 + 2(.05)]. In the same way, the amount of $500 in n years at 5% per annum will be $500[1 + n(.05)].

In this example, $500 is the principal and .05 is the rate expressed in decimal fraction form.

In a general case, therefore, the amount of P in n years at $100i\%$ simple interest is $P(1 + ni)$; that is

$$A = P(1 + ni)$$

where A is the amount,
  P is the principal,
  n is the number of years, and
  i is the rate expressed in decimal fraction form.

Example 1.   Determine the amount of $250 in 12 years at $4\frac{1}{2}\%$ per annum simple interest.

Solution:

$$P = 250.$$
$$i = .045.$$
$$n = 12.$$
$$A = P(1 + ni)$$
$$= 250(1 + .54)$$
$$= 250(1.54)$$
$$= 385.$$

Therefore, the amount is $385.

Example 2.   If $400 amounts to $560 in ten years, determine the rate of simple interest.

Solution:

$$A = 560.$$
$$P = 400.$$
$$n = 10.$$
$$A = P(1 + ni).$$
$$\therefore 560 = 400(1 + 10i)$$
$$7 = 5(1 + 10i)$$
$$7 = 5 + 50i.$$
$$\therefore 50i = 2$$
$$i = \frac{2}{50}$$
$$= .04.$$

Therefore, the annual interest rate is 4% or .04.

EXERCISE 11.1

1. Obtain the amount in each of the following at simple interest:

Principal	Time	Rate per annum
(a) $100	6 years	$4\frac{1}{2}\%$
(b) $320	8 years	$3\frac{1}{4}\%$
(c) $450	$7\frac{1}{2}$ years	6%
(d) $385	15 years	$2\frac{1}{4}\%$
(e) $216.25	5 years	3%
(f) $1865.50	18 years	$4\frac{1}{4}\%$

2. Obtain the annual rate of simple interest in each of the following:

Principal	Time	Amount
(a) $450	7 years	$544.50
(b) $250	12 years	$400

(c)	$620	8 years	$793.60
(d)	$84.50	6 years	$95.91
(e)	$170	$3\frac{1}{2}$ years	$187.85
(f)	$42.50	5 years	$49.41

3. Obtain the time in years necessary for each of the following principals to accumulate to the given amount at the given annual rate of simple interest:

	Principal	Amount	Rate per annum
(a)	$300	$390	5%
(b)	$440	$704	$7\frac{1}{2}\%$
(c)	$650	$981.50	$4\frac{1}{4}\%$
(d)	$1830	$2166.26	$5\frac{1}{4}\%$
(e)	$77.50	$89.90	4%
(f)	$166.40	$215.90	$3\frac{1}{2}\%$

11.2. Compound Interest

The calculation of an amount at simple interest, as in the previous section, is now used very rarely. With a government bond or company share, the interest is usually paid annually, semi-annually, or quarterly. Only the principal remains to be returned at the end of the loan period.

When the interest is not withdrawn at the end of each period but is left to accumulate, it will be added to the principal giving a new figure on which the interest will be calculated for the next period. This is the most common method of calculating an amount or *accumulated value,* and we say that the amount is calculated at *compound interest.*

Let us consider a bank deposit of $100 when the bank pays interest at the rate of 3% compounded annually. For each $1 on deposit at the beginning of the year and left on deposit during the year, the amount due at the end of the year will be $1.03.

For the principal at the beginning of any year, the accumulated value at the end of the year will be the principal multiplied by 1.03.

The following table shows the amount due at the end of various years:

Year	Amount at start of year	Amount at end of year
1	$100	$100 (1.03)$
2	$100 (1.03)$	$100 (1.03) (1.03)$
3	$100 (1.03)^2$	$100 (1.03)^2 (1.03)$
4	$100 (1.03)^3$	$100 (1.03)^3 (1.03)$
.		
.		
.		
n	$100 (1.03)^{n-1}$	$100 (1.03)^n$

For example, the amount or accumulated value at the end of 8 years will be $100(1.03)^8$.

From this, we see that for a principal of $P and a rate of interest of $100i\%$ compounded annually, the amount at the end of n years is given by the formula

$$A = P(1 + i)^n.$$

Unless it is definitely stated otherwise, we always consider that the interest is calculated annually or *compounded annually*. However, in many cases the interest is compounded semi-annually, quarterly, or monthly. In such cases, the interest rate given is the *nominal* annual rate. If we are told that the rate of interest is 6% compounded semi-annually, for 10 years, then

$$A = P(1.03)^{20}.$$

The semi-annual rate is 3%, and during the 10 years the number of interest periods is 20.

The calculation of the amount by ordinary arithmetical means would obviously be tedious and time-consuming. One improvement would be to make use of the tables of logarithms. For instance,

$$\text{if} \qquad A = 240(1.03)^{20},$$

$$\text{then } \log A = \log 240 + 20 \log 1.03.$$

However, even this would take time and therefore, to simplify the calculations, tables of values for $(1 + i)^n$ have been calculated for various values of i and n (see table, page 410). To obtain the value of $(1.03)^{20}$, we look in the 3% column and 20 year row. The value is 1.80611. This, of course, is accurate only to 5 decimal places, consequently our solution cannot be guaranteed beyond the fifth significant digit and even the fifth figure may not be correct. No result obtained by using these tables should be given to more than 5 significant digits.

Example 1.   Calculate the amount of $240 after 10 years at 6% compounded semi-annually.

Solution:
$$P = 240.$$
$$n = 20.$$
$$i = .03.$$
$$A = P(1 + i)^n$$
$$= 240(1.03)^{20}$$
$$\simeq 240(1.80611)$$
$$\simeq 433.4664.$$

Therefore, the amount is $433.47.

Example 2.   Calculate the interest received on $1250 at the end of 8 years at 4% if the interest is compounded (a) annually, and (b) quarterly.

Solution:

(a) Annually,

$$P = 1250.$$
$$n = 8.$$
$$i = .04.$$
$$A = 1250(1.04)^8$$
$$\simeq 1250(1.36857)$$
$$\simeq 1710.71.$$

Therefore, the amount is $1710.71.
Therefore, the interest is $460.71.

(b) Quarterly,

$$P = 1250.$$
$$n = 32.$$
$$i = .01.$$
$$A = 1250(1.01)^{32}$$
$$\simeq 1718.68.$$

Therefore, the amount is $1718.68.
Therefore, the interest is $468.68.

Example 3.   Calculate the equivalent annual rate (or effective rate) if the rate is 12% compounded monthly.

Solution: For a principal of $1 for 1 year

$$A = (1.01)^{12}$$
$$\simeq 1.12683.$$

Therefore, the equivalent annual rate is 12.683%.

EXERCISE 11.2

1. Complete each row in the following table:

Principal	Rate	Compounded	Time	Amount
$200	4%	Annually	12 years	
$350	5%			$350 (1.025)^{18}$
$480		Quarterly		$480 (1.015)^{28}$
	8%			$1200 (1.04)^{20}$
$640	6%	Monthly	3 years	
	3%			$680\left(1 + \dfrac{.03}{12}\right)^{15}$
		Semi-annually		$900 (1.02)^{16}$
$P	12%			$P\,(1.03)^{40}$
		Semi-annually		$200 (1.025)^{2n}$
			16 years	$P\,(1 + i)^{16}$
			n years	$P\,(1 + i)^{4n}$

2. Calculate the accumulated value of each of the following:
   (a) $200 in 12 years at 4%,
   (b) $350 in 9 years at 5%, compounded semi-annually,
   (c) $480 in 7 years at 6%,
   (d) $480 in 7 years at 6% compounded quarterly,
   (e) $1200 in 9 years at 4% compounded semi-annually,
   (f) $675 in 2 years at 12% compounded monthly,
   (g) $1000 in $6\frac{1}{2}$ years at 3% compounded semi-annually,
   (h) $750 in $6\frac{1}{2}$ years at 4% compounded quarterly,
   (i) $500 in $3\frac{3}{4}$ years at 8% compounded semi-annually,
   (j) $800 in 5 years 1 month at 12% compounded quarterly.
3. Calculate the equivalent annual rate in each of the following:
   (a) 5% compounded semi-annually,
   (b) 8% compounded quarterly,
   (c) 12% compounded monthly,
   (d) 6% compounded quarterly,
   (e) 6% compounded semi-annually,
   (f) 12% compounded quarterly,
   (g) 12% compounded semi-annually.
4. If $100 is deposited in a savings account at the end of each year for 3 years, determine the accumulated value 10 years after the first deposit, if the rate of interest is 3% compounded semi-annually.

11.3.   Present Value

We may wish to have a certain sum of money available at some future date and wish to calculate how much we should deposit now in order that the required sum will be available on that date. We assume that our deposit will be earning compound interest while it is on deposit.

If the rate of interest is 5% compounded annually, let us consider how much must be deposited now in order that $1000 may be available at the end of 10 years.

Using the formula $\qquad$ $A = P(1 + i)^n$

with $\qquad\qquad\qquad\qquad$ $A = 1000.$

$\qquad\qquad\qquad\qquad\qquad$ $i = .05.$

$\qquad\qquad\qquad\qquad\qquad$ $n = 10.$

we see that $\qquad\qquad\qquad$ $1000 = P(1.05)^{10}.$

Therefore, $\qquad\qquad\qquad$ $P = \dfrac{1000}{(1.05)^{10}}.$

This value of P is the sum (in dollars) which must be deposited and is known as the *present value* (*P.V.*) of $1000 in 10 years at 5% compounded annually.

In general, $P.V. = \dfrac{A}{(1 + i)^n}$ is the present value of A in n years at $100i\%$ compounded annually.

To avoid the tedious process of division, we use tables of values of $\dfrac{1}{(1 + i)^n}$ which have been calculated (see table, page 412), and are used in a similar manner to the tables of values of $(1 + i)^n$.

Example 1.   What is the present value of $1000 payable 10 years from now if the rate of interest is 5% compounded annually?

Solution: $A = 1000$, $i = .05$, $n = 10$.

$$P.V. = \frac{A}{(1 + i)^n}$$
$$= 1000 \times \frac{1}{(1.05)^{10}}$$
$$\simeq 1000\,(.61391)$$
$$= 613.91.$$

Therefore the present value is $613.91.

Example 2.   A father wishes to arrange that his son will have $6000 available on his eighteenth birthday to provide for his future education. If the rate of interest is 4% compounded semi-annually, how much must the father deposit in a trust account on his son's sixth birthday?

Solution: $A = 6000$, $i = .02$, $n = 24$.

$$P.V. = \frac{A}{(1 + i)^n}$$
$$= \frac{6000}{(1.02)^{24}}$$
$$\simeq 6000\,(.62172)$$
$$= 3730.32.$$

Therefore the amount to be deposited is $3730.30.
We must remember that the cents value here may be incorrect due to rounding-off errors, and a more precise statement would be that the amount is greater than $3730.25 and less than $3730.35.

EXERCISE 11.3

1. Calculate the present value of:
    (a) $650 due in 7 years at 4%
    (b) $300 due in 6 years at 6% compounded semi-annually
    (c) $300 due in 6 years at 6% compounded quarterly

    (d) $750 due in 18 years at 5% compounded semi-annually
    (e) $25 due in 3 years at 12% compounded monthly
    (f) $1380 due in $7\frac{1}{2}$ years at 3% compounded semi-annually
    (g) $1380 due in $7\frac{1}{2}$ years at 3% compounded annually
    (h) $250 due in $4\frac{1}{4}$ years at 4% compounded semi-annually.

2. A house is purchased by paying $5000 now and $4000 at the end of one year. If the rate of interest is 5% compounded semi-annually, what is the equivalent cash price of the house?

3. A trust fund is set up to provide a boy with $10,000 on his twenty-first birthday. If it is agreed that he receive the money on his eighteenth birthday, and the interest rate is 4% compounded semi-annually, how much will he receive?

4. A car is purchased with a down payment of $1200 and it is agreed to pay a further $200 at the end of each month for four months. If the rate of interest is 24% compounded monthly, what is the equivalent cash price?

11.4.   Annuities

DEFINITION. If a fixed sum of money is payable at any regular interval, the sequence of payments is called an *annuity*. The time interval between any two payments is called the *period* of the annuity and is taken as 1 year unless otherwise stated.

Suppose a man deposits $100 in a bank account at the end of each year for 5 years. The sequence of payments constitutes an annuity and may be represented on a diagram as shown below.

0	1	2	3	4	5
	100	100	100	100	100

In this case, we may say that the annuity *begins now and runs for 5 years.*

    In Section 11.2 we learned that $100 invested at 3% compounded annually accumulates to $100 $(1.03)^5$ at the end of 5 years. This is illustrated in the following diagram:

3% annually

now   5

100 $\longrightarrow$ 100 $(1.03)^5$

Generally, where the principal P is invested at $100i\%$ per annum for n years, the accumulated value A is given by $A = P(1 + i)^n$.

In the case of an annuity, the amounts of the individual payments may be summed by an application of the formula for the sum of a geometric series. Consider the following example.

Example 1.   If a man deposits $100 at the end of each year for 5 years in a bank which pays interest at 3% compounded annually, determine the total amount on deposit immediately after the fifth deposit has been made.

Solution:

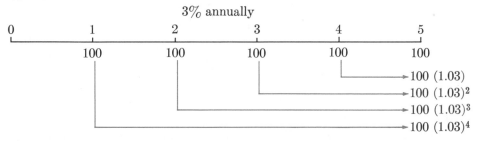

The indicated sum of the five accumulated values forms a geometric series. The amount of the annuity five years hence is $100 + 100\,(1.03) + 100\,(1.03)^2 + 100(1.03)^3 + 100(1.03)^4$.

The sum is obtained from the formula

$$S_n = \frac{a(r^n - 1)}{r - 1},$$

with $\qquad\qquad a = 100,\, r = 1.03,\, n = 5.$

Thus $\qquad\qquad$
$$S_5 = \frac{100[(1.03)^5 - 1]}{1.03 - 1}$$
$$\simeq \frac{100(1.15927 - 1)}{.03} \quad \text{(tables)}$$
$$= \frac{15.927}{.03}$$
$$= 530.9.$$

Therefore, the amount of the annuity is $530.90.

In practice this work can be considerably shortened by making use of additional tables. If the deposit was $R at the end of each period for n periods and the rate of interest was $100i\%$, the total amount on deposit immediately after the last deposit would, in a similar manner, be given by

$$A = \frac{R[(1 + i)^n - 1]}{i}.$$

The value of $\dfrac{(1 + i)^n - 1}{i}$ has been calculated for various values of n and i and is symbolized by $S_{\overline{n}|i}$. These values are given in the tables (page 414).

Example 1 may now be simplified since
$$A = 100\, S_{\overline{5}|\ .03}$$
$$= 100(5.30914).$$

Therefore the amount of annuity is $530.91.

Example 2.   I. Bulger wishes to buy a new colour television set in 4 years time. If the cost of the set is \$800, how much should he deposit in a bank account at the end of each 6-month period in order to have the money available, if the bank interest is 5% per annum compounded semi-annually?

Solution: Let each deposit be \$$R$.

$$800 = RS_{\overline{8}|} \cdot {}_{025}$$
$$800 = R(8.73612)$$
$$R = \frac{800}{8.73612}.$$

Therefore the semi-annual deposit is \$91.57.

It should be noted that the values given in the tables are built on the assumption that payments of the annuity are made at the end of each period and also that the value of the annuity is the value immediately after the last payment is made. If these conditions are altered the procedure has to be modified. This is illustrated in Example 3.

Example 3.   If \$500 is deposited at the beginning of each 6-month period for 12 years, calculate the value after 15 years if the interest rate is 7% per annum compounded semi-annually.

Solution: We can first modify the problem by extending our line diagram to the left for one period and using $-\frac{1}{2}$ as our starting point. This reduces the problem to one in which payments are made at the end of each period.

If we consider the deposits are made at the end of each period until the end of the fifteenth year, the amount would be given by $A = 500\, S_{\overline{31}|}\,._{035}$.

However no deposit was made after year $11\frac{1}{2}$ so that we must subtract the accumulated value of such deposits. The amount of these extra deposits is given by $A = 500\, S_{\overline{7}|}\,._{035}$.

Hence the actual amount is

$$A = 500\, S_{\overline{31}|}\,._{035} - 500\, S_{\overline{7}|}\,._{035}$$
$$= 500\, (S_{\overline{31}|}\,._{035} - S_{\overline{7}|}\,._{035})$$
$$= 500\, (54.42947 - 7.77941)$$
$$= 500\, (46.65006).$$

Therefore the value after 15 years is \$23,325 (nearest dollar).
Note that only 5-figure accuracy is valid in the final result.

If the interest period and the payment period are not identical the use of an annuity table is not valid without considerable modification. In such a case we should, at present, return to first principles as used in the first solution of Example 1.

Example 4. A father makes annual deposits in a trust fund which pays interest at 4% per annum compounded semi-annually. If the first deposit is made on his son's sixth birthday, what should be the amount of the annual deposit so that the fund shall total $5000 when the deposit is made on the boy's eighteenth birthday?

Solution:

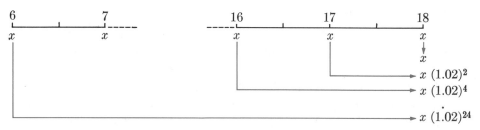

The indicated sum of the accumulated values produces the geometric series

$$x + x(1.02)^2 + x(1.02)^4 + \ldots + x(1.02)^{24}.$$

Now
$$a = x, r = (1.02)^2, n = 13.$$
$$\therefore S_{13} = \frac{x[(1.02)^{26} - 1]}{(1.02)^2 - 1}.$$

But
$$S_{13} = 5000.$$
$$\therefore 5000 = \frac{x[(1.02)^{26} - 1]}{(1.02)^2 - 1}.$$
$$5000 \simeq \frac{x(1.67342 - 1)}{1.0404 - 1}.$$
$$\therefore x(.67342) = 5000(.0404).$$
$$\therefore x = \frac{202}{.67342}$$
$$\simeq 299.961.$$

Therefore the annual deposit is $299.96 (nearest cent).

EXERCISE 11.4

1. A man receives an annuity of $300 each year for 10 years. If he deposits the payments in an account which pays interest at $4\frac{1}{2}\%$ per annum, obtain the total value of the deposits at the end of the 10-year period.
2. An annuity of $500 begins now and runs for 8 years. If the payments are invested at 4% compounded quarterly, what is the total invested at the end of the 8-year period?

3. A person makes 20 annual deposits of $100 each in a trust fund which bears interest at 4% compounded semi-annually. If the first deposit is made on April 1st, 1966, calculate the accumulated value of the deposits on April 1st, 1986.

4. $70 is saved each half year and deposited in a fund which pays 5% compounded semi-annually. If the total number of deposits is 16, what is the accumulated amount on deposit two years after the date of the last deposit?

5. A young man deposits a certain sum of money each half year in a fund which bears interest at 5% compounded semi-annually. What sum must be deposited so that, immediately after the 6th deposit has been made, $350 will be available to buy a motor scooter?

6. What sum of money invested at the beginning of each year for 12 years in a fund which pays 6% per annum compounded annually, will accumulate to $12,000 three years after the date of the last deposit?

7. Obtain the amount deposited annually, in an account paying 5% compounded semi-annually, if the first payment was made on January 1, 1950 and the total value immediately after the deposit on January 1, 1965 was $20,000.

8. An investor deposits $x at the end of each half year in a fund which pays interest at 6% compounded semi-annually. Determine x if the accumulated amount on deposit immediately after the 19th deposit has been made is $5000.

9. Annually on July 1 from 1960 to 1970 inclusive, a man places $1000 in an account which pays interest of 4% per annum compounded semi-annually. Obtain the accumulated value of the account on July 1, 1973.

10. A man invests $1000 per year placing his money at the end of each year in a fund paying an annual rate of 4%. Obtain the number of years needed for the total amount on deposit to accumulate to $20,000. (Use logarithms and obtain an answer correct to one decimal place.)

11. A man pays a premium of $960 at the beginning of each year for a 10-year endowment policy for $10,000, due at the end of 10 years. If the insurance company can invest funds at 5% per annum, compounded annually, what is the accumulated value of these premiums when the policy falls due?

11.5.   Present Value of an Annuity

In Section 11.3 we found that the value now of $100 five years hence is

$$100 \times \frac{1}{(1.03)^5},$$

if money is worth 3% per annum.

This may be shown on a diagram:

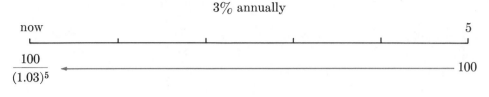

$$\frac{100}{(1.03)^5} \quad \text{(or } 100(1.03)^{-5}\text{) is called the } present\ value \text{ of the \$100 five years hence.}$$

Generally, if the rate is $100i\%$ per annum, the present value $(P.V.)$ of A, n interest periods hence, is given by

$$P.V. = \frac{A}{(1 + i)^n} \text{ or } A(1 + i)^{-n}.$$

Many problems dealing with annuities are concerned with the present value of a sequence of payments. Consider the following examples.

Example 1.   Obtain the present value of an annuity of \$300 which starts now and runs for 10 years, if money is worth $3\frac{1}{2}\%$ per annum.

Solution:

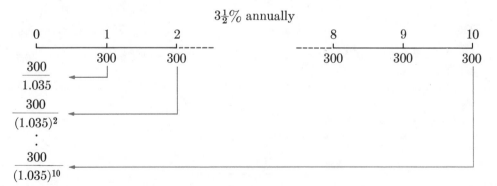

The present value of the annuity may be represented by the geometric series

$$\frac{300}{1.035} \quad + \quad \frac{300}{(1.035)^2} + \cdots + \frac{300}{(1.035)^{10}}.$$

It will be convenient to rewrite this as

$$\frac{300}{(1.035)^{10}} + \frac{300}{(1.035)^9} + \cdots + \frac{300}{1.035},$$

so that $a = \dfrac{300}{(1.035)^{10}}$, $r = 1.035$, $n = 10$.

Therefore $\qquad P.V. = \dfrac{300}{(1.035)^{10}} \times \dfrac{[(1.035)^{10} - 1]}{(1.035) - 1}$

$$= \dfrac{300}{(1.035) - 1} \times \dfrac{(1.035)^{10} - 1}{(1.035)^{10}}$$

$$= \dfrac{300}{.035} \times \left(1 - \dfrac{1}{(1.035)^{10}}\right) \qquad\qquad (1)$$

$$\sim \dfrac{300}{.035} \times (1 - 0.70892) \qquad\qquad \text{(tables)}$$

$$= \dfrac{300\,(0.29108)}{.035}$$

$$= \dfrac{87324}{35}$$

$$\sim 2494.97.$$

The present value of the annuity is \$2495.00 (to 5 significant figures).
The line marked (1) in the above example may be re-written as

$$P.V. = 300\,\dfrac{[1 - (1.035)^{-10}]}{.035}.$$

If the rate of interest is $100i\%$ and the annuity payment is \$R per period, this becomes

$$P.V. = R\left[\dfrac{1 - (1 + i)^{-n}}{i}\right].$$

The value $\dfrac{1 - (1 + i)^{-n}}{i}$ is the present value of an annuity of \$1 for n periods at $100i\%$ per period. This is symbolized as $a_{\overline{n}|\,i}$ and tables of values have been calculated (see page 416).

Again it should be noted that the tables are based on the assumption that the payments are made at the end of each period and that the interest period and payment period are identical.

An alternative, shorter solution is now possible for Example 1.

$$P.V. = 300\,a_{\overline{10}|\,.035}$$
$$= 300(8.31661)$$
$$= 2494.983$$

Therefore the present value is \$2495.00 (5 significant figures).

Example 2. Albert Jones received a bequest of \$20,000 on June 1, 1970 and decided to purchase a 10-year annuity. Equal annual payments will be paid to him on June 1 of each year from 1971 to 1980 inclusive and the rate of interest is 8% per annum. Calculate the value of each payment.

Solution: Let each payment be \$x.

$$20,000 = x\,a_{\overline{10}|\,.08}$$
$$20,000 = x(6.71008)$$

$$x = \frac{20{,}000}{6.71008}$$

$$\simeq 2980.59.$$

Therefore the value of each payment is $2980.60 (5 significant figures).

Again if the interest period and payment period are not identical we will have to return to the first principles as in Example 3.

Example 3.   The price of a house is $6000 down and $2000 per year at the end of each year for five years. What is the equivalent cash price if money is worth 6% per annum compounded semi-annually?

Solution:

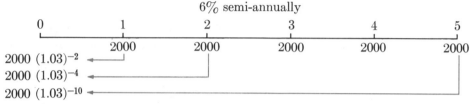

The present value of the five payments is

$$2000(1.03)^{-10} + 2000(1.03)^{-8} + \ldots + 2000(1.03)^{-2}.$$

In this case $a = 2000(1.03)^{-10}$; $r = (1.03)^2$; $n = 5$.

Therefore $\text{P.V.} = 2000(1.03)^{-10} \times \dfrac{[(1.03)^{10} - 1]}{(1.03)^2 - 1}$

$$= \frac{2000}{(1.03)^2 - 1} \times (1.03)^{-10} \, [(1.03)^{10} - 1]$$

$$= \frac{2000}{.06090} \times (1 - .74409) \qquad \text{(tables)}$$

$$= \frac{2000}{.06090} \times (.25591)$$

$$\simeq 8404.269$$

$$= 8404.30 \, (5 \text{ significant figures}).$$

The equivalent cash price of the house is $(6000 + 8404.30)

$$= \$14{,}404.30.$$

EXERCISE 11.5

1. Obtain the present value of an annuity of $300 which begins now and runs for ten years if the rate of interest is 4% per annum compounded semi-annually.

2. A man is to pay back a loan by paying $1000 at the end of each year for six years. What amount in cash would discharge the debt now, if money is worth 5% per annum compounded semi-annually?

3. The purchase price of a summer cottage is $2000 down and $100 at the end of each year for four years. Obtain the equivalent cash price of the cottage if money earns 5% per annum.

4. Obtain the value on June 1, 1967 of an annuity of $50 payable on each June 1 from 1968 to 1977 inclusive. Money earns 6% per annum compounded semi-annually.

5. Obtain the value on May 1, 1965 of annuity of 15 annual payments, the first payment on May 1, 1965. The rate of interest is 4% per annum.

6. If money earns 5% per annum, what is the annual payment of a ten-payment annuity, the first payment one year hence, if $1000 is invested now?

7. $5000 is invested at 4% per annum compounded semi-annually. Calculate the amount of the annual payment of an 8-payment annuity if the first payment is one year hence.

8. You have $10,000 deposited at 5% per annum. Obtain the largest annual withdrawal possible from this fund, if the first of ten withdrawals is made immediately.

9. A man leaves a will stipulating that his son receive $1000 on each of his birthdays from the 21st to the 25th inclusive. What is the present value of these expected sums on the boy's 16th birthday, if money is worth 5% per annum, compounded semi-annually?

10. A man has a 20-year endowment policy on which he has just paid the 17th premium of $420. He learns that the insurance company will allow a discount of 4% per annum, compounded annually, on any premiums paid in advance. What sum paid now would complete his contract with the company?

11.6. Deferred Annuities

When we say that an annuity begins now, the first payment is understood to be one year (or one period) hence.

If an annuity begins in 5 years, the first payment will be at the end of 6 years (or 1 payment period after 5 years). Such an annuity is said to be *deferred* for 5 years. A line diagram will always be of assistance in clarifying such a problem.

Example 1. Obtain the present value of an annuity of $1000 which is deferred for 3 years and runs for 8 years if the interest rate is 6% per annum.

Solution:

0	1	2	3	4	5	6		10	11
				1000	1000	1000		1000	1000

We first calculate the present value of an annuity of $1000 beginning now and running for 11 years. The first 3 payments of this annuity represent an overpayment so we then subtract the present value of these payments to obtain the actual present value.

$$P.V. = 1000\ a_{\overline{11}|}.06 - 1000\ a_{\overline{3}|}.06$$

$$= 1000\ (a_{\overline{11}|}.06 - a_{\overline{3}|}.06)$$

$$= 1000\ (7.88687 - 2.67301)$$
$$= 1000\ (5.21386)$$
$$= 5213.86.$$

Therefore the present value is \$5213.90.

Example 2. I. Gamble at age 51 has won a sweepstake prize of \$30,000. As he does not need the money immediately he decides to invest it in an annuity with payments to begin when he retires at age 60 and to run for 15 years. What annual payment will he receive if the interest rate is 7% per annum?

Solution: Let annual payment be \$x.

51	52		60	61	62		73	74
			x	x	x		x	x

$$30{,}000 = x\ a_{\overline{23}|}\ .07 - x\ a_{\overline{8}|}\ .07$$

$$= x\ (a_{\overline{23}|}\ .07 - a_{\overline{8}|}\ .07)$$

$$= x\ (11.27219 - 5.97130)$$
$$= x\ (5.30089);$$
$$x = \frac{30{.}000}{5{.}30089}$$
$$\simeq 5659.43.$$

Therefore the annual payment is \$5659.40.

Example 3.   Repeat Example 2 but with the rate of interest 7% per annum compounded semi-annually.

Solution: Here the payment period is 1 year but the interest period is $\frac{1}{2}$ year so we must return to first principles.

Let the annual payment be \$x.

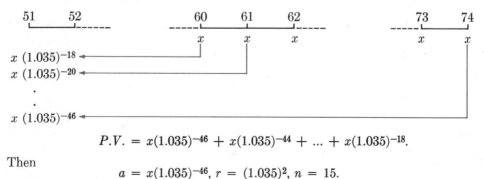

$$P.V. = x(1.035)^{-46} + x(1.035)^{-44} + \ldots + x(1.035)^{-18}.$$

Then

$$a = x(1.035)^{-46},\ r = (1.035)^2,\ n = 15.$$

Therefore $30,000 = x(1.035)^{-46} \times \dfrac{(1.035)^{30} - 1}{(1.035)^2 - 1}$

$$= \frac{x}{(1.035)^2 - 1} \times [(1.035)^{-16} - (1.035)^{-46}]$$

$$= \frac{x}{.07123} (.57671 - .20547)$$

$$= \frac{x(.37124).}{.07123}$$

Therefore $x = \dfrac{30,000(.07123)}{.37124}$

$= \dfrac{2136.9}{.37124}$

$\simeq 5756.11.$

Therefore the annual payment is $5756.10.

EXERCISE 11.6

1. What is the present value of an annuity of $500 which is deferred for 5 years and runs for 4 years, if money earns 4% per annum?

2. Obtain the value now of a 10-payment annuity if the first payment is made 8 years hence and money is worth 5% per annum, compounded semi-annually.

3. A father wishes to give his daughter an annuity of $1000 with the first of 4 payments on her 18th birthday. If money earns 6% per annum, what is the value of the annuity on her 10th birthday?

4. An annuity of $500 is payable every July 1st from 1969 to 1978 inclusive. If the rate of interest is 4% per annum, compounded semi-annually, what is the value of the annuity on July 1, 1966?

5. The first of 12 payments of an annuity of $1000 is made on March 1st, 1972. If money earns 5% per annum, what amount must be invested on March 1st, 1967 to purchase this annuity?

6. What is the annual payment of an annuity of 10 payments which is deferred for 6 years and purchased now for $8000? Money is worth 4% per annum compounded semi-annually.

7. On May 1, 1965, $10,000 is deposited at 5% per annum compounded semi-annually. Obtain the annual payment if this money buys a 10-payment annuity with the first payment on May 1, 1969.

8. Obtain the present value of an annuity of $3000 which is deferred for 5 years and runs for 6 years, if money is worth 6% per annum compounded semi-annually.

9. One person owns an annuity of $500 which is to begin now and last for 16 years. A second person owns an annuity of $1000 which is to be deferred four years and then to run 8 years. By how much do the two annuities differ in present value if money is worth $4\frac{1}{2}\%$ compounded annually?

10. Repeat question 9 if money is worth $3\frac{1}{2}\%$ compounded semi-annually?

11. A man has $20,000 which he does not need. He plans to leave it in the bank for 5 years until all his children have finished school and then to withdraw $3300 annually for a trip to Europe. How much money will be left 13 years from now if money earns 5% compounded semi-annually?

11.7. Amortization

The *amortization of a debt* means simply the paying of the debt by any acceptable set of payments. However, in practice when we state that a debt is amortized at a given rate of interest we usually mean that the liabilities as to principal and interest are liquidated by a sequence of equal payments at equal time intervals. Hence the payments form an annuity whose present value is the original debt.

Example 1. A debt of $8000 is to be paid in 6 equal annual instalments. If the rate of interest is 8% per annum, calculate the annual payment.

Solution: Let each payment be $x.

$$P.V. = x\, a_{\overline{6}|\,.08}$$
$$8000 = x(4.62288)$$
$$x = \frac{8000}{4.62288}$$
$$\simeq 1730.52.$$

Therefore the annual payment is $1730.52.

Note that due to the limitation of accuracy of the tables this should be rounded off to $1730.50. However, if we are now asked to construct an amortization schedule we should keep the extra digit to allow for greater accuracy in the calculations involved. With tables constructed correct to 8 or 10 digits it would be usual to calculate the annual payment correct to the nearest tenth of a cent.

From this calculation an amortization table may be constructed to show the debt situation at any time during the life of the loan.

AMORTIZATION TABLE

Year	Debt at start of year	Total payment	Interest payment	Principal repayment	Debt at end of year
1	8,000.00	1730.52	640.00	1090.52	6909.48
2	6,909.48	1730.52	552.76	1177.76	5731.72
3	5,731.72	1730.52	458.54	1271.98	4459.74
4	4,459.74	1730.52	356.78	1373.74	3086.00
5	3,086.00	1730.52	246.88	1483.64	1602.36
6	1,602.36	1730.52	128.19	1602.33	—

The total payment has been calculated and the interest payment is 8% of the debt at the start of the year. By subtracting the interest payment from the total payment we obtain the amount by which the debt has been reduced during that year. By subtracting this principal repayment from the debt at the start of the year, we obtain the debt remaining at the end of the year. This figure is also the debt at the start of the next year.

Due to rounding-off errors the last principal repayment is unlikely to agree with the outstanding debt exactly to the nearest cent. To ensure exact agreement, more accurate tables would be necessary and all figures maintained to the nearest tenth of a cent.

Example 2.   A debt of $1800 is to be repaid at the rate of $200 per month with a smaller final payment. If the interest rate is 18% per annum, compounded monthly, construct an amortization table and obtain the final payment.

AMORTIZATION TABLE

Month	Debt at start	Total payment	Interest payment	Principal repayment	Debt at end of month
1	1800.00	200.00	27.00	173.00	1627.00
2	1627.00	200.00	24.41	175.59	1451.41
3	1451.41	200.00	21.77	178.23	1273.18
4	1273.18	200.00	19.10	180.90	1092.28
5	1092.28	200.00	16.38	183.62	908.66
6	908.66	200.00	13.63	186.37	722.29
7	722.29	200.00	10.83	189.17	533.12
8	533.12	200.00	8.00	192.00	341.12
9	341.12	200.00	5.12	194.88	146.24
10	146.24	148.43	2.19	146.24	—

Final payment is $148.43

In the tenth month, the debt of $146.24 at the beginning of the month is less than the $200 monthly payment. Consequently we first calculate the interest for the tenth month ($2.19) and add it to the debt to obtain the final payment of $148.43.

EXERCISE 11.7

1. A debt of $6000 with interest at 6% per annum will be discharged by payments of $1500 at the end of each year for as long as necessary. Construct an amortization table for the debt.

2. Construct an amortization table for a debt of $8,000 with interest at 8% per annum compounded semi-annually if the debt is discharged by semi-annual payments of $1000 for as long as necessary. What is the final payment?

3. A debt of $12,000 with interest at 7% per annum is to be discharged in 8 equal annual payments. Calculate the annual payment and construct an amortization table.

4. A mortgage for $15,000 is to be discharged in 8 years by 16 equal semi-annual payments. If the rate of interest is 10% per annum, compounded semi-annually calculate the semi-annual payment and construct an amortization table.

5. A $12,000, 15-year mortgage is to be paid in equal semi-annual payments. If the rate of interest is 8% per annum, compounded semi-annually, calculate the semi-annual payment. Construct an amortization table for the first 5 years and obtain from it the single payment which would clear the debt after 5 years.

11.8. Mortgages and Instalment Buying

In paying off any debt by a sequence of equal payments at equal intervals of time, we can construct an amortization table and from this obtain the state of the debt whenever a payment is made. However, it is possible to calculate this without having to go through the labour of constructing an amortization table each time. Various other problems which arise in mortgage payments and instalment buying may also be solved without having to construct an amortization table.

The usual practice in mortgage repayment is to negotiate for equal payments at equal intervals over a period of years (say 10, 15, 20, or 25 years). However, after 5 years the outstanding debt has either to be paid off or the mortgage renegotiated at the current rate of interest. In such a case a 20-year mortgage may have been obtained at an interest rate of 6% per annum in 1966 but when it comes to renegotiate in 1971 we may find that we have to pay at an interest rate of $9\frac{1}{2}$% per annum.

Example 1.   A mortgage for \$18,000 at 6% per annum compounded semi-annually was obtained in 1966. Calculate the semi-annual payment if the repayment period is 20 years. When the mortgage is renegotiated in 1971, the interest rate is 10% per annum compounded semi-annually.

(a) What cash payment would clear the mortgage in 1971?

(b) What would be the semi-annual payment if the mortgage were renewed for the remaining 15 years.

Solution: Let the semi-annual payment be \$$x$.

Then
$$18{,}000 = x \, a_{\overline{40}|} \, {}_{.03}$$

$$= x(23.11477)$$

$$x = \frac{18000}{23.11477}$$

$$\simeq 778.72.$$

Therefore the semi-annual payment is \$778.72.

(a) In 1971, ten payments have been made and 30 payments remain. The outstanding debt is the present value of these 30 payments.

$$P.V. \text{ of remaining payments} = 778.72 \, a_{\overline{30}|} \, {}_{.03}$$

$$= 778.72(19.60044)$$

$$\simeq 15{,}263.25.$$

Therefore the cash payment to clear mortgage is \$15,263 (5 significant figures).

(b) Let new semi-annual payment be \$$x$.

$$15{,}263.25 = x \, a_{\overline{30}|} \, {}_{.05}$$

$$= x(15.37245)$$

$$x = \frac{15{,}263.25}{15.37245}$$

$$\simeq 992.90.$$

Therefore the new semi-annual payment is \$992.90.

Example 2.   A debt of \$1800 is to be repaid at the rate of \$200 per month with a smaller final payment. If the interest rate is 18% per annum, compounded monthly, calculate the number of \$200 payments and the final payment. (See Example 2, Section 11.7).

Solution: Let number of payments be n.

Then
$$1800 = 200 \, a_{\overline{n}|} \, {}_{.015}$$

$$a_{\overline{n}|} \, {}_{.015} = \frac{1800}{200} = 9$$

From the tables
$$a_{\overline{9}|} \, {}_{.015} = 8.36052$$

$$a_{\overline{10}|} \, {}_{.015} = 9.22218.$$

Hence
$$9 < \quad n \quad < 10.$$

Therefore the number of full payments is 9.

After 9 months, amount of payments	$= 200 \ s_{\overline{9}	} \ {}_{.015}$
	$= 200(9.55933)$
	$= 1911.87.$

Amount of original debt	$= 1800(1.015)^9$
	$= 1800(1.14339)$
	$= \$2,058.10.$

| Therefore the remaining debt | $= \$2,058.10 - 1911.87$ |
| | $= 146.23.$ |

| Therefore the final payment | $= 146.23(1.015)$ |
| | $= \$148.42.$ |

Alternatively,

$$P.V. \text{ of 9 payments} = 200 \ a_{\overline{9}|} \ {}_{.015}$$
$$= 200(8.36052)$$
$$= \$1672.10.$$

| Therefore $P.V.$ of remaining debt | $= \$1800 - \$1672.10$ |
| | $= 127.90.$ |

Therefore the final payment	$= 127.90(1.015)^{10}$
	$= 127.90(1.16054)$
	$= \$148.43.$

Example 3. Otto Basher purchased a used car for which the cash price was \$1500. He was informed that he could obtain it on time payments over 2 years and that the rate of interest was 10% per annum. Hence the interest would be 20% of \$1500 = \$300 and this would make total payments of \$1800 at \$75 per month for 2 years. What was the true rate compounded monthly?

Solution: Let monthly rate be $100i\%$.

$$1500 = 75 \ a_{\overline{24}|} \ {}_{i}$$

$$a_{\overline{24}|} \ {}_{i} = \frac{1500}{75} = 20.$$

At $1\frac{1}{2}\%$

$$a_{\overline{24}|} \ {}_{.015} = 20.03041.$$

At $1\frac{3}{4}\%$

$$a_{\overline{24}|} \ {}_{.0175} = 19.46069.$$
$$20.03041 - 19.46069 = .56972.$$

Monthly rate

$$\simeq 1.5\% + \tfrac{3041}{56972}(1\tfrac{3}{4} - 1\tfrac{1}{2})\%$$
$$= 1.5\% + \tfrac{3041(.25)}{56972}\%$$
$$= 1.513\%.$$

Therefore the true rate is approximately 18.2% per annum compounded monthly.

EXERCISE 11.8 $20,000

1. (a) Calculate the semi-annual payment on a 20-year mortgage if the interest rate is 9% per annum compounded semi-annually.
   (b) If the house is sold for $26,000 after 8 years and the new owner agrees to take over the remaining mortgage payments, what cash payment will he have to give the original owner?

2. (a) A mortgage for $12,000 is paid in equal quarterly instalments for 10 years at an interest rate of 6% per annum compounded quarterly. Calculate the quarterly payment.
   (b) After 5 years, the mortgage is renegotiated at a rate of 8% per annum compounded quarterly. Calculate the new quarterly payment.

3. The sale price of a house is $22,000. A trust company offers a first mortgage for $15,000 at 7% per annum compounded semi-annually with equal semi-annual payments to be paid over 20 years. Since the buyer has only $2,000 available for a down-payment he takes out a second mortgage for $5,000 with an interest rate of 16% per annum compounded semi-annually. If this has to be paid in 5 years, calculate the total semi-annual payment for the first 5 years.

4. Mrs. Newed purchases furniture worth $1800 for her home. If the interest rate on time payments is 1% per month, calculate her monthly payments for 1 year.

5. A debt of $1500 is to be paid by equal monthly instalments of $100 for as long as necessary. If the interest rate is 18% per annum compounded monthly, calculate
   (a) the number of $100 payments made
   (b) the value of the last payment.

6. (a) A mortgage for $8,000 is paid in equal semi-annual instalments for 12 years. If the interest rate is 7% per annum compounded semi-annually, calculate the semi-annual payment.
   (b) What cash payment will clear the mortgage after 5 years of payments?

7. John Jones has accumulated debts amounting to $4200. The Friendly Finance Company offer to pay off his debts and let him repay in easy monthly payments over 3 years. If the rate of interest is 18% per annum compounded monthly, calculate his monthly payment.

8. A car can be purchased for $3,300 or $300 down and the balance by equal monthly payments of $110 for 3 years. Calculate the approximate rate of interest.

9. Renovations to a house will cost $1200 cash or $112.50 per month for 1 year. Calculate the approximate rate of interest.

10. In order to furnish an apartment, $4000 was borrowed from the bank to be repaid in 36 equal semi-annual instalments, the rate of interest being 5% compounded semi-annually. Find the amount of each payment.

11. An automobile cost $2500 and has an estimated life of 5 years, at which time it is likely to re-sell for $800. What semi-annual amount should the owner save at his bank which pays $3\frac{1}{2}$% compounded semi-annually, in order to replace the car, paying cash? (Assume the selling price remains $2500).

11.9. Bonds

Canada Savings Bonds may be purchased in units of various denominations with interest payments made once per year. For recent issues it is possible to leave the interest to accumulate at compound interest for the life of the bond.

Corporation bonds are issued in units of $1,000 and interest payments are normally paid every 6 months. Bond prices are quoted in newspapers under headings "Bid", "Ask". A quotation may be given as

	Bid	Ask
Widgett Inc. 7 15 June 1983	81	86

This means that Widgett Incorporated bonds pay interest at 7% per annum, paid semi-annually and are due to be redeemed on 15 June 1983. Until then interest of $35 will be paid on 15 June and 15 December on each $1000 bond. Prospective buyers of the bond are offering to pay $81 for each $100 face value ($810 for a $1000 bond) and prospective sellers are asking $860 for each $1000 bond. Usually transactions will be made somewhere between the two figures. A person who buys a bond will receive payments of $35 every 6 months until 15 June 1983 when he will receive in addition $1000 for the return of the bond. It should be noted that these figures are independent of the price paid for the bond.

We note that if a $1000 bond paying 8% interest semi-annually is purchased for less than $1000 then the actual yield to the purchaser is greater than 8%. However, if over $1000 is paid for the bond, the yield is less than 8%.

Example 1.   How much should be paid on March 1, 1972 for a $1000, 7% bond due on March 1, 1981 if the purchaser wishes to realize 10% per annum compounded semi-annually on his investment.

Solution: 10% semi-annual rate.

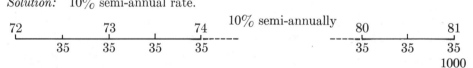

The sequence of payments received by the purchaser is shown in the diagram. The price is the present value of all of these payments at 10% compounded semi-annually.

$$P.V. = 35\ a_{\overline{18}|}\ {}_{.05} + 1000(1.05)^{-18}$$

$$= 35(11.68959) + 1000(.41552)$$

$$= 409.14 + 415.52.$$

Therefore the purchase price = $824.66.

The quoted purchase price of a bond is known as the *flat price* but if a bond is purchased between interest dates, the actual price paid will be the flat price plus the accrued interest since the last interest payment date. If a bond is sold between interest dates the amount received will be the flat price plus the accrued interest.

An additional cost in each case is the stockbroker's commission. At the time of writing this is usually $2.50 per $1000 face value of the bonds bought or sold.

Example 2. Calculate the total cost of $1000, 6% bond quoted at $107\frac{1}{2}$ and purchased on September 15 if the interest dates are July 1 and January 1.

Solution: Flat price = $1075.

Number of days from July 1 to September 15 = 76.

$$\text{Accrued interest} = 1000(.06)\left(\frac{76}{365}\right)$$

$$= \$12.49.$$
Commission = $2.50.
Total cost   = $1089.99.

EXERCISE 11.9

Assume that interest is paid semi-annually in all cases.

1. What would be the flat price of $1,000, 8% bond due in 7 years if the purchaser wishes to obtain a yield of 10% per annum compounded semi-annually?

2. What would be the flat price of a $100, 8% bond due in 7 years if the purchaser wishes to obtain a yield of 6% per annum compounded semi-annually?

3. Calculate the flat price of a $1000, $7\frac{1}{2}$% bond, due in 18 years, to yield the purchaser 9% per annum, compounded semi-annually.

4. Calculate the flat price of $1000, 9% bond, due in 15 years, to yield the purchaser 7% per annum compounded semi-annually.

5. Calculate the total cost of a $1000, 8% bond quoted at 87 and purchased on 16th October if the interest dates are 1st February and 1st August.

6. Calculate the amount received by the seller of bonds with a face value of $8,000 if sold on 3rd March at a quoted price of 95 if the bond interest rate is 7% and the interest dates are 1st January and 1st July (assume that it is not a leap year).

7. Calculate the total cost of 9% bonds worth $15,000 quoted at 105 and bought on 5th December if the interest dates are 15 February and 15th August.

8. Calculate the total cost of the purchase of a $1000, 7% bond on 30th July 1972 if the bond redemption date is 1st May 1983, interest dates are 1st May and 1st November and the purchaser wishes a yield of 9% per annum, compounded semi-annually.

Chapter Summary

Simple Interest: $\qquad A = P(1 + ni)$

Compound Interest: $\qquad A = P(1 + i)^n$

Present Value: $\qquad P.V. = \dfrac{A}{(1 + i)^n} = A(1 + i)^{-n}$

Amount of Annuity: $\qquad A = P \, s_{\overline{n}|\, i}$

Present Value of Annuity: $\qquad P.V. = P \, a_{\overline{n}|\, i}$

REVIEW EXERCISE 11

1. Calculate the amount of $850 for 10 years at
   (a) 4% simple interest   (b) 4% compounded semi-annually.
2. Calculate the equivalent annual rate if the nominal rate is 8% compounded quarterly.
3. Obtain the present value of $1200 due in 15 years if the rate of interest is 5% compounded semi-annually.
4. If $200 is deposited in a bank at the end of each year for 5 years, and the accumulated value is withdrawn 12 years after the first deposit, what is the accumulated value if the rate of interest is 3% compounded annually?
5. Obtain the accumulated value at compound interest of each of the following:
   (a) $250 in 6 years at 4%
   (b) $250 in 6 years at 4% compounded semi-annually
   (c) $850 in $12\frac{1}{2}$ years at 5% compounded semi-annually
   (d) $1000 in 3 years at 15% compounded monthly
   (e) $372.50 in 9 years at 6% compounded quarterly
   (f) $500 in $6\frac{1}{4}$ years at 8%.
6. Obtain the equivalent annual rate in each of the following:
   (a) 18% compounded monthly
   (b) 8% compounded semi-annually
   (c) 4% compounded quarterly
   (d) 18% compounded semi-annually
   (e) 18% compounded quarterly.
7. Obtain the present value of
   (a) $2000 due in 8 years at 5%
   (b) $1500 due in 5 years at 4% compounded quarterly
   (c) $800 due in 2 years at 24% compounded monthly
   (d) $800 due in 2 years at 24% compounded quarterly
   (e) $450 due in $7\frac{1}{2}$ years at 7% compounded semi-annually.

8. $100 is deposited at the end of each year for 10 years in an account which pays interest at 5% per annum. Obtain the accumulated value of the deposits 3 years after the date of the last deposit.

9. What amount invested at the end of each year for 7 years will accumulate to $10,000 immediately after the last deposit if money earns 6% per annum compounded semi-annually?

10. Obtain the present value of an annuity of $1000 which begins now and runs for 8 years, if money is worth 4% compounded quarterly.

11. If money is worth 5% per annum, obtain the annual payment of an annuity which can be bought now for $5000, the first of 6 payments to be 1 year hence.

12. An annuity of $500 is deferred for 6 years and runs for 5 years. Obtain the present value of this annuity if the rate of interest is 4% per annum compounded semi-annually.

13. On each March 1st from 1968 to 1978 inclusive, $1000 is deposited in a fund which pays interest at 6% per annum compounded semi-annually. Determine the accumulated value of these deposits on March 1, 1982.

14. A debt of $6000 is discharged by semi-annual payments of $1000 for as long as necessary. Construct an amortization table for the debt if interest is 8% per annum, compounded semi-annually.

15. Calculate the quarterly payment on a mortgage of $9000 for 8 years, if the rate of interest is 6% per annum compounded quarterly.

16. A ten-year mortgage for $12,000 at 9% per annum compounded semi-annually was assumed on a house on June 1, 1968, payments to be made semi-annually. If the house is sold for $18,000 on June 1, 1972, the new owner agreeing to assume the mortgage and pay the balance in cash, calculate the cash payment due.

17. A car can be purchased for $3800 or $500 down with the balance to be paid in 24 equal monthly instalments of $162.25 for 2 years. Calculate the approximate rate of interest.

18. Calculate the number of equal monthly payments of $200 each required to amortize a debt of $2000 if interest is at the rate of 1% per month. Also calculate the final payment.

19. Calculate the price of a $1000, 6% bond due in 11 years if the purchaser wishes to obtain a yield of 9% per annum, compounded semi-annually.

20. Calculate the total cost of $1000, 9% bond bought on June 20 if the quoted price is $102\frac{1}{2}$ and the interest dates are April 1 and October 1.

Chapter 12

PRESENTATION OF DATA

12.1. Collection of Data

In 1971, the Government of Canada, as it does every ten years, conducted a census of the population of the country. From the census returns a great deal of information about the population was obtained. An obvious first figure was the actual number of Canadians on 1st June 1971. But more than this was asked; what were the numbers in various age groups?; was the population increasing rapidly or slowly?; was the birthrate increasing or decreasing?; what was the average size of home?; what was the average number per family?; and many more such questions.

DEFINITION. Statistics is the science which deals with the collection, tabulation, classification, and analysis of quantitative data.

When a mass of data has been collected it must first be tabulated and organized in a meaningful manner. This organization and presentation of the data is *descriptive statistics*. Once the data has been organized it may then be analysed and conclusions and predictions formulated. This is *inferential statistics* and requires considerable training. In this book we will be concerned with descriptive statistics.

Certain terminology has been used above and we should clarify the meaning of that terminology. The term *data* is applied to the set of numbers which results whenever things are counted or measured. Each number is an *element* or *datum* in the set. The *population* or *universe* is the entire group under consideration and a *sample* is that part of the population which is actually counted or measured.

Once data has been collected the first consideration is how to present that information in a meaningful way. One way is to prepare a graph or chart of the information. Various types of charts are used depending on the nature of the data. Only two of these will be considered here; the pie chart and the histogram.

The *pie chart* consists of a circle divided into sectors with the sector angle proportional to the quantity represented. These sectors are usually arranged in order of magnitude except that any item labelled "Miscellaneous" or "All others" is placed at the end of the set of sectors.

Example 1 Prepare a pie chart to illustrate the sales of the Welcum Supermarket for the week ending September 25, 1971. Meat and fish $12,483.24, Groceries $19,432.37, Fruit and vegetables $4,781.25, Bakery products $5,823.40, Dairy products $8,271.52, Miscellaneous $2,147.82.

Solution.

	Sales	Percentage	Sector Angle
Meat and fish	12,483.24	23.6%	.236 × 360° = 85°
Groceries	19,432.37	36.7%	.367 × 360° = 132°
Fruit and vegetables	4,781.25	9.0%	.09 × 360° = 32°
Bakery products	5,823.40	11.0%	.11 × 360° = 40°
Dairy products	8,271.52	15.6%	.156 × 360° = 56°
Miscellaneous	2,147.82	4.1%	.041 × 360° = 15°
Totals	52,939.60	100.0%	360°

Note that the percentage figures have been taken to 1 decimal place and the angles to the nearest degree. Due to rounding-off errors the totals may not always be exactly 100% and 360° but should approximate these figures.

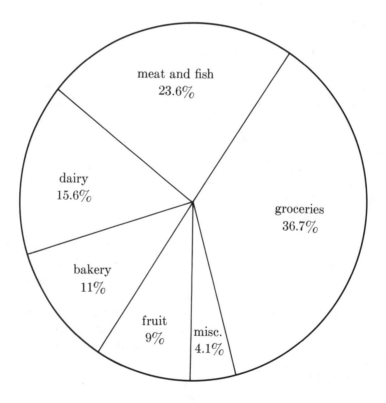

THE HISTOGRAM. In one section of a town the monthly gas bills (in dollars) were tabulated as follows:

10.15	9.40	10.25	10.64	9.25	8.15	9.72	10.10	9.60	10.16
11.87	9.86	13.01	10.18	11.84	9.63	11.55	11.12	8.81	9.49
7.52	8.02	9.15	7.73	9.58	10.86	7.30	10.78	8.30	11.30
8.83	11.05	11.44	8.64	10.47	11.23	9.02	8.76	10.38	9.88
13.95	10.20	9.97	9.95	10.32	10.36	9.86	9.88	11.70	10.46
8.42	9.65	9.83	10.18	12.40	7.87	12.03	9.55	9.44	10.72
12.75	6.82	8.19	10.30	10.02	13.18	10.62	11.23	10.83	9.52
10.51	10.50	13.52	11.79	10.28	9.90	9.14	10.40	11.18	10.10

This mass of figures is rather meaningless as it stands and the first necessity is to arrange it in some sort of order. We note that the lowest figure is $6.82 and the highest is $13.95. The difference between these (that is the *range*) is $7.13.

We could arrange the figures into 15 class intervals, each of length 50¢ as below:

Class Interval	Tally	Frequency
6.80– 7.29	1	1
7.30– 7.79	111	3
7.80– 8.29	1111	4
8.30– 8.79	1111	4
8.80– 9.29	⊦⊦⊦⊦ 1	6
9.30– 9.79	⊦⊦⊦⊦ ⊦⊦⊦⊦	10
9.80–10.29	⊦⊦⊦⊦ ⊦⊦⊦⊦ ⊦⊦⊦⊦ 111	18
10.30–10.79	⊦⊦⊦⊦ ⊦⊦⊦⊦ 111	13
10.80–11.29	⊦⊦⊦⊦ 11	7
11.30–11.79	⊦⊦⊦⊦	5
11.80–12.29	111	3
12.30–12.79	11	2
12.80–13.29	11	2
13.30–13.79	1	1
13.80–14.29	1	1
	Total Frequency	80

Such a table is called a *frequency table* and data have been collected in a *frequency distribution*. The frequency of a class is simply the number in that class. The frequency of the class $8.80 — $9.29 is 6. This frequency distribution is normally the first step in many statistical investigations.

This frequency distribution may be pictured by means of a *histogram* which is simply a graph in which the class intervals are set up on a horizontal line using a convenient scale, while the class frequencies are measured on a vertical line using a convenient scale. The histogram consists of a series of rectangles whose bases represent the class width and whose heights represent the class frequencies.

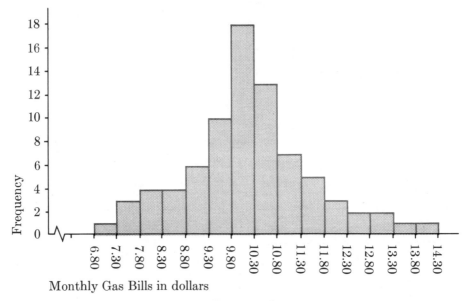

Monthly Gas Bills in dollars

Figure 12.1

The histogram shows us pictorially what the frequency distribution table tells us in numbers. The most frequent bill is in the $9.80 to $10.30 class and the frequencies get less as we go in either direction from this class. This type of symmetrical distribution is very common in statistics.

Example 2. A store selling women's shoes found that over a period of 6 weeks it made the following sales in the different sizes.

Size	2	$2\frac{1}{2}$	3	$3\frac{1}{2}$	4	$4\frac{1}{2}$	5	$5\frac{1}{2}$	6	$6\frac{1}{2}$	7	$7\frac{1}{2}$	8	$8\frac{1}{2}$
Number of sales	1	1	5	8	18	36	54	61	58	32	17	6	0	1

Construct a histogram showing the distribution.

Solution: In this example the class sizes are discrete numbers and not a range of continuously varying numbers. In such a case many statisticians would prefer to use vertical lines in the frequency diagram rather than rectangles. In certain instances, however, it might be useful to construct a histogram. Both forms are shown on the opposite page.

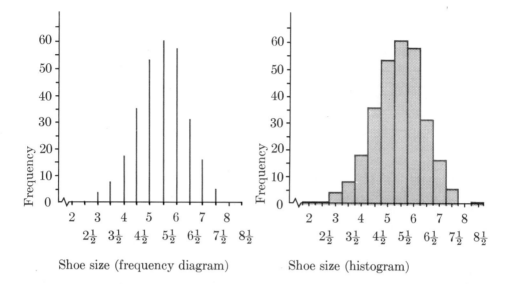

Shoe size (frequency diagram)   Shoe size (histogram)

The frequency diagram on the left indicates that the sizes are discrete numbers. Since the numbers are discrete, there are no class boundaries, so the numbers on the horizontal scale of the histogram are entered in the centres of the bases of the rectangles instead of at the boundaries.

In the example on gas bills we arbitrarily divided the data into 15 classes. In actual practice that number is probably too large. With the example on shoe sizes, there was no difficulty in deciding on the number of classes since each size is automatically a class although it might be possible to combine two or more sizes in one class. When dividing data into classes the main problem is to decide on how many classes we wish. If we choose too many classes the distribution becomes unwieldy, while if we choose too few the differences between the classes would be lost. There is no definite rule regarding the number of classes to be used and experience and examination of the data will often give us an idea as to how many classes to choose.

One rough rule which is frequently used is: obtain the number of elements N and then calculate a number n such that 2^n is approximately equal to N. The number of classes should then lie between $n-1$ and $n+3$. $2^7 = 128$ so that $6 < n < 7$. A suitable number of classes is between $6-1$ and $7+3$ or 5 and 10. We could have made our class interval $1 instead of 50¢ and so used 8 classes instead of 15. It should be remembered that this is *not* a hard and fast rule. It is only a guide and there may be good reasons for not following it in many examples.

If the amount of data is small, the setting up of a frequency distribution in classes is rather pointless. We may as well examine the individual elements. Again it is difficult to lay down a hard and fast rule as to when to divide into classes but one frequently used rough rule is *not* to divide into classes if the number of elements in a set of data is fewer than 50.

In our two previous examples the figures were exact. A gas bill of \$9.84 is exactly \$9.84 and not approximately \$9.84. A shoe size of $4\frac{1}{2}$ is exactly $4\frac{1}{2}$ and not about $4\frac{1}{2}$. However, with figures obtained by measurement the results are only approximations. If a person's weight is 152 lb. we would normally mean that it lies between 151.5 and 152.5 lb. If the smallest figure in a set of such weights were 97 lb. and the largest 230 lb., the range would be $230.5 - 96.5 = 134$ lb. This will be apparent in our next example.

Example 3. The weights of students in first-year mathematics at Utopia University are as given in the following table. All weights are in pounds.

131	147	161	152	159	156	146	142	153	127
185	171	130	145	120	127	137	130	168	158
97	151	178	146	169	163	148	157	148	139
198	134	148	161	145	153	167	150	103	146
112	164	167	168	174	176	117	165	118	165
135	149	141	230	144	135	180	132	172	123
172	166	177	146	186	148	135	159	142	161
146	160	146	170	139	184	173	151	136	140
189	153	188	144	164	221	140	187	163	182
126	170	125	195	183	181	188	156	143	138
151	128	162	152	157	140	166	114	175	166
181	196	184	118	194	190	129	181	128	193
108	143	168	172	128	143	193	160	170	125
163	202	135	180	176	198	152	136	156	145
136	168	204	150	197	141	170	185	194	178
196	192	159	176	162	199	197	144	135	142
143	130	174	153	206	169	133	144	171	153
167	175	182	137	153	182	205	190	168	
156	215	147	206	210	208	166	201	198	
186	159	193	165	157	148	182	158	149	

Construct a frequency table and histogram for the data.

Solution: Smallest weight $= 97$ lb.

Largest weight $= 230$ lb.

Range $= 230.5 - 96.5 = 134$ lb.

Number of entries $= 197$

$2^7 = 128$, $2^8 = 256$, $7 < n < 8$.

Number of classes between 6 and 11.

Choose 9 classes with 15 lb. intervals.

Class Interval	Tally	Frequency
96.5–111.5	111	3
111.5–126.5	ʜʜʟ ʜʜʟ	10
126.5–141.5	ʜʜʟ ʜʜʟ ʜʜʟ ʜʜʟ ʜʜʟ ʜʜʟ 1	31
141.5–156.5	ʜʜʟ ʜʜʟ ʜʜʟ ʜʜʟ ʜʜʟ ʜʜʟ ʜʜʟ ʜʜʟ ʜʜʟ 11	47
156.5–171.5	ʜʜʟ ʜʜʟ ʜʜʟ ʜʜʟ ʜʜʟ ʜʜʟ ʜʜʟ ʜʜʟ 1111	44
171.5–186.5	ʜʜʟ ʜʜʟ ʜʜʟ ʜʜʟ ʜʜʟ ʜʜʟ	30
186.5–201.5	ʜʜʟ ʜʜʟ ʜʜʟ ʜʜʟ 11	22
201.5–216.5	ʜʜʟ 111	8
216.5–231.5	11	2
	Total Frequency	197

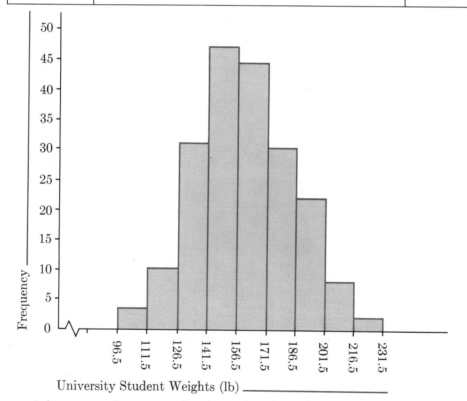

University Student Weights (lb)

A *frequency polygon* may often be preferred to the histogram in picturing the frequency distribution. It may be obtained from the histogram by joining the mid-points of the tops of successive rectangles by straight line segments. However, it is obviously not necessary to construct the histogram first. We may simply use the midpoint of each class interval and join these points.

In Example 3, the midpoint of the 96.5 to 111.5 class is 104; of the 111.5 to 126.5 class is 119 and so on. The frequency polygon for Example 3 is shown below.

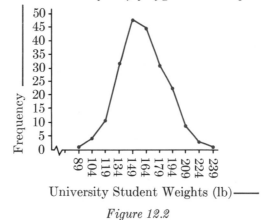

Figure 12.2

Note the midpoint of the first class interval is 104 lb. and the class frequency is 3 but that we start with a frequency of 0 at one class interval below, so that the frequency of the 89 lb. class is 0. Similarly at the upper end the frequency of the 239 lb. class (231.5 to 246.5) is also 0.

EXERCISE 12.1

1. Construct a pie chart to illustrate the distribution of weekly expenses for a manufacturing business as follows.

   Labour $23,472, Raw Materials $12,230, Office $3,824, Shipping $1,852, Maintenance $2,041, Miscellaneous $2,321.

2. The maximum daily temperatures (measured to the nearest degree) in Ottawa during July over a 5-year period were as follows:

Temperature	50–54	55–59	60–64	65–69	70–74	75–79	80–84	85–89	90–94	95–99
Frequency	1	2	13	22	32	44	34	23	11	4

   Construct a histogram of the distribution.

3. Construct a histogram and frequency polygon for the following data. Weekly food bills (in dollars) for families of 4 in a certain community.

Bill	10.00 11.99	12.00 13.99	14.00 15.99	16.00 17.99	18.00 19.99	20.00 21.99	22.00 23.99	24.00 25.99
Frequency	2	4	12	28	51	30	16	3

4. The heights (in inches correct to the nearest inch) of 216 grade 13 male students in the high schools of the town of Brandex were recorded as follows.

65	71	67	71	64	69	70	66	68	65	68
69	66	69	69	71	67	62	69	70	69	63
59	73	72	61	69	72	72	67	63	67	70
70	70	67	72	69	68	67	71	71	73	64
68	67	73	65	74	65	72	61	67	69	72
72	71	64	68	67	69	67	68	71	71	67
61	69	73	72	69	71	70	65	65	62	70
70	73	68	67	70	65	66	70	71	70	66
72	65	63	70	66	68	70	72	68	67	71
70	74	69	74	70	63	71	69	67	60	68
63	72	72	69	69	71	70	72	73	69	74
71	67	74	65	73	70	64	68	63	68	64
71	70	68	73	66	67	70	69	70	71	71
67	74	66	76	68	70	66	73	67	78	65
71	63	70	68	72	71	67	62	70	66	69
68	68	75	71	62	69	70	70	66	68	63
73	71	72	73	74	66	73	71	75	70	
67	76	67	67	68	73	67	74	71	72	
74	70	75	73	69	71	73	70	76	74	
66	73	72	63	72	70	69	67	64	67	

Construct a histogram and frequency polygon of the distribution.

5. Construct a histogram and frequency polygon for the distribution of mathematics marks for 78 grade 12 students as follows.

55	66	64	98	56	69	68	62	52	69	65	63	51
90	69	68	32	66	72	44	80	61	84	74	66	79
61	89	78	63	66	59	75	53	69	23	92	78	73
67	38	65	67	41	75	63	71	57	77	66	56	63
73	100	56	76	71	61	51	46	84	55	63	68	86
65	69	66	60	62	68	82	73	65	76	79	88	44

12.2. Averages

Once a set of data has been arranged in some sort of order, usually by means of a frequency distribution table, the next problem is to extract some useful information from the set. In Example 3 of Section 12.1 where we have a collection of weights, one piece of useful information immediately springs to mind: we could calculate the average weight. However, what precisely do we mean by average? The word average has many meanings, the most common averages being the arithmetic mean, the median, and the mode. Other averages that are sometimes used are the geometric mean and harmonic mean. Most people would understand the word average to mean the arithmetic mean. Because of the possibility of confusion the statistician would avoid using the word average and would use the more precise term for whichever measure he were using. 'Average' encompasses all of the measures of *central tendency.*

The Arithmetic Mean is probably the most commonly used measure of central tendency. So basic is the arithmetic mean in statistics that it is usually known just as the *mean.* The calculation of the mean is intuitively obvious to most people if the data are simple.

Consider the ten numbers

$$7, 13, 12, 18, 25, 43, 27, 16, 32, 24.$$

The mean $\bar{x}$ (x-bar) is

$$\bar{x} = \frac{7+13+12+18+25+43+27+16+32+24}{10} = 21.7.$$

If there are n elements in a set of data we can denote the elements of the set by $x_1, x_2, x_3, \dots , x_n$ and

$$\bar{x} = \frac{1}{n} \sum_{i=1}^{n} x_i$$

The symbol $\sum_{i=1}^{n} x_i$ (read as sigma x_i, i from 1 to n) is a short notation for the sum

of all elements x_i as i takes all integral values from 1 to n or

$$\sum_{i=1}^{n} x_i = x_1 + x_2 + x_3 + \dots + x_n.$$

One more question arises: to how many digits should the mean be calculated? It is difficult to give a hard and fast answer to this as it depends to a large extent on the nature of data, the number of elements in the set of data, and the use to which the mean is to be put! In general, if the set of data is large, the mean is usually calculated to one more significant digit than the common accuracy of the data. If the set of data is small (less than about 30) it is usual to give the mean correct to the same number of significant digits as the data. However, even here many statisticians still prefer to retain one extra digit. In the example of ten numbers above, it would be usual to give the mean as 22 although 21.7 is not unacceptable.

The symbol $\dfrac{1}{n}\displaystyle\sum_{i=1}^{n} x_i$ is usually shortened further to $\dfrac{1}{n}\displaystyle\sum x$ when there is no dubiety about the number of elements.

To calculate the mean of a large number of elements by this method can be very tedious but if these are first arranged in a frequency distribution the principle of the *weighted mean* can be used to shorten the work. As an example we will use the distribution of gas bills from Section 12.1. The table is reproduced below with some additional columns.

Class Interval	x	Frequency(f)	fx
6.80– 7.29	7.045	1	7.045
7.30– 7.79	7.545	3	22.635
7.80– 8.29	8.045	4	32.180
8.30– 8.79	8.545	4	34.180
8.80– 9.29	9.045	6	54.270
9.30– 9.79	9.545	10	95.450
9.80–10.29	10.045	18	180.810
10.30–10.79	10.545	13	137.085
10.80–11.29	11.045	7	77.315
11.30–11.79	11.545	5	57.725
11.80–12.29	12.045	3	36.135
12.30–12.79	12.545	2	25.090
12.80–13.29	13.045	2	26.090
13.30–13.79	13.545	1	13.545
13.80–14.29	14.045	1	14.045
Totals		80	813.600

To obtain a single figure (x) as the representative for each class we simply take the midpoint of the class interval. For the class interval 6.80 — 7.29, the midpoint $\dfrac{6.80+7.29}{2} = 7.045$. This figure is then regarded as a common figure for all elements in that class. The midpoint for the class interval 8.80 — 9.29 is 9.045 and the number of elements in that class is 6. The product (fx) of the frequency and the class value (x) gives us an approximation to the total of all of the figures in that class interval. The weighted mean for the complete data is

$$\bar{x} = \frac{1}{n}\sum fx.$$

In this example $$\bar{x} = \tfrac{1}{80} (813.60)$$

$$= \$10.17.$$

In passing, the actual total of all of gas bills is \$812.54 and

$$\bar{x} = \tfrac{1}{80} (812.54) = \$10.16.$$

Note the method assumes that in any class interval the number of figures below the midpoint and the number above are equal. In practice this will not generally be true but in some intervals there will be more above the midpoint than below while in other intervals the opposite will be true. These two will tend to cancel out and give us a fairly accurate mean. The greater the number of elements in the data set, the more accurate our answer should be.

One way of simplifying the calculations still further is by the use of *coded class values*. We first make an estimate of the possible mean and then calculate the number of classes by which each class value differs from the estimate. If the estimated mean is x_0 and the class value is x_i, then the coded class value (u_i) is

$$u_i = \frac{x_i - x_0}{w} \text{ where } w \text{ is the class width.}$$

In the gas bill example we estimate that the mean value is around \$10.00. Since all class values end in the digits .045 we might decide to use 10.045 as our estimate to make for simpler results. The class width (w) is .50 (in dollars) so that for the class interval 6.80 — 7.29, the class value is 7.045 and

$$u_1 = \frac{7.045 - 10.045}{.5} = \text{-6.}$$

Note that 6 is the number of class widths that 7.045 is below our estimated mean of 10.045.

If we used 10.00 as our estimate then

$$u_1 = \frac{7.045 - 10}{.5} = \text{-5.91}$$

meaning that we are 5.91 class intervals below the estimated mean (x_0).

u_9, the coded mean for the ninth class (10.80 — 11.29) is

$$u_9 = \frac{11.045 - 10.045}{.5} = 2.$$

We will now re-write the table, excluding the class intervals but including the coded values.

Class value(x)	Frequency(f)	Coded value(u)	fu
7.045	1	−6	−6
7.545	3	−5	−15
8.045	4	−4	−16
8.545	4	−3	−12
9.045	6	−2	−12
9.545	10	−1	−10
10.045	18	0	0
10.545	13	1	13
11.045	7	2	14
11.545	5	3	15
12.045	3	4	12
12.545	2	5	10
13.045	2	6	12
13.545	1	7	7
14.045	1	8	8
Totals	80		20

$$x_0 = 10.045. \quad w = .50.$$

The weighted mean of the coded values is

$$\bar{u} = \tfrac{1}{80} \sum fu$$
$$= \tfrac{1}{80} (20) = .25$$

To transform this mean to the required mean $\bar{x}$ we simply reverse the process. Since we subtracted the estimated mean from the original class values and then divided by .50 (the class width) we now multiply $\bar{u}$ by w and then add x_0.

$$\bar{x} = w\bar{u} + x_0$$
$$= .5(.25) + 10.045$$
$$= .125 + 10.045$$
$$= 10.17$$

Note that a judicious selection of x_0 will help to simplify the calculations.

Median. The median is one of the simplest and most obvious measures of central tendency. It is simply the middle number in a set of data.

Consider the numbers 7.2, 8.3, 4.5, 6.7, 11.2, 4.8, 9.4, 2.8, 11.3. There are nine numbers in the set and the fifth number from either the smallest or greatest is the median. By inspection in this case the median is 7.2. The numbers 2.8, 4.5, 4.8, and 6.7 are' smaller while 8.3, 9.4, 11.2, and 11.3 are greater.

In general, if there are n numbers in a set of data and n is *odd*, the median is the number in position $\dfrac{n + 1}{2}$.

If the number of elements is even such as in the set, 4, 11, 5, 6, 18, 21, 7, 3, 12, 9 there is no element exactly in the middle. In this case, with ten elements the fifth and sixth elements are equidistant from the ends. In such a case we take the mean of these two elements as the median. The fifth element is 7 and the sixth is 9 so the median is $\frac{7 + 9}{2} = 8$.

In general, if there are n elements in a set of data and n is *even*, the median is the midpoint of the numbers in positions $\frac{n}{2}$ and $\frac{n}{2} + 1$.

In the case of a large set of data arranged in a frequency distribution it is more difficult to find the median by inspection. However, a very close approximation can be easily obtained.

If we consider the gas bill distribution table we see that there are 80 elements and so the median is midway between the 40th and 41st elements. From 6.80 to 9.79 we have total of 28 bills, and in the 9.80 – 10.29 class we have 18. The 40th and 41st will be in this class. The class width is .50 (dollars) and the median will be in position $40.5 - 28 = 12.5$ in the 9.80 – 10.29 class. Assuming that the 18 elements in this class are evenly distributed, the median is

$$9.79 + \tfrac{12.5}{18} \, (.50) = 9.79 + .35$$
$$= 10.14$$

This means that there are as many gas bills below $10.14 as above.

If the number of data is small (say less than 40) it is usual to round off correct to the same number of digits as the most common number in the data. If the number is large there is some justification in retaining one more digit. However, as with the mean, this is subject to the nature of the data.

The method may be criticized on the grounds that it assumes a symmetrical distribution within the classes and particularly in that class containing the median. This criticism is valid particularly if the total number of elements is small, if the class interval is large, or if the distribution is not reasonably symmetrical. However, for most frequency distributions it is considered to be reasonably satisfactory.

With most distributions the mean and median will be reasonably close. In this case there is a slight but insignificant variation. What would cause the mean to be greater than the median? What would cause the median to be greater than the mean?

Mode. If we consider the set of numbers
$$3, 4, 4, 5, 6, 6, 6, 6, 7, 8, 8, 9, 10,$$
we notice that 6 occurs more frequently than any other number in the set. The number 6 is defined to be the *mode* of this set of data.

DEFINITION: The mode is that number which occurs with greater frequency than any neighbouring number.

It is quite possible to have bimodal or even multimodal sets of data. For example the set

$$5, 7, 8, 8, 8, 9, 10, 11, 12, 12, 12, 13, 13, 14$$

has two distinct modes (8 and 12).

If a set of data has been arranged in a frequency distribution the mode is the point corresponding to the greatest frequency and the *modal class* is that class of greater frequency than any neighbouring class.

Considering the set of data for gas bills we note that the mode is $10.045 or $10.05 since that is the midpoint of the class of greatest frequency. More usefully, the modal class is the class 9.80 – 10.29.

In such a set of data the mode is not a particularly useful average. There is no guarantee, in fact it is most unlikely, that $10.04 or $10.05 occur more frequently than any other bill. The modal class is a little more useful but, even here, the choice of a different class width may cause a difference in the apparent modal class. For such a set of data, the mean and median are more meaningful averages.

A manufacturer of men's shoes may find that the mean size of his sales over a period of time is 8.3, the median is 8.1 and the mode is 8. In his case the mode would be the most useful. Since he does not manufacture sizes 8.1 and 8.3 these are useless as averages. However, the size most frequently in demand is size 8 and he can gear his production accordingly. The mode is the most useful average in this case.

What is the most useful average in a set of data? With the manufacture of men's shoes the mode is the obvious answer but in other cases the answer is not so obvious, particularly when we have to choose between mean and median. In very many cases there is little difference between the two and either will serve equally well. Where there is a significant difference the most suitable may or may not be immediately obvious.

Consider a student who, on five tests, has obtained percentage marks of 46, 53, 60, 81, 81. The mode is 81 but very obviously is not a suitable average. The median is 60 while the mean is 64 (to nearest integer). If all marks are equally weighted it seems that the mean is the best average in such a case.

In a mathematics class of 27 students the marks on a test were as follows:

$$41, 43, 46, 50, 51, 51, 51, 53, 54, 55, 56, 56, 57, 58, 62, 65, 67, 68, 68,$$
$$69, 70, 71, 73, 77, 95, 97, 98.$$

The mode of 51 is obviously not a suitable average, but which is the more suitable; a median of 58 or a mean of 63? In this case the mean has been distorted by the 3 brilliant mathematicians with scores of 95, 97, and 98. Most statisticians would consider the median as the more meaningful. However, it should be pointed out that a few might argue in favour of the mean.

Example 1. Using the frequency table for sizes of women's shoes in Example 2 of Section 12.1, calculate the mean, median, and mode. Which average is the most meaningful?

Solution: In setting up the table we introduce a new column headed cum f (cumulative frequency) to keep a total frequency up to that point as an aid in computing the median.

Class value(x)	Frequency(f)	Cum f	Coded value(u)	fu.
2	1	1	−6	−6
$2\frac{1}{2}$	1	2	−5	−5
3	5	7	−4	−20
$3\frac{1}{2}$	8	15	−3	−24
4	18	33	−2	−36
$4\frac{1}{2}$	36	69	−1	−36
5	54	123	0	0
$5\frac{1}{2}$	61	184	1	61
6	58	242	2	116
$6\frac{1}{2}$	32	274	3	96
7	17	291	4	68
$7\frac{1}{2}$	6	297	5	30
8	0	297	6	0
$8\frac{1}{2}$	1	298	7	7
Totals	298			251

$$x_0 = 5, \; w = \tfrac{1}{2}$$

$$\bar{u} = \tfrac{1}{298}(251)$$

$$= .842$$

$$\bar{x} = w\bar{u} + x_0$$

$$= \tfrac{1}{2}(.842) + 5$$

$$= 5.4.$$

Median is between x_{149} and x_{150}.

$$149.5 - 123 = 26.5.$$

Median is $5 + \frac{26.5}{61}(\tfrac{1}{2}) = 5.2.$

Hence mean is 5.4, median is 5.2 and mode is $5\frac{1}{2}$. The mode is the most meaningful.

Example 2. Using the table of student weights in Example 3 of Section 12.1, calculate the mean, median and mode. Which average is most meaningful?

Solution:

Class Interval	Class value(x)	Frequency	Cum f	Coded value(u)	fu
96.5–111.5	104	3	3	−4	−12
111.5–126.5	119	10	13	−3	−30
126.5–141.5	134	31	44	−2	−62
141.5–156.5	149	47	91	−1	−47
156.5–171.5	164	44	135	0	0
171.5–186.5	179	30	165	1	30
186.5–201.5	194	22	187	2	44
201.5–216.5	209	8	195	3	24
216.5–231.5	224	2	197	4	8
Totals		197			−45

$$x_0 = 164, w = 15.$$
$$\bar{u} = \tfrac{1}{197}(-45)$$
$$= -.228$$
$$\bar{x} = w\bar{u} + x_0$$
$$= 15(-.228) + 164$$
$$= 160.6$$

Median is in position 99.
$$99 - 91 = 8.$$
Median is $\quad 156.5 + \tfrac{8}{44}(15) = 159.2.$
Mean is 160.6 lb., median is 159.2 lb., mode is 149 lb.

The most meaningful average is the median. Note that a good case could be made for the mean as the most meaningful in this case and the choice between median and mean is open to question.

The mode is very inappropriate particularly when the 141.5 – 156.5 and 156.5 – 171.5 class have almost equal frequencies.

EXERCISE 12.2

In questions 1-4, calculate the mean, median and mode and discuss the appropriateness of each average.

1. The first 12 contributions to a university building fund were $10, $20, $5000, $100, $20, $4000, $50, $20, $100, $20, $5, $60.

2. During a 15-day period in June, the maximum temperatures recorded in Ottawa were
75°, 73°, 58°, 67°, 81°, 84°, 92°, 78°, 77°, 75°, 76°, 71°, 75°, 69°, 84°.

3. A sample of 20 washers from a machine had thickness (in centimetres) of
.0105, .0102, .0102, .0101, .0104, .0106, .0101, .0100, .0098,
.0102, .0103, .0099, .0100, .0104, .0102, .0098, .0102, .0104,
.0102, .0104.

4. A baseball player had the following batting averages over 9 seasons.

.213 in 24 games,	.282 in 57 games,	.278 in 68 games,
.295 in 104 games,	.315 in 112 games,	.288 in 110 games,
.326 in 48 games,	.241 in 103 games,	.277 in 114 games.

5. Calculate the mean, median and mode for the frequency distributions in questions 2 to 5 in Exercise 12.1.

12.3. Standard Deviation

The following two sets of numbers each have the same mean and median:

(a) 7, 8, 9, 10, 11, 12, 13, 14, 15, 16, 17, 18, 19, 20, 21.

(b) 12, 12, 12, 13, 13, 13, 14, 14, 14, 15, 15, 15, 16, 16, 16.

However, there is an obvious difference between the two sets. In set (b) the figures are much more closely clustered around the mean. Knowing the mean or median does not tell us everything about the variability of the set.

Range. One easily calculated value is the *range* of the numbers on the set. By simply subtracting the smallest number from the largest we obtain a range of 14 in (a) and of 4 in (b). A doctor would use the range of fluctuations in a patient's temperature and there are several other applications of the range. However, it does have some severe limitations. In particular, a single abnormally high or low value can increase the range considerably. In (b) if one number had been 2, instead of 12, the range would increase from 4 to 14 and both (a) and (b) would have the same range. The mean, of course, would also be affected slightly but the median would remain unaltered. Except for that one abnormal value, set (b) would still be considered more tightly clustered around the mean than (a) but the range does not indicate that.

DEFINITION. *The mean deviation (M.D.) of a set of numbers is the arithmetic mean of the absolute values of their deviations from their arithmetic mean.*

In the set (a) above, the mean of the set is 14 and the absolute values of the individual deviations from this mean are
7, 6, 5, 4, 3, 2, 1, 0, 1, 2, 3, 4, 5, 6, 7,

$$M.D. = \tfrac{1}{15} (7 + 6 + 5 + 4 + 3 + 2 + 1 + 0 + 1 + 2 + 3 + 4 + 5 + 6 + 7)$$
$$= \tfrac{56}{15} = 3.73$$

In set (b)

$$M.D. = \tfrac{1}{15} (2 + 2 + 2 + 1 + 1 + 1 + 0 + 0 + 0 + 1 + 1 + 1 + 2 + 2 + 2)$$
$$= \tfrac{1}{15} (18) = 1.2.$$

The much lower figure in set (b) shows a closer cluster around the mean. Even if one 12 were a 2. The mean deviation would be $\tfrac{1}{15}$ (28) = 1.87 still showing a closer cluster around the mean than (a).

$$M.D. = \frac{1}{n} \sum_{i=1}^{n} |x_i - \bar{x}|$$

or, if no dubiety exists, $M.D. = \dfrac{1}{n} \sum |x - \bar{x}|.$

Standard Deviation. The standard deviation is the most important and most widely used measure of variability. It involves more calculation than the mean deviation but is more amenable to algebraic manipulations and, in more advanced statistical analysis, it leads to useful and interesting results.

DEFINITION. The *standard deviation* of a set of numbers is the square root of the mean of the squares of their deviations from their mean.

In symbols, if the numbers are $x_1, x_2, x_3, \ldots, x_n$ and their mean is $\bar{x}$, then the standard deviation (s) is given by

$$s = \left[\frac{1}{n} \sum_{i=1}^{n} (x_i - \bar{x})^2 \right]^{\frac{1}{2}}$$

or

$$s = \left[\frac{1}{n} \sum (x - \bar{x})^2 \right]^{\frac{1}{2}}$$

One useful theorem, which we will not prove here is that

$$\frac{1}{n} \sum (x - \bar{x})^2 = \frac{1}{n} \sum x^2 - \bar{x}^2$$

so that

$$s = \left[\frac{1}{n} \sum x^2 - \bar{x}^2 \right]^{\frac{1}{2}}$$

In order to demonstrate the equivalence of the two formulae we will calculate the standard deviation for the two sets of numbers (a) and (b) above.

(a)

x	$x-\bar{x}$	$(x-\bar{x})^2$	x^2
7	-7	49	49
8	-6	36	64
9	-5	25	81
10	-4	16	100
11	-3	9	121
12	-2	4	144
13	-1	1	169
14	0	0	196
15	1	1	225
16	2	4	256
17	3	9	289
18	4	16	324
19	5	25	361
20	6	36	400
21	7	49	441
Totals 210	0	280	3220

(b)

x	$x-\bar{x}$	$(x-\bar{x})^2$	x^2
12	-2	4	144
12	-2	4	144
12	-2	4	144
13	-1	1	169
13	-1	1	169
13	-1	1	169
14	0	0	196
14	0	0	196
14	0	0	196
15	1	1	225
15	1	1	225
15	1	1	225
16	2	4	256
16	2	4	256
16	2	4	256
Totals 210	0	30	2970

$$\bar{x} = \tfrac{210}{15} = 14; \ \bar{x}^2 = 196$$
$$s = [\tfrac{1}{15} \Sigma (x-\bar{x})^2]^{\frac{1}{2}}$$
$$= [\tfrac{1}{15} (280)]^{\frac{1}{2}}$$
$$= (18.67)^{\frac{1}{2}}$$
$$= 4.32.$$

$$\bar{x} = 14; \ \bar{x}^2 = 196$$
$$s = [\tfrac{1}{15} \Sigma (x-\bar{x})^2]^{\frac{1}{2}}$$
$$= [\tfrac{1}{15} (30)]^{\frac{1}{2}}$$
$$= 2^{\frac{1}{2}}$$
$$= 1.41.$$

or

$$s = [\tfrac{1}{15} \Sigma x^2 - \bar{x}^2]^{\frac{1}{2}}$$
$$= [\tfrac{1}{15} (3220) - 196]^{\frac{1}{2}}$$
$$= [214.67 - 196]^{\frac{1}{2}}$$
$$= (18.67)^{\frac{1}{2}}$$
$$= 4.32.$$

or

$$s = [\tfrac{1}{15} \Sigma x^2 - \bar{x}^2]^{\frac{1}{2}}$$
$$= [\tfrac{1}{15} (2970) - 196]^{\frac{1}{2}}$$
$$= (198 - 196)^{\frac{1}{2}}$$
$$= 1.41.$$

While the second method avoids the calculation of the differences $(x-\bar{x})$ it does lead usually to larger figures. This disadvantage can be overcome by using coded values as in calculating the mean in Section 12.2. If we represent the standard deviation of the given values by s_x and of the coded values by s_u, we recall from Section 12.2 that

$$u_i = \frac{x_i - x_0}{w} \text{ where } x_0 \text{ is estimated mean.}$$

Hence
$$x_i - x_0 = wu_i.$$

Also
$$\bar{x} - x_0 = w\bar{u}.$$

By subtraction
$$x_i - \bar{x} = wu_i - w\bar{u}$$
$$(x_i - \bar{x})^2 = w^2(u_i - \bar{u})^2$$

$$\frac{1}{n} \sum (x_i - \bar{x})^2 = \frac{1}{n} \sum w^2(u_i - \bar{u})^2$$

$$\left[\frac{1}{n} \sum (x_i - \bar{x})^2 \right]^{\frac{1}{2}} = \left[\frac{1}{n} \cdot w^2 \sum (u_i - \bar{u})^2 \right]^{\frac{1}{2}}$$

$$= w \left[\frac{1}{n} \sum (u_i - \bar{u})^2 \right]^{\frac{1}{2}}$$

That is
$$s_x = ws_u.$$

We will now use this to calculate the mean and standard deviation of the gas bills from Sections 12.1 and 12.2.

x	f	u	u^2	fu	fu^2
7.045	1	-6	36	-6	36
7.545	3	-5	25	-15	75
8.045	4	-4	16	-16	64
8.545	4	-3	9	-12	36
9.045	6	-2	4	-12	24
9.545	10	-1	1	-10	10
10.045	18	0	0	0	0
10.545	13	1	1	13	13
11.045	7	2	4	14	28
11.545	5	3	9	15	45
12.045	3	4	16	12	48
12.545	2	5	25	10	50
13.045	2	6	36	12	72
13.545	1	7	49	7	49
14.045	1	8	64	8	64
Totals	80			20	614

$$x_0 = 10.045, \ w = .50.$$
$$\bar{u} = \frac{1}{80} \Sigma fu$$

$$= \tfrac{1}{80}(20) = .25.$$
$$\bar{x} = w\bar{u} + x_0$$
$$= .5(.25) + 10.045$$
$$= 10.17$$

$$s_u = \left[\frac{1}{n} \sum fu^2 - \bar{u}^2\right]^{\frac{1}{2}}$$
$$= [\tfrac{1}{80}(614) - .0625]^{\frac{1}{2}}$$
$$= (7.675 - .0625)^{\frac{1}{2}}$$
$$= (7.6125)^{\frac{1}{2}} = 2.76$$

$$s_x = .50(2.76)$$
$$= 1.38.$$

Mean is $10.17 and standard deviation is $1.38.

Generally, the standard deviation is given correct to 3 significant digits. However, this again depends to a certain extent on the nature of the data.

With a reasonably normal distribution of data it is usually found that approximately two-thirds of the numbers will lie between the limits $\bar{x} \pm s_x$. In the above example we would expect that about two-thirds of the gas bills would lie between $(10.17 - 1.38)$ and $(10.17 + 1.38)$; that is between $8.79 and $11.55.

Example 1. Using the frequency table for sizes of women's shoes in Example 1 of Section 12.2, calculate the standard deviation.

Solution:

x	f	u	u^2	fu	fu^2
2	1	-6	36	-6	36
$2\frac{1}{2}$	1	-5	25	-5	25
3	5	-4	16	-20	80
$3\frac{1}{2}$	8	-3	9	-24	72
4	18	-2	4	-36	72
$4\frac{1}{2}$	36	-1	1	-36	36
5	54	0	0	0	0
$5\frac{1}{2}$	61	1	1	61	61
6	58	2	4	116	232
$6\frac{1}{2}$	32	3	9	96	288
7	17	4	16	68	272
$7\frac{1}{2}$	6	5	25	30	150
8	0	6	36	0	0
$8\frac{1}{2}$	1	7	49	7	49
Totals	298			251	1373

$$x_0 = 5, w = \tfrac{1}{2}.$$

$$\bar{u} = .842, \bar{x} = 5.4 \text{ (see Section 12.2)}$$

$$s_u = \left[\frac{1}{n} \sum fu^2 - \bar{u}^2 \right]^{\frac{1}{2}}$$

$$= \left[\tfrac{1}{298}(1373) - .709 \right]^{\frac{1}{2}}$$
$$= (4.604 - .709)^{\frac{1}{2}}$$
$$= (3.895)^{\frac{1}{2}}$$
$$\doteq 1.97.$$

$$s_x = ws_u$$
$$= \tfrac{1}{2}(1.97)$$
$$= .99.$$

Standard deviation is .99.

Example 2. Using the distribution of student weights in Example 2 of Section 12.2 calculate the standard deviation.

Solution:

x	f	u	u^2	fu	fu^2
104	3	-4	16	-12	48
119	10	-3	9	-30	90
134	31	-2	4	-62	124
149	47	-1	1	-47	47
164	44	0	0	0	0
179	30	1	1	30	30
194	22	2	4	44	88
209	8	3	9	24	72
224	2	4	16	8	32
Totals	197			-45	531

$$x_0 = 164, w = 15.$$

$$\bar{u} = -.228, \bar{x} = 160.6 \text{ (from Example 2,}$$
$$\text{Section 12.2)}$$

$$s_u = \left[\tfrac{1}{197}(531) - .052 \right]^{\frac{1}{2}}$$
$$= (2.695 - .052)^{\frac{1}{2}}$$
$$= (2.643)^{\frac{1}{2}}$$
$$\doteq 1.625.$$

$$s_x = 15(1.625)$$
$$= 24.4.$$

Standard deviation is 24.4 lb.

When comparing two sets of data where the measurements are radically different, it is difficult to say at a glance which is the more variable. If, for example, the mean weight of elephants is 6000 lb. with a standard deviation of 1200 lb. are elephants more variable in weight than the student sample in Example 2?

A useful comparison is the *co-efficient of variation* (V) where

$$V = \frac{s_x}{\bar{x}}.$$

For students

$$V = \frac{24.4}{160.6} = .152$$

For elephants

$$V = \frac{1200}{6000} = .200.$$

This means that for students the standard deviation is 15.2% of the mean while for elephants it is 20%. Elephant weights are more variable than the student weights.

EXERCISE 12.3

For each of the examples in Exercise 12.2, calculate the standard deviation.

12.4. Quartiles, Deciles, Percentiles

In the gas bill problem, there are 80 elements and we calculated in Section 12.2 that the median was $10.14. This means that half of the bills (40) would be below $10.14 and one half above.

Similarly we can define quartiles, deciles, and percentiles. The median divides the data into 2 equal parts, the quartiles divide the data into 4 equal parts, the deciles into 10 equal parts, and the percentiles into 100 equal parts. Note that for percentiles in particular and for deciles to a lesser extent, the figures will be rather meaningless for small samples. With only 80 samples in the gas bill problem division into percentiles would be rather meaningless.

The first quartile (Q_1) is a figure such that $\frac{1}{4}$ of the figures in the data set are below it and $\frac{3}{4}$ above it. The second quartile is obviously the median, and the third quartile (Q_3) will have $\frac{3}{4}$ of the figures less than it.

The fourth decile (D_4) is a figure such that $\frac{4}{10}$ of the figures in the data set are below it.

The twentieth percentile (P_{20}) is a figure such that 20% of the figures in the data set are below it.

Since there are 80 numbers in the set of gas bills, the first quartile will be in position $\frac{1}{4}(80) = 20$. This figure will come in the $9.30 - $9.79 class. There are

18 figures below \$9.30 and 10 figures in that class. Hence we are looking for the second figure in the \$9.30 — \$9.79 class. The class width is \$.50 and the value of the second figure will be approximately

$$Q_1 = 9.29 + \tfrac{20-18}{10}(.50) = \$9.39.$$

To obtain Q_3 we note that

$$\tfrac{3}{4}(n) = \tfrac{3}{4}(80) = 60.$$
$$Q_3 = 10.79 + \tfrac{60-59}{7}(.50)$$
$$= \$10.86$$

For the fourth decile

$$\tfrac{4}{10}(n) = \tfrac{4}{10}(80) = 32.$$
$$D_4 = 9.79 + \tfrac{32-28}{18}(.50)$$
$$= \$9.90.$$

Statistically, quartiles, deciles and percentiles have limited but important application. If several thousand grade 12 students all write a standard achievement test in mathematics, the fact that Joe Jones scored 256 on the test is rather meaningless. Even knowing that the total possible score was 500 and hence that Joe made 51.2% is rather meaningless. It is more important to know how Joe was placed in relation to the others who wrote the test. If we know that Joe's score is in the 75th percentile (that is between the 74th and 75th percentile scores) we know that 74% of those writing the test made less than Joe and that 25% made more. This gives a much better idea of Joe's achievement. Note that the highest percentile is the 99th.

In the gas bill problem, the first quartile is \$9.39 and the median is \$10.14; all bills between \$9.39 and \$10.14 lie in the second quartile; all bills below \$9.39 in the first quartile; all bills between \$10.14 and \$10.86 in the third quartile; all bills above \$10.86 in the fourth quartile.

Example 1. Using the table of student weights in Example 2 of Section 12.2, calculate the values of Q_1, D_6, P_{35} (35th percentile), P_{80}.

Solution:

$$n = 197.$$

$$\tfrac{1}{4}(n) = 49.25$$

$$Q_1 = 141.5 + \left(\tfrac{49.25-44}{47}\right)(15)$$
$$= 141.5 + 1.68$$
$$= 143.2 \text{ lb.}$$

$$\tfrac{6}{10}(n) = 118.2.$$
$$D_6 = 156.5 + \left(\tfrac{118.2-91}{44}\right)(15)$$
$$= 156.5 + 9.27$$
$$= 165.8 \text{ lb.}$$

$$\tfrac{35}{100}(n) = 68.95$$
$$P_{35} = 141.5 + (\tfrac{68 \cdot 95 - 44}{47})\,(15)$$
$$= 141.5 + 7.96$$
$$= 149.5 \text{ lb.}$$

$$\tfrac{80}{100}(n) = 157.6 \quad -$$
$$P_{80} = 171.5 + (\tfrac{157 \cdot 6 - 135}{30})\,(15)$$
$$= 171.5 + 11.3$$
$$= 182.8 \text{ lb.}$$

Since 50% of the figures in a set of data will lie between the first and third quartiles it would appear that these figures would give a reasonable measure of dispersion about the median. It is not a measure that is often used, the standard deviation is usually more useful, but the quartile deviation (Q) is given by

$$Q = \tfrac{1}{2}(Q_3 - Q_1).$$

In the gas bill problem, $Q_1 = \$9.39$, $Q_3 = \$10.86$ and the quartile deviation is

$$Q = \tfrac{1}{2}(10.86 - 9.39)$$
$$= \$.74.$$

EXERCISE 12.4

1. Using the data in question 2, Exercise 12.2, calculate Q_1, Q_3, D_4.

2. Using the data in question 3, Exercise 12.2, calculate Q_3, D_4, D_6.

3. Using the data in question 2, Exercise 12.1, calculate Q_1, Q_3, Q, D_6, P_{40}, P_{80}.

4. Using the data in question 3, Exercise 12.1, calculate Q_3, D_1, P_{20}, P_{90}.

5. Using the data in question 4, Exercise 12.1, calculate Q_1, D_8, P_{15}, P_{65}.

6. Using the data in question 4, Exercise 12.1, calculate Q_1, Q_3, Q, P_{75}, P_{90}. Which of these two values are equal and why are they equal?

Chapter Summary

Frequency distribution and histogram.
In a set of N elements, the number of classes in a frequency distribution is usually between $n - 1$ and $n + 3$ where n is a positive integer such that $2^n \simeq N$.

Mean:
$$\bar{x} = \frac{1}{n} \sum_{i=1}^{n} x_i$$

Median is middle number in a data set.
Mode is the number occurring with greatest frequency in a set of data.

Coded values:

$$u_i = \frac{x_i - x_0}{w}$$

where x_0 is estimated mean and w is class width.

$$\bar{x} = w\bar{u} + x_0$$

Mean Deviation:

$$M.D. = \frac{1}{n} \sum_{i=1}^{n} x_i - \bar{x}$$

Standard Deviation:

$$s = \left[\frac{1}{n} \sum_{i=1}^{n} (x_i - \bar{x})^2 \right]^{\frac{1}{2}}$$

$$= \left[\frac{1}{n} \sum_{i=1}^{n} x_i^2 - \bar{x}^2 \right]^{\frac{1}{2}}$$

$$s_x = w s_u.$$

REVIEW EXERCISE 12

1. For the following set of figures, calculate the mean, median, Q_1, and the standard deviation.

   3.7, 4.2, 4.5, 6.4, 6.7, 6.9, 7.2, 8.1, 8.4, 8.9, 9.1, 9.2, 9.8, 10.3, 10.5, 10.8, 11.1, 11.8, 12.3.

2. 4,825 students wrote a mathematical ability test with the results distributed as follows.

Score	1-10	11-20	21-30	31-40	41-50	51-60	61-70	71-80	81-90	91-100	101-110	111-120	121-130	131-140	141-150
Number	8	41	93	188	327	455	756	1004	827	422	365	201	95	37	6

Construct a histogram of the distribution and calculate the mean, median, mode, standard deviation, Q_1, Q_3, D_7, P_{41}, P_{81}, P_{82}.

What scores would be in the 81st percentile?

3. The hourly wage for bricklayers in a survey made in a cross-Canada survey produced the following distribution.

2.00-2.49	2.50-2.99	3.00-3.49	3.50-3.99	4.00-4.49	4.50-4.99	5.00-5.49	5.50-5.99
15	38	87	123	98	72	36	8

Construct a histogram and frequency polygon of the distribution, and calculate the mean, median, standard deviation, co-efficient of variation, Q_1, Q_3, Q, D_3, D_8.

4. The chest measurements (correct to the nearest inch) of 160 grade 12 students were recorded as follows:

35	33	37	36	37	36	38	43	37	40	39	38	39	36	39	38
35	38	40	37	35	39	32	35	39	37	33	37	35	39	36	34
39	38	35	39	38	36	39	38	37	34	38	40	41	38	39	37
31	36	38	33	39	37	38	36	39	41	39	38	33	39	38	39
39	41	36	41	36	42	39	38	35	38	36	44	37	35	40	32
37	37	39	37	48	34	37	39	39	37	39	35	39	45	37	39
40	41	40	42	41	40	44	40	43	41	42	41	40	40	42	40
42	44	43	46	41	42	42	44	41	43	40	41	42	40	40	42
41	40	42	43	44	40	43	42	40	41	42	40	40	43	43	41
44	41	45	40	42	44	41	47	42	42	40	46	43	44	40	40

(a) Prepare a frequency distribution table and sketch a frequency polygon of the distribution.
(b) Calculate the mean, median, mode, and standard deviation.
(c) Which of these averages would be most useful to a shirt manufacturer? To the Department of Health?
(d) Calculate Q_1, Q_3, P_{30}, P_{80}.

5. The weekly food bills of a family over a 25-week period were:
$16.43, $12.54, $19.36, $17.83, $11.72, $15.68, $21.40, $13.20, $12.80, $16.54, $18.96, $23.42, $19.47, $13.28, $17.64, $21.85, $32.54, $17.61, $19.27, $12.93, $18.54, $17.83, $18.46, $24.52, $16.75.
Calculate the mean, median, and standard deviation.

6. 288 machinists were timed on a certain operation and the times taken to the nearest second were recorded in the following chart.

140	155	149	145	152	141	156	146	152	146	150	148	137	152	147	145
149	130	157	161	172	154	149	144	157	154	159	158	163	160	156	150
158	163	138	150	147	158	160	159	135	156	145	141	154	146	142	156
144	150	156	154	153	140	152	147	164	151	157	149	148	154	159	146
156	173	148	143	156	162	136	154	150	141	154	155	157	164	145	152
151	154	159	160	147	150	155	142	152	148	146	144	148	149	157	155
146	135	151	146	158	157	149	157	155	153	162	161	158	153	151	142
153	156	146	153	153	144	162	153	146	158	149	151	132	159	166	150
162	153	158	162	140	157	151	140	161	143	159	157	163	146	144	157
142	147	151	139	149	148	146	158	150	165	150	138	150	155	158	146
150	161	155	151	161	156	150	154	162	151	159	156	163	151	148	162
160	149	142	157	145	154	165	144	148	148	140	150	146	151	153	149
153	155	153	149	159	142	146	160	154	170	161	147	153	153	167	138
145	152	156	164	151	168	149	151	163	147	151	160	156	141	147	165
150	159	151	141	155	146	164	169	144	153	166	149	143	158	162	150
157	143	154	162	154	153	151	145	178	164	145	159	169	150	152	166
154	160	167	150	148	166	154	172	154	149	174	142	151	146	174	140
148	152	147	163	169	137	158	152	146	166	154	150	160	159	154	144

Calculate the mean, median, mode, standard deviation, Q_1, D_8, P_{35}, P_{84}.

Chapter 13

ARRANGEMENTS AND SUBSETS

13.1.   Arrangements of a Set

If two sets A and B contain r elements and s elements, respectively, we know that the Cartesian product set $A \times B$ contains rs elements. This could be reworded to state that, if a certain act can be performed in r different ways and if, for each of these ways, a second act can be performed in s different ways, then the two acts can be performed successively in rs different ways.

Consider the set of five elements $A = \{a, b, c, d, e\}$. The number of elements in the subset of $A \times A \times A$, in which no two of the members in each ordered triple are alike, is $5 \times 4 \times 3$ or 60. We can arrive at this by considering that we have 3 spaces ☐☐☐ to fill for each element of $A \times A \times A$. The first space can be filled with any one of the five letters. For each of these ways the second space can be filled with any one of the four remaining letters. Hence the first two spaces can be filled in $5 \times 4 = 20$ different ways. For each of these ways, the third space can be filled with any of the three remaining letters. The three spaces can, therefore, be filled in $5 \times 4 \times 3$ or 60 different ways.

In this case we have sixty 3-arrangements of five objects. We note that the set $A \times A \times A$ contains $5 \times 5 \times 5$ or 125 elements, each of which is an ordered triple, and also includes ordered triples with two or three like letters.

This can be extended to include arrangements of any finite number of elements from any finite set.

DEFINITION.   An r-arrangement of n objects is an *ordered* selection of r of the objects ($r \in W$, $n \in N$).

The number of r-arrangements may be deduced in the same way as we found the number of 3-arrangements of five objects.

n	$n - 1$	$n - 2$	...	$n - (r - 1)$

We may select the first object in n different ways. For each of these ways, the second object can be selected from any one of the remaining $(n - 1)$ objects.

The first two objects can, therefore, be selected in $n(n-1)$ different ways and, for each of these ways, the third object can be selected in $(n-2)$ different ways. The first three objects can be selected in $n(n-1)(n-2)$ ways. Continuing this procedure, the rth object can be selected in $n-(r-1)$ different ways $(r \leq n)$. The r objects can be selected in $n(n-1)(n-2) \ldots (n-r+1)$ different ways.

Therefore, the number of r-arrangements of n objects is

$$n(n-1)(n-2) \ldots (n-r+1) \qquad (r \leq n).$$

Various symbols are used to indicate the number of r-arrangements of n objects taken r at a time. The one we shall use in this text is $n_{(r)}$. Others used are $P(n,r)$, $P\left(\dfrac{n}{r}\right)$, and $_nP_r$. The number of arrangements of five objects taken three at a is $5_{(3)}$ or $5 \times 4 \times 3$.

Example 1. Find the number of 4-arrangements of six objects.

Solution: Number of 4-arrangements $= 6_{(4)}$,
$$= 6 \times 5 \times 4 \times 3,$$
$$= 360.$$

Example 2. How many different licence plates, each containing five digits, can be made using the ten digits 0 to 9 if
(a) the first digit cannot be 0 and repetition of digits is not allowed?
(b) the first digit cannot be 0 but repetitions are allowed?
In how many arrangements in (b) do repetitions actually occur?

Solution:

(a) Since the first digit cannot be 0, there are nine choices for the first digit. The other digits form 4-arrangements of the nine remaining digits. Therefore

$$\text{number of licence plates} = 9 \times 9_{(4)},$$
$$= 9 \times 9 \times 8 \times 7 \times 6,$$
$$= 27{,}216.$$

(b) If repetitions are allowed, there are ten choices for each digit after the first. Therefore

$$\text{number of licence plates} = 9 \times 10^4,$$
$$= 9 \times 10{,}000,$$
$$= 90{,}000.$$

The number of arrangements in which repetitions occur is

$$90{,}000 - 27{,}216 = 62{,}784.$$

Example 3.   How many arrangements of all of the letters of the word *numbers* are possible if

(a) there is no restriction?   (b) the letter *s* must be last?   (c) the vowels must be together?

Solution:

(a) Number of arrangements with no restrictions

$$= 7_{(7)},$$
$$= 7 \times 6 \times 5 \times 4 \times 3 \times 2 \times 1,$$
$$= 5040.$$

(b) Since *s* must be placed last, the other six letters may be arranged in $6_{(6)}$ ways.   Therefore

number of arrangements with *s* last $= 6_{(6)},$
$$= 6 \times 5 \times 4 \times 3 \times 2 \times 1,$$
$$= 720.$$

(c) Since the vowels must be together, they can be considered as one object. Therefore the number of arrangements is $6_{(6)}$. But for each of these arrangements the *u* and *e* may be interchanged without altering the position of the other letters.

Therefore

total number of arrangements with vowels together

$$= 2 \times 6_{(6)},$$
$$= 2 \times 720,$$
$$= 1440.$$

EXERCISE 13.1

1. Evaluate
   (a) $4_{(2)}$ (b) $16_{(2)}$ (c) $7_{(4)}$
   (d) $15_{(3)}$ (e) $5_{(5)}$ (f) $6_{(4)}$.

2. Calculate the number of 3-arrangements of eight objects.

3. Calculate the number of 2-arrangements of seven objects.

4. Calculate the number of 5-arrangements of five objects.

5. Calculate the number of 6-arrangements of six objects.

6. How many three-digit numbers can be made from the digits 1, 2, 3, 4, 5 if repetitions are not allowed?

7. How many three-digit numbers can be made from the digits 0, 1, 2, 3, 4, if repetitions are not allowed?

8. How many three-digit numbers can be made from the digits 0, 1, 2, 3, 4, if repetitions are allowed?

9. If there are five possible routes by which a driver can travel from Toronto to Ottawa and three possible routes from Ottawa to Montreal, how many different ways are there to travel from Toronto to Montreal via Ottawa?

10. If a dime, a nickel, and a quarter are tossed together, in how many different ways can they fall?

11. In how many ways can eight boys be arranged in a row if
    (a) there is no restriction?
    (b) two boys, John and Jim, must be together?
    (c) John and Jim must be kept apart?

12. How many batting orders are possible for a baseball team of nine players if the pitcher must bat in ninth position?

13. How many possible signals can be made using five different signal flags arranged one above the other?

14. In how many ways can a chairman, a vice-chairman, and a secretary be chosen from a committee of nine members?

15. There are four routes between two towns. In how many ways can a driver travel by one route and return by a different route?

16. In how many ways can the letters of the word *factor* be arranged if
    (a) there is no restriction?
    (b) the first letter must be a consonant?
    (c) the second and fifth letters must be vowels?

17. The dial of a combination lock has one hundred different numbers on it. The lock is opened by dialing three different numbers in a particular order. How many different combinations can be produced?

18. There are ten teams in a hockey league. How many games are in the schedule if each team must play each of the other teams once at home and once away from home?

19. There are six teams in another hockey league. Each team must play each of the other teams seven times on home ice and seven times away from home. How many games are played each season?

13.2. Factorials

In Section 13.1 we have seen that the number of 3-arrangements of five objects is

$$5_{(3)} = 5 \times 4 \times 3,$$

and that the number of 5-arrangements of five objects is

$$5_{(5)} = 5 \times 4 \times 3 \times 2 \times 1.$$

In the latter case we have the product of all the natural numbers from 1 to 5 inclusive. Such a product is written as 5! and read as "five factorial". We understand that

$$n_{(n)} = n! = n(n-1)(n-2)\ldots(3)(2)(1)$$

is the product of all the natural numbers from 1 to n inclusive. (Note that we must assume that n is a natural number.)

Probably the most rigorous way to define factorial notation is by a recursive definition,

$$0! = 1,$$
$$(n+1)! = n!(n+1). \qquad (n \geq 0).$$

It may appear strange to define 0! as 1, but the reason for this definition will appear later.

From the recursive definition, we obtain

$$1! = 0!(1) = 1,$$
$$2! = 1!(2) = 1 \times 2,$$
$$3! = 2!(3) = 1 \times 2 \times 3,$$
$$4! = 3!(4) = 1 \times 2 \times 3 \times 4,$$

and so on, in agreement with our more intuitive concept of the product of all the natural numbers from 1 to n inclusive.

The number of r-arrangements of n elements may be expressed in terms of factorials. We know that

$$5_{(3)} = 5 \times 4 \times 3 = \frac{5 \times 4 \times 3 \times 2 \times 1}{2 \times 1},$$
$$= \frac{5!}{2!}.$$
$$16_{(4)} = 16 \times 15 \times 14 \times 13,$$
$$= \frac{16 \times 15 \times 14 \times 13 \times 12!}{12!},$$
$$= \frac{16!}{12!}.$$

Similarly,

$$n_{(r)} = n(n-1)(n-2)\ldots(n-r+1)$$
$$= \frac{n(n-1)(n-2)\ldots(n-r+1)(n-r)!}{(n-r)!}.$$

Therefore,

$$n_{(r)} = \frac{n!}{(n - r)!}.$$

Note: This implies that

$$n_{(n)} = \frac{n!}{(n - n)!},$$
$$= \frac{n!}{0!}.$$

But we know that

$$n_{(n)} = n!.$$

That is,

$$\frac{n!}{0!} = n!.$$

This will only be true if 0! is equal to 1, which agrees with the definition that 0! = 1. With any other definition we would lose consistency.

Example 1.   Evaluate $\dfrac{52!}{50!}$

Solution:

$$\frac{52!}{50!} = \frac{52 \cdot 51 \cdot 50!}{50!},$$
$$= 52 \cdot 51,$$
$$= 2652.$$

Example 2.   Solve for n in $\dfrac{(n + 2)!}{n!} = 56.$

Solution:

$$\frac{(n + 2)!}{n!} = 56.$$
$$\frac{(n + 2)(n + 1)n!}{n!} = 56.$$
$$(n + 2)(n + 1) = 56.$$
$$n^2 + 3n + 2 = 56.$$
$$n^2 + 3n - 54 = 0.$$

Therefore
$$(n + 9)(n - 6) = 0.$$
$$n = 6 \qquad\qquad (n \in N)$$

Example 3.   Prove that $(n + 1)_{(r+1)} = (n + 1)n_{(r)}.$

Solution:
$$(n + 1)_{(r+1)} = \frac{(n + 1)!}{(n + 1 - r - 1)!},$$
$$= \frac{(n + 1)n!}{(n - r)!},$$

$$= (n + 1) \frac{n!}{(n - r)!},$$
$$= (n + 1)n_{(r)}.$$

EXERCISE 13.2

In each of the following questions, $n, r \in N, n \geq r$.

1. Calculate the value of each of the following.

    (a) $\dfrac{8!}{6!}$

    (b) $\dfrac{6!}{3!3!}$

    (c) $\dfrac{20!}{19!}$

    (d) $\dfrac{8!}{5!3!}$

    (e) $\dfrac{7!}{5!2!} + \dfrac{7!}{3!4!}$

    (f) $\dfrac{20!}{17!3!}$

2. Express each of the following as a single factorial expression.

    (a) $(n + 1)n!$

    (b) $\dfrac{(n + 7)!}{n + 7}$

    (c) $(n - r + 1)\, (n - r)!$

3. Simplify the following as far as possible.

    (a) $\dfrac{(n + 5)!}{(n + 3)!}$

    (b) $\dfrac{n!}{(n - 1)!}$

    (c) $\dfrac{(n + 1)!}{n!}$

    (d) $\dfrac{(n - r + 1)!}{(n - r)!}$

    (e) $\dfrac{(n - r)!}{(n - r - 1)!}$

    (f) $\dfrac{(n - r + 1)!}{(n - r - 1)!}$

4. Solve the following equations.

    (a) $\dfrac{(n + 5)!}{(n + 4)!} = 7.$

    (b) $\dfrac{(n + 2)!}{n!} = 20.$

    (c) $n_{(2)} = 30.$

    (d) $\dfrac{n!}{2(n - 2)!} = 6.$

    (e) $\dfrac{(n + 1)!}{(n - 1)!} = 12.$

    (f) $\dfrac{(n - 1)!}{(n - 3)!} = 42.$

5. Prove that $n_{(r+1)} = (n - r)n_{(r)}.$

13.3.   Arrangements with Like Elements

How many six-digit numbers can be made using the digits 1, 1, 1, 2, 2, 3? If the digits were all different, we know that the number of numbers would be 6! In this case, however, certain of the digits are alike and interchanging the position of the three 1's or the two 2's among themselves without altering the positions of the other digits would not produce another number. The number of arrangements must be less than 6! Our problem is to discover the number of distinct arrangements possible. To do this we imagine some means of distinguishing among the like objects. We may, for instance, temporarily label the 1's and 2's with distinctive subscripts $1_1, 1_2, 1_3, 2_1, 2_2$. In this case $1_1 \, 1_2 \, 1_3 \, 2_2 \, 3 \, 2_1$ would be a different arrangement from $1_2 \, 1_1 \, 1_3 \, 2_2 \, 3 \, 2_1$. The three 1's can then be arranged among themselves in 3! ways without altering the position of the other digits. Similarly, the two 2's can be arranged in 2! ways without altering the positions of the other digits. We shall assume that there are x arrangements of the six digits taken all at a time with three alike of one kind (the 1's) and two alike of another (the 2's).

Let the number of arrangements be x. If the three 1's were unlike, then, for each of these x arrangements, the 1's could be arranged among themselves in 3! ways without altering the positions of the other digits.

Therefore the number of arrangements with unlike 1's would be $x \cdot 3!$. Similarly if the two 2's were unlike, they could be rearranged in 2! ways without altering the positions of the other digits.

Therefore the number of arrangements with unlike 1's and 2's would be $x \cdot 3! \cdot 2!$. But if the 1's and 2's were unlike, the number of arrangements would be 6!

Hence
$$x \cdot 3! \cdot 2! = 6!.$$

$$x = \frac{6!}{3!2!},$$

$$= 60.$$

Therefore the number of six-digit numbers is 60.

This process can obviously be extended to arrangements of any number of objects taken all at a time with certain of the objects alike.

To Calculate the Number of Arrangements of n Objects When Some Are Alike

To calculate the number of arrangements of n objects taken all at a time with n_1 alike of one kind, n_2 alike of a second, ..., n_r alike of an rth kind ($n \geq n_1 + n_2 + ... + n_r$), we proceed as follows.

Let the number of arrangements be x. If the n_1 like objects were unlike, then, for each of these x arrangements, the n_1 like objects could be rearranged among themselves in $n_1!$ ways without altering the positions of the other objects.

Therefore the number of arrangements would be $x \cdot n_1!$. Similarly, if the n_2 like objects were unlike, each of these $x \cdot n_1!$ arrangements would give rise to $n_2!$ arrangements.

Therefore the number of arrangements would be $x \cdot n_1! \cdot n_2!$ Similarly, if all the objects were unlike, the number of arrangements would be
$$x \cdot n_1! \cdot n_2! \cdot ... \cdot n_r!$$
But if all n objects were unlike, the number of arrangements would be $n!$

Hence
$$x \cdot n_1! \cdot n_2! \cdots n_r! = n!$$

$$x = \frac{n!}{n_1! \, n_2! \, \dots \, n_r!}$$

$$(n \geq n_1 + n_2 + \dots + n_r).$$

Therefore the number of n-arrangements of n objects, if n_1 are alike of one kind, n_2 alike of a second, ..., n_r alike of an rth, is

$$\frac{n!}{n_1! \, n_2! \, \dots \, n_r!}.$$

Example 1. Calculate the number of ways of arranging the letters of the word *Tennessee* taken all at a time, (a) if there is no restriction, (b) if the first two letters must be e.

Solution:

(a)
$$\text{Number of arrangements} = \frac{9!}{4!2!2!}$$
$$= 3780.$$

(b) Place two e's in the first two positions. Therefore
$$\text{Number of arrangements} = 1 \times \frac{7!}{2!2!2!}$$
$$= 630.$$

Example 2. A man wished to travel from one point in a city to a second point which is five blocks south and six blocks east of his starting point. In how many ways can he make the journey if he always travels either south or east?

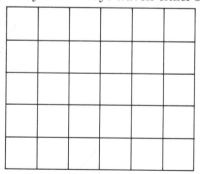

Solution: If we consider a south-going route past one block as being represented by the letter S and an east-going route past one block as being represented by the letter E, then the problem is equivalent to the number of arrangements of eleven letters, five of which are S and six of which are E.

Therefore, the number of routes $= \dfrac{11!}{6!5!} = \dfrac{11 \times 10 \times 9 \times 8 \times 7}{5 \times 4 \times 3 \times 2 \times 1} = 462.$

Example 3. How many five-digit numbers can be formed from the digits 1, 2, 3, 4, 5, if the odd digits must always appear in ascending order?

Solution: Since the order of the odd digits cannot be altered, they may be considered as like digits.

Hence, the number of numbers $= \dfrac{5!}{3!}$

$$= 20.$$

EXERCISE 13.3

1. Evaluate the following.

    (a) $\dfrac{6!}{3!2!}$ (b) $\dfrac{8!}{3!5!}$ (c) $\dfrac{10!}{6!2!}$ (d) $\dfrac{12!}{7!4!}$

2. Calculate the number of arrangements of all the letters of each of the following.
    (a) Ottawa   (b) Toronto   (c) subset
    (d) algebra   (e) Mississippi   (f) element

3. In how many ways can all the letters of the word *factor* be arranged if the consonants must always appear in the order *f, c, t, r*?

4. How many six-digit numbers may be formed from the digits 1, 1, 1, 2, 3, 4?

5. Calculate the number of arrangements of all the letters of the word *parallel*. In how many of the arrangements will the three l's be together?

6. How many numbers greater than 3,000,000 can be formed from the digits 1, 2, 3, 3, 3, 4, 4?

7. How many numbers can be formed using all of the digits 1, 2, 2, 3, 3, 3, 4, if the odd digits must always occupy the odd positions?

8. How many possible routes may a person travel in order to go from one point in a city to a second point which is six blocks south and three blocks east, if he travels always in a southerly or easterly direction?

9. In the arrangements of all of the letters of the word *Toronto*, how many
    (a) start with the letter *o*?
    (b) start with two *o*'s?
    (c) start with one *o* with the second letter other than *o*?
    (d) start with three *o*'s?
    (e) start with two *o*'s with the third letter other than *o*?

10. In the arrangement of all of the letters of the word *Ottawa*, how many
    (a) start with *t*, with the second letter other than *t*?
    (b) start with *ta*?

11. How many numbers can be formed using all of the digits from 1 to 7 if the odd digits must always be in descending order and the even digits in ascending order?

12. How many odd numbers can be formed using all of the digits 1, 3, 4, 4, 5, 5?

13.4.   Subsets of a Set

Consider the set $A = \{a, b, c, d, e\}$. One subset $\emptyset$ contains no elements; one subset, A itself, contains all five elements. It is also fairly obvious that there will be five different subsets each consisting of one element, $\{a\}, \{b\}, \{c\}, \{d\}$, $\{e\}$. However, the number of subsets each consisting of 2 or 3 or 4 elements of A is not so obvious. Since the number of elements in A is 5, it is possible, in this case, to write out all of the subsets consisting of, say, three elements of A. These subsets are $\{a, b, c\}, \{a, b, d\}, \{a, b, e\}, \{a, c, d\}, \{a, c, e\}, \{a, d, e\}, \{b, c, d\}$, $\{b, c, e\}, \{b, d, e\}, \{c, d, e\}$. However, even with just these ten possible subsets, it requires care and is time consuming to have to list all of them in order to find the required number of subsets. It would be rather tedious to find the number of 40-element subsets of a set of one hundred elements in this way!

Returning to our example of the number of 3-element subsets (usually simply called 3-subsets) of a given set of five elements, the subset $\{a, b, c\}$ gives rise to 3! arrangements of its elements all three at a time. This is true for each of the 3-subsets of A, and if we let the number of 3-subsets be x, the number of 3-arrangements of the five elements of A is $x(3!)$. However, we know that the total number of 3-arrangements of five elements is $5_{(3)}$.

Hence
$$x(3!) = 5_{(3)}.$$
$$x = \frac{5_{(3)}}{3!}.$$

Therefore the number of 3-subsets is $\dfrac{5 \times 4 \times 3}{3 \times 2 \times 1} = 10$. This agrees with the result of listing all the 3-subsets as we did above.

Extending this reasoning, we can develop a general method for finding the number of r-subsets of a set of n elements. We note of course, that $\{a, b, c\} = \{a, c, b\} = \{b, a, c\}$, etc. In selecting a subset of a given set, the order in which the elements are selected is immaterial. We can, therefore, define an r-subset as follows.

DEFINITION.   An r-subset of a set of n elements is a selection of r of the elements without regard to order ($r \in W, n \in N$).

We could regard finding the number of r-arrangements of n objects as first finding the number of r-subsets of the set of n elements, and then finding the number of ways of rearranging the element of each of the subsets.

To Calculate the Number of r-Subsets of a Set of n Elements

Let the number of r-subsets be x. Each of the x subsets can be rearranged in $r!$ different orders.

Therefore the number of r-arrangements is $x(r!)$. But the number of r-arrangements of n objects is $n_{(r)}$.

Hence

$$x(r!) = n_{(r)}.$$

$$x = \frac{n_{(r)}}{r!}.$$

Therefore the number of r-subsets is $\dfrac{n_{(r)}}{r!}$.

The symbol used for the number of r-subsets of a set of n elements is $\dbinom{n}{r}$.

Therefore,

$$\binom{n}{r} = \frac{n_{(r)}}{r!}.$$

Other symbols used are $C(n, r)$ and $_nC_r$. Also, since

$$n_{(r)} = \frac{n!}{(n-r)!}.$$

Therefore

$$\binom{n}{r} = \frac{n!}{(n-r)!\,r!}.$$

Example 1. Calculate the number of 2-subsets of a set of twelve elements.

Solution: Number of 2-subsets

$$= \binom{12}{2}.$$

$$= \frac{12 \times 11}{2 \times 1},$$

$$= 66.$$

Example 2. Prove that

$$\binom{n}{r} = \binom{n}{n-r}.$$

Solution:

$$\binom{n}{r} = \frac{n!}{(n-r)!\,r!}.$$

$$\binom{n}{n-r} = \frac{n!}{[n-(n-r)]!\,(n-r)!},$$

$$= \frac{n!}{(n-r)!\,r!}.$$

Therefore,

$$\binom{n}{r} = \binom{n}{n-r}.$$

These examples indicate that in the more practical type of problem where an evaluation is necessary, as in Example 1, it is usually simpler to use the form $\binom{n}{r} = \frac{n_{(r)}}{r!}$, but in the more theoretical type of examples as in Example 2, the factorial form is usually the more useful.

Example 2 also gives a most useful result.

$$\binom{8}{6} = \frac{8 \times 7 \times 6 \times 5 \times 4 \times 3 \times 2!}{6 \times 5 \times 4 \times 3 \times 2 \times 1 \times 2!},$$

$$\binom{8}{6} = \frac{8 \times 7}{2 \times 1}.$$

From Example 2, we know that $\binom{8}{6} = \binom{8}{2}$ and thus to evaluate $\binom{8}{6}$, it is obviously simpler to evaluate $\binom{8}{2}$. This is no accident. For every subset of r elements selected from a set of n elements, there must be a corresponding set of the $(n - r)$ elements which was not selected. In the example of the 3-subsets of the set $A = \{a, b, c, d, e\}$ used at the beginning of this section, corresponding to the subset $\{a, b, c\}$ of the elements selected, there is the subset $\{d, e\}$ of the elements not selected. If we form the corresponding subsets of elements not selected for each subset selected, we will obtain the ten 2-subsets of the set A.

Example 3. Find the number of 18-subsets of a set of twenty elements.

Solution: Number of subsets

$$= \binom{20}{18},$$
$$= \binom{20}{2},$$
$$= \frac{20 \times 19}{2 \times 1},$$
$$= 190.$$

Example 4. In a club with twelve members,
(a) in how many ways can a committee of three be selected?
(b) in how many ways can a president, secretary, and treasurer be appointed?

Solution:

(a) Number of ways of selecting committee

$$= \binom{12}{3},$$
$$= \frac{12 \times 11 \times 10}{3 \times 2 \times 1},$$
$$= 220.$$

(b) Number of ways of appointing officers

$$= 12_{(3)},$$
$$= 12 \times 11 \times 10,$$
$$= 1320.$$

We note that in the first part a committee of John, Jane and Tom is exactly the same committee as Jane, Tom, and John. *The order of selection is unimportant.* This indicates that 3-*subsets* are required.

In the second part the appointment of John as president, Jane as secretary and Tom as treasurer is not the same as Jane as president, Tom as secretary, and John as treasurer. *The order is of importance* and the number of 3-*arrangements* is required.

Example 5. In how many ways can six 3's and four 2's be arranged in a row so that the 2's are always apart?

Solution:

$$\square\ 3\ \square\ 3\ \square\ 3\ \square\ 3\ \square\ 3\ \square\ 3\ \square$$

We can first arrange the 3's in a row. The 2's must now be placed in position. The seven possible positions for the 2's are marked in the diagram and the four 2's may be placed in any four of these seven positions. Thus we require the number of 4-subsets of the seven positions. Therefore, the number of ways of arranging the 3's and 2's is

$$\binom{7}{4} = \frac{7 \times 6 \times 5}{3 \times 2 \times 1}$$
$$= 35.$$

Example 6. Ten boys volunteered to assist in the organization of a school dance. It was agreed that three would be responsible for decorating, two for ticket sales, and the remaining five for clean-up after the dance. In how many ways could the ten boys be chosen for the different groups?

Solution: For the decorating group, 3 are selected from 10 in $\binom{10}{3}$ ways.

For tickets, 2 are selected from the remaining 7 in $\binom{7}{2}$ ways.

For clean-up, 5 are selected from the remaining 5 in $\binom{5}{5}$ ways.

Therefore the number of ways of selecting the group is

$$\binom{10}{3}\binom{7}{2}\binom{5}{5} = \frac{10 \times 9 \times 8}{3 \times 2 \times 1} \times \frac{7 \times 6}{2 \times 1} \times 1,$$
$$= 2520.$$

EXERCISE 13.4

1. Evaluate each of the following.

   (a) $\binom{8}{6}$ (b) $\binom{5}{2}$ (c) $\binom{14}{12}$ (d) $\binom{9}{9}$ (e) $\binom{9}{0}$

   (f) $\binom{21}{3}$ (g) $\binom{52}{50}$ (h) $\binom{100}{99}$ (i) $\binom{600}{1}$ (j) $\binom{15}{6}$

2. Calculate the number of 2-subsets of the set $\{0, 1, 2, 3\}$.

3. Calculate the number of 5-subsets of the set $\{a, b, c, d, e, f, g\}$.

4. For the set $\{1, 2, 3, 4\}$, find the number of 0-subsets, the number of 1-subsets, the number of 2-subsets, the number of 3-subsets, the number of 4-subsets. What is the total number of subsets of the given set?

5. (a) In how many ways can a committee of 3 be selected from 12 students?
   (b) In how many ways can a president, secretary, and treasurer be chosen from twelve students?

6. If fourteen points, no three of which are collinear, are marked on a sheet of paper, how many line segments can be drawn to join pairs of points?

7. How many diagonals has a polygon of twelve sides?

8. How many diagonals has a polygon of n sides?

9. Ten friends attend a reunion. Each shakes hands with each of the others. How many handshakes occur?

10. In how many ways can a committee of three men and two women be selected from eight men and six women?

11. In how many ways can a committee of five be selected from eight men and six women if at least three of the committee members must be men?

12. In how many ways can a committee of five be selected from ten men and seven women if at least one of the committee members must be a man?

13. The student council of Brandex High School consists of twenty members. In how many ways can a committee of four be selected if the president and secretary must be included?

14. In how many ways can a committee of four be selected from eight men and seven women if Miss Jones refuses to serve on the same committee as Mr. Smith?

15. In how many ways can twelve similar books be arranged on three shelves if each shelf must contain at least one book?

16. In how many ways can twelve similar books be arranged on three shelves if there is no restriction and one shelf may receive all of the books?

17. Twelve different books are to be shared so that Tom receives five, Dick receives four, and Harry receives three. In how many different ways can the books be distributed?

18. Solve for x: $\dbinom{x+1}{3} = \dbinom{x}{2}$.

19. Solve for x: $\dbinom{x}{2} = 28$.

20. Solve for x: $\dbinom{x}{3} = 3(x_{(2)})$.

21. Prove that $\dbinom{n}{r} + \dbinom{n}{r+1} = \dbinom{n+1}{r+1}$.

22. Prove that $r\dbinom{n}{r} = n\dbinom{n-1}{r-1}$.

23. In how many ways can a bridge hand of thirteen cards be dealt from a deck of fifty-two cards? (Solution may be left in factorial form!)

24. In how many ways can thirteen cards be dealt to each of four players from a deck of fifty-two cards? (Solution may be left in factorial form!)

25. In how many ways can eight different books be divided into two parcels of five books in one parcel and three in the other?

26. In how many ways can eight different books be divided into parcels of four books in each parcel?

Chapter Summary

DEFINITIONS: An r-arrangement of n objects is an ordered selection of r of the objects ($r \in W$, $n \in N$).

An r-subset of a set of n elements is a selection of r of the elements without regard to order ($r \in W$, $n \in N$).

FORMULAE AND SYMBOLS

1. The number of r-arrangements of n objects is
$$n_{(r)} = n(n-1)(n-2) \ldots (n-r+1),$$
$$(n \geq r)$$
$$= \frac{n!}{(n-r)!}$$
where $n! = n(n-1)(n-2) \ldots 3 \cdot 2 \cdot 1$ and $0! = 1$.

2. The number of r-subsets of a set of n elements is

$$\binom{n}{r} = \frac{n_{(r)}}{r!} = \frac{n!}{r!(n-r)!}.$$

3. The number of n-arrangements of n objects if n_1 are alike of one kind, n_2 alike of a second kind, ..., n_r alike of an rth kind is

$$\frac{n!}{n_1!n_2! \ldots n_r!}, \qquad (n \geq n_1 + n_2 \ldots + n_r)$$

$$\binom{n}{r} = \binom{n}{n-r}.$$

REVIEW EXERCISE 13

1. Evaluate each of the following.

   (a) $7_{(3)}$ (b) $7_{(5)}$ (c) $100_{(2)}$ (d) $12_{(3)}$

   (e) $\binom{7}{3}$ (f) $\binom{8}{8}$ (g) $\binom{100}{99}$ (h) $\binom{12}{5}$

   (i) $\dfrac{12!}{10!}$ (j) $\dfrac{7 \times 5!}{3!}$ (k) $\dfrac{8!}{4!} - \dfrac{7!}{3!}$ (l) $\dfrac{8!}{3!} - \dfrac{7!}{4!}$

2. Simplify as far as possible.

   (a) $\dfrac{x!}{(x-1)!}$ (b) $\dfrac{(x+1)!}{(x-1)!}$ (c) $\dfrac{(n-r)!}{(n-r-1)!}$

3. Prove that $\dfrac{(2n+2)!}{(n+1)!} = \dfrac{2(2n+1)!}{n!}.$

4. Prove that $5\binom{8}{5} = 8\binom{7}{4}.$

5. Prove that $\binom{n+1}{r+1} = \dfrac{n+1}{r+1}\binom{n}{r}$

6. In how many ways can a committee of five be formed from six men and five women if
   (a) there is no restriction?
   (b) the committee must contain exactly three men?
   (c) the committee must contain at least one man?

7. A starting line-up for a hockey team must consist of one goalkeeper, two defencemen, and three forwards.
   (a) In how many ways can a starting line-up be selected from two goalkeepers, five defencemen, and nine forwards?
   (b) In how many ways can the starting line-up be filled if the same two goalkeepers, five defencemen, and nine forwards are available to fill any position?

8. How many different arrangements can be made from all the letters of the word *distinct* if
   (a) there is no restriction?
   (b) the first and last letters must be alike?

9. How many different seven-digit numbers can be formed from the digits 1, 1, 1, 2, 2, 3, 3?

10. How many different seven-digit numbers can be formed from the digits 0, 0, 1, 1, 2, 2, 2?

11. How many different licence plates, each consisting of one letter and either four or five digits, can be formed from the letters H, J, K, L, M, and from the digits 0 to 9, if 0 cannot be the first digit and repetitions are allowed?

12. In how many ways can six different books be arranged in a row if two specified books must always be together?

13. In how many ways can twelve copies of the same book be arranged on three shelves if each shelf must contain at least one copy?

14. How many arrangements can be formed from all the letters of the word *combine* if the vowels must always be in the same order?

15. How many arrangements can be formed from all of the letters of the word *combine* if the vowels must occupy the second, fifth, and seventh positions?

16. An examination consists of three compulsory questions and another six questions of which the candidate may select any four. In how many ways may the candidate select the questions to be answered?

17. In how many ways can a committee of four be selected from twelve members?

18. In how many ways can a committee, consisting of a president, a secretary, and two other members, be chosen from twelve members?

19. In how many ways can twelve people be divided into three groups consisting of four, five, and three individuals?

20. In how many ways can twelve people be divided into three groups, each consisting of four individuals?

21. How many diagonals has an octagon?

22. How many sides has a polygon if it has thirty-five diagonals?

23. Solve the following equations.

   (a) $\dbinom{n}{2} = 45$

   (b) $n_{(3)} = 2\dbinom{n}{2}$

   (c) $n! = 5(n-1)!$

   (d) $10\dbinom{n}{r-1} = 3\dbinom{n}{r}; \ 4\dbinom{n}{r+1} = 9\dbinom{n}{r}$

Chapter 14

THE BINOMIAL THEOREM

14.1. Powers of a Binomial Base

Let us consider the expansion of $(a + b)^3$, using only the axioms of algebra.

$$
\begin{aligned}
(a + b)^3 &= (a + b)\,(a + b)\,(a + b) \\
&= (a + b)\,[(a + b)\,(a + b)] && \text{Associative Law} \\
&= (a + b)\,[(a + b)a + (a + b)b] && \text{Distributive Law} \\
&= (a + b)\,[aa + ba + ab + bb] && \text{(Dist.)} \\
&= a[aa + ba + ab + bb] + b[aa + ba + ab + bb] && \text{(Dist.)} \\
&= \underset{1}{aaa} + \underset{2}{aba} + \underset{3}{aab} + \underset{4}{abb} + \underset{5}{baa} + \underset{6}{bba} + \underset{7}{bab} + \underset{8}{bbb}. && \text{(Dist.)}
\end{aligned}
$$

The eight terms (some, of course, are like terms) have been numbered. Each term is the product of three factors, the first being obtained from the first binomial, the second from the second binomial, and the third from the third binomial in $(a + b)\,(a + b)\,(a + b)$. All such possible selections are included in the eight terms. The third term, aab, is formed by selecting a from each of the first two binomials and b from the third. Each term will, therefore, be the product of three variables, one selected from each of the binomial factors. In the expansion, a^3 appears only once (aaa), a^2b appears three times (aba, aab, baa), ab^2 appears three times (abb, bba, bab), and b^3 appears once (bbb).

Therefore $\qquad\qquad (a + b)^3 = a^3 + 3a^2b + 3ab^2 + b^3.$

We see that each term of this expression is formed by selecting one and only one term from each of the three binomial factors, multiplying these terms together, and adding all like products. We note that we can select either none, one, two, or three b's. If we select no b's, then we must select one a from each factor. This can be done in only one way and gives the first term, a^3. If we select one b, we can select it from any one of the three factors. This can be done in $\binom{3}{1} = 3$ ways. For each of these, we must select one a from each of the other two factors and this can be done in only one way. Hence, we have three terms, each equal to a^2b, giving the second term, $3a^2b$. We may now select two b's from the three factors in $\binom{3}{2} = 3$ ways, and an a must then be selected in one way from the remaining factor. This gives the third term, $3ab^2$. Finally, we may select three b's (one from each factor) in $\binom{3}{3} = 1$ way and we obtain the fourth term, b^3. Therefore,

$$(a + b)^3 = \binom{3}{0}a^3 + \binom{3}{1}a^2b + \binom{3}{2}ab^2 + \binom{3}{3}b^3,$$
$$= a^3 + 3a^2b + 3ab^2 + b^3.$$

We note that this may be written as

$$(a + b)^3 = \sum_{k=0}^{3} \binom{3}{k} a^{3-k}b^k.$$

In the expansion of $(a + b)^6$, each term will be of dimension six in a and b together, since each term will be a product of one variable from each of the six binomial factors; hence it will be of the form $a^{6-r}b^r$, where $r \in \{0, 1, 2, 3, 4, 5, 6\}$. By using a similar argument to that used in the expansion of $(a + b)^3$, we see that

when $r = 0$, the coefficient of a^6 is $\binom{6}{0}$,

when $r = 1$, the coefficient of a^5b is $\binom{6}{1}$,

when $r = 2$, the coefficient of a^4b^2 is $\binom{6}{2}$,

when $r = 3$, the coefficient of a^3b^3 is $\binom{6}{3}$,

when $r = 4$, the coefficient of a^2b^4 is $\binom{6}{4}$,

when $r = 5$, the coefficient of ab^5 is $\binom{6}{5}$,

when $r = 6$, the coefficient of b^6 is $\binom{6}{6}$.

Therefore,

$$(a+b)^6 = \binom{6}{0}a^6 + \binom{6}{1}a^5b + \binom{6}{2}a^4b^2 + \binom{6}{3}a^3b^3 + \binom{6}{4}a^2b^4 + \binom{6}{5}ab^5 + \binom{6}{6}b^6,$$

$$= \sum_{r=0}^{6} \binom{6}{r} a^{6-r}b^r,$$

$$= a^6 + 6a^5b + 15a^4b^2 + 20a^3b^3 + 15a^2b^4 + 6ab^5 + b^6.$$

EXERCISE 14.1

1. If the numerical coefficients are disregarded, terms of the following form will appear in the expansion of $(a + b)^7$. State the value of the exponent r in each case.
   (a) a^5b^r (b) a^2b^r (c) a^rb^4 (d) a^rb^2

2. In each of the following, write the expansion in sigma-notation form, in r-subset notation form $\binom{n}{r}$, and in fully expanded form.
   (a) $(a + b)^4$ (b) $(a + b)^5$ (c) $(x + y)^8$ (d) $(p + q)^7$

3. How many different terms are there in the expansion of each of the binomials in question 2?

4. Without expanding, state the number of different terms in the expansions of
   (a) $(a + b)^{11}$ (b) $(x + y)^{15}$ (c) $(p + q)^{18}$ (d) $(1 + x)^{20}$.

14.2.   Expansion of $(a + b)^n$, $n \in N$

$$(a + b)^n = (a + b)(a + b) \ldots (a + b) \ldots \text{to } n \text{ factors}$$

Each term in the expansion is the product obtained by multiplying together one term from each binomial factor. Each term of the expansion will, therefore, be of the form

$$a^{n-r}b^r, \text{ where } r \in \{0, 1, 2, \ldots, n\}.$$

This general term $a^{n-r}b^r$ is formed by selecting one b from each of r of the n factors. This can be done in $\binom{n}{r}$ ways. For each of these ways, the $(n-r)$ a's can be selected, one from each of the remaining $(n-r)$ binomial factors, in only one way.

Hence, the coefficient of $a^{n-r}b^r$ is $\binom{n}{r}$.

Therefore,
$$(a + b)^n = \sum_{r=0}^{n} \binom{n}{r} a^{n-r}b^r,$$

$$= \binom{n}{0} a^n + \binom{n}{1} a^{n-1}b + \binom{n}{2} a^{n-2}b^2$$
$$+ \ldots + \binom{n}{r} a^{n-r}b^r + \ldots + \binom{n}{n} b^n.$$

We note the following points in this expansion:

(i) The number of different terms is $n + 1$.

(ii) The general term $\binom{n}{r} a^{n-r}b^r$ is the $(r + 1)$ st term.

(iii) The coefficients of terms equidistant from the ends of this expansion are equal.

The following expansions were obtained from the previous section or are known from earlier work.

$(a + b)^0 = 1.$
$(a + b)^1 = a + b.$
$(a + b)^2 = a^2 + 2ab + b^2.$
$(a + b)^3 = a^3 + 3a^2b + 3ab^2 + b^3.$
$(a + b)^4 = a^4 + 4a^3b + 6a^2b^2 + 4ab^3 + b^4.$
$(a + b)^5 = a^5 + 5a^4b + 10a^3b^2 + 10a^2b^3 + 5ab^4 + b^5.$
$(a + b)^6 = a^6 + 6a^5b + 15a^4b^2 + 20a^3b^3 + 15a^2b^4 + 6ab^5 + b^6.$

It can be seen that the coefficients follow a definite pattern which can be most easily demonstrated by means of *Pascal's Triangle.*

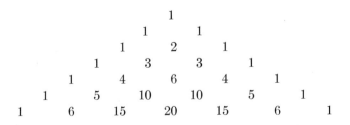

Can you see how the pattern develops? What will be the next two lines in the triangle? In forming the lines in the triangle, we are making use of the identity which you were asked to prove in question 21, Exercise 13.4.

$$\binom{n}{r} + \binom{n}{r+1} = \binom{n+1}{r+1}$$

Example 1. Express (a) $(a + 2b)^4$, (b) $(2a - 3b)^7$ using sigma notation.

Solution:

(a) $(a + 2b)^4 = \sum_{r=0}^{4} \binom{4}{r} a^{4-r}(2b)^r$

$= \sum_{r=0}^{4} \binom{4}{r} 2^r a^{4-r} b^r.$

(b) $(2a - 3b)^7 = \sum_{r=0}^{7} \binom{7}{r} (2a)^{7-r} (-3b)^r$

$= \sum_{r=0}^{7} \binom{7}{r} (-1)^r (2^{7-r}) (3^r) a^{7-r} b^r.$

Example 2. Expand (a) $(a + 2b)^4$,   (b) $(2a - 3b)^7$.

Solution:

(a) $(a + 2b)^4 = \binom{4}{0} a^4 + \binom{4}{1} a^3 (2b) + \binom{4}{2} a^2 (2b)^2 + \binom{4}{3} a (2b)^3$

$+ \binom{4}{4} (2b)^4,$

$= a^4 + 8a^3b + 24a^2b^2 + 32ab^3 + 16b^4.$

(b) $(2a - 3b)^7 = \binom{7}{0} (2a)^7 + \binom{7}{1} (2a)^6 (-3b) + \binom{7}{2} (2a)^5 (-3b)^2,$

$+ \binom{7}{3} (2a)^4 (-3b)^3 + \binom{7}{4} (2a)^3 (-3b)^4$

$+ \binom{7}{5} (2a)^2 (-3b)^5 + \binom{7}{6} (2a) (-3b)^6$

$+ \binom{7}{7} (-3b)^7,$

$= 128a^7 - 1344a^6b + 6048a^5b^2 - 15120a^4b^3 + 22680a^3b^4$

$- 20412a^2b^5 + 10206ab^6 - 2187b^7.$

Example 3. Calculate the first three terms and the seventeenth term in the expansion of $(x - 2y)^{19}$.

Solution:

$$(x - 2y)^{19} = \binom{19}{0} x^{19} + \binom{19}{1} x^{18}(-2y) + \binom{19}{2} x^{17}(-2y)^2 + \dots$$

$$= x^{19} - 38x^{18}y + 684x^{17}y^2 + \dots$$

$$t_{17} = \binom{19}{16} x^3(-2y)^{16},$$

$$= 2^{16} \cdot 969 x^3 y^{16}.$$

Example 4. Write the term containing a^8 in the expansion of $\left(a^2 - \dfrac{b}{2} \right)^6$.

Solution:

Since the required term must contain a^8 or $(a^2)^{6-2}$, the coefficient must be $\binom{6}{2}$.

Hence $\qquad t_3 = \binom{6}{2} (a^2)^4 \left(-\dfrac{b}{2} \right)^2,$

$$= \frac{15a^8b^2}{4}.$$

EXERCISE 14.2

1. Write the following expansions in sigma notation.
    (a) $(x + y)^{12}$
    (b) $(x - y)^9$
    (c) $(2x + y)^7$
    (d) $\left(2x + \dfrac{y}{2} \right)^8$
    (e) $(x^2 + 1)^{10}$
    (f) $(1 - 2x^2)^{15}$

2. Expand each of the following.
    (a) $(a - b)^5$
    (b) $(2a + b)^4$
    (c) $\left(2x - \dfrac{y}{2} \right)^6$
    (d) $\left(x^2 + \dfrac{1}{x} \right)^4$
    (e) $\left(4x^2 - \dfrac{x}{2} \right)^4$
    (f) $\left(3a - \dfrac{2}{b} \right)^5$

3. Write the first three terms of each of the following expansions.
    (a) $(a + b)^{10}$
    (b) $(a - b)^8$
    (c) $(a + 3b)^7$
    (d) $(1 - 3x)^{15}$
    (e) $(3a - 2)^5$
    (f) $(1 + 2b)^{12}$
    (g) $\left(2x - \dfrac{y}{4} \right)^8$
    (h) $\left(x^2 - \dfrac{2}{x} \right)^6$
    (i) $\left(3x^2 - \dfrac{x}{y} \right)^6$

4. Calculate the indicated term in each of the following expansions.

(a) $(a + b)^{10}$, t_7

(b) $(a - 2b)^7$, t_4

(c) $\left(x^2 + \dfrac{x}{2}\right)^6$, t_3

(d) $\left(x^2 - \dfrac{2}{x}\right)^{10}$, t_4

(e) $\left(2x - \dfrac{y}{3}\right)^7$, t_5

(f) $(3x + 2y)^6$, middle term

(g) $\left(\dfrac{2}{a} + \dfrac{a}{2}\right)^8$, t_5

(h) $\left(\dfrac{2}{a} + \dfrac{a}{2}\right)^{2n}$, t_{n+1}

5. Write the term in the expansion of $(x + 2y)^7$ in which the exponent of x is 5.

6. Write the term in the expansion of $(2x^2 - y)^8$ in which the exponent of x is 6.

7. Write the term in the expansion of $\left(3x^2 - \dfrac{2}{y^2}\right)^6$ in which the exponent of y is $- 8$.

8. In the expansion of $(ax + by)^7$, the coefficients of the first two terms are 128 and $- 224$, respectively. Calculate the values of a and b.

9. In the expansion of $(ax + by)^n$, the coefficients of the first three terms are 1, $-\dfrac{16}{3}$, and $\dfrac{112}{9}$, respectively. If $a > 0$, calculate the values of a, b, and n.

14.3.   The General Term

In the expansion of $(a + b)^n$, the general term is $t_{r+1} = \dbinom{n}{r} a^{n-r} b^r$. Once the general term of any particular expansion has been found, it becomes a relatively simple matter to find any particular term in the expansion.

Example 1. Calculate, in simplified form, the general term in the expansion of

$$\left(x^2 + \frac{1}{x}\right)^{10}$$

Solution: In the expansion of $(x^2 + x^{-1})^{10}$,

$$t_{r+1} = \binom{10}{r} (x^2)^{10-r} (x^{-1})^r,$$

$$= \binom{10}{r} x^{20-2r} x^{-r},$$

$$= \binom{10}{r} x^{20-3r}.$$

Example 2. Calculate the coefficients of x^{10}, x^0, and x^{-8} in the expansion of

$$\left(x^3 + \frac{1}{x}\right)^{12}.$$

Solution: In the expansion of $(x^3 + x^{-1})^{12}$,

$$t_{r+1} = \binom{12}{r}(x^3)^{12-r}(x^{-1})^r,$$

$$= \binom{12}{r}x^{36-3r}x^{-r},$$

$$= \binom{12}{r}x^{36-4r}.$$

(i) If $36 - 4r = 10$, then $r = 6\frac{1}{2}$.
   Since $r \in W$, there is no term containing x^{10}.

(ii) If $36 - 4r = 0$, then $r = 9$.
   Hence the coefficient of x^0 is $\binom{12}{9} = 220$.

(iii) If $36 - 4r = -8$, then $r = 11$.
   Thus the coefficient of x^{-8} is $\binom{12}{11} = 12$.

Note that when $r = 9$, $t_{10} = 220x^0 = 220$, and when $r = 11$, $t_{12} = 12x^{-8}$.

Example 3. In the expansion of $\left(a - \frac{2}{a}\right)^8$, calculate the terms containing a^4, a^0,

$\frac{1}{a^2}$.

Solution: In the expansion of $(a - 2a^{-1})^8$

$$t_{r+1} = \binom{8}{r}a^{8-r}(-2a^{-1})^r,$$

$$= \binom{8}{r}(-2)^r a^{8-r}a^{-r},$$

$$= \binom{8}{r}(-2)^r a^{8-2r}.$$

(i) If $8 - 2r = 4$, then $r = 2$.

   Therefore $\qquad t_3 = \binom{8}{2}(-2)^2 a^4,$

$$= (28)(4)a^4,$$
$$= 112a^4.$$

(ii) If $8 - 2r = 0$, then $r = 4$.

$$\text{Therefore} \qquad t_5 = \binom{8}{4}(-2)^4 a^0,$$

$$= (70)\,(16)a^0,$$
$$= 1120 a^0.$$

(iii) If $8 - 2r = -2$, then $r = 5$.

$$\text{Therefore} \qquad t_6 = \binom{8}{5}(-2)^5 a^{-2},$$

$$= (56)\,(-32)a^{-2},$$
$$= -\frac{1792}{a^2}.$$

EXERCISE 14.3

1. Calculate the general term in each of the following expansions.

(a) $(1 + x)^{12}$ (b) $(2 - a)^8$ (c) $(x^2 + x)^7$

(d) $\left(a + \dfrac{1}{a}\right)^7$ (e) $\left(p - \dfrac{1}{p}\right)^8$ (f) $\left(x^2 - \dfrac{1}{x}\right)^{10}$

(g) $\left(2a + \dfrac{1}{a^2}\right)^{10}$ (h) $\left(2a - \dfrac{1}{a^3}\right)^{15}$ (i) $\left(a^3 + \dfrac{2}{a^2}\right)^n$

2. In the expansion of $\left(x + \dfrac{1}{x^2}\right)^{12}$, obtain the coefficients of x^9, x^3, x^{-9}.

3. Calculate the term independent of a in the expansion of $\left(a + \dfrac{1}{a^4}\right)^{15}$.

4. In the expansion of $\left(2x + \dfrac{1}{x}\right)^{10}$, calculate the terms containing x^8, x^0, x^{-4}.

5. In the expansion of $\left(\dfrac{3x}{2} - \dfrac{2}{x^2}\right)^6$, calculate the term independent of x and the term containing x^{-6}.

6. In the expansion of $\left(a^2 - \dfrac{1}{a^3}\right)^9$, calculate the coefficients of a^3, a^{-7}, a^{-10}.

7. Calculate the term independent of x in the expansion of $\left(2x + \dfrac{1}{2\sqrt{x}}\right)^9$.

8. In the expansion of $(x + x^{-1})^n$, the fifth term is independent of x. Calculate the value of n.

9. In the expansion of $\left(\dfrac{3x}{2} + \dfrac{1}{x}\right)^n$, the fourth term contains x^3. Calculate the value of n.

10. In the expansion of $(1 - x)(1 + x)^n$, the third term is $35x^2$. Calculate the value of n.

Chapter Summary

If $n \in N$,

$$(a + b)^n = \sum_{r=0}^{n} \binom{n}{r} a^{n-r}b^r$$

$$= \binom{n}{0} a^n + \binom{n}{1} a^{n-1}b + \binom{n}{2} a^{n-2}b^2 + \dots + \binom{n}{r} a^{n-r}b^r$$

$$+ \dots + \binom{n}{n} b^n.$$

The general term is
$$t_{r+1} = \binom{n}{r} a^{n-r}b^r.$$

REVIEW EXERCISE 14

1. Write the following expansions using sigma notation.
   (a) $(a + b)^7$
   (b) $(x + 2y)^n$
   (c) $(2a - b)^{10}$
   (d) $\left(x^2 - \dfrac{1}{x}\right)^8$
   (e) $\left(2x^2 + \dfrac{1}{2x}\right)^{15}$
   (f) $(2 - x^2)^n$

2. Expand each of the following.
   (a) $(a + b)^6$
   (b) $(a - b)^6$
   (c) $(2a + 3b)^5$

3. Write the first three terms of each of the following expansions.
   (a) $(a + 2b)^{12}$
   (b) $(2x - y)^8$
   (c) $\left(2x^2 + \dfrac{x}{2}\right)^{10}$
   (d) $\left(3x - \dfrac{1}{x}\right)^6$
   (e) $\left(\dfrac{x}{2} + \dfrac{2}{x}\right)^{10}$
   (f) $(ax^2 + b)^{20}$

4. Calculate the eleventh term in the expansion of $\left(3x + \dfrac{1}{x}\right)^{12}$.

5. Calculate the seventh term in the expansion of $\left(x^2 - \dfrac{1}{x} \right)^{10}$.

6. In the expansion of $(2x - 1)^{10}$, calculate the term of containing x^2.

7. Calculate the first three terms in the expansion of $(a + 1)^8 (2a - 1)^5$.

8. Calculate the first three terms in the expansion of $(1 - x)^7 (2 + x)^4$.

9. In the expansion of $\left(3x + \dfrac{x^2}{3} \right)^{10}$, calculate the coefficients of x^{12} and x^{15}.

10. Calculate the term independent of x in the expansion of $\left(2x - \dfrac{1}{x^2} \right)^6$.

11. Calculate the middle term in the expansion of $\left(\dfrac{2}{x} + \dfrac{x}{2} \right)^{10}$.

12. In the expansion of $(1 + px)^n$, the first three terms are $1 - 36x + 594x^2$. Calculate the values of n and p.

13. In the expansion of $(1 + px)^n$, the first three terms are $1 + 5x + \dfrac{45x^2}{4}$. Calculate the values of n and p.

14. In the expansion of $\left(a^2 - \dfrac{1}{a^3} \right)^n$, the fifth term is $70a^{-4}$. Calculate the value of n.

15. In the expansion of $(ax + by)^7$, the coefficients of the first two terms are 128 and -112, respectively. Calculate the values of a and b.

16. In the expansion of $(ax + by)^n$, the coefficients of the first three terms are 729, 486, and 135 respectively. If $a > 0$, calculate the values of a, b, and n.

Chapter **15**

PROBABILITY

15.1. Introduction and Definitions

Most of us already have some intuitive idea as to what is meant by probability. If we toss a coin, we feel certain that it is just as likely to fall "heads" as to fall "tails"; if we roll a die, we feel that one face is just as likely to end up on top as another. In the case of the coin, we consider that "heads" and "tails" have *equal chances* or are *equally likely outcomes.* With the die, we feel that one dot, two dots, three dots, four dots, five dots, or six dots, on top are *equally likely outcomes.*

If a coin is tossed and we consider heads to be a favourable outcome, then we feel that we have one chance in two of having our wish satisfied. If we consider a three to be a favourable outcome in the toss of a die, then we feel that we have one chance in six of being successful.

In more technical language, we would say that, in the case of the coin, the probability of heads is $\frac{1}{2}$, and, in the case of the die, the probability of three on top is $\frac{1}{6}$. This is usually expressed symbolically as

$$P(\text{head}) = \tfrac{1}{2},$$
$$P(3 \text{ on top}) = \tfrac{1}{6}.$$

We note, of course, that we are considering only a "fair" coin or die. If the die were more heavily loaded on one side, then the opposite side would be more likely to appear on top. The six faces would no longer be equally likely.

If we consider the probability of drawing an honour card (ace, king, queen, jack, or ten) from a well-shuffled deck of playing cards, we know that we have fifty-two possible outcomes, and of these, twenty are favourable (an honour card). The probability of drawing an honour card is $\frac{20}{52}$. That is

$$P(\text{honour card}) = \tfrac{20}{52} = \tfrac{5}{13}.$$

That all outcomes are equally likely is not always true but, for the moment, we will consider only cases where they are. In the example of drawing an honour card, there are fifty-two equally likely outcomes. Twenty of these outcomes correspond to the event "honour card drawn" and may be considered as favourable outcomes. In the same way, if n is the number of equally likely outcomes of a specific experiment and exactly m of these outcomes $(m \leq n)$ correspond to an event A, then the probability of A is $\dfrac{m}{n}$. In symbols,

$$P(A) = \frac{m}{n}.$$

This, of course, does not constitute a rigorous definition of an event nor of the probability of an event. It is a useful, intuitive approach and more rigorous definitions will be given in the next section.

Example 1. If one card is drawn at random from a well-shuffled deck of fifty-two playing cards, what is the probability of each of the following events?
(a) drawing a spade,   (b) drawing a king,   (c) drawing a red card,
(d) drawing the queen of spades.

Solution:

$$P(\text{a spade}) = \tfrac{13}{52} = \tfrac{1}{4}.$$

$$P(\text{a king}) = \tfrac{4}{52} = \tfrac{1}{13}.$$

$$P(\text{red card}) = \tfrac{26}{52} = \tfrac{1}{2}.$$

$$P(\text{queen of spades}) = \tfrac{1}{52}.$$

Example 2. A letter is chosen at random from the word *probability*. What is the probability that the letter chosen is
(a) a vowel?   (b) a consonant?   (c) the letter b?   (d) the letter s?

Solution:

$$P(\text{vowel}) = \tfrac{4}{11}.$$

$$P(\text{consonant}) = \tfrac{7}{11}.$$

$$P(\text{b}) = \tfrac{2}{11}.$$

$$P(\text{s}) = \tfrac{0}{11} = 0.$$

Example 3. A group of five men and four women agree that three should be chosen by lot to form a special committee. What is the probability that the committee consists of one man and two women?

Solution: Number of possible committee selections is

$$\binom{9}{3} = \frac{9 \times 8 \times 7}{3 \times 2}$$
$$= 84.$$

Number of possible committee selections consisting of one man and two women is

$$\binom{5}{1}\binom{4}{2} = 5 \times 6$$
$$= 30.$$

Therefore, $P(1 \text{ man and 2 women}) = \frac{30}{84} = \frac{5}{14}$.

Example 4. Twenty tickets are placed in a box and shaken. One ticket is taken from the box and the person whose name is on that ticket receives a prize. What is the probability that Tom wins the prize if his name is on
(a) 4 of the tickets   (b) none of the tickets?   (c) all 20 tickets?

Solution:

(a) $P(\text{Tom wins}) = \frac{4}{20} = \frac{1}{5}.$

(b) $P(\text{Tom wins}) = \frac{0}{20} = 0.$

(c) $P(\text{Tom wins}) = \frac{20}{20} = 1.$

This last example illustrates that the probability of any event A is a real number between 0 and 1, that is,

$$0 \leq P(A) \leq 1.$$

If the event cannot happen, as in Example 4(b), then the probability is zero. If Tom's name does not appear on any of the tickets, he cannot win the prize.
    If $P(A) = 1$, then A is certain. If Tom's name appears on all twenty tickets, then he must win. His success is certain and $P(\text{Tom wins}) = 1$.

EXERCISE 15.1

1. If a die is thrown, what is the probability that the upper face shows
   (a) 4 dots?   (b) more than 4 dots?
   (c) fewer than 4 dots?   (d) an odd number of dots?
   (e) an even number of dots?   (f) more than 3 dots?

2. A bag contains five red balls and three black balls. If one ball is drawn from the bag, what is the probability that it is
   (a) a red ball?   (b) a black ball?

3. A letter is chosen at random from the word *Toronto*. What is the probability that the letter chosen is

   (a) the letter t?   (b) the letter o?   (c) a consonant?

4. From a group of twenty men and sixteen women, one person is chosen by lot. What is the probability that a man is chosen?

5. From a group of twenty men and sixteen women, two persons are chosen by lot. What is the probability that
   (a) both are men?
   (b) both are women?
   (c) one man and one woman are chosen?
   What is the sum of the three probabilities?

6. Six slips of paper, numbered 1 to 6, are placed in a bag and two are drawn out. Find the probability of each of the following events.
   (a) The numbers 2 and 5 are drawn.
   (b) The numbers 2 and 5 are drawn in that order.
   (c) Two even numbers are drawn.

7. A three-digit number is formed by drawing three slips from a box containing nine slips of paper numbered 1 to 9. The first digit drawn is to be the hundreds' digit, the second is to be the tens' digit, and the third is to be the units' digit. The slips are not replaced after being drawn. What is the probability that the number formed

   (a) is even?   (b) is odd?   (c) has units' digit 4?

8. Three books are selected at random from eight different books on a shelf. What is the probability that a specific book is included in the selection?

9. From a group of twelve boys, a selection of three will be made by lot to attend the Stanley Cup final. Tom and Jim are very anxious to win. What is the probability that

   (a) both will be selected?   (b) only one of them will be selected?

10. If two dice are tossed, what is the probability that

    (a) both upper faces show 6?   (b) the upper faces total 4?

11. Assuming that boys and girls have an equal chance of being born, what is the probability that, in a family of three children, all three are girls?

12. If two cards are drawn at random from a well-shuffled deck of fifty-two playing cards, what is the probability of each of the following events?
    (a) Both are clubs.   (b) Both are aces.
    (c) Both are red cards   (d) Both are black aces.

15.2.   Sample Space

If a nickel and a quarter are tossed together, what is the set of all possible outcomes of the experiment? The answer to this question will depend upon what particular aspect of the experiment interests us. If we are interested simply in whether the coins fall alike (both heads or both tails) or differently (one head and one tail), then we have only two possible outcomes, L (like) and D (different). The set of all possible outcomes is

$$S_1 = \{L, D\}.$$

However, we may be interested in the number of heads or the number of tails that show. If we agree to denote x heads and y tails by the ordered pair (x, y), then the set of all possible outcomes is

$$S_2 = \{(2, 0), (1, 1), (0, 2)\}.$$

Any possible outcome of the experiment corresponds to exactly one element of the set S_2.

Again, we may be interested in whether each individual coin falls heads (H) or tails (T). In this case we may list the outcome by the ordered pairs (x, y), in which x represents the outcome for the nickel and y, the outcome for the quarter. The set of all possible outcomes is

$$S_3 = \{(H, H), (H, T), (T, H), (T, T)\}.$$

(T, H) means that the nickel fell tails and the quarter fell heads. All possible outcomes are elements of the set S_3.

Each of the sets S_1, S_2, S_3 is a set of all possible outcomes of the experiment. Each set is called a sample space of the experiment. Note that there may be many possible sample spaces of an experiment so that we talk about *a* sample space rather than *the* sample space.

We should also note that S_3 is a more fundamental sample space than either S_1 or S_2. If we know that (T, H) is the actual outcome in S_3, we also know that D is the outcome in S_1, and $(1, 1)$ is the outcome in S_2. However, if we know that L is the outcome in S_1, we do not know the outcome in S_3. It may be (H, H) or (T, T). If we know that the actual outcome in S_2 is $(2, 0)$, then we know that the outcome in S_3 is (H, H); but if the outcome in S_2 is $(1, 1)$, we do not know whether the outcome in S_3 is (H, T) or (T, H).

DEFINITION. A *sample space* of an experiment is a set of elements such that every possible outcome of the experiment corresponds to exactly one element of the set.

An element in a sample space is often called a *sample point.* Since the sample space is the set of all possible outcomes, there is a tendency in some texts to use the terms *outcome set* and *outcome* in place of sample space and sample point. There is much to be said in favour of this terminology since by definition a sample space is a set of all possible outcomes. Outcome set would seem to be a more descriptive title. However, although there are good reasons for changing to outcome set, we will continue to use the more traditional title of sample space.

This definition of a sample space now enables us to define an event.

DEFINITION. An *event* is a result of an experiment that may be represented by a subset of a sample space of the experiment.

In a sample space $S_3 = \{ (H, H), (H, T), (T, H), (T, T) \}$, the event "both coins fall alike" corresponds to the subset $\{ (H, H), (T, T) \}$. The subset in this case contains two elements of the sample space. Other events in this sample space may contain 1, 2, 3, or 4 elements of the sample space.

Example 1. A bag contains twenty red balls and twenty black balls. If three balls are drawn from the bag one after the other without replacement, list two sample spaces for the experiment. How many elements of the most fundamental sample space correspond to the following events?
(a) drawing two red balls and one black ball?
(b) drawing three red balls.
(c) drawing at least one red ball.

Solution: $S_1 = \{0, 1, 2, 3\}$,
where each element is the number of red balls drawn.

$$S_2 = \{RRR, RRB, RBR, RBB, BRR, BRB, BBR, BBB\}.$$

A useful method of setting up S_2 is by means of a tree diagram.

1st draw	2nd draw	3rd draw	Sample Space
		R	RRR
	R	B	RRB
R		R	RBR
	B	B	RBB
		R	BRR
	R	B	BRB
B		R	BBR
	B	B	BBB

Table 15.1

(a) Three elements of S_2 correspond to drawing two red balls and one black ball.
(b) One element of S_2 corresponds to drawing three red balls.
(c) Seven elements of S_2 correspond to drawing at least one red ball.

Example 2. Two dice, one black and one white, are rolled and the number shown on each die is noted. List a sample space for this experiment.

We note that we are told that the *number* on each die is noted. If only the *total* were required, a suitable sample space would be {2, 3, 4, ..., 12}.

Solution: A tabular arrangement is probably the most suitable way to illustrate the elements of this sample space.

Table 15.2

White die *W*

B \ W	1	2	3	4	5	6
1	(1, 1)	(1, 2)	(1, 3)	(1, 4)	(1, 5)	(1, 6)
2	(2, 1)	(2, 2)	(2, 3)	(2, 4)	(2, 5)	(2, 6)
Black 3	(3, 1)	(3, 2)	(3, 3)	(3, 4)	(3, 5)	(3, 6)
die 4	(4, 1)	(4, 2)	(4, 3)	(4, 4)	(4, 5)	(4, 6)
B 5	(5, 1)	(5, 2)	(5, 3)	(5, 4)	(5, 5)	(5, 6)
6	(6, 1)	(6, 2)	(6, 3)	(6, 4)	(6, 5)	(6, 6)

Note that each row corresponds to a fixed value of the outcome for the black die, and each column, to a fixed value of the outcome for the white die. There are thirty-six elements in the sample space.

Example 3. Using the sample space in Example 2, how many elements of the sample space correspond to the following events?
  (a) Both dice show the same number,
  (b) The number on the white die is two more than the number on the black die,
  (c) The total for the two dice is seven,
  (d) The total for the two dice is eleven.

Solution:
  (a) Six elements show the same number on both dice.
  (b) Four elements correspond to having the number on the white die two more than the number on the black die.
  (c) Six elements correspond to a total of seven for the two dice.
  (d) Two elements correspond to a total of eleven for the two dice.

EXERCISE 15.2

  1. List two sample spaces for an experiment of tossing three coins.

2. Using the sample spaces in question 1, how many elements of each sample space correspond to two heads and one tail?

3. Use a tree diagram to set up a sample space to study the distribution of boys and girls in families having three children. How many elements of the sample space correspond to
   (a) families having three boys?
   (b) families having one boy and two girls?

4. Use a tree diagram to set up a sample space to study the distribution of boys and girls in families having four children. How many elements of the sample space correspond to
   (a) families having three girls and one boy?
   (b) families having two girls and two boys?
   (c) families in which the first two children are girls?

5. A box contains five differently coloured balls: red (R), blue (B), green (G), white (W), and yellow (Y). If three have to be chosen, list a sample space of the $\binom{5}{3}$ possible selections. How many elements of the sample space correspond to
   (a) a selection including Y?
   (b) a selection excluding Y?
   (c) a selection including both B and G?
   (d) a selection including either B or G?

6. A bag contains twenty blue marbles, twenty green marbles, and twenty red marbles, identical except for colour. Two marbles are drawn one after the other with the first being replaced before the second is drawn. List a sample space for the experiment. How many elements of the sample space correspond to
   (a) drawing two marbles of the same colour?
   (b) drawing a blue and a green marble?
   (c) drawing a blue or a green marble?

7. Four cards, numbered 1, 2, 3, and 4, are to be placed in four boxes numbered 1, 2, 3, 4; one card in each box. List a sample space of ordered quadruples that indicate the card in each slot. (For example, 1243 indicates card 1 in box 1, card 2 in box 2, card 4 in box 3, and card 3 in box 4.) How many elements of the sample space correspond to the following events?
   (a) Exactly two card numbers and two box numbers coincide.
   (b) At least two card numbers and two box numbers coincide.
   (c) No card number coincides with its box number.

15.3. Probabilities in a Finite Sample Space

In Section 15.2, we listed three sample spaces for the example of tossing two coins.

$S_1 = \{L, D\}$, where L indicated that both coins fell heads or both fell tails, and D indicated that one fell heads and the other, tails.

$S_2 = \{ (2, 0), (1, 1), (0, 2) \}$, where the ordered pairs (x, y) indicated x heads and y tails.

$S_3 = \{ (H, H), (H, T), (T, H), (T, T) \}$, where the ordered pairs (x, y) indicated the outcome for the nickel (x) and for the quarter (y).

In Section 15.1, we stated that the probability of an event A is $\dfrac{m}{n}$, where n is the number of equally likely outcomes and exactly m of these outcomes correspond to event A.

In the experiment of tossing two coins, what is the probability that one falls heads and the other, tails? Using S_1, the outcome corresponding to a favourable event is D, that is, one outcome of the two possible outcomes. From this it would appear that

$$P \text{ (1 head and 1 tail)} = \tfrac{1}{2}.$$

However, if we consider that the three outcomes in S_2 are equally likely, only the pair $(1, 1)$ corresponds to the favourable event, 1 head and 1 tail. From this it would appear that

$$P \text{ (1 head and 1 tail)} = \tfrac{1}{3}.$$

From S_3, it would appear that

$$P \text{ (1 head and 1 tail)} = \tfrac{2}{4} = \tfrac{1}{2}.$$

The difference arises because the outcomes in S_2 are not equally likely. If we assume that the outcome of one coin is independent of the outcome of the other, then the four outcomes in S_3 are equally likely and each can be assigned a probability of $\tfrac{1}{4}$. In this case the outcomes in S_2 are not equally likely and

$$P (2, 0) = \tfrac{1}{4}, P (1, 1) = \tfrac{1}{2}, P (0, 2) = \tfrac{1}{4}.$$

It is essential when using a sample space either to ensure that each of the outcomes is equally likely or to know the probability of each possible outcome.

In Table 15.2 of the last section, we set up the thirty-six elements of the sample space for the experiment of rolling two dice, one white and one black, noting the number on each die. Naturally we would expect thirty-six elements in this sample space even if they were not listed. If B is the set of all possible outcomes for the black die and W is the set of all possible outcomes for the white die, then

$$B = \{1, 2, 3, 4, 5, 6\} \text{ and } n(B) = 6,$$
$$W = \{1, 2, 3, 4, 5, 6\} \text{ and } n(W) = 6.$$

Note that $n(B)$ is a symbol representing "the number of elements in set B". The set of all possible outcomes of the experiment of rolling both dice is

$$B \times W = \{ (b, w) \mid b \in B \text{ and } w \in W \}$$
$$n(B \times W) = n(B) \times n(W)$$
$$= 6 \times 6$$
$$= 36.$$

Since there are thirty-six equally likely outcomes of the experiment of rolling both dice, we assign a probability of $\frac{1}{36}$ to each possible outcome.

If the sample space contains n *equally likely* outcomes, we assign probability $\frac{1}{n}$ to each element of the sample space.

An event corresponds to a subset of the sample space. For example, if A is the event that both dice show the same number, then A corresponds to the subset $\{ (1, 1), (2, 2), (3, 3), (4, 4), (5, 5), (6, 6) \}$ of S, where S is the sample space in Table 15.2.

Therefore

$$P(\text{A}) = \tfrac{6}{36} = \tfrac{1}{6}.$$

Of course, it may happen that the elements of the sample space are not equally likely outcomes and we prefer to have a definition of the probability of an event that will cover all cases.

In the two-coin experiment, if $S_3 = \{ (H, H), (H, T), (T, H), (T, T) \}$ is the sample space, and if A is the event "at least one coin falls heads", then

$$A = \{ (H, H), (H, T), (T, H) \} \text{ and } P(A) = \tfrac{3}{4}.$$

If we use $S_2 = \{ (2, 0), (1, 1), (0, 2) \}$,

then
$$A = \{ (2, 0), (1, 1) \}.$$
$$P(2, 0) = \tfrac{1}{4}, P(1, 1) = \tfrac{1}{2},$$
$$P(A) = \tfrac{1}{4} + \tfrac{1}{2} = \tfrac{3}{4}.$$

To each element of a sample space, we assign a real number called a *probability*. Every probability must satisfy two conditions.

1. A probability is a real number x such that $0 \leq x \leq 1$.

2. The sum of the probabilities assigned to all the elements of any sample space is 1.

We may now define the probability of an event.

DEFINITION.   If A is an event which corresponds to a subset of a sample space, then the probability of A, $P(A)$, is the sum of the probabilities of the elements of the subset corresponding to A.

Example 1.   List a sample space to study the distribution of boys and girls in a family of three children. What is the probability that
(a) all three children are boys? (b) the first two children are girls? (c) there are two girls and one boy in a family?

Solution:

1st child	2nd child	3rd child	Sample Space
		B	BBB
	B	G	BBG
B		B	BGB
	G	G	BGG
		B	GBB
	B	G	GBG
G		B	GGB
	G	G	GGG

There are 8 elements in the sample space.

$$P(3 \text{ boys}) = \tfrac{1}{8}.$$

$$P(\text{First 2 are girls}) = \tfrac{2}{8} = \tfrac{1}{4}.$$

$$P(2 \text{ girls, 1 boy}) = \tfrac{3}{8}$$

Note that we are assuming that, when a child is born, it is just as likely to be a boy as a girl. By actual count, there are a few more boys born than girls, but for most purposes our assumption is adequate.

Example 2.   Using the sample space in Table 15.2 for the two-dice experiment, what is the probability that,
   (a) the number on the white die is two more than the number on the black die? $(w = b + 2)$
   (b) the total for the two dice is seven? $(b + w = 7)$
   (c) the total for the two dice is eleven? $(b + w = 11)$

Solution:

$$P(w = b + 2) = \tfrac{4}{36} = \tfrac{1}{9}.$$

$$P(b + w = 7) = \tfrac{6}{36} = \tfrac{1}{6}.$$

$$P(b + w = 11) = \tfrac{2}{36} = \tfrac{1}{18}.$$

Example 3. Using the sample space in Table 15.2 for the two-dice experiment state the following probabilities.

(a) $P(A)$, where $A = \{ (b, w) \mid b \geq 3 \}$

(b) $P(B)$, where $B = \{ (b, w) \mid w \leq 3 \}$

(c) $P(A \text{ and } B)$, where A and B are as described above

(d) $P(A \text{ or } B)$ (Note that *or* is inclusive).

Solution:

(a)
$$P(A) = \tfrac{24}{36} = \tfrac{2}{3}$$

(b)
$$P(B) = \tfrac{18}{36} = \tfrac{1}{2}$$

(c)
$$P(A \text{ and } B) = \tfrac{12}{36} = \tfrac{1}{3}$$

(d)
$$P(A \text{ or } B) = \tfrac{30}{36} = \tfrac{5}{6}.$$

Note that
$$P(A) + P(B) - P(A \text{ and } B) = \tfrac{2}{3} + \tfrac{1}{2} - \tfrac{1}{3}$$
$$= \tfrac{5}{6}$$
$$= P(A \text{ or } B).$$

Example 4. A box contains five differently coloured balls: red (R), green (G), blue (B), white (W), and yellow (Y). If a selection of three of the balls is made, state the following probabilities.

(a) The selection includes Y.

(b) The selection excludes Y.

(c) The selection includes both B and G.

(d) The selection includes either B or G.

Solution: $S = \{RGB, RGW, RGY, RBW, RBY, RWY, GBW, GBY, GWY, BWY\}.$

(a)
$$P(Y \text{ included}) = \tfrac{6}{10} = \tfrac{3}{5}.$$

(b)
$$P(Y \text{ excluded}) = \tfrac{4}{10} = \tfrac{2}{5}.$$

(c)
$$P(B \text{ and } G \text{ included}) = \tfrac{3}{10}.$$

(d)
$$P(B \text{ or } G \text{ included}) = \tfrac{9}{10}.$$

Solution (Alternative):

Number of selections without restriction is
$$\binom{5}{3} = 10.$$

Number of selections with Y included is
$$\binom{4}{2} = 6.$$

Number of selections with Y excluded is
$$\binom{4}{3} = 4.$$

Number of selections with both B and G included is

$$\binom{3}{1} = 3.$$

Number of selections with B and G excluded is

$$\binom{3}{3} = 1.$$

Therefore the number of selections with B or G included is 9.

Hence

$$P(Y \text{ included}) = \tfrac{6}{10} = \tfrac{3}{5},$$
$$P(Y \text{ excluded}) = \tfrac{4}{10} = \tfrac{2}{5},$$
$$P(B \text{ and } G \text{ included}) = \tfrac{3}{10},$$
$$P(B \text{ or } G \text{ included}) = \tfrac{9}{10}.$$

EXERCISE 15.3

1. Using the sample space given in Table 15.2 for the two-dice experiment, calculate the following probabilities.
   (a) The numbers on the two dice differ by two.
   (b) The total is ten or greater.
   (c) The total is less than seven.
   (d) The black die shows less than the white die.
   (e) The total is six.
   (f) The black die shows less than two.
   (g) The white die shows greater than four.
   (h) The black die shows less than two and the white die shows greater than four.
   (i) The black die shows less than two or the white die shows greater than four.
   (j) The total on the two dice is a prime number.
   (k) If it is known that the total on the two dice is odd, what is the probability that it is seven?
   (l) If it is known that the total on the two dice is even, what is the probability that it is seven?

2. A coin is tossed three times.
   (a) What is the probability of three heads?
   (b) What is the probability of exactly two heads?
   (c) What is the probability of at least two heads?
   (d) What is the probability of not more than two heads?

3. Six students, John, Jim, Dick, Mary, Helen, and Betty, have the qualifications for an all-expenses paid trip to New York but, unfortunately, only two can

be selected. They agree to make the selection by placing the six names on slips of paper and having the school principal draw two slips at random. What is the probability that

(a) John is selected?
(b) both Mary and Betty are selected?
(c) either Mary or Betty (not both) is selected?
(d) two girls are selected?

4. List a sample space to study the distribution of boys and girls in families having four children. (See question 4, Exercise 15.2.) What is the probability that

(a) a family has three boys and one girl?
(b) a family has two girls and two boys?
(c) the two eldest children are girls?

5. Four cards numbered 1, 2, 3, and 4 are shuffled and placed in four boxes numbered 1, 2, 3, 4, one card to a box. What is the probability that

(a) exactly two card numbers and two box numbers coincide?
(b) at least two card numbers and two box numbers coincide?
(c) no card number coincides with its box number?
(d) all card numbers and box numbers coincide?

6. John, Jim, Dick, Mary, and Helen are candidates for three positions on the students' council. Assuming the selection of any three is equally likely, what is the probability that

(a) Jim is selected?
(b) Mary and Helen are both selected?
(c) Dick is not selected?
(d) either Mary or Helen (or both) is selected?

15.4. Odds

If we consider the sample space in Table 15.2 for the experiment of throwing two dice, we know that it contains thirty-six elements. Any event A will correspond to a subset of the sample space. For any discussion of probabilities in this sample space, the universe of the discussion is the sample space S. If A is the event "throwing a double", the event A is a subset of S.

$$n(S) = 36 \text{ and } n(A) = 6,$$

so that

$$P(A) = \tfrac{6}{36} = \tfrac{1}{6}.$$

The set A' will correspond to the event
not-A or "not throwing a double".

$$n(A') = 30 \text{ and } P(A') = \tfrac{30}{36} = \tfrac{5}{6}.$$

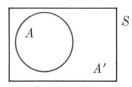

Figure 15.1

In general, if
$$P(A) = \frac{m}{n},$$

$$P(A') = \frac{n-m}{n}$$

$$= 1 - \frac{m}{n}$$

$$= 1 - P(A).$$

The relative probabilities of event A and event *not-A* are frequently expressed in terms of the *odds in favour* of A.

Odds in favour of A are $P(A)$ to $P(A')$

that is,
$$\frac{m}{n} \text{ to } \frac{n-m}{n},$$

or
$$m \text{ to } n - m.$$

Also,   *Odds against A are $P(A')$ to $P(A)$,*

that is, $n - m$ to m.

The odds in favour of throwing a double in the two-dice experiment will be given by

P(throwing a double) to P(not throwing a double),

that is, $\frac{1}{6}$ to $\frac{5}{6}$

or   1 to 5.

If the odds in favour of an event A are a to b, then
$$\frac{P(A)}{P(A')} = \frac{a}{b}.$$

Thus
$$\frac{P(A)}{1 - P(A)} = \frac{a}{b}$$

$$b \cdot P(A) = a - a \cdot P(A)$$

$$(a + b) \, P(A) = a.$$

Therefore,
$$P(A) = \frac{a}{a + b}.$$

Example 1.   If two dice are rolled, what are the odds in favour of throwing
(a) 7? (b) 11?

Solution:
$$P(7) = \tfrac{6}{36} = \tfrac{1}{6}.$$

Therefore the odds in favour of 7 are 1 to $(6 - 1)$ or 1 to 5.
$$P(11) = \tfrac{2}{36} = \tfrac{1}{18}.$$
Therefore the odds in favour of 11 are 1 to 17.

Example 2.   If the odds against a certain event are given as 5 to 2, what is the
probability of the event?

Solution: Denote the event by A.
$$P(A') = \frac{5}{5 + 2} = \tfrac{5}{7}.$$
$$P(A) = 1 - P(A')$$
$$= 1 - \tfrac{5}{7},$$
$$= \tfrac{2}{7}.$$

EXERCISE 15.4

1. A bag contains seven red balls and four black balls. If one ball is drawn from
   the bag, what are the odds in favour of its being
   (a) a red ball?   (b) a black ball?

2. If a die is thrown, what are the odds in favour of the upper face showing
   (a) 4?   (b) more than 4?
   What are the odds against the upper face showing six?

3. If one letter is chosen at random from the word *Toronto*, what are the odds
   in favour of its being the letter *o*? What are the odds against its being the
   letter *t*?

4. A committee of three is to be chosen by lot from seven candidates. What are
   the odds that a particular candidate not be selected?

5. From a group of eight men and five women, two are chosen by lot. What are
   the odds in favour of both chosen individuals being men?

6. If two coins are tossed, what are the odds in favour of both showing heads?

7. In a family of three children, what are the odds against all three being girls?

8. Two cards are drawn at random from a deck of fifty-two playing cards. What are the odds?
   (a) that both cards are red?
   (b) against drawing a king?
   (c) in favour of drawing two aces?

9. If two dice are rolled, what are the odds
   (a) in favour of a total of nine?
   (b) against a total of six?
   (c) in favour of a total of more than seven?
   (d) against a total of less than five?

10. Eight men enter a doubles tennis tournament in which partners are selected by lot. What are the odds against having two specified men, A and B, selected as partners?

11. A committee of five is selected by lot from a group of six men and four women. What are the odds in favour of having a specified man and a specified woman on the committee?

12. A plant breeder crosses two plants each possessing the gene pair Aa. Each parent contributes either A or a to the offspring, where the two are combined. What are the odds in favour of the offspring's being of the same genetic type as the parents, that is, Aa?

15.5.   Addition of Probabilities

In Example 3 of Section 15.3 we discussed the following problem.

Using the sample space given in Table 15.2 for the two-dice experiment, state the following probabilities.

   (a) $P(A)$, where $A = \{ (b, w) \mid b \geq 3\}$
   (b) $P(B)$, where $B = \{ (b, w) \mid w \leq 3\}$
   (c) $P(A$ and $B)$, where A and B are described above
   (d) $P(A$ or $B)$

We note that A and B are subsets of the sample space, and that the set A *and* B may be written in set notation as $A \cap B$, while the set A *or* B may be written as $A \cup B$.

In this particular example, $n(S) = 36$, where S is the sample space, $n(A) = 24$, $n(B) = 18$, and $n(A \cap B) = 12$ as shown in the Venn diagram. We note from the Venn diagram that, when we total the number of elements in the sets A and B, the elements in $A \cap B$ have been counted twice. These twelve elements in this example must then be subtracted in order to obtain the correct number of elements in $A \cup B$.

Therefore,

$$P(A) = \tfrac{24}{36} = \tfrac{2}{3}.$$
$$P(B) = \tfrac{18}{36} = \tfrac{1}{2}.$$
$$P(A \cap B) = \tfrac{12}{36} = \tfrac{1}{3}.$$
$$P(A \cup B) = \tfrac{30}{36} = \tfrac{5}{6}.$$

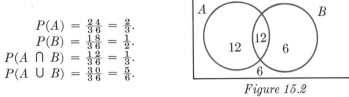

And in this case,

Figure 15.2

$$P(A \cup B) = P(A) + P(B) - P(A \cap B).$$

This result is true in general but will not be proved here.

Example 1. A box contains five differently coloured balls: red (R), green (G), blue (B), white (W), and yellow (Y). If a selection of three of the balls is made, state the probabilities of each of the following:
  (a) The selection includes either Y or G.
  (b) The selection includes Y or both B and G.

Solution: Total number of selections without restriction is

$$\binom{5}{3} = 10.$$

Number of selections which include Y is

$$\binom{4}{2} = 6.$$

Number of selections which include G is

$$\binom{4}{2} = 6.$$

Number of selections which include both Y and G is

$$\binom{3}{1} = 3.$$

Number of selections which include both B and G is

$$\binom{3}{1} = 3.$$

Number of selections which include B, G, and Y is 1.

  (a)
$$P(Y \cup G) = P(Y) + P(G) - P(Y \cap G)$$
$$= \tfrac{6}{10} + \tfrac{6}{10} - \tfrac{3}{10}$$
$$= \tfrac{9}{10}.$$

  (b)
$$P[Y \cup (B \cap G)] = P(Y) + P(B \cap G) - P(Y \cap B \cap G)$$
$$= \tfrac{6}{10} + \tfrac{3}{10} - \tfrac{1}{10}$$
$$= \tfrac{4}{5}.$$

It is suggested that this example should also be solved by forming a sample space as in Example 4 of Section 15.3.

Example 2. One number, x, is selected at random from the set 1, 2, 3, ..., 10. What is the probability that (a) $x < 4$? (b) x is odd? (c) $x < 4$ or x is odd?

Solution:

(a)
$$P(x < 4) = \tfrac{3}{10}.$$

(b)
$$P(x \text{ is odd}) = \tfrac{5}{10} = \tfrac{1}{2}.$$

(c)
$$P(x < 4 \text{ and } x \text{ is odd}) = \tfrac{2}{10} = \tfrac{1}{5}.$$
$$P(x < 4 \text{ or } x \text{ is odd}) = \tfrac{3}{10} + \tfrac{5}{10} - \tfrac{2}{10}$$
$$= \tfrac{3}{5}.$$

EXERCISE 15.5

1. Using the sample space in Table 15.2 for the two-dice experiment, calculate the following probabilities, where b is the number on the black die and w is the number on the white die.
   (a) $b < 3$ and $w > 4$.
   (b) $b < 3$ or $w > 4$.
   (c) $b < 4$ or $w < 4$.
   (d) $b + w = 7$ or $b + w = 11$.

2. One number if selected at random from the set $\{1, 2, 3, ..., 20\}$. If x is the number selected, calculate the following probabilities.
   (a) $P(x > 15)$
   (b) $P(A)$, where $A = \{x \mid x \text{ is even}\}$
   (c) $P(B)$, where $B = \{x \mid x < 12\}$
   (d) $P(A \cup B)$

3. If a bag contains four white balls, five red balls, six green balls, and four yellow balls, and one ball is drawn from the bag at random, what is the probability that
   (a) a red ball is selected?
   (b) the ball selected is either red or green?

4. A committee of three is selected by lot from four men and six women. What is the probability that either Mrs. Smith or Mr. Jones is selected? (Note that we always assume the inclusive *or* unless otherwise stated.)

5. John has been given permission to select any three books from a collection of six books $\{A, B, C, D, E, F\}$. Calculate the following probabilities.
   (a) The selection includes A.

(b) The selection includes either A or B.

(c) The selection includes C or both A and B.

(d) The selection includes both A and C or both E and F.

(e) The selection includes both A and C or both C and D.

6. The four aces and four kings are removed from a pack of cards. If two cards are drawn at random from these eight cards, what is the probability that they are both aces or both red?

7. If two cards are drawn at random from a pack of fifty-two cards, what is the probability that they are both aces or both red?

8. There are three tickets available for an N.H.L. game and ten boys agree to draw lots to decide which three will receive the tickets. Calculate each of the following probabilities.

(a) Either Tom or Jim will be included.

(b) Either Tom and Jim or Jim and Ken will be included.

(c) Either Tom and Jim or Ted and Ken will be included.

9. In a certain school, 15% of the students failed Mathematics, 12% failed English, and 5% failed both Mathematics and English. What is the probability that a particular student, selected at random, failed either English or Mathematics? If there were 550 students who wrote both examinations, how many failed at least one of these subjects?

10. The odds against John's winning a race are 3 to 1 and the odds against Bill's winning are 4 to 1. What is the probability that either Bill or John will win? (Note that a tie is excluded.)

15.6. Mutually Exclusive Events

In question 1(d) of Exercise 15.5, we were asked to find the probability that $b + w = 7$ or $b + w = 11$, using Table 15.2 for the two-dice experiment. If $A = \{ (b,w) | b + w = 7\}$ and $B = \{ (b,w) | b + w = 11\}$, then $n(A) = 6$ and $n(B) = 2$. It is obvious that $A \cap B = \emptyset$ and $n(A \cap B) = 0$.

Hence

$$P(A \cup B) = P(A) + P(B) - P(A \cap B)$$
$$= \tfrac{6}{36} + \tfrac{2}{36} - \tfrac{0}{36}$$
$$= \tfrac{2}{9}.$$

In this instance, $P(A \cup B) = P(A) + P(B)$.

When two events in a given sample space have no elements in common, and their intersection is the empty set, they are said to be mutually exclusive events.

DEFINITION. If two events in a given sample space have no elements in common, they are *mutually exclusive events* or disjoint events.

This definition can be extended to cover any number of events in a given sample space. *n* events are mutually exclusive if no two of them have any elements in common. In the Venn diagram, the events A, B, C, and D are mutually exclusive.

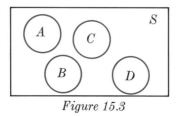

Figure 15.3

Theorem. If two events A and B are mutually exclusive, then

$$P(A \cap B) = 0$$

and

$$P(A \cup B) = P(A) + P(B).$$

Corollary. If A, B, and C are mutually exclusive events, then

$$P(A \cup B \cup C) = P(A) + P(B) + P(C).$$

It must be noted that this applies only if the events are known to be mutually exclusive.

EXERCISE 15.6

1. In an experiment of throwing two dice, one white and one black, state which of the following events are mutually exclusive.
   (a) The total is seven. Black die shows four.
   (b) The total is five. White die shows six.
   (c) White die shows five. Black die shows two.
   (d) White die shows greater than four. Black die shows less than four.
   (e) White die shows greater than four. Total is less than five.

2. If two coins are tossed, which of the following events are mutually exclusive?
   (a) One coin shows heads. Both coins show heads.
   (b) One coin shows heads. Both coins show tails.
   (c) One coin shows tails. The coins fall differently.
   (d) One coin shows heads. The coins fall alike.

3. In a family of three children, which of the following events are mutually exclusive?
   (a) The two eldest are girls. All three are of the same sex.
   (b) The eldest is a boy. The family has two girls.
   (c) Two children are boys. The youngest is a boy.
   (d) Two children are boys. The eldest and youngest are girls.
   (e) All three are girls. The youngest is a boy.

4. In rolling a single die, A is the event "die shows 3", and B is the event "die shows an odd number". Are A and B mutually exclusive? What is $P(A \cup B)$?

5. In rolling a single die, A is the event "die shows 3", and B is the event "die shows an even number". Are A and B mutually exclusive? What is $P(A \cup B)$?

6. In an experiment of rolling two dice, b represents the number on the black die and w, the number on the white die. Find $P(A \cup B)$ for each of the following events A and B.
   (a) $A = \{ (b,w) \mid b + w = 7 \}$, $\qquad$ $B = \{ (b,w) \mid b = 4 \}$.
   (b) $A = \{ (b,w) \mid b + w = 5 \}$, $\qquad$ $B = \{ (b,w) \mid w = 6 \}$.
   (c) $A = \{ (b,w) \mid b + w < 5 \}$, $\qquad$ $B = \{ (b,w) \mid w > 4 \}$.
   (d) $A = \{ (b,w) \mid w = 5 \}$, $\qquad$ $B = \{ (b,w) \mid b = 2 \}$.
   (e) $A = \{ (b,w) \mid w > 4 \}$, $\qquad$ $B = \{ (b,w) \mid b < 4 \}$.
   (f) $A = \{ (b,w) \mid b \text{ is odd} \}$, $\qquad$ $B = \{ (b,w) \mid w = b + 1 \}$.

7. If two coins are tossed, find the probability of each of the following.
   (a) One coin shows heads or both coins show heads.
   (b) One coin shows heads or both coins show tails.
   (c) One coin shows tails or the coins fall differently.
   (d) One coin shows heads or both coins fall alike.

8. Find the probability of the following distributions in families of three children.
   (a) The two eldest are girls or all are of the same sex.
   (b) The eldest is a boy or the family has exactly two girls.
   (c) Exactly two children are boys or the youngest is a boy.
   (d) Exactly two children are boys or the eldest and youngest are girls.
   (e) All three are girls or the youngest is a boy.

9. Two cards are drawn from a pack of fifty-two playing cards. Find the probability of each of the following events.
   (a) Both cards are clubs.
   (b) Both cards are black.
   (c) Both cards are kings.
   (d) Both cards are black kings.
   (e) Both cards are kings or both cards are black.

10. Two cards are drawn from a pack of fifty-two playing cards. What is the probability that the cards drawn are the ace and king of spades or that they are both diamonds?

15.7. Independent Events

If, in considering the distribution of children in families, we understand that *BGB* means that the eldest child is a boy, the second is a girl, and the youngest is a boy, then a sample space, S, of all possible distributions in a family of three is,

$$S = \{BBB, BBG, BGB, BGG, GBB, GBG, GGB, GGG \}.$$

If X is the event "eldest child is a boy", and Y is the event "second child is a girl", then

$$P(X) = \tfrac{4}{8} = \tfrac{1}{2},$$
$$P(Y) = \tfrac{4}{8} = \tfrac{1}{2},$$
$$P(X \cap Y) = \tfrac{2}{8} = \tfrac{1}{4},$$

Here we notice that

$$P(X \cap Y) = P(X) \cdot P(Y).$$

If Z is the event "all three are boys", then

$$P(Z) = \tfrac{1}{8}$$

and

$$P(X \cap Z) = \tfrac{1}{8}.$$

In this case

$$P(X \cap Z) \neq P(X) \cdot P(Z).$$

We note also that

$$P(Y \cap Z) = 0$$

and

$$P(Y \cap Z) \neq P(Y) \cdot P(Z).$$

Intuitively, we feel that events X and Y are independent of each other. The sex of the eldest child has no effect on the sex of the second. These events are independent. The events X and Z cannot be regarded as independent. If all three children are boys, such an event does depend on the eldest's being a boy. The two events are dependent. Events Y and Z are, by definition, mutually exclusive. It is impossible for all three children to be boys and the second child to be a girl.

Event X is one that we expect to occur in about one half of all births of eldest children. About one half of all three-child families will have a boy as the eldest child. Restricting ourselves to this one half, we would expect that one half of this group would have a girl as the second child. The fraction of three-child families having a boy as the eldest child and a girl as second, would therefore be expected to be about $\tfrac{1}{2} \times \tfrac{1}{2}$ or $\tfrac{1}{4}$.

Our intuition agrees with the mathematical result in these cases. Independent events are events which have no effect on each other. However, the rather vague statement "having no effect on each other", is not suitable as a mathematical definition.

The results of our example lead us to a definition which satisfies the requirements of mathematical rigour.

DEFINITION.   Two events, A and B, are *independent* if and only if
$$P(A \cap B) = P(A) \cdot P(B).$$

Note that this allows us to state that, if two events are such that

$$P(A \cap B) = P(A) \cdot P(B),$$

then the events are independent.   Conversely, if we know that two events are independent, we can state that

$$P(A \cap B) = P(A) \cdot P(B).$$

Note: The student sometimes confuses mutually exclusive events with independent events. This is unlikely to happen if he remembers that, in general, *mutually exclusive events cannot be independent.*

If two events A and B are mutually exclusive then they are disjoint and $P(A \cap B) = 0$. For A and B, two independent events with nonzero probabilities, $P(A \cap B) \neq 0$ since $P(A \cap B) = P(A) \cdot P(B)$.

The exception occurs (A and B become *both* mutually exclusive and independent) if either $P(A) = 0$ or $P(B) = 0$ causing $P(A) \cdot P(B)$, which equals $P(A \cap B)$, to equal zero.

DEFINITION.   Two events, A and B, are *dependent* if and only if
$$P(A \cap B) \neq P(A) \cdot P(B) \text{ and } P(A \cap B) \neq 0.$$

In the example of the three-child family,
$$P(X \cap Y) = P(X) \cdot P(Y)$$
so events X and Y are independent.
$$P(X \cap Z) \neq P(X) \cdot P(Z) \text{ and } P(X \cap Z) \neq 0,$$
so events X and Z are dependent.
$$P(Y \cap Z) = 0 \neq P(Y) \cdot P(Z)$$
so events Y and Z are mutually exclusive.

When three or more events are independent, the probability that all occur is the product of their probabilities.

For example, if A, B, and C are independent events, then
$$P(A \cap B \cap C) = P(A) \cdot P(B) \cdot P(C).$$

Example 1. In the two-dice experiment (See Table 15.2), where b represents the number showing on the black die and w, the number showing on the white die, state which of the following pairs of events are independent, dependent, or mutually exclusive.

(a) $b = 3$, $\qquad\qquad\qquad\qquad\qquad$ $w = 4$.
(b) $b + w = 7$, $\qquad\qquad\qquad\qquad$ $b = 3$.
(c) $b + w = 7$, $\qquad\qquad\qquad\qquad$ $b < 3$.
(d) $b + w = 7$, $\qquad\qquad\qquad\qquad$ $b \neq 3$.
(e) $b + w = 11$, $\qquad\qquad\qquad\qquad$ $b \neq 5$.
(f) $b + w = 11$, $\qquad\qquad\qquad\qquad$ $b + w = 7$.

Solution:

(a) Let A be the event $b = 3$ and B, the event $w = 4$.

$$P(A) = \tfrac{6}{36} = \tfrac{1}{6}.$$
$$P(B) = \tfrac{6}{36} = \tfrac{1}{6}.$$
$$P(A \cap B) = \tfrac{1}{36}.$$

Therefore $P(A \cap B) = P(A) \cdot P(B)$ and events A and B are independent.

(b) Let C be the event $b + w = 7$ and D, the event $b = 3$.

$$P(C) = \tfrac{6}{36} = \tfrac{1}{6} \text{ and } P(D) = \tfrac{6}{36} = \tfrac{1}{6}.$$
$$P(C \cap D) = \tfrac{1}{36}.$$

Therefore $P(C \cap D) = P(C) \cdot P(D)$ and events C and D are independent.

(c) Let C be the event $b + w = 7$ and E, the event $b < 3$.

$$P(C) = \tfrac{1}{6} \text{ and } P(E) = \tfrac{12}{36} = \tfrac{1}{3}.$$
$$P(C \cap E) = \tfrac{2}{36} = \tfrac{1}{18}.$$

Therefore $P(C \cap E) = P(C) \cdot P(E)$ and events C and E are independent.

(d) Let C be the event $b + w = 7$ and F, the event $b \neq 3$.

$$P(C) = \tfrac{1}{6} \text{ and } P(F) = \tfrac{30}{36} = \tfrac{5}{6}.$$
$$P(C \cap F) = \tfrac{5}{36}.$$

Therefore $P(C \cap F) = P(C) \cdot P(F)$ and events C and F are independent.

(e) Let G be the event $b + w = 11$ and H, the event $b \neq 5$.

$$P(G) = \tfrac{2}{36} = \tfrac{1}{18} \text{ and } P(H) = \tfrac{30}{36} = \tfrac{5}{6}.$$
$$P(G \cap H) = \tfrac{1}{36}.$$

Therefore $P(G \cap H) \neq P(G) \cdot P(H)$ and events G and H are dependent.

(f) Let G be the event $b + w = 11$ and C, the event $b + w = 7$.
$$P(G) = \tfrac{1}{18} \text{ and } P(C) = \tfrac{1}{6}.$$
$$P(G \cap C) = 0.$$
Therefore events G and C are mutually exclusive.

Example 2.   A bag contains twenty red balls and ten black balls. If one ball is drawn from the bag and returned, and then a second ball is drawn from the bag, what is the probability that the first ball drawn is red and the second, black? (Since the first ball is returned, the events are independent.)

Solution: P (red ball) $= \frac{20}{30} = \frac{2}{3}.$
$\quad\quad\quad\quad P$ (black ball) $= \frac{10}{30} = \frac{1}{3}.$
$\quad\quad\quad\quad P$ (red ball followed by black ball) $= \frac{2}{3} \times \frac{1}{3}$
$\quad\quad\quad\quad\quad\quad\quad\quad\quad\quad\quad\quad\quad\quad\quad\quad = \frac{2}{9}.$

EXERCISE 15.7

1. In the two-dice experiment (see Table 15.2), state whether the following pairs of events are independent, dependent, or mutually exclusive; b represents the number showing on the black die and w, the number showing on the white die.
   (a) $b = 6, \quad w = 6.$
   (b) $w < 3, \quad b + w = 8.$
   (c) $w < 2, \quad b + w = 8.$
   (d) $w \neq 5, \quad b + w = 8.$
   (e) $b = 3$ or $w = 3, \quad b = 5.$
   (f) $b = 3$ or $w = 3, \quad b \neq 5.$

2. A die is thrown three times. Assuming that the throws are independent events, what is the probability that the first throw shows a six, the second shows an even number, and the third shows a five?

3. A coin is tossed six times. Each throw is independent of the other throws. What is the probability of six heads?

4. A bag contains twenty red balls and ten black balls. One ball is drawn from the bag and returned. A second ball is then drawn from the bag. Assuming that the outcomes are independent events, calculate the following probabilities.
   (a) Both balls are red.
   (b) Both balls are black.
   (c) One ball is red and the other is black. (Order is not considered.)

5. Three coins are tossed. Are the following events independent, dependent, or mutually exclusive?
   (a) Heads on first two coins, tails on third coin.
   (b) Heads on first two coins, tails on second two coins.
   (c) Heads on first two coins, heads on all three coins.

6. A bag contains six black balls, four red balls, and five white balls. Three balls are drawn in succession, each one being replaced before the next is drawn. Calculate the following probabilities.
   (a) First is black, second is red, third is white.

  (b) All three are black.
  (c) All three are white.
  (d) First two are black and the third is red.

7. In a family of three children, calculate the following probabilities.
  (a) First is a boy and next two are girls.
  (b) First two are boys and the third is a girl.
  (c) First two are boys or the third is a girl.

8. In a certain school, 15% of the students failed Mathematics, 12% failed English, and 5% failed both English and Mathematics. Are the events "student failed English" and "student failed Mathematics", independent?

9. If two cards are drawn at random from a pack of fifty-two cards, are the events "both cards aces" and "both cards red", independent?

10. If two cards are drawn at random from a pack of fifty-two cards, are the events, "first card an ace" and "second card a king", independent? Assume that the first card is returned to the pack before the second is drawn.

15.8. Binomial Distribution

If a bag contains twenty red balls and ten black balls, and six balls are drawn at random with the ball drawn being replaced and the bag well shaken before the next ball is drawn, what is the probability that exactly two red balls are drawn?

Here we have a case of six independent events in which P (red ball) $= \frac{2}{3}$ and P (black ball) $= \frac{1}{3}$ for each event. If, in drawing six balls, we obtain two red balls and four black balls, we have a successful event. Any other combination is not successful.

One successful event is $RRBBBB$, where R represents a red ball and B, a black ball. The probability of this event is

$$\left(\tfrac{2}{3}\right) \left(\tfrac{2}{3}\right) \left(\tfrac{1}{3}\right) \left(\tfrac{1}{3}\right) \left(\tfrac{1}{3}\right) \left(\tfrac{1}{3}\right) = \left(\tfrac{1}{3}\right)^4 \left(\tfrac{2}{3}\right)^2.$$

However, if a red ball occupies any two of the six positions, we have a successful event. Each of these successful events will have the same probability and all such events are mutually exclusive. The number of such events is $\binom{6}{2}$ and so the probability of exactly two red balls is

$$\binom{6}{2} \left(\tfrac{1}{3}\right)^4 \left(\tfrac{2}{3}\right)^2 = 15 \times \tfrac{1}{81} \times \tfrac{4}{9}$$
$$= \tfrac{20}{243}.$$

In the same way, if there are n independent events for which the probability of success in any one event is p and the probability of failure is $q = 1 - p$, that is, there are only two possible outcomes for each event, then the probability for exactly r successes in the n events is

$$\binom{n}{r} q^{n-r} p^r.$$

This is the $(r + 1)$st term of the binomial expansion of $(q + p)^n$.

In the example of twenty red balls and ten black balls, we were seeking the probability of drawing exactly two red balls in six trials.

$$p = \tfrac{2}{3}, q = \tfrac{1}{3}, n = 6.$$

Therefore

$$(q + p)^n = [(\tfrac{1}{3}) + (\tfrac{2}{3})]^6$$

$$= \binom{6}{0}(\tfrac{1}{3})^6 (\tfrac{2}{3})^0 + \binom{6}{1}(\tfrac{1}{3})^5 (\tfrac{2}{3}) + \binom{6}{2}(\tfrac{1}{3})^4 (\tfrac{2}{3})^2 + \binom{6}{3}(\tfrac{1}{3})^3 (\tfrac{2}{3})^3 +$$

$$\binom{6}{4}(\tfrac{1}{3})^2 (\tfrac{2}{3})^4 + \binom{6}{5}(\tfrac{1}{3}) (\tfrac{2}{3})^5 + \binom{6}{6}(\tfrac{1}{3})^0 (\tfrac{2}{3})^6$$

$$= \tfrac{1}{729} + \tfrac{4}{243} + \tfrac{20}{243} + \tfrac{160}{729} + \tfrac{80}{243} + \tfrac{64}{243} + \tfrac{64}{729}.$$

The successive terms give the probabilities of drawing 0, 1, 2, 3, 4, 5, or 6 red balls, respectively, in any drawing of six balls with replacement between each drawing. It must be emphasized that the events *have to be independent.*

If $P(x)$ represents the drawing of x red balls in any drawing of six balls, then

$$P(0) = \tfrac{1}{729}, P(1) = \tfrac{4}{243}, P(2) = \tfrac{20}{243},$$

$$P(3), = \tfrac{160}{729}, P(4) = \tfrac{80}{243}, P(5) = \tfrac{64}{243}, P(6) = \tfrac{64}{729}.$$

We note that the outcomes, "no red balls", "one red ball", "two red balls", etc., are not equally likely outcomes.

Also, $P(0) + P(1) + P(2) + P(3) + P(4) + P(5) + P(6) = 1.$
This should have been expected since these results give all possible results. Also $q + p = 1$ and hence $(q + p)^n = 1$.

Example 1.   If a bag contains twenty red balls and ten black balls and six balls are drawn at random with the ball drawn being replaced before the next ball is drawn, what is the probability that at least three red balls are drawn?

Solution 1: $P(3) = \binom{6}{3} (\tfrac{1}{3})^3 (\tfrac{2}{3})^3 = \tfrac{160}{729}.$

$$P(4) = \binom{6}{4} (\tfrac{1}{3})^2 (\tfrac{2}{3})^4 = \tfrac{240}{729}.$$

$$P(5) = \binom{6}{5} \left(\tfrac{1}{3}\right) \left(\tfrac{2}{3}\right)^5 = \tfrac{192}{729}.$$

$$P(6) = \binom{6}{6} \left(\tfrac{2}{3}\right)^6 \quad = \tfrac{64}{729}.$$

Therefore

$$P(\text{at least 3 red balls}) = \tfrac{160}{729} + \tfrac{240}{729} + \tfrac{192}{729} + \tfrac{64}{729}.$$
$$= \tfrac{656}{729}.$$

Solution 2:

$$P(0) = \binom{6}{0} \left(\tfrac{1}{3}\right)^6 \quad = \tfrac{1}{729}.$$

$$P(1) = \binom{6}{1} \left(\tfrac{1}{3}\right)^5 \left(\tfrac{2}{3}\right) \quad = \tfrac{12}{729}.$$

$$P(2) = \binom{6}{2} \left(\tfrac{1}{3}\right)^4 \left(\tfrac{2}{3}\right)^2 = \tfrac{60}{729}.$$

$$P(0) + P(1) + P(2) = \tfrac{73}{729}.$$

Therefore

$$P(\text{at least 3 red balls}) = 1 - \tfrac{73}{729}.$$
$$= \tfrac{656}{729}.$$

Depending on the particular problem Solution 1 or Solution 2 may be the quicker method. In this particular example, there is little to choose between the two methods. If we were asked for the probability of at least five red balls, Solution 1 would be the more useful, but, if we were asked for the probability of at least two red balls, Solution 2 would be the more useful.

Example 2. In families of four children, calculate the following probabilities: (a) Exactly three are boys. (b) At least three are boys. (c) At least one is a boy.

Solution:

(a) $p = \tfrac{1}{2}$, $q = \tfrac{1}{2}$, where p is the probability of a boy.

$$P(3 \text{ boys}) = \binom{4}{3} \left(\tfrac{1}{2}\right) \left(\tfrac{1}{2}\right)^3$$
$$= 4 \times \tfrac{1}{16}$$
$$= \tfrac{1}{4}.$$

(b)

$$P(4 \text{ boys}) = \binom{4}{4} \left(\tfrac{1}{2}\right)^0 \left(\tfrac{1}{2}\right)^4$$
$$= \tfrac{1}{16}.$$

Therefore $\quad P(\text{at least 3 boys}) = \tfrac{1}{4} + \tfrac{1}{16}$
$$= \tfrac{5}{16}.$$

(c) $$P(\text{no boys}) = \binom{4}{0} (\tfrac{1}{2})^4 (\tfrac{1}{2})^0$$
$$= \tfrac{1}{16}.$$

Therefore $$P(\text{at least 1 boy}) = 1 - \tfrac{1}{16}$$
$$= \tfrac{15}{16}.$$

Example 3. A student writes a test which contains ten questions. For each question, four possible answers are given and the student has to underline the single, correct solution. Calculate the following probabilities.
(a) He will obtain at least 50% (5 correct answers).
(b) He will obtain 100% (all answers correct).

Solution:
(a) $$p = \tfrac{1}{4}, q = \tfrac{3}{4}, n = 10$$

$$P(5) = \binom{10}{5} (\tfrac{3}{4})^5 (\tfrac{1}{4})^5$$
$$= 252 \left(\tfrac{243}{1024}\right) \left(\tfrac{1}{1024}\right),$$
$$= \frac{61,236}{1,048,576}.$$

$$P(6) = \binom{10}{6} (\tfrac{3}{4})^4 (\tfrac{1}{4})^6,$$
$$= 210 \left(\frac{81}{4^{10}}\right),$$
$$= \frac{17,010}{1,048,576}.$$

$$P(7) = \binom{10}{7} (\tfrac{3}{4})^3 (\tfrac{1}{4})^7,$$
$$= \frac{3,240}{1,048,576}.$$

$$P(8) = \binom{10}{8} (\tfrac{3}{4})^2 (\tfrac{1}{4})^8,$$
$$= \frac{405}{1,048,576}.$$

$$P(9) = \binom{10}{9} (\tfrac{3}{4}) (\tfrac{1}{4})^9,$$
$$= \frac{30}{1,048,576},$$

$$P(10) = \binom{10}{10} (\tfrac{1}{4})^{10},$$
$$= \frac{1}{1,048,576}.$$

Therefore

$$P(\text{at least 5 correct}) = \frac{61,236+17,010+3,240+405+30+1}{1,048,576},$$

$$= \frac{81,922}{1,048,576},$$
$$\simeq .078.$$

(b) $P(\text{perfect } \textbf{paper}) = \binom{10}{10} (\tfrac{1}{4})^{10},$

$$= \frac{1}{1,048,576},$$
$$\simeq .000001.$$

EXERCISE 15.8

1. Four dice are thrown. Calculate each of the following probabilities.
    (a) Two sixes show.
    (b) Three fives show.
    (c) At least one six shows.

2. Five coins are tossed. Calculate each of the following probabilities.
    (a) Three show heads.
    (b) At least three show heads.
    (c) All five show tails.

3. In a family of five children, calculate the following probabilities.
    (a) Three are boys.
    (b) At least three are girls.
    (c) All five are girls.
    (d) At least one is a boy.

4. A baseball player is batting .250. Assuming that this is the probability that he will hit safely any given time at bat, what are the following probabilities?
    (a) He will hit safely on his next two times at bat.
    (b) He will hit safely twice during his next five times at bat.

5. Records show that a certain treatment will successfully cure a particular disease in one third of the cases treated. If six patients are treated, what is the probability that at least three will be cured?

6. A pair of dice is rolled three times. Calculate each of the following probabilities.
    (a) A total of seven is rolled each time.
    (b) A total of seven is obtained once only.
    (c) A total of seven is obtained at least once.
    (d) A total of eleven is obtained at least once.

7. If the probability that a child will inherit a certain disease is 0.25, calculate the following probabilities for a family of four children.
    (a) One child will inherit the disease.
    (b) Three children will inherit the disease.
    (c) At least two of the children will be free of the disease.

(d) All the children will inherit the disease.

8. On a test of ten questions, a student had to select the correct answer from four given possible answers. If the student knew the correct answer to three of the questions and decided to guess at the others, what is the probability that he will pass the test if five correct answers constitute a pass?

9. In a family of five children, it is known that the three eldest are boys. What is the probability that the other two are also boys?

10. If a bag contains six red balls and four black balls, and three balls are drawn without replacement, calculate the probability that all the balls drawn are red.

11. Using the data in question 10, calculate the probability that all the balls drawn are red if the balls are drawn one at a time and replaced before the next is drawn.

12. In a bridge hand of thirteen cards, the probability of obtaining no aces in any one hand is approximately 0.3. What is the probability that a player will obtain no aces in any two of three consecutive hands?

13. Calculate the probability that a bridge player will receive no honour cards (ace, king, queen, jack, or ten) on any two of three consecutive hands.

15.9.   Normal Distribution

If six coins are tossed and the number of heads showing is recorded, the probabilities of the seven possible results are as follows:

$$P(0 \text{ heads}) = \binom{6}{0} (\tfrac{1}{2})^0 (\tfrac{1}{2})^6 = \tfrac{1}{64}$$

$$P(1 \text{ head}) = \binom{6}{1} (\tfrac{1}{2}) (\tfrac{1}{2})^5 = \tfrac{6}{64}$$

$$P(2 \text{ heads}) = \binom{6}{2} (\tfrac{1}{2})^2 (\tfrac{1}{2})^4 = \tfrac{15}{64}$$

$$P(3 \text{ heads}) = \binom{6}{3} (\tfrac{1}{2})^3 (\tfrac{1}{2})^3 = \tfrac{20}{64}$$

$$P(4 \text{ heads}) = \binom{6}{4} (\tfrac{1}{2})^4 (\tfrac{1}{2})^2 = \tfrac{15}{64}$$

$$P(5 \text{ heads}) = \binom{6}{5} (\tfrac{1}{2})^5 (\tfrac{1}{2}) = \tfrac{6}{64}$$

$$P(6 \text{ heads}) = \binom{6}{6} (\tfrac{1}{2})^6 (\tfrac{1}{2})^0 = \tfrac{1}{64}$$

If we tossed these six coins 64 times, the theoretical frequency would be as in the table below. It is extremely unlikely that we would actually obtain the theoretical frequencies in practice. The results of actually carrying out the experiment once are given in the table.

Number of Heads	0	1	2	3	4	5	6
Theoretical Frequency	1	6	15	20	15	6	1
Actual Frequency	1	3	19	20	18	2	1

Another repetition of 64 tosses would probably give a very different actual frequency. If 128 tosses were made, the theoretical frequencies would all be doubled. It is suggested that each member of your class make 64 tosses with 6 coins and the totals of all of the results be compared with the totals of the theoretical frequencies.

Below we have a frequency polygon of the theoretical distribution of the results of tossing 6 coins 64 times and also a graph with a smooth curve drawn through the points.

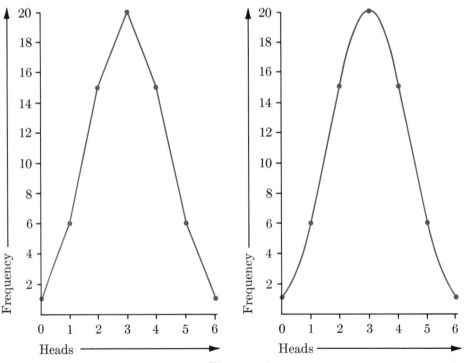

Figure 15.4

In Section 12.1 we constructed a frequency polygon of the weights of 197 students in first-year mathematics at Utopia University. The polygon is reproduced below.

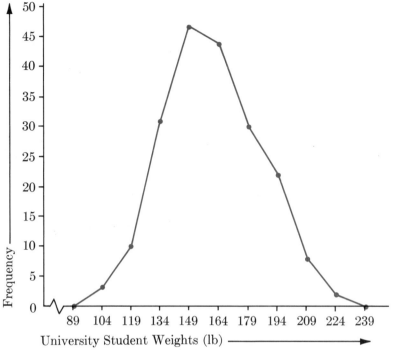

Figure 15.5

We note that the frequency polygon of the weight distribution is very similar to the frequency polygon of the theoretical distribution of tossing the coins. A smooth curve through the points would produce a curve also similar in shape to the curve formed by the theoretical results of the coin tossing. If the histogram of the weight distribution is re-drawn with the class boundaries brought closer and closer together so that instead of a 15 lb. class interval we reduce this figure to 10 lb., 5 lb., or even less, the frequency polygon formed by joining the mid-points of the tops of the rectangles would come closer to forming a smooth bell-shaped curve. If the curve is completely symmetrical about the mean as in the theoretical frequency curve of the coin-tossing, we have what is called a *normal curve*.

When we graph any particular set of data, it is very unlikely that we will obtain a normal curve. The actual frequencies obtained by tossing 6 coins 64 times do not agree exactly with the theoretical frequencies, and so the curve of the actual frequencies does not completely coincide with the normal curve. The distribution for another set of 64 tosses is unlikely to coincide exactly with either the theoretical frequency or with the actual frequency of the first set of tosses.

With any sample, it is unlikely that the frequency distribution will fit a normal curve exactly, but we may feel that the normal curve would be a better description of the whole population than the actual curve formed by the sample. For a normal distribution where the mean and the standard deviation have been calculated, the probability that any random sample lies at a certain distance from the mean has been calculated mathematically, but the actual method of calculation is beyond our scope at the moment. The probability that any sample lies within one standard deviation of the mean has been calculated at .683 (correct to 3 decimal places). This means that .683 or 68.3% or approximately $\frac{2}{3}$ of all the figures will lie between one standard deviation below the mean and one standard deviation above. For the weight distribution of first-year university students which we calculated in Chapter 12, the mean was 160.6 lb. and the standard deviation was 24.4. lb. One standard deviation below the mean is 136.2 lb. and one standard deviation above is 185.0 lb. If the distribution is normal, we would expect 68.3% of the weights to lie between 136.2 lb. and 185.0 lb. Of our 197 weights, approximately 134 or 135 should lie between these limits.

The probabilities that a random sample will lie between various standard deviations of the mean are given in the table below.

Standard Deviation Interval	$\pm\frac{1}{2}$	± 1	$\pm 1\frac{1}{2}$	± 2	$\pm 2\frac{1}{2}$	± 3
Probability that sample is in interval	.383	.683	.866	.954	.988	.997

Note that 99.7% or almost all of the samples of normal distribution will lie between ± 3 standard deviations of the mean.

Example 1. Calculate the probability that a random sample of a normal distribution will lie between 2 and 3 standard deviations of the mean.

Solution:

$$P(\text{within } 3S.D.) = .997$$

$$P(\text{within } 2S.D.) = .954$$

$$P(\text{between 2 and } 3S.D.) = .997 - .954$$

$$= .043.$$

Having the statistics of a sample selected from a large (theoretically infinite) population, it is even then unlikely that the data will fit the normal curve exactly. However, if the sample has been properly selected, we may feel that a normal distribution would give a better picture of the total population. We should, of course, be sure that our sample is a true random selection. This can be a difficult problem. Of what total population is our selection of 197 first-year mathematics students at Utopia University a sample? Is it a representative sample of all first-year students at Utopia? of all first-year students in all universities? of all first-year Mathematics students? Perhaps Utopia students come from an area where nutritional standards are high or low. This would obviously bias the sample. Perhaps Utopia requires 13 years of school before University while other areas require only 12 years. Naturally we know that mathematicians are of higher intelligence than other students! As a consequence, they would have been younger when entering university! These, and many other considerations make it obvious that the total population must be carefully defined and that the sample must be a proper random selection of that population. For the moment, we shall assume that our sample has been so selected and examine the problem of fitting a normal curve to the sample. To do this we shall use our university student weights, set up a table of calculations and then explain each column of the table. We shall make use of the information previously calculated in Chapter 12.

1	2	3	4	5	6
Class Interval	Class value x	Frequency f	$z = \dfrac{x - \bar{x}}{s}$	$g(z)$	Theoretical frequency $f^1 = \dfrac{nw}{s} g(z)$
96.5—111.5	104	3	− 2.3196	.0270	3.3
111.5—126.5	119	10	− 1.7049	.0940	11.4
126.5—141.5	134	31	− 1.0902	.2203	26.7
141.5—156.5	149	47	− .4755	.3555	43.1
156.5—171.5	164	44	.1392	.3951	47.8
171.5—186.5	179	30	.7539	.3011	36.5
186.5—201.5	194	22	1.3686	.1561	18.9
201.5—216.5	209	8	1.9833	.0562	6.8
216.5—231.5	224	2	2.5980	.0136	1.6
Totals		197			196.1
$\bar{x} = 160.6$			0	.3989	48.3

$$\bar{x} = 160.6 \text{ (from Example 2, Section 12.2)}$$
$$s = 24.4 \quad \text{(from Example 2, Section 12.3)}$$

The first three columns are obtained from Chapter 12 and have been discussed there.

In column 4 we calculate the number of standard deviations from the mean of each class value from the mean. Since $\bar{x} = 160.6$, the class value $x_1 = 104$ differs from the mean by $104 - 160.6$ or $- 56.6$. Since $s = 24.4$, this is $= \dfrac{- 56.6}{24.4}$ or

— 2.1396 standard deviations from the mean. One z has been calculated, the remaining values may be easily calculated, since

$$z_{i+1} = \frac{x_{i+1} - \bar{x}}{s},$$

$$= \frac{x_i + w - \bar{x}}{s}, \qquad (w \text{ is class width})$$

$$= \frac{x_i - \bar{x}}{s} + \frac{w}{s},$$

$$= z_i + \frac{w}{s}.$$

In the example, $w = 15$, $s = 24.4$ and $\frac{w}{s} = .6147$. Hence, each value of z is easily obtained by adding .6147 to the previous value. In general, $\frac{w}{s}$ is added to the previous value. For column 5 we require these values correct to only 2 decimal places, but we should maintain at least 3 and preferably 4 decimal places to avoid rounding-off errors. If we took $\frac{w}{s}$ to be .61 instead of .6147 we would quickly run into such errors.

In column 5 we obtain values of $g\,(z) = \frac{1}{\sqrt{2\pi}}e^{-\frac{1}{2}z^2}$ which is one form of the equation of the normal curve. These values are tabulated in the table of Ordinates of the Normal Curve (page 418) from values of $g\,(z)$ correct to 4 decimal places. Since the equation involves z^2, the results will always be positive.

To obtain the theoretical frequency, we now multiply these figures by $\frac{nw}{s}$ where w is the class width and n is the total frequency. In this case, $\frac{nw}{s} = \frac{197 \times 15}{24.4} = 121.1$. The results are rounded-off to one decimal place. The total of the theoretical frequencies should be approximately equal to the total of the actual frequencies. However, due to rounding-off errors, they will rarely be exactly equal.

For the normal curve the maximum point occurs at the mean, hence it is useful to obtain the theoretical frequency for the mean. In this case, of course, $z = 0$ and $g(z) = .3989$ (from the table). Hence the theoretical frequency is .3989 $\times$ 121.1 or 48.3. This is shown in the last row of the table.

Below we show the original histogram with the theoretical normal curve of the distribution superimposed. It should be noted that we assume that the mean and standard deviation of the sample correspond to the same figures for the entire population. If our sample has been carefully selected this assumption should be reasonably accurate.

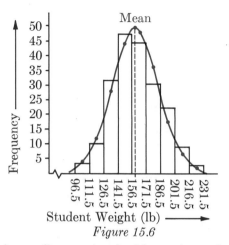

Figure 15.6

A normal curve is usually associated with continuously variable data, but it may be applied to discrete data as with the coin tosses. Our next example will deal with the shoe size problem from Chapter 12.

Example 2. Construct a normal curve to fit the data on sizes of women's shoes as in Example 2 of Section 12.1.

Solution:

Class value x.	Frequency f	$z = \dfrac{x - \bar{x}}{s}$	$g(z)$	Theoretical frequency $f^1 = \dfrac{nw}{s} g(z)$
2	1	−3.4343	.0011	.2
$2\frac{1}{2}$	1	−2.9293	.0055	.8
3	5	−2.4243	.0213	3.2
$3\frac{1}{2}$	8	−1.9193	.0632	9.5
4	18	−1.4143	.1476	22.2
$4\frac{1}{2}$	36	− .9093	.2637	39.7
5	54	− .4043	.3683	55.4
$5\frac{1}{2}$	61	.1007	.3970	59.8
6	58	.6057	.3312	49.8
$6\frac{1}{2}$	32	1.1107	.2155	32.4
7	17	1.6157	.1074	16.2
$7\frac{1}{2}$	6	2.1207	.0422	6.4
8	0	2.6257	.0126	1.9
$8\frac{1}{2}$	1	3.1307	.0030	.5
Totals	298			298.0
$\bar{x} = 5.4$		0	.3989	60.0

$$\bar{x} = 5.4 \text{ (Example 1, Section 12.2)}$$

$$s = .99 \text{ (Example 1, Section 12.3)}$$

$$\frac{w}{s} = \frac{.5}{.99} = .5050$$

$$\frac{nw}{s} = \frac{298 \times .5}{.99} = 150.505$$

Histogram and Normal Curve.

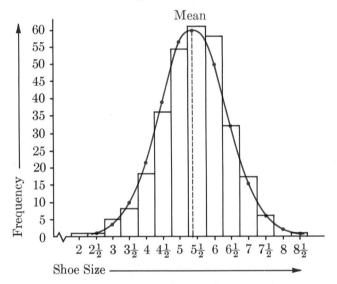

EXERCISE 15.9

1. Calculate the probability that a random sample of a normal distribution will lie between 1 and 2 standard deviations of the mean.

2. How many elements of a normal distribution of 250 elements may be expected to lie between the mean and one standard deviation above the mean?

3. Using the data in questions 2 to 5 of Exercise 12.1, calculate the theoretical frequencies of a normal distribution and sketch the normal curve.

Chapter Summary

DEFINITIONS.   (1) A *sample space* of an experiment is a set of elements such that every outcome of the experiment corresponds to exactly one element of the set.

(2) An *event* is a result of an experiment that may be represented by a subset of a sample space of the experiment.

(3) If A is an event corresponding to a subset of a sample space, then $P(A)$, *the probability of A*, is the sum of the probabilities of the elements of the subset corresponding to A.

(4) *Mutually-exclusive events* or disjoint events are two or more events in a given sample space which have no elements in common.

$$P(A \cap B) = 0.$$

(5) Two events, A and B, are independent if and only if

$$P(A \cap B) = P(A) \cdot P(B).$$

(6) Two events, A and B, are dependent if and only if

$$P(A \cap B) \neq P(A) \cdot P(B) \text{ and } P(A \cap B) \neq 0.$$

FORMULAE.   (1) For any event A,

$$0 \leq P(A) \leq 1.$$

If $P(A) = \dfrac{m}{n}$, then $P(A') = \dfrac{n - m}{n}$

$$= 1 - P(A).$$

(2) Odds in favour of A are

$$P(A) \text{ to } P(A').$$

If $P(A) = \dfrac{m}{n}$, then

$$P(A) \text{ to } P(A') \text{ is to } m \text{ to } n - m.$$

(3) $\qquad\qquad P(A \cup B) = P(A) + P(B) - P(A \cap B).$

(4) If events A and B are mutually exclusive,

$$P(A \cup B) = P(A) + P(B).$$

(5) For n independent events in which the probability of success in any one event is p and the probability of failure is $q = 1 - p$, the probability for exactly r successes in the n events is

$$P(r) = \binom{n}{r} q^{n-r} p^r.$$

(6) Normal curve.

REVIEW EXERCISE 15

1. Construct sample spaces of *equally-likely outcomes* for each of the following.
   (a) Four books are to be chosen at random from six different books, A, B, C, D, E, F.
   (b) The five honour cards in spades (ace, king, queen, jack, and ten) are placed in one bundle and the five honour cards in hearts in a second bundle. One card is drawn from each bundle.

2. John, Jim, Bert, Bill, and Andy form the starting line-up for the school basketball team. The coach has obtained three tickets for a display by the Harlem Globetrotters. It is decided that the five boys will draw lots for the three tickets. Calculate the following probabilities.
   (a) John will be selected.
   (b) John and Bill will be selected.
   (c) John or Bill will be selected.
   (d) John, and Bill or Jim will be selected.
   (e) Jim and Bert, or Bill and Andy will be selected.
   (f) Andy, Jim, and Bill will be selected.

3. If two dice are thrown, state the following probabilities. (b is the number on the black die and w is the number on the white die.)
   (a) Exactly one shows a three.
   (b) Both show three.
   (c) The total is six.
   (d) The total is ten.
   (e) $b < 3$ and $w > 3$.
   (f) $b < 3$ or $w > 3$.
   (g) $b < 3$ and $w > 3$, or $b > 3$ and $w < 3$.

4. If one card is drawn from a pack of fifty-two playing cards, calculate the following probabilities.
   (a) The card is an ace.
   (b) The card is a black ace.
   (c) The card is a diamond.
   (d) The card is an ace or a king.
   (e) The card is an honour card.

5. From a group of fifteen men and ten women, a committee of three is chosen by lot. Calculate the following probabilities.
   (a) The committee contains two specified men.
   (b) The committee consists of two men and one woman.
   (c) The committee consists of three women.

6. A drawer contains eight black socks and six brown socks well-mixed. If a man opens the drawer in the dark and removes two socks, what is the probability

that he has a matched pair? If he removes three socks, what is the probability that he has a matched pair?

7. A bag contains seven red balls and four black balls. If three balls are drawn at random without replacement, calculate the following probabilities.
    (a) All three are red.
    (b) All three are black.
    (c) Two are red and one is black.
    (d) Two are black and one is red.

8. If four cards are drawn from a pack of fifty-two playing cards, what are the odds that none of the cards is an ace?

9. Two balls are drawn without replacement from a bag containing eight red balls and five black balls. What are the odds that both balls are red?

10. Four coins are tossed. Are the following events independent, dependent, or mutually exclusive?
    (a) First three show heads; fourth shows tails.
    (b) First shows heads; first three show heads.
    (c) First three show tails; last three show heads.
    (d) Second shows heads; fourth shows heads.

11. 5% of the population belong to blood group B and 15% of the population have the Rh⁻factor in their blood. What is the probability that an individual is of blood group B and Rh^-?

12. If 40% of the population belong to blood group 0, what is the probability that, of five people chosen at random, at least two belong to group 0?

13. A bag contains ten red balls and five black balls. If six balls are drawn from the bag, each ball being replaced before the next is drawn, calculate the following probabilities.
    (a) Four red and two black balls are drawn.
    (b) Two red and four black balls are drawn.
    (c) At least two red balls are drawn.
    (d) At least four black balls are drawn.

14. In a batch of twenty light bulbs it is known that four are defective. In a selection of five of the bulbs, what is the probability that at least two are defective?

15. In a family of six children, calculate the following probabilities.
    (a) Two are boys and four are girls.
    (b) At least two are boys.
    (c) At least five are boys.
    (d) All are girls.

16. Calculate the number of elements which should lie between 1 and 2 standard deviations of the mean in a normal distribution of 2384 elements.

17. Calculate the theoretical frequencies of a normal distribution and sketch the normal curve for the data in questions 2, 3, 4, and 6 of Review Exercise 12.

POWERS, ROOTS, AND RECIPROCALS 1—100

n	n^2	n^3	$\sqrt{n}$	$\sqrt[3]{n}$	$1/n$	n	n^2	n^3	$\sqrt{n}$	$\sqrt[3]{n}$	$1/n$
1	1	1	1.000	1.000	1.0000	51	2,601	132,651	7.141	3.708	.0196
2	4	8	1.414	1.260	.5000	52	2,704	140,608	7.211	3.733	.0192
3	9	27	1.732	1.442	.3333	53	2,809	148,877	7.280	3.756	.0189
4	16	64	2.000	1.587	.2500	54	2,916	157,464	7.348	3.780	.0185
5	25	125	2.236	1.710	.2000	55	3,025	166,375	7.416	3.803	.0182
6	36	216	2.449	1.817	.1667	56	3,136	175,616	7.483	3.826	.0179
7	49	343	2.646	1.913	.1429	57	3,249	185,193	7.550	3.849	.0175
8	64	512	2.828	2.000	.1250	58	3,364	195,112	7.616	3.871	.0172
9	81	729	3.000	2.080	.1111	59	3,481	205,379	7.681	3.893	.0169
10	100	1,000	3.162	2.154	.1000	60	3,600	216,000	7.746	3.915	.0167
11	121	1,331	3.317	2.224	.0909	61	3,721	226,981	7.810	3.936	.0164
12	144	1,728	3.464	2.289	.0833	62	3,844	238,328	7.874	3.958	.0161
13	169	2,197	3.606	2.351	.0769	63	3,969	250,047	7.937	3.979	.0159
14	196	2,744	3.742	2.410	.0714	64	4,096	262,144	8.000	4.000	.0156
15	225	3,375	3.873	2.466	.0667	65	4,225	274,625	8.062	4.021	.0154
16	256	4,096	4.000	2.520	.0625	66	4,356	287,496	8.124	4.041	.0152
17	289	4,913	4.123	2.571	.0588	67	4,489	300,763	8.185	4.062	.0149
18	324	5,832	4.243	2.621	.0556	68	4,624	314,432	8.246	4.082	.0147
19	361	6,859	4.359	2.668	.0526	69	4,761	328,509	8.307	4.102	.0145
20	400	8,000	4.472	2.714	.0500	70	4,900	343,000	8.367	4.121	.0143
21	441	9,261	4.583	2.759	.0476	71	5,041	357,911	8.426	4.141	.0141
22	484	10,648	4.690	2.802	.0455	72	5,184	373,248	8.485	4.160	.0139
23	529	12,167	4.796	2.844	.0435	73	5,329	389,017	8.544	4.179	.0137
24	576	13,824	4.899	2.884	.0417	74	5,476	405,224	8.602	4.198	.0135
25	625	15,625	5.000	2.924	.0400	75	5,625	421,875	8.660	4.217	.0133
26	676	17,576	5.099	2.962	.0385	76	5,776	438,976	8.718	4.236	.0132
27	729	19,683	5.196	3.000	.0370	77	5,929	456,533	8.775	4.254	.0130
28	784	21,952	5.292	3.037	.0357	78	6,084	474,552	8.832	4.273	.0128
29	841	24,389	5.385	3.072	.0345	79	6,241	493,039	8.888	4.291	.0127
30	900	27,000	5.477	3.107	.0333	80	6,400	512,000	8.944	4.309	.0125
31	961	29,791	5.568	3.141	.0323	81	6,561	531,441	9.000	4.327	.0123
32	1,024	32,768	5.657	3.175	.0312	82	6,724	551,368	9.055	4.344	.0122
33	1,089	35,937	5.745	3.208	.0303	83	6,889	571,787	9.110	4.362	.0120
34	1,156	39,304	5.831	3.240	.0294	84	7,056	592,704	9.165	4.380	.0119
35	1,225	42,875	5.916	3.271	.0286	85	7,225	614,125	9.220	4.397	.0118
36	1,296	46,656	6.000	3.302	.0278	86	7,396	636,056	9.274	4.414	.0116
37	1,369	50,653	6.083	3.332	.0270	87	7,569	658,503	9.327	4.431	.0115
38	1,444	54,872	6.164	3.362	.0263	88	7,744	681,472	9.381	4.448	.0114
39	1,521	59,319	6.245	3.391	.0256	89	7,921	704,969	9.434	4.465	.0112
40	1,600	64,000	6.325	3,420	.0250	90	8,100	729,000	9.487	4.481	.0111
41	1,681	68,921	6.403	3.448	.0244	91	8,281	753,571	9.539	4.498	.0110
42	1,764	74,088	6.481	3.476	.0238	92	8,464	778,688	9.592	4.514	.0109
43	1,849	79,507	6.557	3.503	.0233	93	8,649	804,357	9.644	4.531	.0108
44	1,936	85,184	6.633	3.530	.0227	94	8,836	830,584	9.695	4.547	.0106
45	2,025	91,125	6.708	3.557	.0222	95	9,025	857,375	9.747	4.563	.0105
46	2,116	97,336	6.782	3.583	.0217	96	9,216	884,736	9.798	4.579	.0104
47	2,209	103,823	6.856	3.609	.0213	97	9,409	912,673	9.849	4.595	.0103
48	2,304	110,592	6.928	3.634	.0208	98	9,604	941,192	9.899	4.610	.0102
49	2,401	117,649	7.000	3.659	.0204	99	9,801	970,299	9.950	4.626	.0101
50	2,500	125,000	7.071	3.684	.0200	100	10,000	1,000,000	10.000	4.642	.0100

COMPOUND AMOUNT OF 1

$$(1 + i)^n$$

n \ i	1%	1¼%	1½%	1¾%	2%	2½%	3%	3½%
1	1.01000	1.01250	1.01500	1.01750	1.02000	1.02500	1.03000	1.03500
2	1.02010	1.02516	1.03023	1.03531	1.04040	1.05063	1.06090	1.07123
3	1.03030	1.03797	1.04568	1.05342	1.06121	1.07689	1.09273	1.10872
4	1.04060	1.05094	1.06136	1.07185	1.08243	1.10381	1.12551	1.14752
5	1.05101	1.06408	1.07728	1.09062	1.10408	1.13141	1.15927	1.18769
6	1.06152	1.07738	1.09344	1.10970	1.12616	1.15969	1.19405	1.22926
7	1.07214	1.09085	1.10985	1.12912	1.14869	1.18869	1.22987	1.27228
8	1.08286	1.10449	1.12649	1.14888	1.17166	1.21840	1.26677	1.31681
9	1.09369	1.11829	1.14339	1.16899	1.19509	1.24886	1.30477	1.36290
10	1.10462	1.13227	1.16054	1.18944	1.21899	1.28008	1.34392	1.41060
11	1.11567	1.14642	1.17795	1.21026	1.24337	1.31209	1.38423	1.45997
12	1.12683	1.16075	1.19562	1.23144	1.26824	1.34489	1.42576	1.51107
13	1.13809	1.17526	1.21355	1.25299	1.29361	1.37851	1.46853	1.56396
14	1.14947	1.18995	1.23176	1.27492	1.31948	1.41297	1.51259	1.61869
15	1.16097	1.20483	1.25023	1.29723	1.34587	1.44830	1.55797	1.67535
16	1.17258	1.21989	1.26899	1.31993	1.37279	1.48451	1.60471	1.73399
17	1.18430	1.23514	1.28802	1.34303	1.40024	1.52162	1.65285	1.79468
18	1.19615	1.25058	1.30734	1.36653	1.42825	1.55966	1.70243	1.85749
19	1.20811	1.26621	1.32695	1.39044	1.45681	1.59865	1.75351	1.92250
20	1.22019	1.28204	1.34686	1.41478	1.48595	1.63862	1.80611	1.98979
21	1.23239	1.29806	1.36706	1.43954	1.51567	1.67958	1.86029	2.05943
22	1.24472	1.31429	1.38756	1.46473	1.54598	1.72157	1.91610	2.13151
23	1.25716	1.33072	1.40838	1.49036	1.57690	1.76461	1.97359	2.20611
24	1.26973	1.34735	1.42950	1.51644	1.60844	1.80873	2.03279	2.28333
25	1.28243	1.36419	1.45095	1.54298	1.64060	1.85394	2.09378	2.36324
26	1.29526	1.38124	1.47271	1.56998	1.67342	1.90029	2.15659	2.44596
27	1.30821	1.39851	1.49480	1.59746	1.70689	1.94780	2.22129	2.53157
28	1.32129	1.41599	1.51722	1.62541	1.74102	1.99650	2.28793	2.62017
29	1.33450	1.43369	1.53998	1.65386	1.77584	2.04641	2.35657	2.71188
30	1.34785	1.45161	1.56308	1.68280	1.81136	2.09757	2.42726	2.80679
31	1.36133	1.46976	1.58653	1.71225	1.84759	2.15001	2.50008	2.90503
32	1.37494	1.48813	1.61032	1.74221	1.88454	2.20376	2.57508	3.00671
33	1.38869	1.50673	1.63448	1.77270	1.92223	2.25885	2.65234	3.11194
34	1.40258	1.52557	1.65900	1.80372	1.96068	2.31532	2.73191	3.22086
35	1.41660	1.54464	1.68388	1.83529	1.99988	2.37320	2.81386	3.33359
36	1.43077	1.56394	1.70914	1.86741	2.03988	2.43253	2.89827	3.45026
37	1.44508	1.58349	1.73478	1.90009	2.08068	2.49334	2.98522	3.57102
38	1.45953	1.60329	1.76080	1.93334	2.12229	2.55568	3.07478	3.69601
39	1.47412	1.62333	1.78721	1.96717	2.16474	2.61957	3.16702	3.82537
40	1.48886	1.64362	1.81402	2.00160	2.20803	2.68506	3.26203	3.95925

COMPOUND AMOUNT OF 1

$$(1 + i)^n$$

n \ i	4%	4½%	5%	6%	7%	8%	9%	10%
1	1.04000	1.04500	1.05000	1.06000	1.07000	1.08000	1.09000	1.10000
2	1.08160	1.09203	1.10250	1.12360	1.14490	1.16640	1.18810	1.21000
3	1.12486	1.14117	1.15763	1.19021	1.22504	1.25971	1.29503	1.33100
4	1.16986	1.19252	1.21551	1.26248	1.31080	1.36049	1.41158	1.46410
5	1.21665	1.24618	1.27628	1.33823	1.40255	1.46933	1.53862	1.61051
6	1.26532	1.30226	1.34010	1.41852	1.50073	1.58687	1.67710	1.77156
7	1.31593	1.36086	1.40710	1.50363	1.60578	1.71382	1.82804	1.94872
8	1.36857	1.42210	1.47746	1.59385	1.71819	1.85093	1.99256	2.14359
9	1.42331	1.48610	1.55133	1.68948	1.83846	1.99900	2.17189	2.35795
10	1.48024	1.55297	1.62889	1.79085	1.96715	2.15893	2.36736	2.59374
11	1.53945	1.62285	1.71034	1.89830	2.10485	2.33164	2.58043	2.85312
12	1.60103	1.69588	1.79586	2.01220	2.25219	2.51817	2.81266	3.13843
13	1.66507	1.77220	1.88565	2.13293	2.40985	2.71962	3.06580	3.45227
14	1.73168	1.85194	1.97993	2.26090	2.57853	2.93719	3.34173	3.79750
15	1.80094	1.93528	2.07893	2.39656	2.75903	3.17217	3.64248	4.17725
16	1.87298	2.02237	2.18287	2.54035	2.95126	3.42594	3.97031	4.59497
17	1.94790	2.11338	2.29202	2.69277	3.15882	3.70002	4.32763	5.05447
18	2.02582	2.20848	2.40662	2.85434	3.37993	3.99602	4.71712	5.55992
19	2.10685	2.30786	2.52695	3.02560	3.61653	4.31570	5.14166	6.11591
20	2.19112	2.41171	2.65330	3.20714	3.86968	4.66096	5.60441	6.72750
21	2.27877	2.52024	2.78596	3.39956	4.14056	5.03383	6.10881	7.40025
22	2.36992	2.63365	2.92526	3.60354	4.43040	5.43654	6.65860	8.14027
23	2.46472	2.75217	3.07152	3.81975	4.74053	5.87146	7.25787	8.95430
24	2.56330	2.87601	3.22510	4.04893	5.07237	6.34118	7.91108	9.84973
25	2.66584	3.00543	3.38635	4.29187	5.42743	6.84848	8.62308	10.83471
26	2.77247	3.14068	3.55567	4.54938	5.80735	7.39635	9.39916	11.91818
27	2.88337	3.28201	3.73346	4.82235	6.21387	7.98806	10.24508	13.10999
28	2.99870	3.42970	3.92013	5.11169	6.64884	8.62711	11.16714	14.42099
29	3.11865	3.58404	4.11614	5.41839	7.11426	9.31727	12.17218	15.86309
30	3.24340	3.74532	4.32194	5.74349	7.61226	10.06266	13.26768	17.44940
31	3.37313	3.91386	4.53804	6.08810	8.14511	10.86767	14.46177	19.19434
32	3.50806	4.08998	4.76494	6.45339	8.71527	11.73708	15.76333	21.11378
33	3.64838	4.27403	5.00319	6.84059	9.32534	12.67605	17.18203	23.22515
34	3.79432	4.46636	5.25335	7.25103	9.97811	13.69013	18.72841	25.54767
35	3.94608	4.66734	5.51601	7.68609	10.67658	14.78534	20.41397	28.10244
36	4.10393	4.87737	5.79181	8.14725	11.42394	15.96817	22.25122	30.91268
37	4.26808	5.09686	6.08140	8.63609	12.22362	17.24562	24.25383	34.00395
38	4.43881	5.32621	6.38547	9.15425	13.07927	18.62527	26.43668	37.40434
39	4.61636	5.56589	6.70475	9.70351	13.99482	20.11529	28.81598	41.14478
40	4.80102	5.81636	7.03998	10.28572	14.97446	21.72452	31.40942	45.25926

PRESENT VALUE OF 1

$$(1 + i)^{-n}$$

$\diagdown\ i$ n	1%	1¼%	1½%	1¾%	2%	2½%	3%	3½%
1	0.99010	0.98765	0.98522	0.98280	0.98039	0.97561	0.97087	0.96618
2	0.98030	0.97546	0.97066	0.96590	0.96117	0.95181	0.94260	0.93351
3	0.97059	0.96342	0.95632	0.94928	0.94232	0.92860	0.91514	0.90194
4	0.96098	0.95152	0.94218	0.93296	0.92385	0.90595	0.88849	0.87144
5	0.95147	0.93978	0.92826	0.91691	0.90573	0.88385	0.86261	0.84197
6	0.94204	0.92817	0.91454	0.90114	0.88797	0.86230	0.83748	0.81350
7	0.93272	0.91672	0.90103	0.88565	0.87056	0.84127	0.81309	0.78599
8	0.92348	0.90540	0.88771	0.87041	0.85349	0.82075	0.78941	0.75941
9	0.91434	0.89422	0.87459	0.85544	0.83675	0.80073	0.76642	0.73373
10	0.90529	0.88318	0.86167	0.84073	0.82035	0.78120	0.74409	0.70892
11	0.89632	0.87228	0.84893	0.82627	0.80426	0.76214	0.72242	0.68495
12	0.88745	0.86151	0.83639	0.81206	0.78849	0.74356	0.70138	0.66178
13	0.87866	0.85087	0.82403	0.79809	0.77303	0.72542	0.68095	0.63940
14	0.86996	0.84037	0.81185	0.78436	0.75788	0.70773	0.66112	0.61778
15	0.86135	0.82999	0.79985	0.77087	0.74302	0.69047	0.64186	0.59869
16	0.85282	0.81975	0.78803	0.75762	0.72845	0.67363	0.62317	0.57671
17	0.84438	0.80963	0.77639	0.74459	0.71416	0.65720	0.60502	0.55720
18	0.83602	0.79963	0.76491	0.73178	0.70016	0.64117	0.58739	0.53836
19	0.82774	0.78976	0.75361	0.71919	0.68643	0.62553	0.57029	0.52016
20	0.81954	0.78001	0.74247	0.70682	0.67297	0.61027	0.55368	0.50257
21	0.81143	0.77038	0.73150	0.69467	0.65978	0.59539	0.53755	0.48557
22	0.80340	0.76087	0.72069	0.68272	0.64684	0.58087	0.52189	0.46915
23	0.79544	0.75147	0.71004	0.67098	0.63416	0.56670	0.50669	0.45329
24	0.78757	0.74220	0.69954	0.65944	0.62172	0.55288	0.49193	0.43796
25	0.77977	0.73303	0.68921	0.64810	0.60953	0.53939	0.47761	0.42315
26	0.77205	0.72398	0.67902	0.63695	0.59758	0.52624	0.46369	0.40884
27	0.76440	0.71505	0.66899	0.62599	0.58586	0.51340	0.45019	0.39501
28	0.75684	0.70622	0.65910	0.61523	0.57438	0.50088	0.43708	0.38165
29	0.74934	0.69750	0.64936	0.60465	0.56311	0.48866	0.42435	0.36875
30	0.74192	0.68889	0.63976	0.59425	0.55207	0.47674	0.41199	0.35628
31	0.73458	0.68004	0.63031	0.58403	0.54125	0.46512	0.39999	0.34423
32	0.72730	0.67198	0.62099	0.57398	0.53063	0.45377	0.38834	0.33259
33	0.72010	0.66369	0.61182	0.56411	0.52023	0.44270	0.37703	0.32134
34	0.71297	0.65549	0.60277	0.55441	0.51003	0.43191	0.36605	0.31048
35	0.70591	0.64740	0.59387	0.54487	0.50003	0.42137	0.35538	0.29998
36	0.69893	0.63941	0.58509	0.53550	0.49022	0.41109	0.34503	0.28983
37	0.69201	0.63151	0.57644	0.52629	0.48061	0.40107	0.33498	0.28003
38	0.68515	0.62372	0.56792	0.51724	0.47119	0.39129	0.32523	0.27057
39	0.67837	0.61602	0.55953	0.50834	0.46195	0.38174	0.31575	0.26141
40	0.67165	0.60841	0.55126	0.49960	0.45289	0.37243	0.30656	0.25257

PRESENT VALUE OF 1

$$(1 + i)^{-n}$$

n	4%	4½%	5%	6%	7%	8%	9%	10%
1	0.96154	0.95694	0.95238	0.94340	0.93458	0.92593	0.91743	0.90909
2	0.92456	0.91573	0.90703	0.89000	0.87344	0.85734	0.84168	0.82645
3	0.88900	0.87630	0.86384	0.83962	0.81630	0.79383	0.77218	0.75131
4	0.85480	0.83856	0.82270	0.79209	0.76290	0.73503	0.70842	0.68301
5	0.82193	0.80245	0.78353	0.74726	0.71299	0.68058	0.64993	0.62092
6	0.79031	0.76790	0.74622	0.70496	0.66634	0.63017	0.59627	0.56447
7	0.75992	0.73483	0.71068	0.66506	0.62275	0.58349	0.54703	0.51316
8	0.73069	0.70319	0.67684	0.62741	0.58201	0.54027	0.50187	0.46651
9	0.70259	0.67290	0.64461	0.59190	0.54393	0.50025	0.46043	0.42410
10	0.67556	0.64393	0.61391	0.55840	0.50835	0.46319	0.42241	0.38554
11	0.64958	0.61620	0.58468	0.52679	0.47509	0.42888	0.38753	0.35049
12	0.62460	0.58966	0.55684	0.49697	0.44401	0.39711	0.35553	0.31863
13	0.60057	0.56427	0.53032	0.46884	0.41496	0.36770	0.32618	0.28966
14	0.57748	0.53997	0.50507	0.44230	0.38782	0.34046	0.29925	0.26333
15	0.55526	0.51672	0.48102	0.41727	0.36245	0.31524	0.27454	0.23939
16	0.53391	0.49447	0.45811	0.39365	0.33874	0.29189	0.25187	0.21763
17	0.51337	0.47318	0.43630	0.37136	0.31657	0.27027	0.23107	0.19784
18	0.49363	0.45280	0.41552	0.35034	0.29586	0.25025	0.21199	0.17986
19	0.47464	0.43330	0.39573	0.33051	0.27651	0.23171	0.19449	0.16351
20	0.45639	0.41464	0.37689	0.31181	0.25842	0.21455	0.17843	0.14864
21	0.43883	0.39679	0.35894	0.29416	0.24151	0.19866	0.16370	0.13513
22	0.42196	0.37970	0.34185	0.27751	0.22571	0.18394	0.15018	0.12285
23	0.40573	0.36335	0.32557	0.26180	0.21095	0.17032	0.13778	0.11168
24	0.39012	0.34770	0.31007	0.24698	0.19715	0.15770	0.12640	0.10153
25	0.37512	0.33273	0.29530	0.23300	0.18425	0.14602	0.11597	0.09230
26	0.36069	0.31840	0.28124	0.21981	0.17220	0.13520	0.10639	0.08390
27	0.34682	0.30469	0.26785	0.20737	0.16093	0.12519	0.09761	0.07628
28	0.33348	0.29157	0.25509	0.19563	0.15040	0.11591	0.08955	0.06934
29	0.32065	0.27902	0.24295	0.18456	0.14056	0.10733	0.08215	0.06304
30	0.30832	0.26700	0.23138	0.17411	0.13137	0.09938	0.07537	0.05731
31	0.29646	0.25550	0.22036	0.16426	0.12277	0.09202	0.06915	0.05210
32	0.28506	0.24450	0.20987	0.15496	0.11474	0.08520	0.06344	0.04736
33	0.27409	0.23397	0.19987	0.14619	0.10724	0.07889	0.05820	0.04306
34	0.26355	0.22390	0.19036	0.13791	0.10022	0.07305	0.05339	0.03914
35	0.25341	0.21425	0.18129	0.13011	0.09366	0.06763	0.04899	0.03558
36	0.24367	0.20503	0.17266	0.12274	0.08754	0.06263	0.04494	0.03235
37	0.23430	0.19620	0.16444	0.11579	0.08181	0.05799	0.04123	0.02941
38	0.22529	0.18775	0.15661	0.10924	0.07646	0.05369	0.03783	0.02673
39	0.21662	0.17967	0.14915	0.10306	0.07146	0.04971	0.03470	0.02430
40	0.20829	0.17193	0.14205	0.09722	0.06678	0.04603	0.03184	0.02209

AMOUNT OF AN ANNUITY

$$s_{\overline{n}|i} = \frac{(1 + i)^n - 1}{i}$$

n i	1%	1¼%	1½%	1¾%	2%	2½%	3%
1	1.00000	1.00000	1.00000	1.00000	1.00000	1.00000	1.00000
2	2.01000	2.01250	2.01500	2.01750	2.02000	2.02500	2.03000
3	3.03010	3.03766	3.04523	3.05281	3.06040	3.07563	3.09090
4	4.06040	4.07563	4.09090	4.10623	4.12161	4.15252	4.18363
5	5.10101	5.12657	5.15227	5.17809	5.20404	5.25633	5.30914
6	6.15202	6.19065	6.22955	6.26871	6.30812	6.38774	6.46841
7	7.21354	7.26804	7.32299	7.37841	7.43428	7.54743	7.66246
8	8.28567	8.35889	8.43281	8.50753	8.58297	8.73612	8.89234
9	9.36853	9.46337	9.55933	9.65641	9.75463	9.95452	10.15911
10	10.46221	10.58167	10.70272	10.82540	10.94972	11.20338	11.46388
11	11.56683	11.71394	11.86326	12.01484	12.16872	12.48347	12.80780
12	12.68250	12.86036	13.04121	13.22510	13.41209	13.79555	14.19203
13	13.80933	14.02112	14.23683	14.45654	14.68033	15.14044	15.61779
14	14.94742	15.19638	15.45038	15.70953	15.97394	16.51895	17.08632
15	16.09690	16.38633	16.68214	16.98445	17.29342	17.93193	18.59891
16	17.25786	17.59116	17.93237	18.28168	18.63929	19.38022	20.15688
17	18.43044	18.81105	19.20136	19.60161	20.01207	20.86473	21.76159
18	19.61475	20.04619	20.48938	20.94463	21.41231	22.38635	23.41444
19	20.81090	21.29677	21.76972	22.31117	22.84056	23.94601	25.11687
20	22.01900	22.56298	23.12367	23.70161	24.29737	25.54466	26.87037
21	23.23919	23.84502	24.47052	25.11639	25.78332	27.18327	28.67649
22	24.47159	25.14308	25.83758	26.55593	27.29898	28.86286	30.53678
23	25.71630	26.45737	27.22514	28.02065	28.84496	30.58443	32.45288
24	26.97346	27.78808	28.63352	29.51102	30.42186	32.34904	34.42647
25	28.24320	29.13544	30.06302	31.02746	32.03030	34.15776	36.45926
26	29.52563	30.49963	31.51397	32.57044	33.67091	36.01171	38.55304
27	30.82089	31.88087	32.98668	34.14042	35.34432	37.91200	40.70963
28	32.12910	33.27938	34.48148	35.73788	37.05121	39.85980	42.93092
29	33.45039	34.69538	35.99870	37.36329	38.79223	41.85630	45.21885
30	34.78489	36.12907	37.53868	39.01715	40.56808	43.90270	47.57542
31	36.13274	37.58068	39.10176	40.69995	42.37944	46.00027	50.00268
32	37.49407	39.05044	40.68829	42.41220	44.22703	48.15028	52.50276
33	38.86901	40.53857	42.29861	44.15441	46.11157	50.35403	55.07784
34	40.25770	42.04530	43.93309	45.92712	48.03380	52.61289	57.73018
35	41.66028	43.57087	45.59209	47.73084	49.99448	54.92821	60.46208
36	43.07688	45.11551	47.27597	49.56613	51.99437	57.30141	63.27594
37	44.50765	46.67945	48.98511	51.43354	54.03425	59.73395	66.17422
38	45.95272	48.26294	50.71989	53.33362	56.11494	62.22730	69.15945
39	47.41225	49.86623	52.48068	55.26696	58.23724	64.78298	72.23423
40	48.88637	51.48956	54.26789	57.23413	60.40198	67.40255	75.40126

AMOUNT OF ANNUITY

$$s_{\overline{n}|i} = \frac{(1+i)^n - 1}{i}$$

n \ i	3½	4%	4½%	5%	6%	7%	8%
1	1.00000	1.00000	1.00000	1.00000	1.00000	1.00000	1.00000
2	2.03500	2.04000	2.04500	2.05000	2.06000	2.07000	2.08000
3	3.10627	3.12160	3.13703	3.15250	3.18360	3.21490	3.24640
4	4.21494	4.24646	4.27819	4.31013	4.37462	4.43994	4.50611
5	5.36247	5.41632	5.47071	5.52563	5.63709	5.75074	5.86660
6	6.55015	6.63298	6.71689	6.80191	6.97532	7.15329	7.33593
7	7.77941	7.89829	8.01915	8.14201	8.39384	8.65402	8.92280
8	9.05169	9.21423	9.38001	9.54911	9.89747	10.25980	10.63663
9	10.36850	10.58280	10.80211	11.02656	11.49132	11.97799	12.48756
10	11.73140	12.00611	12.28821	12.57789	13.18079	13.81645	14.48656
11	13.14199	13.48635	13.84118	14.20679	14.97164	15.78360	16.64549
12	14.60196	15.02581	15.46403	15.91713	16.86994	17.88845	18.97713
13	16.11303	16.62684	17.15991	17.71298	18.88214	20.14064	21.49530
14	17.67699	18.29191	18.93211	19.59863	21.01507	22.55049	24.21492
15	19.29568	20.02359	20.78405	21.57856	23.27597	25.12902	27.15211
16	20.97103	21.82453	22.71934	23.65749	25.67253	27.88805	30.32428
17	22.70502	23.69751	24.74171	25.84037	28.21288	30.84022	33.75023
18	24.49969	25.64541	26.85508	28.13238	30.90565	33.99903	37.45024
19	26.35718	27.67123	29.06356	30.53900	33.75999	37.37896	41.44626
20	28.27968	29.77808	31.37142	33.06595	36.78559	40.99549	45.76196
21	30.26947	31.96920	33.78314	35.71925	39.99273	44.86518	50.42292
22	32.32890	34.24797	36.30338	38.50521	43.39229	49.00574	55.45676
23	34.46041	36.61789	38.93703	41.43048	46.99583	53.43614	60.89330
24	36.66653	39.08260	41.68920	44.50200	50.81558	58.17667	66.76476
25	38.94986	41.64591	44.56521	47.72710	54.86451	63.24903	73.10594
26	41.31310	44.31174	47.57064	51.11345	59.15638	68.67647	79.95442
27	43.75906	47.08421	50.71132	54.66913	63.70577	74.48382	87.35077
28	46.29063	49.96758	53.99333	58.40258	68.52811	80.69769	95.33883
29	48.91080	52.96629	57.42303	62.32271	73.63980	87.34653	103.96594
30	51.62268	56.08494	61.00707	66.43885	79.05819	94.46079	113.28321
31	54.42947	59.32834	64.75239	70.76079	84.80168	102.07304	123.34587
32	57.33450	62.70147	68.66625	75.29883	90.88978	110.21815	134.21354
33	60.34121	66.20953	72.75623	80.06377	97.34316	118.93343	145.95062
34	63.45315	69.85791	77.03026	85.06696	104.18375	128.25876	158.62667
35	66.67401	73.65222	81.49662	90.32031	111.43478	138.23688	172.31680
36	70.00760	77.59831	86.16397	95.83632	119.12087	148.91346	187.10215
37	73.45787	81.70225	91.04134	101.62814	127.26812	160.33740	203.07032
38	77.02889	85.97034	96.13820	107.70955	135.90421	172.56102	220.31595
39	80.72491	90.40915	101.46442	114.09502	145.05846	185.64029	238.94122
40	84.55028	95.02551	107.03032	120.79977	154.76197	199.63511	259.05652

PRESENT VALUE OF AN ANNUITY

$$a_{\overline{n}|i} = \frac{1 - (1 + i)^{-n}}{i}$$

i / n	1%	1¼%	1½%	1¾%	2%	2½%	3%
1	.99010	.98765	.98522	.98280	.98039	.97561	.97087
2	1.97040	1.96312	1.95588	1.94870	1.94156	1.92742	1.91347
3	2.94099	2.92653	2.91220	2.89798	2.88388	2.85602	2.82861
4	3.90197	3.87806	3.85438	3.83094	3.80773	3.76197	3.71710
5	4.85343	4.81784	4.78264	4.74786	4.71346	4.64583	4.57971
6	5.79547	5.76401	5.69719	5.64900	5.60143	5.50813	5.41719
7	6.72819	6.66273	6.59821	6.53464	6.47199	6.34939	6.23028
8	7.65168	7.56812	7.48593	7.40505	7.32548	7.17014	7.01969
9	8.56602	8.46234	8.36052	8.26049	8.16224	7.97087	7.78611
10	9.47130	9.34553	9.22218	9.10122	8.98259	8.75206	8.53020
11	10.36763	10.21780	10.07112	9.92749	9.78685	9.51421	9.25262
12	11.25508	11.07931	10.90751	10.73955	10.57534	10.25776	9.95400
13	12.13374	11.93018	11.73153	11.53764	11.34837	10.98318	10.63496
14	13.00370	12.77055	12.54338	12.32201	12.10625	11.69091	11.29607
15	13.86505	13.60055	13.34323	13.09288	12.84926	12.38138	11.93794
16	14.71787	14.42029	14.13126	13.85050	13.57771	13.05500	12.56110
17	15.56225	15.22992	14.90765	14.59508	14.29187	13.71220	13.16612
18	16.39827	16.02955	15.67256	15.32686	14.99203	14.35336	13.75351
19	17.22601	16.81931	16.42617	16.04606	15.67846	14.97889	14.32380
20	18.04555	17.59932	17.16864	16.75288	16.35143	15.58916	14.87747
21	18.85698	18.36969	17.90014	17.44755	17.01121	16.18455	15.41502
22	19.66038	19.13056	18.62082	18.13027	17.65805	16.76541	15.93692
23	20.45582	19.88204	19.33086	18.80125	18.29220	17.33211	16.44361
24	21.24339	20.62423	20.03041	19.46069	18.91393	17.88499	16.93554
25	22.02316	21.35727	20.71961	20.10878	19.52346	18.42438	17.41315
26	22.79520	22.01225	21.39863	20.74573	20.12104	18.95061	17.87684
27	23.55961	22.79630	22.06762	21.37173	20.70690	19.46401	18.32703
28	24.31644	23.50252	22.72672	21.98695	21.28127	19.96489	18.76411
29	25.06579	24.20002	23.37608	22.59160	21.84438	20.45355	19.18845
30	25.80771	24.88891	24.01584	23.18585	22.39646	20.93029	19.60044
31	26.54229	25.56929	24.64615	23.76988	22.93770	21.39541	20.00043
32	27.26959	26.24127	25.26714	24.34386	23.46833	21.84918	20.38877
33	27.98969	26.90496	25.87895	24.90797	23.98856	22.29188	20.76579
34	28.70267	27.56046	26.48173	25.46238	24.49859	22.72379	21.13184
35	29.40858	28.20786	27.07559	26.00725	24.99862	23.14516	21.48722
36	30.10751	28.84727	27.66068	26.54275	25.48884	23.55625	21.83225
37	30.79951	29.47878	28.23713	27.06904	25.96945	23.95732	22.16724
38	31.48466	30.10250	28.80505	27.58628	26.44064	24.34860	22.49246
39	32.16303	30.71852	29.36458	28.09463	26.90259	24.73034	22.80822
40	32.83469	31.32693	29.91585	28.59423	27.35548	25.10278	23.11477

PRESENT VALUE OF AN ANNUITY

$$a_{\overline{n}|i} = \frac{1 - (1 + i)^{-n}}{i}$$

n \ i	3½%	4%	4½%	5%	6%	7%	8%
1	.99618	.96154	.95694	.95238	.94340	.93458	.92593
2	1.89969	1.88609	1.87267	1.85941	1.83339	1.80802	1.78326
3	2.80164	2.77509	2.74896	2.72325	2.67301	2.62432	2.57710
4	3.67308	3.62990	3.58753	3.54595	3.46511	3.38721	3.31213
5	4.51505	4.45182	4.38998	4.32948	4.21236	4.10020	3.99271
6	5.32855	5.24214	5.15787	5.07569	4.91732	4.76654	4.62288
7	6.11454	6.00205	5.89270	5.78637	5.58238	5.38929	5.20637
8	6.87396	6.73274	6.59589	6.46321	6.20979	5.97130	5.74664
9	7.60769	7.43533	7.26879	7.10782	6.80169	6.51523	6.24689
10	8.31661	8.11090	7.91272	7.72173	7.36009	7.02358	6.71008
11	9.00155	8.76048	8.52892	8.30641	7.88687	7.49867	7.13896
12	9.66333	9.38507	9.11858	8.86325	8.38384	7.94269	7.53608
13	10.30274	9.98565	9.68285	9.39357	8.85268	8.35765	7.90378
14	10.92052	10.56312	10.22282	9.89864	9.29498	8.74547	8.24424
15	11.51741	11.11839	10.73955	10.37966	9.71225	9.10791	8.55948
16	12.09412	11.65230	11.23402	10.83777	10.10590	9.44665	8.85137
17	12.65132	12.16567	11.70719	11.27407	10.47726	9.76322	9.12164
18	13.18968	12.65930	12.15999	11.68959	10.82760	10.05909	9.37189
19	13.70984	13.13394	12.59329	12.08532	11.15812	10.33560	9.60360
20	14.21240	13.59033	13.00794	12.46221	11.46992	10.59401	9.81815
21	14.69797	14.02916	13.40472	12.82115	11.76408	10.83553	10.01680
22	15.16712	14.45112	13.78442	13.16300	12.04158	11.06124	10.20074
23	15.62041	14.85684	14.14777	13.48857	12.30338	11.27219	10.37106
24	16.05837	15.24696	14.49548	13.79864	12.55036	11.46933	10.52876
25	16.48151	15.62208	14.82821	14.09394	12.78336	11.65358	10.67478
26	16.89035	15.98277	15.14661	14.37519	13.00317	11.82578	10.80998
27	17.28536	16.32959	15.45130	14.64303	13.21053	11.98671	10.93516
28	17.66702	16.66306	15.74287	14.89813	13.40616	12.13711	11.05108
29	18.03577	16.98371	16.02189	15.14107	13.59072	12.27767	11.15841
30	18.39205	17.29203	16.28889	15.37245	13.76483	12.40904	11.25778
31	18.73628	17.58849	16.54439	15.59281	13.92909	12.53181	11.34980
32	19.06887	17.87355	16.78889	15.80268	14.08404	12.64656	11.43500
33	19.39021	18.14765	17.02286	16.00255	14.23023	12.75379	11.51389
34	19.70068	18.41120	17.24676	16.91290	14.36814	12.85401	11.58693
35	20.00066	18.66461	17.46101	16.37419	14.49825	12.94767	11.65457
36	20.29049	18.90828	17.66604	16.54685	14.62099	13.03521	11.71719
37	20.57053	19.14258	17.86224	16.71129	14.73678	13.11702	11.77518
38	20.84109	19.36786	18.04999	16.86789	14.84602	13.19347	11.82887
39	21.10250	19.58448	18.22966	17.01704	14.94907	13.26493	11.87858
40	21.35507	19.79277	18.40158	17.15909	15.04630	13.33171	11.92461

TRIGONOMETRIC FUNCTIONS

Angle Degrees	Angle Radians	Sine	Cosine	Tangent	Cotangent	Secant	Cosecant
0°	.0000	.0000	1.0000	.0000	undefined	1.000	undefined
1°	.0175	.0175	.9998	.0175	57.2900	1.000	57.30
2°	.0349	.0349	.9994	.0349	28.6363	1.001	28.65
3°	.0524	.0523	.9986	.0524	19.0811	1.001	19.11
4°	.0698	.0698	.9976	.0699	14.3007	1.002	14.34
5°	.0873	.0872	.9962	.0875	11.4301	1.004	11.47
6°	.1047	.1045	.9945	.1051	9.5144	1.006	9.567
7°	.1222	.1219	.9925	.1228	8.1443	1.008	8.206
8°	.1396	.1392	.9903	.1405	7.1154	1.010	7.185
9°	.1571	.1564	.9877	.1584	6.3138	1.012	6.392
10°	.1745	.1736	.9848	.1763	5.6713	1.015	5.759
11°	.1920	.1908	.9816	.1944	5 1446	1.019	5.241
12°	.2094	.2079	.9781	.2126	4.7046	1.022	4.810
13°	.2269	.2250	.9744	.2309	4.3315	1.026	4.445
14°	.2443	.2419	.9703	.2493	4.0108	1.031	4.134
15°	.2618	.2588	.9659	.2679	3.7321	1.035	3.864
16°	.2793	.2756	.9613	.2867	3.4874	1.040	3.628
17°	.2967	.2924	.9563	.3057	3.2709	1.046	3.420
18°	.3142	.3090	.9511	.3249	3.0777	1.051	3.236
19°	.3316	.3256	.9455	.3443	2.9042	1.058	3.072
20°	.3491	.3420	.9397	.3640	2.7475	1.064	2.924
21°	.3665	.3584	.9336	.3839	2.6051	1.071	2.790
22°	.3840	.3746	.9272	.4040	2.4751	1.079	2.669
23°	.4014	.3907	.9205	.4245	2.3559	1.086	2.559
24°	.4189	.4067	.9135	.4452	2.2460	1.095	2.459
25°	.4363	.4226	.9063	.4663	2.1445	1.103	2.366
26°	.4538	.4384	.8988	.4877	2.0503	1.113	2.281
27°	.4712	.4540	.8910	.5095	1.9626	1.122	2.203
28°	.4887	.4695	.8829	.5317	1.8807	1.133	2.130
29°	.5061	.4848	.8746	.5543	1.8040	1.143	2.063
30°	.5236	.5000	.8660	.5774	1.7321	1.155	2.000
31°	.5411	.5150	.8572	.6009	1.6643	1.167	1.942
32°	.5585	.5299	.8480	.6249	1.6003	1.179	1.887
33°	.5760	.5446	.8387	.6494	1.5399	1.192	1.836
34°	.5934	.5592	.8290	.6745	1.4826	1.206	1.788
35°	.6109	.5736	.8192	.7002	1.4281	1.221	1.743
36°	.6283	.5878	.8090	.7265	1.3764	1.236	1.701
37°	.6458	.6018	.7986	.7536	1.3270	1.252	1.662
38°	.6632	.6157	.7880	.7813	1.2799	1.269	1.624
39°	.6807	.6293	.7771	.8098	1.2349	1.287	1.589
40°	.6981	.6428	.7660	.8391	1.1918	1.305	1.556
41°	.7156	.6561	.7547	.8693	1.1504	1.325	1.524
42°	.7330	.6691	.7431	.9004	1.1106	1.346	1.494
43°	.7505	.6820	.7314	.9325	1.0724	1.367	1.466
44°	.7679	.6947	.7193	.9657	1.0355	1.390	1.440
45°	.7854	.7071	.7071	1.0000	1.0000	1.414	1.414

TRIGONOMETRIC FUNCTIONS

Angle		Sine	Cosine	Tangent	Cotangent	Secant	Cosecant
Degrees	Radians						
45°	.7854	.7071	.7071	1.0000	1.0000	1.414	1.414
46°	.8029	.7193	.6947	1.0355	.9657	1.440	1.390
47°	.8203	.7314	.6820	1.0724	.9325	1.466	1.367
48°	.8378	.7431	.6691	1.1106	.9004	1.494	1.346
49°	.8552	.7547	.6561	1.1504	.8693	1.524	1.325
50°	.8727	.7660	.6428	1.1918	.8391	1.556	1.305
51°	.8901	.7771	.6293	1.2349	.8098	1.589	1.287
52°	.9076	.7880	.6157	1.2799	.7813	1.624	1.269
53°	.9250	.7986	.6018	1.3270	.7536	1.662	1.252
54°	.9425	.8090	.5878	1.3764	.7265	1.701	1.236
55°	.9599	.8192	.5736	1.4281	.7002	1.743	1.221
56°	.9774	.8290	.5592	1.4826	.6745	1.788	1.206
57°	.9948	.8387	.5446	1.5399	.6494	1.836	1.192
58°	1.0123	.8480	.5299	1.6003	.6249	1.887	1.179
59°	1.0297	.8572	.5150	1.6643	.6009	1.942	1.167
60°	1.0472	.8660	.5000	1.7321	.5774	2.000	1.155
61°	1.0647	.8746	.4848	1.8040	.5543	2.063	1.143
62°	1.0821	.8829	.4695	1.8807	.5317	2.130	1.133
63°	1.0996	.8910	.4540	1.9626	.5095	2.203	1.122
64°	1.1170	.8988	.4384	2.0503	.4877	2.281	1.113
65°	1.1345	.9063	.4226	2.1445	.4663	2.366	1.103
66°	1.1519	.9135	.4067	2.2460	.4452	2.459	1.095
67°	1.1694	.9205	.3907	2.3559	.4245	2.559	1.086
68°	1.1868	.9272	.3746	2.4751	.4040	2.669	1.079
69°	1.2043	.9336	.3584	2.6051	.3839	2.790	1.071
70°	1.2217	.9397	.3420	2.7475	.3640	2.924	1.064
71°	1.2392	.9455	.3256	2.9042	.3443	3.072	1.058
72°	1.2566	.9511	.3090	3.0777	.3249	3.236	1.051
73°	1.2741	.9563	.2924	3.2709	.3057	3.420	1.046
74°	1.2915	.9613	.2756	3.4874	.2867	3.628	1.040
75°	1.3090	.9659	.2588	3.7321	.2679	3.864	1.035
76°	1.3265	.9703	.2419	4.0108	.2493	4.134	1.031
77°	1.3439	.9744	.2250	4.3315	.2309	4.445	1.026
78°	1.3614	.9781	.2079	4.7046	.2126	4.810	1.022
79°	1.3788	.9816	.1908	5.1446	.1944	5.241	1.019
80°	1.3963	.9848	.1736	5.6713	.1763	5.759	1.015
81°	1.4137	.9877	.1564	6.3138	.1584	6.392	1.012
82°	1.4312	.9903	.1392	7.1154	.1405	7.185	1.010
83°	1.4486	.9925	.1219	8.1443	.1228	8.206	1.008
84°	1.4661	.9945	.1045	9.5144	.1051	9.567	1.006
85°	1.4835	.9962	.0872	11.4301	.0875	11.47	1.004
86°	1.5010	.9976	.0698	14.3007	.0699	14.34	1.002
87°	1.5184	.9986	.0523	19.0811	.0524	19.11	1.001
88°	1.5359	.9994	.0349	28.6363	.0349	28.65	1.001
89°	1.5533	.9998	.0175	57.2900	.0175	57.30	1.000
90°	1.5708	1.0000	.0000	undefined	.0000	undefined	1.000

ORDINATES OF NORMAL CURVE

$$g(z)$$

z	.00	.01	.02	.03	.04	.05	.06	.07	.08	.09
.0	.3989	.3989	.3989	.3988	.3986	.3984	.3982	.3980	.3977	.3973
.1	.3970	.3965	.3961	.3956	.3951	.3945	.3939	.3932	.3925	.3918
.2	.3910	.3902	.3894	.3885	.3876	.3867	.3857	.3847	.3836	.3825
.3	.3814	.3802	.3790	.3778	.3765	.3752	.3739	.3725	.3712	.3697
.4	.3683	.3668	.3653	.3637	.3621	.3605	.3589	.3572	.3555	.3538
.5	.3521	.3503	.3485	.3467	.3448	.3429	.3410	.3391	.3372	.3352
.6	.3332	.3312	.3292	.3271	.3251	.3230	.3209	.3187	.3166	.3144
.7	.3123	.3101	.3079	.3056	.3034	.3011	.2989	.2966	.2943	.2920
.8	.2897	.2874	.2850	.2827	.2803	.2780	.2756	.2732	.2709	.2685
.9	.2661	.2637	.2613	.2589	.2565	.2541	.2516	.2492	.2468	.2444
1.0	.2420	.2396	.2371	.2347	.2323	.2299	.2275	.2251	.2227	.2203
1.1	.2179	.2155	.2131	.2107	.2083	.2059	.2036	.2012	.1989	.1965
1.2	.1942	.1919	.1895	.1872	.1849	.1826	.1804	.1781	.1758	.1736
1.3	.1714	.1691	.1669	.1647	.1626	.1604	.1582	.1561	.1539	.1518
1.4	.1497	.1476	.1456	.1435	.1415	.1394	.1374	.1354	.1334	.1315
1.5	.1295	.1276	.1257	.1238	.1219	.1220	.1182	.1163	.1145	.1127
1.6	.1109	.1092	.1074	.1057	.1040	.1023	.1006	.0989	.0973	.0957
1.7	.0940	.0925	.0909	.0893	.0878	.0863	.0848	.0833	.0818	.0804
1.8	.0790	.0775	.0761	.0748	.0734	.0721	.0707	.0694	.0681	.0669
1.9	.0656	.0644	.0632	.0620	.0608	.0596	.0584	.0573	.0562	.0551
2.0	.0540	.0529	.0519	.0508	.0498	.0488	.0478	.0468	.0459	.0449
2.1	.0440	.0431	.0422	.0413	.0404	.0396	.0387	.0379	.0371	.0363
2.2	.0355	.0347	.0339	.0332	.0325	.0317	.0310	.0303	.0297	.0290
2.3	.0283	.0277	.0270	.0264	.0258	.0252	.0246	.0241	.0235	.0229
2.4	.0224	.0219	.0213	.0208	.0203	.0198	.0194	.0189	.0184	.0180
2.5	.0175	.0171	.0167	.0163	.0158	.0154	.0151	.0147	.0143	.0139
2.6	.0136	.0132	.0129	.0126	.0122	.0119	.0116	.0113	.0110	.0107
2.7	.0104	.0101	.0099	.0096	.0093	.0091	.0088	.0086	.0084	.0081
2.8	.0079	.0077	.0075	.0073	.0071	.0069	.0067	.0065	.0063	.0061
2.9	.0060	.0058	.0056	.0055	.0053	.0051	.0050	.0048	.0047	.0046
3.0	.0044	.0043	.0042	.0040	.0039	.0038	.0037	.0036	.0035	.0034
3.1	.0033	.0032	.0031	.0030	.0029	.0028	.0027	.0026	.0025	.0025
3.2	.0024	.0023	.0022	.0022	.0021	.0020	.0020	.0019	.0018	.0018
3.3	.0017	.0017	.0016	.0016	.0015	.0015	.0014	.0014	.0013	.0013
3.4	.0012	.0012	.0012	.0011	.0011	.0010	.0010	.0010	.0009	.0009
3.5	.0009	.0008	.0008	.0008	.0008	.0007	.0007	.0007	.0007	.0006
3.6	.0006	.0006	.0006	.0005	.0005	.0005	.0005	.0005	.0005	.0004
3.7	.0004	.0004	.0004	.0004	.0004	.0004	.0003	.0003	.0003	.0003
3.8	.0003	.0003	.0003	.0003	.0003	.0002	.0002	.0002	.0002	.0002
3.9	.0002	.0002	.0002	.0002	.0002	.0002	.0002	.0002	.0002	.0001
4.0	.0001	.0001	.0001	.0001	.0001	.0001	.0001	.0001	.0001	.0001

ANSWERS

Chapter 1

	Set	Domain	Range
1. (a)	$\{(3,2),(3,1)\,(3,0)\}$	$\{3\}$.	$\{0,1,2\}$.
(b)	$\{(4,5),(5,6),(6,7),(7,8)\}$	$\{4,5,6,7\}$.	$\{5,6,7,8\}$.
(c)	$\{(x,y) \mid x, y \in N$ and $x + y < 6\}$	$\{1,2,3,4,5\}$.	$\{1,2,3,4,5\}$.
(d)	$\{(x,y) \mid x, y \in I, xy = 4\}$	$\{\pm 1, \pm 2, \pm 4\}$.	$\{\pm 1, \pm 2, \pm 4\}$.

2. (a) $(1, \frac{1}{2}), (0, -1), (-4, 2), (1, -5)$.   (b) $(-3, 0)$.

3. $M = \{-2, 0, 2\}, \quad N = \{3, 5, 7, 9\}$

$$M \times N = \begin{cases} (-2,3), (-2,5), (-2,7), (-2,9), \\ (0,3), (0,5), (0,7), (0,9), \\ (2,3), (2,5), (2,7), (2,9). \end{cases}$$

4. $M \cap N = \phi$, the null set   **5.** $P = \{(-2,3), (0,5), (2,7)\}$
   $M \cup N = \{-2, 0, 3, 5, 7, 9, 2\}$. $D_P = \{-2, 0, 2\}$
                                       $R_P = \{3, 5, 7\}$.

6. (a) $\{1, -1\}$.   (b) $\{0\}$.   (c) $\{1, -1\}$.   (d) ϕ.
    (e) $\{x \mid x \in N, \sqrt{x} \in N\} \cup \{0\}$. (f) I.   (g) $\{0\}$.
    (h) $N \cup \{0\}$.   (i) I.   (j) $\{x \mid x \leq 0, \sqrt{-x} \in I\}$.

7. (a) $(1,3), (3,1), (0,2), (2,0)$.   (b) $(0,1), (1,4), (2,7), (3,10)$.
    (c) $(1,0), (2,0), (3,0), (4,0)$.   (d) $(0,0), (1,1), (2,2), (3,3)$.
    (e) $(4,16), (3.5, 12.25), (3.25, 10.5625), (4.5, 20.25)$.
    (f) $(2,2), (1,1), (-1,1), (0,0)$.

1. (i) $x > 0, y > 0$.   (ii) $x < 0, y > 0$.   (iii) $x < 0, y < 0$.   (iv) $x > 0, y < 0$.

		x-intercept	y-intercept
2. (a)	$x + y = 1$	$x = 1$	$y = 1$.
(b)	$2x + y = 5$	$x = 2.5$	$y = 5$.
(c)	$y = x^2$	$x = 0$	$y = 0$.
(d)	$y - 1 = 3(x - 2)^2$	---	$y = 13$.
(e)	$x^2 + y^2 = 30$	$x = \pm\sqrt{30}$	$y = \pm\sqrt{30}$.
(f)	$xy = 0$	$x \in Re$	$y \in Re$.

3. (a) A straight line parallel to the x-axis with $y = 4$.
    (b) A straight line parallel to the y-axis with $x = -2$.
    (c) The x-axis.   (d) The y-axis.
    (e) The first and second quadrants.   (f) The first and fourth quadrants.
    (g) The first quadrant.   (h) The third quadrant.

4. (a) $\{(-4, 16), (-2, 4), (0, 0), (2, 4), (4, 16)\}$.
(b) $\{(-4, 4), (-2, 2), (0, 0), (2, 2), (4, 4)\}$.
(c) $\{(-4, -7), (-2, -3), (0, 1), (2, 5), (4, 9)\}$.
(d) $\{(-4, 4), (-2, 2), (0, 0), (2, -2), (4, -4)\}$.

EXERCISE 1.3 (page 10)

1. (a) $g(1) = -3$.   (b) $g(0) = -5$.   (c) $g(-1) = -7$.
(d) $g(\sqrt{2}) = 2\sqrt{2} - 5$.   (e) $g(13) = 21$.   (f) $g(-40) = -85$.
(g) $g(2x) = 4x - 5$.   (h) $g(x + 1) = 2x - 3$.   (i) $g[g(x)] = 4x - 15$.
(j) $g(k) = 2k - 5$.   (k) $g(x + a) = 2x + 2a - 5$.   (l) $g(\pi^2) = 2\pi^2 - 5$.
2. (a) 1.   (b) -1.   (c) -8.   (d) $+1$.   (e) 1.   (f) 1.   (g) 9.   (h) -1.
3. The left and middle mappings are functions; the right mapping is not. From left to right, the sets of ordered pairs are $\{(6, -1), (5, -1), (4, -2), (3, -2), (2, -6), (1, -6), (0, -6)\}$, $\{(12, 0), (10, -2), (8, -4), (6, -6), (4, -8), (2, -10), (0, -12)\}$, and $\{(9, 7), (8, 7), (7, 7), (6, 7), (5, 6), (5, 4), (4, 4), (3, 4), (3, 3)\}$.
4. (a) is a function but (b) is not.
6. (a) $\{-6, -3, 0, 3, 6\}$.   (b) $\{7, 6, 5, 4, 3\}$.   (c) $\{-\frac{3}{2}, -3, 3, \frac{3}{2}\}$.
(d) $\{0, -3, -4\}$.
8. (a) $\{x \mid -8 \le x \le 27\}$.   (b) $\{x \mid 0 \le x \le 3\}$.   **9.** $\{x \mid f(x) = g(x)\} = \{3, -2\}$.
10. (a) $(0, 17), (1, 8), (2, 5), (3, 8), (4, 17)$.
(b) $(1, 8), (2, 4), (3, \frac{8}{3}), (4, 2), (8, 1)$.
(c) $(0, 4), (1, 5), (-1, 3), (-2, 4), (3, 7)$.
(d) $(1, -2), (2, -\frac{3}{2}), (5, 0), (9, 2), (11, 3)$.
13. (a), (b), (c), (d), (f).   **14.** $\{x \mid 1 \le x \le 2\}$.   **15.** $\{x \mid 0 \le x \le 18\}$.
16. $\{\ldots, -14, -7, 0, 7, 14, \ldots\}$
17. (a) 0, 1.   (b) none.   (c) 0.   (d) the integers.

EXERCISE 1.4 (page 16)

1. (i) $\{(-2, -8), (-1, -3), (0, 2), (1, 7), (2, 12)\}$.
(ii) $\{(-2, -8), (-1, -1), (0, 0), (1, 1), (2, 8)\}$.
(iii) $\{(-2, 2), (-1, 1), (0, 0), (1, 1), (2, 2)\}$.
2. (i) $\{(-8, -2), (-3, -1), (2, 0), (7, 1), (12, 2)\}$ Yes.
(ii) $\{(-8, -2), (-1, -1), (0, 0), (1, 1), (8, 2)\}$ Yes.
(iii) $\{(2, -2), (1, -1), (0, 0), (1, 1), (2, 2)\}$ No.
3. Pairs in $A^{-1} \{(3, 4), (3, 5), (3, 6)\}$ A^{-1} is not a function.

4. (a) $3y = 2x - 1$.   (b) $y = x^{1/3}$.   (c) $b = a + 3$.   (d) $t^2 - s^2 = 16$.

5. (a) 9.   (b) 7.   (c) -4.   (d) 6.   (e) 2.5.   (f) -5.
6. The defining sentence for g^{-1} is $g^{-1} = \{(x, y) \mid 2y = x + 5\}$.
g is a function. g^{-1} is a function.

     (a) 6.   (b) 13.   (c) $\dfrac{11}{+4}$.   (d) 9.   (e) -5.   (f) 2.5.

7. The inverse of f is f.   **8.** (a) f.   (b) ϕ.
9. (b) and (d).   **10.** Yes.   **11.** No.   **12.** Yes.
13. (b) Domain $\{x \mid x \in Re, \ x \ne -2\}$ Range $\{y \mid y \in Re, \ y \ne 0\}$.
(c) Domain $\{x \mid x \in Re, \ x \ne 0\}$ Range $\{y \mid y \in Re, \ y \ne -2\}$.
(d) Yes.   **14.** (a) $\{1, -1\}, \{0\}, \phi$.   (b) $\{3\}, \phi$.

15. (a) $f^{-1}(\{x \mid 0 < x < 1\}) = \{x \mid 0 < x < 1\}$.
  (b) $f^{-1}(\{x \mid -1.5 < x < 3.7\}) = \{x \mid -2 < x < 4\}$.

EXERCISE 1.5 (page 21)

1. (a) $\{(6, 2), (4, 3), (1, 4), (0, 5)\}$.   (b) $\{(1, 0), (0, 4)\}$.
  (c) $\{(3, -4), (5, 4), (-6, 0)\}$.

2. (a) $f(x) \in Re$.   (b) $f^{-1}(x) = \dfrac{x+4}{5}$.   (c) $f^{-1}(x) \in Re$ for $x \in Re$.

3. (a) $f(x) \in Re$.   (b) $f^{-1}(x) = \dfrac{2x+5}{3}$.   (c) $f^{-1}(x) \in Re$ for $x \in Re$.

4. (a) $f(x) \in Re, f(x) \geq 0$. (b) $f^{-1}(x) = \sqrt{x^2 + 16}$.
  (c) $f^{-1}(x) \in Re, f^{-1}(x) \geq 4$ for $x \in Re, x \geq 0$.

5. (a) $f(x) \in Re - \{0\}$. (b) $f^{-1}(x) = 1 - \dfrac{1}{x}$.
  (c) $f^{-1}(x) \in Re$ for $x \in Re, x \neq 0$; $f^{-1}(x) \neq 1$.

6. (a) $f(x) \in Re, f(x) \geq 0$. (b) $f^{-1}(x) = 3 + \sqrt{x}$.
  (c) $f^{-1}(x) \in Re, f^{-1}(x) \geq 3$ for $x \in Re, x \geq 0$.

7. (a) $f(x) \in Re^{+} \cup \{0\}$. (b) $f^{-1}(x) = \sqrt{x+3}$.
  (c) for $x \in Re, x \geq 0, f^{-}(x) \in Re, f^{-1}(x) \geq \sqrt{3}$.

8. Range $\{f(x) \mid f(x) \in Re, f(x) \geq -4\}$. **9.** Range $\{g(x) \mid g(x) \in Re, g(x) \leq 27\}$.

10. Range $\{h(x) \mid 0 \leq h(x) \leq 9\}$.   **11.** (8) Yes. (9) Yes. (10) No.

12. (2) $1 - 1$.   (3) $1 - 1$.   (4) Not $1 - 1$.   (5) $1 - 1$.   (6) Not $1 - 1$.
  (7) Not $1 - 1$.   (8) $1 - 1$.   (9) $1 - 1$.   (10) Not $1 - 1$.

13. Identical.   **15.** Both functions are identical with their inverses.

16. (a) $\{(x, y) \mid x^2 + y^2 = 25\}$ (b) $\{(x, y) \mid xy = 8\}$.

REVIEW EXERCISE 1 (page 22)

2. $A \cap B = \{3\}$ $A \cup B = \{1, 2, 3, 4, 5, 7\}$.

3. (a) -3. (b) -3. (c) $-\frac{9}{2}$. (d) $| |x| - 5 | - 5$. (e) $x^2 - 5$.
  (f) $|a - b| - 5 = b - a - 5$.

4. (a) $\{x \mid x \in Re\}$ $\{f(x) \mid f(x) \in Re, f(x) \geq -2\}$.
  (b) $\{x \mid x \in Re, x \neq 0\}$ $\{f(x) \mid f(x) \in Re\}$.
  (c) $\{x \mid x \in Re, x \geq 0\}$ $\{f(x) \mid f(x) \in Re, f(x) \geq 0\}$.
  (d) $\{x \mid x \in Re\}$ $\{f(x) \mid f(x) \in Re, f(x) \geq 1\}$.
  (e) $\{x \mid x \in Re\}$ $\{f(x) \mid f(x) \leq 0\}$.
  (f) $\{x \mid x \in Re\}$ $\{f(x) \mid 0 \leq f(x) \leq \frac{1}{5}\}$.

8. (a) 2. (b) 2. (c) 5. (d) $\sqrt[3]{16}$. (e) 1. (f) 5.

9. $B^{-1} = \{(3, 2), (4, 7), (5, 8)\}$. B^{-1} is a function.

10. (a) $|y| \leq 6$. (b) $7 \leq y \leq 119$.   **11.** (a) Yes. (b) No.   **13.** $8, -6$.

16. Domain of $t : x \in Re$. Range of $t : y \in Re, y \geq -11$. $t^{-1} : x \rightarrow t + \sqrt{11} - x$.
  Domain $\{x \mid x \in Re, x \leq 11\}$. Range of $t : y \in Re, y \geq 6$.

17. (b) $\{x \mid x \in Re\}$ $\{f \mid f \in Re, 0 < f \leq 1\}$.
  (d) $\{x \mid x \in Re, x \neq 0\}$ $\{f \mid f \in Re\}$.   (e) No.

19. The second inclusion is proper for $f : Re \rightarrow Re, f(x) = x^2$,
  $A = \{x \mid 10 \leq x \leq 3\}, B = \{x \mid 1 \leq x \leq 5\}$.

20. The first inclusion is proper for $f : Re \rightarrow Re, f(x) = x^2, D = \{x \mid 0 \leq x \leq 1\}$.
  The second inclusion is proper for $f : Re \rightarrow Re, f(x) = x^2, H = \{1, -1\}$.

Chapter 2

EXERCISE 2.1 (page 30)

1. (a) $x^2 + y^2 = 16$.   (b) $25x^2 + 25y^2 = 9$.   (c) $x^2 + y^2 = 8$.
   (d) $3x^2 + 3y^2 = 1$.   (e) $16x^2 + 16y^2 = 7$.

2. (a) $x^2 + y^2 = 169$.   (b) $x^2 + y^2 = 5$.   (c) $x^2 + y^2 = 27$.
   (d) $x^2 + y^2 = 29$.   (e) $x^2 + y^2 = 41$.   (f) $x^2 + y^2 = 100$.

3. (a) 7.   (b) $2\sqrt{3}$.   (c) $\frac{9}{2}$.   (d) $\dfrac{3\sqrt{2}}{5}$.

4. (a) $(0, \pm 2)$; $(\pm 2, 0)$; $-2 \le x \le 2$; $-2 \le y \le 2$.

    (b) $\left(0, \pm\dfrac{\sqrt{3}}{3}\right)$; $\left(\pm\dfrac{\sqrt{3}}{3}, 0\right)$; $-\frac{1}{3}\sqrt{3} \le x \le \frac{1}{3}\sqrt{3}$; $-\frac{1}{3}\sqrt{3} \le y \le \frac{1}{3}\sqrt{3}$.

    (c) $(0, \pm\frac{8}{5})$; $(\pm\frac{8}{5}, 0)$; $-\frac{8}{5} \le x \le \frac{8}{5}$; $-\frac{8}{5} \le y \le \frac{8}{5}$.

    (d) $(0, \pm\sqrt{6})$; $(\pm\sqrt{6}, 0)$; $-\sqrt{6} \le x \le \sqrt{6}$; $-\sqrt{6} \le y \le \sqrt{6}$.

5. (a) x-axis, y-axis, origin.   (b) y-axis.   (c) Origin.
   (d) None.   (e) x-axis.   (f) x-axis, y-axis, origin.
   (g) y-axis.   (h) Origin.

6. (a) On. (b) Inside. (c) On. (d) On. (e) On. (f) Outside.

	x-intercept	y-intercept	Domain	Range	Symmetry
9. (a)	$(\pm 4, 0)$	None	$1 < \lvert x \rvert \le 4$	$\lvert y \rvert \le 4$	x-axis, y-axis, origin.
(b)	$\pm\sqrt{5}$	$-1, +5$	$\lvert x \rvert \le 3$	$-1 \le y \le 5$	y-axis.
(c)	$-4, 2$	$\pm 2\sqrt{2}$	$-4 \le x \le 2$	$\lvert y \rvert \le 3$	x-axis.

EXERCISE 2.2 (page 32)

1. $3\sqrt{2}$.   2. $x^2 + y^2 = 25$.

	Length of chord	Equation of chord
3. (a)	6	$y = 4$
(b)	$4\sqrt{5}$	$x + 2y = 5$
(c)	4.14	$8x - 10y = -41$
(d)	No solution.	

4. The point $(5, 6)$ is outside the circle.

5. (a) 6. (b) $\sqrt{71}$. (c) $\sqrt{55}$. (d) $4\sqrt{22}$. (e) No solution.

6. Point $(3, 4)$ is inside the circle.   7. $\sqrt{x_1^2 + y_1^2 - r^2}$; $x_1^2 + y_1^2 - r^2 \ge 0$.

10. $x^2 + y^2 - 4x - 2y = 20$.   11. $2\sqrt{15}$.

EXERCISE 2.3 (page 35)

	x-intercept	y-intercept	Domain	Range	Symmetry
1.	0	0	$x \in Re$	$y \le 0$	y-axis
2.	0	0	$x \in Re$	$y \ge 0$	y-axis
3.	0	0	$x \in Re$	$y \ge 0$	y-axis
4.	0	0	$x \in Re$	$y \ge 0$	y-axis
5.	0	0	$x \in Re$	$y \le 0$	y-axis
6.	0	0	$x \in Re$	$y \ge 0$	y-axis

13. $k = 8$.   **14.** y-axis.   **16.** $y + 5 = 3(x - 2)^2$.   **17.** $y - 2 = -4(x + 3)^2$.

18. The graph changes from a straight line for $a = 0$ to a parabola for $a > 0$; as a increases the parabola becomes "narrower." As $a \to \infty$, the graph approaches (but never becomes) that of the upper half of the y-axis.

EXERCISE 2.4   (page 40)

	x-intercepts	y-intercepts	Domain	Range	Symmetry
1.	± 5	± 4	$\lvert x \rvert \leq 5$	$\lvert y \rvert \leq 4$	x-axis, y-axis, origin.
2.	± 5	$\pm 2\sqrt{3}$	$\lvert x \rvert \leq 5$	$\lvert y \rvert \leq 2\sqrt{3}$	x-axis, y-axis, origin.
3.	± 3	± 1	$\lvert x \rvert \leq 3$	$\lvert y \rvert \leq 1$	x-axis, y-axis, origin.
4.	$\pm 2\sqrt{5}$	$\pm 2\sqrt{2}$	$\lvert x \rvert \leq 2\sqrt{5}$	$\lvert y \rvert \leq 2\sqrt{2}$	x-axis, y-axis, origin.
5.	$\pm \sqrt{3}$	± 1	$\lvert x \rvert \leq \sqrt{3}$	$\lvert y \rvert \leq 1$	x-axis, y-axis, origin.
6.	± 8	± 3	$\lvert x \rvert \leq 8$	$\lvert y \rvert \leq 3$	x-axis, y-axis, origin.

7. (a)

	1	2	3	4	5	6
Semi-major	5	5	3	$2\sqrt{5}$	$\sqrt{3}$	8
Semi-minor	4	$2\sqrt{3}$	1	$2\sqrt{2}$	1	3

(b) $(\pm 5, 0)$, $(\pm 5, 0)$, $(\pm 3, 0)$, $(\pm 2\sqrt{5}, 0)$, $(\pm \sqrt{3}, 0)$, $(\pm 8, 0)$
$(0, \pm 4)$, $(0, \pm 2\sqrt{3})$, $(0, \pm 1)$, $(0, \pm 2\sqrt{2})$, $(0, \pm 1)$, $(0, \pm 3)$.

14. $k = 2$.   **15.** Circle, $x^2 + y^2 = 16$.

16. (a) Inside.   **(b)** Outside.   **(c)** Inside.   **(d)** On.

EXERCISE 2.5   (page 44)

	x-intercepts	y-intercepts	Domain	Range	Symmetry
1.	± 5	---	$\lvert x \rvert \geq 5$	$y \in Re$	x-axis, y-axis, origin.
2.	± 2	---	$\lvert x \rvert \geq 2$	$y \in Re$	x-axis, y-axis, origin.
3.	± 2	---	$\lvert x \rvert \geq 2$	$y \in Re$	x-axis, y-axis, origin.
4.	$\pm 2\sqrt{5}$	---	$\lvert x \rvert \geq 2\sqrt{5}$	$y \in Re$	x-axis, y-axis, origin.
5.	$\pm \frac{1}{2}$	---	$\lvert x \rvert \geq \frac{1}{2}$	$y \in Re$	x-axis, y-axis, origin.
6.	± 5	---	$\lvert x \rvert \geq 5$	$y \in Re$	x-axis, y-axis, origin.

7.

	Semi-transverse	Semi-conjugate	Vertices
(1)	5	4	$(\pm 5, 0)$
(2)	2	5	$(\pm 2, 0)$
(3)	2	$2\sqrt{5}$	$(\pm 2, 0)$
(4)	$2\sqrt{5}$	7	$(\pm 2\sqrt{5}, 0)$
(5)	$\frac{1}{2}$	1	$(\pm \frac{1}{2}, 0)$
(6)	5	5	$(\pm 5, 0)$

8. The transverse and conjugate axes are equal in length.

15. $k = 1$.   **16.** Ellipse, hyperbola.

EXERCISE 2.6 (page 48)

11. $xy = \dfrac{a^2}{2}$ is a rotation of the graph of $x^2 - y^2 = a^2$ through $\dfrac{\pi}{4}$ radians.

19. First draw the asymptotes and then sketch the hyperbola so that the asymptotes are the limiting cases of the hyperbola.

REVIEW EXERCISE 2 (page 49)

1. (a) $x^2 + y^2 = 100$.   (b) $81x^2 + 81y^2 = 16$.
   (c) $x^2 + y^2 = 5$.   (d) $9x^2 + 9y^2 = 13$.
2. (a) $x^2 + y^2 = 100$.   (b) $x^2 + y^2 = 29$.   (c) $x^2 + y^2 = 18$.
3. (a) $\frac{5}{2}$ (b) $2\sqrt{7}$.   (c) $\sqrt{\frac{35}{6}}$.   (d) $\dfrac{\sqrt{2}}{10}$.
4. (a) x-axis, y-axis, origin.   (b) x-axis, y-axis, origin.
   (c) y-axis.   (d) Origin.   (e) Origin.   (f) y-axis.
   (g) y-axis.   (h) x-axis, y-axis, origin.
27. $k = 3$.   28. $k = 16$.   29. $k = 4$.   30. $k = \frac{18}{5}$.
32. (a) $5 < m < 30$.   (b) $m > 30$ or $m < 5$.

Chapter 3

EXERCISE 3.1 (page 53)

1. (a) $x^2 + y^2 = 0$, conic degenerates to single point (origin). (b) Division by zero is not defined.   4. $x = \dfrac{a}{e}$; 2 directrices possible in each case.

EXERCISE 3.2 (page 56)

1. $(0, 2), y = -2, \frac{1}{2}$.   2. $(0, \frac{3}{5}), y = -\frac{3}{5}, \frac{5}{3}$.   3. $(0, -\frac{15}{16}), y = \frac{15}{16}, -\frac{16}{15}$.
4. $(0, -.01), y = .01, -100$.   5. $x^2 = -16y$.   6. $x^2 = -20y$.
7. $x^2 = 12y$.   8. $x^2 = 30y$.   9. 1.   10. $-\frac{1}{4}$.
11. -1.   12. -1.   15. $(5, 0), (x + 5) = 0, \frac{5}{4}$.   16. $(-\frac{15}{6}, 0). \; x = \frac{15}{16}, -\frac{20}{3}$.
17. $(-\frac{1}{32}, 0); x = \frac{1}{32}; -200$.   18. $(\frac{5}{8}, 0); x = -\frac{5}{8}; 10$.
19. $y^2 = -40x$.   20. $y^2 = -\frac{4}{3}x$.   21. $y^2 = \frac{28}{5}x$.
22. $y^2 = -\frac{5}{2}x$.   23. $-\frac{1}{2}$.   24. $-\frac{1}{2}$.
25. $\frac{1}{2}$.   26. $-\frac{1}{128}$.   27. $(3, 0); y^2 = 12$.
28. $(0, -\frac{12}{7}); x^2 = -\frac{48}{7}y$.   30. $y^2 - 4y = 16x - 20$.   31. $y^2 = -4px + 4p^2$.

EXERCISE 3.3 (page 60)

1. $(\pm 3, 0); x = \pm\frac{25}{3}; \frac{3}{5}$ 2. $(\pm 3\sqrt{3}, 0); x = \pm\,4\sqrt{3}; \frac{1}{2}\sqrt{3}$

3. $(\pm 2, 0); x = \pm 10; \frac{1}{5}\sqrt{5}$ 4. $(\pm\sqrt{2}, 0); x = \pm\dfrac{5\sqrt{2}}{2}; \frac{1}{5}\sqrt{10}$

5. $\dfrac{x^2}{100} + \dfrac{y^2}{75} = 1$ 6. $\dfrac{x^2}{36} + \dfrac{y^2}{32} = 1$ 7. $\dfrac{x^2}{25} + \dfrac{y^2}{16} = 1$

8. $\dfrac{x^2}{49} + \dfrac{16y^2}{343} = 1$ 9. $\dfrac{x^2}{16} + \dfrac{25y^2}{336} = 1$

10. $\dfrac{(x-1)^2}{16} + \dfrac{(y-1)^2}{15} = 1$

EXERCISE 3.4 (page 63)

1. $(\pm 2\sqrt{23},0)$; $x = \pm\dfrac{32\sqrt{23}}{23}$; $\tfrac{1}{4}\sqrt{23}$ 2. $(\pm 5,0)$; $x = \pm\tfrac{9}{5}$; $\tfrac{5}{3}$

3. $(\pm\sqrt{10},0)$; $x = \pm\tfrac{9}{10}\sqrt{10}$; $\tfrac{1}{3}\sqrt{10}$ 4. $(\pm 3,0)$; $x = \pm\tfrac{5}{3}$; $\tfrac{3}{5}\sqrt{5}$

5. $\dfrac{x^2}{9} - \dfrac{y^2}{16} = 1$ 6. $\dfrac{x^2}{4} - \dfrac{4y^2}{9} = 1$ 7. $\dfrac{4x^2}{169} - \dfrac{4y^2}{507} = 1$

8. $\dfrac{4x^2}{49} - \dfrac{y^2}{18} = 1$ 9. 231   10. 8   11. 3   12. $\tfrac{5}{13}$

13. $\dfrac{x^2}{2} - \dfrac{y^2}{2} = 1$ 14. $\dfrac{20(x + \frac{15}{4})^2}{405} - \dfrac{16(y + 4)^2}{405} = 1$

EXERCISE 3.5 (page 67)

1. (a) $\dfrac{x^2}{25} + \dfrac{y^2}{9} = 1$.   (b) $\dfrac{x^2}{64} + \dfrac{y^2}{28} = 1$.   (c) $\dfrac{x^2}{49} + \dfrac{y^2}{13} = 1$.

   (d) $\dfrac{x^2}{676} + \dfrac{y^2}{144} = 1$.

2. (a) $\dfrac{x^2}{36} - \dfrac{y^2}{9} = 1$.   (b) $\dfrac{x^2}{16} - \dfrac{y^2}{9} = 1$.   (c) $\dfrac{x^2}{64} - \dfrac{y^2}{36} = 1$.

   (d) $\dfrac{x^2}{27} - \dfrac{y^2}{9} = 1$.

3. $\dfrac{x^2}{169} + \dfrac{y^2}{25} = 1$.   4. $\dfrac{x^2}{49} + \dfrac{y^2}{16} = 1$.   5. $\dfrac{3x^2}{35} + \dfrac{2y^2}{35} = 1$.

6. $\dfrac{x^2}{27} + \dfrac{y^2}{18} = 1$.

7. $\dfrac{x^2}{36} - \dfrac{y^2}{64} = 1$.   8. $\dfrac{x^2}{14} - \dfrac{y^2}{22} = 1$.   9. $\dfrac{x^2}{24} - \dfrac{y^2}{96} = 1$.

10. $\dfrac{x^2}{10} - \dfrac{3y^2}{20} = 1$.

	11.	12.	13.	14.	15.	16.
Semi-transverse	3	4	$4\sqrt{2}$	13	4	$\tfrac{1}{8}$
Semi-conjugate	5	2	$4\sqrt{2}$	5	$\sqrt{3}$	$\tfrac{1}{12}$
Foci	$(\pm\sqrt{34}, 0)$	$(\pm 2\sqrt{3},0)$	$(\pm 8, 0)$	$(\pm 12, 0)$	$(\pm\sqrt{19}, 0)$	$\left(\pm\dfrac{\sqrt{5}}{24}, 0\right)$
Eccentricity	$\dfrac{\sqrt{34}}{3}$	$\dfrac{\sqrt{3}}{2}$	$\sqrt{2}$	$\dfrac{\sqrt{12}}{13}$	$\dfrac{\sqrt{19}}{4}$	$\dfrac{\sqrt{5}}{3}$

18. $\dfrac{x^2}{73} + \dfrac{16y^2}{73} = 1$.   19. $\dfrac{x^2}{25} + \dfrac{y^2}{9} = 1$.   20. $3x^2 + 4y^2 = 8x + 8y - 8$.

21. $\dfrac{x^2}{9} - \dfrac{y^2}{4} = 1$.   22. $4x^2 - y^2 = 100$.   23. $\dfrac{x^2}{3025} - \dfrac{y^2}{86975} = 1$.

25. $\dfrac{x^2}{5625} - \dfrac{y^2}{34375} = 1$.

EXERCISE 3.6 (page 73)

Vertices	Foci	Eccentricity
1. $(0, \pm 5)$	$(0, \pm\sqrt{21})$	$\dfrac{\sqrt{21}}{5}$
2. $(0, \pm 3)$	$(0, \pm 2\sqrt{2})$	$\dfrac{2\sqrt{2}}{3}$
3. $(0, \pm 2)$	$(0, \pm 1)$	$\frac{1}{2}$
4. $(0, \pm\frac{1}{4})$	$\left(0, \pm\dfrac{\sqrt{65}}{36}\right)$	$\dfrac{\sqrt{65}}{9}$

5. $\dfrac{x^2}{9} + \dfrac{y^2}{25} = 1.$ 6. $\dfrac{x^2}{288} + \dfrac{y^2}{324} = 1.$ 7. $\dfrac{x^2}{24} + \dfrac{y^2}{25} = 1.$

8. $\dfrac{x^2}{289} + \dfrac{y^2}{64} = 1.$ 9. $\dfrac{x^2}{32} + \dfrac{7y^2}{128} = 1.$ 10. $\dfrac{3x^2}{35} + \dfrac{2y^2}{35} = 1.$

11. $(0, \pm 5)$; $(0, \pm\sqrt{34})$; $\frac{1}{5}\sqrt{34}$. 12. $(0, \pm 2)$; $(0, \pm\sqrt{13})$; $\dfrac{\sqrt{13}}{2}$.

13. $(0, \pm 2)$; $(0, \pm 2\sqrt{2})$; $\sqrt{2}$. 14. $(0, \pm\sqrt{3})$; $(0, \pm 2\sqrt{3})$; 2.

15. $\dfrac{y^2}{9} - \dfrac{x^2}{16} = 1.$ 16. $\dfrac{y^2}{16} - \dfrac{x^2}{20} = 1.$ 17. $\dfrac{y^2}{18} - \dfrac{x^2}{16} = 1.$

18. $\dfrac{y^2}{12} - \dfrac{x^2}{12} = 1.$ 19. $\dfrac{x^2}{24} - \dfrac{y^2}{96} = 1.$ 20. $\dfrac{255y^2}{503} - \dfrac{112x^2}{503} = 1.$

25. $\dfrac{x^2}{12} + \dfrac{y^2}{16} = 1.$ 26. $\dfrac{9y^2}{400} - \dfrac{9x^2}{500} = 1.$ 29. 22 feet.

EXERCISE 3.7 (page 77)

1. $(0, 0)$, $(4, 4)$. 2. $(\frac{1}{2}, 2)$, $(8, -8)$. 3. $(6, 1)$, $(2, 3)$.

4. $(\pm\sqrt{\frac{45}{23}}, \pm\sqrt{\frac{72}{23}})$. 5. $(\pm 3, -\frac{16}{5})$. 6. None.

7. $(1, 1)$, $(-3, 5)$. 8. $(5.53, \pm 6.65)$, $(.87, \pm 2.64)$ 19. $(\pm 4, \pm 4)$, 64.

20. $\dfrac{x^2}{144} + \dfrac{y^2}{16} = 1.$ 21. $\frac{1}{2}\sqrt{2}$. 22. $\dfrac{x^2}{a^2} + \dfrac{y^2}{b^2} = \dfrac{x}{a}.$

23. (a) $X = \dfrac{x_1 + x_2}{2}, Y = \dfrac{y_1 + y_2}{2}.$ (d) $9y + 32x = 0.$

EXERCISE 3.8 (page 81)

1. $3x - 4y = 25.$ 2. $x\sqrt{2} = y + 4.$ 3. $-8x + y = 10.$

4. $4x - y = 15.$ 5. $y = -\frac{1}{2}x \pm \sqrt{5}.$ 6. $y = -\frac{3}{4}x + 4.$

7. $y = \frac{1}{3}x \pm \frac{11}{3}.$ 8. $y = 2x \pm \frac{1}{2}.$

9. $y = -3x + 10$; $y = \frac{1}{3}x - \frac{10}{3}.$ 10. $y = 5x - 25$; $x + y + 1 = 0.$

11. $y = -1$; $x = 2.$ 12. $y = 2x - 1$; $y = \frac{7}{4}x - \frac{1}{4}.$

13. $k = \pm 7.$ 17. $\left(-\dfrac{3}{26}\sqrt{65}, \dfrac{4\sqrt{195}}{78}\right), \left(\dfrac{3}{26}\sqrt{65}, \dfrac{-4\sqrt{195}}{78}\right).$

21. (a) $(3, 1)$, $(1, -3)$. (b) $y = 2x - 5.$ (d) $x_1 x + y_1 y = r^2.$

22. (a) $k^2 - 8k + 4 = 0.$ (b) $k_1 + k_2 = 8$, $k_1 k_2 = 4.$

23. (b) $(\frac{2}{3}, -2)$.   **26.** (a) $3y + 2x = 0$.   (b) $(3, -2), (-3, 2)$.

30. The second theorem implies the first.

EXERCISE 3.9   (page 86)

1. $3y = \pm 2x$.   **2.** $x = \pm y$.   **3.** $7x = \pm y$.   **4.** $x = \pm y$.

5. $\sqrt{14}x = \pm 5y$.   **6.** $12x = \pm 5y$.   **10.** $x = \pm y$.

13. $xy = -32; x = 0, y = 0$.   **14.** $16x^2 - 25y^2 = 39$.

REVIEW EXERCISE 3   (page 88)

1. $(0, \frac{2}{3}); y = -\frac{2}{3}; \pm\frac{4}{3}\sqrt{3}$.   **2.** $(\frac{3}{8}, 0); x = -\frac{3}{8}; \frac{8}{3}$.

3. $(0, \frac{15}{16}); y = -\frac{15}{16}; \pm\frac{1}{2}\sqrt{30}$.   **4.** $(-\frac{7}{6}, 0); x = \frac{7}{6}, -\frac{6}{7}$.

5. $x^2 = -20y$.   **6.** $\dfrac{x^2}{40} + \dfrac{y^2}{24} = 1$.   **7.** $\dfrac{x^2}{100} + \dfrac{y^2}{84} = 1$.

8. $x^2 + \frac{64}{39}y^2 = 25$.   **9.** $\dfrac{x^2}{16} - \dfrac{y^2}{9} = -1$.   **10.** $\dfrac{x^2}{15} - y^2 = -64$.

11. $x^2 - y^2 = -\frac{9}{8}$.   **12.** $\dfrac{x^2}{25} + \dfrac{y^2}{16} = 1$.   **13.** $\dfrac{x^2}{200} - \dfrac{y^2}{25} = -1$.

14. $\dfrac{y^2}{25} + \dfrac{64x^2}{975} = 1$.   **15.** $\dfrac{16x^2}{799} - \dfrac{16y^2}{225} = -1$.   **16.** $\dfrac{x^2}{10} - \dfrac{3y^2}{20} = 1$.

17. $\dfrac{x^2}{4} + \dfrac{y^2}{16} = 1$.   **18.** $\dfrac{x^2}{50} - \dfrac{y^2}{50} = -1$.   **24.** $2x + 3y = 13$.

25. $y = 2x - 2$.   **26.** $(8, 8)$.   **27.** $k = -\frac{5}{4}$.

28. $y = \frac{3}{4}x, y = \frac{5}{4}x - 8$.   **29.** $3x^2 = 4000y$.

31. $y = mx - pm^2$.   **32.** $y = \frac{1}{2}x - \frac{1}{6}$.   **33.** k^2.

34. $y = -\frac{1}{2}x - 2$.   **35.** (a) $X = \frac{1}{2}(x_1 + x_2)$ $Y = \frac{1}{2}(y_1 + y_2)$.
(c) $y = \frac{3}{40}x$.

36. (d) $(-30, 10)$.

37. (a) $5x = \pm 4y$.   (b) $6x = \pm y$.   (c) $x = \pm y$.
(d) $x\sqrt{5} = \pm y$.   (e) $9x = \pm 13y$.   (f) $x = 0; y = 0$.

38. $9x^2 - 64y^2 = 65$.

Chapter 4

EXERCISE 4.1   (page 99)

1. (a) $(4, -3), (-3, 5), (-1, -3), (4, 4)$.
(b) $(1, -1), (-6, 7), (-4, -1), (1, 6)$.
(c) $(6, -7), (-1, 1), (1, -7), (6, 0)$.
(d) $(0, -10), (-7, -2), (-5, -10), (0, -3)$.

2. (a) $(-3, 0), (-1, 3), (1, 6), (5, 12)$.
(b) $(-4, -4), (-2, -1), (0, 2), (4, 9)$.
(c) $(0, -4), (2, -1), (4, 2), (8, 8)$.
(d) $(2, 5), (4, 8), (6, 11), (10, 17)$.

3. (a) $(-1, -3)$, $(0, 0)$, $(-6, 1)$, $(-7, -2)$.
(b) $(6, -1)$, $(7, 2)$, $(1, 3)$, $(0, 0)$.
4. (a) $(0, 0)$, $(-3, 2)$, $(-2, -4)$.
(b) $(2, 4)$, $(-1, 6)$, $(0, 0)$.

EXERCISE 4.2 (page 103)

1. $AB = 4$, $BC = 3$, $CA = 5$.   **2.** Slope $AC = \frac{3}{4}$.

EXERCISE 4.3 (page 109)

1. $v = 3u + 7$.   **2.** $v = -2u + 5$.   **3.** $v = 4u$.   **4.** $v = 2u$.
5. $v = -u$.   **6.** $2v = 3u$.   **7.** $2v = 3u$.   **8.** $v = 4 - u$.
9. $v = 2 - u$.   **10.** $v = 2u$.   **11.** $h = 0$, $k = -3$ or $h = \frac{3}{2}$, $k = 0$.
12. $h = 0$, $k = 1$ or $h = 1$, $k = 5$.   **13.** $h = 1$, $k = 6$ or $h = -1$, $k = 1$.
14. $h = -1$, $k = 1$ or $h = 2$, $k = -3$. **15.** $h = -1$, $k = 1$ or $h = -5$, $k = -5$.
16. $h = -2$, $k = 0$ or $h = 1$, $k = 2$.   **17.** $h = 0$, $k = -3$ or $h = -2$, $k = 0$.
18. $h = 0$, $k = -\dfrac{3}{\pi}$ or $h = \dfrac{3}{\sqrt{2}}$, $k = 0$.   **19.** No.   **20.** Yes.

21. (a) $u + 2v < 5$; yes.   (b) $3u + 2v < 16$; yes.

22. The property of being above, below, to the right of, or to the left of a line is invariant under a translation.

23. (a) $x > 1$, $y < -1$.   (b) $3y - 2x \le 33$, $2x - y < -11$.
(c) $y - x < 3$, $x + 2y > -9$, $3x + 2y < -15$.

EXERCISE 4.4 (page 113)

1. $(0, 0) \to (-\frac{3}{2}, -\frac{3}{2})$ $(3, 0) \to (\frac{3}{2}, -\frac{3}{2})$.
$(0, 3) \to (-\frac{3}{2}, \frac{3}{2})$ $(3 ,3) \to (\frac{3}{2}, \frac{3}{2})$.
3. Centre is $(3, -4)$.   Centre in $v - u$ plane is $(0, 0)$ $(x, y) \to (x - 3, y + 4)$
$= u, v$.
4. $(x, y) \to (x - 3, y + 2) = (u, v)$; $u^2 + v^2 = 1$.
5. $(x, y) \to (x - 2, y - 3) = (u, v)$; $u^2 + v^2 = 31$.
6. $(x, y) \to (x + 3, y - 4) = (u, v)$; $u^2 + v^2 = 49$.
7. $(x, y) \to (x - 12, y - 5) = (u, v)$; $u^2 + v^2 = 169$.
8. $(x, y) \to (x + 2\sqrt{2}, y + 1) = (u, v)$; $u^2 + v^2 = 9$.
9. $(x, y) \to (x - 1), y - 3) = (u, v)$.

EXERCISE 4.5 (page 117)

	Curve	Image
1.	Parabola	$y^2 - 4x = 0$.
2.	Hyperbola	$y^2 - 2x^2 = \frac{17}{2}$.
3.	Pair of straight lines	$x^2 - 4y^2 = 0$.

4. Ellipse $\qquad\qquad 2x^2 + 3y^2 = 6.$

5. Hyperbola $\qquad\qquad 9x^2 - 4y^2 = 118.$

6. Pair of straight lines $\quad 3x^2 - y^2 = 0.$

7. Parabola $\qquad\qquad x^2 = y.$

8. Ellipse $\qquad\qquad x^2 + 4y^2 = 54.$

9. Ellipse $\qquad\qquad 4x^2 + 9y^2 = 36.$

10. Hyperbola $\qquad\qquad 9y^2 - 4x^2 = 13.$

EXERCISE 4.6 (page 119)

Translation	Curve
1. $(x, y) \to (x + 1, y - 2)$	Parabola.
2. $(x, y) \to (x + 4, y + \frac{77}{4})$	Parabola.
3. $(x, y) \to (x - 2, y - 4)$	Parabola.
4. $(x, y) \to (x - 3, y + \frac{1}{4})$	Parabola.
5. $(x, y) \to (x + 6, y - 2)$	Hyperbola.
6. $(x, y) \to (x + 2, y + \frac{3}{4})$	Ellipse.
7. $(x, y) \to (x + \frac{3}{2}, y - 5)$	Ellipse.
8. $(x, y) \to (x + 4, y + 7)$	Hyperbola.
9. $(x, y) \to (x + 2, y - 3)$	Ellipse.
10. $(x, y) \to (x - 1, y - 4)$	Hyperbola.

11. (i) $ab = 0 \Rightarrow$ straight line or parabola. (ii) $ab > 0 \Rightarrow$ ellipse.

(iii) $ab < 0 \Rightarrow$ hyperbola. **12.** $h = \dfrac{g}{a}, \; k = \dfrac{f}{b}.$

REVIEW EXERCISE 4 (page 120)

1. $A'(4, 2), B'(3, -3), C'(-1, -23).$

2. Triangle. $A'(-1, 2), B'(-4, -2), C'(2, -2).$

3. $A'(0, 0), B'(-1, 1 - \sqrt{3}), C'(3, -2\sqrt{3}).$

5. $3v = 2u - 30.$

6. $h = -\frac{3}{4}, k = 0$ **7.** $h = -2, k = -1$ **8.** $h = 0, = k \; -4.$

9. $h = 0, k = -1.$

10. $3u - 5v < 14.$

11. (b) $3v < u + 10$; yes.

12. $4u^2 - 24u + 4v^2 + 16v + 27 = 0.$

13. $(x, y) \to (x - 5, y + 3); \; x^2 + y^2 = 12.$

14. $(x, y) \to (x - \frac{1}{2}, y + \frac{3}{2}); \; 4x^2 + 4y^2 = 25.$

15. $4x^2 - 9y^2 = 36;$ hyperbola with foci on x-axis.

16. $x^2 + 4y^2 = \frac{25}{4};$ ellipse with foci on x-axis.

17. $(x, y) \to (x + 3, y - 4);$ parabola opening to the left.

18. $(x, y) \to (x - 5, y - 1);$ ellipse with foci on x-axis.

19. $(x, y) \to (x - 3, y + 5);$ ellipse with foci on y-axis.

20. $(x, y) \to (x - 1, y + 2);$ ellipse with foci on y-axis.

21. $(x, y) \to (x - \frac{3}{2}, y + \frac{1}{2});$ parabola opening upwards.

Chapter 5

EXERCISE 5.1   (page 127)

1. (a) $(3, -2)$, $(7, -3)$, $(4, 0)$.   (d) $y = 0$.
2. (a) $A'(-3, -5)$, $B'(-1, -2)$, $C'(-8, -1)$.
3. (a) $A'(2, 8)$, $B'(2, 2)$, $C'(-1, 2)$.   (b) $x = 3$.
4. (a) $M'(0, 1)$, $N'(1, 2)$, $P'(4, 7)$.   (b) $x = y$.
5. (a) $A'(1, -9)$, $B'(3, -6)$, $C'(5, -3)$, $A''(-1, -9)$, $B''(-3, -6)$, $C''(-5, -3)$.
(c) $x = 0$, $y = 0$.   (d) $(x, y) \rightarrow (-x, -y)$.
6. (a) $A''(-3, -9)$, $B''(-5, -6)$, $C''(-7, -3)$.   (b) $x = -1$.
(c) $(x, y) \rightarrow (-x - 2, -y)$.   (d) Point is $(-1, 0)$.
7. (a) $V(W(3, 1)) = (-2, -4)$, $V(W(-6, -1)) = (7, -2)$,
$V(W(2, -4)) = (-1, 1)$, $W(V(3, 1)) = (-4, 2)$, $W(V(-6, -1)) = (5, 4)$,
$W(V(2, -4)) = (-3, 7)$.

EXERCISE 5.2   (page 132)

1. $R_1 : -2x + 3y = -6$. $R_2 : +2x + 3y = +6$.   **2.** Image: $(-2, \frac{7}{3}) \rightarrow (2, -\frac{7}{3})$.
3. Image: $x^2 + y^2 + 10y = 0$.   **4.** $-2x + 3y < -6$.
5. $x^2 + y^2 \leq 16$, $3x - 5y \geq 15$.   **6.** $x + y < -2$, $x + y > -6$.
7. (a) (i) $x^2 - y^2 = 16$. (ii) $x^2 - y^2 = 16$. (iii) $x^2 - y^2 = 16$.
(b) (i) $xy = -8$. (ii) $xy = -8$. (iii) $xy = 8$.   (c) Two hyperbolas.
8. $\dfrac{(x - 4)^2}{16} + \dfrac{y^2}{9} = 1$.   **9.** (a) $y^2 = -4x$.   (c) $x = 1$.
10. $R_1 : \dfrac{(y - 12)^2}{144} + \dfrac{x^2}{25} = 1$. $R_2 : \dfrac{(x + 12)^2}{144} + \dfrac{y^2}{25} = 1$.   **11.** $y = \dfrac{-6}{x^2 + 2}$.
12. $y < \dfrac{-6}{x^2 + 2}$, $x^2 + y^2 < 9$.

EXERCISE 5.3   (page 137)

1. (a) $A'(4, 4)$, $B'(-4, 4)$, $C'(-4, -4)$, $D'(4, -4)$.
2. (a) $A'(28, 36)$, $B'(20, 36)$, $C'(20, 28)$, $D'(28, 28)$.
3. (a) $A'(2, \frac{1}{2})$, $B'(-2, \frac{1}{2})$, $C'(-2, -\frac{1}{2})$, $D'(2, -\frac{1}{2})$.   (c) Rectangle.
4. (a) $A'(\sqrt{3}, 0)$, $B'(-\sqrt{3}, 0)$, $C'(0, -3)$.
5. (a) $A'(2, 0)$. $B'(-2, 0)$, $C'\left(0, -\dfrac{\sqrt{3}}{3}\right)$.
6. $M'(6, 6)$, $O'(0, 0)$, $N'(-9, 9)$, $P'(-9, -6)$, $Q'(6, -6)$.
7. (a) $M'(6, 4)$, $O'(0, 0)$, $N'(-9, 6)$, $P'(-9, -4)$, $Q'(6, -4)$.

EXERCISE 5.4   (page 142)

1. (a) $u + v + 2 = 0$. $2s + t + 4 = 0$.   **2.** (a) $u^2 + v^2 = 9$, $\dfrac{s^2}{9} + \dfrac{t^2}{25} = 1$.
3. $x^2 - 6x + y^2 + 18y = -9$, $(3, -9)$, $(3, -9)$.
4. (a) $4u^2 = -5v$.   (b) Original: $F(0, -\frac{1}{4})$. Image: $F(0, -\frac{5}{16})$.

5. $\dfrac{u^2}{49} + \dfrac{v^2}{49} = 1$ or $(u^2 + v^2 = 49)$.   **6.** $36x^2 + 36y^2 + 576x - 84y + 589 = 0$.

7. $D_1 \dfrac{u^2}{9} - \dfrac{v^2}{4} = 1$. $D_2\, m^2 - n^2 = 1$.

8. (a) $\dfrac{x^2}{25} - \dfrac{y^2}{49} = -1$.   (b) $\dfrac{x^2}{100} - y^2 = -1$.

9. (a) $\dfrac{x^2}{10} + \dfrac{y^2}{2} = 1$.   (b) Semi-major axis $\dfrac{\sqrt{5}}{2}$, semi-minor axis $\dfrac{\sqrt{5}}{5}$.

10. (b) $\dfrac{x^2}{3} - \dfrac{y^2}{2} = 1$.   (c) $e = \dfrac{\sqrt{15}}{3}$.   (d) Hyperbola. $e = \dfrac{\sqrt{13}}{3}$

11. $v = \dfrac{-5}{4u^2 + 1}$.

REVIEW EXERCISE 5   (page 145)

1. (a) $A'(-4, 1)$, $B'(-6, 5)$, $C'(-9, -1)$.
2. (a) $y = -|x|$.   (c) $(4, 4) \to (4, -4)$, $(0, 0) \to (0, 0)$, $(-2, 2) \to (-2, -2)$.
3. $P'(-1, -7)$, $(0, -5)$, $(6, -9)$ axis: $y = -1$.
4. $A'(-2, 1)$, $B'(-1, 3)$, $C'(-6, 5)$.
5. $x + y + 1 < 0$; $x - 5y - 5 > 0$; $x < 5$.   **6.** $4x^2 + y^2 \le 36$; $2x + y \le -6$.
7. $9x^2 - 16y^2 - 256y = 1168$, axis: $y = -4$.
9. $A'(0, 6)$, $B'(0, -6)$, $C'(9, -6)$, $D'(9, 6)$.
10. (a) $A'(0, 8)$, $B'(0, -8)$, $C'(3, -8)$, $D'(3, 8)$.
11. $A'(-9, 6)$, $B'(-9, -6)$, $C'(0, -6)$, $D'(0, 6)$.
12. $P'(15, 0)$, $Q'(15, -18)$, $R'(27, -9)$.   **13.** $P'(\tfrac{5}{2}, 0)$, $Q'(\tfrac{5}{2}, -2)$, $R'(\tfrac{9}{21}, -1)$.
14. $D_1: 4u^2 + 25v^2 = 25$. $D_2: u^2 + v^2 = 1$.   **15.** $u^2 - v^2 = -400$.
16. $4u^2 - 9v^2 = -25$.
17. $(x, y) \to \left(\dfrac{3x - y}{\sqrt{10}}, \dfrac{x + 3y}{\sqrt{10}}\right)$, $6x^2 + y^2 = 9$, ellipse with foci on y-axis, reflection is $11x^2 + 6xy + 3y^2 - 18 = 0$.

Chapter 6

EXERCISE 6.1   (page 152)

1. .74314.   **2.** −.17365.   **3.** .30573.   **4.** −.74314.
5. −.17365.   **6.** −.30573.   **7.** .26795.   **8.** .95106.
9. .98481.   **10.** .26795.   **11.** −.95106.   **12.** −.98481.
13. .29237.   **14.** −.45399.   **15.** −.70021.   **16.** −.81915.
17. .34202.   **18.** 2.7475.   **19.** $\tfrac{1}{2}$.   **20.** $\sqrt{2}$.   **21.** $\sqrt{3}$.
22. $\tfrac{1}{2}\sqrt{3}$.   **23.** $-\tfrac{1}{2}\sqrt{2}$.   **24.** $-\tfrac{1}{3}\sqrt{3}$.   **25.** $-\tfrac{2}{3}\sqrt{3}$.
26. $-\tfrac{1}{2}\sqrt{2}$.   **27.** $\tfrac{1}{2}\sqrt{3}$.   **28.** -1.   **29.** $-\tfrac{1}{2}\sqrt{3}$.
30. $-\tfrac{2}{3}\sqrt{3}$.   **31.** $\tfrac{1}{2}\sqrt{2}$.   **32.** $\sqrt{3}$.   **33.** 2.
34. $27°, 153°$.   **35.** $32°, 328°$.   **36.** $47°, 227°$.   **37.** $47°, 313°$.
38. $230°, 310°$.   **39.** $116°, 296°$.   **40.** $43°, 317°$.   **41.** $15°, 165°$.
42. $102°, 282°$.
45. (a) $-\tfrac{1}{2}\sqrt{3}$.   (b) −.64279.   (c) −.36397.   (d) −.17365.
   (e) $-\tfrac{1}{3}\sqrt{3}$.   (f) 5.7588.

EXERCISE 6.2 (page 158)

2. (a) 1. (b) $0°, 360°, -360°$. (c) -1. (d) $-180°, 180°$. (e) $-\dfrac{3\pi}{2}, -\dfrac{\pi}{2}, \dfrac{\pi}{2}, \dfrac{3\pi}{2}$.

4. (a) About lines $x = (k + \frac{1}{2})\pi, k \in I$.
   (b) About origin, and about lines $x = k\pi, k \in I$.

5. (a) $0°, 360°, 720°, 1080°$.　　(b) $-30°, 330°, 690°, 1050°$.
   (c) $45°, 405°, 765°, 1125°$.　　(d) $-90°, 270°, 630°, 990°$.

6. (a) $135°, 495°, 855°, 1215°$.　　(b) $60°, 420°, 780°, 1140°$.
   (c) $150°, 510°, 870°, 1230°$.　　(d) $140°, 500°, 860°, 1220°$.

7. (a) $\theta = 45°, 225°$.　　(b) $\theta = 135°, 315°$.　　(c) $\theta = 0°, 90°, 360°$.
   (d) No value.　　(e) No value.　　(f) $\theta = 0°, 270°, 360°$.

8. (a) 1. (b) 1.　　**9.** (a) 3. (b) k.

EXERCISE 6.3 (page 160)

2. (a) No maximum or minimum.
   (b) Domain: $\theta \in Re: \theta \neq \pi k, k \in I$.　Range: $\cot \theta \in Re$.
   (c) $\theta = (k + \frac{1}{2})\pi, k \in I$.　　(d) $180°$.　(e) $\theta = 45°, 225°, 405°, 585°$.

7. All values, and the amplitude, are 3 times as great.

8. All values, and the amplitude, are half as great.

9. The period is twice as great.

EXERCISE 6.4 (page 164)

4. (a) 2　　(b) $\frac{1}{2}$　　(c) 2π　　**5.** (a) $\frac{1}{2}\pi$　　(b) 6π　　(c) 2

9. (a) $4; \frac{2}{3}\pi; -\frac{1}{6}\pi$　　(b) $\frac{1}{3}; \pi; +\frac{1}{2}\pi$

REVIEW EXERCISE 6 (page 170)

1. (a) $\frac{5}{6}\pi$　　(b) $-\frac{11}{6}\pi$　　(c) $\frac{25}{6}\pi$　　(d) $-\frac{245}{36}\pi$　　(e) 20π
   (f) $\frac{5}{2}\pi$　　**2.** (a) $225°$　　(b) $-210°$　　(c) $2385°$　　(d) $-5400°$

3. (a) $-\dfrac{\sqrt{3}}{2}$　　(b) $+\frac{1}{2}$　　(c) $+\dfrac{1}{\sqrt{3}}$　　(d) $-\dfrac{1}{\sqrt{2}}$　　(e) undefined

   (f) $-\dfrac{2}{\sqrt{3}}$.

4. (a) $1, 2\pi, 0$　　(b) $2, \frac{2}{3}\pi, 0$　　(c) $\frac{5}{2}, \frac{2}{3}\pi, +\frac{1}{2}\pi$　　(d) $4, \frac{2}{3}\pi, -\frac{1}{6}\pi$
   (e) $4, \frac{2}{3}\pi, -\frac{1}{2}\pi$　　(f) $2, 4\pi, +2\pi$　　(g) $\frac{1}{3}, \frac{1}{2}\pi, +\frac{1}{3}\pi$
   (h) $5, \frac{1}{2}\pi, +\frac{1}{12}\pi$

10.

	Minimum	θ	Maximum	θ	
(a)	0	$\dfrac{\pi}{2}(3 + 4n)$	2	$\dfrac{\pi}{2}(1 + 4n)$	$n \in I$
(b)	-1	$\dfrac{2\pi(1 + n)}{5}$	5	$\dfrac{\pi(1 + 2n)}{5}$	
(c)	$\dfrac{1}{2}$	$\pi(1 + 2n)$	2	$2\pi n$	

(d)	.5403	πn	1	$\dfrac{\pi}{2}(1 + 2n)$
(e)	8.0806	$\dfrac{\pi}{2}(1 + 2n)$	9	πn

Chapter 7

EXERCISE 7.1   (page 177)

1. $\dfrac{\sqrt{2}}{4}(\sqrt{3} + 1).$ **2.** $\dfrac{\sqrt{2}}{4}(\sqrt{3} + 1).$ **3.** $-\tfrac{1}{2}.$ **4.** $2 - \sqrt{3}.$

5. $\dfrac{\sqrt{2}}{4}(\sqrt{3} - 1).$ **6.** $2 - \sqrt{3}.$ **7.** $\tfrac{1}{39}(10 + 12\sqrt{5}).$

8. $\tfrac{1}{39}(5\sqrt{5} - 24).$ **9.** $\dfrac{-540 - 338\sqrt{5}}{451}.$ **10.** $\dfrac{270 - 169\sqrt{5}}{310}.$

11. $\tfrac{1}{39}(10 - 12\sqrt{5}).$ **12.** $\tfrac{1}{39}(5\sqrt{5} + 24).$ **13.** $\dfrac{-4}{(39)^2}(30 + 119\sqrt{5}).$

14. $\dfrac{480\sqrt{5} - 119}{1521}.$ **15.** $\dfrac{540 - 338\sqrt{5}}{451}.$ **29.** $\dfrac{\sqrt{2} - \sqrt{6}}{4}.$

30. $\dfrac{\sqrt{2} - \sqrt{6}}{4}.$ **31.** $2 - \sqrt{3}.$ **32.** $\dfrac{\sqrt{2} - \sqrt{6}}{4}.$

33. $\dfrac{\sqrt{2}}{4}(\sqrt{3} - 1).$ **34.** $-\sqrt{3}.$ **35.** $\dfrac{\sqrt{3}}{2}.$ **36.** $\dfrac{\sqrt{2}}{2}(\cos 2A - \sin 2A).$

37. $\cos 2A.$ **38.** $\tfrac{1}{2}.$ **39.** $2 \cos A \cos B.$

40. $-2 \sin A \sin B.$ **41.** $2 \sin A \cos B.$ **42.** $2 \cos A \sin B.$

43. $\dfrac{\cot A \cot B - 1}{\cot A + \cot B}; \ \dfrac{\cot A \cot B + 1}{\cot B - \cot A}.$

EXERCISE 7.2   (page 180)

1. $2 \cos \dfrac{x + y}{2} \cos \dfrac{x - y}{2}; \ -2 \sin \dfrac{x + y}{2} \sin \dfrac{x - y}{2}.$

2. (a) $2 \sin 4x \cos 2x.$ (b) $2 \cos 4x \cos 2x.$ (c) $-2 \cos \dfrac{3A}{2} \sin \dfrac{A}{2}.$

(d) $2 \sin \dfrac{3A}{2} \sin \dfrac{A}{2}.$ (e) $2 \sin 4\theta \cos \theta.$ (f) $2 \cos 4\theta \cos \theta.$

(g) $2 \cos \dfrac{2A + B}{2} \sin \dfrac{B}{2}.$ (h) $-2 \sin \dfrac{2A + B}{2} \sin \dfrac{B}{2}.$

3. (a) $\dfrac{\sqrt{2}}{2}.$ (b) $\dfrac{-\sqrt{2}}{2}.$ (c) $\dfrac{-\sqrt{2}}{2}.$ (d) $\dfrac{\sqrt{6}}{2}.$

EXERCISE 7.3   (page 183)

1. $11°.$ **2.** $14°.$ **3.** $59°.$ **4.** $80°.$ **5.** $45°.$
6. $80°.$ **7.** $\tfrac{5}{3}.$ **8.** $\pm 5\sqrt{3} - 8.$ **9.** $2y = x + 11.$

EXERCISE 7.4 (page 186)

1. $\cos^2 2A - \sin^2 2A$.

2. $2\cos 2A \sin 2A$.

3. $\dfrac{2\tan 2A}{1 - \tan^2 2A}$.

4. $2\sin 6A \cos 6A$.

5. $\cos^2 6A - \sin^2 6A$.

6. $2\cos 5\pi \sin 5\pi$.

7. $2\cos^2 \dfrac{\pi}{8} - 1$.

8. $2\cos^2 \dfrac{7\pi}{4} - 1$.

9. $\dfrac{2\tan 120°}{1 - \tan^2 120°}$.

10. $\frac{120}{169}; \frac{119}{169}; \frac{120}{119}$; 1st quadrant.

11. $\frac{4}{5}; -\frac{3}{5}; -\frac{4}{3}$; second quadrant.

12. $4\cos^3 A - 3\cos A$.

13. $-\frac{44}{125}$.

14. (a) $\dfrac{1 - \tan^2 A}{2\tan A}$. (b) $\dfrac{\cot^2 A - 1}{2\cot A}$.

15. $\dfrac{3\sqrt{10}}{10}, \dfrac{\sqrt{10}}{10}$.

16. $\dfrac{\sqrt{3}}{2}, \frac{1}{2}$.

18. $\pm\sqrt{\dfrac{1 + \cos\theta}{2}}; \pm\sqrt{\dfrac{1 - \cos\theta}{1 + \cos\theta}}$.

EXERCISE 7.5 (page 190)

1 and 2.

	Period	Amplitude	Phase angle w.r.t. sin	Phase angle w.r.t. cos
(a)	2π	2	$\dfrac{\pi}{3}$	$-\dfrac{\pi}{6}$
(b)	2π	5	$127°$	$37°$
(c)	2π	13	$67°$	$-23°$
(d)	2π	$\sqrt{5}$	$-27°$	$-117°$
(e)	π	2	$\dfrac{\pi}{3}$	$-\dfrac{\pi}{6}$
(f)	$\frac{2}{3}$	$\sqrt{5}$	$63°$	$-27°$

REVIEW EXERCISE 7 (page 191)

1. $59°$.

2. $82°$.

4. $\dfrac{\sqrt{3}}{2}$.

17.

	Period	Amplitude	Phase angle
(a)	2π	2	$30°$.
(b)	2π	2	$-30°$.
(c)	2π	5	$-37°$.
(d)	2π	$2\sqrt{2}$	$45°$.

Chapter 8

EXERCISE 8.1 (page 197)

1. (a) A: $\left(\dfrac{\sqrt{2}}{2}, \dfrac{7\sqrt{2}}{2}\right)$ $\theta = 45°$.   B: $(-2\sqrt{2}, \sqrt{2})$ $\theta = 45°$.

C: $\left(\dfrac{\sqrt{2}}{2}, -\dfrac{3\sqrt{2}}{2}\right)$ $\theta = 45°$.   D: $(3\sqrt{2}, \sqrt{2})$ $\theta = 45°$.

1. (b) $\left(-\dfrac{7\sqrt{2}}{2}, \dfrac{3\sqrt{2}}{2}\right)$ $(-\sqrt{2}, -2\sqrt{2})$ $\left(\dfrac{\sqrt{2}}{2}, \dfrac{\sqrt{2}}{2}\right)$ $(-\sqrt{2}, 3\sqrt{2})$ $\theta = 135°$.

(c) $\left(2 - \dfrac{3}{2}\sqrt{3}, 2\sqrt{3} + \dfrac{3}{2}\right) \left(-\dfrac{1}{2} - \dfrac{3}{2}\sqrt{3}, -\dfrac{\sqrt{3}}{2} + \dfrac{3}{2}\right) \left(-\dfrac{1}{2} + \sqrt{3}, -\dfrac{1}{2}\sqrt{3} - 1\right)$

$(2 + \sqrt{3}, 2\sqrt{3} - 1)$ $\theta = 60°$.

(d) $(-3, 4)$ $(-3, -1)$ $(2, -1)$ $(+2, 4)$ $\theta = 90°$.

2. (a) $\left(\dfrac{-2\sqrt{3} + 1}{2}, \dfrac{-2 - \sqrt{3}}{2}\right)$, $(0, 0)$, $\left(\dfrac{2\sqrt{3} - 1}{2}, \dfrac{2 + \sqrt{3}}{2}\right)$,

$\left(\dfrac{6\sqrt{3} - 3}{2}, \dfrac{6 + 3\sqrt{3}}{2}\right)$, $\theta = 30°$.

(b) $\left(\dfrac{-3}{\sqrt{2}}, \dfrac{1}{\sqrt{2}}\right)$, $(0, 0)$, $\left(\dfrac{3}{\sqrt{2}}, \dfrac{-1}{\sqrt{2}}\right)$, $\left(\dfrac{9}{\sqrt{2}}, \dfrac{-3}{\sqrt{2}}\right)$, $\theta = -45°$.

(c) $(2, 1)$ $(0, 0)$, $(-2, -1)$ $(-6, -3)$ $\theta = 180°$.

(d) $\left(\dfrac{2 + \sqrt{3}}{2}, \dfrac{-2\sqrt{3} + 1}{2}\right)$, $(0, 0)$, $\left(\dfrac{-2 - \sqrt{3}}{2}, \dfrac{2\sqrt{3} - 1}{2}\right)$,

$\left(\dfrac{-6 - 3\sqrt{3}}{2}, \dfrac{6\sqrt{3} - 3}{2}\right)$, $\theta = 120°$. Distance and angles are preserved.

3. $AB = \sqrt{13}$, $AD = \sqrt{17}$

4. $\theta = 120°$ $(x, y) \rightarrow \left(-\dfrac{x}{2} - \dfrac{y\sqrt{3}}{2}, \dfrac{x\sqrt{3}}{2} - \dfrac{y}{2}\right)$.

$\theta = 240°$ $(x, y) \rightarrow \left(-\dfrac{x}{2} + \dfrac{y\sqrt{3}}{2}, \dfrac{-x\sqrt{3}}{2} - \dfrac{y}{2}\right)$.

EXERCISE 8.2   (page 202)

2. (a) $(0, -2)$, $(4, -2)$, $(4, 2)$, $(0, 2)$.

3. (a) $(-1, \sqrt{3})$, $(-2, 0)$, $(-1, -\sqrt{3})$, $(1, -\sqrt{3})$, $(2, 0)$, $(1, \sqrt{3})$, $\theta = 120°$.

(b) $\theta = 60°$ $(x, y) \rightarrow \left(\dfrac{x}{2} - \dfrac{y\sqrt{3}}{2}, \dfrac{x\sqrt{3}}{2} + \dfrac{y}{2}\right)$.

$\theta = 180°$ $(x, y) \rightarrow (-x, -y)$.

$\theta = 240°$ $(x, y) \rightarrow \left(-\dfrac{x}{2} + \dfrac{y\sqrt{3}}{2}, -\dfrac{x\sqrt{3}}{2} - \dfrac{y}{2}\right)$.

$\theta = 300°$ $(x, y) \rightarrow \left(\dfrac{x}{2} + \dfrac{y\sqrt{3}}{2}, -\dfrac{x\sqrt{3}}{2} + \dfrac{y}{2}\right)$.

4. $u = \dfrac{x - y}{\sqrt{2}}$, $v = \dfrac{x + y}{\sqrt{2}}$, $x = y$. $u = 0$, $v = \dfrac{2x}{\sqrt{2}} = \sqrt{2}x$. $u = 0$.

5. $u = 0$.

6. $x = y$.

7. $x = \dfrac{u + v}{\sqrt{2}}$, $\dfrac{-u + v}{\sqrt{2}} - \left(\dfrac{u + v}{\sqrt{2}}\right) = 4$. $y = \dfrac{-u + v}{\sqrt{2}}$, $2u = -4\sqrt{2}$,

$u = -2\sqrt{2}$.

8. $x = \dfrac{-u - v}{\sqrt{2}}$, $y = \dfrac{u - v}{\sqrt{2}}$, $-\sqrt{2}v + \sqrt{2} = 0$. $v = 1$.

9. $x = \dfrac{3u + 4v}{5}$, $\dfrac{-4u + 3v}{5} = 4$. $y = \dfrac{-4u + 3v}{5}$, $-4u + 3v = 20$.

$4u - 3v + 20 = 0$.

10. $x = \dfrac{3u - 4v}{5}$, $y = \dfrac{4u + 3v}{5}$, $4\left(\dfrac{3u - 4v}{5}\right) + 3\left(\dfrac{4u + 3v}{5}\right) = 5$;

$3\left(\dfrac{3u - 4v}{5}\right) - 4\left(\dfrac{4u + 3v}{5}\right) = -5$. $12u - 16v + 12u + 9v = 25$;

$9u - 12v - (16u + 12v) = -25$. $24u - 7v = 25$; $+7u + 24v = +25$.

11. $u^2 + v^2 = 4$.

12. $x = \dfrac{u + v}{\sqrt{2}}, \quad y = \dfrac{-u + v}{\sqrt{2}}, \quad 4u^2 + v^2 = 16,$ Semi-axes, 4,2 ;

Foci $(0, \pm 2\sqrt{3})$.

13. $x = \dfrac{u - v}{\sqrt{2}}, \quad y = \dfrac{u + v}{\sqrt{2}}. \quad v^2 = -\frac{16}{3}.$

There exists no real v satisfying this last equation; therefore the image is the null set. Note that $3x^2 - 6xy + 3y^2 = 3(x - y)^2 = -32$ has no solution for x and y; the original curve is also the null set.

14. $x = \dfrac{\sqrt{3}u - v}{2}, \quad y = \dfrac{u + \sqrt{3}v}{2}. \quad \dfrac{2u^2}{3} - 2v^2 = 1.$

$a^2 = \frac{3}{2},\ b^2 = \frac{1}{2},\ c^2 = 2 = a^2 + b^2,\ e = \dfrac{c}{a} = \dfrac{2}{\sqrt{3}} = \frac{2}{3}\sqrt{3}.$ Foci $(\pm\sqrt{2}, 0)$.

15. $x = \dfrac{u - v}{\sqrt{2}}, \quad y = \dfrac{u + v}{\sqrt{2}}. \quad v^2 = \dfrac{1}{\sqrt{2}}u.$

16. $x = \dfrac{u + v}{\sqrt{2}}, \quad y = \dfrac{-u + v}{\sqrt{2}}. \quad uv = 2.$

17. $xy = 4.\ x = \dfrac{u - v}{\sqrt{2}}, y = \dfrac{u + v}{\sqrt{2}}.\ \dfrac{u^2}{8} - \dfrac{v^2}{8} = 1.$

$c^2 = a^2 + b^2 = 16.$ Foci are $(\pm 4, 0)$, vertices are $(\pm 2\sqrt{2}, 0)$.

18. $\dfrac{x^2}{16} + \dfrac{y^2}{9} = 1,\ x = \dfrac{4u + 3v}{5}, \quad y = \dfrac{-3u + 4v}{5}.\ 288u^2 + 337v^2 - 168uv = 3600.$

19. $x = \dfrac{\sqrt{3}u + v}{2}, \quad y = \dfrac{-u + \sqrt{3}v}{2}.\ 3u^2 + v^2 + 2\sqrt{3}uv = -4u + 4\sqrt{3}v.$

20. $x = \dfrac{3u + 4v}{5}, y = \dfrac{3v - 4u}{5}.\ u^2 = v.$

21. $x = \dfrac{2u + 3v}{\sqrt{13}};$ so $\dfrac{2u + 3v}{\sqrt{13}} < 2$ or $2u + 3v < 2\sqrt{13}.$

This region is that to the left of (or, equivalently, "under") the line $2u + 3v = 2\sqrt{13}$.

22. $y < x \le y + 1\ x = \dfrac{-5u + 12v}{13}, \quad y = \dfrac{-12u - 5v}{13}.$

$\dfrac{-12u - 5v}{13} < \dfrac{-5u + 12v}{13} \le \dfrac{-12u - 5v}{13} + 1\quad 0 < 7u + 17v \le 13.$

This gives the area between $7u + 17v = 0$ and $7u + 17v = 13$, including the line $7u + 17v = 13$.

23. $-y < x + 1 < y < 1\quad x = \dfrac{-u - \sqrt{7}v}{2\sqrt{2}}, \quad y = \dfrac{+\sqrt{7}u - v}{2\sqrt{2}},$

$v - \sqrt{7}u < -u - \sqrt{7}v + 2\sqrt{2} < \sqrt{7}u - v < 2\sqrt{2}.$
The result is a triangle congruent to the original triangle.

EXERCISE 8.3   (page 210)

1. $\theta = 45°.\ (x, y) \to \left(\dfrac{x - y}{\sqrt{2}}, \dfrac{x + y}{\sqrt{2}}\right).\ x = \dfrac{u + v}{\sqrt{2}}, y = \dfrac{-u + v}{\sqrt{2}}.$

$(x - y)^2 = 12(x + y).\ (\sqrt{2}u)^2 = 12(\sqrt{2}v),\ 2u^2 = 12\sqrt{2}u,\ u^2 = 6\sqrt{2}v.$

2. $\theta = 60°$. $(x, y) \to \left(\dfrac{x - \sqrt{3}y}{2}, \dfrac{\sqrt{3}x + y}{2} \right)$.

$x = \dfrac{u + \sqrt{3}v}{2}$, $y = \dfrac{-\sqrt{3}u + v}{2}$. $\dfrac{v^2}{2} - \dfrac{u^2}{2} = 1$.

3. $\tan 2\theta = \dfrac{4\sqrt{3}}{-4} = -\sqrt{3}$, $\theta = -30°$, $(x, y) \to \left(\dfrac{\sqrt{3}x + y}{2}, \dfrac{-x + \sqrt{3}y}{2} \right)$.

$x = \dfrac{\sqrt{3}u - v}{2}$, $y = \dfrac{+u + \sqrt{3}v}{2}$. $5u^2 - 3v^2 = 9$.

4. $\theta = 45°$, $(x, y) \to \left(\dfrac{x - y}{\sqrt{2}}, \dfrac{x + y}{\sqrt{2}} \right)$. $x = \dfrac{u + v}{\sqrt{2}}$, $y = \dfrac{-u + v}{\sqrt{2}}$. $\dfrac{u^2}{25} + \dfrac{v^2}{9} = 1$.

5. $\theta = 45°$, $(x, y) \to \left(\dfrac{x - y}{\sqrt{2}}, \dfrac{x + y}{\sqrt{2}} \right)$, $x = \dfrac{u + v}{\sqrt{2}}$, $y = \dfrac{-u + v}{\sqrt{2}}$. $\dfrac{3u^2}{16} - \dfrac{v^2}{16} = 1$.

6. $\theta = 45°$. $(x, y) \to \left(\dfrac{x - y}{\sqrt{2}}, \dfrac{x + y}{\sqrt{2}} \right)$. $x = \dfrac{u + v}{\sqrt{2}}$, $y = \dfrac{-u + v}{\sqrt{2}}$.

$v^2 - u^2 = 18$.

7. $\theta = 45°$. $x = \dfrac{u + v}{\sqrt{2}}$, $y = \dfrac{-u + v}{\sqrt{2}}$. $\dfrac{8^2}{25} - \dfrac{2u^2}{25} = 1$.

8. $\theta = 45°$, $x = \dfrac{u + v}{\sqrt{2}}$, $y = \dfrac{-u + v}{\sqrt{2}}$. $\dfrac{u^2}{9} + \dfrac{v^2}{16} = 1$.

9. $\theta = 45°$, $x = \dfrac{u + v}{\sqrt{2}}$, $y = \dfrac{-u + v}{\sqrt{2}}$. $u = \dfrac{x - y}{\sqrt{2}}$, $v = \dfrac{x + y}{\sqrt{2}}$.

$2u^2 - 2\sqrt{2}v + 1 = 0$.

10. $\tan 2\theta = \dfrac{2\sqrt{3}}{2} = \sqrt{3}$, $\theta = 30°$. $(x, y) \to \left(\dfrac{\sqrt{3}x - y}{2}, \dfrac{x + \sqrt{3}y}{2} \right)$.

$x = \dfrac{\sqrt{3}u + v}{2}$, $y = \dfrac{-u + \sqrt{3}v}{2}$. $v^2 + u + \sqrt{3}v = 0$.

11. $\theta = 45°$. $(x, y) \to \left(\dfrac{x - y}{\sqrt{2}}, \dfrac{x + y}{\sqrt{2}} \right)$ $x = \dfrac{u + v}{\sqrt{2}}$, $y = \dfrac{-u + v}{\sqrt{2}}$

$\dfrac{(u - \sqrt{\frac{9}{2}})^2}{39} - \dfrac{(v - \sqrt{\frac{1}{2}})^2}{13} = 1$. $\dfrac{s^2}{39} - \dfrac{t^2}{13} = 1$.

12. $\theta = 45°$. $(x, y) \to \left(\dfrac{x - y}{\sqrt{2}}, \dfrac{x + y}{\sqrt{2}} \right)$, $x = \dfrac{u + v}{\sqrt{2}}$, $y = \dfrac{-u + v}{\sqrt{2}}$.

$\dfrac{32(u + \frac{9}{4}\sqrt{2})^2}{3} + \dfrac{128(v - \frac{3}{16}\sqrt{2})^2}{3} = -1$.

This equation has no solution; the original and image curves are both the empty set.

13. $\theta = 45°$. $(x, y) \to \left(\dfrac{x - y}{\sqrt{2}}, \dfrac{x + y}{\sqrt{2}} \right)$. $x = \dfrac{u + v}{\sqrt{2}}$, $y = \dfrac{-u + v}{\sqrt{2}}$.

$(x - y)^2 + 5x = 0$. $\left(u + \dfrac{5}{4\sqrt{2}} \right)^2 + \dfrac{5}{2\sqrt{2}}v = \dfrac{25}{32}$.

$\left(u + \dfrac{5}{4\sqrt{2}} \right)^2 = -\dfrac{5}{2\sqrt{2}} \left(v - \dfrac{5\sqrt{2}}{16} \right)$. $s^2 = -\dfrac{5}{2\sqrt{2}}t$.

14. $(x + 3)^2 - 3y + 6 = 9$. $(x + 3)^2 = 3(y + 1)$. $s^2 = 3t$.

15. $(\sqrt{3}x - y)^2 + 4(x - \sqrt{3}y) = 0.$ $\theta = 30°.$ $(x, y) \to \left(\dfrac{\sqrt{3}x - y}{2}, \dfrac{x + \sqrt{3}y}{2}\right).$

$x = \dfrac{\sqrt{3}u + v}{2}, \; y = \dfrac{-u + \sqrt{3}v}{2}.$ $u^2 + \sqrt{3}u = v.$

$\left(u + \dfrac{\sqrt{3}}{2}\right)^2 = v + \tfrac{3}{4}.$ $s^2 = t.$

16.

	Semi-major or semi-transverse axis	Semi-minor or semi-conjugate axis	Vertices
11.	$\sqrt{39}$	$\sqrt{13}$	$\left(\dfrac{\sqrt{78} + 10}{2}, -\dfrac{\sqrt{78} - 8}{2}\right), \left(-\dfrac{\sqrt{78} + 10}{2}, \dfrac{\sqrt{78} - 8}{2}\right).$
12.	See the answer for question 12.		
13.	Not defined		$\left(\dfrac{-5}{16}, \dfrac{15}{16}\right)$
14.	Not defined		$(-3, -1)$
15.	Not defined		$\left(\dfrac{-9}{8}, \dfrac{-\sqrt{3}}{8}\right)$

17. (b) $\tan 2\theta = \dfrac{2h}{b - a}.$

18. $\tan 2\theta = \sqrt{3}, \; 2\theta = 60°, \; \theta = 30°.$ $\sin \theta = \tfrac{1}{2}, \cos \theta = \tfrac{1}{2}\sqrt{3}.$

19. $2\theta = 90°, \; \theta = 45°.$

REVIEW EXERCISE 8 (page 211)

1. (a) $\left(\dfrac{2\sqrt{3} + 1}{2}, \dfrac{2 - \sqrt{3}}{2}\right), \left(\dfrac{3\sqrt{3} - 4}{2}, \dfrac{3 + 4\sqrt{3}}{2}\right), \left(\dfrac{-5}{2}, \dfrac{5\sqrt{3}}{2}\right),$

$\left(\dfrac{1 - \sqrt{3}}{2}, \dfrac{-1 - \sqrt{3}}{2}\right), \theta = 30°.$

(b) $(-2, +1), (-3, -4), (0, -5), (1, +1).$ $\theta = 180°.$

(c) $(\sqrt{5}, 0) \left(\dfrac{2}{\sqrt{5}}, \dfrac{11}{\sqrt{5}}\right) (-\sqrt{5}, 2\sqrt{5}) \left(\dfrac{-1}{\sqrt{5}}, \dfrac{-3}{\sqrt{5}}\right).$

$\sin \theta = \dfrac{1}{\sqrt{5}} = \dfrac{1}{5}\sqrt{5}.$ $\sin \theta = (.2)(2.236) = .447.$ $\theta = 27°.$

2. $(x, y) \to \left(\dfrac{x - \sqrt{3}y}{2}, \dfrac{\sqrt{3}x + y}{2}\right).$ $(0, 0) \to (0, 0).$ $(5, 0) \to (\tfrac{5}{2}, \tfrac{5}{2}\sqrt{3}).$

$(4, 3) \to \left(\dfrac{4 - 3\sqrt{3}}{2}, \dfrac{4\sqrt{3} + 3}{2}\right).$

3. $(x, y) \to \left(\dfrac{x - y}{\sqrt{2}}, \dfrac{x + y}{\sqrt{2}}\right) = (u, v).$ $x = \dfrac{u + v}{\sqrt{2}}, y = \dfrac{v - u}{\sqrt{2}}$

$\dfrac{u + v}{\sqrt{2}} = \dfrac{v - u}{\sqrt{2}}; u = 0.$

4. $v = -\dfrac{5}{\sqrt{2}}.$

5. $6u - 8v = -15.$

6. $u^2 + v^2 = 9.$

7. $\dfrac{v^2}{16} - \dfrac{u^2}{16} = 1.$

8. $\dfrac{v^2}{4} - \dfrac{u^2}{25} = 1.$

17. $a = \sqrt{3}, b = \sqrt{2}, c^2 = a^2 + b^2 = 5, c = \sqrt{5}.$
Foci: $(\pm\sqrt{5}, 0).$

18. $\tan 2\theta = \dfrac{3}{-4} = \dfrac{2T}{1 - T^2}.$ $3 - 3T^2 = -8T.$ $3T^2 - 8T - 3 = 0.$

$T = \dfrac{8 \pm \sqrt{64 + 36}}{6} = \dfrac{8 \pm 10}{6} = 3$ or $-\frac{1}{3}.$ $\tan \theta = 3.$ Let $0 < 2\theta < 180°.$

$(x, y) \to \left(\dfrac{x - 3y}{\sqrt{10}}, \dfrac{3x + y}{\sqrt{10}} \right),$ $x = \dfrac{u + 3v}{\sqrt{10}}, y = \dfrac{-3u + v}{\sqrt{10}}.$

$\dfrac{u^2}{26} + \dfrac{v^2}{6} = 1.$ Ellipse. Eccentricity: $\dfrac{\sqrt{130}}{13}.$ Image foci: $(2\sqrt{5}, 0), (-2\sqrt{5}, 0).$
Original foci: $(\sqrt{2}, -3\sqrt{2}), (-\sqrt{2}, 3\sqrt{2}).$

Chapter 9

EXERCISE 9.1   (page 215)

1. (a) $3, -, 2.$ (b) $6, 0, 5.$ (c) $4, -, 6.$ (d) $1, 3, -.$
(e) $5, -, -.$ (f) $4, -1, 5.$

2. (a) $2 \times 2.$ (b) $2 \times 3.$ (c) $3 \times 2.$ (d) $1 \times 4.$
(e) $4 \times 1.$ (f) $3 \times 3.$

3. No.   **4.** $a = 5, b = -1.$ **5.** Never.

6. (a) $11.$ (b) $-1.$ (c) $-10.$ (d) $-5.$

7. (a) $-15.$ (b) $10.$ (c) $11.$ (d) $10.$

EXERCISE 9.2   (page 217)

1. (a) $\begin{bmatrix} 4 & 2 \\ -2 & 3 \end{bmatrix}.$ (b) $\begin{bmatrix} 4 & 7 \\ -9 & 2 \end{bmatrix}.$ (c) $\begin{bmatrix} 8 & 3 \\ 3 & 3 \end{bmatrix}.$ (d) $\begin{bmatrix} 4 & 2 \\ -2 & 3 \end{bmatrix}.$

(e) $\begin{bmatrix} 4 & 7 \\ -9 & 2 \end{bmatrix}.$ (f) $\begin{bmatrix} 8 & 3 \\ 3 & 3 \end{bmatrix}.$ (g) $\begin{bmatrix} 8 & 6 \\ -4 & 4 \end{bmatrix}.$ (h) $\begin{bmatrix} 8 & 6 \\ -4 & 4 \end{bmatrix}.$

2. (a) $\begin{bmatrix} 7 & -8 \\ 4 & 3 \end{bmatrix}.$ (b) $\begin{bmatrix} -3 & -3 \\ 6 & 6 \end{bmatrix}.$ (c) $\begin{bmatrix} 0 & 3 \\ 0 & 9 \end{bmatrix}.$ (d) $\begin{bmatrix} 7 & -8 \\ 4 & 3 \end{bmatrix}.$

(e) $\begin{bmatrix} -3 & -3 \\ 6 & 6 \end{bmatrix}.$ (f) $\begin{bmatrix} 0 & 3 \\ 0 & 9 \end{bmatrix}.$ (g) $\begin{bmatrix} 2 & -4 \\ 5 & 9 \end{bmatrix}.$ (h) $\begin{bmatrix} 2 & -4 \\ 5 & 9 \end{bmatrix}.$

3. (a) $\begin{bmatrix} 30 & -6 \\ -6 & 18 \end{bmatrix}.$ (b) $\begin{bmatrix} -6 & 21 \\ -15 & 0 \end{bmatrix}.$ (c) $\begin{bmatrix} \frac{-5}{2} & 2 \\ \frac{1}{2} & 3 \end{bmatrix}.$

4. (a) $\begin{bmatrix} 19 & -17 \\ 7 & 9 \end{bmatrix}.$ (b) $\begin{bmatrix} -35 & 22 \\ 7 & 24 \end{bmatrix}.$ (c) $\begin{bmatrix} -1 & -22 \\ 11 & -30 \end{bmatrix}.$

5. (a) $\begin{bmatrix} 3 & 3 \\ -2 & 6 \end{bmatrix}.$ (b) $\begin{bmatrix} 9 & -5 \\ 9 & 6 \end{bmatrix}.$ (c) $\begin{bmatrix} 9 & -5 \\ 9 & 6 \end{bmatrix}.$ (d) $\begin{bmatrix} 17 & -8 \\ 9 & 15 \end{bmatrix}.$

(e) $\begin{bmatrix} 19 & -9 \\ 20 & 7 \end{bmatrix}.$ (f) $\begin{bmatrix} 1 & 1 \\ -6 & 16 \end{bmatrix}.$ (g) $\begin{bmatrix} 18 & 12 \\ 1 & 2 \end{bmatrix}.$ (h) $\begin{bmatrix} 17 & 10 \\ 10 & 12 \end{bmatrix}.$

9. $\theta = 45°$. $(x, y) \rightarrow \left(\dfrac{x - y}{\sqrt{2}}, \dfrac{x + y}{\sqrt{2}}\right)$. $x = \dfrac{u + v}{\sqrt{2}}, y = \dfrac{-u + v}{\sqrt{2}}$. $\dfrac{u^2}{2} + \dfrac{v^2}{4} = 1$

$(0, \sqrt{2}) \frac{1}{2}(0)^2 + \frac{1}{4}(\sqrt{2})^2 = \frac{1}{2} < 1$, inside.

$\left(-\dfrac{3\sqrt{2}}{2}, \dfrac{\sqrt{2}}{2}\right) \frac{1}{2}(\frac{9}{2}) + \frac{1}{4}(\frac{1}{2}) = \frac{9}{4} + \frac{1}{8} > 1$, outside.

10. $\tan 2\theta = \dfrac{24}{-7}$; $\tan 2\theta = \dfrac{2 \tan \theta}{1 - \tan^2\theta} = \dfrac{2T}{1 - T^2} = \dfrac{-24}{7}$.

$T = \dfrac{7 \pm \sqrt{49 + 4(144)}}{24} = \dfrac{7 \pm 25}{24}$. $\tan \theta = \frac{4}{3}$ or $-\frac{3}{4}$.

Let $0 < 2\theta < 180°$. Then, $0 < \theta < 90°$.

Then, $\tan \theta = \frac{4}{3}$, $\sin \theta = \frac{4}{5}$, $\cos \theta = \frac{3}{5}$.

$(x, y) \rightarrow \left(\dfrac{3x - 4y}{5}, \dfrac{4x + 3y}{5}\right)$, $x = \dfrac{3u + 4v}{5}, y = \dfrac{-4u + 3v}{5}$.

$x = \dfrac{3u + 4v}{5}, y = \dfrac{-4u + 3v}{5}$. $\dfrac{u^2}{10} + \dfrac{3v^2}{20} = 1$.

$(-\frac{9}{5}, -\frac{13}{5})$, $\dfrac{162 + 507}{500} > 1$, outside. $\left(-\frac{11}{5}, \frac{-2}{5}\right)$ $\dfrac{242 + 12}{500} < 1$, inside.

11. $\theta = 45°$, $(x, y) \rightarrow \left(\dfrac{x - y}{\sqrt{2}}, \dfrac{x + y}{\sqrt{2}}\right)$.   12. $\theta = 45°$, $(x, y) \rightarrow \left(\dfrac{x - y}{\sqrt{2}}, \dfrac{x + y}{\sqrt{2}}\right)$.

13. $\tan 2\theta = \frac{12}{5}$, $\frac{12}{5} = \dfrac{2 \tan \theta}{1 - \tan^2\theta} = \dfrac{2T}{1 - T^2}$. Choose $0 < 2\theta < 180°$. So $0 < \theta < 90°$.

$T = \dfrac{-5 \pm \sqrt{25 + 144}}{12} = \dfrac{-5 \pm 13}{12} = \frac{2}{3}$ or $-\frac{3}{2}$.

$\tan \theta = 34°$. $.66666 \cdots$, $(x, y) \rightarrow \left(\dfrac{3x - 2y}{\sqrt{13}}, \dfrac{2x + 3y}{\sqrt{13}}\right)$.

14. $\tan 2\theta = \dfrac{-20}{21} = \dfrac{2T}{1 - T^2}$. $-20 + 20T^2 = 42T$.   Let $0 < 2\theta < 180°$.

So $0 < \theta < 90°$. $20T^2 - 42T - 20 = 0$. $10T^2 - 21T - 10 = 0$.

$T = \dfrac{21 \pm \sqrt{441 + 400}}{20} = \dfrac{21 \pm 29}{20} = 2.5, -.4$. $\tan \theta = 2.5$.

$(x, y) \rightarrow \left(\dfrac{2x - 5y}{\sqrt{29}}, \dfrac{5x + 2y}{\sqrt{29}}\right)$.

16. (a) $\tan 2\theta = \dfrac{24}{-7}$, $\tan \theta = \frac{4}{3}$ or $-\frac{3}{4}$ from question (10).

Choose $\tan \theta = \frac{4}{3}$ and $0 < \theta < 90°$.

$(x, y) = \left(\dfrac{3x - 4y}{5}, \dfrac{4x + 3y}{5}\right)$. $x = \dfrac{3u + 4v}{5}, y = \dfrac{-4u + 3v}{5}$.

$10u^2 + 28u - 15v^2 - 6v - 11 = 0$. $\dfrac{(u + \frac{7}{5})^2}{3} - \dfrac{(v + \frac{1}{5})^2}{2} = 1$.

$\dfrac{s^2}{3} - \dfrac{t^2}{2} = 1$. Hyperbola.

(b) $(x, y) \rightarrow (x + 1, y - 1)$, $6u^2 + 24uv - v^2 + 30 = 0$, same final curve as in (a)

(c) Hyperbola.

6. (a) $3, 4, 6, -4$.   (b) $-\frac{4}{3}, -2, -\frac{13}{3}, 3$.   (c) $5, \frac{20}{3}, 10, -\frac{20}{3}$.

8. (a) $\begin{bmatrix} 0 & -2 & 7 \\ 8 & 4 & 1 \end{bmatrix}$.   (b) $\begin{bmatrix} 8 & 0 \\ -4 & 0 \\ -1 & 7 \end{bmatrix}$.   (c) $\begin{bmatrix} 5 & -2 \\ -1 & 3 \\ 6 & 0 \\ 7 & 1 \end{bmatrix}$.

(d) $\begin{bmatrix} 9 & 2 & 1 \\ -5 & 5 & 0 \\ 5 & 0 & 0 \end{bmatrix}$.   (e) $\begin{bmatrix} 1 & 5 & 3 \\ 7 & -4 & 6 \\ 4 & 2 & -1 \end{bmatrix}$.   (f) No sum.

9. (a) Yes.   (b) Yes.   (c) Yes.

EXERCISE 9.3 (page 221)

5. $-A = \begin{bmatrix} -1 & -7 \\ 3 & -5 \end{bmatrix}$; $-B = \begin{bmatrix} 3 & 3 \\ -5 & 2 \end{bmatrix}$; $-C = \begin{bmatrix} -4 & 2 \\ -1 & -7 \end{bmatrix}$.

6. (a) $\begin{bmatrix} 13 & 25 \\ -18 & 26 \end{bmatrix}$. (b) $\begin{bmatrix} 8 & 26 \\ -30 & 1 \end{bmatrix}$. (c) $\begin{bmatrix} 11 & 35 \\ -30 & 16 \end{bmatrix}$.   **9.** Yes.

EXERCISE 9.4 (page 225)

1. (a) $\begin{bmatrix} 0 \\ 0 \end{bmatrix}$.   (b) $\begin{bmatrix} 4 \\ 1 \end{bmatrix}$.   (c) $\begin{bmatrix} 11 \\ 1 \end{bmatrix}$.   (d) $\begin{bmatrix} -3 \\ -6 \end{bmatrix}$.   (e) $\begin{bmatrix} 5 \\ 10 \end{bmatrix}$.

(f) $\begin{bmatrix} -9 \\ 3 \end{bmatrix}$.   (g) $\begin{bmatrix} -16 \\ 3 \end{bmatrix}$.   (h) $\begin{bmatrix} -3 \\ 8 \end{bmatrix}$.

2. (a) $(0, 0)$.   (b) $(\frac{8}{7}, -\frac{5}{7})$.   (c) $(\frac{5}{7}, \frac{10}{7})$.   (d) $(\frac{10}{7}, -\frac{8}{7})$.

3. (a) $R = \begin{bmatrix} 3 & -1 \\ 5 & 2 \end{bmatrix}$.   (b) $S = \begin{bmatrix} 1 & 1 \\ 2 & -3 \end{bmatrix}$.   (c) $T = \begin{bmatrix} 1 & 4 \\ 2 & 1 \end{bmatrix}$.

(d) $U = \begin{bmatrix} 1 & 0 \\ 0 & 1 \end{bmatrix}$.   (e) $V = \begin{bmatrix} 3 & 0 \\ 0 & 5 \end{bmatrix}$.   (f) $W = \begin{bmatrix} 1 & 1 \\ 0 & 2 \end{bmatrix}$.

4. (a) $\begin{aligned} u &= 5x - y \\ v &= x + y \end{aligned}$.   (b) $\begin{aligned} u &= 2x - 3y \\ v &= x \end{aligned}$.   (c) $\begin{aligned} u &= 5x + 5y \\ v &= -2x + 3y \end{aligned}$.

(d) $\begin{aligned} u &= x - y \\ v &= y \end{aligned}$.   (e) $\begin{aligned} u &= x \\ v &= y \end{aligned}$.   (f) $\begin{aligned} u &= y \\ v &= x \end{aligned}$.

5. (a) $\begin{bmatrix} -5 \\ -1 \end{bmatrix}$. (b) $\begin{bmatrix} -1 \\ -2 \end{bmatrix}$. (c) $\begin{bmatrix} 20 \\ 12 \end{bmatrix}$. (d) $\begin{bmatrix} -2 \\ -3 \end{bmatrix}$. (e) $\begin{bmatrix} -15 \\ 25 \end{bmatrix}$. (f) $\begin{bmatrix} -3 \\ -6 \end{bmatrix}$.

6. (a) $(\frac{12}{11}, -\frac{19}{11})$.   (b) $(-\frac{2}{5}, -\frac{8}{5})$.   (c) $(\frac{1}{7}, -\frac{2}{7})$.
(d) $(4, -3)$.   (e) $(\frac{1}{3}, \frac{1}{5})$.   (f) $(-\frac{7}{2}, \frac{3}{2})$.

7. (a) $\begin{bmatrix} 22 \\ -6 \end{bmatrix}$.   (b) $\begin{bmatrix} -\frac{1}{4} \\ \frac{9}{8} \end{bmatrix}$.

8. $T\begin{bmatrix} \dfrac{a + 2b}{11} \\ \dfrac{-4a + 3b}{11} \end{bmatrix} = \begin{bmatrix} a \\ b \end{bmatrix}$.   **9.** $T\begin{bmatrix} \dfrac{a + b}{4} \\ \dfrac{-a + 3b}{8} \end{bmatrix} = \begin{bmatrix} a \\ b \end{bmatrix}$.   **10.** $T\begin{bmatrix} \dfrac{5b - a}{7} \\ \dfrac{2a - 3b}{7} \end{bmatrix} = \begin{bmatrix} a \\ b \end{bmatrix}$.

EXERCISE 9.5 (page 230)

1. All images lie on the line $v = 3u$.   2. All images lie on the line $v = 2u$.

3. All images lie on the line $v = -2u$.   4. All images lie on the line $v = -\frac{1}{3}u$

5. All images lie on the line $v = 2u$.   6. All images lie on the line $v = 4u$.

7. All images lie on the line $v = -u$.   8. All images lie on the line $v = 0$.

9. All images lie on the line $u = 0$.   10. $\{(2k - 1, k) \mid k \in Re\}$.

11. $\{(4k - 14, k) \mid k \in Re\}$.   12. $\left\{\left(\dfrac{k + 15}{3}, k\right) \,\middle|\, k \in Re\right\}$.

13. $\left\{\left(\dfrac{k - 8}{3}, k\right) \,\middle|\, k \in Re\right\}$.   14. $\left\{\left(\dfrac{k + 2}{4}, k\right) \,\middle|\, k \in Re\right\}$.

15. (1) $x - 2y = k$, $(k, 3k)$.   (2) $\frac{1}{2}x + y = k$, $(k, 2k)$.
    (3) $-x + 4y = k$, $(k, -2k)$.   (4) $3x - 2y = k$, $(k, -\frac{1}{3}k)$.
    (5) $3x - y = k$, $(k, 2k)$.   (6) $x + y = k$, $(k, 4k)$.
    (7) $-x + \frac{1}{3}y = k$, $(k, -k)$.   (8) $x + 2y = k$, $(k, 0)$.
    (9) $4x - y = k$, $(0, k)$.   16. $ad - bc \neq 0$.

EXERCISE 9.6 (page 234)

F, R, U, W do not have inverses.

1. $x = -\frac{1}{8}u + \frac{3}{8}v$ 2. $x = \frac{1}{5}u + \frac{2}{5}v$ 3. $x = \frac{2}{5}u - \frac{1}{5}v$
   $y = \frac{3}{8}u - \frac{1}{8}v$ $y = \frac{1}{5}u - \frac{3}{5}v$ $y = \frac{1}{5}u - \frac{3}{5}v$

4. $x = \dfrac{u}{3}$ 5. $x = \dfrac{v}{2}$ 8. $x = \dfrac{v}{3}$

   $y = \dfrac{v}{2}$ $y = \dfrac{u}{3}$ $y = u - \dfrac{v}{3}$

9. $x = \frac{3}{4}u + \frac{1}{2}v$ 11. $x = \frac{1}{5}u + \frac{1}{5}v$
   $y = \frac{1}{2}u$ $y = \frac{2}{5}u - \frac{3}{5}v$

13. (a) $(7, 5)$, $(7, -1)$, $(1, -3)$, $(3, 4)$, $(6, 2)$, $(3, 3)$, $(4, -4)$, $(5, 0)$.
    (b) $(-3, -9)$, $(-9, -3)$, $(-9, -3)$, $(-9, 0)$, $(0, -6)$, $(-3, -9)$, $(0, -6)$, $(-9, -6)$.
    (c) $(-13, 1)$, $(-4, 7)$, $(11, 12)$, $(6, -10)$, $(-15, 4)$, $(-3, 6)$, $(-10, 19)$, $(1, 9)$.
    (d) $(-10, 2)$, $(-2, 6)$, $(10, 10)$, $(6, -8)$, $(-12, 4)$, $(-2, 6)$, $(-8, 16)$, $(2, 8)$.

EXERCISE 9.7 (page 237)

1. (a) $\begin{bmatrix} -6 \\ 1 \end{bmatrix}$, $\begin{bmatrix} -19 \\ -5 \end{bmatrix}$.   (b) $\begin{bmatrix} 1 \\ -2 \end{bmatrix}$, $\begin{bmatrix} -1 \\ -5 \end{bmatrix}$.   (c) $\begin{bmatrix} 3 \\ -6 \end{bmatrix}$, $\begin{bmatrix} -27 \\ 15 \end{bmatrix}$.

   (d) $\begin{bmatrix} -2 \\ -6 \end{bmatrix}$, $\begin{bmatrix} 2 \\ -6 \end{bmatrix}$.

2. (a) $\begin{bmatrix} 13 \\ -4 \end{bmatrix}, \begin{bmatrix} 43 \\ 9 \end{bmatrix}.$ (b) $\begin{bmatrix} -5 \\ 5 \end{bmatrix}, \begin{bmatrix} -5 \\ 15 \end{bmatrix}.$ (c) $\begin{bmatrix} -8 \\ 16 \end{bmatrix}, \begin{bmatrix} 72 \\ -40 \end{bmatrix}.$

(d) $\begin{bmatrix} 3 \\ 17 \end{bmatrix}, \begin{bmatrix} -11 \\ 33 \end{bmatrix}.$

3. (a) $\begin{aligned} r &= 14x - 5y \\ s &= 6x + y \end{aligned}.$ (b) $\begin{aligned} r &= 8x + 7y \\ s &= -5y \end{aligned}.$ (c) $\begin{aligned} r &= 9x - 18y \\ s &= -5x + 10y \end{aligned}.$

(d) $\begin{aligned} r &= 5x + 7y \\ s &= -15x - 21y \end{aligned}$

4. $\begin{aligned} r &= 10x - 3y \\ s &= 5x - 7y \end{aligned}.$ **5.** $A^{-1}\begin{cases} x \doteq \frac{3}{11}u + \frac{2}{11}v \\ y = \frac{-1}{11}u + \frac{3}{11}v \end{cases}, \; B^{-1}\begin{cases} u = \frac{1}{5}r + \frac{1}{5}s \\ v = \frac{2}{5}r - \frac{3}{5}s \end{cases}.$

6. $(BA)^{-1}\begin{cases} x = \frac{7}{55}r - \frac{3}{55}s \\ y = \frac{1}{11}r - \frac{2}{11}s \end{cases}.$ **7.** $A^{-1}B^{-1}\begin{cases} x = \frac{7}{55}r - \frac{3}{55}s \\ y = \frac{1}{11}r - \frac{2}{11}s \end{cases}.$

8. $BA\begin{cases} r = 6x \\ s = 7x + y \end{cases}; \; A^{-1}\begin{cases} x = \frac{v}{2} \\ y = u - \frac{5}{2}v \end{cases}; \; B^{-1}\begin{cases} u = -\frac{1}{3}r + s \\ v = \frac{1}{3}r \end{cases};$

$(BA)^{-1}\begin{cases} x = \frac{1}{6}r \\ y = -\frac{7}{6}r + s \end{cases}; \; A^{-1}B^{-1} = (BA)^{-1}.$

REVIEW EXERCISE 9   (page 238)

1. (a) $-1, -1, 3.$ (b) $18.$

2. (a) $\begin{bmatrix} 7 & -1 \\ 4 & 5 \end{bmatrix}.$ (b) $\begin{bmatrix} -4 & 0 \\ 1 & -3 \end{bmatrix}.$ (c) $\begin{bmatrix} 17 & -3 \\ 13 & 12 \end{bmatrix}.$

4. $\begin{bmatrix} 4 & -5 \\ 5 & 6 \end{bmatrix}.$

5. (a) $\begin{aligned} r &= -x + 3y \\ s &= 5x + 2y \end{aligned}.$ (b) $\begin{bmatrix} 8 \\ -23 \end{bmatrix}.$ (c) $\begin{bmatrix} \frac{13}{17} \\ \frac{-24}{17} \end{bmatrix}.$

(d) $T\begin{bmatrix} \frac{3}{17}n - \frac{2}{17}m \\ \frac{n}{17} + \frac{5}{17}m \end{bmatrix} = \begin{bmatrix} m \\ n \end{bmatrix}.$

6. (a) All image points lie on the line $v = -3u.$

(b) Line $-x + 4y = k \leftrightarrow$ point $(k, -3k).$

7. (a) $\begin{aligned} x &= \frac{1}{6}u + \frac{1}{6}v \\ y &= \frac{1}{4}u - \frac{1}{4}v \end{aligned}.$ (b) $\begin{aligned} x &= -\frac{1}{3}u + \frac{1}{3}v \\ y &= 2u - v \end{aligned}.$ (c) None.

8. (a) $\begin{aligned} r &= 12x + y \\ s &= 15x + 5y \end{aligned}.$ (b) $\begin{aligned} w &= 24x + 2y \\ z &= 45x + 15y \end{aligned}.$ (c) $\begin{aligned} w &= 6u + 4v \\ z &= 18u + 3v \end{aligned}.$

(d) $\begin{aligned} w &= 24x + 2y \\ z &= 45x + 15y \end{aligned}.$

Chapter 10

EXERCISE 10.1   (page 242)

1. $\begin{bmatrix} -10 & 7 \\ 5 & 2 \end{bmatrix}, \begin{bmatrix} -15 & -2 \\ 25 & 7 \end{bmatrix}.$ **2.** $\begin{bmatrix} 18 & 9 \\ -3 & 0 \end{bmatrix}, \begin{bmatrix} 13 & 19 \\ 2 & 5 \end{bmatrix}.$

3. $\begin{bmatrix} 4 & -3 \\ 1 & 2 \end{bmatrix}, \begin{bmatrix} 4 & -3 \\ 1 & 2 \end{bmatrix}.$ **4.** $\begin{bmatrix} 2 & -8 \\ 11 & 26 \end{bmatrix}, \begin{bmatrix} -1 & -13 \\ 13 & 29 \end{bmatrix}.$

5. $\begin{bmatrix} 1 & 0 \\ 0 & 1 \end{bmatrix}, \begin{bmatrix} 1 & 0 \\ 0 & 1 \end{bmatrix}.$ **6.** $\begin{bmatrix} 1 & 0 \\ 0 & 1 \end{bmatrix}, \begin{bmatrix} 1 & 0 \\ 0 & 1 \end{bmatrix}.$

EXERCISE 10.2 (page 247)

1. (a) $\begin{bmatrix} 4 & -2 \\ 23 & -9 \end{bmatrix}.$ (b) $\begin{bmatrix} -7 & -2 \\ 12 & 2 \end{bmatrix}.$ (c) $\begin{bmatrix} 2 & 12 \\ -6 & 14 \end{bmatrix}.$

(d) $\begin{bmatrix} 14 & -5 \\ -25 & 9 \end{bmatrix}.$ (e) $\begin{bmatrix} 56 & -10 \\ 82 & -20 \end{bmatrix}.$

2. (a) $\begin{bmatrix} 22 & 7 \\ 26 & 0 \end{bmatrix}.$ (b) $\begin{bmatrix} -7 & 7 \\ -3 & 29 \end{bmatrix}.$ (c) $\begin{bmatrix} 11 & 15 \\ 6 & 26 \end{bmatrix}.$

(d) $\begin{bmatrix} 19 & 115 \\ 46 & 134 \end{bmatrix}.$ (e) $\begin{bmatrix} 211 & 555 \\ 222 & 766 \end{bmatrix}.$

3. (a) $\begin{bmatrix} -2 & 5 \\ 4 & 16 \end{bmatrix}.$ (b) $\begin{bmatrix} -5 & 5 \\ 19 & 7 \end{bmatrix}.$ (c) $\begin{bmatrix} 3 & -1 \\ 4 & 12 \end{bmatrix}.$

(d) $\begin{bmatrix} 11 & 6 \\ 1 & 33 \end{bmatrix}.$ (e) $\begin{bmatrix} 6 & -4 \\ -19 & -3 \end{bmatrix}.$

4. (a) $\begin{bmatrix} 3 & -2 \\ 5 & 4 \end{bmatrix}.$ (b) $\begin{bmatrix} 3 & -2 \\ 5 & 4 \end{bmatrix}.$ (c) $\begin{bmatrix} 1 & 0 \\ 0 & 1 \end{bmatrix}.$

(d) $\begin{bmatrix} -1 & -14 \\ 35 & 6 \end{bmatrix}.$ (e) $\begin{bmatrix} -1 & -14 \\ 35 & 6 \end{bmatrix}.$

5. (a) $\begin{bmatrix} -1 & 3 \\ -2 & 5 \end{bmatrix}.$ (b) $\begin{bmatrix} 5 & -2 \\ 3 & -1 \end{bmatrix}.$ (c) $\begin{bmatrix} 1 & 0 \\ 0 & 1 \end{bmatrix}.$

(d) $\begin{bmatrix} 4 & -1 \\ 5 & -1 \end{bmatrix}.$ (e) $\begin{bmatrix} 5 & -1 \\ 4 & -1 \end{bmatrix}.$

6. $AB = \begin{bmatrix} 1 & 0 \\ 0 & 1 \end{bmatrix} = BA.$

7. (a) $\begin{bmatrix} 16 \\ 34 \end{bmatrix}.$ (b) $[-2 \ \ 23].$ (c) Not possible. (d) Not possible.

(e) $\begin{bmatrix} 0 \\ 31 \end{bmatrix}.$ (f) $[-3].$ (g) $\begin{bmatrix} 9 & -8 \\ 34 & -7 \end{bmatrix}.$ (h) $[-14 \ \ -6].$

(i) $\begin{bmatrix} 8 \\ 1 \\ 10 \end{bmatrix}.$ (j) $\begin{bmatrix} -5 & 1 & -5 \\ 6 & 12 & 4 \\ -2 & 8 & -4 \end{bmatrix}.$

8. $A^2 = \begin{bmatrix} 1 & 0 \\ 0 & 1 \end{bmatrix} = B^2; \ \ C^2 = \begin{bmatrix} 0 & 0 \\ 0 & 0 \end{bmatrix} = 0.$

If $a^2 = b^2$, $a, b \in Re$, then $a = \pm b$. But $A \neq B$.

If $a^2 = 0$, $a \in Re$, then $a = 0$. But $C \neq 0$.

9. (a) AB yes, BA no. (b) AB yes, BA no. (c) Yes. (d) Yes. (e) No.

10. BA if $n = r$; AB if $s = m$.

EXERCISE 10.3   (page 252)

1. (a) and (b) $\begin{bmatrix} -12 & -10 \\ 39 & 15 \end{bmatrix}$;   (c) and (d) $\begin{bmatrix} -7 & 0 \\ 28 & 0 \end{bmatrix}$.

2. (a) and (b) $\begin{bmatrix} -2 & -6 \\ 34 & 62 \end{bmatrix}$;   (c) and (d) $\begin{bmatrix} -6 & 4 \\ 32 & 12 \end{bmatrix}$.

3. (a) and (b) $\begin{bmatrix} -1 & 0 \\ 5 & 2 \end{bmatrix}$;   (c) and (d) $\begin{bmatrix} 11 & 6 \\ 7 & 5 \end{bmatrix}$.

4. (a) and (b) $\begin{bmatrix} 88 & 16 \\ -2 & 28 \end{bmatrix}$;   (c) and (d) $\begin{bmatrix} 20 & 36 \\ 33 & -11 \end{bmatrix}$.

5. $A(AB) = A^2B = \begin{bmatrix} 51 & -13 \\ -34 & 71 \end{bmatrix}$; $A(A + B) = A^2 + AB = \begin{bmatrix} 24 & 0 \\ -16 & 34 \end{bmatrix}$.

6. $B = \begin{bmatrix} 0 & 0 \\ 1 & 1 \end{bmatrix}$.   7. $B = \begin{bmatrix} 1 & 0 \\ 2 & 0 \end{bmatrix}$.   8. $B = \begin{bmatrix} 1 & 1 \\ 2 & 2 \end{bmatrix}$.

EXERCISE 10.4   (page 257)

1. $\begin{bmatrix} \frac{4}{15} & \frac{1}{15} \\ \frac{1}{15} & \frac{4}{15} \end{bmatrix}$.   2. $\begin{bmatrix} 0 & \frac{1}{5} \\ 1 & \frac{3}{5} \end{bmatrix}$.   3. $\begin{bmatrix} \frac{3}{8} & -\frac{2}{8} \\ \frac{1}{8} & \frac{2}{8} \end{bmatrix}$.   4. $\begin{bmatrix} \frac{2}{9} & \frac{5}{9} \\ -\frac{1}{9} & \frac{2}{9} \end{bmatrix}$.

5. No inverse.   6. $\begin{bmatrix} \frac{1}{8} & -\frac{3}{40} \\ \frac{3}{8} & -\frac{1}{40} \end{bmatrix}$.   7. $\begin{bmatrix} -\frac{1}{8} & -\frac{3}{40} \\ -\frac{3}{8} & -\frac{1}{40} \end{bmatrix}$.   8. No inverse.

9. $\begin{bmatrix} 0 & -1 \\ \frac{1}{2} & 1 \end{bmatrix}$.   10. $\begin{bmatrix} \frac{1}{3} & 0 \\ -\frac{4}{3} & 1 \end{bmatrix}$.   11. $\begin{bmatrix} \frac{1}{5} & 0 \\ 0 & 1 \end{bmatrix}$.   12. $\begin{bmatrix} 0 & -\frac{1}{3} \\ \frac{1}{4} & 0 \end{bmatrix}$.

13. No inverse.   14. No inverse.   15. $\begin{bmatrix} \frac{1}{2} & -\frac{1}{2} \\ \frac{1}{2} & \frac{1}{2} \end{bmatrix}$.   16. $\begin{bmatrix} \frac{6}{23} & \frac{-3}{23} \\ \frac{-2}{23} & \frac{24}{23} \end{bmatrix}$.

17. $\begin{bmatrix} \frac{1}{a} & 0 \\ 0 & \frac{1}{d} \end{bmatrix}$.   18. $\begin{bmatrix} 0 & \frac{1}{c} \\ \frac{1}{b} & 0 \end{bmatrix}$.

19. (a) $\begin{bmatrix} 2 & 6 \\ -10 & 12 \end{bmatrix}$.   (b) $\begin{bmatrix} \frac{1}{7} & -\frac{1}{14} \\ \frac{5}{42} & \frac{1}{42} \end{bmatrix}$.   (c) $\begin{bmatrix} \frac{2}{3} & -\frac{1}{6} \\ \frac{1}{3} & \frac{1}{6} \end{bmatrix}$.

(d) $\begin{bmatrix} \frac{2}{7} & -\frac{1}{7} \\ \frac{1}{14} & \frac{3}{14} \end{bmatrix}$.

EXERCISE 10.5   (page 260)

1. (a) $\begin{bmatrix} 17 \\ 22 \end{bmatrix}$.   (b) $\begin{bmatrix} 31 \\ 16 \end{bmatrix}$.   (c) $\begin{bmatrix} 41 \\ -2 \end{bmatrix}$.   (d) $\begin{bmatrix} 12 \\ 15 \end{bmatrix}$.

(e) $\begin{bmatrix} -2 \\ 13 \end{bmatrix}$.   (f) $\begin{bmatrix} -5 \\ -4 \end{bmatrix}$.   (g) $\begin{bmatrix} 5a + 3b \\ -a + 4b \end{bmatrix}$.   (h) $\begin{bmatrix} 3x + 2y \\ -2x + 3y \end{bmatrix}$.

(i) $\begin{bmatrix} 4s \\ -s + 3t \end{bmatrix}$.   (j) $\begin{bmatrix} 6m - n \\ 4m + 5n \end{bmatrix}$.

2. (a) $\begin{bmatrix} 6 & -1 \\ 1 & 4 \end{bmatrix} \begin{bmatrix} x_1 \\ x_2 \end{bmatrix} = \begin{bmatrix} 3 \\ 5 \end{bmatrix}$.   (b) $\begin{bmatrix} 2 & 5 \\ 1 & -4 \end{bmatrix} \begin{bmatrix} x \\ y \end{bmatrix} = \begin{bmatrix} 6 \\ -3 \end{bmatrix}$.

(c) $\begin{bmatrix} 3 & 2 \\ 1 & -6 \end{bmatrix} \begin{bmatrix} a \\ b \end{bmatrix} = \begin{bmatrix} 5 \\ -2 \end{bmatrix}$.   (d) $\begin{bmatrix} 2 & -7 \\ 5 & 1 \end{bmatrix} \begin{bmatrix} m \\ n \end{bmatrix} = \begin{bmatrix} 0 \\ -3 \end{bmatrix}$.

(e) $\begin{bmatrix} 4 & -1 \\ 1 & 3 \end{bmatrix} \begin{bmatrix} r \\ s \end{bmatrix} = \begin{bmatrix} 0 \\ 0 \end{bmatrix}$.   (f) $\begin{bmatrix} 5 & -2 \\ 2 & 3 \end{bmatrix} \begin{bmatrix} u \\ v \end{bmatrix} = \begin{bmatrix} -1 \\ 5 \end{bmatrix}$.

3. (a) -2.   (b) No value.   (c) -3.

4. $WA = [0 \ 19]$; AW is not defined.

EXERCISE 10.6   (page 263)

1. $\{(\frac{28}{13}, \frac{9}{13})\}$.   **2.** $\{(\frac{13}{7}, \frac{10}{7})\}$.   **3.** $\{(\frac{5}{9}, \frac{26}{9})\}$.   **4.** Inconsistent.

5. $\{(\frac{31}{24}, -\frac{75}{24})\}$.   **6.** $\{(-1, 4)\}$.   **7.** $\{(\frac{-8}{17}, \frac{22}{17})\}$.   **8.** $\{(\frac{-4}{13}, \frac{-12}{13})\}$.

9. $\{(\frac{3}{5}, \frac{8}{5})\}$.   **10.** $\left\{\left(\dfrac{2m + 3n}{23}, \dfrac{5m - 4n}{23}\right)\right\}$.

EXERCISE 10.7   (page 267)

1. $\begin{bmatrix} -\frac{7}{8} & \frac{3}{8} \\ \frac{5}{8} & -\frac{1}{8} \end{bmatrix}$.   **2.** $\begin{bmatrix} \frac{-3}{2} & \frac{1}{2} \\ 1 & 0 \end{bmatrix}$.   **3.** No inverse.   **4.** $\begin{bmatrix} \frac{2}{9} & \frac{1}{3} \\ -\frac{1}{18} & \frac{1}{6} \end{bmatrix}$.

5. $\begin{bmatrix} \frac{1}{6} & \frac{1}{2} \\ -\frac{1}{12} & \frac{1}{4} \end{bmatrix}$.   **6.** No inverse.   **7.** $\begin{bmatrix} \frac{8}{5} & \frac{-4}{5} \\ \frac{4}{5} & \frac{8}{5} \end{bmatrix}$.   **8.** $\begin{bmatrix} 3 & -5 \\ 2 & -3 \end{bmatrix}$.

9. $\begin{bmatrix} \frac{1}{6} & 0 \\ \frac{1}{4} & \frac{1}{2} \end{bmatrix}$.

EXERCISE 10.8   (page 272)

1. (a) V_2', V_2'.   (b) V_2', V_2'.   (c) V_2', V_2'.

(d) V_2', $\left\{\begin{bmatrix} a \\ b \end{bmatrix} \ \middle| \ a, b \in Re, a = b\right\}$.   (e) V_2', V_2'.   (f) V_2', V_2'.

(g) V_2', V_2'.   (h) V_2', $\left\{\begin{bmatrix} a \\ b \end{bmatrix} \ \middle| \ a, b \in Re, b = -3a\right\}$.

EXERCISE 10.9 (page 277)

1. (a) $\begin{bmatrix} 1 & 0 \\ 0 & 1 \end{bmatrix}$.

(b) $\begin{bmatrix} \dfrac{\sqrt{3}}{2} & -\dfrac{1}{2} \\ \dfrac{1}{2} & \dfrac{\sqrt{3}}{2} \end{bmatrix}$.

(c) $\begin{bmatrix} \dfrac{1}{\sqrt{2}} & -\dfrac{1}{\sqrt{2}} \\ \dfrac{1}{\sqrt{2}} & \dfrac{1}{\sqrt{2}} \end{bmatrix}$.

(d) $\begin{bmatrix} \dfrac{1}{2} & -\dfrac{\sqrt{3}}{2} \\ \dfrac{\sqrt{3}}{2} & \dfrac{1}{2} \end{bmatrix}$.

(e) $\begin{bmatrix} 0 & -1 \\ 1 & 0 \end{bmatrix}$.

(f) $\begin{bmatrix} -\dfrac{1}{2} & -\dfrac{\sqrt{3}}{2} \\ \dfrac{\sqrt{3}}{2} & -\dfrac{1}{2} \end{bmatrix}$.

(g) $\begin{bmatrix} -1 & 0 \\ 0 & -1 \end{bmatrix}$.

(h) $\begin{bmatrix} 0 & 1 \\ -1 & 0 \end{bmatrix}$.

3. $(-\sqrt{3}, 1)$, $(-1 + \dfrac{\sqrt{3}}{2}, -\sqrt{3} - \frac{1}{2})$, $(1 + \dfrac{\sqrt{3}}{2}, \sqrt{3} - \frac{1}{2})$.

4. $(0, 4)$, $(-4, -2)$, $(4, -2)$.

5. (a) $\begin{bmatrix} 2 & 0 \\ 0 & 1 \end{bmatrix}$; $\begin{bmatrix} -2 & 0 \\ 0 & 1 \end{bmatrix}$. (b) $(2, 2)$, $(6, 2)$, $(10, 7)$.
(c) $(-3, 2)$, $(-9, 2)$, $(-15, 7)$.

6. (a) $\begin{bmatrix} 1 & 0 \\ 0 & 3 \end{bmatrix}$; $\begin{bmatrix} 1 & 0 \\ 0 & -1 \end{bmatrix}$. (b) $(1, -9)$, $(1, 15)$, $(2, 24)$.
(c) $(1, 3)$, $(1, -5)$, $(2, -8)$.

7. (a) $\begin{bmatrix} 1 & 0 \\ 0 & 0 \end{bmatrix}$.

(b) $\begin{bmatrix} 0 & 0 \\ 0 & 1 \end{bmatrix}$.

8. (a) $\begin{bmatrix} -1 & 0 \\ 0 & 1 \end{bmatrix}$; $\begin{bmatrix} 1 & 0 \\ 0 & -1 \end{bmatrix}$; $\begin{bmatrix} -1 & 0 \\ 0 & -1 \end{bmatrix}$.   (b) $(-1, 3)$, $(-2, 5)$, $(-3, 7)$.
(c) $(1, -3)$, $(2, -5)$, $(3, -7)$.   (d) $(-1, -3)$, $(-2, -5)$, $(-3, -7)$.

9. (a) $\begin{bmatrix} 1 & a \\ 0 & 1 \end{bmatrix}$; $\begin{bmatrix} 1 & 0 \\ a & 1 \end{bmatrix}$.   (b) $(0, 0)$, $(3, 0)$, $(13, 4)$.
(c) $(0, 0)$, $(3, -6)$, $(1, 2)$.

10. If the magnification in the y-direction is $u = x + 0y$, $v = 0x + ky$, the required transformation is $u = x + 0y$, $v = 0x - ky$.

11. $\begin{bmatrix} k & ka \\ 0 & 0 \end{bmatrix}$, k from the uniform magnification and a from the shear.

12. $\begin{bmatrix} -1 & -ka \\ 0 & -k \end{bmatrix}$, k from the uniform magnification and a from the shear.

REVIEW EXERCISE 10 (page 279)

1. $BA = \begin{bmatrix} 20 & 8 \\ -18 & -2 \end{bmatrix}$.   **2.** $AB = \begin{bmatrix} 14 & 2 \\ -24 & 4 \end{bmatrix}$.

4. (a) $\begin{bmatrix} -3 & 12 \\ 7 & -7 \end{bmatrix}$. (b) $\begin{bmatrix} -6 & -15 \\ 4 & 3 \end{bmatrix}$. (c) $\begin{bmatrix} 6 & 6 \\ 3 & -6 \end{bmatrix}$. (d) $\begin{bmatrix} 29 & -5 \\ -13 & 21 \end{bmatrix}$.

5. (a) No.   (b) Yes.   (c) No.   (d) Yes.

7. $\begin{bmatrix} 0 & 0 \\ 0 & 0 \end{bmatrix}$; A and B are divisors of zero.   8. $\begin{bmatrix} \frac{2}{9} & \frac{1}{27} \\ -\frac{1}{9} & \frac{4}{27} \end{bmatrix}$.

9. (a) $\begin{bmatrix} \frac{2}{5} & -\frac{1}{5} \\ \frac{1}{15} & \frac{2}{15} \end{bmatrix}$. (b) $\begin{bmatrix} \frac{1}{7} & \frac{5}{7} \\ -\frac{1}{7} & \frac{2}{7} \end{bmatrix}$. (c) $\begin{bmatrix} 7 & -7 \\ 4 & 11 \end{bmatrix}$. (d) $\begin{bmatrix} \frac{11}{105} & \frac{1}{15} \\ \frac{-4}{105} & \frac{1}{15} \end{bmatrix}$.

10. (a) $\begin{bmatrix} 16 & 4 \\ -8 & 3 \end{bmatrix}$. (b) $\begin{bmatrix} \frac{3}{80} & \frac{-1}{20} \\ \frac{1}{10} & \frac{1}{5} \end{bmatrix}$. (c) $\begin{bmatrix} \frac{1}{5} & 0 \\ \frac{1}{5} & 1 \end{bmatrix}$.

11. (a) $\begin{bmatrix} 40 \\ 10 \end{bmatrix}$; $\begin{bmatrix} 20 \\ -1 \end{bmatrix}$; $\begin{bmatrix} 20 \\ 15 \end{bmatrix}$.   12. $\begin{bmatrix} 3 & -2 \\ 1 & 5 \end{bmatrix}\begin{bmatrix} x \\ y \end{bmatrix} = \begin{bmatrix} 4 \\ -3 \end{bmatrix}$.

Chapter 11

EXERCISE 11.1   (page 282) Answers to *five* significant figures.

1. (a) \$127.00
    (b) \$403.20
    (c) \$652.50
    (d) \$514.94
    (e) \$248.69
    (f) \$3292.60 ·

2. (a) 3%
    (b) 5%
    (c) $3\frac{1}{2}$%
    (d) $2\frac{1}{4}$%
    (e) 3%
    (f) $3\frac{1}{4}$%

3. (a) 6 years
    (b) 8 years
    (c) 12 years
    (d) 3.5 years
    (e) 4 years
    (f) 8.5 years

EXERCISE 11.2   (page 285)

1. $200(1.04)^{12}$
    Semi-annually, 9 years
    6%, 7 years
    \$1200, semi-annually, 10 years
    $640(1.005)^{36}$
    \$680, monthly, $1\frac{1}{4}$ years
    \$900, 4%, 8 years
    Quarterly, 10 years.
    \$200, 5% n years.
    \$$P$, i%, annually
    \$$P$, $4i$%, quarterly

2. (a) \$320.21
    (b) \$545.88
    (c) \$721.74
    (d) \$728.27
    (e) \$1713.90
    (f) \$857.07
    (g) \$1213.60
    (h) \$971.45
    (i) \$671.13
    (j) \$1459.30

3. (a) 5.063%   (b) 8.243%   (c) 12.683%   (d) 6.136%
    (e) 6.090%   (f) 12.551%   (g) 12.360%

4. \$392.32

EXERCISE 11.3   (page 287)

1. (a) \$493.95   (b) \$210.41   (c) \$209.86   (d) \$308.32

(e) $17.47   (f) $1103.80   (g) $1105.70   (h) $211.28

2. $8807.20   3. $8879.70   4. $1961.54

EXERCISE 11.4 (page 291)

1. $3686.50
2. $4617.50
3. $2990.17
4. $1497.45

5. $54.79
6. $597.24
7. $922.58
8. $199.06

9. $13,545
10. 15.0 years
11. $12,075

EXERCISE 11.5 (page 295)

1. $2428.40
2. $5065.00
3. $2354.60
4. $366.43

5. 11.563x$
6. $129.54
7. $743.87

8. $1233.40
9. $3546.90
10. $1165.50

EXERCISE 11.6 (page 298)

1. $1491.80
2. 5.4478x$
3. $2304.50

4. $3739.20
5. $7291.80
6. $1253.40

7. $1506.50
8. $10,946.00
9. $585.96

10. $557.54
11. $6427.60

EXERCISE 11.7 (page 301)

1.

Year	Beginning Debt	Total Payment	Interest Payment	Principal Repayment	End Debt
1	$6000.00	$1500.00	$360.00	$1140.00	$4860.00
2	$4860.00	$1500.00	$291.60	$1208.40	$3651.60
3	$3651.60	$1500.00	$219.10	$1280.90	$2370.70
4	$2370.70	$1500.00	$142.24	$1357.76	$1012.94
5	$1012.94	$1073.72	$ 60.78	$1012.94	—

2.

6-Month Period	Beginning Debt	Total Payment	Interest Payment	Principal Repayment	End Debt
1	$8000.00	$1000.00	$320.00	$680.00	$7320.00
2	$7320.00	$1000.00	$292.80	$707.20	$6612.80
3	$6612.80	$1000.00	$264.51	$735.49	$5877.31
4	$5877.31	$1000.00	$235.09	$764.91	$5112.40

5	$5112.40	$1000.00	$204.50	$795.50	$4316.90
6	$4316.90	$1000.00	$172.68	$827.32	$3489.58
7	$3489.58	$1000.00	$139.58	$860.42	$2629.16
8	$2629.16	$1000.00	$105.17	$894.83	$1734.33
9	$1734.33	$1000.00	$ 69.37	$930.63	$ 803.70
10	$ 803.70	$ 835.85	$ 32.15	$803.70	—

3. Annual Payment: $2009.61

Year	Beginning Debt	Total Payment	Interest Payment	Principal Repayment	End Debt
1	$12,000.00	$2009.61	$840.00	$1169.61	$10,830.39
2	$10,830.39	$2009.61	$758.12	$1251.49	$ 9,578.90
3	$ 9,578.90	$2009.61	$670.52	$1339.09	$ 8,239.81
4	$ 8,239.81	$2009.61	$576.79	$1432.82	$ 6,806.99
5	$ 6,806.99	$2009.61	$476.49	$1533.12	$ 5,273.87
6	$ 5,273.87	$2009.61	$369.17	$1640.44	$ 3,633.43
7	$ 3,633.43	$2009.61	$254.34	$1755.27	$ 1,878.16
8	$ 1,878.16	$2008.63	$130.47	$1878.16	—

4. Semi-Annual Payment: $1384.05

6-Month Period	Beginning Debt	Total Payment	Interest Payment	Principal Repayment	End Debt
1	$15,000.00	$1384.05	$750.00	$ 634.05	$14,365.95
2	$14,365.95	$1384.05	$718.30	$ 665.75	$13,700.20
3	$13,700.20	$1384.05	$685.01	$ 699.04	$13,001.16
4	$13,001.16	$1384.05	$650.06	$ 733.99	$12,267.17
5	$12,267.17	$1384.05	$613.36	$ 770.69	$11,496.48
6	$11,496.48	$1384.05	$574.82	$ 809.23	$10,687.25
7	$10,687.25	$1384.05	$534.36	$ 849.69	$ 9,837.56
8	$ 9,837.56	$1384.05	$491.88	$ 892.17	$ 8,945.39
9	$ 8,945.39	$1384.05	$447.27	$ 936.78	$ 8,008.61
10	$ 8,008.61	$1384.05	$400.43	$ 983.62	$ 7,024.99
11	$ 7,024.99	$1384.05	$351.25	$1032.80	$ 5,992.19
12	$ 5,992.19	$1384.05	$299.61	$1084.44	$ 4,907.75
13	$ 4,907.75	$1384.05	$245.39	$1138.66	$ 3,769.09
14	$ 3,769.09	$1384.05	$188.45	$1195.60	$ 2,573.49
15	$ 2,573.49	$1384.05	$128.67	$1255.38	$ 1,318.11
16	$ 1,318.11	$1384.02	$ 65.91	$1318.11	—

5. Semi-Annual Payment: $693.96   Clearing Payment: $9431.16

6-Month Period	Beginning Debt	Total Payment	Interest Payment	Principal Repayment	End Debt
1	$12,000.00	$693.96	$480.00	$213.96	$11,786.04
2	$11,786.04	$693.96	$471.44	$222.52	$11,563.52
3	$11,563.52	$693.96	$462.54	$231.42	$11,332.10
4	$11,332.10	$693.96	$453.28	$240.68	$11,091.42
5	$11,091.42	$693.96	$443.66	$250.30	$10,841.12
6	$10,841.12	$693.96	$433.64	$260.32	$10,580.80
7	$10,580.80	$693.96	$423.23	$270.73	$10,310.07
8	$10,310.07	$693.96	$412.40	$281.56	$10,028.51
9	$10,028.51	$693.96	$401.14	$292.82	$ 9,735.69
10	$ 9,735.69	$693.96	$389.43	$304.53	$ 9,431.16

EXERCISE 11.8   (page 304)

1. (a) $x = \dfrac{P.V.}{a_{\overline{40}|}\ .045}$

    (b) $\$(26{,}000 - x.a_{\overline{24}|}\ .045)$

2. (a) $401.12

    (b) $421.17

✱ 3. $1800.56   *1447.56*

4. $159.92

5. (a) $n = 17$

    (b) $12.07

6. (a) $498.18

    (b) $5440.38

7. $151.84
    1.73

8. 1.58% monthly

9. 1.86% monthly

10. $169.81

11. $186.79
    157.04

EXERCISE 11.9   (page 306)

1. $901.02

2. $111.29

3. $867.51

4. $1183.92

5. $889.10

6. $7713.60

7. $16,198.05

8. $883.78

REVIEW EXERCISE 11   (page 307)

1. (a) $1190.00

    (b) $1263.10

2. 8.243%

3. $572.09

4. $1345.10

6. (a) 19.562%

    (b) 8.160%

    (c) 4.06%

    (d) 18.81%

    (e) 19.252%

5. (a) $316.33

    (b) $317.06

    (c) $1575.80

    (d) $1563.90

7. (a) $1353.70

    (b) $1229.30

    (c) $497.38

    (d) $501.93

    (e) $269.41

    (e) $636.65

    (f) $809.31

8. $1456.05

9. $1188.10

10. $6716.70

11. $985.10

12. $1753.10

13. $17,962.00   15. $356.19   16. $14,653.15   17. 1.37%

18. 10 full + $117.97   19. $793.23   20. $1047.29

14.

6-Month Period	Beginning Debt	Total Payment	Interest Payment	Principal Repayment	End Debt
1	$6000.00	$1000.00	$240.00	$760.00	$5240.00
2	$5240.00	$1000.00	$209.60	$790.40	$4449.60
3	$4449.60	$1000.00	$177.98	$822.02	$3627.58
4	$3627.58	$1000.00	$145.10	$854.90	$2772.68
5	$2772.68	$1000.00	$110.90	$889.10	$1883.58
6	$1883.58	$1000.00	$ 75.34	$924.66	$ 958.92
7	$ 958.92	$ 997.28	$ 38.36	$958.92	—

Chapter 12

EXERCISES 12.2 and 12.3   (page 325, 332)

Question	Mean	Median	Mode	Standard Deviation
1	$783.75	$35.00	$20.00	1675
2	75.7°	75°	75°	7.428
3	.01020	.0102	.0102	.00024
4	.283	.288	.277	.027

EXERCISE 12.4   (page 334)

1. $Q_1 = 71.3$, $Q_3 = 78.8$, $D_4 = 73.5$.
2. $Q_3 = .010325$, $D_4 = .010166$, $D_6 = .01023$.
3. $Q_1 = 69.75$, $Q_3 = 80.9$, $Q = 76.1$, $D_6 = 77.8$, $P_{40} = 74.4$, $P_{80} = 74.1$.
4. $Q_3 = 20.82$, $D_1 = 15.42$, $P_{20} = 16.78$, $P_{90} = 22.54$.

REVIEW EXERCISE 12 (PAGE 335)

	Mean	Median	Mode	Standard Deviation	
1	8.42	8.9		2.48	$Q_1 = 6.63$
2	75.8	70.93	75.5	23.1	$Q_1 = 61.25$, $Q_3 = 89.03$, $D_7 = 80.61$, $P_{41} = 71.10$, $P_{81} = 94.96$, $P_{82} = 96.1$
3	3.93	3.89	3.745	0.77	$Q_1 = 3.37$, $Q_3 = 4.47$, $Q = 3.89$, $D_3 = 3.50$, $D_8 = 4.63$, $V = 0.196$
4	39.48	39	39 or 40	3.13	$Q_1 = 36.69$, $Q_3 = 40.88$, $P_{30} = 37.20$, $P_{80} = 41.33$
5	$18.02	$17.83		$4.45	
6	152.71	151.96	149	8.14	$Q_1 = 146.74$, $D_8 = 158.77$, $P_{35} = 148.80$, $P_{84} = 160.16$

Chapter 13

EXERCISE 13.1   (page 339)

1. (i) 12   3. 42   10. 8   15. 12
    (ii) 240   4. 120   11. (a) 40,320   16. (a) 720

(iii) 840
(iv) 2730
(v) 120
(vi) 360
2. 336

5. 720
6. 60
7. 48
8. 100
9. 15

(b) 10,080
(c) 30,240
12. 40,320
13. 120
14. 504

(b) 480
(c) 48
17. 970,200
18. 90
19. 210

EXERCISE 13.2 (page 343)

1. (a) 56
   (b) 20
   (c) 20
   (d) 56
   (e) 56
   (f) 1140

2. (a) $(n + 1)!$
   (b) $(n + 6)!$
   (c) $(n - r + 1)!$
3. (a) $(n + 5)(n + 4)$
   (b) n
   (c) $n + 1$

(d) $n - r + 1$
(e) $n - r$
(f) $(n - r + 1)(n - r)$

4. (a) $n = 2$
   (b) $n = +3$
   (c) $n = 6$

(d) $n = 4$
(e) $n = 3$
(f) $n = 8$

EXERCISE 13.3 (page 346)

1. (a) 60
   (b) 56
   (c) 2520
   (d) 3960
2. (a) 180
   (b) 420

(c) 360
(d) 2520
(e) 3465
(f) 840
3. 30
4. 120

5. 3360; 360
6. 300
7. 12
8. 84
9. (a) 180
   (b) 60

(c) 120
(d) 12
(e) 48
10. (a) 48
    (b) 24
11. 35
12. 120

EXERCISE 13.4 (page 351)

1. (a) 28
   (b) 10
   (c) 91
   (d) 1
   (e) 1
   (f) 1330
   (g) 1326
   (h) 100
   (i) 600

(j) 5005
2. 6
3. 21
4. $1 + 4 + 6 + 4 + 1 = 16$
5. (a) 220
   (b) 1320
6. 91
7. 54
8. $\frac{1}{2}(n^2 - 3n)$

9. 45
10. 840
11. 1316
12. 6167
13. 153
14. 1287
15. 55
16. 91

17. 27,720
18. $x = 2$
19. $x = 8$
20. $x = 20$
23. $52! \div 13! \, 39!$
24. $52! \div 13! \, 13! \, 13! \, 13!$
25. 56
26. 35

REVIEW EXERCISE 13 (page 353)

1. (a) 210
   (b) 2520
   (c) 9900
   (d) 1320
   (e) 35
   (f) 1

2. (a) x
   (b) $x(x + 1)$
   (c) $n - r$
6. (a) 462
   (b) 200
   (c) 461

10. 150
11. 495,000
12. 240
13. 55
14. 840
15. 144

22. $n = 10$
23. (a) $n = 10$
    (b) $n = 3$
    (c) $n = 5$
    (d) $n = 12, r = 3$

(g) 100   7. (a) 1680   16. 15
(h) 792   (b) 8008   17. 495
(i) 132   18. 5940
(j) 140   8. (a) 10,080   19. 27,720
(k) 840   (b) 720   20. 5775
(l) 6510   9. 210   21. 20

Chapter 14

EXERCISE 14.1   (page 357)

1. (a) 2   (b) 5   (c) 3   (d) 5

2. (a) $(a + b)^4 = \sum_{k=0}^{4} \binom{4}{k} a^{4-k} b^k$

$$= \binom{4}{0} a^4 b^0 + \binom{4}{1} a^3 b^1 + \binom{4}{2} a^2 b^2 + \binom{4}{3} a^1 b^3 + \binom{4}{4} a^0 b^4$$

$$= a^4 + 4a^3 b + 6a^2 b^2 + 4ab^3 + b^4.$$

(b) $(a + b)^5 = \sum_{k=0}^{5} \binom{5}{k} a^{5-k} b^k$

$$= \binom{5}{0} a^5 b^0 + \binom{5}{1} a^4 b^1 + \binom{5}{2} a^3 b^2 + \binom{5}{3} a^2 b^3 + \binom{5}{4} a^1 b^4$$

$$+ \binom{5}{5} a^0 b^5$$

$$= a^5 + 5a^4 b + 10a^3 b^2 + 10a^2 b^3 + 5ab^4 + b^5.$$

(c) $(x + y)^8 = \sum_{k=0}^{8} \binom{8}{k} x^{8-k} y^k$

$$= \binom{8}{0} x^8 y^0 + \binom{8}{1} x^7 y^1 + \binom{8}{2} x^6 y^2 + \binom{8}{3} x^5 y^3 + \binom{8}{4} x^4 y^4$$

$$+ \binom{8}{5} x^3 y^5 + \binom{8}{6} x^2 y^6 + \binom{8}{7} x^1 y^7 + \binom{8}{8} x^0 y^8$$

$$= x^8 + 8x^7 y + 28x^6 y^2 + 56x^5 y^3 + 70x^4 y^4 + 56x^3 y^5$$

$$+ 28x^2 y^6 + 8xy^7 + y^8.$$

(d) $(p + q)^7 = \sum_{k=0}^{7} \binom{7}{k} p^{7-k} q^k$

$$= \binom{7}{0} p^7 q^0 + \binom{7}{1} p^6 q^1 + \binom{7}{2} p^5 q^2 + \binom{7}{3} p^4 q^3 + \binom{7}{4} p^3 q^4$$

$$+ \binom{7}{5} p^2 q^5 + \binom{7}{6} p^1 q^6 + \binom{7}{7} p^0 q^7$$

$$= p^7 + 7p^6q + 21p^5q^2 + 35p^4q^3 + 35p^3q^4 + 21p^2q^5 + 7pq^6$$
$$+ q^7.$$

3. (a) 5   (b) 6   (c) 9   (d) 8

4. (a) 12   (b) 16   (c) 19   (d) 21

EXERCISE 14.2 (page 360)

1. (a) $(x + y)^{12} = \displaystyle\sum_{k=0}^{12} \binom{12}{k} x^{12-k}y^k.$

 (b) $(x - y)^9 = \displaystyle\sum_{k=0}^{9} \binom{9}{k} x^{9-k}(-y)^k = \sum_{k=0}^{9} (-1)^k \binom{9}{k} x^{9-k}y^k.$

 (c) $(2x + y)^7 = \displaystyle\sum_{k=0}^{7} \binom{7}{k} (2x)^{7-k}(y)^k = \sum_{k=0}^{7} 2^{7-k} \binom{7}{k} x^{7-k}y^k.$

 (d) $\left(2x + \dfrac{y}{2}\right)^8 = \displaystyle\sum_{k=0}^{8} \binom{8}{k} (2x)^{8-k}\left(\dfrac{y}{2}\right)^k = \sum_{k=0}^{8} 2^{8-2k} \binom{8}{k} x^{8-k}y^k.$

 (e) $(x^2 + 1)^{10} = \displaystyle\sum_{k=0}^{10} \binom{10}{k} (x^2)^{10-k}(1)^k = \sum_{k=0}^{10} \binom{10}{k} x^{20-2k}.$

 (f) $(1 - 2x^2)^{15} = \displaystyle\sum_{k=0}^{15} \binom{15}{k} (1)^{15-k}(-2x^2)^k = \sum_{k=0}^{15} (-2)^k \binom{15}{k} x^{2k}.$

2. (a) $(a - b)^5 = a^5 - 5a^4b + 10a^3b^2 - 10a^2b^3 + 5ab^4 - b^5.$

 (b) $(2a + b)^4 = 16a^4 + 32a^3b + 24a^2b^2 + 8ab^3 + b^4.$

 (c) $\left(2x - \dfrac{y}{2}\right)^6 = 64x^6 - 96x^5y + 60x^4y^2 - 20x^3y^3 + \dfrac{15}{4}x^2y^4 - \dfrac{3}{8}xy^5$
 $+ \dfrac{1}{64}y^6.$

 (d) $\left(x^2 + \dfrac{1}{x}\right)^4 = x^8 + 4x^5 + 6x^2 + 4x^{-1} + x^{-4}.$

 (e) $\left(4x^2 - \dfrac{x}{2}\right)^4 = 256x^8 - 128x^7 + 24x^6 - 2x^5 + \dfrac{1}{16}x^4.$

 (f) $\left(3a - \dfrac{2}{b}\right)^5 = 243a^5 - 810a^4b^{-1} + 1080a^3b^{-2} - 720a^2b^{-3} + 240ab^{-4}$
 $- 32b^{-5}.$

3. (a) $(a + b)^{10} = a^{10} + 10a^9b + 45\,a^8b^2 + \ldots$

 (b) $(a - b)^8 = a^8 - 8a^7b + 28a^6b^2 - \ldots$

 (c) $(a + 3b)^7 = a^7 + 21a^6b + 189a^5b^2 + \ldots$

 (d) $(1 - 3x)^{15} = 1 - 45x + 945x^2 - \ldots$

 (e) $(3a - 2)^5 = 243a^5 - 810a^4 + 1080a^3 - \ldots$

 (f) $(1 + 2b)^{12} = 1 + 24b + 264b^2 + \ldots$

(g) $\left(2x - \dfrac{y}{4}\right)^8 = 256x^8 - 256x^7y + 112x^6y^2 - \ldots$

(h) $\left(x^2 - \dfrac{2}{x}\right)^6 = x^{12} - 12x^9 + 60x^6 - \ldots$

(i) $\left(3x^2 - \dfrac{x}{y}\right)^6 = 729x^{12} - 1458x^{11}y^{-1} + 1215x^{10}y^{-2} - \ldots$

4. (a) $210a^4b^6$

    (b) $-280a^4b^3$

    (c) $\frac{15}{4}x^{10}$

    (d) $-960x^{11}$

    (e) $\frac{280}{81}x^3y^4$

    (f) $4320x^3y^3$

    (g) 70

    (h) $(2n)! \div (n!)^2$

5. $84x^5y^2$

6. $-448x^6y^5$

7. $2160x^4y^{-8}$

8. $a = 2, \ b = -\frac{1}{2}$

9. $a = 1, \ n = 8, \ b = -\frac{2}{3}$

EXERCISE 14.3 (page 363)

1. (a) $\dbinom{12}{r} x^r$

    (b) $\dbinom{8}{r} 2^{8-r}(-a)^r$

    (c) $\dbinom{7}{r} x^{14-r}$

    (d) $\dbinom{7}{r} a^{7-2r}$

    (e) $(-1)^r \dbinom{8}{r} p^{8-2r}$

    (f) $(-1)^r \dbinom{10}{r} x^{20-3r}$

    (g) $2^{10-r} \dbinom{10}{r} a^{10-3r}$

    (h) $(-1)^r (2^{15-r}) \dbinom{15}{r} a^{15-4r}$

    (i) $2^r \dbinom{n}{r} a^{3n-5r}$

2. (a) 12

    (b) 220

    (c) 792

3. 455

4. (a) $5(2^{10})x^8$

    (b) $63(2^7)x^0$

    (c) $15(2^6)x^{-4}$

5. (a) $\frac{1215}{4}$

    (b) $540x^{-6}$

6. (a) -84

    (b) -126

    (c) no solution

7. $\frac{21}{2}$

8. 8

9. 9

10. 10

REVIEW EXERCISE 14 (page 364)

1. (a) $(a + b)^7 = \displaystyle\sum_{k=0}^{7} \dbinom{7}{k} a^{7-k}b^k.$

    (b) $(x + 2y)^n = \displaystyle\sum_{k=0}^{n} \dbinom{n}{k} (x)^{n-k} (2y)^k = \displaystyle\sum_{k=0}^{n} \dbinom{n}{k} 2^k \, x^{n-k}y^k.$

(c) $(2a - b)^{10}$ $= \sum_{k=0}^{10} \binom{10}{k} (2a)^{10-k}(-b)^k = \sum_{k=0}^{10} \binom{10}{k}(-1)^k 2^{10-k}a^{10-k}b^k.$

(d) $\left(x^2 - \dfrac{1}{x}\right)^8$ $= \sum_{k=0}^{8} \binom{8}{k} (x^2)^{8-k}(-x^{-1})^k = \sum_{k=0}^{8} \binom{8}{k}(-1)^k x^{16-3k}.$

(e) $\left(2x^2 + \dfrac{1}{2x}\right)^{15} = \sum_{k=0}^{15} \binom{15}{k}(2x^2)^{15-k}\left(\dfrac{1}{2}x^{-1}\right)^k = \sum_{k=0}^{15} \binom{15}{k} 2^{15-2k}\, x^{30-3k}.$

(f) $(2 - x^2)^n$ $= \sum_{k=0}^{n} \binom{n}{k}(2)^{n-k}(-x^2)^k = \sum_{k=0}^{n} \binom{n}{k} 2^{n-k}(-1)^k x^{2k}.$

2. (a) $(a + b)^6$ $= a^6 + 6a^5b + 15a^4b^2 + 20a^3b^3 + 15a^2b^4 + 6ab^5 + b^6.$
   (b) $(a - b)^6$ $= a^6 - 6a^5b + 15a^4b^2 - 20a^3b^3 + 15a^2b^4 - 6ab^5 + b^6.$
   (c) $(2a + 3b)^5$ $= 32a^5 + 240a^4b + 720a^3b^2 + 1080a^2b^3 + 810ab^4 + 243b^5.$
3. (a) $(a + 2b)^{12}$ $= a^{12} + 24a^{11}b + 264a^{10}b^2 + \dots$
   (b) $(2x - y)^8$ $= 256x^8 - 1024x^7y + 1792x^6y^2 - \dots$
   (c) $\left(2x^2 + \dfrac{x}{2}\right)^{10}$ $= 1024x^{20} + 2560x^{19} + 2880x^{18} + \dots$
   (d) $\left(3x - \dfrac{1}{x}\right)^6$ $= 729x^6 - 1458x^4 + 1215x^2 - \dots$
   (e) $\left(\dfrac{x}{2} + \dfrac{2}{x}\right)^{10}$ $= \dfrac{x^{10}}{2^{10}} + 10\,\dfrac{x^8}{2^8} + 45\,\dfrac{x^6}{2^6} + \dots$
   (f) $(ax^2 + b)^{20}$ $= a^{20}x^{40} + 20a^{19}bx^{38} + 190a^{18}b^2x^{36} + \dots$
4. $594x^{-8}$ 5. $210x^2$
6. $t_9 = 180x^2$ 7. $32a^{13} + 176a^{12} + 336a^{11} + \dots$
8. $16 - 80x + 136x^2 - \dots$ 9. $32805, 252$
10. 240 11. 252
12. $n = 12, p = -3$ 13. $n = 10, p = \frac{1}{2}$
14. $n = 8$ 15. $a = 2, b = -\frac{1}{4}$
16. $a = 3, b = \frac{1}{3}, n = 6$

Chapter 15

EXERCISE 15.1   (page 368)

1. (a) $\frac{1}{6}$
   (b) $\frac{1}{3}$
   (c) $\frac{1}{2}$
   (d) $\frac{1}{2}$
   (e) $\frac{1}{2}$
   (f) $\frac{1}{2}$

2. (a) $\frac{5}{8}$
   (b) $\frac{3}{8}$
3. (a) $\frac{2}{7}$
   (b) $\frac{3}{7}$
   (c) $\frac{4}{7}$
4. $\frac{5}{9}$

5. (a) $\frac{19}{63}$
   (b) $\frac{4}{21}$
   (c) $\frac{32}{63}$
6. (a) $\frac{2}{6}$
   (b) $\frac{1}{15}$
   (c) $\frac{1}{30}$

7. (a) $\frac{28}{63}$
   (b) $\frac{35}{63}$
   (c) $\frac{7}{63}$
8. $\frac{3}{8}$
9. (a) $\frac{5}{11}$
   (b) $\frac{9}{22}$

10. (a) $\frac{1}{36}$
    (b) $\frac{1}{12}$
11. $\frac{1}{8}$
12. (a) $\frac{3}{51}$
    (b) $\frac{1}{221}$
    (c) $\frac{25}{102}$
    (d) $\frac{1}{1326}$

EXERCISE 15.2 (page 372)

1. $\{(3, 0), (2, 1), (1, 2), (0, 3)\}$
   $\{(HHH), (HHT), (HTH), (HTT), (THH), (THT), (TTH), (TTT)\}$
2. one, three
3. one, three
4. (a) four
   (b) six
   (c) four
5. (a) six
   (b) four
   (c) three
   (d) nine
6. (a) three
   (b) two
   (c) eight
7. (a) six
   (b) seven
   (c) nine

EXERCISE 15.3 (page 378)

1. (a) $\frac{2}{9}$
   (b) $\frac{1}{6}$
   (c) $\frac{5}{12}$
   (d) $\frac{5}{12}$
   (e) $\frac{5}{36}$
   (f) $\frac{1}{6}$
   (g) $\frac{1}{3}$
   (h) $\frac{1}{18}$
   (i) $\frac{4}{9}$
   (j) $\frac{5}{12}$
   (k) $\frac{1}{3}$
   (l) 0
2. (a) $\frac{1}{8}$
   (b) $\frac{3}{8}$
   (c) $\frac{1}{2}$
   (d) $\frac{7}{8}$
3. (a) $\frac{1}{3}$
   (b) $\frac{1}{15}$
   (c) $\frac{8}{15}$
   (d) $\frac{1}{5}$
4. (a) $\frac{1}{4}$
   (b) $\frac{3}{8}$
   (c) $\frac{1}{4}$
5. (a) $\frac{1}{6}$
   (b) $\frac{5}{24}$
   (c) $\frac{3}{8}$
   (d) $\frac{1}{24}$
6. (a) $\frac{3}{5}$
   (b) $\frac{3}{10}$
   (c) $\frac{2}{5}$
   (d) $\frac{9}{10}$

EXERCISE 15.4   (page 381)

1. (a) 7:4
   (b) 4:7
2. (a) 1:5
   (b) 2:4
   (c) 5:1
3. (a) 3:4
   (b) 5:2
4. 4:3
5. 14:25
6. 1:3
7. 7:1
8. (a) 25:77
   (b) 220:1
   (c) 1:220
9. (a) 1:8
   (b) 31:5
   (c) 5:7
   (d) 5:1
10. 27:1
11. 33:28
12. 1:2

EXERCISE 15.5 (page 384)

1. (a) $\frac{1}{9}$
   (b) $\frac{5}{9}$
   (c) $\frac{3}{4}$
   (d) $\frac{2}{9}$
2. (a) $\frac{1}{4}$
   (b) $\frac{1}{2}$
   (c) $\frac{11}{20}$
   (d) $\frac{4}{5}$
3. (a) $\frac{5}{19}$
   (b) $\frac{11}{19}$
4. $\frac{8}{15}$
5. (a) $\frac{1}{2}$
   (b) $\frac{4}{5}$
   (c) $\frac{13}{20}$
   (d) $\frac{2}{5}$
   (e) $\frac{7}{20}$
6. $\frac{11}{28}$
7. $\frac{165}{663}$
8. (a) $\frac{8}{15}$
   (b) $\frac{1}{8}$
9. (a) $\frac{11}{50}$
   (b) 121
   (c) $\frac{2}{15}$
10. $\frac{9}{20}$

EXERCISE 15.6 (page 386)

1. (a) No
   (b) Yes
   (c) No
   (d) No
   (e) Yes
2. (a) No
   (b) Yes
   (c) No
   (d) No
   (e) Yes
3. (a) No
   (b) No
   (c) No
   (d) Yes
   (e) Yes
4. No, $\frac{1}{2}$
5. Yes, 0
6. (a) $\frac{11}{36}$
   (b) $\frac{5}{6}$
   (c) $\frac{1}{2}$
   (d) $\frac{11}{36}$
   (e) $\frac{2}{3}$
   (f) $\frac{5}{9}$
7. (a) $\frac{3}{4}$
   (b) 1
   (c) $\frac{3}{4}$
   (d) 1
8. (a) $\frac{3}{8}$
   (b) $\frac{3}{4}$
   (c) $\frac{5}{8}$
   (d) $\frac{1}{2}$
   (e) $\frac{5}{8}$
9. (a) $\frac{1}{17}$
   (b) $\frac{25}{102}$
   (c) $\frac{1}{221}$
   (d) $\frac{1}{1326}$
   (e) $\frac{55}{221}$
10. $\frac{79}{1326}$

EXERCISE 15.7   (page 391)

1. (a) independent
   (b) dependent
   (c) mutually exclusive
   (d) dependent
   (e) dependent
   (f) dependent

2. $\frac{1}{72}$

3. $\frac{1}{64}$

4. (a) $\frac{4}{9}$
   (b) $\frac{1}{9}$
   (c) $\frac{2}{9}$

5. (a) independent

   (b) mutually exclusive
   (c) dependent

6. (a) $\frac{8}{225}$
   (b) $\frac{8}{125}$
   (c) $\frac{1}{27}$
   (d) $\frac{16}{375}$

7. (a) $\frac{1}{8}$
   (b) $\frac{1}{8}$
   (c) $\frac{5}{8}$

8. dependent
9. dependent
10. independent

EXERCISE 15.8   (page 396)

1. (a) $\frac{25}{216}$
   (b) $\frac{5}{324}$
   (c) $\frac{671}{1296}$

2. (a) $\frac{5}{16}$
   (b) $\frac{1}{2}$
   (c) $\frac{1}{32}$

3. (a) $\frac{5}{16}$
   (b) $\frac{1}{2}$
   (c) $\frac{1}{32}$
   (d) $\frac{31}{32}$

4. (a) $\frac{1}{16}$
   (b) $\frac{135}{592}$

5. $\frac{160}{729}$

6. (a) $\frac{1}{216}$
   (b) $\frac{25}{72}$
   (c) $\frac{91}{216}$
   (d) $\frac{4913}{5832}$

7. (a) $\frac{27}{64}$

8. $\simeq .55$

9. $\frac{1}{4}$

10. $\frac{1}{6}$

(b) $\frac{3}{64}$
(c) $\frac{243}{256}$
(d) $\frac{1}{256}$

11. $\frac{27}{125}$

12. .189

13. 3.03×10^{-7}

EXERCISE 15.9   (page 404)

1. 0.271

2. 85

REVIEW EXERCISE 15   (page 406)

1. (a) $\{(ABCD), (ABCE), (ABCF), (ABDE), (ABDF), (ABEF), (ACDE),$
       $(ACDF), (ACEF), (BCDE), (BCDF), (BCEF), (CDEF), (DEFA),$
       $(DEFB)\}$

   (b) $\{A_S A_H, A_S K_H, A_S Q_H, A_S J_H, A_S T_H$
       $K_S A_H, K_S K_H, K_S Q_H, K_S J_H, K_S T_H$
       $Q_S A_H, Q_S K_H, Q_S Q_H, Q_S J_H, Q_S T_H$
       $J_S A_H, J_S K_H, J_S Q_H, J_S J_H, J_S T_H$
       $T_S A_H, T_S K_H, T_S Q_H, T_S J_H, T_S T_H\}$

2. (a) $\frac{3}{10}$
   (b) $\frac{3}{10}$
   (c) $\frac{3}{10}$
   (d) $\frac{1}{2}$
   (e) $\frac{3}{5}$
   (f) $\frac{1}{10}$

3. (a) $\frac{5}{18}$
   (b) $\frac{1}{36}$
   (c) $\frac{5}{36}$
   (d) $\frac{1}{12}$

3. (e) $\frac{1}{6}$
   (f) $\frac{2}{3}$
   (g) $\frac{1}{3}$

4. (a) $\frac{1}{13}$
   (b) $\frac{1}{26}$
   (c) $\frac{1}{4}$
   (d) $\frac{2}{13}$

5. (a) $\frac{1}{100}$
   (b) $\frac{21}{46}$
   (c) $\frac{6}{115}$

6. $\frac{43}{91}$, 1

7. (a) $\frac{7}{33}$
   (b) $\frac{4}{165}$

(e) $\frac{5}{13}$
(d) $\frac{14}{55}$

8. $\simeq .72$

9. $\frac{14}{25}$

10. (a) independent
    (b) dependent
    (c) mutually exclusive

(c) $\frac{28}{55}$

(d) independent

11. $\frac{3}{400}$

12. $\simeq .66$

13. (a) $\frac{240}{729}$
    (b) $\frac{60}{729}$
    (c) $\frac{716}{729}$
    (d) $\frac{73}{729}$

14. $\frac{821}{3125}$

15. (a) $\frac{15}{64}$
    (b) $\frac{57}{64}$
    (c) $\frac{7}{64}$

16. $\simeq 646$

INDEX